"Davidowitz's theories on track bias are worth many times the price of the book." —*New York Post*

"The only thing harder to find than a man of Davidowitz's wealth of handicapping knowledge is the horse player who couldn't learn something new from him." —*Las Vegas Review-Journal*

"A classic of handicapping literature." —*San Francisco Examiner*

"The most accessible and clear-headed work on the subject." —*The New Yorker*

"A great book just got better. This is much stronger, more comprehensive than the original classic." —Andrew Beyer

"Wow! A remarkable revision. . . . Every vital aspect of modern handicapping has been scrutinized by one of the country's best players." —James Quinn, author of *Figure Handicapping*

"Written for every level player by one of the most respected racing columnists and handicappers in the nation." —*Gaming Today*

STEVEN DAVIDOWITZ, one of the most respected racing writers in the country, has covered the sport's most prestigious events for *Racing Times*, the *Philadelphia Inquirer*, the *Minneapolis Star Tribune*, *Sport* magazine, and other publications. Among his many accomplishments, Davidowitz has picked a world-record 13 winners in succession, 20 out of 22, and the 1-2-3 order of eight Belmont Stakes. He also owns the two highest finishes of any public handicapper in the history of the World Series of Handicapping at Penn National Racecourse. He lives in Corte Madera, California.

BETTING THOROUGHBREDS

A Professional's Guide for the Horseplayer

SECOND REVISED EDITION

Steven Davidowitz

A PLUME BOOK

PLUME
Published by the Penguin Group
Penguin Books USA Inc., 375 Hudson Street, New York, New York 10014, U.S.A.
Penguin Books Ltd, 27 Wrights Lane, London W8 5TZ, England
Penguin Books Australia Ltd, Ringwood, Victoria, Australia
Penguin Books Canada Ltd, 10 Alcorn Avenue, Toronto, Ontario, Canada M4V 3B2
Penguin Books (N.Z.) Ltd, 182–190 Wairau Road, Auckland 10, New Zealand

Penguin Books Ltd, Registered Offices: Harmondsworth, Middlesex, England

Published by Plume, an imprint of Dutton Signet,
a division of Penguin Books USA Inc.
Previously published in a Dutton edition.

First Plume Printing, Second Revised Edition, April, 1997
10 9 8

Ⓟ REGISTERED TRADEMARK—MARCA REGISTRADA

The Library of Congress has catalogued the Dutton edition as follows:
Davidowitz, Steven.
     Betting thoroughbreds : a professional's guide for the horseplayer
 / Steven Davidowitz.—2nd rev. ed.
          p.   cm.
     ISBN 0-525-93951-2 (hc.)
     ISBN 0-452-27042-1 (pbk.)
     1. Horse racing—Betting.   I. Title.
 SF331.D36   1995
 798.401—dc20   94–34539
                                                            CIP

Printed in the United States of America
Original hardcover design by Stanley S. Drate/Folio Graphics Co., Inc.

BOOKS ARE AVAILABLE AT QUANTITY DISCOUNTS WHEN USED TO PROMOTE PRODUCTS
OR SERVICES. FOR INFORMATION PLEASE WRITE TO PREMIUM MARKETING DIVISION,
PENGUIN BOOKS USA INC., 375 HUDSON STREET, NEW YORK, NY 10014.

For my mother, my father, my son, and for Saul Rosen, a good man who may have been the best editor *Daily Racing Form* ever had.

Contents

Acknowledgments   *xiii*

Foreword *by Andrew Beyer*   *xv*

Introduction   *xvii*

1   Through the Looking Glasses   *1*
How to watch a race properly

2   A B.A. in Handicapping   *7*
The author's college education at the track

3   The Horseplayer's Bible   *12*
The improved *Daily Racing Form* and the extraordinary value of result charts

4   The Bias of the Racing Surface   *20*
How and when the racing surface itself influences horse performance along with advanced applications of this phenomenon

5   The Money Tree   *39*
The winning strategy of an obscure trainer

6   The Trainer's Window   *42*
The role of the trainer in the conditioning process as described and illustrated by some of the finest trainers of all time, including Allen Jerkens, Woody Stephens, Frank Whiteley, Jr., Charles Whittingham and Jack Van Berg

7 Who's Hot and Who's Not

Dealing with trainers on winning and losing streaks—a look at D. Wayne Lukas' methods

58

8 What's He Doing in Today's Race?

How to glean the most clues from past-performance profiles

69

9 The Key Race Method Revisited

The research technique to uncover important information not available in past-performance or result charts. New applications and variations to identify races of significant strength and depth

84

10 An Edge in Class

Minor track handicapping—the classification code—new applications to claiming races at major tracks

93

11 The Mystery of Allowance Races

The hidden class dropdown and other tools to solve the handicapping riddles of better-class races

100

12 Speed Handicapping 101

Basics of speed handicapping—what's wrong with *Daily Racing Form* speed ratings and when to make use of them

111

13 $E = MC^2$

Class pars—parallel time charts—making Beyer figures, the best speed-figure method ever created

116

14 The Race Is to the Swift

When to use Beyer figures or your own and when to throw them in the wastebasket

130

15 Pace: The New-Old Frontier

Basics of pace as it makes the race—the importance of early speed, middle moves and late bursts of speed—Bill Quirin's speed-point method revised—positive moves in grass races

141

16 **Pace as Science and Pseudoscience**   *157*

Sartin methodology velocity ratings—the different values for ⅕
seconds and one length—estimated pace lines—weaknesses in
pace handicapping's mathematics

17 **Converting Beyer Figures for Pace
Analysis**   *164*

The value of par charts and the weakness of the Beyer rating scale
for pace analysis—a new method for making pace ratings using
Beyer speed figures in *Daily Racing Form*—different approaches
to beaten lengths and track variants

18 **Pace and the Single Race Bias**   *173*

Analyzing races by their "shapes."—the power of pace analysis in
races already run—limits of pace handicapping

19 **Theory Versus Experience**   *182*

Hundreds of practical hints on weight, sex, running styles and the
distance factor, optional equipment, horseshoes, bandages,
physical appearance and evaluating jockeys

20 **Working With Workouts**   *203*

Detailed explanations and dozens of examples of how to interpret
workouts—when to trust the workout line and when to regard it
suspiciously—how to spot pending improvement, live first-time
starters or absentees

21 **It's in the Blood**   *221*

Master turf sires—mud breeding—"early win sires" and speed
breeding—the Chef-de-Race sires' list—Dr. Steve Roman's Dosage
Index system to spot sprint speed and/or stamina in the
racehorse—Dosage and the Kentucky Derby

22 **The Drug Factor**   *235*

The key facts about racetrack drugs and how they affect the
horseplayer—when Lasix is likely to improve performance

23 **To Bet or Not to Bet . . . and How Much**   *243*

Recognizing winning situations—sensible money
management—making an accurate morning line and the value line

24   Promising Exotic Plays   *252*

When and how to take advantage of daily doubles, exactas, trifectas, the pick three and pick six—wagering strategies for prime bets, action bets, reasonable longshots and the exotics—how to cure losing streaks

25   La Prevoyante to Win, My Wife to Place   *262*

Bonus profits in the place and show pools

26   Betting Myths and Longshot Angles   *266*

"Smart money" and sucker bets—going against the grain of common racetrack wisdom—dozens of invaluable hints on how to spot live longshots

27   The Best Handicapping Tool Ever Invented   *281*

Using the video home recorder to dramatically improve your handicapping—studying the Triple Crown

28   The Winning Horseplayer   *286*

A recap of major handicapping factors with key examples—assessing the wagering favorite—the best performance and best bet of all time

APPENDIX **A**   *303*
Guide to *Daily Racing Form* Past Performances

Symbols and abbreviations; purse values at North American tracks; "points of call" in result charts; post position surveys; morning line percentage tables; how to compute place and show prices; modern handicapping aids

APPENDIX **B**   *315*
Speed Figures

Complete parallel time charts for sprints and routes; computing Beyer speed figures and track variants; the projection method; class and speed pars for selected turf courses

APPENDIX **C**   *323*

Pace Figures

Fractional clockings and pace pars; complete six-furlong pace pars
for a New York track; sample pace lines for six-and-a-half furlongs,
seven furlongs, one mile, 1⅛ miles and other two-turn routes;
sample par times and pace lines for Santa Anita; mathematical
errors in traditional beaten length charts; "too fast" preliminary
fractions for two-turn routes

APPENDIX **D**   *331*

Exotic Wagering Strategies

Numerous examples of sound strategies for playing all exotic wagers
including the Pick Six; recommended books, tapes and computer
services

Recommended Reading and Resources   *346*

Acknowledgments

The charts appearing on pages 1, 2, 3, 12, 13, 14, 15, 17, 18, 23, 24, 29, 30, 31, 32, 33, 34, 35, 37, 38, 39, 45, 46, 47, 48, 49, 50, 51, 52, 53, 55, 56, 59, 61, 62, 63, 65, 66, 67, 70, 72, 73, 75, 76, 77, 78, 79, 80, 81, 82, 85, 86, 87, 89, 91, 95, 100, 101, 102, 104, 105, 106, 107, 108, 109, 110, 113, 120, 132, 133, 134, 135, 137, 138, 139, 140, 142, 143, 147, 151, 152, 154, 175, 177, 183, 184, 187, 188, 190, 191, 192, 193, 194, 195, 197, 204, 206, 207, 209, 210, 211, 212, 213, 214, 215, 216, 217, 218, 219, 224, 225, 235, 239, 240, 241, 267, 269, 270, 271, 275, 276, 277, 279, 280, 291, 292, 294, 295, 297, 298, 299, 302, 303, 304, 305, 306, 307 of this book are reprinted by special arrangement with Daily Racing Form, Inc. Copyright, 1957, 1962, 1963, 1968, 1969, 1972, 1973, 1974, 1975, 1976, 1980, 1981, 1982, 1986, 1987, 1988, 1989, 1990, 1991, 1992, 1993, 1994, by Daily Racing Form. Reprinted with permission of the copyright owner.

The past-performance illustration on page 155 and the jockey-trainer statistics on pages 313–314 are reprinted with permission of Equibase Corp. and the New York Racing Association.

Gratitude also is extended to Ron Cox and Dan Montilion, publishers and editor of the *Northern California Track Record;* Bloodstock Research Information Services in Lexington, Kentucky; *Handicapper's Report,* published by Jeff Siegel and Bob Selvin in Los Angeles for permission to use samples of their products.

Further, I wish to thank Mark Berner of *Newsday* newspaper in New York, Scott McMannis of Arlington International Racecourse, the staff of the Kentucky Derby Museum and the Keeneland Library for locating back issues of *Daily Racing Form* needed for this work, and a special thanks to Andy Beyer for his support and suggestions in the final stages of the manuscript.

Foreword

All gamblers, even the most rational ones, will acknowledge that luck influences their destinies. It did for me. One of the most important events in my life as a horseplayer was a fortuitous meeting on a bench at Saratoga Race Track in 1970. When Steve Davidowitz and I struck up a conversation, we learned that we shared the same passion for the game and the art of handicapping.

At that time, however, I was in the same position that many readers may be as they pick up this book. I loved racing and I desperately wanted to become a successful player, but I didn't know how to proceed. I wasn't sure the goal was even obtainable. I had never met a professional bettor—until this chance encounter under the elm trees.

Steve became my mentor.

The great lesson he taught me was one forged from practical play at dozens of the nation's racetracks and as a handicapper for the *Daily Racing Form*, which required him to study races from coast to coast. What struck him most was the diversity of the game. Other bettors approached racing as a quest for the Rosetta Stone, for a system that would explain all of the mysteries of horseracing. But Steve perceived that successful methods can vary greatly from time to time and place to place. At one track, the central factor may be the methodology of certain trainers; at another, a bias in the racing surface may be of paramount importance. The winning horseplayer is one who can observe and adapt to the conditions around him.

The combination of Steve's lessons and my own discovery of the potency of speed figures, made me a successful horseplayer for the first time. It spurred me to write the book, *Picking Winners*. That book included the first discussion of track biases that had ever appeared in a book, although I credit Steve for both the concept and the term. He did not have a chance to expound on the subject until the publication of the original *Betting Thoroughbreds* in 1977.

While the first edition of that book has remained one of the best primers on thoroughbred handicapping, it makes an interesting comparison with this stronger, greatly expanded second—revised edition. The differences underscore another reason why the author is such an adept student of the game: There is a tendency for any horseplayer—once he or she has achieved a measure of success—to become wedded to the methods that have been successful. But the best players continually reevaluate their handicapping tools, polishing the useful ones, discarding the ones that are outdated, and making additions to their arsenal when necessary.

Steve's views of some subjects have needed little revision; his treatment of track bias in this book is just as strong as it was in his first one, with new illustrations and applications. But in the original *Betting Thoroughbreds,* there was scarcely a mention of the word "pace." In the intervening years, Steve has recognized (as I have) that this is one of the game's most interesting new frontiers, and his experiences while based in northern California strengthened his belief in the importance of this factor. His treatment of the subject in this book is exhaustive. He emphasizes commonsense approaches to the subject—such as his discussion of what he calls the "single race pace bias"—because he has a personal disinclination to employ mathematical systems. He recognizes, however, that pace is a subject whose complexity demands more sophisticated approaches, and he explains an advanced method for calculating pace figures that may be built upon Beyer speed figures in the *Daily Racing Form.*

Steve acknowledges too, that "the state of the art of pace handicapping is incomplete" and—if his own past performances are any guide—he will keep working to understand more of the mysteries of the game. In the meantime, the book you are holding is packed with Steve's insights on every facet of the game, and is sure to stand among the most comprehensive, most valuable books on handicapping ever published. . . . Perhaps we can also look forward to a *Betting Thoroughbreds in the 21st Century?*

—ANDREW BEYER

Introduction

Although the original edition of *Betting Thoroughbreds* is among the few handicapping books that still provide workable clues to the race-track puzzle, there have been enough changes to the fabric of racing to mandate a substantially revised and expanded version.

Racing has become a twelve-month, nonstop season in most regions of the country. New tracks have been opened (and closed) in new markets, while old ones in traditional locales have been lavishly rebuilt from the ashes. The betting mix has dramatically changed, with an explosion of exotic bets that include the pick six, pick three, twin trifecta, pick seven and pick nine. Where such exotics had once been novelties to complement win, place and show wagering, now they dominate betting menus at most tracks, including ultra-conservative Oaklawn Park in Arkansas, which had resisted exactas as recently as 1988.

The expansion of offtrack betting [OTB] and simulcast wagering has changed the way the game is played, or at least its accessibility and its economics. Available only in New York during the 1970s, offtrack, inter-track and satellite wagering now is fundamental to the wagering experience in virtually every racing state. By the end of the 1990s, most players probably will be able to wager on several tracks at home via telephone wagering systems or at least at nearby multitrack satellite sites.

Offtrack Betting (OTB) is sure to force some tracks to close, but it certainly has the potential to mute the impact of severe nationwide horse shortages caused by financial problems in the breeding industry, while making larger wagering pools more accessible to thousands of players in numerous states.

Through satellite television transmissions that debuted in the early 1980s, numerous races in one region of the country are now playable in other regions. Fans in Ohio, Florida and everywhere else wager legally on the Kentucky Derby, Preakness, and Belmont Stakes, among dozens of other stakes, including the spectacular $10 million Breeders' Cup Day, created in 1984.

The Breeders' Cup, featuring seven championship style races worth a hefty $1–3 million apiece, already overshadows the Triple Crown in national importance and has brought an unparalleled surge of international competition to dozens of other stakes, especially grass events in California, New York, Maryland, and Illinois. All of this has changed since *Betting Thoroughbreds* first was published in 1977 and modestly revised in 1982.

Yet, the most important reason for a new and expanded *Betting Thoroughbreds* is the revolution in the dissemination of vital handicapping information.

During the early 1990s, the *Daily Racing Form (DRF)* was bought and sold twice, while rebuffing several competitive challenges to its monopolistic control of racing statistics. The challenges—first from the brilliant, but ill-fated *Racing Times* and subsequently from a host of racetrack-sponsored past performance publications—finally forced *DRF* to open the floodgates to a wide range of handicapping data that it had persistently shielded from view.

The *Racing Times* had the most immediate impact. Born in April 1991, it was shut down and its assets sold to *DRF* in February, 1992, four months after its controversial founder, Robert Maxwell, died mysteriously at sea. But during its brief run, the *Racing Times* made an indelible mark, combining refreshing, energetic editorial content tailored specifically for horseplayers, while unveiling numerous improvements in past performance data, much of which subsequently has been incorporated into the *Form*.

Following the death of the *Racing Times*, many racetracks moved quickly to publish expanded track programs, complete with their own past performance lines. No doubt this kept the burr on the backside of *DRF*'s new owners (K-3 Corporation), who earned credibility in the marketplace by fighting the competitive threats with an improved product.

There are other trends to note, including the open access to Andy Beyer's Speed Figures, first in the *Racing Times*, then in the *Form*, plus the commercial availability of several first-class newsletters, featuring workout reports, performance ratings, and sophisticated trip notes for every horse in every race in selected markets. Where such newsletters rarely provided useful information in the 1970s, a handful of contemporary newsletters in every region truly do offer professional insights on their respective meets in progress.

The wealth of material available on one's personal home computer also has increased logarithmically to include in-depth trainer and jockey records, as well as esoteric breeding and track stats that, properly used, can give the most sophisticated handicappers in the country clear-cut advantages over less industrious players.

As stated in the original introduction, _Betting Thoroughbreds_ first was written to provide clues to the most intellectually challenging pastime man has ever invented. In this new and enlarged edition, _Betting Thoroughbreds_ keeps that promise intact. While I have tinkered very little with the first few chapters and left undisturbed a few more, this edition includes vastly expanded and wholly new sections about trainers, speed, pace, workouts, Key Races, drugs, breeding and wagering concepts, plus a wide spectrum of new ideas and more than 150 new illustrations.

Changes were made to advance new ideas and where modern realities commanded them. Original illustrations remain because they still provide maximum illumination to key points.

Drugs, nutrition, extensive travel, night racing and twelve-month seasons have affected the race horse form cycle, but the trick in handicapping is to master a method to detect the trends in progress—to be among the first on your block to spot winning and losing patterns. While pace analysis, which is covered in four new chapters, offers considerable practical possibilities, the expanded chapters on trainer patterns provide fertile handicapping territory to uncover generous price winners. Indeed, there are dozens of winning ideas and practical applications in the new chapters on long-shot angles, promising exotic wagers and breeding concepts.

The original _Betting Thoroughbreds_ was a good book because it stemmed from private discovery and genuine professional insight. Its design was not to provide unalterable truths, but to offer interested fans sufficient windows to see the racing game more clearly. Workable tools were provided so that any player at any level of skill or experience could build a solid plan of attack. This book has a similar intent: to guide players toward practical handicapping and betting strategies with powerful tools that will help solve the modern riddles of the racetrack puzzle. In effect, this new edition of *Betting Thoroughbreds* is not just the son of the first edition, but its cousin, uncle and brother all in one. Good luck and I sincerely hope it helps your game.

Through the
Looking Glasses

Thanks to television's annual coverage of the Triple Crown events, almost everyone with the vaguest interest in horseracing knows that the horse whose lifetime record is shown above was one of a kind, a champion of his age and one of the greatest racehorses ever to appear on this planet.

As a two-year-old, before the TV cameras discovered him, Secretariat was just as spectacular to watch, officially winning eight races in ten starts, including a defeat only the stewards could hang on him in the Champagne Stakes. But it is his other defeat I want to tell you about. His first lifetime start.

Secretariat	113	Ch. c (1970), by Bold Ruler—Somethingroyal, by Princequillo. Breeder, Meadow Stud, Inc. (Va.). 1972 0 M 0 0 (——)
Owner, Meadow Stable. Trainer, L. Laurin.		
June 29 Bel 3f ft :35h	June 24 Bel 6f sly 1:12⅖h	June 15 Bel 5f ft 1:00⅕hg

One, two, three strides out of the starting gate with inexperienced Paul Feliciano barely able to stay in the saddle, Secretariat was welcomed to the sport of kings with a bang. Make that two bangs. One from the left and one from the right.

"Forget *that* horse," I said to console myself and made a mental note to see him a bit later in the race. Ten lengths to the front, a pack of expensively bred two-year-old maidens were trying to win the first race of their careers. It was time to see how the race was taking shape.

I love two-year-old racing. I'm fascinated by its freshness and its promise, and I've gained valuable insights about speed, class, distance potential, and trainers through watching these young horses progress from race to race. Besides, the better ones run fast, very formfully, and provide some of the best bets in all of racing.

When the great filly Ruffian, for example, made her debut in 1974, I was absolutely astonished to get a $10.40 payoff (see next page). Her trainer, Frank Whiteley, Jr., is one of the deadliest trainers of first-time starters in the history of racing—a man who wins upward of 40 percent of all such attempts, a man who trains horses like they are put together with Swiss-clockwork efficiency.

Not only did Ruffian score by fifteen lengths in track record time, but she was the third straight first-time starter Whiteley put over in three early season attempts. It also turned out to be a typical Ruffian performance.

Throughout her two-year-old season Ruffian was never defeated, never threatened, never pushed to race any faster than she was willing to give on her own. But I'm not at all sure that pushing would have produced anything more than she was already willing to give.

Ruffian's striding action was incredibly powerful and remarkably smooth, resembling the top human sprinter, Valery Borzov, the Russian who won the gold medal in the 100-meter dash at the 1972 Munich

THIRD RACE
Belmont
MAY 22, 1974

5 ½ FURLONGS. (1.03) MAIDEN SPECIAL WEIGHTS. Purse $9,000. Fillies, 2-year-olds, weights, 116 lbs.

Value of race $9,000, value to winner $5,400, second $1,980, third $1,080, fourth $540. Mutuel pool $144,330, OTB pool $47,785. Track Exacta Pool $182,574. OTB Exacta Pool $83,829.

Last Raced	Horse	Eqt.	A.	Wt	PP	St	¼	½	Str	Fin	Jockey	Odds $1
	Ruffian		2	116	9	8	1^{3}	1^{5}	1^{8}	1^{15}	Vasquez J	4.20
	Suzest		2	113	3	3	3^{hd}	2^{4}	2^{5}	2^{5}	Wallis T3	1.50
	Garden Quad		2	116	10	9	5^{2}	$4^{\frac{1}{2}}$	4^{3}	$3^{\frac{1}{2}}$	Baltazar C	26.20
	Fierce Ruler		2	116	7	5	$6^{1\frac{1}{2}}$	5^{1}	3^{1}	$4^{3\frac{1}{2}}$	Rivera M A	20.80
	Flower Basket		2	116	8	6	8^{3}	$7^{\frac{1}{2}}$	$5^{\frac{1}{2}}$	$5^{\frac{1}{2}}$	Turcotte R	45.30
	Curlique	b	2	116	5	7	$7^{\frac{1}{2}}$	8^{4}	6^{3}	6^{nk}	Maple E	14.10
4May74 ^{6}CD^{12}	Funny Cat		2	116	6	10	10	10	$8^{\frac{1}{2}}$	7^{5}	Hole M	32.70
14May74 ^{4}Bel^{3}	Merrie Lassie		2	116	4	4	9^{6}	9^{5}	9^{4}	$8^{4\frac{1}{2}}$	Gustines H	13.90
	Precious Elaine		2	116	1	1	2^{hd}	3^{1}	$7^{\frac{1}{2}}$	$9^{6\frac{1}{2}}$	Castaneda M	4.50
28Feb74 ^{3}GP^{2}	Great Grandma Rose		2	116	2	2	4^{2}	$6^{1\frac{1}{2}}$	10	10	Cordero A Jr	4.60

OFF AT 2:32 EDT. Start good, Won ridden out. Time, :22⅕, :45, :57, 1:03 Track fast.

Equals track record.

$2 Mutuel Prices:				
	9-(L)-RUFFIAN	10.40	4.60	3.80
	3-(D)-SUZEST		3.20	3.00
	10-(M)-GARDEN QUAD			7.00

$2 EXACTA 9-3 PAID $35.20.

dk b or br. f, by Reviewer—Shenanigans, by Native Dancer. Trainer Whiteley F Y Jr. Bred by Janney Jr Mrs & S S (Ky).

RUFFIAN, rushed to the front from the outside at the turn, quickly sprinted away to a good lead and continued to increase her advantage while being ridden out. SUZEST, prominent from the start, was no match for the winner while easily besting the others. GARDEN QUAD hustled along after breaking slowly, failed to seriously menace. FIERCE RULER had no excuse. FUNNY CAT was off slowly. PRECIOUS ELAINE had brief speed. GREAT GRANDMA ROSE was through early.

Owners— 1, Locust Hill Farm; 2, Olin J M; 3, Irving R; 4, LaCroix J W; 5, Reineman R L; 6, Calumet Farm; 7, Whitney C V; 8, T-Square Stable; 9, Brodsky A J; 10, Five Friends Farm.

Trainers— 1, Whiteley F Y Jr; 2, Stephens W C; 3, Johnson P G; 4, Toner J J; 5, Freeman W C; 6, Cornell R; 7, Poole G T; 8, Cincotta V J; 9, Conway J P; 10, Donato R A.

Scratched—Cross Words; Footsie (14May74 ^{4}Bel^{4}); French Rule.

Olympics. Perfect rhythm. Maximum efficiency. Ruffian just came out of the gate running and never stopped, never missed a beat. Indeed, at six furlongs (three-quarters of a mile), I am convinced she could have beaten any horse that ever lived, including Secretariat, the fast-working son of Bold Ruler I had come to watch and bet in his debut, the colt we left in a tangle three steps out of the starting gate.

A few inches more to the left, a few more pounds of pressure, and we might never have heard about Secretariat. My notebooks are full of horses whose careers were terminated by less severe blows. But somehow this greenhorn kept his balance and settled slowly into stride far back of his field in the run down the backstretch.

On the turn I could see all the horses clearly at once, but the image I remember is that of the reddish brown colt going by three horses so fast it made me blink. Twice he changed gears to avoid further trouble.

Twice more Feliciano choked him down to avoid running up on the heels of a tandem of horses that looked cloddish by comparison.

At the top of the stretch he moved again, into a higher gear, angling sharply to the inside, looking for room, shifting leads to gain better traction, losing precious time in the bargain. "A freak," I said to myself, but I had barely completed the thought when the copper-toned chestnut colt with three white feet exploded in midstretch with a force that almost jiggled my binoculars right out of focus. He finished fourth, beaten about 1½ lengths, but it was the most electric exhibition of split-second acceleration I had seen since the mighty Kelso exploded seventy yards from the wire to gobble up front-running Malicious in a Saratoga stakes nine years earlier.

It was only the beginning, only the tip of the iceberg; but being there, watching the race, knowing WHAT I was watching was a thrill—the kind of thrill that reaches the mind bringing awareness and awe.

Maybe your aim is to become a successful handicapper. Or perhaps you are reading this book just to improve your understanding of horseracing, putting it on a par with your comprehension of other hobbies and sports. In either case, the quickest, straightest line to the goal begins with the race itself and how to watch it. Unfortunately, all too many racing fans, it seems to me, do not know how to do that.

There are three simultaneous disciplines involved.

For one thing, you must see as much of the race as possible—the development of it, the flow of it, and the battle to the wire down the stretch. For another, your mind controls a switch for a focusing device like the zoom lens of a camera. You must train your mind to operate that switch—to zoom in and zoom out—the moment anything unusual hits the retina.

Combining these two disciplines into a smooth two-gear transmission takes practice. You will have to learn when to switch away from the action in the front of the pack or away from the horse your money is riding on.

There are different ways to facilitate the learning process; but because the inclination of most horseplayers is to watch their bet, I suggest starting with that.

When the field hits the turn, when your grandstand vantage point makes it easy to see the entire field, without moving your binoculars, pull back on the zoom lens in your mind and see if you can spot the fastest-moving horses, the horses in trouble, the horses on the rail, the horses stuck on the outside.

Don't be concerned if you are not able to identify more than a couple of horses at once. Later you can use the videotape replays and result charts to put it all together.

In my judgment, the turn is the most important part of the race. It is the place where the majority of races are won and lost, the place where jockeys show their greatest skill and commit the most atrocious errors, the place where the fan can glean the most knowledge for the future.

Horses get into the most trouble on the turn. Centrifugal force pulls them naturally to the outside, and the ones that are weakly ridden, out of shape, or hurting are unable to hold their line as they turn the corner into the stretch.

Sometimes the player will see a horse who was by far the best, but was simply unable to get free of traffic. Sometimes a good or bad effort can be explained by the way the rider uses (or doesn't use) his whip.

On the turn, every well-meant horse in the race should be making its move or else trying to hold its position. On the turn, a jockey in the race may show if he is afraid to go inside, or if he has a particular strength or weakness.

Does the horse only do its best when it's given lots of running room? Does the jockey do his best only when he's aboard a front-running type? Is the horse in the clear, or suspiciously placed behind a wall of horses?

These observations will help the player in his quest for solid insights. They will provide meaningful clues to compare contenders. But even more important, as described later in greater detail, the action on the turn often reveals the true nature of the racetrack as it tends to influence the ultimate result.

There is no need for me to describe any further steps in the process of learning how to watch a race properly. If you master the turn, your ability to focus and shift focus to significant happenings will be firmly established. You will be able to use that skill anytime—at the start or in the stretch—at any stage of the race. After some practice you will even find yourself doing it automatically. Believe me, no other racetrack skill will ever be more useful.

For example, carefully reviewing the action at the start, at specific distances, may also provide clues about the way the track is playing.

At some tracks, especially in races around two turns, horses break-ing from inside post positions may get into their natural stride much faster than their rivals. This may be sheer coincidence, or it may be because of the way the top soil is repeatedly packed down by heavy roll-ing machines. On such days the player should be doing more than just watching individual races. He or she should be charting events, noting patterns, or dramatic changes in the way a series of races may be run, a subject we intend to cover in considerable depth.

The third discipline you need to master while watching races has nothing to do with the function of sight. In all sincerity it is what the rest of this book is about, the discipline that all your racetrack judg-ments are based on—the discipline of enlightened insight.

Watching a race properly is only one of the ways you can acquire greater knowledge about particular horses. To make maximum use of the skill, to put yourself in a position to recognize the unusual, impor-tant things that take place, you must first have some clear ideas about the limits of thoroughbred performance, some understanding of the rel-ative importance of track condition, trainers, class, and all the other pieces that make up the racetrack puzzle.

As I hinted in the introduction, most of the better players in the game have acquired that kind of knowledge only after many years of struggle. For some the effort was roughly equivalent to the pursuit of a college-level education. My own education was a case in point. And I mean that literally.

A B.A. in Handicapping

The first race in my life took place at Aqueduct on April 18, 1960. I was an eighteen-year-old freshman at Rutgers University and I needed $100 to make it to Fort Lauderdale for spring recess. But I only had $42.

A few of my friends paid for the bus ticket, pushed me through the turnstiles, and armed me with a program and Jack's Little Green Card (a tout sheet). I bet $5 to show on Jack's best bet of the day—Happy Lion in the first race—but when I realized that wouldn't get me past the Delaware Memorial Bridge, I went back and bet a wheel in the daily double. Twice.

Of course, when Happy Lion sent me and my crazy friends barreling down the pike to a week of girl chasing in the Florida sun, I thought I had found the secret to a rich and easy life. Naturally, I became a devout believer in Jack's Little Green Card.

But the romance didn't last very long. Every time I skipped classes to go out to the track, Jack's Card would surely have three or four winners listed; but who could figure which of the three choices per race would turn out to be the right choice. It was my misfortune that the winner was rarely the top choice.

So I switched cards; bet the secret code selections of Ken Kling in the New York *Daily Mirror*; made a system founded on *Racing Form* consensus picks; bet repeaters; bet the top speed rating; followed the "horses to watch" list in *Turf and Sport Digest*; bought an assortment of systems and other gadgets at $5, $10, and $20 a pop; and then began to bet with a bookie.

At minus $1,200, it didn't take much of a handicapper to predict where I was headed; but the final straw was a last-place finish by my old friend Happy Lion. The irony of it all did not escape me.

My father, bless his heart, picked up the tab with the New Brunswick bookie and made me promise never to bet another horserace again. It was a promise I wasn't sure I wanted to keep, but I knew there wasn't much future in going out to the track just to lose. I was determined to find out if, in fact, it was possible to win.

For the next six months I stayed away from the track and bought, borrowed, and read everything I could find about the inner workings of the sport.

The history of it was fascinating enough: the stuff about Man O' War and Citation, Arcaro and Shoemaker. But I was appalled at the lack of good material in the field of handicapping. So much of it was so badly written, so illogical, so poorly documented that I became discouraged and abandoned the project. I was convinced that racing was nothing more than a game of roulette on horseback, a sucker's game of pure chance, and I might very well have held that view forever. An assignment my statistics professor handed out a few weeks later changed my mind. "Analyze the winning tendencies of post positions at Monmouth Park," he said. And the irony of *that* did not escape me either.

The task, simple enough, revealed very little useful information the first time through. But when I introduced track condition and distance into the equation, there were powerful indicators that suggested the need for more intensive research. My statistics professor—no fool, to be sure—probably took the hint and spent the rest of the summer buried in his *Racing Form*.

He wasn't the only one.

I looked up horses', trainers', and jockeys' records. I studied result charts and workouts diligently and kept a file on all the best horses and stakes races on the East Coast. I made endless comparisons and was not surprised when some patterns began to emerge, patterns that were never mentioned by the so-called experts who were publishing and selling their empty-headed systems and books to a starved racing public.

I discovered that each type of race had its own set of key clues, its own major factors. I discovered that some trainers were consistently more successful than others and that most successful trainers were specialists who tended to repeat winning strategies. These strategies, I found, were frequently revealed in the past performance records of the horses they trained. By comparing these horses—comparing the dates between races, the workout lines, the distance and class manipulations—I began to gain some important insights into the conditioning process. The effort also cost me a failing grade in German 201, and I damn near flunked out of school. But it was worth it. I had begun to realize that there was a logic to the sport, and I suspected that I would be able to put all this time and effort to good use in the not-too-distant future. And I didn't have to wait very long to test out my thesis.

In late spring 1961 I spotted a horse named Nasomo in the past performance charts for Gulfstream Park. The half-mile workout from the starting gate attached to the bottom of his chart (.47bg) leaped off the page at me.

Nasomo hadn't shown such gate speed in any of his prior workouts, a deficiency he was content to carry over into his races. By habit he was a slow-breaking, Silky Sullivan type whose late burst of speed had earned him absolutely nothing in eight tries. But my research into workout patterns had already convinced me that such a dramatic change in behavior on the training track invariably meant a vastly improved effort in competition. Barring bad racing luck—which is something that frequently plagues slow-breaking types—I was sure Nasomo would run the race of his life.

At 28–1 Nasomo turned in a spectacular performance, a nose defeat by the stakes prospect Jay Fox. Although that didn't score too many points with Nasomo's betting friends at the track, it was the first time I had ever felt confident about the performance of a horse before a race, the first time I began to think seriously about racing as a career.

Several weeks and several silent winning picks later, I broke my maiden on a horse called Flying Mercury. He was a retread sprinter that had once met top-class stock, but few people in the stands were able to appreciate his virtues (six outstanding workouts stretching back over a four-week period, all but one missing from the past performance records). Flying Mercury paid $78 to win, and I bought back my promise to my father with the proceeds of a $40 wager.

For the next two years I continued my studies into the mysteries of handicapping, keeping my losses to a minimum and my bets in perspective. But the Rutgers Dean of Men was not very pleased about my ragged classroom attendance, and he gave me a year off from school in September 1962, at the beginning of my senior year. In the true sense of the cliché, it turned out to be a blessing in disguise.

I visited racetracks in West Virginia, Louisiana, Ohio, Florida, New England, Michigan, Arkansas, Illinois, Maryland, California, New York, and New Jersey. Through those varied exposures and continued research, I detected two basic racetrack realities that seemed fundamental to handicapping. Yet I was sure that too few people in the stands were giving either of them the thought they deserved.

In the first place, I was surprised to learn that at many racetracks there was no way to measure the true class of horses by the claiming prices or race labels.

At most minor tracks, for example, a careful reading of result charts and race eligibility conditions suggested that there were five, six, or even seven separate class levels lumped into each claiming price. Moving up in company within a particular claiming price was frequently more difficult than ascending to the next claiming level.

At the major one-mile racetracks I frequently observed variations of this phenomenon in lower-level claiming events, maiden races, and non-claiming (allowance) races. Very often these observations pointed out winners that were not otherwise discernible.

Second, because each racing surface—man-made and considerably different—had specific peculiarities, some race results were predetermined, or at least heavily influenced, by those characteristics.

In sprints at Monmouth Park, for example, post positions were of no consequence on fast-track racing days, but following any rain the track did not (and still does not) dry out evenly.

On days like that the rail was so deep and tiring that posts one, two, and three were at a terrible disadvantage. Stretch runners breaking from the outer post positions won everything. (At the Fair Grounds in New Orleans, where water can be found less than ten feet below the surface, the drainage system created precisely the opposite effect.)

Indeed, at every racetrack on my itinerary I noticed an influential track bias at work at one or more distances. And at some tracks a particular bias was so strong and so predictable that all handicapping questions had to be directed toward finding out which horse would be helped, hurt, or eliminated by the peculiarities of the running surface.

Of course, most handicappers seemed well aware of the difference between sloppy, fast, and other moisture-related track conditions, and a few even knew that Aqueduct in July favored speedy, front-running types while Belmont in September seemed to be deeper, slower, and kinder to stretch runners; but my observations about track bias suggested a stronger relationship between the track and actual horse performance. What I discovered was a relationship that sometimes eliminated the best horse in the race from contention, or else helped to promote an otherwise modestly qualified contender into a logical race winner.

By thinking first in these terms, before trying to compare the relative talents of the horses in a specific race, I found myself consistently able to recognize solid horses at every racetrack, horses that frequently went to post at generous odds. *It was also possible to interpret results and past-performance lines more accurately when these horses ran back at a later date.*

With the first consistent profits of my handicapping career, I returned to Rutgers full of confidence.

On May 24, 1964, I finally did graduate from Rutgers, with a B.A. in psychology; but in truth it was only through the grace of my music professor, who raised my cumulative average to the passing level by changing a C to a B on the final day. Three weeks earlier the two of us accidentally met at Garden State Park, and he had a $280 reason to remember the event.

"I'm not doing this as a reward for your touting services," Professor Broome said while making the change of grade, "but I think you deserve some academic credit for your racing studies and this is the best I can do."

It was just enough.

3

The Horseplayer's Bible

In the early morning hours at racetracks coast to coast, from January to December, thousands of horses of varying abilities are out on the training track. In the afternoons and evenings thousands more compete in races for fillies, colts, sprinters, routers, maidens, claimers, allowances, and stakes. Some races are on the grass course, some on the dirt. Some tracks are fast; some are sloppy, muddy, or something in between. The possibilities are endless, the data voluminous. And at $3.00 per copy, most of it is all there in the *Daily Racing Form* in black and white.

Supah Gem
Own: Perez & Stephen

B. f. 3 (Mar)
Sire: Gold Meridian (Seattle Slew)
Dam: Jenny's Nandy (Great Above)
Br: Bush John (Fla)
Tr: Dollase Wallace (7 0 3 2 .00)

120

Lifetime Record:	18	5	2	5	$274,499						
1993	7	1	1	2	$56,509	Turf	2	0	1	0	$15,509
1992	11	4	1	3	$217,990	Wet	1	1	0	0	$7,100
SA	0	0	0	0		Dist	0	0	0	0	

21Oct93-8SA	fm	1 Ⓣ	:23^{3}	:47^{2}	1:11^{1}	1:35	3↑ ⒻAlw 55000N$mY	96	4	1	1½	1½	1^{hd}	2^{hd}	Nakatani C S	LB 113	17.70	90-10	Sacramentada117^{hd} Supah Gem113$^{1\frac{1}{2}}$ Euphonic117^{2}	Game try	5
15Sep93-3Dmr	fst	1$\frac{1}{16}$	:23	:46^{3}	1:11^{1}	1:42^{1}	· ⒻⓇTorrey Pines 55k	72	7	3	3$^{1\frac{1}{2}}$	3$^{1\frac{1}{2}}$	7^{9}	7$^{11\frac{3}{4}}$	Nakatani C S	LB 122	7.80	79-15	Adorydar115^{1} Glass Ceiling115½ Golden Klair116^{nk}	5 Wide stretch	7
15Aug93-10Crc	gd	*1⅛ Ⓣ				1:46^{4}	ⒻOffice Qn H 70k	77	2	2	2$^{2\frac{1}{2}}$	2$^{1\frac{1}{2}}$	4$^{1\frac{3}{4}}$	4$^{2\frac{3}{4}}$	Madrid S O	L 114 b	2.90	82-14	Urus114^{nk} Courageous Belle111^{nk} Koollanna111$^{2\frac{1}{4}}$	Faded	8
17Jly93-11Crc	fst	1^{70}	:23^{3}	:47	1:12^{1}	1:43	ⒻJudys R S H 50k	89	3	1	3^{1}	1^{hd}	2^{hd}	3^{2}	Lopez R D	L 117 b	2.40e	94-05	Kimscountrydiamond116$^{1\frac{1}{4}}$ ADemonADay113$^{\frac{3}{4}}$ SuphGem117^{3}	Weakened	8
3Feb93-9GP	fst	7f	:22^{1}	:45^{1}	1:10^{1}	1:23^{3}	ⒻFwd Gal B C-G2	67	3	6	5$^{2\frac{3}{4}}$	5$^{7\frac{1}{2}}$	7^{11}	8^{13}	Madrid S O	L 118 b	7.90	72-19	Sum Runner118$^{2\frac{1}{2}}$ Boots 'n Jackie121½ Lunar Spook118$^{3\frac{1}{2}}$	Faltered	9
17Jan93-10GP	fst	1$\frac{1}{16}$ ⊗	:22^{4}	:46^{2}	1:11^{4}	1:45^{3}	ⒻHcmsbrde 50k	82	7	3	2^{7}	2^{4}	2½	3^{2}	Madrid S O	L 116 b	2.60	80-21	Sigrun116$^{1\frac{1}{2}}$ So Say All Of Us112½ Supah Gem116^{4}		8
Brushed on final turn, brushed top of stretch																					
1Jan93-10Crc	gd	1$\frac{1}{16}$ ⊗	:24^{1}	:49^{2}	1:15	1:48^{2}	ⒻTro Pk Oaks 50k	88	2	1	1½	1^{1}	2^{hd}	1no	Madrid S O	L 117 b	2.70	79-19	Supah Gem117^{no} Sigrun117$^{4\frac{1}{2}}$ Miss Gold Peace117$^{1\frac{3}{4}}$	Fully extended	9
12Dec92-10Crc	fst	1$\frac{1}{16}$	:23^{4}	:49	1:14^{4}	1:47^{1}	ⒻBoca Raton 50k	79	4	4	4$^{3\frac{1}{2}}$	4^{2}	3$^{1\frac{1}{2}}$	3^{6}	Madrid S O	L 120 b	2.20	79-13	Sigrun115^{4} Lunar Spook120^{2} Supah Gem120$^{1\frac{1}{4}}$		10
Brushed stretch, lacked response																					
31Oct92-5GP	fst	1$\frac{1}{16}$	:23^{1}	:47	1:10^{3}	1:42^{4}	ⒻB C Juv Fil-G1	80	6	6	6$^{4\frac{3}{4}}$	6$^{7\frac{1}{4}}$	5$^{5\frac{3}{4}}$	4^{7}	Madrid S O	L 119 b	75.50	91-03	Eliza119^{1} Educated Risk119½ Boots 'n Jackie119$^{5\frac{1}{2}}$	Lugged in late	12
17Oct92-10Crc	fst	1$\frac{1}{16}$	:23^{3}	:48^{2}	1:13^{3}	1:46^{4}	ⒻⓇFla Stalion 410k	84	11	3	2^{hd}	1½	1^{2}	2$^{2\frac{1}{2}}$	Madrid S O	L 120 b	3.60	90-11	Boots 'n Jackie120$^{2\frac{1}{2}}$ Supah Gem120 Sigrun120	2nd best	13
The My Dear Girl Division																					
27Sep92-10Crc	fst	1^{70}	:23^{4}	:48^{2}	1:14^{1}	1:45	ⒻGardenia 76k	78	2	2	4$^{3\frac{1}{4}}$	4^{2}	1$^{3\frac{1}{2}}$	1^{2}	Madrid S O	L 114 b	10.00	88-12	Supah Gem114^{2} Boots 'n Jackie116^{6} Near the Edge112	Driving	11
7Sep92-7Crc	fst	7f	:22^{2}	:45^{2}	1:11^{4}	1:26	ⒻClm c-40000	69	2	6	4^{7}	4$^{5\frac{1}{2}}$	2½	1^{4}	Olivero C A^{5}	L 109 b	*1.70	85-09	Supah Gem109^{4} A Demon A Day116½ American Me112	Driving	6
Claimed from Bee Bee Stables Inc, Tortora Emanuel Trainer																					

WORKOUTS: ●Oct 17 **SA 5f fst :58^{4} H** *1/41* Oct 12 **SA 5f fst 1:00^{3} H** *17/51* Oct 6 **SA 4f fst :47^{1} H** *3/28* ●**Aug 31 Crc 5f fst 1:00 H** *1/17* **Aug 11 Crc Ⓣ 4f fm :46^{2} H** *1/1*

Most racegoers have no trouble recognizing the importance of past-performance profiles. The *DRF* p.p. shown on the previous page is a season's worth of racing history at a glance: the date, track, distance and track condition for every start; the fractional times of the leader and

EIGHTH RACE
Churchill
MAY 7, 1994

1¼ MILES. (1.59²) 120th Running of THE KENTUCKY DERBY. Grade I. Purse $500,000 Added. 3-year-olds. Entry fee of $10,000 each and a starting fee of $10,000 each. Supplemental nominations may be made in a ce with the rules upon payment of $150,000. All fees will be paid to the winner.

Value of Race: $878,800 Winner $628,800; second $145,000; third $70,000; fourth $35,000. Mutuel Pool $10,871,550.00 Exacta Pool $4,996,082.00 Trifecta Pool $2,779,675.00

Last Raced	Horse	M/Eqt.	A.	Wt	PP	¼	½	¾	1	Str	Fin	Jockey	Odds $1
16Apr94 9Aqu2	Go For Gin		3	126	8	2½	1½	11½	11½	14	12	McCarron C J	9.10
9Apr94 5SA3	Strodes Creek	Lb	3	126	7	7½	8hd	91	7hd	2hd	22½	Delahoussaye E	7.90
23Apr94 9OP2	Blumin Affair	L	3	126	13	10½	113	8½	61	5½	3¾	Bailey J D	14.90
9Apr94 5SA1	Brocco	L	3	126	10	91½	61	7½	4½	3½	41¼	Stevens G L	4.30
24Apr94 8Kee2	Soul Of The Matter	L	3	126	1	125	10½	102½	82	61	52½	Desormeaux K J	16.90
9Apr94 5SA2	Tabasco Cat	Lb	3	126	9	4½	41	51	51½	72	61¼	Day P	6.10
24Apr94 8Kee1	Southern Rhythm	Lf	3	126	12	14	134	133½	10½	93	71½	Gomez G K	20.00
2Apr94 11TP2	Powis Castle	Lb	3	126	3	31	3½	31	21	4hd	82	Antley C W	20.30
16Apr94 9Kee3	Mahogany Hall	L	3	126	6	13½	14	14	121½	11½	9½	Martinez W	f-16.70
9Apr94 8RP1	Smilin Singin Sam	Lb	3	126	11	11hd	91	2hd	31½	8½	102	Melancon L	f-16.70
3Apr94 11Hia1	Meadow Flight	L	3	126	14	81	122	11½	111½	10½	112	Sellers S J	f-16.70
16Apr94 9Kee1	Holy Bull		3	126	4	61½	51½	61½	92	124	122	Smith M E	2.20
16Apr94 9Kee2	Valiant Nature		3	126	2	5½	7½	123	138	1316	1315	Pincay L Jr	12.00
24Apr94 8Kee3	Ulises		3	126	5	1hd	21½	4hd	14	14	14	Chavez J F	f-16.70

f-Mutuel Field: Mahogany Hall and Smilin Singin Sam and Meadow Flight and Ulises.

OFF AT 5:34 Start Good. Won driving. Time, :22⁴, :47¹, 1:11⁴, 1:37³, 2:03³ Track sloppy.

$2 Mutuel Prices:				
	6–GO FOR GIN	20.20	8.40	5.80
	5–STRODES CREEK		7.80	6.00
	10–BLUMIN AFFAIR			8.00

EXACTA 6–5 PAID $184.80 TRIFECTA 6–5–10 PAID $2,351.40

B. c, (Apr), by Cormorant–Never Knock, by Stage Door Johnny. Trainer Zito Nicholas P. Bred by Darmstadt Pamela duPont (Ky).

GO FOR GIN ducked out after the start forcing TABASCO CAT into BROCCO, quickly reached contention when straightened away, took over entering the backstretch, was well in hand while managing a clear lead into the upper stretch, drew off quickly when roused, then held sway while drifting out in the final sixteenth as his rider took hold nearing the wire. STRODES CREEK, allowed to settle into the backstretch, angled out while rallying leaving the far turn, then finished well to best the others while racing six wide. BLUMIN AFFAIR commenced his rally approaching the end of the backstretch, made a run from between foes nearing midstretch but failed to sustain his bid. BROCCO, squeezed back at the start, moved within easy striking distance entering the backstretch, loomed a strong factor inside the leaders entering the stretch then weakened under pressure. SOUL OF THE MATTER, outrun to the far turn, made a mild bid between rivals through the upper stretch and flattened out. TABASCO CAT, forced into BROCCO at the start, quickly reached a striking position outside horses, remained a factor after moving inside on the second turn, but gave way in the drive. SOUTHERN RHYTHM broke to the inside and was outrun for a mile, then failed to threaten while finishing seven wide. POWIS CASTLE came out after bobbling at the start putting HOLY BULL in tight quarters, raced forwardly until the upper stretch and tired. MAHOGANY HALL, never close, clipped the heels of MEADOW FLIGHT after entering the stretch and stumbled badly. SMILIN SINGIN SAM lacked room after the start, advanced steadily approaching the far turn to make his bid but was finished entering the stretch. MEADOW FLIGHT was finished early. HOLY BULL, in tight after failing to break alertly, raced within easy striking distance to the far turn, then tired badly. VALIANT NATURE, away in good order, took up sharply along the inside racing into the first turn to avoid clipping heels, then gave way readily. ULISES showed speed until near the end of the backstretch and stopped badly. KANDALY WAS SCRATCHED AFTER THE FIFTH RACE BECAUSE OF TRACK CONDITION. ALL WAGERS IN THE STRAIGHT, PLACE, SHOW, EXACTA AND TRIFECTA POOLS WERE ORDERED REFUNDED. ALL PICK-THREE AND PICK-SIX WAGERS INVOLVING KANDALY WERE SWITCHED TO THE FAVORITE, HOLY BULL.

Owners— 1, Condren William & Cornacchia J; 2, Hancock & Rose Hill Stb & Whittgham; 3, Bowman Leroy & Vogel Arthur; 4, Broccoli Mr & Mrs Albert; 5, Bacharach Burt; 6, Overbrook Farm & Reynolds D P; 7, Heiligbrodt B & Keefer R & New W; 8, Vista Stable; 9, Hoeweler Robert; 10, Dogwood Stable; 11, Aliyuee Ben J Stables; 12, Croll Warren A Jr; 13, Winchell Verne H; 14, Perez Robert

Trainers—1, Zito Nicholas P; 2, Whittingham Charles; 3, Van Berg Jack C; 4, Winick Randy; 5, Mandella Richard; 6, Lukas D Wayne; 7, Keefer James O; 8, Rash Rodney; 9, Baker James E; 10, O'Callaghan Niall M; 11, Ryerson James T; 12, Croll Warren A Jr; 13, McAnally Ronald; 14, Callejas Alfredo

Scratched— Kandaly (16Apr94 9KEE4)

finishing time of the race winner; the class of the race, including the age and/or sex of the horses, the claiming price, or allowance purse and/or eligibility codes; the name, grade and/or purse of the stakes race; the Beyer speed figure; the post position, followed by the running line and finishing position, with margins and beaten lengths at each point of call; the jockey; the presence of legal drugs (Lasix and/or Butazolidin); the weight carried and special equipment used—such as blinkers, or front leg bandages; the post-time odds; *DRF* speed figures and track variants; first three finishers with margins and weights; plus a short "trip note" about how the horse performed, or if there had been traffic problems. Obviously, this is an incredible amount of information and it is presented in a powerfully compact format that has improved dramatically in recent years. But the p.p. is not the complete picture provided by other sources of information published in the same newspaper. The *Result Chart* (see previous page) is even more comprehensive and far more valuable.

While every race is being run in North America, a sharp-eyed *DRF* employee known as the "Trackman" gives a horse-by-horse call of the fast-paced action on the track to an attentive assistant. Presto, the result chart is born. Flash, it's over the wires to Hightstown, New Jersey; Phoenix, Arizona, Lexington, Kentucky and other cities where editions of the *Form* are put together.

At the chart desk at *DRF* offices each horse's running line is extracted from the chart and then added to its past-performance profile.

What many fans do not realize about this process hurts them every time they go out to the track.

Because of space limitations, much important information is lost in the transmission from chart to profile. Yet there is no reason any of this information should be lost to the player. Saving a set of chronologically dated result charts for the track(s) in your area is all that's required to fill in the missing information.

FIFTH RACE
Hollywood
JUNE 6, 1993

1⅛ MILES. (Turf) (1.57^{3}) CLAIMING. Purse $40,000. 4-year-olds and upward. Weight, 122 lbs. Non-winners of two races at a mile or over since April 18, allowed 3 lbs. Such a race since then, 6 lbs. Claiming Price $50,000 for each $2,500 to $45,000, 2 lbs. (Races when entered for $40,000 or less not considered)

Value of Race: $40,000 Winner $22,000; second $8,000; third $6,000; fourth $3,000; fifth $1,000. Mutuel Pool $342,522.00 Exacta Pool $318,283.00 Trifecta Pool $405,380.00

Last Raced	Horse	M/Eqt.	A.	Wt	PP	¼	½	¾	1	Str	Fin	Jockey	Cl'g Pr	Odds $1
7May93 ^{3}Hol^{3}	Military Shot	LB	6	116	11	11	11	11	10^{1}	5½	1^{nk}	Delahoussaye E	50000	5.20
1May93 ^{3}Hol^{7}	Intelligently	LBb	7	116	6	8^{2}	$8^{2\frac{1}{2}}$	$8^{1\frac{1}{2}}$	8½	7½	2¾	Solis A	50000	7.10
12Mar93 ^{5}SA^{11}	Very Vigors	LB	7	107	9	3½	2^{1}	2½	2½	1½	3½	Gulas L L^{5}	45000	82.00
30Apr93 ^{7}Hol^{4}	Fabulous Teaser-Fr	LBf	6	116	8	6^{2}	6^{3}	5^{hd}	6^{1}	4½	4^{2}	Black C A	50000	12.50
14May93 ^{8}Hol^{3}	Fire Top-GB	B	8	117	1	1^{1}	1^{1}	1½	1^{hd}	2^{hd}	5^{1}	Pincay L Jr	50000	6.10
14May93 ^{8}Hol^{5}	Cannon Man	LBb	7	113	4	5^{hd}	5½	6^{2}	5^{hd}	6½	6^{nk}	Flores D R	45000	13.70
13May93 ^{8}Hol^{4}	Scheimer-Fr	B	5	116	7	9^{2}	9^{3}	9^{2}	7^{1}	8½	7no	Nakatani C S	50000	2.30
29May93 ^{2}Hol^{2}	King Alain	LB	6	112	5	2^{hd}	$4^{1\frac{1}{2}}$	4^{1}	4^{1}	$9^{1\frac{1}{2}}$	$8^{1\frac{1}{4}}$	Garcia J A	45000	28.20
7May93 ^{3}Hol^{7}	Single Dawn	L	6	116	10	7½	7^{hd}	7^{hd}	9^{1}	10½	$9^{1\frac{1}{2}}$	Almeida G F	50000	15.70
21May93 ^{5}Hol^{6}	Kopelman-Fr	LB	5	114	3	10½	10^{hd}	10^{1}	11	11	10no	Lopez A D	45000	46.10
2Sep92 ^{5}Dmr^{8}	Houmayoun-Fr	LB	6	117	2	4^{2}	$3^{1\frac{1}{2}}$	$3^{1\frac{1}{2}}$	3½	3^{1}	11	Desormeaux K J	50000	4.20

OFF AT 3:38 Start Good. Won driving. Time, :24^{2}, :48^{4}, 1:13^{2}, 1:38, 2:02^{4} Course good.

$2 Mutuel Prices:			
12–MILITARY SHOT	12.40	5.80	4.40
7–INTELLIGENTLY		7.00	5.00
10–VERY VIGORS			16.00

$2 EXACTA 12-7 PAID $77.00 $2 TRIFECTA 12-7-10 PAID $4,595.40

B. g, by Lyphard's Wish-Fr–Pavahra, by Mummy's Pet. Trainer Harte Michael G. Bred by Ransom Richard K (Ky).

MILITARY SHOT, far back early and wide down the backstretch, came into the stretch seven wide, closed strongly and prevailed by a small margin. INTELLIGENTLY, devoid of early speed, was boxed in turning into the stretch, rallied in the drive and lost a close decision. VERY VIGORS, always prominent, entered the stretch five wide and gained the show in a good effort. FABULOUS TEASER, outrun early but not far back, loomed menacingly on the far turn, was boxed in turning into the stretch, entered the stretch four wide, threatened through the drive but did not have the needed late response. FIRE TOP, a pace factor from the beginning, weakened a bit late. CANNON MAN, never far back, lacked the needed punch in the drive. SCHEIMER, devoid of early speed, failed to generate the required rally and was four wide into the stretch. KING ALAIN, in contention early and wide down the backstretch, did not have the needed response in the final quarter and was six wide into the stretch. SINGLE DAWN was five wide into the stretch. KOPELMAN was six wide into the stretch. HOUMAYOUN, close up early, pressed the issue on the far turn and early in the drive before he gave way. PALOS VERDES (6) was scratched by the stewards. All wagers on him in the mutuel, exacta and trifecta pools were ordered refunded and all of his pick six, place pick nine and triple selections were switched to the favorite, SCHEIMER (8).

Owners— 1, Dye Jr & Tabor Trust; 2, Gann Edmund A; 3, Meredith Helen; 4, Segal & Sloan & Xitco; 5, Clear Valley Stables; 6, Chow & Heflin; 7, Craig Sidney H; 8, Sahl China L; 9, Cooke Jack Kent; 10, Flying A Farms; 11, Blue Vista Inc

Trainers—1, Harte Michael G; 2, Frankel Robert; 3, Meredith Derek; 4, Canani Julio C; 5, Shulman Sanford; 6, Hess R B Jr; 7, McAnally Ronald; 8, Van Berg Jack C; 9, Smithwick Daniel M Jr; 10, Hess R B Jr; 11, Frankel Robert

Overweight: Fire Top-GB (1), Cannon Man (1), Kopelman-Fr (2), Houmayoun-Fr (1).

Scratched— Palos Verdes (16May93 ^{6}GG^{3})

If you give a careful reading to the chart and compare it with Fabulous Teaser's June 6 running line, you will discover several missing facts to complement the expanded past-performance lines:

1. Specific eligibility conditions for the race
2. Fractional clockings for *each* quarter mile, plus up to three addi-

tional fractional clockings depending on their availability and/or the distance involved. (p.p.'s show only three fractional splits and the final time, regardless of distance.)

3. The relative running position at the start of the race in races up to 1³⁄₁₆ miles, or the first ½-mile running position for races up to 1⅝ miles. (In past performances, the start only is included in sprint race running lines. In routes beyond 1⅝ miles, the start *and* first ¼-mile call are eliminated in the p.p.'s.)

4. In result charts, the first point of call includes the horse's position and a margin notation (lengths ahead of the field, or in front of the next horse). In p.p.'s, margins for the first call only appear in sprint running lines.

5. Exact age, weight, odds, jockey, owner, running pattern, finishing position for the entire field.

6. Index date, track, race number and finishing position for the entire field's most recent races.

7. Purse value of all races including claiming, maiden and stakes races, which are sometimes missing from the p.p.'s. (Purses are included only for allowance races and stakes in p.p.'s.)

8. Complete trackman's commentary, on how the race was run, plus stewards' rulings and scratches, if any, are included in the footnotes to the chart.

9. Opportunity to compare a day's worth of result charts for the relative speed of the racing surface, or to get more specific weather information, or to detect potential patterns as to the way races are being run.

10. An assortment of additional facts, including complete pari-mutuel payouts.

NOTE: *In result charts, the margins at each call refer to the margin* in front of the next horse. *In past performance profiles, the margins* indicate *lengths behind the leader. For an easy reference guide to all symbols found in* DRF *result charts and past performances, see the expanded Appendix A at the end of this book.*

While each edition of the *Form* publishes complete result charts for all tracks covered by past performances plus out-of-town stakes, the cost-conscious, once-a-week horseplayer can keep pace with the doings at his favorite track through condensed charts appearing in the sports section of a good local newspaper. By ignoring these charts, you will forfeit your best chance to advance your game.

Fine-line decisions are intrinsic to the handicapping process, and result charts invariably present more clues to the right side of the line than the p.p.'s. Sometimes these additional clues provide an insight or an excuse for a recent defeat, or force a reappraisal of a horse's physical condition. Sometimes they point out an extra dimension of quality not otherwise detectable from the past performances. The following two race result charts speak volumes to the point I am making. The first is one of my all-time favorites. The salient points are underlined.

SIXTH RACE
Garden State
NOVEMBER 9, 1972

1 1/16 MILES. (1.41) ALLOWANCE. Purse $6,000. 3-year-olds and upward which have not wontwo races of $5,200 at a mile or over since June 15. 3-year-olds, 119 lbs. Older 122 lbs. Non-winners of three races of $4,225 at a mile or over since May 15 allowed 3 lbs. such a race of $3,900 since then, 5 lbs. such a race of $4,225 since April 15, 7 lbs. (Maiden, claiming and starter races not considered). (Originally carded to be run at 1 1/16 Miles, Turf.)

Value of race $6,000, value to winner $3,600, second $1,200, third $660, fourth $360, fifth $180. Mutuel pool $114,235.

Last Raced	Horse	Eqt.A.Wt	PP	St	¼	½	¾	Str	Fin	Jockey	Odds $1
23Oct72 ^{8}GS^{6}	Laplander	b 5 119	5	5	6	5^{hd}	5^{6}	4^{4}	$1^{3\frac{1}{2}}$	Barrera C	2.70
21Oct72 ^{9}CT^{6}	Test Run	6 119	3	1	2^{2}	2^{3}	4^{hd}	2^{hd}	$2\frac{1}{2}$	Keene J	20.50
21Oct72 ^{8}Lrl^{2}	Seminole Joe	4 119	4	3	$3^{1\frac{1}{2}}$	4^{6}	$1\frac{1}{2}$	$1\frac{1}{2}$	3^{1}	Iannelli F	7.30
21Oct72 ^{6}Lrl^{1}	Duc by Right	b 5 119	2	2	1^{2}	1^{2}	$2\frac{1}{2}$	3^{hd}	$4\frac{1}{2}$	Moseley J W	4.40
27Oct72 ^{8}GS^{6}	Warino	b 4 119	7	4	4^{2}	$3\frac{1}{2}$	$3^{1\frac{1}{2}}$	5^{6}	5^{6}	Hole M	3.30
27Sep72 ^{8}Atl^{6}	Roundhouse	b 4 119	1	6	5^{2}	6	6	6	6	Tejeira J	16.70
23Oct72 ^{8}Aqu^{3}	Prince of Truth	b 4 122	6	7	—	—	—	—	—	Blum W	2.20

Prince of Truth, Lost rider.

Time, :23⅘, :47⅕, 1:12⅗, 1:39⅕, 1:45⅘ Track slow.

$2 Mutuel Prices:				
	5-LAPLANDER	7.40	4.20	2.80
	3-TEST RUN		11.00	4.60
	4-SEMINOLE JOE			4.20

B. g, by Assemblyman—Reindeer, by Polynesian. Trainer Kulina J. Bred by Fowler A (Md).
IN GATE AT 2:55; OFF AT 2:55 EASTERN STANDARD TIME Start Good For All But PRINCE OF TRUTH Won Driving

LAPLANDER, forced to steady and steer wide to avoid a loose horse inside of him entering the clubhouse turn, fell back, recovered gradually nearing the end of the backstretch, circled rivals rallying into the stretch, again steadied and moved inside to miss the loose horse, gained command leaving the furlong grounds and gradually drew clear. TEST RUN pressed the early pace, reached close contention from the inside in upper stretch was in tight a furlong out and faltered. SEMINOLE JOE was forced to check lightly by the loose horse entering the clubhouse turn, recovered quickly, reached the lead from the outside nearing the stretch, came in when intimidated by the loose horse a furlong out, was straightened away and faltered. DUC BY RIGHT went to the front at once, drew clear and was tiring when placed in close quarters between horses by SEMINOLE JOE in the drive. A claim of foul lodged by the rider of DUC BY RIGHT against the rider of SEMINOLE JOE was not allowed. WARINO was forced wide into the first turn, was taken in hand, rallied to reach close contention from the outside entering the stretch and tired. ROUNDHOUSE was never a factor. PRINCE OF TRUTH stumbled and unseated his rider at the start, raced with his field and caused repeated interference.

Owners— 1, Buckingham Farm; 2, Oliver & Stanley; 3, Sugar Mill Farm; 4, Haffner Mrs H Y; 5, Nesbitt H J; 6, Brandywine Stable; 7, Tucker J R.
Trainers— 1, Kulina J; 2, Oliver D; 3, Stirling W Jr; 4, Wahler C; 5, Cocks W; 6, Raines V W; 7, Jennings L W.
Scratched—Best Go (18Sep72 ^{8}Atl^{8}); Vif (27Oct72 ^{8}GS^{8}).

On the day Laplander was playing tag with a riderless horse at Garden State Park, a claiming horse named Third Law was giving Maryland racing fans a first-class impersonation of Emmitt Smith.

Armed with the Trackman's notes about the winner in each of these two races, we should have no difficulty imagining that Laplander and Third Law were able to step up sharply in company and win with ridiculous ease shortly thereafter. It is not stretching the point to say that a few equally revealing charts a season could more than pay for the cost of a subscription to the *Form*.

FOURTH RACE
Laurel
NOVEMBER 9, 1972

7 FURLONGS. ($1.22\frac{1}{5}$) CLAIMING. Purse $7,150, of which $650 to breeder of winner. 3-year-olds, Registered Maryland-Breds. Weights, 122 lbs. Non-winners of two races since September 18, allowed 2 lbs. A race since then, 4 lbs. A race since September 11, 6 lbs. Claiming price $12,500; for each $1,000 to $10,500, 2 lbs. (Races where entered for $9,500 or less not considered.)

Value of race $7,150, value to winner $3,900, second $1,430, third $780, fourth $390; $650 to Breeder of Winner. Mutuel pool $87,225.

Last Raced	Horse	Eqt.	A. Wt	PP	St	¼	½	Str	Fin	Jockey	Cl'g Pr	Odds $1
20Oct72 ^{4}Lrl^{6}	Third Law		3 116	7	2	7^{hd}	$7\frac{1}{2}$	$4\frac{1}{2}$	1^{1}	Jimenez C	12500	40.60
29Sep72 ^{8}Bel^{6}	Admiral Kelly	b	3 118	1	8	$2\frac{1}{2}$	1^{hd}	2^{2}	$2\frac{1}{2}$	Turcotte R L	12500	4.10
24Oct72 ^{6}Lrl^{1}	All Above		3 119	3	1	1^{hd}	$2^{1\frac{1}{2}}$	1^{hd}	3^{hd}	Feliciano B M	12500	1.40
24Oct72 ^{5}Lrl^{7}	Rigel	b	3 116	4	6	$5\frac{1}{2}$	$3\frac{1}{2}$	3^{hd}	$4\frac{3}{4}$	Passmore W J	12500	6.10
4Nov72 ^{4}Lrl^{1}	Gunner's Mate	b	3 113	8	3	6^{4}	6^{2}	6^{3}	5^{1}	Cusimano G	10500	4.90
24Oct72 ^{5}Lrl^{8}	Go Bet		3 116	2	4	$3\frac{1}{2}$	4^{hd}	5^{hd}	$6^{2\frac{1}{4}}$	Kurtz J	12500	22.70
2Nov72 ^{8}Lrl^{5}	Hoosier Grand		3 116	6	7	8	8	7^{3}	$7^{3\frac{1}{2}}$	Wright D R	12500	6.40
3Nov72 ^{5}Lrl^{7}	Sky Flight		3 116	5	5	$4\frac{1}{2}$	$5^{2\frac{1}{2}}$	8	8	Alberts B	11500	12.90

Time, :$23\frac{3}{5}$, :47, 1:13, 1:26 Track fast.

$2 Mutuel Prices:

7-THIRD LAW	83.20	20.60	5.80
1-ADMIRAL KELLY		5.80	3.60
3-ALL ABOVE			3.20

B. g, by Quadrangle—Flighty Jane, by Count Fleet. Trainer Green P F. Bred by Kelly Mrs L C (Md).
IN GATE AT 2:28; OFF AT 2:28 EASTERN STANDARD TIME. Start Good. Won Driving.

THIRD LAW, away in good order but without early speed, had to check stoutly behind horses on the stretch turn, went to the rail entering the stretch, responded strongly when set down, had to pull sharply outside ADMIRAL KELLY for racing room a furlong out but continued strongly to gain command and draw clear in the final seventy yards. ADMIRAL KELLY, away a bit slowly, was hustled up to force the pace inside all above before a quarter, got the lead leaving the backstretch, lost and regained it inside all above in the stretch, then could not resist the winner's closing bid while tiring near the end. ALL ABOVE set or forced the pace outside ADMIRAL KELLY throughout but hung slightly near the end. RIGEL, always in contention, responded between horses in the final quarter but was not good enough. GUNNER'S MATE did not threaten with a mild closing response. GO BET gave an even effort. HOOSIER GRAND showed little. SKY FLIGHT had only brief early speed.

Owners— 1, Master's Cave; 2, Audley Farm Stable; 3, Lee C; 4, Leonard R A; 5, Green Lantern Stable; 6, DiNatale J; 7, Hunt R R; 8, Berry C T Jr.

Trainers— 1, Green P F; 2, Thomas G; 3, Lee C; 4, Hacker B P; 5, Delp G G; 6, Bannon J T; 7, Vogelman R E Jr; 8, Simpson J P.

Overweight: Gunner's Mate 1 pound.

Good chartcallers are easy to spot because they clearly report the flow of the race while spelling out which horses were blocked or lucky to get through, or which ones made runs four and five wide, and/or were on the inside part of the racetrack.

Jack Wilson, field supervisor for the *DRF*, who still calls the Kentucky Derby chart, was one of the most precise chartcallers I have ever read, while Jon White, the southern California chartcaller who left the *DRF* in 1993, was by far the most descriptive. Retired Bill Phillips of Maryland was the most insightful. Most contemporary chartcallers do an adequate job, but seem to lose their zest for the task after four or five years of calling 9, 10, or 11 races per day, 300 or more days a year. In today's game, the player should be prepared to supplement all chartcaller footnotes with his or her own observations gleaned from live viewings and examination of the video tape replays.

We are barely scratching the surface. With a little research and a few investigative tools, we may improve the power of result charts; we may add information to them, or supplement them with other clues and insights. Through these supplemental tools we will increase our understanding of the horse, the track and the nature of the game.

The Bias of the Racing Surface

Suppose someone walked up to you and said he knew a roulette wheel in a Las Vegas casino that was rigged in the player's favor. The wheel paid the customary 32–1 odds for a correct number but seldom stopped on any number higher than 20. I am sure you would have trouble believing it.

With a few important variations, that is precisely what I am about to tell you about the majority of racetracks in America. *Some numbers rarely win.*

At Pimlico racecourse in Baltimore, Maryland, where the first turn is less than a stone's throw from the starting gate in 1$\frac{1}{16}$-mile races, horses with sprint speed and inside post positions have a ready-made shot at saving ground and a clear-cut winning edge. Conversely, horses forced to break from post positions nine, ten, eleven, or twelve in such races have to be far superior and perfectly ridden to remain in contention. And there are many racetracks in America with a bias like that. Aqueduct in New York (1$\frac{1}{8}$ miles on the main track, 1$\frac{1}{16}$ miles on the winterized inner dirt track) is a well-known example. But the Fair Grounds in New Orleans and Churchill Downs in Louisville are rarely considered in similar light.

Most players approach two-turn races at these two racetracks with an eye toward the fast-closing distance-type runner. It's hard to think otherwise while two of the longest stretch runs in American racing are in full view (each is in excess of 1250 feet). But these are two extremely elongated racetracks, with radically sharp turns. And the starting gate is frequently positioned so close to the first bend that the race is over before the stretch comes into play. A player who knows that about the Fair Grounds and Churchill may not pick the winner of every two-turn race, but very often he will be able to plot the way a race is likely to be run. In addition, he will catch many well-meant speed types outrunning their apparent distance limitations.

And there are other kinds of biases worth knowing about. At Philadelphia Park in Pennsylvania, and at all other cold-weather tracks, extra layers of topsoil are frequently mixed with antifreeze agents to keep the racing surface from turning into a sheet of ice. The effort usually is successful, but not always; sometimes the rail is like a paved highway, and sometimes it's a slushy path to a quick and certain defeat.

No doubt it would be superfluous to spell out the impact such aberrant track conditions have on horse performance, so I won't. But I will say that a handicapper will probably think about throwing away his *Racing Form* if he doesn't take note of them. Indeed, if there is one pervasive influence on the handicapping experience, *track bias* comes very close to filling the bill. While it isn't fair to say that all races are won and lost because of the influence of a biased racing strip, the player can hardly hope to make consistently accurate predictions without weighing its significance. For instance, at Bay Meadows Racetrack in northern California, through much of the 1992–93 meeting, there was an on-again, off-again track bias favorable to outside runners. This compromised the chances of every horse who was forced to race along the deeper footing nearest the inner rail. These conditions, relatively rare in American racing, practically replicated conditions encountered during the 1960s and 1970s at Saratoga, the beautiful track in upstate New York which annually runs an historic 30-34-day August meet.

The Saratoga of the 1960s and 1970s featured a soft, deep racing surface biased in the extreme toward outer post positions and stretch-running types. This not only contrasted dramatically with the front-running, relatively fast track in use at Aqueduct during that era, it contributed greatly to Saratoga's reputation as a "graveyard for favorites."

Confronted with a typical Saratoga race, too many players were overly impressed with front-running winners shipping up from Aqueduct, a track that was usually pasteboard hard and front-running fast during July. At Saratoga, however, very few front runners were able to duplicate their Aqueduct form, as race after race went to horses with the best late kick. In those days it was relatively easy to eliminate many short-priced front runners in favor of underbet late movers. Unfortunately, this clear-cut tendency did not last forever, and the shift that occurred in the mid-1970s totally changed the handicapping game at the nation's oldest track.

In 1974, a new, faster racing strip was installed, which turned Saratoga into a front-runner's paradise. Suddenly the Saratoga player had to respect horses with Aqueduct form; the two tracks were nearly identical. Both favored fast-breaking types—horses able to get a clear trip on the faster rail path.

This edge to fast-breaking runners has persisted at Saratoga through two decades and is the predominant tendency influencing form at most American tracks—especially west of the Rocky Mountains, where racing is conducted on glib surfaces that do not get as much rainfall as Eastern tracks. As fellow author Bill Quirin aptly noted in a 1983 seminar in Los Angeles, "early speed is the universal track bias of contemporary American racing."

Quirin's theorem seems especially true during specific time periods in long seasons, or when the track cushion—about 3½ inches of top soil—is routinely sealed, or packed down with heavy rollers to protect it from impending rainfall. The technique also is utilized to speed up a racing surface, to create artificially fast race clockings, a dubious practice as old as the game itself.

Rolling the track to assist drainage may be sound maintenance strategy, but packing it down to produce aberrently fast clockings is potentially dangerous to horses and jockeys. Sadly, this latter practice is tacitly approved by track stewards and racing commissions in every state.

Good handicappers may adjust their overall selection methods to incorporate an unusually fast, severely biased racing strip, but only the most alert players in the crowd will anticipate the defeat of a highly fancied favorite in a major stakes. In 1991 there were two dramatic instances a continent apart which made national headlines, each demonstrating the extreme power of a one-dimensional, artificially induced track bias.

The 1991 Super Derby, represented by the chart below, was won by Louisiana-bred Free Spirit's Joy, who hugged an extremely fast inside path every step of the 1¼ miles to defeat the classy Olympio. Olympio may have been tons the best horse and as fit as a Stradivarius, but he was powerless to overcome a modestly talented front-running rival who was perfectly ridden by local jockey Calvin Borel.

Borel was in tune with the tricked-up Louisiana Downs' racing strip which had produced numerous wire-to-wire winners all day.

---

1 ¼ MILES. (2.00¹) 12th Running SUPER DERBY

Value of race $1,000,000; value to winner $600,000; second $200,000; third $110,000; fourth $60,000; fifth $30,000. Mutuel pool $280,286. Exacta pool $190,288. Trifecta pool $55,440.

Last Raced	Horse	M/Eqt.A.Wt	PP	¼	½	¾	1	Str	Fin	Jockey	Odds $1
13Sep91 9LaD1	Free Spirit's Joy	Lb	3 126	5	2⁵	2¹⁰	2⁴	1½	1²	12½	Borel C H	28.50
2Sep91 8AP2	Olympio	L	3 126	3	1½	11½	1hd	2²	21½	2¹	Delahoussaye E	1.90
11Sep91 8AP2	Zeeruler	L	3 126	2	41½	5¹	5¹	4½	3½	3³	Pettinger D R	53.40
10Aug91 3Dmr1	Best Pal	L	3 126	4	3⁵	3⁵	3⁷	3²	4⁵	4⁶	Valenzuela P A	.90
2Sep91 8Bel4	Lost Mountain	b	3 126	6	51½	4½	4hd	6⁸	5¹	53½	Perret C	10.20
1Sep91 8Dmr3	Lite Light	L	3 123	7	6⁴	6⁴	6⁵	51½	6⁵	61½	Nakatani C S	3.80
2Sep91 10LaD3	Far Out Wadleigh	L	3 126	1	7	7	7	7	7	7	Walker B J Jr	92.60

OFF AT 4:45. Start good. Won driving. Time, :23¹, :46², 1:11 , 1:36 , 2:00⁴ Track fast.

$2 Mutuel Prices:

5-FREE SPIRIT'S JOY	59.00	10.40	5.20
3-OLYMPIO		3.80	3.40
2-ZEERULER			8.00

$3 EXACTA (5-3) PAID $253.80. $3 TRIFECTA (5-3-2) PAID $2,608.20.

B. g, (Apr), by Joey Bob—Rays Joy, by Staunch Avenger. Trainer Picou Clarence E. Bred by Karabaic N–Bucsko R & Lane J (La).

FREE SPIRIT'S JOY sprinted clear and to the inside, allowed OLYMPIO the advantage before a quarter, moved up inside that one with a half mile to go, challenged, shook off OLYMPIO in upper stretch, and drew clear under steady urging. OLYMPIO eased back a bit and angled outside FREE SPIRIT'S JOY in the initial furlongs, moved up outside that one before a quarter to gain a short lead, opened a clear advantage before a half, responded willingly when engaged by that same rival with a half mile to go, continued well to the stretch, could not stay with the winner, and held sway for the place. ZEERULER, reserved for six furlongs off the inside, commenced his rally inside on the second turn, was angled out a bit approaching the stretch, bumped BEST PAL in midstretch, then lacked a late bid. BEST PAL, behind the leaders off the inside approaching the second turn, continued off the inside into the stretch, was bumped by ZEERULER in midstretch, and tired. LOST MOUNTAIN made a run between rivals after six furlongs, but could not sustain the bid. LITE LIGHT, unhurried early, made a run three wide to within striking distance approaching the stretch, but gave way. FAR OUT WADLEIGH was outrun.

Owners— 1, Free Spirit's Stable; 2, Winchell Verne H Jr; 3, J & J Racing Stable; 4, Golden Eagle Farm; 5, Loblolly Stable; 6, Oaktown Stable; 7, Wadleigh Ralph.

Trainers— 1, Picou Clarence E; 2, McAnally Ronald; 3, Von Hemel Donnie K; 4, Jones Gary; 5, Bohannan Thomas; 6, Hollendorfer Jerry; 7, Frederick Raymond.

A few weeks after the Super Derby, at Bay Meadows, longshot Admirallus and Charts dueled with each other throughout 1⅛ miles on a racetrack that had produced a succession of front-running winners for nearly a week. (This was the same Bay Meadows track that would produce a succession of outside, stretch-running winners for more than two months the following season.) Try as he might, 2–5 shot Sea Cadet floundered in third place in the middle of the course on a stone-cold, inside-speed-favoring track that left trainer Ron McAnally shaking his head after enduring another bias-induced defeat. McAnally, you see, also trained Olympio.

It is interesting to add that Sea Cadet resumed his winning ways when McAnally shipped him to Florida for two convincing scores over top Eastern handicap horses at Gulfstream Park, and Olympio posted a sharp victory in a top level Graded stakes when shipped back to southern California. Free Spirit's Joy, however, was through for the year, injuring himself in training shortly after his Super Derby triumph. Admirallus too, failed to win a race for more than a year.

```
Sea Cadet                         B. c. 4, by Bolger—Hattab Gal, by Al Hattab                 Lifetime      1992  5  3  1  1   $932,500
                                  Br.—Winchell V H–Katalpa Farm (Ky)                          23 10  4  5   1991 10  4  1  3   $679,800
Own.—Winchell V H                 Tr.—McAnally Ronald  (—)                            121     $1,705,150
16Oct92-10Medfst 1⅛  :461 1:094 1:48  3↑Med Cup H   108 6 3 31  1hd 13  11¾ Solis A       L  120  1.90e  92-13 SeCdet1201¾VlleyCrossing1114AmericnChnc109 Driving 10
    16Oct92-Grade I
11Apr92- 8OP fst 1⅛  :46  1:094 1:48    Oaklawn H     119 3 3 31½ 31½ 2½  21½ Solis A       L  120  4.30   94-20 BestPal1251½SeaCadet120½TwilightAgend123 4 wide 1/4 7
    11Apr92-Grade I
7Mar92-10GP fst 1¼   :473 1:363 2:013 3↑G'strm Pk H 120 4 2 22  12  15  17  Solis A       L  119  *1.20  93-14 SeCdt1197StrikthGold1152½SunnySunris114 Ridden out 6
    7Mar92-Grade I
1Feb92- 9GP fst 1⅛   :464 1:101 1:48  3↑Donn H      116 1 2 23  22  11½ 13  Solis A       L  115  2.50   97-12 SeCdet1153OutofPlce114nkSunnySunrise115 Drew clear 8
    1Feb92-Grade I
11Jan92- 9BM gd 1⅛   :462 1:103 1:492   W P Kyne H    108 6 5 42½ 33  35  37  Solis A       LB 124  *.40   82-27 Admirallus115hd Charts1137 Sea Cadet124 Wide, evenly 7
    11Jan92-Grade III
24Nov91- 8Hol fst 1 1/16 :451 1:094 1:421 L S Barra H  103 7 4 34½ 1hd 16  18  Pedroza M A   LB 122  *.50   90-19 SeCdet1228Multiengin116noWhtASpll116 Class showed 7
    .24Nov91-Grade III
18Oct91-10Medfst 1⅛  :463 1:101 1:463 3↑Med Cup H   113 6 2 21  2hd 1hd 31¾ Solis A       L  115  7.80   100-06 Twilight Agenda121nk Scan1161½ Sea Cadet115 Tired 9
    18Oct91-Grade I
20Sep91- 9Medfst 1⅛  :46  1:093 1:462   Pegasus H     113 8 2 1hd 2hd 21½ 21¾ Solis A       L  119  1.90   101-07 Scan1191¾ Sea Cadet1194 Sultry Song114 Game effort 8
    20Sep91-Grade I
11Aug91-10Lga fst 1 3/16 :464 1:11 1:551  Lga Dby      115 6 2 31½ 1hd 13  111½ Solis A      LB 123  *.40   97-24 SeaCdet123111½MjorHowey1234IceInSpce123 Much best 6
13Jly91- 8Hol fst 1 1/16 :452 1:09 1:401 3↑Bel Air H  109 5 3 32½ 31½ 33½ 33¾ McCarron C J LB 114  3.40   96-06 TwilightAgend116¾Timebnk1183SCdt114 5-wide stretch 5
    13Jly91-Grade II
LATEST WORKOUTS   Nov 18 SA  5f fst :591 H     ●Nov 13 SA  7f fst 1:261 H     Oct 11 Bel  7f fst 1:252 H
```

```
Admirallus                Dk. b. or br. g. 6, by Hail Emperor—Sailing Leader, by Mr Leader           Lifetime     1993  1  0  0  1    $6,300
BLACK C A (61 5 9 5 .08)      $62,500  Br.—Manfuso Robert T (Md)                                      22 5 5 5     1992  5  1  1  1   $67,200
Own.—Lansdburg & Waranch               Tr.—Cerin Vladimir  (16 2 3 4 .13)                     115     $173,515     Turf  5  0  0  2   $14,025
3Jan93- 2SA gd 1     :462 1:111 1:371     Clm 75000    92 4 2 2hd 11  1½  31½ Black C A        LB 115 *2.10  82-18 EmplrLdr1171½DrOfF-Ir115noAdrlls115 Nipped for 2nd 7
    3Jan93-Originally scheduled on turf
11Dec92- 8Hol fst 1 1/16 :461 1:104 1:42  3↑Clm 80000  96 1 3 2½  1hd 1hd 21¾ Valenzuela P A   LB 117 *1.40  89-13 TrtTobtyft1151¾Admrllus1175½Journlsm119 Good effort 5
26Nov92- 7Hol fm 1⅛ Ⓣ:48 1:112 1:472  3↑Clm 62500    92 3 3 31½ 31½ 41½ 34¼ Valenzuela P A   LB 118 7.70   83-14 DrmOfFm-Ir1192¾PrdOfArby1191½Admrllus118 Rail trip 6
8Nov92- 5SA fm *6½f Ⓣ:213 :44 1:133   3↑Clm 80000    71 8 7 63  73¼ 98½ 911 Valenzuela P A   LB 118 13.60  80-09 ThGd-NZ116nkSftshSrSt1162½Trts-Fr116 5-wide stretch 11
7Jun92- 8Hol fst 1⅛  :461 1:10  1:48  3↑Californian  65 2 5 54¼ 64  69½ 724¼ Alvarado F T    LB 115 21.60  70-14 AnotherReview1191¾DfnsivPly1202Ibro-Ar119 Gave way 7
    7Jun92-Grade I
11Jan92- 9BM gd 1⅛   :462 1:103 1:492     W P Kyne H  119 2 2 31  22  2hd 1hd Judice J C       LB 115 13.30  89-27 Admirallus115hdCharts1137SeaCadet124 Closed gamely 7
    11Jan92-Grade III
21Dec91- 7Hol fst 1 1/16 :454 1:094 1:413 3↑Handicap 103 2 3 34  31½ 2hd 31¼ Stevens G L      B  115 6.20   92-15 Tokatee119¾ Perforce118½ Admirallus115 Hung 8
20Nov91- 8Hol fst 7½f :231 :454 1:282 3↑Alw 36000     93 2 4 2hd 1hd 11  13  Valenzuela P A   B  116 *1.90  — — Admirallus1163QuiDnzig115hdHoofer119 Driving, inside 7
6Nov91- 7SA fm 1⅛ Ⓣ:47 1:101 1:461    3↑Alw 40000   100 2 3 31½ 31½ 32  31  Desormeaux K J   B  115 8.90   92-07 MdumCool115½PrdOfArby119½Admrllus115 Good effort 6
20Oct91-11Fno fst 1⅛ :474 1:114 1:482 3↑Harvest H     85 1 3 2hd 2hd 53½ 54  Judice J C       B  116 5.30   92-10 CoolGoldMood1201DsrtLovr1111CbrClssc118 Weakened 8
LATEST WORKOUTS   Dec 24 SA  5f fst 1:011 H     Dec 5 SA  5f fst 1:01 H     ●Nov 19 SA  5f fst :59 H
```

Although many players have gained an understanding of track bias since the concept was detailed in the original *Betting Thoroughbreds* in 1978, some also have come to overemphasize it in their handicapping. Spotting two or three wire-to-wire winners in a row does not constitute inviolate evidence of a bias in action. Nor should it be concluded from a pair of stretch-running winners that the reverse is true. Yet it is a simple fact that every racing surface has clearly defined peculiarities and biases that come into periodic play at varying strength. Far from posing an insurmountable handicapping problem, these tendencies or biases provide observent horseplayers with sound reasons to upgrade, downgrade, or eliminate numerous horses in many races.

After fine-tuning this concept for nearly 30 years, it is my conviction that players who prepare in advance will be in the best position to detect a true track bias. For instance, knowing which horses have fainthearted speed and which ones have wire-to-wire speed is fundamental to assessing the strength of a speed-favoring track. If three or four fainthearted types stick around much longer than they usually do in each of the first two races on the card, I would be willing to make an immediate adjustment in my handicapping to reflect the tendency. When a bias is asserting itself, it is virtually impossible to handicap races effectively without taking it into account. But why worry? A true track bias of any strength is the player's best friend.

Knowledge of the way a track is playing will help underline the weaknesses of those who perform well when conditions are in their favor. It will help point out hidden strengths of horses who may have had to overcome a post position, or running-style bias. Armed with such insight, players will find past-performance lines easier to interpret. Lacking it, players will find themselves tossing away their *Forms* in disgust after a series of inexplicable defeats.

Make no mistake, biases are part of the racing mix, but there is no rule of thumb, no law of nature that says that a given bias must remain the same from day to day, week to week, season to season. On the contrary, as shown by the transformation of the Saratoga racing surface three decades ago and the Bay Meadows strip in the 1990s, any bias can be dramatically altered by changes in track design, track maintenance, or sudden shifts in weather.

When Calder Racetrack in Florida installed an artificial racing strip in the 1960s, I made a special note to follow any horse who ran the first half mile of a sprint in 46 seconds and change—which is not especially fast. Such horses couldn't win many races at Calder—the track was powerfully tilted toward stretch-running speed—but if and when the stable kept such a speedball fit enough to get a crack at Hialeah or Gulfstream Park, it was fat city.

Today, the Calder to Gulfstream angle still works because Gulfstream has the kind of glib racing surface speed horses dream about. At the same time, a fit front-running Calder horse no longer is an automatic throwout; a half mile in 46⅗ seconds no longer is a viable yardstick for excellence there. Times change, people change, and so do track biases.

Every racetrack has its peculiarities. Some have pasteboard-hard running surfaces such as Turf Paradise in Arizona, which annually produces some of the world's fastest clockings. Some are 1⅛ miles in circumference, including Atlantic City, Aqueduct, Hialeah, Hollywood Park, Saratoga and Arlington International Racecourse, while others measure one mile around. In either configuration, the prevailing track bias will depend on the relative position of the starting gate to the first turn, the general climate of the region, the track's drainage system and/ or the banking of its turns.

Fairplex Park in Pomona, California, is a relatively small, ⅝ths of a mile track which compensates for its extremely tight turns with steeply banked curves. This apparently nullifies the logical advantage inside posts should have, and sometimes tilts the bias in the opposite direction in three-turn route races.

In recent years, Bay Meadows has had two distinctly different bias periods each session. During the early portion of the meet, when the weather is warmer, outside posts dominate. In mid-December, to protect the track from seasonably cooler weather, sand is added to the soil mixture before it is packed down and manicured differently, which collectively produces a bias shift toward neutral, or inside speed.

Nothing helps to change or create a bias as effectively as a shift in weather conditions or a decision to manicure the track differently.

A sudden rainstorm on an otherwise normal racetrack is odds-on to place a premium on early speed. A few days of rain, a thaw after a sudden frost, a period of extreme heat, or very severe crosswinds can institute a new track bias or have totally unpredictable effects.

A normal, or slightly speed-favoring track bias can be accentuated severely if the track maintenance crew scrapes soil away from the inside rail and seals the "cushion" in anticipation of rain. Conversely, there may not be any speed bias at all if track officials rake the top soil with "harrows" and permit the surface to go through a normal drying-out process.

When the modern Saratoga racing strip gets hit with heavy rains, sealing may hold the speed bias intact during the storm, but shortly afterward no amount of sealing may prevent the biases of the early 1970s from reappearing. A drying-out or muddy Saratoga racing strip can be a sticky, tiring surface that favors outside runners and/or those with a clear-cut edge in conditioning. After heavy rains Saratoga also dries out much slower than most tracks. Under such trying conditions—often mislabeled as "good"—horses who have demonstrated speed at longer distances frequently will outfinish rivals who would dominate on less tiring tracks. (The accent toward stamina types occurs at most other tracks during the "good" portion of a normal drying-out cycle, but it can disappear before a complete racing card is played out.)

At some tracks, players who study the way races are being run certainly will find days when there is a dual track bias—two distinctly different biases at work for one-turn and two-turn races, respectively. These dual biases may be induced by mid-card weather shifts, rapid drainage, extreme track maintenance, the banking of the turns, the relative positions of the starting gate at different distances, and/or aberrant wind conditions. On such days front runners may dominate sprints, while deep-closing stretch runners will win every route. (Routes are races at one mile or longer, usually around two turns.)

While some of the above trends may be safely anticipated via weather forecasts, it is important to fine-tune your race-watching skills as described in Chapter 1, because it is relatively easy to spot and evaluate any track bias if you:

- Watch the turns.
- Observe the running patterns. Are horses able to make up ground going to the outside or is the rail the only place to be?
- Watch the break from the gate. Are horses in certain post positions always a bit late getting into the hunt?
- Watch the run to the first turn (especially in route races). Are horses able to settle into contending positions from outer post positions without undue effort?
- And watch the top jockeys. Do they consistently steer their horses to one part of the track over another?

Frankly, I used to hesitate to mention jockeys in this context, because all but a handful seemed incapable of recognizing a bias until they lost a bunch of races because of it. This is changing.

Hall of Famer Angel Cordero, Jr., who retired in 1992, still ranks as the best bias interpreter I have seen. But in recent years, as track bias has become widely accepted as a handicapping reality, many more jockeys have become adept at finding the best lanes on the track. Among the best to watch are Richard Migliore, Mike Smith and Gary Stevens, Eddie Delahoussaye and Kent Desormeaux, Kerwin Clark, Julie Krone, Pat Day, Jeffrey Lloyd, and Chris Antley. If you are at a track where any of these jockeys are riding, watch them. They will spot a favorable path on the racing surface in two or three runs of the course.

If you are unable to attend races regularly or are planning an assault on a new track, the only way to spot a bias is through careful reading of the result charts. But even if your on-track observations have detected a bias—it's hard not to notice the presence of one when six races in a row are won wire-to-wire—you will need to refer to the charts to note those horses that were stuck on the outside, blocked, left at the gate, or handed the race on a silver platter.

A horse stuck on the rail on a dead rail day will have a ready-made excuse. A speed horse that cruised to a front-running victory because it drew into a favorable post may not be as good as it seems. By way of example I am including trackman Jack Wilson's comments and the charts for the first four main-track races run at Saratoga on August 21, 1976.

FIRST RACE
Sar
August 21. 1976

6 FURLONGS. (1:08). MAIDENS. CLAIMING. Purse $7,500. Fillies. 2-year-olds. Weight, 119 lbs. Claiming price, $20,000; 2 lbs. allowed for each $1,000 to $18,000. Value to winner $4,500; second, $1,650; third, $900; fourth, $450. Mutuel Pool, $93,694. Off-track betting, $82,077.

Last Raced	Horse	EqtAWt	PP	St	1/4	1/2	Str	Fin	Jockeys	Owners	Odds to $1
13 Aug76 1Sar3	By by Chicken	b2 115	8	1	1$\frac{1}{2}$	2^3	1^h	1^h	JVelasquez	Harbor View Farm	1.70
13 Aug76 1Sar9	Sun Bank	b2 119	5	2	2^h	1^h	2^2	2$^2\frac{1}{2}$	MVenezia	B Rose	b-4.30
13 Aug76 1Sar8	Mean Katrine	b2 115	1	3	5^2	5$\frac{1}{2}$	4^2	3$^2\frac{3}{4}$	ASantiago	Robdarich Stable	7.50
	Peach Flambeau	2 117	4	5	4^h	4$^1\frac{1}{2}$	3$\frac{1}{2}$	4$^1\frac{3}{4}$	DMcHargue	J W LaCroix	a-7.40
	I Gogo	b2 112	6	9	6^h	6$\frac{1}{2}$	6^1	5$^2\frac{1}{2}$	KWhitley7	Brookfield Farm	18.50
13 Aug76 9Sar6	Good Party	2 115	3	4	3^2	3$\frac{1}{2}$	5$\frac{1}{2}$	6no	EMaple	N A Martini	12.50
25 Jly 76 2Del5	Tootwright	b2 119	2	10	7$\frac{1}{2}$	7^3	7^4	7^5	PDay†	D Sturgill	3.00
	North Ribot	2 115	7	8	8^2	8^1	8$\frac{1}{2}$	8^h	MPerrotta	Betty Rose	b-4.30
27 Jun76 9Bel8	Hot Dogger	b2 117	9	6	9^1	9$\frac{1}{2}$	9$^1\frac{1}{2}$	9$\frac{1}{2}$	TWallis	Judith McClung	21.20
13 Aug76 9Sar4	Behavingaise	b2 117	10	7	10	10	10	10	RTurcotte	J W LaCroix	a-7.40

†Seven pounds apprentice allowance waived.
b-Coupled, Sun Bank and North Ribot; a-Peach Flambeau and Behavingaise.
OFF AT 1:30 EDT. Start good. Won driving. Time, :22⅗, :46⅗, 1:12⅗. Track fast.
Official Program Numbers ↘

$2 Mutuel Prices:

7-BY BY CHICKEN	5.40	3.40	2.80
2-SUN BANK (b-Entry)		4.60	3.40
3-MEAN KATRINE			3.60

B. f, by The Pruner—Chicken Little, by Olympia. Trainer, Lazaro S. Barrera. Bred by Carl L. Broughton (Fla.).

BY BY CHICKEN saved ground while vying for the lead with SUN BANK and prevailed in a stiff drive. The latter raced outside BY BY CHICKEN while dueling for command and narrowly missed. MEAN KATRINE finished evenly while saving ground. PEACH FLAMBEAU rallied approaching midstretch but hung. I GOGO failed to seriously menace while racing wide. GOOD PARTY tired from her early efforts. TOOTWRIGHT, off slowly, failed to be a serious factor. NORTH RIBOT was always outrun. BEHAVINGAISE showed nothing.
Claiming Prices (in order finish)—$18000, 20000, 18000, 19000, 20000, 18000, 20000, 18000, 19000, 19000.
Scratched—Lots of Flair.

SECOND RACE
Sar
August 21, 1976

1⅛ MILES. (1:47). CLAIMING. Purse $8,500. 3-year-olds and upward. 3-year-olds, 117 lbs.; older, 122 lbs. Non-winners of a race at a mile and a furlong or over since Aug. 1 allowed 3 lbs.; of such a race since July 15, 5 lbs. Claiming price, $12,500; 2 lbs. allowed for each $1,000 to $10,500. (Races when entered to be claimed for $8,500 or less not considered.)
Value to winner $5,100; second, $1,870; third, $1,020; fourth, $510. Mutuel Pool, $131,999.
Off-track betting, $95,870.

Last Raced	Horse	EqtAWt	PP	St	¼	½	¾	Str	Fin	Jockeys	Owners	Odds to $1
7 Aug76 ^{1}Sar^{6}	Tingle King	b4 114	1	3	$2^{\frac{1}{2}}$	3^{4}	$1^{1\frac{1}{2}}$	1^{5}	1^{6}	RTurcotte	Vendome Stable	5.40
7 Aug76 ^{1}Sar^{4}	O'Rei	7 113	4	5	4^{h}	4^{h}	4^{4}	3^{3}	2^{4}	TWallis	Mrs L I Miller	3.40
13 Aug76 ^{3}Sar^{1}	Mycerinus	b5 122	8	7	7	7	6^{2}	4^{7}	3no	MVenezia	Audley Farm Stable	3.40
7 Aug76 ^{2}Sar^{7}	Good and Bold	5 117	5	2	3^{4}	$2^{\frac{1}{2}}$	2^{3}	$2^{\frac{1}{2}}$	$4^{9\frac{1}{2}}$	EMaple	S Sommer	4.00
18 Aug76 ^{7}Sar^{8}	Slaw	3 107	7	4	6^{2}	$6^{\frac{1}{2}}$	7	5^{2}	5^{8}	RD'g'diceJr^{5}†	Betty Anne King	26.40
7 Aug76 ^{1}Sar^{9}	Gene's Legacy	b4 106	6	6	5^{1}	5^{6}	$5^{1\frac{1}{2}}$	6^{1}	$6^{6\frac{1}{2}}$	KWhitley^{7}	Beau-G Stable	10.40
13 Aug76 ^{3}Sar^{2}	Mister Breezy	4 113	3	1	$1^{1\frac{1}{2}}$	$1^{\frac{1}{2}}$	$3^{1\frac{1}{2}}$	7	7	JCruguet‡	M M Garren	2.50

†Two pounds apprentice allowance waived. ‡Five pounds apprentice allowance waived.
OFF AT 2:05 EDT. Start good. Won handily. Time, :23⅗, :47, 1:11⅕, 1:36⅘, 1:50⅖. Track fast.

$2 Mutuel Prices:

2-TINGLE KING	12.80	5.80	4.20
3-O'REI II.		5.20	4.00
7-MYCERINUS			3.40

B. c, by Bold Legend—Miss Tingle, by Avant Garde. Trainer, Flint S. Schulhofer. Bred by D. Shaer (Md.).
TINGLE KING raced forwardly into the backstretch, took over while saving ground into the far turn and drew away while being mildly encouraged. O'REI II., never far back, finished well to be second best without menacing the winner. MYCERINUS, void of early foot, passed tired horses. GOOD AND BOLD, a factor to the stretch, tired. MISTER BREEZY stopped badly after showing speed to the far turn.
Overweight—Tingle King, 1.
Claiming Prices (in order of finish)—$10500, 10500, 12500, 12500, 12500, 10500, 10500.
Scratched—Campaigner.

Daily Double (7-2) Paid $56.60; Double Pool, $303,256; OTB Pool, $515,166.

THIRD RACE
Sar
August 21, 1976

6 FURLONGS. (1:08). CLAIMING. Purse $9,000. 3-year-olds and upward. 3-year-olds, 117 lbs.; older, 122 lbs. Non-winners of two races since Aug. 1 allowed 3 lbs.; of a race since then, 5 lbs. Claiming price, $20,000; 2 lbs. allowed for each $1,000 to $18,000. (Races when entered to be claimed for $16,000 or less not considered.)
Value to winner $5.400; second, $1,980; third, $1,080; fourth, $540.
Mutuel Pool, $157.960. Off-track betting, $94,849. Exacta Pool, $158,817. Off-track betting Exacta Pool, $231,460.

Last Raced	Horse	EqtAWt	PP	St	¼	½	Str	Fin	Jockeys	Owners	Odds to $1
26 Apr76 ^{6}Aqu^{8}	Gabilan	4 117	7	2	1^{h}	1^{2}	1^{5}	1^{3}	EMaple	S Sommer	6.20
7 Aug76 ^{2}Sar^{2}	Rare Joel	b4 117	1	7	$7^{1\frac{1}{2}}$	$7^{\frac{1}{2}}$	$6^{\frac{1}{2}}$	2^{h}	JVelasquez	Elysa M Alibrandi	5.40
25 Jly 76 ^{3}Aqu^{5}	Snappy Chatter	b4 117	5	5	5^{h}	4^{1}	$2^{\frac{1}{2}}$	$3^{\frac{3}{4}}$	JAmy	May-Don Stable	8.80
7 Aug76 ^{2}Sar^{1}	Commercial Pilot	b4 113	2	4	$4^{\frac{1}{2}}$	5^{2}	3^{h}	$4^{1\frac{3}{4}}$	DMcHargue	Lovir Stable	6.50
10 Jly 76 ^{2}Aqu^{6}	Odds and Evens	5 108	8	8	8	6^{h}	$7^{1\frac{1}{2}}$	5^{3}	RDelq'riceJr^{5}	Colvie Stable	17.10
7 Aug76 ^{4}Sar^{2}	Native Blend	b6 108	4	3	3^{3}	2^{1}	4^{1}	6^{3}	KWhitley^{7}	Hobeau Farm	1.60
23 Jun76 ^{7}Bel^{9}	Chaulky Long	b4 118	3	6	6^{5}	8	8	$7^{2\frac{1}{2}}$	BBaeza	A Rosoff	4.40
7 Aug76 ^{4}Sar^{4}	What A Lucky Star	b4 117	6	1	$2^{\frac{1}{2}}$	3^{2}	5^{1}	8	PDay	J W LaCroix	14.90

OFF AT 2:45 EDT. Start good for all but ODDS AND EVENS. Won ridden out.
Time, :21⅘, :44⅗, 1:09⅘. Track fast.

$2 Mutuel Prices:

7-GABILAN	14.40	6.20	4.20
1-RARE JOEL		6.00	4.40
5-SNAPPY CHATTER			5.20

$2 EXACTA (7-1) PAID $89.60.

Dk. b. or br. c, by Penowa Rullah—Little Buzzy, by Royal Coinage. Trainer, Frank Martin. Bred by L. P. Sasso (Md.).
GABILAN sprinted clear approaching the stretch and, after opening a good lead, was ridden out to hold sway. RARE JOEL, void of early foot, finished full of run. SNAPPY CHATTER rallied from the outside entering the stretch, lugged in near the final furlong and continued on with good energy. COMMERCIAL PILOT split horses nearing midstretch but lacked the needed late response. ODDS AND EVENS broke in the air. NATIVE BLEND, a factor to the stretch, gave way. CHAULKY LONG was always outrun. WHAT A LUCKY STAR stopped badly after entering the stretch.
Overweight—Chaulky Long, 1.
Claiming Prices (in order of finish)—$20000, 20000, 20000, 18000, 18000, 19000, 20000, 20000.

FOURTH RACE
Sar
August 21, 1976

6 FURLONGS. (1:08). MAIDENS. SPECIAL WEIGHTS. Purse $9,000. Fillies and mares. 3-year-olds and upward. 3-year-olds, 117 lbs.; older, 122 lbs.
Value to winner $5,400; second, $1,980; third, $1,080; fourth, $540.
Mutuel Pool, $223,335.

Last Raced	Horse	EqtAWt	PP	St	1/4	1/2	Str	Fin	Jockeys	Owners	Odds to $1
	Love for Love	3 117	2	4	2^1	$2\frac{1}{2}$	$22\frac{1}{2}$	1^2	PDay	Rokeby Stable	1.10
13 Aug76 5Sar7	Solo Dance	3 117	1	3	7^2	$7^1\frac{1}{2}$	$5\frac{1}{2}$	2no	JVelasquez	Elmendorf	5.60
13 Aug76 5Sar8	Ready Again	b3 117	5	1	1^2	1^1	1^h	$31\frac{1}{2}$	MVenezia	Dogwood Stable	21.10
13 Aug76 5Sar3	Cornish Pet	3 117	6	6	$5\frac{1}{2}$	$3\frac{1}{2}$	$3\frac{1}{2}$	4^h	JCruguet	Verulam Farm	5.00
	Skater's Waltz	3 117	4	5	$3\frac{1}{2}$	4^1	6^1	5^h	RCSmith	A G Vanderbilt	16.60
13 Aug76 5Sar2	Like for Like.	3 117	3	2	$4\frac{1}{2}$	$5^1\frac{1}{2}$	$4\frac{1}{2}$	6no	JARodriguez	Waldemar Farm	6.10
	Naivasha	3 110	8	8	6^1	8	$7^1\frac{1}{2}$	$76\frac{3}{4}$	KWhitley7	King Ranch	28.50
13 Aug76 5Sar4	Artful Levee	3 117	7	7	8	$6\frac{1}{2}$	8	8	RLTurcotte	Whitney Stone	5.90

OFF AT 3:21½ EDT. Start good. Won handily. Time, :22⅗, :46⅖, 1:12⅕. Track fast.

$2 Mutuel Prices:

2–LOVE FOR LOVE	4.20	3.20	3.40
1–SOLO DANCE		4.80	4.40
5–READY AGAIN			6.40

Dk. b. or br. f, by Cornish Prince—Rare Exchange, by Swaps. Tr., Elliott Burch. Bred by Mellon Paul (Va.).
LOVE FOR LOVE prompted the pace into the stretch, took over from READY AGAIN just inside the final furlong and proved clearly best under confident handling. SOLO DANCE, eased back along the inside early, finished well to gain the place. READY AGAIN saved ground while making the pace and weakened under pressure. CORNISH PET made a bid from the outside leaving the turn but hung. SKATER'S WALTZ, between horses much of the way, lacked a late response. LIKE FOR LIKE rallied along the inside leaving the turn but failed to sustain her bid. ARTFUL LEVEE failed to be a serious factor.

This was the 107th Travers Day and the concept of Track Bias was not yet accepted by the majority of handicappers. But if players had reviewed the charts from preceeding days, the strong front-running accent that has dominated Saratoga racing for two decades would have been hard to miss. On August 18, 19 and 20, the inside part of the racetrack was faster than the outside. The charts for August 21 indicate that the tendency toward inside speed was overpowering.

I must confess that I was not at Saratoga on August 21, 1976. I was in Maryland writing the original *Betting Thoroughbreds*. At the time I vowed never to miss another Saratoga meet, but that promise was to be broken several times after moving to Minnesota to become racing columnist for the *Minneapolis Star Tribune* in 1985 and then to San Francisco for the *Racing Times* and other publications in 1991. I still miss Saratoga very much and plan to spend at least one week there each August for the rest of my life.

Saratoga is a special place, a racetrack where grass grows in the parking lot, where the trees outnumber people, where the Hall of Fame of Racing is located across the street from the antique wooden grandstand that has played host to Man o' War and Citation, Count Fleet and Secretariat, Alydar and Affirmed, Shoemaker and Arcaro, Cordero and Pincay, Sunny Jim Fitzsimmons and Max Hirsch, Woody Stephens, Laz

6th Saratoga

AUGUST 21, 1976

1¼ MILES. (2:01). 107th running TRAVERS. SCALE WEIGHTS. $100,000 added. 3-year-olds. Weight, 126 lbs. By subscription of $200 each, which shall accompany the nomination; $500 to start, with $100,000 added. The added money and all fees to be divided: 60% to the winner, 22% to second, 12% to third, and 6% to fourth. The winner shall have his name inscribed on the Man o' War Cup and a gold plated replica will be presented to the owner. Trophies will also be presented to the winning trainer and jockey. Closed with 22 nominations.

McKenzie Bridge 126

B. c (1973), by Le Fabuleux—Nanticious, by Nantallah.
Breeder, Carver Stable (Ky.). 1976 . . 9 2 1 1 $82,566
Owner, Mrs. Douglas Carver. Trainer, J. S. Dunn. 1975 . . 4 1 1 0 $9,626

11 Aug76 8Sar	1⅛	:461 1:103 1:484 gd	3	114	1017	96¾	42½	43	McHeDM6	AlwS 88	FatherHogan114	DanceSpell	10
27 Jun76 8Hol	1¼	:452 1:093 1:591 ft	5¾	114	912	66½	56	59¼	McHeDG5	AlwS 86	MajsticLight114	CrystlWatr	9
5 Jun76 7Bel	1½	:47 1:111 2:29 ft	6½	126	922	712	37½	2nk	McHgeD2	ScwS 75	BoldForbes126	McKzeBrdge	10
24 May76 7Bel	1 1/16	:462 1:104 1:423 ft	3	113	77½	66	51¼	12¼	VasquezJ7	Alw 89	McKnzieBridge113	FthrHgn	7
2 May76 6Hol	Ⓣ 1 1/16	:471 1:124 1:424 fm	3-2	118	55	21½	54½	53¾	ShoakerW6	Alw 81	Delta Junction 121	Lean To	6
17 Apr76 8Hol	1⅛	:46 1:093 1:482 ft	152	122	913	78	66½	44½	AlvarezF9	SpwS 85	CrystalWater122	Life'sHope	11
28 Mar76 8SA	1⅛	:46 1:101 1:48 ft	16	120	813	99	915	921	HawleyS6	SpwS 71	An Act 120	Double Discount	9
17 Mar76 8SA	1⅛	:471 1:114 1:484 ft	3-2	▲118	812	63½	55	36¾	ShakerW3	SpwS 81	June's Blazer 118	Pindoro	8
24 Jan76 6SA	1 1/16	:454 1:104 1:43 ft	3½	114	410	41	2h	14	ShoakerW7	Alw 87	McKenzieBrdge114	Spoonwd	7
2 Nov75 8SA	1 1/16	:461 1:104 1:433 ft	21	118	88	86½	67	56¾	OlivresF7	SpwS 77	Telly'sPop118	Imcrnishprnce	8
25 Oct75 6SA	6½ f	:214 :444 1:161 ft	4½	118	710	45	42½	24¾	ToroF1	Alw 87	PntedWgn115	McKnzieBdge	7

Aug 19 Sar 4f ft :48⅗b   Aug 10 Sar 4f sy :50⅕b   Aug 5 Sar 4f ft :49b

---

Quiet Little Table 126

Gr. g (1973), by Mr. Leader—Grey Table, by Grey Sovereign.
Breeder, Meadowhill (Ky.). 1976 9 5 1 2 $104,781
Owner, Meadowhill. Trainer, P. G. Johnson. 1975 1 1 0 0 $5.400

11 Aug76 8Sar	1⅛	:461 1:103 1:484 gd	2½	▲123	57½	31	63¼	68¾	MapleE8	AlwS 82	FatherHogan114	DanceSpell	10
10 Jly 76 8Aqu	1⅛	:464 1:361 1:49 ft	2½	▲111	2h	1½	15	12½	MapleE7	HcpS 90	Quiet Lttle Tble 111	Sir Lstr	8
30 Jun76 8Aqu	1	:451 1:084 1:341 ft	2	114	32	51¾	32	31½	TurctteR1	AlwS 93	Dance Spell 114	Zen	6
5 Jun76 8Bel	1 1/16	:452 1:10 1:421 ft	4¼	119	1½	1½	14	12¾	MapleE4	Alw 91	QuietLittleTable119	KirbyLe	7
26 May76 6Bel	1⅛	:46 1:103 1:491 ft	3¼	112	24	21½	1h	1nk	MapleE4	Alw 81	QuietLittleTable112	Christn	5
17 May76 5Bel	1	:453 1:094 1:351 ft	4-5	▲115	22½	21½	11½	13	MapleE5	Alw 92	QuietLittleTble115	RdAnchr	6
10 May76 6Bel	1 1/16	:46 1:10 1:423 ft	6	111	2½	1h	2½	22	MapleE8	Alw 87	Sawbones110	QuietLttleTble	8
20 Apr76 8Aqu	6 f	:222 :451 1:101 ft	1	▲110	42	45	34	11¾	MapleE4	Alw 92	QuietLittleTble110	Balancer	7
10 Apr76 5Aqu	6 f	:223 :461 1:104 ft	3½	▲117	44	44	44½	33¼	MapleE5	Alw 86	Bonge 117	Distinctively	9
5 Oct75 5Bel	6 f	:23 :463 1:114 ft	2	122	3½	2h	1½	12	CstedaM2	Mdn 83	QuietLittleTable122	PvtThts	9

Aug 18 Sar 6f ft 1:12⅖h   Aug 5 Sar 1⅛m ft 1:53⅗b   July 26 Bel 6f ft 1:14⅕h

---

Majestic Light 126

B. c (1973), by Majestic Prince—Irradiate, by Ribot.
Breeder, O. M. Phipps (Ky.). 1976 13 6 1 3 $229.123
Owner, Ogden M. Phipps. Trainer, John Russell. 1975 7 1 0 2 $8.400

7 Aug76 8Mth	1⅛	:46 1:10 1:47 ft	5¼	122	712	54	1½	16	HawleyS3	InvH 105	MajesticLight122	Appssnato	10
18 Jly 76 8Hol	Ⓣ 1⅛	:48 1:12 1:481 fm	2	▲121	78½	64	2½	11	HawleyS5	HcpS 95	MajesticLight121	L'Heureux	10
4 Jly 76 6AP	Ⓣ 1⅛	:481 1:122 1:491 fm	2½	121	109	85½	35½	21½	CrdoAJr1	HcpS 89	Ffth Mrine 121	Mjstic Lght	11
27 Jun76 8Hol	1¼	:452 1:093 1:591 ft	20	114	710	54	31½	13¼	HawleyS7	AlwS 95	MajesticLght114	CrystlWatr	9
5 Jun76 7Bel	1½	:47 1:111 2:29 ft	14	126	616	59½	412	49	VelasqzJ6	ScwS 66	BoldForbes126	McKzeBrdge	10
15 May76 8GS	Ⓣ 1 1/16	1:431 fm	6¾	117	915	79½	51¾	1½	BarreraC9	HcpS 89	Majestic Light 117	Chati	12
5 May76 8GS	Ⓣ 1	1:393 fm	2½	115	75½	64	41½	13½	BarreraC7	Alw 75	MajsticLight115	NobleAdml	8
16 Apr76 5Aqu	1	:461 1:102 1:36 ft	27	117	89	710	710	69	BaezaB6	Alw 77	BestLaidPlns119	Practitionr	8
11 Mar76 8Aqu	1	:464 1:12 1:371 sy	5	113	2½	21½	33½	58¼	CrdroAJr2	Alw 72	Be-A-Son 113	Cabriolet II.	6
28 Feb76 6Aqu	1	:482 1:133 1:391 ft	7-5	▲117	31	2h	1h	11½	CordroAJr6	Alw 70	MajesticLight117	Resilient	6
20 Feb76 8Aqu	1	:463 1:113 1:372 ft	6-5	▲119	68	46	44	31¼	CordroAJr3	Alw 78	Kupper 115	Distinctively	8

Aug 17 Sar 7f ft 1:26b

Honest Pleasure 126

Dk b. or br. c (1973), by What a Pleasure—Tularia, by Tulyar.
Breeder, Waldemar Farms, Inc. (Fla.). 1976 8 4 2 1 $229.172
Owner, B. R. Firestone. Trainer, LeRoy Jolley. 1975 8 6 2 0 $370.227

7 Aug76 8Mth	1⅛	:46 1:10 1:47 ft	1	▲126	21½	11½	2½	36	PerretC4	InvH 99	MajesticLight122	Appssnato	10
27 Jly 76 8Mth	1 1/16	:46 1:10 1:411 ft	1-10	▲115	13½	11½	2h	21½	BaezaB1	Alw 97	PeppyAddy119	HonestPlsure	6
15 May76 8Pim	1 3/16	:45 1:09 1:55 ft	4-5	▲126	22	22	42	57¼	BaezaB6	ScwS 87	Elocutionist126	Play theRed	6
1 May76 8CD	1¼	:454 1:102 2:013 ft	2-5	▲126	25	2½	2½	21	BaezaB5	ScwS 88	BoldForbes126	HonestPlesre	9
22 Apr76 7Kee	1⅛	:48 1:123 1:492 ft	1-10	▲121	14	15	12	11½	BaezaB2	SpwS 90	HontPlease121	CertnRoman	7
3 Apr76 9GP	1⅛	:464 1:103 1:474 ft	1-20	▲122	13	13	13	13	BaezaB3	AlwS 95	HonestPlsre122	GrtContrctr	6
28 Feb76 9Hia	1⅛	:454 1:09 1:464 ft	1-3	▲122	12	18	18	111	BaezaB7	ScwS 98	HonestPleasure122	IncaRoca	8
11 Feb76 Hia	7 f	:23 :452 1:222 ft		122	11	14	110	114	BaezaB4	SpwS 93	HonestPlease122	ParcForiln	4
Exhibition race; no wagering.													
1 Nov75 8Lrl	1 1/16	:454 1:103 1:424 ft	1-5	▲122	11	13	11½	12½	BaezaB3	ScwS 99	HonestPlasure122	Whtsyrple	7
18 Oct75 8Bel	1	:45 1:101 1:362 sy	6-5	▲122	1½	11½	15	17	BaezaB9	ScwS 86	HonestPleasre122	DnceSpell	14
8 Oct75 8Bel	7 f	:224 :452 1:223 ft	2¾	121	13	14	15	18	BaezaB7	AlwS 89	HnestPlsre121	Whtsyrplsure	7

Aug 19 Sar 4f ft :46⅕h   Aug 14 Sar 7f ft 1:25h

Romeo 126 B. c (1973), by T. V. Lark—Gallizzie, by Tiger Wander.
Breeder, P. Madden (Ky.). 1976 17 3 2 3 $53,760
Ownre, Mary Lou Cashman. Trainer, Paul Adwell.
7 Aug76 7AP Ⓣ 1 1/16 :4741:1241:441fm 9 114 1210 74½ 710 811 GavdiaW2 HcpS 77 Effervescing113 Rule theRge 13
29 Jly 76 9AP 1 1/16 :4711:1121:421sy 6-5 ▲115 41 21 1½ 1¾ GavidiaW6 Alw 101 Romeo 115 Auberge 7
17 Jly 76 6AP Ⓣ 1 1/16 :4811:1211:434fm 2¼ 115 45½ 21 31½ 43¼ GavidiaW7 Alw 87 NatvePraise117 Fightmaster 9
4 Jly 76 6AP Ⓣ 1⅛ :4811:1221:491fm 12e 111 34 32 68 69½ SnyderL9 HcpS 81 Ffth Mrine 121 Mjstic Lght 11
27 Jun76 8Hol 1¼ :4521:0931:591ft 8¾ 115 37 43½ 45½ 49¼ PincyLJr8 AlwS 86 MajesticLight114 Crystl Wtr 9
13 Jun76 8Hol 1⅛ :4631:1021:472ft 31 115 68 53 32 22 VergraO7 HcpS 93 L'Heureux 119 Romeo 7
23 May76 5Hol Ⓣ 1 1/16 :4641:1121:423fm 7¼ 118 74 41¼ 2½ 1no VergaraO7 Alw 86 Romeo 118 Electric Flag 12
8 May76 2Hol Ⓣ 1 1/16 :4831:1231:431fm 2 ▲120 43 32 42 43½ McHgeDG9 Alw 79 PrinceBoynton115 GasEnrgy 9
25 Apr76 9Hol Ⓣ 1 1/16 :4721:1141:424fm 9 120 64½ 53 53 34½ VergaraO5 Alw 80 Today n'Tmrrw117 HdnWrld 10
17 Apr76 5Hol Ⓣ 1 1/16 :4731:1131:43 fm 7½ 120 42 52½ 33 35½ VergaraO9 Alw 78 DeltaJnctn120 Tody n'Tmrw 12
Aug 18 Sar 5f ft 1:00h July 28 AP 3f ft :37b July 24 AP 6f ft 1:15⅘b

---

El Portugues * 126 Ch. c (1973), by Gallant Romeo—Miss Swoon, by Swoon's Son.
Breeder, Copelan & Thornbury (Ky.). 1976..20 2 6 2 $66.593
Owner, E. Ubarri. Trainer, Lazaro S. Barrera. 1975.. 1 M 0 0 $152
11 Aug76 8Sar 1⅛ :4611:1031:484gd 4¾ 114 611 52 3½ 33 CrdoAJr7 AlwS 88 FatherHogan114 DanceSpell 10
31 Jly 76 8Aqu Ⓣ 1⅛ :4721:1121:492fm 8 112 38½ 510 59½ 69¼ VelasqzJ5 HcpS Mcdred 117 Dream 'n BeLky 7
17 Jly 76 8Pim 1⅛ :4631:1041:484ft 7¼e 110 76 58 53¾ 43¾ VelezRI4 HcpS 89 AmericanTradr109 OnTheSly 7
4 Jly 76 6AP Ⓣ 1⅛ :4811:1221:491fm 15 114 76¾ 74½ 911 910 GvidiaW10 HcpS 81 Ffth Mrine 121 Mjstic Lght 11
27 Jun76 10Tdn 1⅛ :46 1:1031:494ft 5½e 112 53¼ 3½ 31 43 VelezRI14 AlwS 88 Return of a Native115 Cojak 14
14 Jun76 8Bel 1 1/16 :47 1:1131:434ft 3-5 ▲110 52¼ 33 33 23¾ CordroAJr1 Alw 79 Brown Cat 117 El Portugues 6
23 May76 8Bel 1 :4531:1011:36 ft 8-5 ▲116 64¾ 53 51¾ 2½† CrdroAJr6 AlwS 87 Sir Lister114 El Portugues 9
†Disqualified and placed third.
8 May76 8Bel 1 :4531:10 1:35 ft 8¼ 126 67 54 22 2½ CrdroAJr2 ScwS 92 Sonkisser 126 El Portugues 6
1 May76 6Aqu 1 :45 1:09 1:343sy 5½ 110 53¼ 45½ 38 28½ AmyJ7 Alw 84 Cinteelo 104 El Portugues 7
24 Apr76 6Aqu 1 :4521:09 1:35 ft 9½ 113 58½ 57½ 56½ 54¾ VelasquzJ3 Alw 86 NewCllection112 Cplet'sSng 7
June 24 Tdn 5f ft 1:02b

Legendaire 126 Ch. c (1973), by Le Fabuleux—Native Guide, by Raise a Native.
Breeder, W. P. Little (Ky.). 1976 .. 8 2 1 0 $15,157
Owner, Silk Willoughby Farm. Trainer, J. P. Conway. 1975.. 4 1 0 0 $5,400
11 Aug76 8Sar 1⅛ :4611:1031:484gd 19 114 916 108¾ 98¾ 710 TurctteR4 AlwS 81 FatherHogan114 DanceSpell 10
31 Jly 76 6Aqu Ⓣ 1⅛ :4721:12 1:50 fm 11 112 33 1h 66¼ 63¾ TurctteR1 HcpS FabledMonrch114 Effrvscing 8
10 Jly 76 8Aqu 1⅛ :4641:3611:49 ft 9 112 67½ 711 716 715 VasquzJ4 HcpS 75 Quiet Lttle Tble 111 Sir Lstr 8
26 Jun76 8Bel 1 1/16 :4621:11 1:42 ft 6 113 74½ 31 11 12¾ VasquezJ2 Alw 92 Legendaire113 RedAnchor 7
13 Apr76 7Kee 1 1/16 :4711:1111:431ft 7 113 63¾ 69 612 620 BrumfldD5 Alw 70 No Link 121 Inca Roca 6
24 Mar76 8GP Ⓣ a 1 1:39 fm 6 116 89½ 63½ 53¾ 44† MarquzC5 Alw 82 Hall ofRean114 Fightmaster 10
†Placed third through disqualification.
6 Mar76 6GP 1 1/16 :4721:1121:434ft 2¼ ▲122 45 33 2½ 1¾ RuaneJ5 Alw 82 Legendaire122 ArchieBmish 11
20 Feb76 7Hia 7 f :224 :4611:24 ft 62 115 109 66 31½ 2nk MapleE3 Alw 85 Sonkisser 122 Legendaire 11
21 Nov75 7Aqu 1 :4441:0841:344sy 11 122 918 930 932 940 CastandaK5 Alw 52 Cinteelo 117 Play the Red 9
Aug 17 Sar 1 ft 1:43b Aug 10 Sar 3f sy :36b Aug 7 Sar 5f ft 1:07b

---

Dance Spell 126 B. c (1973), by Northern Dancer—Obeah, by Cyane.
Breeder, Christiana Stables (Ky.). 1976.. 7 3 1 1 $72,702
Owner, Christiana Stables. Trainer, J. W. Maloney. 1975..10 2 6 1 $93,846
11 Aug76 8Sar 1⅛ :4611:1031:484gd 3½e 121 25 11 1h 21 VasquzJ5 AlwS 90 FatherHogan114 DanceSpell 10
10 Jly 76 8Aqu 1⅛ :4641:3611:49 ft 3½ 117 31 2½ 35 32¾ CrdoAJr8 HcpS 87 Quiet Lttle Tble 111 Sir Lstr 8
30 Jun76 8Aqu 1 :4511:0841:341ft 3¼e 114 1½ 11 12 11¼ CdroAJr3 AlwS 95 Dance Spell 114 Zen 6
12 Jun76 6Bel 6 f :223 :4531:093ft 2¾ 112 21½ 32 68 611 CruguetJ3 Alw 83 QueenCityLd115 VlidAppeal 6
8 May76 8Bel 1 :4531:10 1:35 ft 1 ▲126 2½ 2½ 44 49 CruguetJ3 ScwS 84 Sonkisser 126 El Portugues 6
21 Apr76 6Aqu 7 f :224 :4541:22 ft 2¼ 110 21½ 21½ 11½ 12¾ CruguetJ1 Alw 91 DanceSpll 110 GabeBnzur 7
31 Mar76 7Aqu 7 f :23 :4541:223ft 8-5 ▲111 31½ 1h 1h 1½ CruguetJ3 Alw 88 DanceSpel 111 Kohoutek 7
29 Nov75 8Aqu 1⅛ :4631:1041:491ft 9-5 ▲113 35 31½ 22½ 2½ CrugutJ10 AlwS 88 Hang Ten 116 Dance Spell 12
19 Nov75 8Aqu 6 f :221 :4511:094ft 2½ 115 21½ 2h 22½ 22¼ CruguetJ3 AlwS 92 LordHenribee117 DanceSpell 6
1 Nov75 8Lrl 1 1/16 :4541:1031:424ft 7½ 122 31½ 33½ 33½ 36 CruguetJ7 SpwS 93 HonestPlsre122 Whatsyrplse 7
Aug 20 Sar 3f ft :36b Aug 17 Sar 5f ft :58⅗h Aug 8 Sar 5f sy 1:02⅕b

Barrera and the best racing has offered for more than 130 years. Oh, it gets hot in Saratoga Springs. Very hot. But with the ghosts of racing's past in the air and a track bias like the one you are about to contemplate, a good player will tell time by the coming of the Saratoga season.

While it's not necessary to handicap this prestigious stakes race in depth to select Honest Pleasure as a front-running stickout, I am also including (below) the chart of the Monmouth Invitational, the race Majestic Light won over Honest Pleasure by six lengths. The Trackman's comments clearly show that Honest Pleasure was regaining his early season form.

Leroy Jolley wisely stopped on Honest Pleasure after the Preakness debacle (May 15) and was patiently reestablishing the horse's speed and staying power. The recent workouts indicate further progress.

Majestic Light is a slow-breaking, fast-closing three-year-old that appreciates true distance racing. Trainer John Russell has done an excellent job, and there is very little doubt that Majestic Light is fit enough

EIGHTH RACE
Mth
August 7, 1976

1⅛ MILES. (1:48). Ninth running MONMOUTH INVITATIONAL HANDICAP. Purse $100,000. 3-year-olds. by invitation only, with no nomination or starting fees. The winner to receive $65,000, with $20,000 to second; $10,000 to third; and $5,000 to fourth. A representative field of those weighted will be invited to participate. The Monmouth Park Jockey Club reserves the right to reassign weight to any horse after the release of the weights. Owner of the winner to receive a trophy.

Value to winner $65,000; second, $20,000; third, $10,000; fourth, $5,000. Mutuel Pool, $349,197.

Last Raced	Horse	EqtAWt	PP	St	¼	½	¾	Str	Fin	Jockeys	Owners	Odds to $1
18 Jly 76 ⁸Hol¹	Majestic Light	3 122	3	2	7²	7²	5¹½	1½	1⁶	SHawley	O M Phipps	5.30
31 Jly 76 ⁸Aqu⁵	Appassionato	3 113	7	9	9¹½	9²	9²	5¹½	2ⁿᵒ	RHernandez	F A Luro	27.10
27 Jly 76 ⁸Mth²	Honest Pleasure	3 126	4	1	2²	2⁴	1¹½	2²½	3½	CPerrtt	B R Firestone	1.10
17 Jly 76 ⁸Pim³	Zen	3 118	6	7	6ʰ	5¹½	4½	3³	4²½	JVasquez	Pen-Y-Bryn Farm	3.10
25 Jly 76 ⁸Del¹	On The Sly	3 115	2	8	8⁷	8⁶	8⁶	4²	5¹½	GMcCarron	Balmak Stable	6.00
31 Jly 76 ⁸Aqu²	Dream 'N Be Lucky	3 114	5	10	10	10	10	7⁵	6⁶	MSolomone	G A Zimmerman	33.00
17 Jly 76 ⁸Mth⁶	Wardlaw	b3 115	1	3	3ʰ	3²½	3²	6ʰ	7⁴	JTejeira	D Lasater	39.30
27 Jly 76 ⁷Mth¹	Best Bee	b3 113	10	6	5¹½	6¹½	7½	8⁴	8⁶	RWilson	Dixiana	65.10
31 Jly 76 ⁷Aks²	Joachim	b3 117	8	5	4²½	4¹	6²	9ʰ	9ʰ	SMaple	E Pratt-J C Van Berg	18.90
17 Jly 76 ⁸Pim¹	American Trader	b3 114	9	4	1³	1¹½	2ʰ	10	10	AAgnello	Mrs B Cohen	19.60

OFF AT 5:57 EDT. Start good. Won driving. Time, :22⅗, :46, 1:10, 1:34⅗, 1:47 (new track record). Track fast.

4-HONEST PLEASURE	2.80

B. c, by Majestic Prince—Irradiate. by Ribot. Trainer. J. W. Russell. Bred by O. M. Phipps (Ky.).

$2 Mutuel Prices:

3-MAJESTIC LIGHT	12.60	6.80	4.20
7-APPASIONATO		19.40	6.20

MAJESTIC LIGHT, taken in hand after the start, angled to the outside leaving the clubhouse turn, remained outside when roused under a flurry of right-handed whipping at the far turn, brushed lightly with ZEN on the stretch turn but continued strongly to gain the lead in the upper stretch, swerved out when struck left-handed at the eighth-pole but continued to draw off with authority and was under only mild encouragement in the final seventy yards. APPASSIONATO, outrun for three-quatrers, rallied gamely outside the leaders when roused for the drive but could not threaten the winner. HONEST PLEASURE, reserved off the early pace outside AMERICAN TRADER, moved willingly to the lead when asked at the far turn, resisted the winner gamely in the stretch but hung in the closing yards. ZEN rallied just inside MAJESTIC LIGHT at the far turn, brushed with that one but finished with good courage. ON THE SLY did not reach contention with a mild closing rally. JOACHIM and AMERICAN TRADER were finished after three-quarters.
Overweight—Dream 'N Be Lucky, 1 pound.

or good enough to win. Thus, a good performance, despite the bias, is possible; however, it's not likely. Much depends on whether Majestic Light can get clear sailing on the rail for an uninterrupted rally. Unfortunately, he will need an unusual degree of cooperation from the rest of the field to get that kind of running room. Finally, he will still have to run faster than Honest Pleasure, who is on the improve and likely to have the rail and the lead for the entire race!

Quiet Little Table, a well-managed speed horse, would have a fine winning chance in any good field. But with Honest Pleasure in the race, Quiet Little Table has virtually no chance at all. It is further doubtful that he has enough speed to stop Honest Pleasure from getting a clear lead over the field in the run to the first turn. That's important for two reasons: (1) most front-running types tend to race better when they are able to relax in front of the pack; (2) everything in Honest Pleasure's record says he is a horse that improves dramatically when he is able to make the lead without undue stress.

Dance Spell has generally good form and cannot be completely eliminated.

SIXTH RACE
Sar
August 21, 1976

1¼ MILES. (2:01). 107th running TRAVERS. SCALE WEIGHTS. $100,000 added. 3-year-olds. Weight, 126 lbs. By subscription of $200 each, which shall accompany the nomination; $500 to start, with $100,000 added. The added money and all fees to be divided: 60% to the winner, 22% to second, 12% to third, and 6% to fourth. The winner shall have his name inscribed on the Man o' War Cup and a gold plated replica will be presented to the owner. Trophies will also be presented to the winning trainer and jockey. Closed with 22 nominations.

Value of race $108,400. Value to winner $65,040; second, $23,848; third, $13,008; fourth, $6,504. Mutuel Pool, $328,104. Off-track betting, $342,517.

Last Raced	Horse	EqtAWt	PP	¼	½	¾	1	Str	Fin	Jockeys	Owners	Odds to $1
7 Aug76 ^{8}Mth^{3}	Honest Pleasure	3 126	4	1^{2}	1^{6}	1^{4}	1^{2}	1^{3}	1^{4}	CPerret	B R Firestone	2.10
7 Aug76 ^{7}AP^{8}	Romeo	b3 126	5	$5^{1\frac{1}{2}}$	$5^{1\frac{1}{2}}$	5^{1}	4^{1}	2^{h}	$2^{1\frac{1}{2}}$	BBaeza	Mary L Cashman	49.30
11 Aug76 ^{8}Sar^{2}	Dance Spell	3 126	8	4^{1}	4^{1}	$3^{1\frac{1}{2}}$	$3^{\frac{1}{2}}$	3^{1}	3^{3}	JCruguet	Christiana Stable	14.70
11 Aug76 ^{8}Sar^{6}	Quiet Little Table	3 126	2	3^{1}	$3^{1\frac{1}{2}}$	2^{1}	$2^{1\frac{1}{2}}$	4^{2}	4^{nk}	EMaple	Meadowhill	12.50
11 Aug76 ^{6}Sar^{3}	El Portugues	b3 126	6	2^{1}	2^{h}	$4^{1\frac{1}{2}}$	$5^{\frac{1}{2}}$	$5^{\frac{1}{2}}$	$5^{1\frac{1}{2}}$	JVelasquez	E Ubarri	23.60
11 Aug76 ^{8}Sar^{4}	McKenzie Bridge	3 126	1	8	$7^{\frac{1}{2}}$	7^{3}	7^{12}	7^{24}	$6^{\frac{3}{4}}$	DMcHargue	Mrs D Carter	4.60
7 Aug76 ^{8}Mth^{1}	Majestic Light	3 126	3	$7^{\frac{1}{2}}$	$6^{\frac{1}{2}}$	6^{2}	$6^{1\frac{1}{2}}$	$6^{\frac{1}{2}}$	7^{30}	SHawley	O M Phipps	1.00
11 Aug76 ^{8}Sar^{7}	Legendaire	b3 126	7	6^{h}	8	8	8	8	8	RTurcotte	Silk Willoughby Fm	64.40

OFF AT 4:34 EDT. Start good. Won ridden out. Time, :23$\frac{2}{5}$, :46$\frac{3}{5}$, 1:10$\frac{2}{5}$, 1:35, 2:00$\frac{1}{5}$ (new track record). Track fast.

$2 Mutuel Prices:			
4–HONEST PLEASURE	6.20	5.00	4.20
5–ROMEO		2 .1 00	6.80
8–DANCE SPELL			5.40

Dk. b. or br. c, by What a Pleasure—Tularia, by Tlyar. Trainer, LeRoy Jolley. Bred by Waldemar Farms, Inc. (Fla.).

HONEST PLEASURE dropped over to save ground after outrunning QUIET LITTLE TABLE into the turn, quickly opened a long lead, made thepace while going easily, was roused soon after entering the stretch and drew away under a hand ride. ROMEO, unhurried early, rallied along the inside leaving the far turn and finished with good energy to be second best. DANCE SPELL, reserved early while saving ground, moved outside QUIET LITTLE TABLE to launch a bid at the far turn, raced forwardly into the stretch but weakened during the drive. QUIET LITTLE TABLE, well placed early, went after HONEST PLEASURE approaching the stretch but had nothing left for the drive. EL PORTUGUES, hustled along after the start, was finished approaching the end of the backstretch. McKENZIE BRIDGE was never close. MAJESTIC LIGHT, void of early foot, was sent up outside horses midway of the far turn but lacked a further response. LEGENDAIRE wasn't able to keep pace.

The shipper Romeo is a stretch runner that has never beaten a good field.

In summary, what we have here is a fit front-running racehorse of obvious quality getting a track he should absolutely relish. The betting crowd made the wrong favorite.

As a footnote to the Travers result chart, you might be interested to know that Dance Spell—the colt that moved outside to launch his bid against the Saratoga bias—came back to win the Jerome Mile in his next start, paying $17.60. That price was inflated by Dance Spell's number-one post position, generally interpreted by most Belmont fans as an unfavorable post. I can well understand that interpretation because the rail is usually dead at Belmont during the fall meeting. Nevertheless, it is my experience with track biases that logic still prevails in such conditions.

A dead rail only eliminates horses that race on the dead rail.

A front runner breaking from post one should be automatically downgraded if not eliminated under such conditions.

A stretch runner breaking from post one may have to give up a length

---

EIGHTH RACE
Bel
Septemb'r 6, 1976

1 MILE. (1:33⅗). One hundred and seventh running JEROME HANDICAP. $100,000 added. 3-year-olds. By subscription of $100 each, which shall accompany the nomination; $500 to start, with $100,000 added. The added money and fees to be divided: 60% to the winner, 22% to second, 12% to third and 6% to fourth. Trophies will be presented to the winning owner, trainer and jockey. Closed with 30 nominations.

Value of race $111,000. Value to winner $66,600; second, $24,420; third, $13,320; fourth, $6,660.
Mutuel Pool, $560,376. Off-track betting, $193,704.

Last Raceu	Horse	EqtA	Wt	PP	St	¼	½	¾	Str	Fin	Jockeys	Owners	Odds to $1
21 Aug76 ^{6}Sar^{3}	Dance Spell	3	117	1	4	3½	2½	1^{1}	$1^{1\frac{1}{2}}$	$1^{3\frac{3}{4}}$	RHernandez	Christiana Stable	7.80
30 Aug76 ^{6}Bel^{3}	Soy Numero Uno	3	117	7	2	4½	4^{1}	$3^{1\frac{1}{2}}$	$3^{1\frac{1}{2}}$	2no	PDay	Strapro Stable	3.00
26 Aug76 ^{8}Sar^{1}	Clean Bill	3	112	5	10	1^{1}	1^{2}	2^{h}	2^{1}	3^{2}	JImparato	Tartan Stable	30.60
19 Aug76 ^{8}Mth^{3}	Full Out	3	116	4	1	5^{h}	5^{h}	5^{h}	4½	4^{nk}	DMontoya	Buckland Farm	61.90
17 Jly 76 ^{8}Rkm^{6}	Life's Hope	3	117	3	7	7½	6½	4½	5½	5^{h}	MSolomone	Harbor View Farm	31.50
21 Aug76 ^{6}Sar^{4}	Quiet Little Table	3	117	2	3	2^{h}	3½	6^{1}	6½	6^{3}	EMaple	Meadowhill	7.20
18 Aug76 ^{6}Sar^{1}	Sawbones	3	113	10	8	10	9½	$8^{1\frac{1}{2}}$	7^{1}	7¾	HGustines	Greentree Stable	5.20
18 Aug76 ^{8}Mth^{2}	Sonkisser	3	122	6	6	6½	7^{h}	9½	9^{1}	8^{h}	BBaeza	H I Snyder	3.10
30 Aug76 ^{6}Bel^{2}	Kirby Lane	3	112	8	5	$8^{1\frac{1}{2}}$	8^{1}	7½	8½	9½	ACorderoJr	Gedney Farms	6.30
11 Aug76 ^{8}Sar^{1}	Father Hogan	b3	115	9	9	9^{h}	10	10	10	10	MVenezia	Sea Spray Farms	8.00

Uncoupled for betting purposes: LIFE'S HOPE and KIRBY LANE.

OFF AT 5:53½ EDT. Start good. Won driving. Time, :23⅘, :46⅗, 1:10⅗, 1:35. Track fast.

$2 Mutuel Prices:			
1-DANCE SPELL	17.60	7.60	4.60
7-SOY NUMERO UNO		6.00	3.60
5-CLEAN BILL			9.00

B. c, by Northern Dancer—Obeah, by Cyane. Trainer, James W. Maloney. Bred by Christiana Stable (Ky.).

DANCE SPELL, away in good order, moved to the fore when ready while racing well out in the track approaching the stretch and drew away under brisk handling while continuing wide. SOY NUMERO UNO, reserved behind the early leaders, made a bid while racing wide nearing the stretch, lugged in slightly approaching the final furlong and was just up for the place. A foul claim against SOY NUMERO UNO by the rider of FULL OUT, for alleged interference through the stretch, was not allowed. CLEAN BILL, off slowly, rushed through along the rail to take over before going a quarter, remained a factor to midstretch and weakened. FULL OUT, never far back, remained a factor into the stretch but lacked a late response while drifting out. LIFE'S HOPE made a mild bid along the inside leaving the turn but hung. QUIET LITTLE TABLE tired from his early efforts. SAWBONES, outrun early, was sent up between horses leaving the far turn but failed to be a serious factor. SONKISSER, steadied along while in close quarters between horses approaching the end of the backstretch, lacked a further response. KIRBY LANE failed to seriously menace while racing very wide. FATHER HOGAN showed nothing.

Scratched—Fighting Bill.

or two at the start. That of course is frequently reason enough to eliminate many stretch runners.

Horses like Dance Spell—those that have tractable speed, speed that frequently permits maneuverability—may yet get trapped along the rail if the jockey is not alert. That's a smaller risk factor, but it cannot be overlooked. Several issues must be balanced against that risk:

How superior is the horse breaking from post one?
How many horses figure to break with him?
How good is the jockey?
Have most of the riders been breaking toward the outside in order to
    avoid the rail, thus leaving post one with room to maneuver?
What kind of odds are available for the risk?

In my judgment, a set of encouraging answers to these questions, especially to the first and last questions, would suggest buying into the risk.

Dance Spell's next start was in Forego's Woodward Stakes on September 18. Honest Pleasure was also in the field, making his first start since the Travers. Honest Pleasure drew the rail, Dance Spell the extreme outside post in a ten-horse field. There was really no betting issue involved. Forego was a stickout with a tempting 1–1 price, considering his tendency to go off at 1–2. But there is just no margin for profit or error playing horses at those odds.

Because of the post position draw, the second-best horse looked convincingly like Dance Spell; the third choice depended on how much post one would actually cost Honest Pleasure. As the chart on the following page indicates, the Woodward was no less formful than the other two races we have examined in this series of Saratoga-Belmont stakes races.

At Del Mar, near San Diego in southern California, which also runs a high-caliber late summer meet, there were streaks of speed and stretch-running biases to play with in the 1990s. At Golden Gate in the spring of 1993, four weekends out of the final five produced some of the strongest one-dimensional speed tracks of the year. In all such instances, which pop up periodically at every track in America, the astute player must realize that he or she suddenly has been given a terrific advantage that would be foolish to ignore. Indeed, while biases do not exist as often as impatient players believe, there is no better time to play the game aggressively than when the racing surface is helping to identify which

EIGHTH RACE
Bel
Sept'ber 18, 1976

1⅛ MILES (chute). (1:45⅖). Twenty-third running WOODWARD HANDICAP. $150,000 added. 3-year-olds and upward. By subscription of $100 each, which shall accompany the nomination; $500 to pass the entry box, $1,500 to start, with $150,000 added. The added money and all fees to be divided 60% to the winner, 22% to second, 12% to third and 6% to fourth. Mrs. William Woodward has donated a trophy to be presented to the owner of the winner and trophies will also be presented to the winning trainer and jockey. Closed with 27 nominations.
Value of race, $173,200. Value to winner $103,920; second, $38,104; thirds, $15,588 each. Mutuel Pool, $550,396.

Last Raced	Horse	EqtA	Wt	PP	St	¼	½	¾	Str	Fin	Jockeys	Owners	Odds to $1
21 Aug76 ^{8}Mth^{3}	Forego	6	135	2	10	7^{h}	7^{h}	7^{2}	4^{3}	$1^{1\frac{1}{4}}$	WShoemaker	Lazy F Ranch	1.10
6 Sep76 ^{8}Del^{4}	Dance Spell	3	115	10	1	6^{4}	$5^{1\frac{1}{2}}$	$2^{\frac{1}{2}}$	1^{h}	$2^{2\frac{3}{4}}$	RHernandez	Christiana Stable	7.10
21 Aug76 ^{6}Sar^{1}	DH Honest Pleasure	3	121	1	2	1^{1}	$1^{1\frac{1}{2}}$	1^{1}	3^{2}	3	CPerret	B R Firestone	2.10
14 Sep76 ^{4}Bel^{1}	DH Stumping	b6	109	4	7	5^{1}	6^{2}	5^{1}	5^{7}	$3^{\frac{1}{2}}$	JAmy	Hobeau Farm	27.80
6 Sep76 ^{8}Bel^{2}	Soy Numero Uno	3	112	5	4	3^{1}	$3^{\frac{1}{2}}$	3^{2}	$2^{\frac{1}{2}}$	$5^{8\frac{1}{4}}$	EMaple	Strapro Stable	11.20
21 Aug76 ^{8}Mth^{1}	Hatchet Man	b5	114	3	9	10	10	$8^{\frac{1}{2}}$	7^{1}	6no	HGustines	Greentree Stable	11.30
21 Aug76 ^{8}Mth^{8}	El Pitirre	4	112	7	5	9^{4}	$9^{\frac{1}{2}}$	9^{h}	$6^{\frac{1}{2}}$	7^{3}	ASantiago	E Ubarri	29.20
6 Sep76 ^{8}Del^{4}	Dancing Gun	b4	112	8	2	$2^{1\frac{1}{2}}$	2^{h}	6^{h}	$8^{\frac{1}{2}}$	8^{h}	JVelasquez	Gedney Farms	37.30
6 Sep76 ^{8}Bel^{8}	Sonkisser	3	117	6	8	$4^{\frac{1}{2}}$	$4^{\frac{1}{2}}$	4^{2}	$9^{1\frac{1}{2}}$	9^{nk}	BBaeza	H I Snyder	37.40
7 Sep76 ^{8}Bel^{8}	Right Mind	5	114	9	6	8^{h}	8^{5}	10	10	10	RTurcotte	Deronjo Stable	70.90

DH Dead-heat.

OFF AT 5:45 EDT. Start good. Won ridden out. Time, :23, :45⅗, 1:09⅕, 1:33⅗, 1:45⅘. Track fast.

$2 Mutuel Prices:

2–FOREGO	4.20	3.00	2.20
11–DANCE SPELL		5.40	3.00
1–HONEST PLEASURE (Dead-heat)			2.20
4–STUMPING (Dead-heat)			2.80

B. g, by Forli—Lady Golconda, by Hasty Road. Trainer, Frank Y. Whitley, Jr. Bred by Lazy F. Ranch (Ky.).
FOREGO, unhurried after breaking slowly, was steadied along while racing along the inside to the turn, eased out for room approaching the three-eighths pole, moved fast while continuing wide after entering the stretch, caught DANCE SPELL inside the final sixteenth and drew clear under good handling. DANCE SPELL, eased back after breaking in front, moved fast to make his bid while racing well out in the track leaving the turn, took over from SOY NUMERO UNO with a furlong remaining but wasn't able to withstand the winner while besting the others. HONEST PLEASURE sprinted to the front along the inside soon after the start, made the pace while racing well out from the rail, held on well to midstretch and finished on even terms with STUMPING while weakening. STUMPING, never far back, finished with good energy. SOY NUMERO UNO, reserved behind the early leaders, moved through along the inside to gain a narrow advantage nearing the stretch, remained prominent to the final furlong and gave way. HATCHET MAN was always outrun. EL PITIRRE was never close. DANCING GUN was finished soon after going five furlongs. SONKISSER gave way after racing forwardly for six furlongs. RIGHT MIND was always outrun.

horses have a built-in advantage and which ones should be seriously downgraded or tossed out.

Track bias is one of the fundamental realities of racing. There really is a logic to the race, a surprisingly consistent stream of logic. But it can rarely be appreciated without understanding the role of the racetrack as it influences the flow of the action from start to finish.

A SAMPLE RACE: The Schuyerville Stakes, July 29, 1974. Opening day at Saratoga. Five of the first six races were main track sprints and all were won wire to wire. Not one horse made a move on the outside all day, and no horse was passed in the stretch.

No speed figures are needed to handicap this race, no pace numbers, no race charts either. The logical front runner is easy to discern and she paid $22.40. I'll give you one hint and one guess. Hint: The best two-year-old filly in racing history . . . The winner will be revealed in Chapter 14.

JULY 29, 1974

7th SARATOGA

6 FURLONGS. (1:08) Fifty-seventh running SCHUYLERVILLE (1st Division).

My Compliments 116 B. f (1972), by Delta Judge—Granny's Pride, by Roman.
Breeder, R. L. Reineman (Ky.). 1974 3 2 1 0 $11,580
Owner, R. L. Reineman. Trainer, W. C. Freeman.
Jly 20-743Mth 5½ f 1:05⅘sft 9-5 *119 42 2½ 1h 12¾ RuaneJ5 Alw 91 ⒻMyComplim'ts119 Q Up Myst'ryM'd 6
Jly 6-743Aqu 5½ f 1:05 ft 6-5 *117 1½ 13 13 12 VeneziaM6 Mdn 88 ⒻMyC'mpliments117 Awarr Q'n'sTurf 7
Jun25-743Aqu 5½ f 1:05 ft 15 117 63¾ 63½ 3½ 2no VeneziaM8 Mdn 88 ⒻLadyP'tia117 MyC'plim'ts M'lyB'ne 10
July 27 Sar 4f ft :49⅗b July 17 Aqu 4f ft :47⅗h July 13 Aqu 4f ft :51b

---

Our Dancing Girl 116 B. f (1972), by Solo Landing—Amber Dancer, by Native Dancer.
Breeder, Elcee-H Stable (Fla.). 1974 5 1 1 2 $11,793
Owner, Elcee-H Stable. Trainer, J. Rigione.
Jly 10-748Aqu 5½ f 1:02⅘sft 11 115 31 39 314 321 HoleM3 AlwS 78 ⒻRuff'n118 L'gh'gB'dge OurD'c'gGirl 4
Jly 1-747Mth 5½ f 1:06 ft 7½ 117 14 1h 21 33 GallitanoG6 Alw 84 PropMan118 Prev ier OurDanc'gGirl 7
Jun15-743Bel 5½ f 1:06 ft 3½ 116 14 15 16 14½ HoleM4 Mdn 85 ⒻO'rD'c'gG'l 116 Tricks Bl'de ofR's 10
Jun 7-743Bel 5½ f 1:05⅘sft 3½ 116 12 12 11½ 21 HoleM2 M40000 86 ⒻCurlique116 OurD'c'gGirl SwiftImp 10
May30-743Bel 5½ f 1:06 ft 4½ 114 31 11 21½ 47½ HoleM3 M35000 77 ⒻCurtainCall 116 M'snM'se Cl's'gM't 8
July 24 Bel 5f ft :59⅘sh July 8 Bel 4f ft :47⅗h June 29 Bel 4f ft 48⅗b

---

La Bourresque 116 Dk. b. or br. f (1972), by Victoria Park—Nearanna, by Nearctic.
Breeder, J. L. Levesque (Can.). 1974 6 1 2 2 $7,164
Owner, J. L. Levesque. Trainer, J. Starr.
Jly 14-746WO 6 f 1:11⅗sft 8e 119 54 55½ 54¾ 2no TurcotteN1 Alw 86 R'son'bleWin119 LaB'r'sque Dap'rS'dy 12
Jly 6-746WO 6 f 1:11⅗sft 15 112 3nk 1h 2½ 32½ D'tfashH4 HcpS 83 ⒻDeepstar112 M'dowsw't LaB'r'sque 8
Jun27-746WO 6 f 1:13⅗ssl 9½ 116 5 253¼ 56 59¾ RogersC4 InvH 65 P'sleyPal 117 H'pe forS'shine Petrus 7
Jun 8-744WO 5½ f 1:04⅘sft 1 *119 3½ 32 33½ 39 RogersC6 Alw 87 ⒻKn'tlyPr's119 M'd'sw't LaB'r'sque 6

Some Swinger 116 Ch. f (1972), by Tirreno—Batting a Thousand, by Hitting Away.
Breeder, H. T. Mangurian, Jr. (Ky.). 1972 4 2 0 1 $6,475
Owner, H. T. Magurian, Jr. Trainer, T. F. Root, Sr.
Jly 8-746Crc 6 f 1:13⅘sft 4-5 *118 4½ 41½ 2½ 14 GuerinE1 Alw 85 ⒻSomeSw'g'r118 B'lPrineR'se Whirl It 8
Jun29-749Crc 5 f 1:00⅘sft 17 118 85¾ 83½ 53 31½ GuerinE5 HcpS 89 ⒻMyM'mN'h113 W'd a.L'l'g S'eS'g'r 12
Jun17-742Crc 5½ f 1:07⅘sft 9 118 3nk 11½ 14 13 Gr'nst'nB3 Mdn 91 ⒻS'eS'g'r118 Fl'daN'dies H'K andEve 10
Jun 5-742Crc 5½ f 1:07⅘ssy 18 118 910 911 916 913 StLeonG3 Mdn 78 ⒻSoloRoyal 118 Sm'l theRoses OldH'n 9
July 25 Bel 4f sy :46hg July 21 Bel 6f ft 1:16b July 17 Bel 3f ft :37b

---

Secret's Out 119 Lt. ch. f (1972), by Royal Saxon—Secret Verdict, by Clandestine.
Breeder, Mrs. M. W. Schott (Fla.). 1974 4 3 0 0 $24,503
Owner, Marcia Schott. Trainer, J. E. Picou.
Jun19-748Mth 5½ f 1:04 ft 6 119 21 74¾ 69¾ 59½ B'mf'ldD2 AlwS 88 ⒻF'rWind 115 Copernica Fant'ticMiss 7
May26-749Suf 5 f 1:00⅗sm 3-5 *121 1½ 12 13½ 13½ W'dh'eR9 HcpS 85 Secret'sOut121 Incniq'l'ah Wh't aT'k't 9
Apr24-747Kee 4½ f :53⅕sft 1 *119 2 13 11 14½ B'f'ldD1 AlwS 89 ⒻS'cr't'sOut119 Fl'Prince's Ain'tE'sy 8
Mar15-743Hia 3 f :33⅖ssy 2½ *117 3 11 13½ W'dh'seR1 Mdn 95 ⒻS'cr't'sO't117 Ebo'lite W'tATr'nk't 14
July 17 Bel 6f ft 1:12⅘sh July 11 Bel 6f ft 1:13h June 29 4f ft :48⅘sb

---

Precious Elaine 112 Dk. b. or br. f (1972), by Tom Fool or Advocator—Imgoinaway, by
On-and-On. Br., Mrs. J. R. Pancoast (Fla.) 1974 3 M 1 0 $1,980
(Formerly named Idontlikehim).
Owner, A. J. Brodsky. Trainer, J. P. Conway.
Jly 15-743Aqu 6 f 1:12 ft 10 117 11½ 11½ 1½ 21¾ S'nt'goA1 Mdn 76 ⒻGoldB'x117 Pr'ciousE'l'ne G'rd nQu'd 11
Jun12-748Bel 5½ f 1:03 ft 18 112 64 611 623 630 Cast'daM5 AlwS 70 ⒻRuffian 117 Copernica Jan Verzal 6
May22-743Bel 5½ f 1:03 ft 4½ 116 23 39 721 934 Cast'daM1 Mdn 66 ⒻRuffian 116 Suzest Garden Quad 10
July 24 Bel 4f ft :49b July 10 Bel 5f ft 1:00⅕h July 5 Bel 3f ft :36⅘sb

---

But Exclusive 116 Ch. f (1972), by Exclusive Native—Royal Bit, by Alcibiades II.
Breeder, L. Combs II. (Ky.). 1974 3 1 2 0 $9,470
Owner, W. A. Levin. Trainer, D. A. Imperio.
Jly 12-744Aqu 5½ f 1:05⅖sft 3 118 65½ 47½ 36 24 VeneziaM1 Alw 82 ⒻSc't'shM'l'dy118 B'tExcl've C's'nlvy 8
Jun22-743Bel 5½ f 1:05⅕sft 3-2 *116 64½ 22 2½ 1h VeneziaM5 Mdn 89 ⒻButExclu've116 Aw'ra Sc't'shM'l'dy 9
Jun10-744Bel 5½ f 1:05⅕sft 7½ 116 57½ 45 42 23½ Ven'ziaM3 Mdn 85 ⒻFr'chR'le116 B'tExcl've M'ivB'l'tine 10
July 26 Bel 4f ft :48⅕h July 19 Bel 4f ft :47⅖hg July 11 Bel trt 3f ft :35⅘sh

5

The Money Tree

Trainer Glenn C. Smith will never make the Hall of Fame at Saratoga. But I doubt seriously that he cares.

Mr. Smith, never more than a part-time claiming-horse trainer with few horses and no following, did quite well during the winter meets at Bowie a decade ago. He also helped to teach a particular struggling student of handicapping an important lesson: You can't really understand this game without taking the role of the trainer into account.

It was February 1, 1963, and I had just had a miserable afternoon at Bowie, a zero-for-nine afternoon, and I was not enjoying the four-hour bus ride back to New Jersey one bit. My handicapping had been awful, but the fellow in the back of the bus who had done considerably better was bent on giving me a headache. He was succeeding more than I cared to admit. In exasperation, I opened up the *Racing Form*—half to punish myself, half to get out of his range. What I saw is what you see below—Trojan Seth, the wire-to-wire winner of the sixth race. A 3–1 stickout trained by Mr. Smith.

Trojan Seth * 112 B. h (1958), by Trojan Monarch—Cedquest, by Alquest.
Breeder C B. Caldwell.

Owner, G. C Smith. Trainer, G. C Smith. $7.500

1962	8	4	0	4	$10.422
1961	13	2	3	1	$7,240

Apr27-62⁷Lrl	7 f	1:24⅗ft	5	114•	12	1½	22	32	AddesaE5	10000	88	Cycount103	C'ch a'dF'r109	Troj'nSeth	6
Apr18-62⁶Lrl	6 f	1:12⅘ft	3½	114•	1½	2½	2h	3¾	AddesaE5	10000	90	Klinkh'se116	C'h andF'r108	Tr'j'nSeth	10
Apr 7-62⁶Lrl	6 f	1:11⅕sy	3	114•	2h	2½	2½	32¼	AddesaE1	12000	97	Adorette115	Polyn'nB'ly115	Tr'nSeth	7
Mar28-62⁷Bow	6 f	1:11 ft	6-5	112‡	15	16	16	15	AddesaE1	Alw	96	Tr'j'nS'th112	S'r andC'm107	En'shS'le	6
Mar17-62⁷Bow	6 f	1:11⅘ft	3-2e	113	1h	2½	21	34†	McKeeC2	Alw	88	Yeuxdoux115	Adorette119	TrojanSeth	7
†Dead heat.															
Mar 5-62⁷Bow	5½ f	1:05⅗ft	2½	▲117‡	12	1½	1h	1no	AddesaE2	9000	92	TrojanSeth 117	Dollmaker 117	OleKel	6
Feb20-62⁷Bow	6 f	1:14⅗m	2¾	▲113‡	13	1½	1h	1¾	AddesaE6	8000	79	Trojan Seth 113	Dollmaker 112	Ji-Jo	6
Feb14-62⁷Bow	6 f	1:14 sy	6-5	▲108‡	11½	14	11	12¼	AddesaE2	7000	81	TrojanSeth108	Dalsax1'4	Tourdan	8
Dec13-61⁶P.m	6 f	1:13 m	12	107‡	21	22	43½	56	AddesaE5	9000	79	Ano rArt114	Giewith116	Barb'raLeeG.	7

Jan 30 Bow 1m ft 1:45⅗b

According to all the rules of traditional handicapping theory, Trojan Seth should have been a throwout on the grounds of physical condition. The colt had not been out on the track for a race in over nine months. The workout, a single slow mile just two days before the race, could hardly have sharpened the colt's speed. And as the race shaped up, it was not an easy spot.

There were four recent winners shipping in from the South and two confirmed $8,500 horses dropping down in class. Now, when it was too late, the bottom two races in Trojan Seth's chart barked out their message.

Instantly, it was clear that Trojan Seth was not a horse that needed to be raced into shape. Was Smith, I wondered, the kind of man who made a habit of such doings?

The answer, along with the cure for my headache, came later that night when I compared the past-performance records of all Smith's starters from the previous winter. Nine horses. Thirty-two starts. Ten total victories. An excellent 30 percent win record. But there was more, much more. I checked back over the prior year just to be sure.

There was no doubt about it; this little-known trainer brought considerable skill to his craft. Smith had a pattern. An amazing 60 percent win record with first-time starters and absentees, only one of which was a post-time favorite. But the most astounding part of the pattern was the long, slow workout that accompanied six out of his seven absentee winners. All were sprinters, all showed early speed in their past performances, and all but one scored after several months of inactivity.

The lone exception raced in a route, finished out of the money, and then came back five days later to score in a sprint at 16–1. Mr. Smith was a horseplayer's dream. A veritable money tree. He trained all his horses back on the farm, away from the prying eyes of the clockers and the competition. And the long, slow workout was just the final touch of a well-thought-out training regimen.

Each year Smith invaded Bowie with a stableful of razor-sharp claimers, got the money, went back to the farm, and smiled a lot.

I was smiling too. By meeting's end Smith won nine more races to lead the Bowie trainers. His overall win record was an excellent 30 percent. But he was five for nine with the pattern, and I was four for eight. But the moral of the story is not complete without sharing one additional detail.

One of the nonpattern horses that won for Mr. Smith was a cheap but useful three-year-old named Cedar Key. Smith lost him via the claim box for $5,000, took him back for $6,500, and then lost him again at the end of the meeting for $6,500 to Don McCoy, the same trainer who had taken him away from Smith the first time.

McCoy wanted this colt as badly as Smith, but for a very different reason. McCoy's New York client owned a bakery shop with the identical name—the Cedar Key Bakery. Of such motives are champions made.

Over the next two years, while Smith was breaking his back to win $100,000 in purses with his band of hobbled platers, Cedar Key was winning nearly $200,000 in turf stakes coast to coast. That may be one reason Mr. Smith will never make the Hall of Fame at Saratoga. For what it's worth, he has my vote.

The Trainer's Window

There are many successful trainers like Glenn C. Smith. Every racetrack has its aces, and each horseman brings to his craft one or more special skills (or winning strategies) that separate him from the rest of the crowd.

Some are small-time operators, patient men who spend months getting cheap, sore-legged horses fit enough to deliver one or two sharp efforts. Others travel the racing circuit first class, commanding large armies of horses on several fronts. And there are a few—throwbacks to the days when racing was truly the sport of kings—who deal only with the best-bred racing stock money can buy.

Because of these vastly different economic situations, because different trainers have rather personal methods, preferences, and skills, there is no single, simplistic formula that can be applied to a reading of physical condition. Although we all tend to forget it from time to time, the Thoroughbred racehorse is an athlete in the purest sense of the word. And to a far greater degree than most people think, the trainer is its coach.

From dawn until well after dusk, 365 days a year, the trainer must watch over the feed tub, consult the veterinarian, study the *Racing Form*, plan the workout schedule, saddle the horses, watch the day's races, make travel arrangements, supervise the stable help, reassure the owners, select the class, distance, jockey, equipment, and date of the race. The horse is a wonderfully fast, woefully fragile creature, and it takes considerable skill, timing, and patience to keep it in competition. (It also costs the owner about $18,000 a year per horse.)

"I can usually tell when a horse is a race away from losing its form," said Hall of Fame trainer Allen Jerkens, master of the upset and one of the best coaches a thoroughbred athlete could possibly have. Few trainers in racing history have been more effective with recently acquired stock and few have been better at monitoring the subtle day-to-day changes of the horses in his care.

"There are many signs," explained Jerkens. "Every horse has his own habits. You get to know them pretty well. The ankle doesn't respond as quickly, or the hair on the coat begins to lose its sheen, or he leaves some feed in the tub. You've got to look them over very carefully. Any change makes an impression." Later, Jerkens added, "If you want to save a horse for future racing, the time to stop is *before* they stop on you."

Not all trainers can afford the luxury of long-range planning. Where cheap horses are concerned, most goals begin and end with the here and now. Nevertheless, at every racetrack there are a few claiming horse trainers who seem to have as much patience and a better sense of timing than most stakes-class horsemen. One such trainer is Jerry Hollendorfer, who has dominated northern California racing for nearly a decade. Hollendorfer has won every meet title at Golden Gate Fields and Bay Meadows from 1985 through the winter of 1994, with no end in sight.

"There's not much sense putting a horse in a race he can't win," Hollendorfer said. "I don't drill my horses that fast, but we get them ready through a balanced program of regularly spaced workouts and gallops. When they're fit, they go, and when they're not, they stay in the barn. Every trainer and handicapper should remember that every race takes something out of a horse, or puts something into him. All I try to do is run them where they best fit because the owners deserve as much. Besides," he added, "the horse is only going to learn how to lose if you keep running him over his head or at the wrong distance."

Under the care of one trainer, a horse with good recent form might be an excellent wager; in the care of another, the horse might be ready to fall apart at the seams.

In the hands of an ace, a horse stepping up sharply in company or stretching out in distance might well be expected to handle the task; in the care of a lesser talent, such a maneuver might only be an experiment or an unnecessary risk.

While many trainers like to wager on their own horses, the player is misled to believe that poor trainers are any better at handicapping than they are at their chosen craft.

The horse may have a fine turn of speed or suddenly show signs of life, but if the trainer is impatient, sloppy or incompetent, he or she will find ways to lose control and blow the best of opportunities.

Maybe the horse is bred for distance races on the turf, or needs a better jockey to harness his speed; perhaps a change in equipment will improve its manners at the starting gate. Maybe the horse has been ambitiously placed, or has been asked to work too fast, too often, and has left his best race on the training track. You would be amazed how many horses are mismanaged in that fashion.

The positive and negative impact of the trainer on horse performance is all too rarely taken into account by the average horseplayer, who, at best, glances at the leading trainers' list and automatically assumes universal competence.

But the mistake is easily corrected, and it is great fun.

After all, the past-performance profile is not only a summation of horse performance but a window through which the talents, habits, and strategies of the trainer can be seen.

For example, by comparing the past performances of a dozen or so winners (and losers) trained by Hall of Famer Woody Stephens, the player will know for a certainty that Stephens was an absolute master with an improving three-year-old as well as with stakes-class fillies and mares on and off the grass course. Stephens, who endured emphysema and several other major illnesses and injuries during the 1980s, nevertheless reached the pinnacle of his glorious career during that decade.

Stephens' approach, which was developed in part by studying Max Hirsch, Sunny Jim Fittzimmons and other top horsemen of the 1940s and 1950s, blended extraordinary patience with the boldness of a bank robber.

When Woody Stephens set a horse down for a series of hard races, the signs were unmistakable and the player could anticipate *two, three, or four solid efforts in succession.* While no task seemed impossible, few of Stephens' horses ever were asked to attempt something physically beyond their capabilities.

Forty Niner *

Own.—Claiborne Farm

Ch. c. 3, by Mr Prospector—File, by Tom Rolfe
Br.—Claiborne Farm (Ky) **1988 11 5 5 0 $1,540,892**
Tr.—Stephens Woodford C **1987 6 5 0 0 $634,908**
Lifetime 17 10 5 0 $2,175,800

17Sep88-8Bel	1¼	:47^3	1:35	1:59^{2}ft	2¾	119	2½	1^{hd}	1^{hd}	2^{nk}	PncLJr^2	Woodward H	101-08	Alysheba, Forty Niner, Waquoit	8
17Sep88—Grade I															
20Aug88-8Sar	1¼	:48^3	1:37^4	2:01^{2}ft	2¼	126	1½	1½	1^2	1no	McCrrnCJ^5	Travers	93-09	FortyNiner,SekingthGold,Brin'sTim	6
20Aug88—Grade I															
30Jly88-9Mth	1⅛	:47^3	1:11^2	1:47^{3}ft	*4-5	126	2^{1½}	1^{hd}	1^{hd}	1no	PincyLJr^1	Haskell H	96-10	Forty Niner,SeekingtheGold,Primal	5
30Jly88—Grade I															
16Jly88-8Mth	1	:45^2	1:09^1	1:33^{4}ft	*1-3	114	2^2	2^1	1^{2½}	1^{7¼}	Krone J A^4	Aw30000	104-09	FortyNiner,SlwCitySlw,BluBuckroo	6
21May88-9Pim	1 3/16	:47	1:11^1	1:56^{1}gd	2¼	126	1^{hd}	1^{hd}	7^8	7^{14¼}	Day P^4	Preakness	72-11	RisenStr,Brin'sTime,WinningColors	9
21May88—Grade I; Brushed rival															
7May88-8CD	1¼	:46^4	1:36	2:02^{1}ft	5e	126	3^{4½}	5^7	3^4	2^{nk}	Day P^{17}	Ky Derby	86-11	WinningColors,FortyNiner,RisnStr	17
7May88—Grade I															
16Apr88-8Kee	1 1/16	:48	1:12^2	1:42^{4}ft	*2-5	121	3^1	2^{1½}	1½	2^{hd}	Day P^4	Lexington	92-18	Risen Star, Forty Niner, Stalwars	5
16Apr88—Grade II															
8Apr88-8Kee	7f	:23	:45^2	1:22 ft	*1-2	121	4^{2½}	3½	1^1	1^5	Day P^7	Lafayette	96-21	Forty Niner, Buoy,AlohaProspector	8
5Mar88-10GP	1⅛	:46^3	1:10^4	1:49^{4}ft	3	122	1½	1^{1½}	1^2	2^{nk}	Maple E^9	Fla Derby	83-16	Brian'sTime,FortyNiner,Notebook	10
5Mar88—Grade I															
15Feb88-10GP	1 1/16	:46^3	1:10^4	1:43^{1}ft	*4-5	122	1^{hd}	1^{hd}	1^{hd}	1no	Maple E^7	Fountin Yth	85-21	Forty Niner, Notebook, Buoy	9
15Feb88—Grade II															
3Feb88-9GP	7f	:21^4	:44^3	1:23 ft	*2-3	122	2^{hd}	2½	2^{1½}	2^1	Maple E^5	Hutcheson	88-24	Perfect Spy, Forty Niner,Notebook	7
3Feb88—Grade III															
30Oct87-8Kee	1 1/16	:46^4	1:11	1:43^{4}ft	*2-5	121	2^1	2^{hd}	2^{hd}	1no	Maple E^2	Brd Fut	87-18	Forty Niner, Hey Pat, Sea Trek	7
30Oct87—Grade II															

Oct 16 Bel 6f ft 1:14^1 b ●Oct 12 Bel 6f ft 1:11 h Oct 10 Bel 4f gd :50^2 b Oct 5 Bel 1 ft 1:42 b

The remarkable but predictable development of Conquistador Cielo—the first of Stephens' record-smashing five straight Belmont Stakes winners—is worth repeated study. Below are this superior colt's past performances as they appeared in *Daily Racing Form*, prior to his track record victory in the Metropolitan Mile, on May 31, 1982, less than one week before the 1½-mile Belmont Stakes. The Met, one of my favorite races of the year, is a prestigious handicap for three-year-olds and up, contested around one turn at Belmont Park on Memorial Day.

Conquistador Cielo

Own.—deKwiatkowski H **111**

B. c. 3, by Mr Prospector—K D Princess, by Bold Commander
Br.—Landoli L E (Fla) **1982 4 3 0 0 $46,300**
Tr.—Stephens Woodford C **1981 4 2 0 1 $49,668**
Lifetime 8 5 0 1 $95,968

19May82-7Bel	1	:45^4	1:09^4	1:34^{1}ft	*2-3	113	1^{hd}	1^3	1^7	1^{11}	Maple E^4	Aw35000	95	ConqstdorClo,SwngngLght,BchlorB	7
8May82-7Pim	1 1/16	:47^3	1:11^3	1:44^{1}ft	*1-2	112	2^2	2^1	1^{1½}	1^3	Maple E^3	Aw27000	84	ConquistdorCielo,DoubleNo,SixSils	5
26Feb82-7Hia	7f	:22^4	:45^1	1:22^{1}ft	*3-5	116	1½	1^{1½}	1^{2½}	1^4	Maple E^1	Aw14000	92	ConquistdorCilo,Hostg,MysticSqur	7
16Feb82-9Hia	7f	:22^3	:44^3	1:23 ft	5¼	116	5^{3½}	6^{7½}	4^4	4^{7¾}	Maple E^1	Aw14000	81	Star Gallant, CutAway,Rex'sProfile	7
12Aug81-8Sar	6f	:21^3	:45	1:11^{1}gd	3¾	122	6^{4½}	7^8	5^{4½}	4^{nk}	Maple E^2	Sanford	84	Mayanesian,ShippingMgnte,Lejoli	10
3Aug81-8Sar	6f	:22^1	:45^3	1:10^{3}ft	8¼	117	6^{3¾}	2^{hd}	1^{hd}	1½	Maple E^2	Sar Spec'l	87	ConqstdorCl,Hrschlwlkr,TmlyWrtr	10
10Jly81-6Bel	5½f	:23	:46^4	1:05 ft	*8-5	118	3^2	2^1	1^3	1^8	Saumell L^7	Mdn	90	ConquistdorCilo,HghAscnt,Grrs'Ldr	9
29Jun81-4Bel	5½f	:22^4	:46^4	1:06^{2}ft	4½	118	4^{4¼}	5^3	2^3	3^{3¾}	Saumell L^9	Mdn	82	AntgBrd,Commodty,ConqstdorClo	10

●May 26 Bel 6f ft 1:10^2 h ●May 16 Bel 5f ft :59 h May 6 Bel 4f ft :47 h May 2 Bel 5f ft 1:00 h

Stephens knew he had an outstanding colt in the summer of 1981, when C.C. ran a great race to finish fourth in the Sanford stakes at Saratoga, despite suffering a minor leg fracture and a world of traffic trouble.

Instead of rushing his prize colt into the Triple Crown chase the following spring, Woody took special care to give C.C. lessons in a variety of racing situations, including a race around two turns at Pimlico one week prior to the Preakness and a rather convincing win over older rivals in an allowance race at Belmont, May 19. "I skipped over the Preakness," Stephens explained, "because it was just one notch tougher than he was ready for, and he was one race light in getting ready for a Triple Crown race."

Sadly, too many trainers fail to appreciate the need for restraint when good horses are close but not quite ready to compete in tough stakes. As a result they prematurely burn up horses who might become stars.

Following Conquistador Cielo's awesome victory in the Met, Stephens had all the evidence he needed to become characteristically aggressive, throwing the razor-sharp budding superhorse into the grueling 1½ mile Belmont Stakes five days later.

The betting public and most of the public handicappers focused on doubts about C.C.'s breeding limitations and let him go off at a relatively generous 4–1 price. Few apparently believed this son of the ultrafast Mr. Prospector would hold his form over the demanding 1½-mile distance. But these same critics ignored the colt's overpowering final quarter-mile clockings, which hovered around 24 seconds for each of his last three races at one mile and longer. Such final clockings tend to signal above-average ability, but in C.C.'s case there was the added fact that he had run that fast after setting a brisk pace in through the first six furlongs in the Met.

"I thought my colt had developed perfectly," Stephens said. "He was big and strong and racing on the pace in quick fractions and finishing better than any of those stretch runners behind him. I also remembered how [Hall of Fame trainer] Elliot Burch twice used the Met Mile against older horses as key prep races for Quadrangle (1964) and Arts and Letters (1969) to win their Belmonts. So I told Henry [Conquistador Cielo's owner, Henry deKwiatkowski] to bet his money and put some champagne on ice."

Such immaculate horsemanship literally serves as textbook material for trainers and players alike. Players should take special note of every nuance, every ounce of information. Indeed, there is considerable value in studying the best work of outstanding horsemen. Many gained universal insights studying other masters while adding their own special touches through years of trial and error.

Frank Whiteley, Jr., who trained Forego, Damascus and Ruffian certainly fits into this category, as do contemporary Hall of Famers Charley Whittingham, Allen Jerkens, Jack Van Berg, LeRoy Jolley, Ron McAnally and the late, great Lazaro S. Barrera.

A casual look below at the performances of Forego and Ruffian (and Honorable Miss on page 187) provide ample peeks at the conservative, direct Whiteley training method. No frills, no tricks, no wild experiments. A sprinter is kept sprinting, a stakes horse is given a balanced, well-spaced campaign and a first-time starter is well prepared and well meant. (See Ruffian's debut p.p.'s in Chapter 1.)

Mistakes are made but seldom repeated. Experiments are tried but quickly abandoned when they do not produce satisfactory results. A horseplayer can learn a lot about good horsemanship by looking through Frank Whiteley, Jr.'s, window.

Charles Whittingham is another amazing trainer who set standards for others to follow and study. The West Coast's answer to Woody Ste-

Forego **137** B. g (1970) by Forli—Lady Golconda by Hasty Road.
Breeder. Lazy F Ranch (Ky.). 1976 7 5 1 1 $321,481
Owner, Lazy F Ranch. Trainer, Frank Y. Whiteley. Jr. 1975 9 6 1 1 $429.521

18 Sep76 8Bel	1⅛	$:45^{3}$ $1:09^{1}$ $1:45^{4}$ ft	1	▲135	7^{6}	$7^{6\frac{1}{2}}$	$4^{2\frac{1}{2}}$	$1^{1\frac{1}{4}}$	$ShmkrW^{2}$	HcpS 98	Forego 135	Dance Spell 10
21 Aug76 8Mth	1¼	$:47^{2}$ $1:11^{2}$ $2:00^{3}$ ft	3-5	▲136	3^{3}	2^{2}	2^{1}	3^{1}	$VasquzJ^{7}$	HcpS 98	HatchetMan112	IntrepidHro 8
24 Jly 76 8Aqu	1¼	$:46^{4}$ $1:11^{1}$ $2:01^{1}$ ft	2-3	▲134	$6^{8\frac{1}{2}}$	$2^{1\frac{1}{2}}$	2^{h}	1^{2}	$CustinsH^{4}$	HcpS 90	Forego 134	Lord Rebeau 8
5 Jly 76 8Aqu	$1\frac{3}{16}$	$:47^{4}$ $1:11^{2}$ $1:55^{2}$ ft	2-5	▲134	$3^{2\frac{1}{2}}$	$2^{1\frac{1}{2}}$	$3^{1\frac{1}{2}}$	2no	$GustinsH^{2}$	HcpS 85	Foolish Pleasure 125	Forego 4
13 Jun76 8Bel	1⅛	$:47^{2}$ $1:11^{2}$ $1:48^{3}$ ft	4-5	▲132	$4^{2\frac{1}{2}}$	3^{2}	1^{h}	$1^{2\frac{3}{4}}$	$VsquezJ^{1}$	HcpS 84	Forego 132	El Pitirre 5
31 May76 8Bel	1	$:45^{3}$ $1:09^{2}$ $1:34^{4}$ ft	1	▲130	$5^{4\frac{1}{2}}$	4^{4}	$4^{1\frac{1}{2}}$	1^{h}	$GustinsH^{4}$	HcpS 94	Forego 130	Master Derby 6
20 May76 8Bel	7 f	$:23^{4}$ $:46^{4}$ 1:22 ft	1-3	▲126	$4^{1\frac{1}{2}}$	$3^{\frac{1}{2}}$	1^{h}	$1^{1\frac{1}{4}}$	$GustinesH^{2}$	Alw 92	Forego 126	Wishing Stone 4

Oct 1 Bel 4f sy :46h   Sept 27 Bel 1f ft 1:43⅕b   Sept 25 Bel 5f ft 1:05b

Ruffian Dk. b. or br. f. 3, by Reviewer—Shenanigans, by Native Dancer
Br.—Janney Mr-Mrs S S Jr (Ky)
Own.—Locust Hill Farm Tr.—Whiteley F Y Jr

	St.	1st	2nd	3rd	Amt.
1975	6	5	0	0	$179,356
1974	5	5	0	0	$134,073

6Jly75- 8Bel	fst	1¼	:44⅗	1:08⅗	2:02⅘	Match Race	1	1	—				Vasquez J	121	*.40	— —	Foolish Pleasure 126 Ruffian 121	Broke down 2
21Jun75- 8Bel	fst	1½	:49	1:13⅖	2:27⅘	ⓕC C A Oaks	5	1	1^{4}	$1^{1\frac{1}{2}}$	1^{3}	$1^{2\frac{3}{4}}$	Vasquez J	121	*.05	81-12	$Ruffin121^{2\frac{3}{4}}EqulChnge121^{9}LetMeLinger121^{2\frac{1}{2}}$	Confidently ridden 7
31May75- 8Aqu	fst	1⅛	:47⅗	1:11⅗	1:47⅘	ⓕMotherGoose	6	1	$1^{1\frac{1}{2}}$	1^{2}	1^{8}	1^{14}	Vasquez J	121	*.10	96-07	$Ruffian\ 121^{13\frac{1}{2}}$ Sweet Old Girl 121^{2} $SunandSnow121^{2\frac{1}{2}}$	Easy score 7
10May75- 8Aqu	fst	1	:45⅗	1:09⅗	1:34⅖	ⓕAcorn	3	1	1^{1}	1^{3}	1^{7}	$1^{8\frac{1}{4}}$	Vasquez J	121	*.10	94-08	$Ruffian\ 121^{8\frac{1}{4}}$ Somethingregal 121no Gallant Trial 121^{1}	In hand 7
30Apr75- 8Aqu	fst	7f	:22⅘	:45	1:21⅕	ⓕComely	3	5	1^{1}	$1^{1\frac{1}{2}}$	1^{6}	$1^{7\frac{3}{4}}$	Vasquez J	113	*.05	95-16	$Ruffian\ 113^{7\frac{3}{4}}$ Aunt Jin $113^{2\frac{1}{2}}$ $PointInTime113^{2}$	Slow start,handily 5
14Apr75- 8Aqu	fst	6f	:23	:45⅘	1:09⅖	ⓕAllowance	2	3	1^{1}	$1^{\frac{1}{2}}$	1^{2}	$1^{4\frac{3}{4}}$	Vasquez J	122	*.10	96-17	$Ruffian\ 122^{4\frac{3}{4}}$ Sir Ivor's Sorrow 113^{hd} Channelette 113^{2}	Easily 5
23Aug74- 8Sar	fst	6f	:22⅕	:44⅘	1:08⅗	ⓕSpinaway	2	1	1^{2}	1^{3}	1^{7}	1^{13}	Bracciale V Jr	120	*.20	97-10	$Ruffian\ 120^{13}$ Laughing Bridge $120^{1\frac{1}{2}}$ Scottish $Melody120^{5}$	Easily 4
27Jly74- 8Mth	fst	6f	:21⅗	:44⅕	1:09	ⓕSorority	3	3	$1^{\frac{1}{2}}$	1^{hd}	$1^{\frac{1}{2}}$	$1^{2\frac{1}{4}}$	Vasquez J	119	*.30	95-15	$Ruffian\ 119^{2\frac{1}{4}}$ Hot N Nasty 119^{22} Stream Across 119^{4}	Driving 4
10Jly74- 8Aqu	fst	5½f	:21⅘	:44⅖	1:02⅘	ⓕAstoria	2	2	1^{1}	1^{3}	1^{6}	1^{9}	Bracciale V Jr	118	*.10	99-15	$Ruffin118^{9}LughingBridg115^{12}OurDncingGirl115^{3\frac{1}{2}}$	Speed to spare 4
12Jun74- 8Bel	fst	5½f	:22⅖	:45⅕	1:03	ⓕFashion	3	4	$1^{1\frac{1}{2}}$	$1^{1\frac{1}{2}}$	1^{4}	$1^{6\frac{3}{4}}$	Vasquez J	117	*.40	100-12	$Ruffian\ 117^{6\frac{3}{4}}$ Copernica 117^{13} Jan Verzal 117^{nk}	Ridden out 6
22May74- 3Bel	fst	5½f	:22⅕	:45	1:03	ⓕMd Sp Wt	9	8	1^{3}	1^{5}	1^{8}	1^{15}	Vasquez J	116	4.20	100-15	$Ruffian\ 116^{15}$ Suzest 113^{5} Garden Quad $116^{\frac{1}{2}}$	Ridden out 10

LATEST WORKOUTS Jly 5 Bel 3f fst :35 b ● Jly 1 Bel 5f fst :58⅕ b Jun 27 Bel 4f fst :47 b Jun 19 Bel 4f fst :46⅖ b

Golden Pheasant Ro. c. 4, by Caro—Perfect Pigeon, by Round Table
Br.—CarelaineFarm&VintageMeadowFarm (Ky)
Own.—Gretzky & Summa Stable Tr.—Whittingham Charles
Lifetime 11 5 3 1 $965,470 | 1990 5 3 0 1 $790,500 | 1989 6 2 3 0 $174,970 | Turf 11 5 3 1 $965,470

2Sep90- 8AP fm 1¼ Ⓣ:48⅗ 1:36⅕ 1:59⅗ 3↑Arl Million 1 5 66 53¾ 3½ 11¼ Stevens G L 126 6.60 114 — GoldenPheasant1261¼WithApprovl1265¼Steinlen126nk Driving 11
2Sep90-Grade I
12Aug90- 8Dmr fm 1⅛ Ⓣ:48⅗ 1:12⅖ 1:48⅕ 3↑E Read H 3 4 53½ 64 43 31¾ Stevens G L B 122 2.40 95-06 FlyTillDwn112hdClssicFme1191¾GoldenPhesnt1221 No mishap 8
12Aug90-Grade I
28May90- 8Hol gd 1¼ Ⓣ:48⅗ 1:37⅘ 2:03 3↑Hol Turf H 5 4 36 32½ 34½ 45¾ McCarron C J 122 *1.00 72-22 Steinlen124nk Hawkster1225½ Santangelo110hd Bid, weakened 6
28May90-Grade I
13May90- 8Hol fm 1⅛ Ⓣ:48⅘ 1:12⅕ 1:47 3↑Jhn Henry H 3 4 44 41¾ 3½ 11¾ McCarron C J 120 *1.40 93-09 GoldenPhesnt1201¾ClssicFme117nkSteinln1261¾ Bumped start 5
13May90-Grade II
22Apr90- 5SA fm 1⅛ Ⓣ:45⅘ 1:09⅗ 1:45⅕ Alw 42000 1 10 109¼ 88 22 11¾ McCarron C J 116 *.90 96 — GoldnPhsnt1161¾FlyTillDwn1181Kntiyr1185 Broke slowly wid 10
22Apr90-Broke slowly; wide
8Oct89♦5Longchamp(Fra) gd*1½ 2:30⅘ Ⓣ Arc de Triomphe(Gr1) 14 Cruz A S 123 10.00 — — CarrollHouse 1301½ Behera 120nk SaintAndrews130nk Outrun 19
17Sep89♦4Longchamp(Fra) yl*1½ 2:32⅖ Ⓣ Prix Niel (Gr2) 11½ Cruz A S 123 7.10 — — GoldenPleasant1231½ FrenchGlory123½ Nshwn130nk Bid,drvg 8
2Jly89♦4StCloud(Fra) gd*1½ 2:35⅘ Ⓣ GrandPrix de StCloud(Gr1) 2hd Cruz A S 121 7.75 — — Sheriff'sStar134hd GoldenPheasant121hd Boytino1341 Cl.well 6
11Jun89♦7Chantilly(Fra) gd*1½ 2:33⅘ Ⓣ Prix du Lys(Gr3) 2no Cruz A S 121 *1.75 — — HrvestTime124no GoldnPlsnt1212½ Spiritsil1242½ Outfinished 8
9May89♦3Chester(Eng) gd*1½ 2:34⅕ Ⓣ Chester Vase Stks 22½ Roberts M 123 6.00 — — OldVic1232½ GoldenPheasant12312 Warrshn1237 Prom,no exc 5

Speed Index: Last Race: +14.0 3–Race Avg.: +3.0 5–Race Avg.: +1.4 Overall Avg.: +1.4
LATEST WORKOUTS ●Aug 30 AP Ⓣ 4f fm :51 B Aug 25 Dmr Ⓣ 1 fm 1:39⅗ H (d) Aug 20 Dmr Ⓣ 5f fm 1:04⅘ B (d)

phens, Whittingham has been a prolific winner of rich stakes for four decades. Among his lengthy list of important horses, Whittingham developed Ferdinand and Sunday Silence, each winners of the Kentucky Derby and the $3 million Breeders Cup Classic, plus three winners of the prestigious Arlington Million—Perrault, Estrapade and Golden Pheasant.

For most of his distinguished career, Whittingham's horses resembled his Arlington Million winners—late developers, long-distance specialists, most imported from Europe or South America, or infused with the best stamina bloodlines in the American stud book.

Estrapade Ch. m. 6, by Vaguely Noble—Klepto, by No Robbery
Br.—Hunt N B (Ky) | 1986 7 3 2 1 $968,800
Own.—Paulson A E Tr.—Whitti..gham Charles | 1985 11 5 2 1 $601,800
Lifetime 28 12 5 4 $1,708,556 | Turf 25 12 5 3 $1,663,556

12Oct86-8SA 1½Ⓣ:4642:0032:26 fm*2-5e 123 11½ 12 12 12¼ Toro F6 Oak Tree Iv 85-12 Estrapade,Theatrical,UptownSwell 10
12Oct86—Grade I
31Aug86-8AP 1¼Ⓣ:4711:3712:004fm *2e 122 64½ 1hd 11½ 15 Toro F7 Bud Mil 90-11 Estrapade, Divulge, Pennine Walk 14
31Aug86—Grade I
9Aug86-8Dmr 1 Ⓣ:4611:1041:342fm*4-5e 124 32 41 44½ 65¾ Toro F3 ⒻPlmr H 94-04 Aberuschka, Sauna,Fran'sValentine 9
9Aug86—Grade II; Crowded, steadied 3/8 turn
29Jun86-8Hol 1¼Ⓣ:4641:3411:59 fm*4-5e 122 25 11½ 11½ 1½ Toro F3 ⒻBv Hlls H 112-02 Estrapade, Treizieme, Sauna 7
29Jun86—Grade II
8Jun86-8Hol 1⅛Ⓣ:4611:10 1:454fm*2-3 123 32 31½ 31 21¾ ShmrW5 ⒻGmly H 101 — La Koumia, Estrapade, Tax Dodge 8
8Jun86—Grade I; Crowded 3/8 turn, early stretch; steadied 3/16
25May86-8Hol 1$\frac{1}{16}$Ⓣ:4841:1211:413fm*3-5 124 2½ 2hd 3nk 3nk ShmrW5 ⒻWlshr H 96-03 Outstandingly,LaKoumia,Estrapade 5
25May86—Grade II
30Mar86-8SA 1¼Ⓣ:4811:3632:01 fm*4-5e 124 41½ 3½ 21½ 2½ ShmrW7 ⒻSta Brb H 81-16 MountainBear,Estrapade,RoylRegtt 8
30Mar86—Grade I
24Nov85-8Hol 1⅛Ⓣ:4641:1041:481fm*3-5e 123 21 1hd 1hd 41¾ ShmrW5 ⒻMtrch Inv — — FactFinder,Tamarind,PossibleMte 10
24Nov85—Grade I
10Nov85-8SA 1¼Ⓣ:4731:3522:002fm*4-5 123 31½ 31 11 1¾ ShrW8 ⒻYlw Rbn Iv 85-18 Estrapade,Alydar'sBest,LaKoumia 11
10Nov85—Grade I
19Oct85-8SA 1⅛Ⓣ:4531:0941:471fm *1e 124 42½ 31 13 13½ ShrW7 ⒻLs Plms H 91-12 Estrapade, L'Attrayante, Johnica 11
19Oct85—Grade II

●Oct 9 SA Ⓣ 5f fm 1:002 h (d) ●Oct 4 SA Ⓣ 1 fm 1:413 h (d) ●Sep 28 SA Ⓣ 6f fm 1:131 h (d) Sep 22 SA 5f ft 1:013 b

"Why put so much pressure on those young knees and legs?" Whittingham once explained to a reporter who wondered why he chose not to run most of his top juvenile prospects in stakes races.

Some Whittingham trademarks:

- A long series of workouts, perhaps a few at racing speed and at least one, probably two, works at one mile or longer
- A carefully chosen prep race a few weeks prior to the main objective, with victory not as important as a good effort against decent competition. This to be followed by a finishing series of workouts, including one or two at the scene where the big race is scheduled to be run

WINNER OF THE 1993 SANTA ANITA HANDICAP, SIR BEAUFORT

Sir Beaufort — Gr. h. 6, by Pleasant Colony—Carolina Saga, by Caro (Ire)
VALENZUELA P A (173 26 24 22 .15) — Br.—Buckland Farm (Va)
Own.—Calantoni Victoria — Tr.—Whittingham Charles (59 4 7 8 .07) — **119**

Lifetime						
30 9 10 4	1993	2	1	1	0	$112,900
$562,255	1992	9	3	4	0	$244,250
	Turf	4	0	1	0	$7,800
	Wet	3	2	0	0	$80,500

14Feb93- 8SA	fst	1⅛	$:46^4$	$1{:}10^4$	$1{:}48^4$	Sn Antnio H	101	3	3	3^2	2^1	1^{hd}	2^{hd}	McCarron C J	LB	120	*1.00	86–16	$Marquetry117^{hd}SirBeaufort120^2ReignRod116$	Erratic 1/8	6
14Feb93-Grade II																					
9Jan93- 8SA	my	7f	$:22^1$	$:44^4$	$1{:}22^1$	Sn Carlos H	109	5	5	3^3	3^1	$1^{1\frac{1}{2}}$	1^5	McCarron C J	LB	120	2.20e	92–14	$SirBeaufort120^5Cardmania117\frac{1}{2}Excavate114$	Ridden out	6
9Jan93-Grade II																					
6Dec92- 8Hol	fst	1⅛	$:47^1$	$1{:}11^3$	$1{:}47^4$	3↑ Ntv Dvr H	109	5	2	2^1	2^1	2^{hd}	$1^{\frac{3}{4}}$	McCarron C J	LB	119	1.70	95–14	$SirBufort119\frac{3}{4}Mmo\text{-}Ch115^8Brillon\text{-}GB115$	Determinedly	5
6Dec92-Grade III																					
11Oct92- 8SA	fst	1⅛	$:46^2$	1:10	$1{:}48^1$	3↑ Goodwood H	107	5	4	4^1	$4^{\frac{3}{4}}$	$1^{\frac{1}{2}}$	$2^{1\frac{1}{2}}$	Solis A	LB	116	6.50	87–18	$ReignRoad116^{1\frac{1}{2}}SirBeaufort116^2Mrquetry120$	Wide trip	6
11Oct92-Grade II																					
13Sep92- 8Dmr	fst	1	$:44^3$	$1{:}09^2$	$1{:}35^1$	3↑ Bd Br Cp H	99	1	8	$7^{4\frac{1}{4}}$	$4^{1\frac{1}{2}}$	3^1	2^1	McCarron C J	LB	116	10.60	90–11	$RgnRod114^1SrBfort116^{1\frac{3}{4}}Chrmonnr115$	Boxed in 1/4-1/8	10
13Sep92-Grade II																					
24Aug92- 8Dmr	fst	1 1/16	:46	1:10	$1{:}41^1$	3↑ Wndy Snds H	93	3	3	$3^{1\frac{1}{2}}$	3^1	$2^{\frac{1}{2}}$	$2^{3\frac{1}{2}}$	McCarron C J	LB	120	*.60e	91–09	$RglGrom117^{3\frac{1}{2}}SrBfrt120\frac{1}{2}BckngBrd114$	Not enough late	7
7Jun92- 8Hol	fst	1⅛	$:46^1$	1:10	1:48	3↑ Californian	94	5	4	3^{nk}	$3^{\frac{1}{2}}$	$2^{1\frac{1}{2}}$	$4^{6\frac{3}{4}}$	McCarron C J	L	116	4.00e	87–14	$AnothrRviw119^{1\frac{3}{4}}DfnsivPly120^2Ibro\text{-}Ar119$	Balked gate	7
7Jun92-Grade I																					
17May92- 8Hol	fst	1 1/16	$:46^3$	$1{:}10^1$	$1{:}41^1$	3↑ Mrvn Lery H	105	2	3	$2^{\frac{1}{2}}$	2^{hd}	$2^{\frac{1}{2}}$	$2^{2\frac{3}{4}}$	Delahoussaye E	LB	116	8.60	92–13	$AnothrRviw116^{2\frac{3}{4}}SirBufort116^4Mrqutry119$	Balked gate	5
17May92-Grade II																					
15Feb92- 8SA	my	1⅛	$:47^1$	$1{:}10^3$	1:47	San Antno H	94	6	4	$4^{2\frac{1}{2}}$	4^2	7^7	$7^{10\frac{1}{4}}$	McCarron C J	LB	115	5.20	85–08	$Ibro\text{-}Ar115\frac{3}{4}InExcss\text{-}Ir123^2CobrClssc114$	4-wide stretch	8
15Feb92-Grade II																					
15Jan92- 7SA	fst	1 1/16	$:47^2$	$1{:}11^1$	1:42	Royal Owl H	112	3	4	4^2	3^1	1^{hd}	1^{hd}	McCarron C J	L	117	2.40	93–12	$SirBeaufort117^{hd}AnotherRviw117\frac{1}{2}Tokt118$	Jostled start	7

LATEST WORKOUTS Mar 2 SA 5f fst $:59^4$ H — Feb 25 SA 6f gd $1{:}12^2$ H — Feb 21 SA 3f gd $:35^4$ B — Feb 8 SA tr.t 5f gd $1{:}04^2$ B

The past performances of a Whittingham-trained horse aimed at a major stakes will make so much sense they will practically leap off the page at you. Virtually every last horse—even his longshots—can be expected to run to their potential.

Would you believe eight Hollywood Gold Cup victories, nine Santa Anita's "Big 'Caps" and 14 runnings of the San Juan Capristrano through 1993? Does it surprise you that Whittingham has scored some of his most impressive victories in these stakes without any prep races?

"It makes no difference to me, there are ways to win with workouts, or prep races," Whittingham explained while preparing Ferdinand for the 1986 Kentucky Derby. "Sometimes you can control the situation better by using workmates (in a series of long workouts)," he said. "A couple of good long workouts can condition a horse as well as a race and there's less risk of injury."

Ferdinand — Ch. c. 3, by Nijinsky II—Banja Luka, by Double Jay
Br.—Keck H B (Ky) — 1986 4 1 2 1 $162,250
Own.—Keck Mrs H B — 126 — Tr.—Whittingham Charles — 1985 5 1 1 2 $178,650
Lifetime 9 2 3 3 $340,900

6Apr86-5SA	1⅛	:47^1	1:11	1:48^{3}ft	5¼	122	5^5	5^4	$5^{4\frac{1}{2}}$	3^7	ShmkrW^2	S A Dby	79-15	Snow Chief, Icy Groom, Ferdinand	7
6Apr86—Grade I															
22Feb86-8SA	1	:45^3	1:10^2	1:35^{3}ft	*9-5	116	$7^{7\frac{1}{4}}$	$4^{1\frac{1}{2}}$	1^2	$2^{\frac{1}{2}}$	ShmkrW^9	Sn Rafael	89-16	VarietyRoad,Ferdinnd,JettingHome	9
22Feb86—Grade II															
29Jan86-8SA	1$\frac{1}{16}$	:46^2	1:11	1:43 ft	2¼	114	$6^{4\frac{3}{4}}$	$6^{4\frac{1}{2}}$	3^2	$1^{\frac{1}{2}}$	ShmkrW^6	Ⓡ Sta Ctlna	86-15	Ferdinand,VrietyRod,GrndAllegince	8
29Jan86—Lacked room, steadied at intervals 5/16 to 1/8															
4Jan86-8SA	1	:45^3	1:10^3	1:36^{1}ft	*4-5	114	$3^{2\frac{1}{2}}$	$3^{\frac{1}{2}}$	$1^{1\frac{1}{2}}$	2^{hd}	ShoemkrW^3	Ⓡ Ls Feliz	87-13	Badger Land,Ferdinand,CutByGlass	7
4Jan86—3-wide into stretch															
15Dec85-8Hol	1	:44^3	1:09	1:34^{1}ft	34	121	$9^{5\frac{3}{4}}$	$3^{5\frac{1}{2}}$	$3^{5\frac{1}{2}}$	$3^{6\frac{1}{2}}$	ShomkrW^2	Hol Fut	85-09	SnowChief,ElectricBlue,Ferdinand	10
15Dec85—Grade I															
3Nov85-1SA	1	:47^1	1:12	1:37^{2}ft	*2-5	117	$3^{2\frac{1}{2}}$	1^1	1^1	$1^{2\frac{1}{4}}$	Ward W A^1	Mdn	81-15	Ferdinand,StrRibot,ImperiousSpirit	6
20Oct85-6SA	1	:46^3	1:12	1:37^{3}ft	*2¼	117	$5^{3\frac{1}{4}}$	$2^{\frac{1}{2}}$	2^{hd}	2no	Toro F^7	Mdn	80-17	AcksLikRuler,Frdinnd,Frnkinstrlli	10
20Oct85—Lugged in stretch, bumped late															
6Oct85-6SA	6f	:21^4	:45^1	1:10^{1}ft	19	117	9^6	$5^{6\frac{3}{4}}$	4^8	3^{11}	Shoemaker W^3	Mdn	76-16	JudgeSmells,OurGreyFox,Frdinnd	12
8Sep85-6Dmr	6f	:22^3	:46	1:10^{2}ft	4¼	118	10^{12}	10^{12}	$8^{9\frac{1}{2}}$	$8^{11\frac{1}{2}}$	Shoemaker W^5	Mdn	74-08	DonB.Blue,ElCorzon,AuBonMrche	11

●Apr 29 CD 5f ft :58^3 h Apr 24 CD 1 ft 1:38^4 h Apr 17 SA 7f ft 1:24^3 h Apr 13 SA 4f ft :52 b

"Charlie used the top filly Hidden Light as a workmate—a prompter for Ferdinand's workouts at Churchill," explained Hall of Fame jockey Bill Shoemaker, who worked closely with Whittingham and has become an astute trainer since suffering a paralyzing injury in a tragic car accident in April 1991.

"We always thought Ferdinand had raw talent," Shoemaker said. "He was big and gawky as a two-year-old and only really matured when Charlie set him down in those Churchill works before the Derby. I never saw anything like it. Every day leading up to the race he seemed to get stronger and more confident. Charlie made that colt into a real racehorse—almost on command."

Three years after winning that Derby with considerable assistance from Shoemaker, who rode a spectacular race, Whittingham was back in Louisville with the exceptionally gifted Sunday Silence, who came to Churchill labeled only as a probable foil for the Eastern-based juvenile champion Easy Goer.

Easy Goer was an awesomely built, copper-coated, chestnut son of Alydar who might have won the 1989 Triple Crown without the presence of Sunday Silence. The reverse certainly applied to Sunday Silence, who lost the Belmont Stakes to Easy Goer after winning the first two legs.

Sunday Silence X — Dk. b. or br. c. 3(Mar), by Halo—Wishing Well, by Understanding
Own.—Gaillard–Hancock III–Whttghm — Br.—Oak Cliff Thoroughbreds Ltd (Ky) — Tr.—Whittingham Charles
Lifetime 11 7 4 0 $3,250,154 — 1989 8 6 2 0 $3,228,454 — 1988 3 1 2 0 $21,700

24Sep89-10LaD fst 1¼ :47⅕ 1:37⅘ 2:03⅕ Super Derby 7 5 4 2½ 1hd 14 16 Valenzuela P A 126 *.40 85-15 Sunday Silence 126⁶ Big Earl 126hd Awe Inspiring126nk Drew out 8
24Sep89-Grade I
23Jly89- 8Hol fst 1¼ :47⅗ 1:36⅖ 2:01⅗ Swaps 2 1 1 1½ 1 2½ 14 2¾ Valenzuela P A 126 *.20 82-18 Prized 120¾ Sunday Silence 126¹⁰ Endow 1231¼ Lugged out late 5
23Jly89-Grade II
10Jun89- 8Bel fst 1½ :47 2:00⅘ 2:26 Belmont 6 3 2 1½ 21 2 4½ 28 Valenzuela P A 126 *.90 82-13 EasyGoer126⁸SundySilence126¹LeVoygeur126¹² Brief lead, wknd 10
10Jun89-Grade I
20May89-10Pim fst 1³⁄₁₆ :46⅖ 1:09⅗ 1:53⅕ Preakness 7 4 33 32 1hd 1no Valenzuela P A 126 2.10 98-10 SundySilence126noEsyGoer126⁵RockPoint126² Bmpd,stead'd,brsh 8
20May89-Grade I
6May89- 8CD my 1¼ :46⅘ 1:37⅘ 2:05 Ky Derby 10 4 4 6½ 31 1 1½ 1 2½ Valenzuela P A 126 3.10 72-17 SundySilenc126²½EsyGor126hdAwInspiring126¾ Stead'd st, swrvd 15
6May89-Grade I
8Apr89- 5SA fst 1⅛ :45⅗ 1:09⅗ 1:47⅗ S A Derby 4 3 32 2½ 16 111 Valenzuela P A 122 2.40 91-12 SundySilnc122¹¹FlyingContinntl122¾MusicMrci122½ Jostled start 6
8Apr89-Grade I
19Mar89- 8SA fst 1¹⁄₁₆ :45⅕ 1:09⅕ 1:42⅗ S Felipe H 5 4 24 24 12 1 1¾ Valenzuela P A 119 2.90 88-16 SndySlnc119¹¾FlyngCntnntl118³½MscMrc124³½ Broke awkwardly 5
19Mar89-Grade II
2Mar89- 7SA sly 6½f :21⅗ :44⅗ 1:15⅖ Alw 32000 5 2 1hd 11 1 3½ 1 4½ Valenzuela P A 119 *.90 93-18 Sunday Silence 119⁴½ HeroicType119¾MightBeRight119³½ Driving 7
3Dec88- 3Hol fst 6½f :22 :44⅗ 1:16⅗ Alw 24000 1 5 3 1½ 1½ 1 1½ 2hd Gryder A T 120 1.80 92-12 Houston120hdSundySilence120¹¼ThreeTimsOldr117² Lug'd out lt. 7
13Nov88- 2Hol fst 6f :22 :44⅘ 1:09⅖ Md Sp Wt 9 2 2 1½ 1½ 14 110 Valenzuela P A 118 *.70 95-13 SundySlnc118¹⁰MomntOfTm118¾NorthrnDrm118¹¼ Veered out st. 10
30Oct88- 6SA fst 6½f :21⅘ :45⅕ 1:17 Md Sp Wt 11 7 32 2hd 11 2nk Valenzuela P A 118 *1.50 85-13 CroLover118nkSundySilence118⁷½GrenStorm118hd Raced greenly 12

Speed Index: Last Race: 0.0 3-Race Avg.: -1.6 7-Race Avg.: -0.1 Overall Avg.: +1.8
LATEST WORKOUTS ●Sep 21 LaD 5f fst :59⅘ B Sep 16 SA 5f fst 1:00⅕ B ●Sep 9 Dmr 1 fst 1:33⅖ H Sep 4 Dmr 1 fst 1:39⅘ H

Easy Goer — Ch. c. 3(Mar), by Alydar—Relaxing, by Buckpasser
Own.—Phipps O — Br.—Phipps O (Ky) — Tr.—McGaughey Claude III
Lifetime 16 12 4 0 $3,859,650 — 1989 10 8 2 0 $3,162,150 — 1988 6 4 2 0 $697,500

7Oct89- 8Bel fst 1½ :48⅗ 2:05 2:29⅕ 3↑J C Gold Cp 3 4 3 5½ 11 12 14 Day P 121 *.10 74-23 EasyGoer121⁴Cryptoclearnce126¹⁹½ForeverSilver126¾ Ridden out 7
7Oct89-Grade I
16Sep89- 8Bel my 1¼ :48⅕ 1:36⅕ 2:01 3↑Woodward H 1 4 4 5½ 43 1hd 12 Day P 122 *.30 92-17 Easy Goer 122² Its Acedemic 109¾ Forever Silver119⁵ Ridden out 5
16Sep89-Grade I
19Aug89- 8Sar fst 1¼ :46⅘ 1:35⅗ 2:00⅘ Travers 5 4 3 4½ 21 1 1½ 13 Day P 126 *.20 96-04 Easy Goer 126³ Clever Trevor 126⁹ShyTom126⁵¾ Dckd in, rdn out 6
19Aug89-Grade I
5Aug89- 8Sar fst 1⅛ :48⅕ 1:12 1:47⅖ 3↑Whitney H 1 4 43 4 2½ 1½ 1 4½ Day P 119 *.30 98-12 EsyGoer119⁴½ForeverSilver120½Cryptoclernc122⁴ Steadied, easily 6
5Aug89-Grade I
10Jun89- 8Bel fst 1½ :47 2:00⅘ 2:26 Belmont 7 5 4 2½ 11 1 4½ 18 Day P 126 1.60e 90-13 Easy Goer 126⁸ Sunday Silence 126¹LeVoyageur126¹² Ridden out 10
10Jun89-Grade I
20May89-10Pim fst 1³⁄₁₆ :46⅖ 1:09⅗ 1:53⅘ Preakness 2 5 5 4½ 1hd 2hd 2no Day P 126 *.60 98-10 SundaySilence126noEasyGoer126⁵RockPoint126² Brk in air,brshd 8
20May89-Grade I
6May89- 8CD my 1¼ :46⅘ 1:37⅘ 2:05 Ky Derby 13 6 58 5 2½ 6 3½ 2 2½ Day P 126 *.80e 69-17 SundySilence126²½EsyGoer126hdAwInspiring126¾ B'thrd st,rallied 15
6May89-Grade I
22Apr89- 8Aqu fst 1⅛ :48⅗ 1:13⅘ 1:50⅗ Wood Mem 3 2 2½ 2½ 11 13 Day P 126 *.10 82-29 Easy Goer 126³ Rock Point 126hd Triple Buck 126¹¹½ Ridden out 6
22Apr89-Grade I
8Apr89- 7Aqu fst 1 :44⅕ 1:08⅗ 1:32⅖ Gotham 5 2 4 2¼ 2 1½ 1 2½ 113 Day P 123 *.05 104-14 EsyGoer123¹³DimondDonnie114⁷½ExpensiveDcision118⁷½ Handily 5
8Apr89-Grade II
4Mar89-11GP fst 7f :21⅘ :44⅗ 1:22⅕ Swale 1 6 511 310 1½ 1 8¾ Day P 122 *.30 93-18 Easy Goer 122⁸¾ Trion 112nk Tricky Creek 122⁷½ Handily 6
5Nov88- 8CD my 1¹⁄₁₆ :47⅕ 1:12⅕ 1:46⅗ Br Cp Juv 9 7 7 7¾ 66 23 2 1¼ Day P 122 *.30 74-20 Is It True 122¹¼ Easy Goer 122⁸ Tagel 122³ Bmpd st.,jmpd trks 10
5Nov88-Grade I
15Oct88- 8Bel fst 1 :45⅗ 1:10 1:34⅘ Champagne 1 2 2½ 2 1½ 1 1½ 14 Day P 122 *.10 91-17 Easy Goer 122⁴ Is It True 122¹⁵½ Irish Actor 122¹¼ Ridden out 4
15Oct88-Grade I

Speed Index: Last Race: -3.0 3-Race Avg.: +2.0 11-Race Avg.: +4.0 Overall Avg.: +4.5
LATEST WORKOUTS ●Oct 17 Bel 4f fst :47⅗ B Oct 5 Bel 4f fst :49 B Sep 30 Bel 6f fst 1:12⅗ H Sep 24 Bel 4f fst :51 B

For the Derby, McGaughey seemed to baby Easy Goer through a relatively weak series of prep races, including an empty renewal of the Wood Memorial. Six months later he put Easy Goer into an excessively tough stakes against older horses at the awkward 1½-mile distance in his final prep for the 1¼-mile Breeders' Cup.

By contrast, Whittingham did the reverse, using the Santa Anita Derby—the toughest prep race in America—to prepare Sunday Silence for the Kentucky Derby and opted for the weaker Super Derby at 1¼ miles at Louisiana Downs for the colt's major Breeders' Cup prep.

All racehorses from the lowest of the low to the top of the line are high-strung, fragile creatures of great muscle power who may be finely tuned or weakly prepared by their trainers. Sunday Silence was naturally more nimble than Easy Goer, a classy, long-striding colt who needed to build up momentum before he could reach his best running gear. Sunday Silence was slightly sharper for their first meeting in the Kentucky Derby, and there was no question he was at his absolute career best for their championship match in the Breeders' Cup.

While the past performances of all Whittingham-trained marathon runners provide continual insights into the proper training of the long-distance turf specialist, the past performances of Sunday Silence reveal Whittingham's unique brilliance in handling a classic performer. Moreover, there is little question that many of the best trainers on the West Coast, including turf ace Robert Frankel and the English-born Neil Drysdale, have borrowed repeatedly from the Whittingham school of horse training. Compare for yourself the past performances of A.P. Indy prior to his victory in the Breeders' Cup Classic with the p.p.'s of Sunday Silence, or any Frankel-trained turf runners with Whittingham's major turf stars.

A.P. Indy Dk. b. or br. rig. 3(Mar), by Seattle Slew—Weekend Surprise, by Secretariat
DELAHOUSSAYE E (—) Br.—Farish III W S & Kilroy W S (Ky)
Own.—Frish-Goodmn-Kilroy&Tsurumk Tr.—Drysdale Neil (—) 121
Lifetime 10 7 0 1 $1,419,815
1992 6 4 0 1 $1,062,560
1991 4 3 0 0 $357,255
Wet 1 1 0 0 $13,750

10Oct92- 8Bel gd 1¼ :46¹ 1:35 1:58⁴ 3↑J C Gold Cp 107 5 7 7¹⁵ 6²¾ 5⁴ 3⁶¾ Delahoussaye E 121 2.90 90–04 PlsntTp126⁴½StrthGld126²¼APInd121 Bobbled pnchd br 7
10Oct92-Grade I
13Sep92- 8WO fst 1⅛ :47³ 1:12² 1:51³ Molson Mil 93 2 3 3²½ 5⁵½ 6³¾ 5²½ Delahoussaye E 126 *.70 85–18 Benburb119½ Elated Guy117½ VyingVictor119 Gave way 7
13Sep92-Grade II
6Jun92- 8Bel gd 1½ :47 2:01¹ 2:26 Belmont 111 1 2 4² 3½ 2½ 1¾ Delahoussaye E 126 *1.10 100 — A.P.Ind126¾MMmrs-GB126ⁿᵏPnBlff126 Strong handling 11
6Jun92-Grade I
24May92- 8Bel fst 1⅛ :45³ 1:10 1:47² Peter Pan 108 6 5 5³½ 1½ 1²½ 1⁵½ Delahoussaye E 126 *.50 92–08 A.P.Indy126⁵½ColonyLight114⁴¾BrklyFitz114 Ridden out 7
24May92-Grade II
4Apr92- 5SA fst 1⅛ :46¹ 1:10² 1:49¹ S A Derby 95 3 4 4²½ 4³ 3¹ 1¹¾ Delahoussaye E B 122 *.90 84–11 A.P.Indy122¹¾Bertrando122ⁿᵏCsulLies122 Wide, driving 7
4Apr92-Grade I
29Feb92- 8SA fst 1 :46 1:10 1:35² San Rafael 100 5 3 3¹½ 2½ 2²½ 1¾ Delahoussaye E B 121 *.50 90–12 A.P.Indy121¾Treekster116⁹PrinceWild118 Determinedly 6
29Feb92-Grade II
22Dec91- 5Hol fst 1¹⁄₁₆ :46⁴ 1:11 1:42⁴ Hol Fut 96 11 9 9⁵¾ 6³¼ 1ʰᵈ 1ⁿᵏ Delahoussaye E B 121 3.20 87–17 A. P. Indy121ⁿᵏ Dance Floor121⁵½ Casual Lies121 14
22Dec91-Grade I; Wide trip, ridden out
4Dec91- 8BM fst 1 :46⁴ 1:11² 1:36² Alw 21000 82 1 1 1ʰᵈ 1ʰᵈ 1¹ 1³ Delahoussaye E B 117 *.20 88–19 A.P.Indy117³KlooknBoy117³½FbulousPol117 Ridden out 8
27Oct91- 6SA sl 6½f :21⁴ :45³ 1:18¹ Md Sp Wt 88 4 8 8⁷¼ 6³½ 3¹½ 1⁴ Delahoussaye E B 117 *1.30 79–24 A. P. Indy117⁴ Dr Pain117³½ Hickman Creek117 9
27Oct91-Lacked room 1/4, swung out, handily
24Aug91- 4Dmr fst 6f :22¹ :45¹ 1:10¹ Md Sp Wt 71 2 5 5⁴½ 4⁶½ 4⁷ 4⁵½ Delahoussaye E B 117 *2.30 82–11 ShrpBndt117²½Annsl117²¾RchrdOfEnld117 Gaining late 7
LATEST WORKOUTS Oct 26 GP 6f fst 1:13⁴ B Oct 21 GP 4f fst :48³ B Oct 16 Bel 4f fst :51¹ B Oct 5 Bel 6f fst 1:14⁴ H

Toussaud
Own: Juddmonte Farms
DESORMEAUX K J (256 64 62 30 .25)

Dk. b or br f. 4
Sire: El Gran Senor (Northern Dancer)
Dam: Image of Reality (In Reality)
Br: Juddmonte Farms Inc (Ky)
Tr: Frankel Robert (74 17 15 6 .23)

111

Lifetime Record: 10 5 2 2 $233,033

1993	3	2	0	1	$167,800	Turf	10	5	2	2	$233,033
1992	6	3	1	1	$62,748	Wet	0	0	0	0	
Hol (T)	2	2	0	0	$161,200	Dist (T)	2	1	0	0	$107,700

30May93-8Hol fm 1 1/8 (T) :463 1:094 1:33 1:45 3↑ (F)Gamely H-G1 106 8 5 55 54 32 1/2 11 Desormeaux K J B 116 1.90e 99-02 Toussaud1161 Gold Fleece1141 Bel's Starlet1162 1/2 9
Ridden out, returned with cut on left front leg
2May93-8Hol fm 1 1/16 (T) :232 :471 1:103 1:40 3↑ (F)Willshire H-G2 100 2 4 43 43 1/2 22 1 3/4 Desormeaux K J B 116 *2.00 96-05 Toussaud116 3/4 Visible Gold1171 1/2 Wedding Ring1151 Late surge 7
8Apr93-8SA fm 1 (T) :23 :464 1:104 1:35 (F)Alw 44000N3X 95 1 6 67 1/2 67 54 1/2 3 1/2 Desormeaux K J B 114 *1.20 90-10 Gumpher109hd Potridee115nk Toussaud1144 6 Wide stretch 8
24Oct92-8Kee fm 1 1/8 (T) :464 1:104 1:354 1:483 (F)Q Eliz C Cp-G1 96 1 10 1010 108 75 3/4 41 1/2 Flores D R 121 16.40 97-01 Captive Miss121nk Suivi1211 Trampoli121 In stride late 10
27Jly92♦ Newcastle(GB) gd 7f (T)Str 1:271 3↑ Stk 53500 35 Eddery Paul 122 *1.00 — — Casteddu1195 Sure Sharp132hd Toussaud122 3/4 7
Tr: John Gosden Beeswing Stakes-G3 *Tracked in 3rd, short-lived effort 2f out, no late response*
11Jly92♦ Lingfield(GB) gd *7 1/2f (T)Str 1:282 3↑ Stk 36500 2no Eddery Pat 119 *2.00 — — Thourios119no Toussaud1197 Casteddu1192 1/2 6
Silver Trophy (Listed) *Patiently ridden, bid over 1f out, dueled final 16th, just failed*
27Jun92♦ Newmarket(GB) gd 7f (T)Str 1:244 3↑ Stk 53500 1 1/2 Eddery Pat 116 7.00 — — Toussaud116 3/4 Prince Ferdinand124nk Casteddu1191 7
Van Geest Criterion Stakes-G3 *Raced in 4th, rallied to lead 1f out, won driving*
13Jun92♦ Nottingham(GB) gd *6f (T)Str 1:122 Alw 7400 1 1/2 Eddery Paul 128 *1.00 — — Toussaud128 1/2 Storm Dove1285 Alsaarm1336 7
BBC Radio N'ham Graduation Stk *Reserved in 6th, roused to lead over 1f out, driving*
3Jun92♦ Yarmouth(GB) gd *6f (T)Str 1:151 Maiden 5700 11 1/2 Holland D 121 *.50 — — Toussaud1211 1/2 Nagida1215 Alkarif1268 6
Breckland Maiden Stakes *Led virtually throughout, drifted and hit rail 2f out, very game*

WORKOUTS: Jun 30 SA 6f fst 1:13 Hg *3/13* Jun 23 SA 6f fst 1:143 Bg *4/12* Jun 16 SA 5f fst 1:00 Hg *7/41* Jun 9 SA 4f fst :484 H *9/63* May 28 SA 4f fst :473 Hg *4/51* May 22 SA 6f fst 1:142 H *4/10*

When I was a budding horseplayer, the past performances of horses trained by another Hall of Famer, Jack Van Berg, taught me more about how to spot a live contender in a claiming race than any other trainer. Van Berg, one of three trainers to win more than 5,000 races (along with Dale Baird and King Leatherbury), began his career in the 1960s, helping his late father, Marion H. Van Berg, set winning records that still persist.

For more than 20 years—before winning his first Triple Crown race with Gate Dancer in the 1984 Preakness—Jack Van Berg was a steady 25 percent winner with an arsenal of maneuvers at a half-dozen tracks simultaneously. For six straight seasons in the 1970s, Van Berg averaged 350 winners a year, while setting a national record of 496 winners in 1976. Astounding perhaps, but Van Berg's three most productive winning patterns accounted for more than half of his claiming race victories and produced a flat bet profit for more than 15 years.

Along with such rising stars as Ron Ellis and Mike Mitchell in southern California, Lonnie Arterburn in northern California, Mike Hushion in New York, Donnie Von Hemel in the Midwest, Tim Ritchey in Pennsylvania, Mark Reid in New Jersey, Barclay Tagg in Maryland and a sprinkling of fine horsemen throughout the country, Van Berg is deadly with recent winners stepping up in class and with recently claimed or privately purchased runners. On the other hand, a Van Berg-trained winner attempting a repeat victory at the same class level or lower usually is a poor risk (approximately one win for every eight attempts). The same usually is true for other horsemen who tend to win going up the ladder.

It takes considerable horsemanship to know that a horse is fit and fast enough to beat better competition. It takes no less skill to spot genuine value in another man's horse. It costs money to claim a horse. Not Monopoly money—*real* money: $5,000, $10,000, $20,000 and up. If a trainer at your favorite track seems particularly skillful with recent claims, it would be worthwhile to pull out a few past-performance profiles and compare them. Possibly he likes to give his recent claims a few weeks off, or else break them in with an easy race. Some trainers prefer to wait out the thirty-day "jail" period which most states require. (After a claim, the trainer is forced to race the horse at a price at least 25 percent higher for a period of thirty days.) Perhaps you will conclude that there is no apparent pattern. Don't believe it. That is rarely the case. You're probably not looking at the right clues. For example, the third and most significant Van Berg pattern had nothing to do with past performance records as they appeared in the *Daily Racing Form*. It merely had to do with where he was!

To a far greater extent than any horseman I have ever seen, the young Jack Van Berg was prone to go on incredible winning binges, seemingly at will. In amazing Ripley-like fashion, these streaks invariably coincided with his travel itinerary.

Van Berg had many horses under his wing and operated at two or three tracks simultaneously, often leading the trainers' standings at each racetrack. But if he was not on the grounds to personally supervise the training regimen of his stock, only his recent claims and repeaters won more than their share of races. If he was on the grounds, however, and had indicated control over the situation by winning two races back to back or three out of five, the odds said he'd win fifteen more before he saddled thirty or thirty-five to the post. Sometimes such a streak would last a month or more; sometimes it was the only clue a player would get.

During his career, Van Berg orchestrated at least three dozen such explosions at racetracks all over the country. Aside from the extraordinary reliability of his repeaters stepping up in company, there was no concrete theory of handicapping or insight into the conditioning process to explain some of his wins. But can you imagine the kind of bets that could have been made on Exclusive Enough in November 1986 and again in October 1987 when he was moving up in class off recent victories in the middle of Van Berg streaks?

Exclusive Enough B. c. 3, by Exclusive Native—One Is Enough, by Three Martinis
Br.—Mandysland Farm (Ky) 1987 5 2 0 0 $114,760
Own.—Scharbauer Dorothy 124 Tr.—Van Berg Jack C 1986 4 2 0 1 $59,900
Lifetime 9 4 0 1 $174,660
16Oct87-8Kee 6f :22 :432 1:082ft 18 111 2hd 11 12 1½ SthME6 Cmwth Br Cp 100-09 ExclusiveEnough,LzrShow,HighBrit 8
3Sep87-7Dmr 6f :212 :441 1:091ft 8¾ 115 45 42 22 11 Baze G5 Aw25000 92-18 EclsvEngh,AsInEgls,OlympcPrspct 7
3Sep87—Bumped hard start; lugged out badly down backstretch; 3/8 turn
20Jun87-7Hol 7f :22 :442 1:224ft 6¾ 114 51¾ 12 32 610 Stevens G L 6 Aw25000 80-11 TommyTheHwk,FleetSudn,DonDieg 8
24May87-7Hol 6f :214 :45 1:10 ft 6 114 821 814 813 — ShoemkerW2 Aw25000 — — W.D.Jacks,CaptainValid,ThunderCt 8
24May87—Eased; Lugged out early
22Apr87-8Hol 7f :214 :442 1:221ft 6½ 119 42 41½ 78½ 718¼ McCrronCJ6 Debonair 75-18 Jmoke,Persevered,HonkyTonkDncr 7
22Apr87—Lugged out, wide
14Dec86-8Hol 1 :444 1:093 1:361ft 6½e 121 85 75½ 1012 1016¾ Snyder L2 Hol Fut'y 65-18 TempertSil,Alyshb,MstrfulAdvoct 12
14Dec86—Grade I
15Nov86-8Hol 7f :22 :444 1:23 ft 14 112 11½ 11½ 12 1½ ShmkrW3 Hol Prvu 89-14 ExclusivEnough,Prsvrd,GoldOnGrn 8
15Nov86—Grade III; Erratic 3/16 to 1/16
2Nov86-6SA 6f :212 :442 1:102ft *3-2 118 23½ 2½ 12 14 Day P1 Mdn 86-10 ExclusivEnough,BrgntnDncr Clvnst 8
2Nov86—Green in stretch
11Oct86-6SA 6½f :214 :444 1:172ft 5¾ 117 11½ 2½ 2hd 33¾ Solis A3 Mdn 79-17 JustBobby,Brb'sRlc,ExclusvEnogh 12
11Oct86—Drifted out late
Oct 27 SA tr.t 3f ft :362 h Oct 10 SA 4f ft :483 b Oct 4 SA 5f ft 1:03 h

No mention of Van Berg is possible without reference to the classy Alysheba.

Alysheba was a remarkable talent, one of the most popular horses in racing history—a sure-fire Hall of Famer who helped Hall of Famer Van Berg achieve his greatest goals. Two sets of past performances are shown below to illustrate the quality work that went into developing a three-year-old classics winner and champion Horse of the Year 18 months later.

1987 KENTUCKY DERBY-PREAKNESS WINNER, ALYSHEBA

Alysheba B. c. 3, by Alydar—Bel Sheba, by Lt Stevens
Br.—Madden P (Ky) 1987 9 3 2 1 $1,836,156
Own.—Scharbauer Dorothy&Pamela 122 Tr.—Van Berg Jack C 1986 7 1 4 1 $359,486
Lifetime 16 4 6 2 $2,195,642
27Sep87-10LaD 1¼ :47 1:362 2:031ft *1-2 126 76½ 32½ 21 1½ McCrrCJ 2 Super Dby 85-19 Alysheba, Candi's Gold, Parochial 8
27Sep87—Grade I; Brushed rival
22Aug87-8Sar 1¼ :461 1:362 2:02 sy *2½ 126 712 78½ 69 620¼ McCrrnCJ 6 Travers 70-16 JavaGold,Cryptoclearnce,PolishNvy 9
22Aug87—Grade I
1Aug87-9Mth 1⅛ :463 1:093 1:47 ft 3-2 126 32½ 21 32½ 2nk McCrrCJ 4 Haskell H 1 99-07 Bet Twice, Alysheba, Lost Code 5
1Aug87—In close turn
6Jun87-8Bel 1½ :492 2:03 2:281ft *4-5 126 47 47 39 414¼ McCrrCJ 3 Belmont 65-15 Bet Twice, Cryptoclearance, Gulch 9
6Jun87—Grade I; Rough trip
16May87-9Pim 1 3/16 :471 1:113 1:554ft *2 126 56½ 43 2hd 1½ McCrrCJ 6 Preakness 88-18 Alysheba,BetTwice,Cryptoclearnce 9
16May87—Grade I
2May87-8CD 1¼ :462 1:364 2:032ft 8½ 126 1312 31½ 21 1¾ McCrrCJ 3 Ky Dby 80-09 Alysheba, Bet Twice, Avies Copy 17
2May87—Grade I; Stumbled
23Apr87-7Kee 1⅛ :464 1:102 1:482ft *4-5 121 32 42½ 2hd 1hd † McCrrnCJ 4 B Grass 95-13 ‡Alysheba, War, Leo Castelli 5
23Apr87—Grade I; †Disqualified and placed third
22Mar87-8SA 1 1/16 :462 1:104 1:43 gd 3¼ 120 76½ 63½ 4¾ 2¾ Day P 3 Sn Flpe H 85-23 ChartTheStrs,Alysheb,TemperteSil 8
22Mar87—Grade I; Lugged in stretch
8Mar87-9SA 1 1/16 :464 1:112 1:43 ft *2-3 114 44½ 45 44 45 Day P 6 Aw30000 81-15 Barb's Relic, Blanco, Rakaposhi 9
14Dec86-8Hol 1 :444 1:093 1:361ft 6½e 121 41¾ 22½ 2½ 2nk Day P 12 Hol Fut'y 82-18 TempertSil,Alyshb,MstrfulAdvoct 12
14Dec86—Grade I
●Oct 28 SA 1 ft 1:353 h Oct 20 SA 7f ft 1:28 h Oct 14 SA 5f ft 1:003 h ●Sep 23 LaD 6f ft 1:123 b

Note the intelligent use of prep races and the sustained gradual improvement to the Derby and the recovery of the horse's good form on cue in the fall. This is Van Berg's finest career work, equaled by his handling of the same horse the following year when Alysheba matured into one of the most powerful horses of the decade and 1988 Horse of the Year. Quite a long way for the trainer who was best known for working with 200 claiming horses at one time at five or six tracks during the 1970s.

1988 BREEDERS' CUP CLASSIC WINNER, ALYSHEBA

Alysheba — B. c. 4, by Alydar—Bel Sheba, by Lt Stevens
MCCARRON C J 126 — Br.—Madden Preston (Ky) — 1988 8 6 1 0 $2,458,600
Own.—Scharbauer Dorothy & Pam — Tr.—Van Berg Jack C — 1987 10 3 3 1 $2,511,156
Lifetime 25 10 8 2 $5,329,242

14Oct88-10Med	$1\frac{1}{4}$	:46^1	1:33^4	1:58^{4}ft	*1-2	127	3^7	2^1	1^{hd}	1^{nk}	McCrrCJ^3	Med Cup	108-05	Alysheb,SlewCitySlw,PlsntVirginin	5
14Oct88—Grade I															
17Sep88-8Bel	$1\frac{1}{4}$	:47^3	1:35	1:59^{2}ft	*9-5	126	3^1	3$^{\frac{1}{2}}$	3$^{\frac{1}{2}}$	1^{nk}	McCrrCJ^4	WoodwrdH	101-08	Alysheba, Forty Niner, Waquoit	8
17Sep88—Grade I															
27Aug88-9Mth	$1\frac{1}{8}$	:46^2	1:09^4	1:47^{4}ft	*1	124	5^{11}	4^5	2$^{2\frac{1}{2}}$	1$^{\frac{3}{4}}$	McCrrnCJ^4	P Iselin H	95-12	Alysheba, Bet Twice, Gulch	6
27Aug88—Grade I															
26Jun88-8Hol	$1\frac{1}{4}$	:45^4	1:34^2	1:59^{2}ft	*1	126	5^8	3$^{1\frac{1}{2}}$	2^4	2$^{6\frac{1}{2}}$	McCrrCJ^6	Hol GdCpH	88-07	Cutlass Reality,Alysheba,Ferdinand	6
26Jun88—Grade I															
14May88-8Pim	$1\frac{3}{16}$	:46^2	1:10^2	1:54^{1}ft	*3-5	127	3^2	2$^{\frac{1}{2}}$	4$^{4\frac{1}{2}}$	4$^{4\frac{1}{4}}$	McCrrCJ^2	PimSpec'lH	92-19	BetTwice,LostCode,Cryptoclearnce	6
17Apr88-8SA	$1\frac{1}{8}$	:46^2	1:09^4	1:47^{1}ft	*4-5	127	2$^{1\frac{1}{2}}$	1^{hd}	2^{hd}	1no	McCrrCJ^1	Sn Brndo H	93 —	Alysheba, Ferdinand, Good Taste	5
17Apr88—Grade II															
6Mar88-8SA	$1\frac{1}{4}$	:46^3	1:34^3	1:59^{4}ft	*1	126	3^3	1$^{\frac{1}{2}}$	1^1	1$^{\frac{1}{2}}$	McCrrnCJ^2	S A H	90-13	Alysheba, Ferdinand,SuperDiamond	4
6Mar88—Grade I															
7Feb88-8SA	$1\frac{1}{4}$	:45^3	1:35^1	2:00^{2}ft	*4-5	126	5$^{8\frac{1}{2}}$	1^{hd}	1^{hd}	1^3	McCrrCJ^3	C H Strb	87-16	Alysheba, Candi's Gold, OnTheLine	6
7Feb88—Grade I															
21Nov87-7Hol	$1\frac{1}{4}$	:46^2	1:35^2	2:01^{2}ft	$3\frac{1}{2}$	122	9$^{8\frac{1}{4}}$	5^4	4^1	2no	McCrrCJ^9	Br Cp Clsc	85-12	Ferdinnd,Alysheb,JudgeAngelucci	12
21Nov87—Grade I															
27Sep87-10LaD	$1\frac{1}{4}$	:47	1:36^2	2:03^{1}ft	*1-2	126	7$^{6\frac{1}{2}}$	3$^{2\frac{1}{2}}$	2^1	1$^{\frac{1}{2}}$	McCrrCJ^2	Super Dby	85-19	Alysheba, Candi's Gold, Parochial	8
27Sep87—Grade I; Brushed rival															

●Nov 3 CD 4f ft :47^3 h ●Oct 26 CD 1 ft 1:40 h Oct 11 Med 5f ft :59^3 b Oct 6 Bel 4f ft :48^2 h

Van Berg remains one of the cagiest horsemen in the game, and during the 1994 Santa Anita meet he turned in one of his longshot streaks. But he no longer has a monopoly on such binges, certainly not in southern California, where he has been based since the Alysheba days.

In the 1990s, sharp horseplayers expect to see two or three trainers at every track suddenly go on 30 percent winning streaks almost overnight. The name of the game often is to spot the hot trainer or the newly emerging star during the earliest days of the streak. In California, Mitchell, R. B. Hess, Jr., Ellis, Arterburn, and Vladmir Cerin have been prone to get Van Berg-hot; in the East it may be Hushion, Gasper Moschera, Gary Odintz or Robert Klesaris who dominate this month, while Peter Ferriola and Gary Sciacca take over in the next.

According to the *American Racing Manual* and other authoritative sources, there were approximately 8,500 licensed trainers in North America at the start of 1993. More than 4,000 failed to win a single race in 1992, and about 2,500 more failed to win at least 10.

Looking at this picture from the opposite perspective, the top 600 trainers in America won approximately 30 percent of all purse money distributed during the first three years of the 1990s. Barely 200 were good enough to win at least one race in every five attempts.

For his or her own protection, the player should know which trainers in their region have winning skill, what that skill is, and which ones cannot train their way out of a paper bag.

Who's Hot and Who's Not

All good trainers tend to get hot from time to time. It's important to be able to detect such patterns in the making. Sometimes a trainer will point for a particular meeting, à la Glenn C. Smith at Bowie in the 1960s. And sometimes a trainer has to sacrifice a month or two to get ready.

When New York-based trainer Frank Martin went to California for the 1974–75 winter season, he had nothing but Aqueduct on his mind. Martin won only two races in fifty-odd starts at Santa Anita, but returned to New York with a barnful of tigers. Barely three weeks into his 1975 Aqueduct winter invasion, Martin had 19 winners; eight weeks later he had fifty.

An astute player in New York or California who watched Martin's early results at either track might have gotten the message by the third racing day. Hall of Famer Allen Jerkens, who upset Secretariat twice with different horses in 1973 and has remained a major force in New York into the 1990s, almost dropped out of sight for much of the 1980s, except for an annual sojourn to Saratoga. Inspired by the surroundings and the classy caliber of racing, Jerkens consistently unleashed his best runners in August to remain among the Saratoga leaders every season.

In the early 1990s, a variation of this pattern repeated itself among several trainers who used to split the season between Longacres in Washington state and the northern California racing circuit.

Season after season, trainer Larry Ross had quiet Bay Meadows meets in the fall after enjoying solid success at Longacres during the summer. A few months of R&R and Ross was ready to unleash a barrage of fast and fit runners in the spring. These would include first-time starters, absentees and horses getting important equipment changes or sanctioned drugs such as Lasix, the controversial diuretic that seems to impact horse performance in addition to curbing pulmonary bleeding under stress.

You could set your clock to the beginning of Ross' win streaks midway through the Golden Gate Fields' meet. Below, for instance, are two of the four horses he won with on the same day, May 5, 1993. Cut 'N Set was returning from a six-month layoff after having shown her fondness for Golden Gate in April and May 1992, while Canadian Mischief won a sprint off a layoff in March and was ready to do it again.

Cut 'N Set
HANSEN R D (336 55 64 46 .16)
Own.—Ann Marie Stable
Dk. b. or br. f. 4, by Relaunch—Divisional, by Halo
$16,000 Br.—Glen Hill Farm (Fla)
Tr.—Ross Larry (113 10 21 13 .09)
116
Lifetime 17 5 1 3 $36,212
1992 12 4 1 3 $30,950
1991 5 1 0 0 $5,262
Turf 1 1 0 0 $8,250

26Sep92- 3BM	fst	1	:46	1:11	1:364	ⒻClm 25000	48	5	5	53	65	69	615	Gonzalez R M	LB	116	4.00	71-17	LsLeder1161½AWildBuy1162½ScrltFrindship116	Far wide	6
5Sep92- 9BM	fm	1 Ⓣ	:473	1:131	1:38	ⒻClm 20000	74	6	1	2hd	11	1½	1no	Hansen R D	LB	116	3.20	89-05	Cut'NSet116noDawnMirnd1167LsLeder116	Held gamely	8
12Aug92-11Bmf	fst	6f	:221	:45	1:11	ⒻClm 18000	74	1	5	53½	55½	54½	1hd	Gonzalez R M	LB	115	9.80	81-15	Cut'NSt115hdMdmPrt116½MrtsWyHolm116	Rallied wide	6
9Jly92-10Pln	fst	6f	:223	:451	1:11	ⒻClm 12500	63	1	6	76½	78½	54	31½	Boulanger G	LB	114	4.50	86-09	CrfrWondr1151PowrBurst112½Cut'NSt114	Wide stretch	8
14Jun92- 1GG	fst	6f	:214	:444	1:111	ⒻClm 10000	64	6	6	67½	66½	45	2nk	Hansen R D	LB	116	*2.30	82-15	LdingPric116nkCut'NSt1163PrclssWnch116	Rallied wide	7
20May92- 4GG	fst	6f	:22	:45	1:111	ⒻClm 7000	63	5	5	43½	42½	2hd	16	Hansen R D	LB	117	8.60	82-19	Ct'NSt1176Copln'sDbl1161½SprngDrlng116	Rallied wide	12
24Apr92- 4GG	fst	6f	:22	:452	1:113	ⒻClm 6250	65	10	1	88	76¾	34	13½	Hansen R D	LB	118	8.00	80-20	Cut'NSt1183½Gothrthhrdwy118½Mlogrb118	Rallied wide	12
2Apr92- 4GG	fst	6f	:214	:451	1:11	ⒻClm 6250	46	4	5	53½	64½	1011	97¾	Castaneda M	LB	118	8.70	75-17	Cpln'sDbl1183Gthrthhrdy118nkJnryFr118	Through early	10
12Mar92- 5GG	fst	6f	:214	:45	1:103	ⒻClm 8000	50	1	6	31½	2½	33½	44½	Meza R Q	LB	116	5.50	81-15	Fabricus116¾ JanuaryFour1161½JustRightBaby118	Tired	12
5Feb92- 3GG	fst	1	:461	1:12	1:39	ⒻClm 10500	51	6	4	3nk	1½	2½	52¾	Velasquez DWJr5	LB	111	4.00	72-23	StkBy118½AsGoodAsEvr1161FunLovngGrl118	Gave way	10

LATEST WORKOUTS ●May 1 GG 3f fst :352 H   Apr 25 GG 5f fst 1:01 H   Apr 19 GG 3f fst :364 H   Apr 7 GG 5f fst 1:011 H

Canadian Mischief
HANSEN R D (336 55 64 46 .16)
Own.—CarriganAndy&Brbr&RossShron
B. m. 6, by Chief to Earn—Reserve Account, by Jim J
$32,000 Br.—Kenny&Salishan&Meadows&Valceschini (BC-C)
Tr.—Ross Larry (113 10 21 13 .09)
116
Lifetime 32 5 9 4 $174,095
1993 3 1 1 0 $15,800
1992 8 1 2 4 $27,870
Turf 3 0 0 1 $5,400
Wet 5 1 2 1 $42,760

14Apr93- 4GG	fm	1 1/16 Ⓣ	:482	1:12	1:432 +	ⒻClm 40000	75	2	2	33½	43½	43½	65¼	Hansen R D	LBb	116	9.60	84-11	HtAHmrHny116noMssBrt1171SctDll116	Broke in tangle	7
24Mar93- 6GG	gd	1 1/16	:464	1:111	1:44	ⒻClm 32000	71	5	2	2½	2½	41½	26	Hansen R D	LBb	117	4.40e	71-23	ThanksPp1166CndinMischief117¾MissBeret118	2nd best	8
4Mar93- 7GG	fst	6f	:214	:45	1:104	ⒻClm 25000	78	1	9	99¼	99¼	64¾	1hd	Hansen R D	LBb	116	12.20	86-17	CndnMschf116hdMndMck1163OldTmRmnc116	Far wide	9
4Jly92- 7Lga	sly	1 1/16	:461	1:112	1:443	ⒻClm 40000	75	4	4	411	47½	37½	32¾	Hansen R D	LBb	112	*1.10e	82-08	ThnksPp1151½WildKri1121½CndinMischif112	Evenly late	7
3Jun92- 3GG	fst	1	:461	1:103	1:364	ⒻClm 20000	82	6	2	21	2hd	11	12½	Hansen R D	LBb	116	6.20	86-27	CndMschf1162½SpclCct118½ThDchssVr117	Steady drive	6
1May92- 8GG	fst	1	:462	1:103	1:36	ⒻClm 20000	76	4	3	31½	51¾	22	31	Hansen R D	LBb	116	*1.70	89-16	SpclCnnctn1161NrADbt116noCdMschf116	Brushed lane	6
17Apr92- 6GG	fm	1 1/16 Ⓣ	:471	1:112	1:434 +	ⒻClm 25000	75	5	4	48½	49	38	35	Hansen R D	LBb	117	3.80	88-07	HstssLdy1161½Sntmntllst1163½CndnMschf117	Wide trip	5
28Mar92- 9GG	fst	1	:453	1:101	1:363	ⒻClm 20000	75	7	5	55	45	43	22	Boulanger G	LBb	116	*2.10	85-17	HstssLd1162CdMscf1161MssPrtts114	Bumped break,wide	8
12Mar92- 3GG	fst	1	:454	1:102	1:353	ⒻClm 25000	75	6	6	65½	64½	42½	33½	Hansen R D	LBb	116	9.70	88-12	ThnsPp1162½Sntntllst1161CndMschf116	Lugged in lane	6
20Feb92- 6GG	my	1	:473	1:14	1:403	ⒻClm 20000	69	1	3	23	12	1hd	22	Hansen R D	LBb	117	4.60	65-33	LovlyRulr1162CndinMischf1171½CshInNow116	Game try	6

LATEST WORKOUTS May 1 GG 4f fst :494 H   Apr 23 GG 5f fst 1:03 H   Apr 10 GG 3f fst :382 H   Apr 3 GG 5f fst 1:024 H

Kathy Walsh is another Longacres-based trainer who favored the spring meet at Golden Gate Fields, winning more than 25 percent of her absentees, first-timers and recent acquisitions and claims. But, three rival trainers from Longacres, Mike Chambers, Bill McLean and Howard

Belvoir, never waited for Golden Gate, improving on their good Longacres numbers upon arrival at Bay Meadows.

Northern California players who were tuned into the apparent form-cycle patterns of these trainers caught more than their share of longshot shippers until Longacres was shut down by the Boeing aircraft company after the 1992 season. But even after this disruption Ross and Walsh continued to follow their own form cycle in 1993 and 1994 to win many more races at Golden Gate Fields than Bay Meadows.

While top trainers tend to point for specific meets or are prone to enjoy red-hot winning streaks, they also must endure occasional losing streaks. Fortunately, the attentive player may be able to detect these losing patterns before they drain the bankroll.

Has the trainer abandoned a successful strategy? Perhaps he pushed his horses very hard in pursuit of extra victories and is due for a letdown at the next meet. Or maybe the trainer is trying to shake off the effects of a disastrous personal tragedy or costly mistake.

Several years ago, New York-based trainer John Parisella had his entire barn wiped out by fire. Even after acquiring new stock it took Parisella a full year to get back in the groove. Nearly the same thing happened to Maryland-based Buddy Delp, who needed several months to hit full stride after restocking his depleted barn in the mid-1980s.

D. Wayne Lukas is a more prominent example to consider. A three-time Eclipse Award winner, Lukas set records for stakes wins and purse earnings for six straight seasons through 1991. While he also led the nation in purse earnings in 1992—for the 10th straight year—he was beginning a deep slump that would extend through 1993, failing to win a single Grade 1 stakes or major Kentucky Derby prep race for the first time in a decade. The trend was exacerbated by the death of Union City in the 1993 Preakness and later by the nearly fatal accident suffered by his son and number one assistant Jeff, a superior horsemen in his own right who was run over by a loose horse (the talented Tabasco Cat) near the Lukas barn at Hollywood Park in December 1993.

Specific reasons for Lukas' earliest difficulties never were explained publicly, but astute horseplayers knew his changing financial circumstances were crucial underlying factors at the root of his slump.

In 1989, Lukas lost his number one patron Eugene V. Klein, who had bankrolled him into the premier American-based buyer of blue-blooded yearlings at the priciest yearling sales.

Lukas was left with fewer good horses and no one to replace Klein's bottomless checkbook to replenish his stock. At every key marking post—in the Triple Crown preps, in the major stakes for older horses, in the Breeders' Cup races—Lukas' presence was diminished.

An awesome force in Graded stakes for more than a decade, suddenly horseplayers had to downplay Lukas-trained horses in races he used to dominate.

Ironically, things began to turn around on January 22, 1994, the day Tabasco Cat won the 1994 El Camino Real Derby at Bay Meadows. "Why blame the horse for what happened to Jeff?" Lukas asked. "It could have been any horse; now my job is to develop this one into a champion."

From such a steel spirit comes the Lukas life force and his resolve to lead the nation in earnings again. "Anyone who thinks this is a permanent change in our fortunes doesn't know me very well," Lukas said in the midst of his slump. "We've consolidated a few things, we are reorganizing, and no one will have to wait very long for us to be back with contenders in all the major races."

Lukas was correct as usual and at his career best again while shaking off the traumatic events of the winter to develop the high-strung Tabasco Cat into the winner of the 1994 Preakness and Belmont stakes, (see past-performance profile in Chapter 12.) Yet Lukas has never been an easy trainer to appreciate. Even during his successful run through

Twilight Agenda B. h. 6, by Devil's Bag—Grenzen, by Grenfall
MCCARRON C J (146 24 28 28 .16)
Own.—Moyglare Stud
Br.—Moyglare Stud Farm Ltd (Ky)
Tr.—Lukas D Wayne (63 9 11 6 .14)
121

Lifetime					
28 12 5 4	1992	6	1	1 2	$446,000
$2,057,459	1991	11	6	3 1	$1,563,600
	Turf	12	5	2 1	$59,859
	Wet	2	0	0 1	$8,250

6Jun92- 7Bel	my	1⅛	:44^4	1:08^2	1:46^3	3↑Nassau Ct H	87	4	2	3$^{1\frac{1}{2}}$	3^2	7^5	8$^{12\frac{1}{4}}$	McCarron C J	b	120	3.50e	84-08	StrkthGld116^{nk}PlsntTp119$^{1\frac{1}{2}}$SltrSng111	Dueled outside	9
6Jun92-Grade II																					
25May92- 8Bel	fst	1	:44^4	1:08^2	1:33^3	3↑Metropoln H	103	11	4	3^2	4$^{2\frac{1}{2}}$	5$^{4\frac{1}{4}}$	4$^{4\frac{1}{4}}$	McCarron C J	b	121	*2.20	98-05	DixieBrss107$^{2\frac{1}{2}}$PlsntTp119$^{1\frac{1}{2}}$InExcss-Ir121	Lacked rally	11
25May92-Grade I																					
9May92- 10Pim	fst	1$\frac{3}{16}$	:47^3	1:11^2	1:54^4	Pim Spcl H	108	2	4	4^2	5$^{1\frac{3}{4}}$	6$^{3\frac{3}{4}}$	3^2	McCarron C J	Lb	122	4.40	86-23	StrikethGold114$\frac{3}{4}$FlySoFr116$^{1\frac{1}{4}}$TwilightAgnd122	Rallied	7
9May92-Grade I																					
11Apr92- 8OP	fst	1⅛	:46	1:09^4	1:48	Oaklawn H	117	7	2	2^{hd}	1^{hd}	3^1	3^2	McCarron C J	Lb	123	3.80	94-20	Best Pal125$^{1\frac{1}{2}}$ SeaCadet120$\frac{1}{2}$TwilightAgenda123	Gamely	7
11Apr92-Grade I																					
7Mar92- 5SA	fst	1¼	:46	1:34	1:59	Sta Anita H	115	5	3	4$^{1\frac{3}{4}}$	2$\frac{1}{2}$	2^3	2$^{5\frac{1}{2}}$	McCarron C J	LBb	124	2.20	93-10	Best Pal124$^{5\frac{1}{2}}$ Twilight Agenda124$^{2\frac{1}{2}}$ DefensivePlay115		7
7Mar92-Grade I; Brushed twice backstretch																					
25Jan92- 8SA	fst	1$\frac{1}{16}$	:47^3	1:11^2	1:42^1	Sn Psqual H	110	4	2	1^{hd}	1^{hd}	1$\frac{1}{2}$	1$^{3\frac{1}{2}}$	Desormeaux KJ	LBb	125	*.80	92-18	TwilightAgend125$^{3\frac{1}{2}}$Ibero-Ar116^{nk}AnswerDo118	Handily	5
25Jan92-Grade II																					
8Dec91- 8Hol	fst	1⅛	:47^1	1:11	1:49	3↑Ntv Diver H	109	3	1	1$\frac{1}{2}$	2^{hd}	1$\frac{1}{2}$	1$^{3\frac{1}{2}}$	McCarron C J	LBb	124	*.40	89-18	TwilightAgend124$^{3\frac{1}{2}}$Ibro-Ar117^{hd}CobrClssic117	Driving	4
8Dec91-Grade III																					
2Nov91- 8CD	fst	1¼	:48^2	1:38	2:02^4	3↑B C Classic	118	9	5	4^3	2^1	2^1	2$^{1\frac{1}{4}}$	McCarron C J	LBb	126	13.90	95-09	BlckTAffr-Ir126$^{1\frac{1}{4}}$TlghtAgnd126$^{2\frac{1}{2}}$Unbrdld126	Good try	11
2Nov91-Grade I																					
18Oct91- 10Med	fst	1⅛	:46^3	1:10^1	1:46^3	3↑Med Cup H	116	4	3	4^2	4$^{1\frac{3}{4}}$	3^{nk}	1^{nk}	McCarron C J	Lb	121	2.20	102-06	TwilightAgend121^{nk}Scn116$^{1\frac{1}{2}}$SeCdet115	Boxed in, drvg	9
18Oct91-Grade I																					
5Oct91- 7Bel	fst	1¼	:47^3	1:36	2:00^3	3↑J C Gold Cp	109	3	1	1$^{2\frac{1}{2}}$	1^1	1^{hd}	4$^{3\frac{1}{4}}$	Bailey J D	b	126	*1.60	91-07	Festin-Ar126$^{1\frac{1}{2}}$ChiefHoncho126^{nk}StrikethGold121	Tired	5
5Oct91-Grade I																					

LATEX WORKOUTS ●Jun 22 SA 6f fst 1:13^1 H May 20 Bel 5f fst 1:01^1 B ●May 5 CD 6f fst 1:13^3 H ●Apr 28 CD 6f fst 1:14 H

North Sider

Dk. b. or br. m. 5, by Topsider—Back Ack, by Ack Ack

Br.—Levy & Cisley Stable (Ky) 1987 16 7 3 1 $837,107

Own.—Paternostro & Lukas 123 Tr.—Lukas D Wayne 1986 11 2 3 3 $156,838

Lifetime 35 15 7 5 $1,116,400 Turf 3 0 0 1 $23,000

31Oct87-8Kee 1⅛ :462 1:101 1:483ft *7-5e 123 62¼ 53½ 87¾ 911½ PerretC3 Ⓕ Spinster 82-14 Sacahuista, Ms. Margi, Tall Poppy 13
31Oct87—Grade I

27Sep87-8Bel 1⅛ :462 1:092 1:483ft *2-5e 122 64½ 63¼ 78 106¼ PncLJr7 Ⓕ Ruffian H 78-19 ‡Sachuist,CoupDeFusil,ClbberGirl 12
27Sep87—Grade I

12Sep87-8Bel 1 :444 1:092 1:35 ft 6-5e 123 32 2hd 2hd 1nk CrdrAJr6 Ⓕ Maskette 90-19 North Sider, Wisla, Funistrada 7
12Sep87—Grade I

14Aug87-8Sar 7f :213 :44 1:223ft *4-5e 122 34½ 33½ 3nk 44 RomrRP4 Ⓕ Ballerina 85-21 I'mSwts,StormAndSunshin,PinTrLn 5
14Aug87—Grade II

19Jly87-8Hol 1¼ :453 1:344 2:003ft 3 121 11 12 2½ 26½ PncLJr7 Ⓕ Vnty Iv H 82-07 Infinidad, North Sider, Clabber Girl 7
19Jly87—Grade I

28Jun87-8Bel 7f :222 :454 1:241ft 2¼ 121 31½ 31 11 12 CrdrAJr1 Ⓕ VagrancyH 81-19 NorthSdr,StormAndSunshn,Fnstrd 6
28Jun87—Grade III

20Jun87-9Mth 170 :464 1:101 1:393ft *4-5 120 11 12½ 13 12½ PerrtC 3 Ⓕ Bud Brds' H 98-13 NorthSider,BrbicueSuc,CoupDFusil 7

5Jun87-8Bel 1⅛ :481 1:121 1:50 gd *4-5 120 12 13 1½ 54 CrdrAJr2 Ⓕ HempstdH 73-19 Catatonic, Ms. Eloise, Steal A Kiss 7
5Jun87—Grade I

16May87-8Bel 1 1/16 :453 1:102 1:414ft *9-5 120 22½ 2hd 11½ 2no Day P10 Ⓕ Shuvee H 93-18 Ms.Eloise,NorthSider,Clmnn'sRos 10
16May87—Grade I

1May87-7CD 1 1/16 :48 1:113 1:424ft *2-5e 123 42½ 2½ 22½ 46 CrdrAJr2 Ⓕ Bd Br CpH 88-12 QueenAlexandr,Infinidd,I'mSweets 6

●Oct 26 CD 4f ft :482 b Sep 22 Bel 4f ft :53 b

Dance Floor

Dk. b. or br. c. 3(Feb), by Star de Naskra—Dance Troupe, by Native Charger

Lifetime 15 4 4 1 $751,099 1992 7 1 1 1 $377,498 1991 8 3 3 0 $373,601 Wet 1 0 0 0

ANTLEY C W (115 25 18 15 .22) Br.—Purdey William A (NJ) 126

Own.—Oaktown Stable Tr.—Lukas D Wayne (39 8 6 4 .21)

2Aug92-10Mth fst 1⅛ :461 1:094 1:483 Haskell H 61 5 7 64¾ 77 923 928 Stevens G L L 121 8.10 68-10 Technology1201¾ NinesWild1125¼Scudan113 Dull effort 9
2Aug92-Grade II

6Jun92- 7Bel my 1⅛ :444 1:082 1:463 3↑Nassau Co H 79 1 1 1½ 1½ 97 918¾ Smith M E 109 3.50e 77-08 StrkthGld116nkPlsntTp1191½SltrySng111 Dueled inside 9
6Jun92-Grade II

16May92-10Pim gd 1 3/16 :461 1:104 1:553 Preakness 99 14 4 45½ 31½ 22 43 Antley C W L 126 9.20 81-18 PineBluff126¾Alydeed1261½CsulLies126 Brshd str, wknd 14
16May92-Grade I

2May92- 8CD fst 1¼ :464 1:363 2:03 Ky Derby 101 16 5 1½ 11½ 31 34½ Antley C W LB 126 33.30e 91-06 LilE.Tee1261CsulLies1263½DncFloor126 Brshd str,wknd 18
2May92-Grade I

11Apr92- 9Kee fst 1⅛ :471 1:112 1:49 Blue Grass 96 6 3 52¼ 31½ 42¼ 44¾ Antley C W LB 121 *1.20 85-10 PstlsndRss121nkCntDS1212½EcsttcRd121 Bid, four wide 11
11Apr92-Grade II

14Mar92-10GP fst 1⅛ :46 1:104 1:503 Fla Derby 94 11 6 48½ 31½ 21 24½ Antley C W 122 *.80 79-17 Tchnology1224½DncFlr122hdPstlsndRss122 Saved place 12
14Mar92-Grade I

22Feb92-10GP fst 1 1/16 :464 1:111 1:451 Ftn O Youth 98 1 3 22½ 11 13½ 14½ Antley C W 122 *1.50e 86-19 DncFlor1224½ⒹCrflGstr113noPstlsndRss119 Ridden out 11
22Feb92-Grade II

22Dec91- 5Hol fst 1 1/16 :464 1:11 1:424 Hol Fut 96 1 5 64 52¾ 2hd 2nk Antley C W B 121 *3.00 87-17 A.P.Indy121nkDnceFloor1215½CsuilLies121 Saved ground 14
22Dec91-Grade I

30Nov91- 9CD fst 1 1/16 :473 1:124 1:451 Brwn & Wllm 93 8 3 46½ 23½ 13½ 16 Antley C W B 121 *1.10 89-09 Dance Floor1216 Waki Warrior116hd ChoctawRidge116 10
30Nov91-Grade III; Bobbled start, driving

2Nov91- 6CD fst 1 1/16 :463 1:12 1:443 Br Cp Juv 78 12 11 118¾ 98½ 713 613½ Day P B 122 3.70 78-09 Arzi1225Brtrndo1223½SnppyLnding122 Steadied far trn 14
2Nov91-Grade I

LATEST WORKOUTS ●Aug 18 Sar tr.t 5f gd 1:01 H ●Aug 13 Sar tr.t 5f fst 1:024 B ●Jly 28 Bel 5f fst 1:00 H Jly 22 Bel 5f fst :593 H

Salt Lake

B. c. 3(Mar), by Deputy Minister—Take Lady Anne, by Queen City Lad

Lifetime 21 7 3 4 $536,218 1992 12 3 2 3 $232,108 1991 9 4 1 1 $304,110 Turf 1 0 0 0 Wet 2 1 0 0 $68,190

Br.—Crook Investment Co (Ky)

Own.—Lukas & Overbrook Farm Tr.—Lukas D Wayne (—)

27Nov92- 8Hol fm 5½f Ⓣ:214 :442 1:02 3↑Trf Exprss H 82 5 9 117½116¾109½106¼ Solis A LB 118 14.20 89-05 Answer Do121no Repriced118no Gundaghia117 Outrun 11

31Oct92- 4GP fst 6f :213 :433 1:081 3↑Br Cp Sprnt 82 12 3 127¾131213121311 Smith M E 123 7.00 91 — ThirtySlews126nkMeafar1203Rubino126 Bobbled st., wd 14
31Oct92-Grade I; Bobbled at start, far wide into lane

3Oct92- 6Bel fst 7f :223 :452 1:224 3↑Vosburgh 107 2 3 2½ 1½ 1½ 32 Smith M E 123 7.00 88-17 Rubiano126¾SheikhAlbadou-GB1261¼SltLke123 Gamely 8
3Oct92-Grade I

13Sep92- 8Bel fst 6f :221 :444 1:09 3↑Fall Hiwt H 107 2 1 21½ 2hd 1½ 12½ Smith M E 128 3.50 95-12 Salt Lake1282½ Burn Fair126¾ Belong to Me122 Driving 6
13Sep92-Grade II

22Aug92- 8Sar fst 7f :212 :434 1:212 Kngs Bishop 105 9 2 54 31½ 11 13 Smith M E 117 8.50e 98 — Salt Lake1173 Binalong1151¼ Agincourt122 Wide, drvng 10
22Aug92-Grade II

8Aug92- 8Sar fst 6f :224 :45 1:091 Clarinet Kng 98 1 2 1½ 1½ 2hd 3¾ Madrid A Jr 122 *2.00 97-07 BelongtoMe122nkWildHrmony115½SltLke122 Weakened 6

28Jun92- 4Atl fst 7f :221 :444 1:214 Jersey Shore 95 2 4 2hd 2hd 21½ 33½ Solis A 119 3.00 94-06 SurelySix112½Superstrike-GB1223SltLke119 Weakened 8

20Jun92- 9Mth gd 6f :213 :44 1:084 Select 100 3 1 3½ 3½ 2hd 1¾ Santagata N 122 4.10 97-03 SltLke122¾BelongtoMe1224¼Concord'sFutur118 Driving 6

7Jun92-10Mth fst 5f :213 :442 :564 3↑Wolf Hill 93 5 1 2½ 21 21½ 21 Gryder A T 111 2.80 96-09 JunkBondKing1131SltLke111noFrndlyLovr117 Willingly 7
7Jun92-Originally scheduled on turf

the 1980s, there was one more Lukas trait serious horseplayers had to keep in mind. In numerous instances, Lukas resisted slowing down horses in decline, often running them long past the point of no return. The past-performance examples displayed on the previous pages deserve a close look and resemble at least two dozen other examples from his remarkable career. In each instance they illustrate the best and worst of this prolific trainer's methods. One can only wonder if the exceptional horsemanship he displayed with the high-strung Tabasco Cat will mark a reversal of the trend. (See Chapter 11 for Capote's p.p.'s.)

While many trainers emerge from losing streaks or personal tragedies with renewed confidence, others need no disaster or emotional trauma to expose weaknesses in their game. Some may even rank among the meet leaders yet telegraph their worst defeats through glaring mistakes of judgment in repetitious situations, or lose control of good horses just when they seem on the verge of stardom. No trainer can succeed with such tentative management, and I seriously doubt anyone had more difficulty with that than Reggie Cornell, who first rose to prominence as the man behind the incredible Silky Sullivan in the late 1950s.

Although Silky was a total flop in the Kentucky Derby and never challenged for a divisional championship, he was one of the most remarkable horses in racing history, a colt who developed a large, loyal fan club for his seemingly impossible whirlwind finishes in California stakes, including the Santa Anita Derby.

Through the courtesy of the Kentucky Derby Museum and *Daily Racing Form* I am republishing Silky's mind-bending past performances strictly for its entertainment value. Can you believe this horse once won a 6½-furlong race at Santa Anita after breaking 41 lengths behind his field? That is no misprint—41 lengths is more than 1/16 mile!

Silky Sullivan × 112 Ch. c. 4, by Sullivan—Lady N Silk, by Ambrose Light.
Br., Mrs. N. F. & Dr. R. H. Roberts. 1958 12 5 1 1 $110,225
Owner, Ross & Klipstein. Trainer, R. Cornell.

Dec 4-58^{7}Tan	6 f	1:10⅗ft	2	▴122	9^{11}	8^{10}	$5^{1¼}$	1½	PierceD^3	Alw	95	C'p deV't112	L'dF't'roy112	On theL'ke	9
Jly 1-58^{6}Hol	7 f	1:23⅗ft	6-5	▴120	$5^{2¾}$	1½	1^2	1^2	Sh'akerW^4	Alw	81	Orbital 112	Hit theTr'l 112	Rise 'nSh'e	5
Jun20-58^{7}Hol	6 f	1:09⅗ft	11	119	10^{45}	10^{38}	10^{24}	9^{16}	Har'atzW^1	Alw	79	Aliwar 122	StrongBay 11	ElCajon	10
May17-58^{8}Pim	1 3/16	1:57⅕ft	6½	126	12^{29}	11^{15}	8^{12}	8^{15}	Sh'kerW^4	ScwS	72	TimTam126	Linc'nR'd126	GoneFishin'	12
May 3-58^{7}C.D	1 1-4	2:05 m	2	126	14^{27}	12^{17}	11^{19}	12^{20}	Sh'erW^{12}	ScwS	62	TimTam126	LincolnRoad126	N'reddin	14
Apr26-58^{7}C.D	7 f	1:22⅘gd	2½	▴122	6^{32}	6^{31}	6^{14}	$4^{2¼}$	Sho'akerW^2	Alw	97	B'l'uCh'f119	G'neFishin'119	L'c'lnR'd	6
Apr11-58^{8}G.G	1	1:34⅘ft	1-3	▴122	7^{22}	6^{11}	5^8	$3^{5½}$	Sh'akerW^6	Alw	88	GoneFishin' 110	Furyvan 113	Tabmoc	7
Mar 8-58^{7}S.A	1 1-8	1:49⅗ft	6-5e	▴118	10^{26}	9^{11}	3^5	$1^{3½}$	Sh'kerW^7	SpwS	90	Harcall 118	Aliwar 118	OldPueblo	10
Feb25-58^{5}S.A	6½ f	1:17⅗gd	2-3e	▴120	9^{41}	9^{27}	7^7	1½	Sh'akerW^8	Alw		S'ly'sBoy114	M'sicManFox120	Revada	9
Feb 5-58^{7}S.A	1 1/16	1:45⅕hy	4	118	7^{32}	7^{31}	7^{14}	2^{nk}	Har'tzW^1	SpwS	76	OldPueblo118	TheShoe118	Disdainful	7

A few years after Silky retired, Cornell was given the top training job at fabled Calumet Farm, once the nation's premier racing stable, but the relationship turned out to be disastrous.

Cornell inherited a stable loaded with talent, a stable destined to provide him with a steady flow of top-class racing prospects—horses such as Gleaming, Bold And Able, Eastern Fleet, Prince Turian, Turn To Turia and the freakishly fast Raise A Cup, who set a Belmont track record for 5½ furlongs that lasted nearly 20 years. While all these horses signaled championship potential by winning at least one stakes race very impressively, at least a half-dozen more showed similar precocity in their first or second starts. Every spring Calumet seemed loaded for bear, ready to dominate the racing calendar. But by August almost every last horse worthy of note was on the sidelines for repairs or on the verge of breaking down. Most, it seemed to me, were being kept out of races that were theirs to win and were being pushed instead to the breaking point on the training track.

With first-time starters and absentees, Reggie Cornell was a reliable 20 percent winner, but two or three races and/or a dozen fast workouts later and the player would read the predictable note in *Daily Racing Form* announcing the horse's sudden departure from competition. Trainers who take fast young stock and burn them up on the training track must be viewed cautiously by players who believe in good recent form and fast workouts. All too often these horses reach peak form shortly after dawn a few days before an important race and never live up to their advance billing.

John Gaver, Sr., a genuine Hall of Famer, was another who seemed to put excessive pressure on his horses during training hours.

Although Gaver's training accomplishments included Stop The Music (second best two-year-old during Secretariat's debut season in 1972) and the beautifully prepared 1968 Belmont stakes winner, Stage Door Johnny, I am three-quarters convinced he believed every horse in his barn was the reincarnation of Tom Fool, the rugged handicap champion Gaver developed in the early 1950s.

Tom Fool would often work near track record time between starts and then on race day he'd run his eyeballs out, winning twenty-one out of thirty lifetime starts, including his last eleven in succession under 126–136 pounds.

Some horses thrive on a training regimen that pushes them constantly against their limits. Most, however, will buckle under the punishment and sulk or break down, losing their interest or giving in to pain, never to be heard from again.

Frankly, my mind boggles at the number of races trainers—patient trainers—such as Frank Whiteley, Jr., Woody Stephens or Charles Whittingham would have won with horses trained by Gaver and Cornell, horses who showed signs of brilliance and horses you and I never will hear about.

On the other hand, give a promising young horse to patient Ron McAnally and you might see an early win, or even a late-season stakes victory during the two-year-old campaign, but it is doubtful you will see the true ability of the horse until it turns three on New Year's Day. McAnally, whose style closely resembles the Eastern-based Elliot Burch of the 1960s, is among a group of well-rounded horsemen who come from a completely different orientation than the trainer who seeks a quick score with a promising two-year-old in an early season sprint stakes. McAnally trains horses to run far and to last from one season to the next.

Fast workouts? Definitely. But each workout is designed to complement the horse's progress in actual races—to advance it toward a longer

1990 AND 1989 BREEDERS' CUP DISTAFF WINNER, BAYAKOA

Bayakoa-Ar ⊗
Own.—Whitham Mr-Mrs F E

B. m. 6, by Consultant's Bid—Arlucea, by Good Manners
Br.—Haras Principal (Arg)
Tr.—McAnally Ronald

Lifetime						
35 20 8 0	1990	9	6	2	0	$784,407
$2,296,274	1989	11	9	1	0	$1,406,403
	Turf	8	2	2	0	$46,746

6Oct90- 8Kee	fst	1 1/8	:47	1:10 3/5	1:47	3↑ⒻSpinster	7	2	2^{hd}	1^2	1^3	1^3	Pincay L Jr	LB	123	*.80	99-11	Bayako-Ar123^3Gorgeous123^6Luthier'sLunch123^{no}	Ridden out	8
6Oct90-Grade I																				
1Sep90- 8Dmr	fst	1 1/16	:46 2/5	1:10	1:40 3/5	3↑ⒻChla Vsta H	4	1	1^1	2^{hd}	2^{hd}	1no	Pincay L Jr	LB	127	*.40	98-02	Bayakoa127^{no}FantasticLook$113^{4\frac{1}{2}}$FormidbleLdy$112^{1\frac{3}{4}}$	Gamely	5
1Sep90-Grade II																				
4Aug90- 8Dmr	fst	1 1/16	:46 3/5	1:10	1:40 2/5	3↑San Diego H	5	1	$1^{\frac{1}{2}}$	$1^{\frac{1}{2}}$	$2^{2\frac{1}{2}}$	$2^{2\frac{1}{4}}$	Pincay L Jr	L	122	*.50	97-05	QuietAmerican$115^{2\frac{1}{4}}$Bayako$122^{3\frac{1}{2}}$Bosphorus$112^{\frac{1}{2}}$	Second best	6
4Aug90-Grade III																				
16Jun90- 8Hol	fst	1 1/16	:46 2/5	1:10	1:41 1/5	3↑ⒻMilady H	2	2	$2^{1\frac{1}{2}}$	2^1	$2^{\frac{1}{2}}$	$1^{2\frac{1}{4}}$	Pincay L Jr		127	*.10	94-08	Bayakoa$127^{2\frac{1}{4}}$ Fantastic Look$113^{7\frac{1}{2}}$ Kelly110^8	Ridden out	4
16Jun90-Grade I																				
19May90- 8Hol	fst	1	:44 2/5	1:08 3/5	1:34	3↑ⒻHawthorne H	5	4	$3^{\frac{1}{2}}$	$3^{\frac{1}{2}}$	1^1	1^4	Pincay L Jr		125	*.50	94-12	Bayakoa125^4 Stormy ButValid$119^{3\frac{1}{2}}$FantasticLook$115^{1\frac{1}{4}}$	Wide	5
19May90-Grade II																				
18Apr90- 9OP	gd	1 1/16	:46 3/5	1:10 3/5	1:40 2/5	ⒻA Blossom H	1	1	1^2	1^2	$1^{\frac{1}{2}}$	$2^{2\frac{3}{4}}$	Pincay L Jr		126	*.10	97-21	Gorgeous$122^{2\frac{3}{4}}$ Bayakoa$126^{10\frac{1}{2}}$ Affirmed Classic112^{10}	Gamely	4
18Apr90-Grade II																				
4Mar90- 8SA	fst	1 1/4	:45 4/5	1:34 4/5	2:01 1/5	S Anita H	3	3	$5^{5\frac{1}{2}}$	9^{13}	9^{17}	10^{29}	Pincay L Jr		122	*1.90	59-18	Ruhlmann$121^{1\frac{3}{4}}$CriminalType119^{hd}FlyingContinentl$121^{\frac{1}{2}}$	Wide	10
4Mar90-Grade I																				
18Feb90- 8SA	sly	1 1/8	:46 3/5	1:10 4/5	1:48 3/5	ⒻS Margita H	4	2	1^{hd}	1^2	$1^{3\frac{1}{2}}$	1^6	McCarron C J		127	*.50	94-18	Bayakoa127^6 Gorgeous125^5 Luthier'sLaunch113^5	Easy winner	4
18Feb90-Grade I																				
4Feb90- 5SA	gd	1 1/16	:47 3/5	1:11 3/5	1:43	ⒻS Maria H	2	1	$1^{\frac{1}{2}}$	$1^{1\frac{1}{2}}$	1^4	$1^{3\frac{1}{2}}$	McCarron C J		126	*.30	88-18	Bayakoa$126^{3\frac{1}{2}}$ Nikishka$117^{2\frac{1}{2}}$ Carita Tostada$112^{4\frac{1}{2}}$	Much best	4
4Feb90-Grade I																				
4Nov89- 6GP	fst	1 1/8	:46 2/5	1:11 1/5	1:47 2/5	3↑ⒻBr Cp Dstff	1	2	2^1	$1^{1\frac{1}{2}}$	1^2	$1^{1\frac{1}{2}}$	Pincay L Jr		123	*.70	107-01	Bayakoa$123^{1\frac{1}{2}}$ Gorgeous$119^{2\frac{1}{4}}$ Open Mind119^5	Driving	10
4Nov89-Grade I																				

Speed Index: **Last Race: +10.0** **3-Race Avg.: +4.0** **10-Race Avg.: +4.1** **Overall Avg.: +4.1**

LATEST WORKOUTS ●Oct 5 Kee 3f gd :33 3/5 H

1991 ARLINGTON MILLION WINNER, TIGHT SPOT

Tight Spot — B. c. 4, by His Majesty—Premium Win, by Lyphard
Br.—Winchell Verne H (Ky)
Tr.—McAnally Ronald
126 — Lifetime 17 10 3 1 $1,403,350 — 1991 5 5 0 0 $1,008,800 — 1990 7 4 1 0 $367,150 — Turf 8 8 0 0 $1,282,050

Own.—Winchell V H et al

1Sep91- 9AP fm 1¼ Ⓣ:473 1:354 1:592 3↑Arl Million 7 3 21½ 21 2½ 1hd Pincay L Jr L 126 *1.80 101-07 Tight Spot126hd Algenib-Ar122nk Kartajana-Ir123nk All out 10
1Sep91-Grade I

11Aug91- 8Dmr fm 1⅛ Ⓣ:472 1:112 1:471 3↑Ed Read H 7 1 13½ 11½ 12½ 13½ Pincay L Jr LB 125 *1.10 102-02 TightSpot1253½ValDesBois-Fr115nkMdjristn116nk Ridden out 7
11Aug91-Grade I

4Jly91- 8Hol fm 1⅛ Ⓣ:472 1:102 1:46 3↑American H 1 1 11½ 11½ 11½ 11 Pincay L Jr LB 123 *1.70 100-08 Tight Spot1231 Exbourne1223 Super May118½ Ridden out 8
4Jly91-Grade II

8Jun91- 8Hol fm 1 1/16 Ⓣ:473 1:11 1:401 3↑Inglewood H 3 1 12½ 13 14 14½ Pincay L Jr LB 121 *.80 94-07 TightSpot1214½Somethingdifferent116hdRzn114no Ridden out 6
8Jun91-Grade II

8May91- 8Hol fm 1⅛ Ⓣ:47 1:101 1:444 Alw 50000 2 1 11½ 11½ 11 1nk Pincay L Jr LB 117 *1.40 106-01 Tight Spot117nk High Rank1155 Tarsho-Ir1141¼ Held gamely 5

19Aug90- 8Dmr fm 1⅛ Ⓣ:483 1:131 1:493 Dmr Derby 9 1 11½ 11½ 12½ 13 Pincay L Jr LB 122 *1.10e[D] 90-08 [D]TightSpot1223Itsllgreektome1221¾Prdcssor122¾ Came over 10
19Aug90-Grade II; Disqualified and placed tenth; ruling rescinded 9/26/90

5Aug90- 8Dmr fm 1 1/16 Ⓣ:48 1:112 1:414 La Jolla H 6 2 2½ 2hd 12 1no Delahoussaye E L 118 2.30 98-04 TightSpot118noItsllgreektom1194MusicProspctor1181 Driving 6
5Aug90-Grade III

22Jun90- 7Hol fm 1 1/16 Ⓣ:472 1:112 1:413 [R]Star Dust 5 1 1½ 1½ 11½ 12 Delahoussaye E 117 2.60 87-15 Tight Spot1172 Predecessor114hd Kept His Cool112no Driving 7

21Apr90- 8GG fst 1⅛ :444 1:083 1:464 Cal Derby 9 4 42 43½ 49½ 413¾ Black C A 115 2.70 77-14 StlwrtChrgr1152¼MuscProspctor1178Ts'sDwnng1173½ Evenly 12
21Apr90-Grade III

31Mar90-10TP my 1⅛ :463 1:112 1:492 Jim Beam 10 3 2hd 2½ 48 518 Black C A 121 4.50 80-20 Summer Squall1212½ Bright Again1218 Yonder1216 Gave way. 10
31Mar90-Grade II

3Mar90- 8SA fst 1 :464 1:111 1:363 San Rafael 7 2 21½ 21 22½ 22½ Black C A 115 13.70 81-22 Mister Frisky1152½TightSpot1152LandRush1156½ Good effort 7
3Mar90-Grade II

Speed Index: Last Race: +8.0 3-Race Avg.: +6.6 8-Race Avg.: +3.7 Overall Avg.: +2.1

LATEST WORKOUTS Oct 17 Kee Ⓣ 7f fm 1:302 H Aug 25 Dmr Ⓣ 7f fm 1:272 H (d)

distance, sharpen its speed, or just keep it within range of McAnally's control between important engagements. Once top form has been achieved, McAnally will stop, or decrease the frequency or the speed, or the distance of the workouts (or all three), in direct proportion to the horse's actual racing opportunities. With that kind of sensible management, McAnally, like Burch before him and other contemporary masters, will get two, three, or four topflight races in succession out of his best-grade stock. The player who knows that about McAnally can string along for a very profitable ride.

NOTE: *In addition to the two McAnally-trained champions displayed above, McAnally's Sea Cadet can be found on page 24 in Chapter 4.*

1992 HOLLYWOOD DERBY WINNER PARADISE CREEK

Paradise Creek — Dk. b. or br. c. 3(Feb), by Irish River-Fr—North Of Eden, by Northfields
Br.—Firestone Mr-Mrs B R (Va)
Tr.—Mott William I (—)
Lifetime 9 5 3 0 $630,590 — 1992 7 4 3 0 $604,190 — 1991 2 1 0 0 $26,400 — Turf 8 5 3 0 $618,590

Own.—Firestone Bertram R

22Nov92- 8Hol fm 1⅛ Ⓣ:453 1:093 1:471 Hol Derby 99 5 3 2½ 1½ 1½ 1no Day P LB 122 *1.50 88-15 Paradise Creek122no BienBien1221½Kitwood122 Gamely 12
22Nov92-Grade I

31Oct92- 7GP fm 1 Ⓣ:454 1:09 1:324 3↑Br Cp Mile 106 11 6 63¾ 53¾ 44 23 Day P 122 30.30f 106 — Lure1223ParadiseCreek122nkBriefTruce122 Good effort 14
31Oct92-Grade I

3Oct92- 9Med fm 1 1/16 Ⓣ:463 1:101 1:402 Palis Brd H 98 4 2 21½ 21 2½ 21 Smith M E 119 *.40 95-01 BddngPrd1161PrdsCrk119nkMrlndMn114 No match late 6

7Sep92- 9AP fm 1¼ Ⓣ:482 1:373 2:01 Secretariat 97 3 4 32 42 32½ 2½ Smith M E 123 *2.40 91-05 Ghazi114½PardiseCreek1231¾TngoChrlie117 Strong rally 10
7Sep92-Grade I

6Aug92- 8Sar fm 1⅛ Ⓣ:47 1:101 1:463 Hall Of Fam 100 4 1 1½ 11½ 12 11 Smith M E 115 *1.30 97-03 PrdsCrk1151SmlngAndDncn1191¾SpctculrTd122 Driving 8
6Aug92-Grade II

22Jly92- 7Bel fm 1 1/16 Ⓣ:463 1:10 1:40 3↑Alw 31000 99 5 2 21½ 21 1hd 12¼ Smith M E 113 *.50 96-15 PrdiseCreek1132¼VictoryCross1176TimberCt111 Driving 9

18Jun92- 7Bel fm 1 1/16 Ⓣ:461 1:10 1:402 3↑Alw 29000 97 10 2 21 11 14 14 Perret C b 112 *1.00 94-11 Paradise Creek1124Scuffleburg1136Alfaares117 Handily 11

1987 BREEDERS' CUP TURF WINNER, THEATRICAL

***Theatrical**

Own.—Firestone & Paulson **126**

B. h. 5, by Nureyev—Tree of Knowledge, by Sassafras
Br.—Firestone Mr–Mrs B R (Ire)
Tr.—Mott William I
Lifetime 21 9 4 2 $2,043,627

1987	8	6	0	1	$1,335,500
1986	6	0	3	1	$627,738
Turf 21	9	4	2		$2,043,627

24Oct87-8Aqu	1⅜ (T) :50^{1} 1:38^{2} 2:15^{2} fm	*1-3	126	2^{2}	2^{hd}	1^{hd}	$1^{2\frac{1}{2}}$	Day P^{5}	Man O' War	94-07	Thetricl,LeGloriux,MidnightCousins	8
24Oct87—Grade I												
26Sep87-8Bel	1½ (T) :49^{1} 2:04^{4} 2:29^{1} sf	*1	126	2^{7}	$1^{\frac{1}{2}}$	1^{2}	$1^{3\frac{3}{4}}$	Day P^{5}	Trf Classic	78-25	Theatrical,RiverMemories,Talakeno	6
26Sep87—Grade I												
6Sep87-8AP	1¼ (T) :48^{2} 1:38^{3} 2:02^{2} fm	2¼	126	$2^{\frac{1}{2}}$	1^{1}	2^{3}	$3^{4\frac{3}{4}}$	Day P^{4}	Bud Arl Mil	77-27	Manila, Sharrood, Theatrical	8
6Sep87—Grade I												
1Aug87-8Bel	1½ (T) :49^{1} 2:02^{4} 2:26 fm	*2-5	124	1^{hd}	$2^{1\frac{1}{2}}$	$2^{3\frac{1}{2}}$	2^{3}	Day P^{2}	Swrd Dncr H	91-10	‡Dance of Life, Theatrical, Akabir	4
1Aug87—Grade I; Checked; Placed first through disqualification												
13Jun87-8Bel	1⅜ [T] :50 1:38^{1} 2:14 fm	*6-5	123	3^{3}	3^{3}	2^{hd}	1^{1}	Day P^{1}	Bowlng Gr H	87-24	Theatrical, Akabir, Dance of Life	10
13Jun87—Grade I												
30May87-8Bel	1¼ [T] :48^{1} 1:36^{2} 2:00^{4} fm	2¾	122	3^{2}	$4^{2\frac{1}{4}}$	3^{1}	$1^{1\frac{3}{4}}$	Day P^{5}	Red Smith H	90-24	Theatrical, Dance of Life,Equalize	11
30May87—Grade II												
21Feb87-10Hia	1½ (T) 2:28^{3} fm	*6-5	121	1^{hd}	1^{1}	$1^{\frac{1}{2}}$	1^{nk}	Day P^{6}	Turf Cup H	87-14	Theatrical,LongMick,CremeFraiche	8
21Feb87—Grade I												
31Jan87-10Hia	$1\frac{3}{16}$ (T) 1:54 fm	*8-5	122	8^{5}	$6^{2\frac{1}{4}}$	$3^{3\frac{1}{2}}$	2^{2} †	Day P^{11}	B'gnvilla H	85-14	Akabir, ‡Theatrical,FlyingPidgeon	14
31Jan87—Grade II; Bore in; †Disqualified and placed fourteenth												
7Dec86-8Hol	1½ (T) :47^{4} 2:01 2:25^{4} fm	*6-5e	126	2^{hd}	$1^{\frac{1}{2}}$	1^{1}	3^{nk}	StevnsGL^{2}	Tf Cp Inv	93-09	Alphabatim, Dahar, Theatrical	8
7Dec86—Grade I; Lost whip late												
1Nov86-6SA	1½ (T) :47^{2} 2:00^{3} 2:25^{2} fm	2¾e	126	$2^{2\frac{1}{2}}$	2^{1}	1^{hd}	2^{nk}	StvnsGL^{1}	Br Cp Turf	88-07	Manila, Theatrical, Estrapade	9
1Nov86—Grade I												

Nov 6 Hol 5f gd 1:02^{4} h **Oct 20 Bel 5f ft 1:01^{3} b** **Oct 14 Bel 7f ft 1:31 b** **Oct 9 Bel 6f ft 1:15^{4} b**

Trainer Billy Mott, a former protégé of Jack Van Berg, is another trainer whose work may be viewed as textbook material well into the 21st century. Developer of the millionare sprinter Taylor's Special during the 1980s, Mott has matured into one of the nation's most respected horsemen since moving to New York to handle well-bred runners for Bert Firestone and other patrons.

Mott's brilliant handling of Theatrical, Paradise Creek (and 1992 Breeders' Cup Turf champ Fraise) through well-spaced campaigns is reminiscent of another rock-reliable trainer, Mackenzie Miller, at his best. Miller, who won the 1993 Kentucky Derby with Sea Hero, has been the acknowledged master of East Coast grass racing since the early 1970s, when he was among the first to appreciate that a horse's form on a dirt track is not usually transferable to the grass course. Miller also seemed quickest to note that the sons and daughters of top-notch imports from Europe, South America, Australia and South Africa are more likely to run well on grass than horses who lack such foreign influences in their pedigrees.

To my surprise, the profusion of grass racing during the past two decades has not muted the utility of breeding as a primary handicapping factor in turf racing, especially when it is used in tandem with trainers who have a winning history with lightly raced horses making their first or second starts on the grass. (See Chapter 21 for a master sires list.) Otherwise, the opposite is equally true: Many trainers have no clue what to do with grass horses, or sprinters or routers or fillies or in a variety of situations, even though they may be among the best on the grounds in one or more limited situations. While most handicappers accept the notion that a racehorse must go through various cycles of positive and negative form each season, many players underestimate the equally important truth that trainers tend to have their own reliable preferences or form cycles. Certainly there is money to be made detecting specific trainer patterns and their specialized skills and weaknesses.

How can a player uncover the special winning abilities of new trainers operating at any racetrack, or simply formulate intelligent judgments about the present form of any horse entered in any race at any track?

In the 1990s, many players regularly rely on statistical studies provided by Bloodstock Research of Lexington, Kentucky (see Appendix A), and other compilations sold through the mails or included in publications designed to supplement *Daily Racing Form* past performances. These are useful starting points, but the best players inevitably seek more precise answers through comparisons of past-performance profiles such as we have been examining. Indeed, a single past performance may well answer all the fundamental questions. The trick is to recognize the implications of the evidence. The examples in the next chapter should help illustrate the point.

What's He Doing in Today's Race?

The horse has had ten starts; his last race was a strong performance; the trainer is somebody we have never heard of, or somebody who wins a few races now and then but we don't know how he wins them. How do we decide whether the horse is going to improve, run the same race, or fail to make an impression? What clues in the past performances will help us rate this horse in this field today?

The answer is all the clues we can get—the result charts, the workout listings, and the past-performance records of other horses trained by this man or woman. If we had occasion to do that kind of research before we came out to the track, we would be able to make a confident assessment.

In a single past-performance profile there are important clues about the fitness of the horse, its class, distance capabilities, and soundness. And in fact about the trainer too.

In the following past-performance examples, including a few from the original edition of *Betting Thoroughbreds*, we shall look closely to glean as much information about each horse as possible, attempting to get a fix on the skill of the trainer and to find the answer to an important handicapping question: *What's he doing in today's race?*

6 FURLONGS-$50,000 MAIDEN CLAIMING, 2-YEAR-OLD FILLIES, HOLLYWOOD PARK, DECEMBER 10, 1992

Melrose Park				Ch. f. 2(Mar), by Talinum—Red Lady, by Northjet					Lifetime	1992	5	M	0	2	$7,500
STEVENS G L (95 12 13 16 .13)				$50,000	Br.—Calumet Farm (Ky)					5 0 0 2					
Own.—Overbrook Farm					Tr.—Lukas D Wayne (19 1 1 6 .05)			**119**	$7,500				
14Nov92- 4Hol fst 6f	:22	:45	1:10³	ⒻMd 50000	73 8 1 2¹½ 2¹½ 2¹½ 3³½	Stevens G L	LB 118	5.30	84-11 SmplyGrvy118²⅜BrngSl118½MlrsPrk118	Weakened a bit 8
21Oct92- 6SA fst 6f	:214	:444	1:10⁴	ⒻMd 32000	68 8 2 1ʰᵈ 1ʰᵈ 2ʰᵈ 3⁵	Stevens G L	LB 117	*2.20	77-16 GldOnThIsld117⁵GrdItIs117ʰᵈMlrsPr117	Edged for 2nd 11
2Aug92- 4Dmr fst 5½f	:21	:443	1:03⁴	ⒻMd Sp Wt	8 7 1 2¹½ 2¹½ 7¹¹ 7²⁴¾	Valenzuela P A	B 117	4.20	67-08 UnchndPrcss117⁴IAIss117⁵PrspctRr117	Not urged late 7
18Jly92- 4Hol fst 6f	:214	:444	1:10²	ⒻMd Sp Wt	38 5 2 1¹½ 3² 6¹⁰ 7¹⁵¾	Pincay L Jr	B 117	7.30	72-07 BrHrtd-GB117²½FbsGlr117⁶½Ctch117	Bumpedstart,wide 8
24Jun92- 4Hol fst 5½f	:214	:452	1:04³	ⒻMd Sp Wt	51 4 2 1¹½ 1¹¹ 2ʰᵈ 4⁸½	Solis A	B 117	21.00	81-12 LilyLBelle117⁷PssingVice117¹AvilblAvnu117	Weakened 7
LATEST WORKOUTS	Dec 2 SA	4f fst :48⁴ H			Nov 25 SA	4f fst :47¹ H		Nov 6 SA	5f fst 1:00¹ H	Oct 17 SA	4f fst :51 H

The past-performance profile for the horse above has a familiar look. It resembles past performances seen in maiden races at various claiming prices every few days at tracks from coast to coast. Only the names of the horses, jockeys and trainers are different.

There is nothing earth-shattering here, but the logic contained within a single past-performance profile often reveals the intent of the trainer as well as the probability of a good or poor performance.

Note the early speed and the poor finishes for Melrose Park in her summer 1992 races and the ten-week gap before trainer D. Wayne Lukas brought her back to competition at the $32,000 maiden-claiming level. That's close to the bottom of the barrel in southern California.

Perhaps the 2½-month vacation, plus the addition of the anti-bleeder drug Lasix (L) and the drop in class helped Melrose Park carry her speed a bit further in her October 21 comeback race. Even so, the performance was not much better than her career debut in June.

Lukas did see enough, however, to move Melrose Park back up a notch in class to the $50,000 maiden-claiming level for her second outing since returning to competition. The November 6 workout at Santa Anita was another encouraging sign, validated by a third-place finish that was subtly better than her third on October 21. Note the improved Beyer speed figure of 73 for this race versus 68 earned in her prior race. Beyer speed figures will be explained in greater detail in Chapters 13, 14 and 15, but they purport to measure the actual speed of a given performance regardless of distance or track conditions. Thus, a higher Beyer figure will suggest a faster performance than a slower one, even if the final clocking indicates otherwise. Similarly, a Beyer figure of 80 at one mile at Oaklawn Park roughly equals a Beyer figure of 80 earned in a six-furlong race at Louisiana Downs or any other track or distance.

Without even consulting Beyer figures, note the way Melrose Park chased the leader from start to finish and held on much better than ever, losing only 1¾ lengths during the final furlong. This was an unmistakable positive sign of improvement.

To take advantage, Lukas now is matching Melrose Park against another group of $50,000 maiden claimers and he has put some polish on the package, working her twice. Putting all this information together is not difficult: Melrose Park clearly is approaching a new peak performance in her limited career. We may not know what that peak will be, or how long Melrose Park will maintain it, or even if she will actually reach it today, but we do know she already is competitive at this level, and we have every right to believe she's going to run a stronger race, her best to date.

Our optimism for this horse's winning chances would be tempered by other strong contenders, but this is a typical maiden-claiming race in which only a handful of horses in the field look like they can run. One has faded badly in all four starts; another has three okay races in four outings, but was beaten by Melrose Park on November 14; another weakened noticeably in four outings with weaker, state-bred rivals and has only one relatively slow workout in 3½ weeks.

Melrose Park need not improve at all to win this race unless one of the first-time starters in the field is ready for an unusually strong debut performance. The best of these newcomers is Fine Impression, trained by Ron McAnally.

Fine Impression has had one encouraging workout and did run very well in this race at 8–1 odds, but she was not strong enough to stop Melrose Park. The latter dueled for the lead and edged clear under a hand ride in the final furlong to pay a relatively generous $8.20 as the third betting choice. Fine Impression finished second to complete a very playable $58 exacta.

While the Lukas of the 1980s rarely wasted time with claiming horses or borderline allowance runners like this one, Melrose Park provided ample evidence that the man who has won more money and more stakes than anyone in history can deliver a dose of blue-collar training work just as well as anyone on the southern California circuit.

As a footnote to this race, I probably do not need to tell you that McAnally's Fine Impression used the experience gained from this race to win a maiden race of her own in her second career start.

1-1/16 MILES, $12,500 CLAIMING, 3-YEAR-OLDS, NON WINNERS OF TWO RACES, BAY MEADOWS, OCTOBER 31, 1992

Pleasantly Round — Gr. g. 3(May), by Spectacular Round—Cachua-Ar, by Dancing Moss — Lifetime 8 1 0 1 $5,725 — 1992 8 1 0 1 $5,725; 1991 0 M 0 0; Turf 2 0 0 0

DOOCY T T (112 11 12 14 .10) — $12,500 — Br.—Danene Thoroughbreds Ltd (Cal) — 118

Own.—McCarthy Daniel — Tr.—Aime Ronald D (13 2 1 1 .15)

10Oct92-10BM	fm	*1⅛ Ⓣ	:48	$1:12^4$	$1:47^3$	Hcp 12500s	63	1	6	6^5	$7^{4\frac{1}{4}}$	9^{12}	$8^{11\frac{3}{4}}$	Belmonte J F	LBb	111	85.70	82-06	DbnrAstr116$^{4\frac{1}{2}}$UndrcvrStng122$^{\frac{1}{2}}$BttlsWhrf115	No threat	11
18Sep92- 3BM	fm	1 1/16 Ⓣ	$:47^3$	$1:12^3$	$1:45^1$	Hcp 12500s	69	9	4	4^3	$6^{3\frac{1}{4}}$	6^5	$7^{5\frac{1}{2}}$	Castaneda M	LBb	115	70.70	78-16	SpcyNtiv117^{hd}Romo'sRoylty118$^{1\frac{1}{2}}$CshLgcy115	Wide trip	11
7Sep92- 7BM	fst	1 1/16	$:48^3$	1:13	$1:43^4$	Clm 12500	74	5	4	5^3	$7^{4\frac{3}{4}}$	$5^{4\frac{1}{4}}$	4^5	Campbell B C	LBb	117	12.70	75-21	VlidTry117$^{1\frac{1}{2}}$SpcyNtive117$^{\frac{1}{2}}$GenerlDmges119	Wide early	9
11Aug92- 8Bmf	fst	1 1/16	$:46^4$	$1:12^2$	1:45	Md 12500	65	3	4	5^3	$4^{1\frac{3}{4}}$	2^1	1^1	Baze R A	LBb	120	6.70	74-23	PlsntlRnd120^{1}HjjsHrn120$^{1\frac{1}{2}}$OrPrcNc115	Bumped break	12
29Jly92- 7SR	fst	1 1/16	$:47^4$	$1:12^4$	$1:45^1$	Md 12500	52	2	3	$3^{2\frac{1}{2}}$	2^3	2^4	3^7	Baze R A	Bb	118	5.40	74-19	VlorosAffr118^{5}OrPrncNck113^{2}PlsntlyRnd118	Weakened	10
28Jun92- 5GG	fst	6f	$:22^2$	$:45^4$	$1:11^2$	Ⓢ Md 12500	40	9	3	3^2	5^6	6^9	$6^{8\frac{1}{4}}$	Martinez O A Jr	B	118	15.00	73-17	FnrFhd118^{2}MystclFlwrs118^{6}EmrMgc118	Through early	9
18Jun92- 4GG	fst	6f	$:21^4$	$:44^3$	1:10	Ⓢ Md 12500	44	2	11	$7^{9\frac{1}{4}}$	7^{14}	7^{11}	$6^{8\frac{1}{4}}$	Campbell B C	B	118	55.60	80-10	SrKnnth118$^{\frac{1}{4}}$DnntEs118^{2}PppDRnRn118	Ducked in start	11
26Apr92- 3TuP	fst	5½f	$:21^4$	$:44^4$	$1:02^4$	Md 12500	1	2	7	$6^{8\frac{1}{4}}$	7^{11}	7^{15}	$7^{25\frac{1}{2}}$	Guerrero A		120	8.90	70-09	MdtnEprss120^{5}StdNrdc120$^{8\frac{1}{2}}$MrtsLgnd120	Broke slowly	7

LATEST WORKOUTS Oct 26 GG 5f fst $1:01^1$ H — Oct 20 GG 6f fst $1:13^2$ H — Oct 3 GG 7f fst $1:28^1$ H — Sep 26 GG 6f fst $1:14^2$ H

Pleasantly Round is relatively inexperienced, with only eight career starts, but already has demonstrated a strong preference for a route of ground (one mile or more), on the main dirt track. Surely he improved in his first route race at Santa Rosa on July 29, following two sprint races at Golden Gate Fields. (Santa Rosa is one of several summer fair stopovers on the northern California racing circuit.)

Look at his progress in his second route try—a winning run at the same class and distance at the Bay Meadows Fair on August 11—and there was nothing wrong with his rallying fourth in his first try with winners during the regular Bay Meadows meet on September 7. If we use Beyer speed figures to help us assess performance, we could conclude that Pleasantly Round has continued the upward movement in his form cycle by earning a 75 Beyer figure, compared to the 65 he earned in his victory over maidens. (Again, Beyer speed figures will be dissected in detail in Chapters 13, 14 and Appendix B.)

We do not need to consult result charts to determine that Pleasantly Round's last two races on the grass were significantly tougher than today's race against horses who have won only one race apiece. "Hcp 12,500" races are *starter handicap* races that invite horses who have started for the stated claiming price sometime during a specified time period. Under these flexible conditions, the field may contain a wide range of horses, including some who may have competed in allowance races or stakes. Usually, it pays to double the estimated value of a given starter handicap to approximate the true claiming class of these races, or else consult speed figures or performance histories of the horses who actually competed in the race. Pleasantly Round's last two races were against much stiffer opposition on alien racing surfaces. Today he is back on his preferred racing surface meeting much weaker foes. While that is no guarantee for victory, it is an excellent reason to make a bet.

The workout line gives us additional confidence: six furlongs in 1:14⅖ on September 26 and seven in 1:28⅕ on October 3, plus two more highly encouraging workouts since his most recent race.

Conclusion: Pleasantly Round is in terrific shape, ready to fire one of his better races, if not improve over anything he has shown to date.

Our lone concern is his running style: Horses who rally from deep in the pack are always vulnerable to a soft, uncontested pace. If a front-running type can jump out to set a relaxed pace, Pleasantly Round would find it difficult to cut into the leader's advantage late in the race. Relaxed front runners use up much less energy than front runners who get pushed into faster fractions during the early and middle stages. In this race, however, there is no such dilemma. Four different horses have shown sufficient early speed to contribute to a hot pace. The pace scenario could not be more favorable if we had recruited the competition ourselves.

Trainer Ronald Aime may not be ready to challenge for a meet championship, but we can conclude from this single past performance that he knows how to darken a horse's form just enough to improve the price, while gaining an edge in conditioning. That is a lethal combination, and it boggles the mind to recall that Pleasantly Round won this race with incredible ease at 9–1 odds! He should have been a solid 8–5 wagering favorite.

---

6 FURLONGS—$20,000 ALLOWANCE PURSE, BELMONT PARK, JUNE 7, 1976

Desert Boots **107** B. f (1973), by Ridan—Signal Flag, by Restless Wind.
Breeder, Mrs. Barbara Joslin (Fla.). 1976 7 1 4 1 $16.300
Owner, W. M. Joslin. Trainer, S. DiMauro. 1975 2 1 0 0 $5.940

17 May76 ^{7}Bel	6 f	:22	:44^{4}1:10^{3}ft	7¾	106^5	1^{1½}	1^{1½}	1^2	2½	MartinJE^4	Alw 88	ⒻFurling 114	Desert Boots	7
4 May76 ^{7}Bel	6 f	:22^4	:45^{3}1:11 ft	6½	105^5	1½	1^h	2^h	2^{1¼}	VelezRI^6	Alw 86	ⒻFurling 113	Desert Boots	10
9 Apr76 ^{7}Aqu	6 f	:23	:46^{2}1:11^{4}ft	2	▲113^5	1^2	1^4	1^5	2^h	VelezRI^6	Alw 84	ⒻIn theOffing114	DesertBts	6
15 Mar76 ^{7}Aqu	6 f	:22^1	:45^{3}1:11^{1}ft	2½	118	1½	1^2	1^3	3^2	BaezaB^3	Alw 85	ⒻAncntFbles114	Rsn frTrce	9
3 Mar76 ^{8}Aqu	6 f	:22^2	:45^{2}1:10^{1}ft	4¾	114	1½	2^h	2^4	7^{8¼}	HoleM^4	AlwS 84	ⒻToughElsie116	LightFrost	13
14 Feb76 ^{6}Hia	6 f	:21^3	:44^{3}1:11^{2}ft	4-5	▲116	1½	1^3	1^4	1^{1½}	BaezaB^5	Alw 86	ⒻDesertBoots116	She'sTrble	8
31 Jan76 ^{6}Hia	6 f	:22	:45^{1}1:11^{1}ft	2¾	114	1½	1^3	1^{1½}	2^{2½}	MapleE^8	Alw 84	ⒻDaltonRoad114	DesrtBccts	12
1 Sep75 ^{3}Bel	5 f	:22^1	:45^{4}1:1^{2}ft	3	▲119	1^{1½}	1^4	1^7	1^{8½}	BracleVJr^9	Mdn 85	ⒻDesertB'ts119	Sw'tB'rn'e	12

June 3 Bel trt 1m ft 1:46⅖b May 29 Bel trt 1m ft 1:45⅕b May 23 Bel trt 1m ft 1:46⅖b

---

The example above does not include Andy Beyer's speed figures because it was taken from a 1976 edition of the *Daily Racing Form*. Andy and I were using his figures jointly at the time, and I can tell you they were no help with this horse, as they will not be in any similar situation. Take a close look at the past performances of Desert Boots, a rather quick filly who was in the money for six of her seven 1976 races, with two wins in nine lifetime starts.

With national three-year-old champion Wajima and juvenile filly champ Dearly Precious in his barn, Steve DiMauro had the best year of a good career in 1975. Things were not quite that good in 1976, but this particular filly must have driven DiMauro crazy.

Although an apparent money *earner*, Desert Boots is a classic money burner, a one-dimensional speedball who simply refuses to keep something in reserve for the stretch run. DiMauro was trying to solve her problem through a program of long, slow, stamina-building workouts. The prescription was sensible but it didn't work.

Perhaps a route race would have gotten the message across better than workouts alone. But there is a chance too that nothing will help a horse like this. Desert Boots may have congenital wind problems, which will always keep her from beating quality horses at six furlongs.

In a game like racing we have a right to go our separate ways with a fast-breaking horse like Desert Boots. A horse like that is always eligible to keep right on going all the way to the finish. And some players might be willing to give trainer DiMauro the benefit of the doubt, on the evidence of those interesting long workouts.

I prefer not to be so generous, not unless there is a strong speed-favoring track bias operating in the horse's favor. I want proof that the trainer has solved such a serious problem, or insurance if he hasn't— insurance of a track bias, or proof only a recent winning race can provide. Horses that tire in race after race are notorious money burners.

The next few examples underscore fundamental considerations in the claiming game, an integral part of racing from coast to coast. The claiming game is for shrewd business-minded trainers and poker-playing types. And if you've never encountered José Martin, his Hall of Fame father, Frank, or his son, Carlos, the following examples should be enough to convince you of the family's precise mastery over that aspect of the game.

On the morning before the 1973 Kentucky Derby, in which Frank Martin would saddle second choice Sham against Secretariat, Martin was observed walking in front of his horse, staring straight at the ground all the way from Sham's stall on the Churchill Downs backstretch to the racetrack. Asked what he was looking for, Martin replied: *"Loose stones . . . I do not want anything in my horse's way."*

Powerless to prevent Secretariat from getting one leg up on the Triple Crown, Martin's "no-stone-unturned" training approach was the basis for his rise to stardom with much cheaper stock on the New York circuit. Martin won ten straight New York training titles between 1973 and 1982. The 1992 past performance seen below is clear proof he never lost his touch.

Royal Eagle — B. g. 7, by Beau's Eagle—Growing On Trees, by Big Spruce
ZUNIGA E (10 1 3 1 .10) — $25,000 — Br.—Kinderhill Corp–General Partner (Cal)
Own.—Sommer Viola — Tr.—Martin Frank (7 1 1 1 .14) — 112^5

Lifetime						
33 13 6 3	1992	3	2	0	0	$21,000
$214,650	1991	14	6	2	3	$96,800
	Turf	1	0	0	0	
	Wet	2	1	0	0	$17,600

22Jan92- 6Aqu	fst	6f	⊡:22^4	:45^4	1:11	Clm 35000	98	8	1	$1^{1\frac{1}{2}}$	1^1	1^3	$1^{2\frac{3}{4}}$	Samyn J L	b	117	*2.20	88-23	RoyalEgle117$^{2\frac{3}{4}}$CrftyMn113^{3}LeftyPriolo115	Ridden out	9
11Jan92- 9Aqu	fst	6f	⊡:23^1	:46^2	1:11^3	Clm 16500	93	5	1	$1^{1\frac{1}{2}}$	1^5	$1^{5\frac{1}{2}}$	$1^{3\frac{3}{4}}$	Gryder A T	b	115	3.50	85-24	RoyalEgle115$^{3\frac{3}{4}}$MjorMccllum113^{1}PpInChrge117	Handily	8
1Jan92- 5Aqu	fst	6f	⊡:22^2	:45^1	1:10^3	Clm 25000	76	6	1	5^6	6^8	6^7	5^9	Cordero A Jr	b	117	*1.70	81-13	Buna Lite117$^{2\frac{1}{2}}$AllSilver117^1[DH]RiverPatriot117	No rally	7
20Nov91- 3Aqu	fst	6f	:22	:45^1	1:10^1	3↑Clm 25000	94	6	3	$4^{1\frac{1}{2}}$	$3^{\frac{1}{2}}$	$1^{\frac{1}{2}}$	$2^{1\frac{3}{4}}$	Cruguet J	b	117	4.80	88-14	SeportMc117$^{1\frac{3}{4}}$RoylEgle117$^{\frac{3}{4}}$DncingMinstrl113	2nd best	6
27Oct91- 9Aqu	fst	6f	:22^1	:45^1	1:09^4	3↑Clm 14000	94	1	—	—	—	—	1^4	Cordero A Jr	b	119	*1.70	92-14	RoylEgl119^{4}RomnRport115$^{\frac{1}{2}}$ScrcrdHrry117	Fog, driving	14
2Oct91- 9Bel	fst	6f	:22	:45^3	1:10^1	3↑Clm 17500	92	5	4	$5^{3\frac{3}{4}}$	$2^{\frac{1}{2}}$	1^2	1^1	Cordero A Jr	b	117	*2.70	89-14	RoyalEagle117^{1}Reappeal117$^{2\frac{3}{4}}$TooTrue112	Wide driving	12
15Sep91- 3Bel	fst	6f	:22^2	:45^2	1:10^2	3↑Clm 25000	68	1	4	1^{hd}	1^{hd}	2^1	8^6	Santiago A	b	117	*1.60	82-13	TonyCool108^{1}MjorMccllm117^{1}AlwysAshly117	Gave way	8
21Aug91- 5Sar	sly	6½f	:22	:44^4	1:16^2	3↑Clm 45000	80	5	1	$3^{3\frac{1}{2}}$	3^3	$6^{5\frac{3}{4}}$	5^{10}	Antley C W	b	115	3.10	83-10	ScttshMn117^{nk}MnstrlDncr119$^{6\frac{3}{4}}$ShtsArRngng117	4-wide	7
11Aug91- 1Sar	fst	7f	:22^2	:45	1:22^2	3↑Clm 47500	92	3	2	$2^{2\frac{1}{2}}$	$2^{\frac{1}{2}}$	$1^{\frac{1}{2}}$	$1^{\frac{3}{4}}$	Antley C W	b	115	3.00	93-09	RoylEgl115$^{\frac{3}{4}}$DrummondLn115$^{\frac{1}{2}}$Wingrshk117	Drftd, drvg	7
31Jly91- 2Sar	fst	6f	:21^4	:44^3	1:09^1	3↑Clm 50000	92	4	4	$2^{\frac{1}{2}}$	2^{hd}	$3^{\frac{1}{2}}$	4^5	Cordero A Jr	b	117	*1.50	93-10	MinstrelDancer113$^{3\frac{1}{2}}$SeaportMac117^{no}Furicno115	Tired	6

LATEST WORKOUTS Oct 28 Bel 4f fst :48 H ●Oct 20 Bel 4f fst :46^1 H Oct 13 Bel 3f fst :35 H

Note the effectiveness of a drop in class from July 31 to August 11, 1991, and the consecutive wins on drops in October and the seven-week vacation Royal Eagle was given after he failed to enter contention in a $25,000 claiming race on November 20. Note the sharp victory at a reduced class level in the second start after the vacation. Martin then *doubled* this horse's claiming price for another convincing score 11 days later.

Frank Martin and other skilled claiming horse trainers, such as Sanford Shulman, Lonnie Arterburn and Ron Ellis on the West Coast, do not need to drop horses in class to win; they know how to do it without losing all their best horses to other trainers, and they are just as deadly with recent winners stepping up sharply in class. In this case, a sharp betting crowd made Royal Eagle the legit 2–1 favorite in his repeat score at $35,000 claiming.

As indicated by Panda Bear below (from the original *Betting Thoroughbreds*), José Martin inherited many of his father's shrewd moves in the claiming arena.

6 FURLONGS—$10,500 CLAIMING, BELMONT PARK, SEPTEMBER 1, 1976

Panda Bear **113** B. g (1973), by My Dad George—Gold Threat, by Infidel.
Breeder, Martha Broadbent (Fla.). **$10,500**

1976	7	2	1	1	$12,770
1975	3	1	1	1	$5,865

Owner, B. Combs II. Trainer, J. Martin.

11 Aug76	2Sar	6 f	:222	:462	1:112m	4¼	119	32½	31½	52¼	53¼	BaezaB4	12500	80	Chompchomp 117	I'mProud	7
18 Jly 76	2Aqu	6 f	:224	:463	1:122ft	8-5	▲117	31½	32½	22	1nk	BaezaB7	10000	81	PandaBear117	TakeYourBts	7
16 Jun76	9Bel	7 f	:23	:464	1:252ft	3	117	21½	21½	3nk	36¼	CrdroAJr6	12500	69	Fling 119	Spotted Gem	8
22 May76	9Bel	6 f	:223	:46	1:113ft	4½	119	3nk	3½	42¼	76½	CrdoAJr8	16000	77	Cayman Isle117	Mgie'sPride	11
13 May76	2Bel	6 f	:223	:462	1:113ft	2½	117	11½	11½	1h	1½	CdroAJr5	12500	84	PandaBear117	CaymanIsie	9
8 May76	4Bel	6 f	:224	:461	1:113ft	2¼	▲1125	41¼	41¼	52	43	MrtinJE8	14000	81	HowiesHeat117	TakeYrBoots	8
15 Apr76	7Aqu	6 f	:223	:46	1:122ft	2¾	▲117	31	1h	2h	21½	HerndzR7	12500	79	Break theLock115	PndaBear	11
12 Jly 75	9Tdn	5 f	:232	:48	1:003ft	2½	114	21	1h	3nk	32¼	WeilerD3	AlwS	85	FierceRuffian115	HpyMircle	7
2 Jly 75	9RD	5½ f	:22	:45	1:041ft	3½	113	2h	21	3nk	27	RieraRJr3	AlwS	87	ChanningRoad113	PndaBear	9
21 May75	3CD	5 f	:222	:47	:594ft	5½e	122	2½	11½	1½	1h	RieraRJr7	Mdn	90	Panda Bear 122	Sam's Act	11

Aug 30 Bel trt 3f ft :37b   Aug 24 Sar trt 3f ft :37⅖b   Aug 19 Sar trt 4f ft :54b

In the spring of 1976 Panda Bear was a solid $12,000 racehorse. During the summer Martin found out she was able to beat only $10,000 stock.

Up and down the class ladder Panda Bear won two races and $12,770. Each time Martin dropped the horse to her proper level, she delivered an improved effort.

Three workouts on the deeper training track leading up to today's race assure us of Panda Bear's fitness. Today's drop in class tells us Martin is thinking win. If you're thinking the same thing after you get through with the rest of the field, you'll catch a $9 mutuel.

1-⅛ MILES, $25,000 CLAIMING, 3-YEAR-OLDS AND UP, FAST TRACK, AQUEDUCT, NOVEMBER 8, 1992

Lightning Runner Ch. c. 4, by At The Threshold—Magnolia Lass, by Cutlass
CHAVEZ J F (58 9 8 5 .16) **$25,000** Br.—Fernung & Franks (Fla)
Own.—Corr John Tr.—Martin Carlos F (10 1 1 0 .10) **117**

Lifetime 23 4 1 6 $77,755

1992	12	0	1	2	$13,735
1991	10	3	0	4	$56,820
Turf	5	1	0	1	$16,160
Wet	1	0	0	1	$2,730

25Oct92- 3Aqu	fst	1⅛	:474	1:123	1:512	3+Clm 45000	78	2	4	45	74¼	77	79½	Bruin J E	b	114	28.60	69–21 TwothTwst1171¼DmndAnchr113noDsrtPrspctr111	Tired	7
4Oct92- 2Bel	fm	1¼ [T]	:484	1:374	2:014	3+Clm c-35000	78	8	7	75½	72¾	84¼	96	Smith M E	b	117	6.00	75–17 Imprsontr117hdCmmssnrBrt117½Cntnr117	Broke slowly	9
4Oct92-Claimed from Rosenberg A, Hough Stanley M Trainer																				
29Aug92- 7Crc	fst	170	:48	1:13	1:432	3+Clm 50000	76	4	6	511	58	59	611	Hosang G J	Lb	112	10.50	85–05 S.W.Wildcard114hdMumbai1122FlconMr118	Never close	6
15Aug92- 7Crc	fst	1 1/16	:49	1:131	1:461	3+Clm 50000	87	5	4	44½	43	31½	42½	Hosang G J	Lb	116	6.60	93–04 Falcon Mar1182 Mumbai116½ Without A Plot116	Faded	6
25Jly92- 7Crc	fst	1 1/16	:501	1:134	1:454	3+Alw 21000	85	3	1	1hd	2hd	2hd	33½	Hosang G J	Lb	116	*.70	94–04 ExplodngDwn1163Mmb116½LghtnngRnnr116	Weakened	4
11Jly92- 7Crc	fst	7f	:224	:451	1:241	3+Clm 50000	88	2	6	21	2hd	2½	2no	Hosang G J	Lb	116	8.80	94–08 SunnyCook108noLghtnngRunnr1161½Mn109	Just missed	6
24May92-10Crc	fst	1	:483	1:134	1:393	3+Alw 18000	84	5	1	12½	1hd	21½	47	Velez J A Jr	Lb	119	5.40	90–12 PlesntSmil1192WithoutAPlot1213SirOtto119	Weakened	5
3May92- 8Crc	fm	*1⅛ Ⓣ			1:443	3+Clm 55000	84	4	5	57	56	44	43¼	Ferrer J C	Lb	117	4.20	109–01 PrsnBr115½LnPn115noThsnshsbrht115	Failed to menace	6
15Apr92- 8Crc	fm	*1⅛ Ⓣ			1:462	3+Handicap	80	3	2	22	43½	36	57¾	Velez J A Jr	b	113	11.00	95 — Firme1143½ Without A Plot110½TeesProspect112	Faded	6
8Apr92-10Crc	fst	7f	:223	:452	1:23	3+Sunny Isle H	86	1	8	79¾	77	89¼	512¾	Ferrer J C	b	111	49.90	92–10 DrmmndLn1121¼Grmstck1145½FrnRny114	Passed faders	8

LATEST WORKOUTS   Oct 18 Bel tr.t 4f fst :482 H   Oct 1 Bel 3f fst :361 H   Sep 24 Bel 5f fst :592 H   Sep 17 Bel 4f fst :52 B

Given the success Frank and José Martin have had with the drop-down pattern seen in the two previous examples—16 years apart—just what odds would you have been happy to get on grandson Carlos Martin-trained Lightning Runner in a $25,000 claiming route, on November 8, 1992?

Would you believe 9–1!

And how about the 5–1 payoff for Lightning Runner's repeat tally 11 days later, or the incredible $11.70–$1 he paid two starts after that when Carlos triple-jumped this horse up to a $70,000 claiming race on November 30. Apparently the Martins' skill with claiming horses is in their genes.

1-1/16 MILES, $12,500 CLAIMING, FILLIES AND MARES, 3-YEAR-OLDS AND UP, THE MEADOWLANDS, NEW JERSEY, NOVEMBER 7, 1992

Dented — Dk. b. or br. f. 3(May), by Aloma's Ruler—Crushem, by Hard Crush

$12,500 Br.—Spiegel Robert (NY)

Own.—Spiegel Robert — Tr.—Schaeffer Stephen W (4 0 0 0 .00) — 111

Lifetime						
18 1 4 2	1992	17	1	4	2	$37,130
$37,130	1991	1	M	0	0	
	Turf	2	0	0	0	$520
	Wet	2	1	1	0	$17,800

6Oct92- 5Med	fst	$1\frac{1}{16}$	:47^3	1:12^1	1:45^3	ⒻClm 16000	17	2	5	7^9	7^{14}	7^{16}	7^{32}	Lopez C	b	111	23.70	47-19	MissNnybuck114$^{2\frac{3}{4}}$SilencSpks114^{1}Snsitiz112	Thru early	7
25Sep92- 4Med	fm	1^{70} Ⓣ	:44^4	1:10^1	1:39^3	ⒻClm 20000	69	7	8	9^{11}	7$^{4\frac{1}{4}}$	4^5	4^{13}	Lopez C	b	111	43.80	80-11	LsrFt116^{11}Dt'sStnMnr112^{2}Smthngscndls114	Some gain	10
1Sep92- 3Mth	fst	1^{70}	:46^4	1:13^4	1:45^2	ⒻClm 15000	45	8	4	4^5	4^3	3^6	3$^{12\frac{1}{2}}$	Santagata N	b	112	3.50	56-23	Belle of theNight114$^{4\frac{3}{4}}$CrockRock114$^{7\frac{3}{4}}$Dented112	Tired	8
12Aug92- 2Mth	gd	$1\frac{1}{16}$	:47^4	1:13	1:46^3	ⒻClm 22500	39	7	6	5$^{5\frac{1}{2}}$	7$^{8\frac{3}{4}}$	6^{13}	6$^{14\frac{3}{4}}$	Ferrer J C	b	112	3.30	61-20	MissVlidFund114$^{1\frac{1}{4}}$Alxg112$^{1\frac{1}{2}}$RvrOrchd114	Showed little	7
12Aug92-Originally scheduled on turf																						
31Jly92- 7Mth	sly	1	:47	1:13^1	1:41^2	ⒻClm 19000	60	6	6	5$^{4\frac{1}{2}}$	4$^{2\frac{1}{2}}$	3^2	2no	Santagata N	b	113	3.30	65-30	Alexage115^{no} Dented113$^{5\frac{3}{4}}$ Half Moon Hotel109	Gamely	7
31Jly92-Originally scheduled on turf																						
22Jly92- 8Mth	fst	1	:47^4	1:12^2	1:39^2	ⒻClm 20000	58	2	4	5$^{4\frac{1}{2}}$	5$^{6\frac{3}{4}}$	4$^{5\frac{1}{2}}$	3^4	Santagata N	b	112	24.50	71-25	Caro Lure112$^{2\frac{3}{4}}$ Stoly114$^{1\frac{1}{4}}$ Dented112	Willingly	7
6Jly92- 9Bel	fst	$1\frac{1}{16}$	:46^1	1:10^4	1:43^3	ⒻClm 20000	54	9	9	9^9	7$^{8\frac{3}{4}}$	5^{13}	5$^{16\frac{1}{4}}$	Chavez J F	b	112	26.50	68-11	Hesitant Lady114^3 Alice Key116$^{5\frac{3}{4}}$ I'm Proud116	Wide	9
29Jun92- 7Bel	fst	7f	:23^1	:46^2	1:23^4	3↑Ⓕ[S]Alw 27000	52	6	8	10$^{5\frac{3}{4}}$	6$^{2\frac{3}{4}}$	6$^{5\frac{1}{2}}$	7$^{11\frac{3}{4}}$	Chavez J F	b	109	58.90	73-12	Mrs.PMinister114^{hd}DrkPltt114^{4}StplQun111	No menace	11
30May92- 5Bel	fm	$1\frac{1}{16}$ Ⓣ	:45^3	1:09^2	1:42	3↑Ⓕ[S]Alw 29000	37	11	3	4$^{3\frac{1}{2}}$	5^4	11^{14}	12$^{23\frac{1}{2}}$	Pezua J M	b	112	49.40	62-13	[DH]Thtmfdnslf110^{nk}[DH]ShrMDrs110^{nk}DRb115	Gave way	12
1May92- 7Aqu	fst	1	:46^2	1:11^2	1:38^1	3↑Ⓕ[S]Alw 29000	45	4	3	4$^{3\frac{1}{2}}$	4$^{3\frac{1}{2}}$	6^7	6$^{13\frac{3}{4}}$	Chavez J F	b	110	6.20	57-30	Mckymcknn114$^{4\frac{1}{2}}$TitnsBll119^{nk}StickyRid114	Done early	7

LATEST WORKOUTS Nov 1 Bel tr.t 3f fst :38^2 B Oct 24 Bel tr.t 4f fst :49 B Oct 17 Bel tr.t 3f fst :36^2 H Oct 4 Bel tr.t 3f fst :37 B

Back in May and June, Dented was unable to make a dent in allowance races against older rivals bred in New York state. Next came a similar weak performance in an open $20,000 claiming route for three-year-olds, which actually was about the same class race as the state-bred allowance race. State-bred races tend to be significantly weaker than corresponding "open" races that do not restrict entries. Anyway, Dented's next two races were noticeably improved—a third-place finish against similar opposition at Monmouth Park in New Jersey and a sharp nine days later over a sloppy Monmouth racing strip.

Note that the July 31 race in the slop had been scheduled for the infield turf course, but was moved to the main track due to wet weather. Also note Dented's improvement in these two starts coincided with his first two attempts around two turns—which would not be apparent in the past performances unless you knew that the one-mile and $1\frac{1}{16}$-mile races at Aqueduct and Belmont are always contested around a single turn, with the start from an elongated chute on the backstretch as illustrated below.

Dented's two-race improvement stalled when trainer Stephen Schaeffer moved her up a small notch in claiming class on August 12. Barely three weeks later, Dented could only manage a weak third when she was dropped to $15,000 on September 1. The last two races in her chart are very discouraging for several reasons. There was nothing in her prior turf race on May 30 to indicate that she suddenly would improve on grass. Her best races of the summer came when she was forced off the turf onto a wet racing strip.

Allowing for the possibility that Schaeffer might have entered Dented in a turf race hoping for rain, the subsequent move back up to $20,000 on October 6 was too aggressive, and there was nothing positive in her seventh sluggish performance.

What is Dented doing in today's $12,500 claiming race against older fillies and mares? Nothing she would choose to be doing if she had any say in the affair. Schaeffer missed the boat when he pushed this filly up in class following her sharp second in the slop, and he may have compounded the error by the second move into a turf race.

Today's drop in class will not compensate for this filly's current lack of spirit or possible physical problems. Rest would seem in order.

While each handicapping situation requires considerable interpretation, claiming horses tend to have relatively short form cycles or specific distance limitations that sometimes can be measured in half furlongs. This point is vividly illustrated by the complete past performances of the horse below.

1 MILE, 70 YARDS, $24,000 ALLOWANCE, NON-WINNERS OF $11,500 TWICE SINCE APRIL 30, THE MEADOWLANDS, NOVEMBER 28, 1992

Rega — Dk. b. or br. c. 4, by Danzig—Kashan, by Damascus
Br.—Claiborne Farm & Gamely Corp (Ky)
Own.—Kaufman Robert — Tr.—Carlesimo Charles Jr (30 7 6 2 .23) — **117**

Lifetime								
23 4 3 4	1992	6	1	2	0	$20,585
$73,685	1991	12	3	0	1	$36,540
	Turf	6	0	1	2	$11,890
	Wet	3	0	1	1	$8,760

30Oct92- 6Med	fst	1	:47	1:112	1:363	3↑Alw 20000	93	2	2	2hd	1hd	1hd	1½	Marquez C HJr	Lb	116	5.10	97-13 Rega116½LuckyVirginian1132½ReglConquest116	Driving	8
24Oct92- 3Med	gd	170	[T]:452	1:101	1:411	3↑Alw 19000	84	2	4	43½	42	52¾	42½	Gryder A T	Lb	116	5.30	87-10 Maston1111 Amberfax1161½ River Wolf116	Even trip	8
14Oct92- 9Med	fm	1 1/16	[T]:462	1:104	1:42	3↑Alw 19000	87	1	2	22	21½	2hd	22¾	Gryder A T	Lb	116	17.40	90-15 Be Nimble1162¾ Rega116¾ Amberfax116	Held place	8
25Sep92- 8Med	fst	6f	:22	:443	1:084	3↑Skip Trial	76	1	8	87	810	77¾	610½	Marquez C HJr	Lb	113	48.90	88-10 Arrowtown1131½Dontclosyrys1174½Mr.Nsty113	No rally	8
17Mar92-10Crc	fm	1 1/16	(T):463	1:101	1:424	Alw 18000	79	11	7	612	812	811	66	Ferrer J C	Lb	112	13.00	— — Mxgroom1152GoldnExplosv1171Mr.Explsv115	No factor	11
29Feb92- 9GP	fst	7f	:23	:454	1:232	Alw 21000	89	5	7	2hd	21	2½	21½	Krone J A	Lb	112b	27.10	87-10 Fiercely1151½[DH]Rega112[DH]SentorSchu120	Bid, otfnshd	8
29Feb92-Dead heat																				
28Dec91-10Lrl	fst	1¼	:471	1:371	2:021	3↑Congress H	50	1	1	1hd	917	924	937¾	Douglas F G	Lb	111	112.20	59-17 Manlove1131¾ Valley Crossing1143 Midas113	Faltered	9
14Dec91- 9Pha	my	170	:454	1:104	1:422	Flintlock	60	2	2	31	35	614	720½	Lloyd J S	Lb	115	35.10	63-30 Riflery11510 L. J.'sTerminator1151½Arrowtown117	Tired	8
16Nov91- 8Med	fst	170	:46	1:113	1:412	Stockton	56	2	4	46	36	412	421¾	Gryder A T	Lb	115	7.20	69-21 Arrowtwn1141½VchfrM11415½L.J.'sTrmntr115	Even trip	6
12Oct91- 7Med	fst	170	:463	1:114	1:42	3↑Alw 17000	79	1	2	21½	21	11½	1½	Gryder A T	Lb	113	3.40	88-12 Rega113½ Three Chopt Road1162QuiteNoble116	Driving	7

LATEST WORKOUTS Nov 17 Med 5f fst 1:01 B — Oct 6 Med 1 fst 1:42 B

Carefully note one crucial fact above all others: When this horse was entered in a one-mile race, around two turns at the Meadowlands on October 30, 1992, he was getting his first opportunity to race in conditions similar to his most recent victory, one that was obscured by the intervening races during the past 12 months. Note that the October 30 victory was at virtually the same class, distance and track condition.

Chronologically since the 1991 win at the Meadowlands, Rega was seriously overmatched in three consecutive stakes, was second in a one-turn sprint following a layoff at Gulfstream Park, was unimpressive in a turf race, and badly outrun in still another stakes before he finished second and fourth in two more turf races.

On October 30, 1992, after so many races which did not play to this horse's strength, trainer Charles Carlesimo slipped Rega back into a modest-grade allowance race on the dirt at a comfortable distance. Lo and behold, Rega responded with a victory at 5–1 odds.

While some might have predicted a dull performance, the two recent turf races say otherwise. In both instances Rega held his form relatively well, finishing second and fourth on surfaces he had not handled well in prior attempts. Note also that the victorious October 30 race was only *six days* after the second turf race. All this says that October 30 was the day to cash in on this horse, not today.

Rega is entered today in a much tougher allowance race at the one-mile, 70-yard distance at the Meadowlands. He fits the distance requirement, but has shown on several occasions that he does not have the depth of talent to compete with high-quality runners. The eligibility conditions of this allowance race are too strong and are likely to attract horses who may have won or done well in stakes. In fact, there were two horses with bankrolls over $200,000 and $400,000, respectively, and

---

Rush Chairman Bill Dk. b. or br. g. 2(Feb), by Count Prospector—La Broker, by Blues Alley
ROMERO R P (98 12 14 12 .12) Br.—Garbarini William N (NY)
Own.—Martin Michael T Tr.—Schosberg Richard (28 6 3 2 .21) 115
Lifetime 2 2 0 0 $62,400 1992 2 2 0 0 $62,400
25Oct92- 6Aqu fst 6f :223 :463 1:111 ⓇNy Stallion 88 11 3 21 11 13 16½ Romero R P 115 *.70 85-19 RushChairmnBill1156½SkyCrr1132Auspex113 Ridden out 11
25Oct92-Colts and Geldings Divison
7Oct92- 6Bel fst 6f :223 :462 1:104 ⓈMd Sp Wt 90 9 2 11 11 16 111½ Romero R P 118 5.30 86-16 RushChirmnBill11811½Itk1186½BoldDoer118 Ridden out 13
LATEST WORKOUTS Nov 24 Bel tr.t 4f my :481 B ●Nov 18 Bel tr.t 6f fst 1:141 B Nov 12 Bel tr.t 5f fst 1:04 B Nov 7 Bel tr.t 5f gd 1:01 B

Nine Holes B. c. 2(Mar), by Dr Blum—Bon Vie, by Bon Mot
VELASQUEZ J (39 3 7 4 .08) Br.—Michael T. Martin Racing Stable (NY)
Own.—Martin Michael T Tr.—Schosberg Richard (28 6 3 2 .21) 115
Lifetime 1 1 0 0 $9,000 Wet 1 1 0 0 $9,000
3Nov92- 4Aqu sly 1 :483 1:144 1:421 Md 50000 55 8 1 2hd 1hd 11 12½ Bailey J D 118 8.50 51-39 Nine Holes1182½ Sky Dr.114nk Stack Um Up114 Driving 8
LATEST WORKOUTS Nov 24 Bel tr.t 4f my :481 H Nov 18 Bel tr.t 5f fst 1:031 B Nov 12 Bel tr.t 4f fst :511 B Oct 29 Bel tr.t 5f fst 1:04 B

Lord Beer Dk. b. or br. c. 2(May), by Cormorant—Bright Tribute, by Barrera
MADRID A JR (97 7 19 6 .07) Br.—Nielsen Gerald A (NY)
Own.—Heatherwood Farm Tr.—Schosberg Richard (28 6 3 2 .21) 115
Lifetime 2 1 0 0 $14,400 1992 2 1 0 0 $14,400
13Nov92- 6Aqu gd 7f :223 :454 1:241 ⓈMd Sp Wt 76 12 1 2½ 2hd 15 15¾ Romero R P 118 17.30e 84-17 Lord Beer1185¾ Alanne1185¼ Sweet Ralph118 Driving 12
11Oct92- 4Bel gd 6f :222 :46 1:113 ⓈMd Sp Wt 64 10 7 41½ 2hd 4nk 53½ Smith M E 118 3.20 78-18 ScrletAgent1181DringFly1181¼PerfectWrning118 4-wide 11
LATEST WORKOUTS Nov 9 Bel tr.t 5f fst 1:042 B Nov 4 Bel tr.t 4f sly :53 B Oct 28 Bel tr.t 5f fst 1:04 B ●Oct 8 Bel tr.t 3f fst :361 H

three others who earned more than double Rega's career bankroll. Each had won 6, 8, 12, 14 and 16 races, respectively. Rega's chances are dim, yet we should also have learned through this past-performance profile that Rega might be a solid play on another day. Trainer Carlesimo is distance-conscious and can deliver a well-meant horse at a fair and square price. We will watch for a drop in class a few races down the road.

After checking the three examples on the previous page—Rush Chairman Bill, Nine Holes, and Lord Beer—is there any doubt that trainer Richard Schosberg is an ace with New York-bred two-year-olds, especially first-time starters?

Unbridled
Own.—Genter F A

B. c. 4, by Fappiano—Gana Facil, by Le Fabuleux
Br.—Tartan Farms Corp (Fla)
Tr.—Nafzger Carl

Lifetime				1990	11	4	3	2	$3,718,149
17	6	5	4	1989	6	2	2	2	$174,546
$3,892,695				Turf	1	0	1	0	$50,000

27Oct90- 9Bel 27Oct90-Grade I	fst	1¼	:45^4	1:35^3	2:02^1	3↑B C Classic	14	13	13^{12}	96¾	32½	1^1	Day P		121	6.60e	95-15	Unbridled121^{1}IbnBey-En126^{1}ThirtySixRed121^{no}	Strong drive	14
23Sep90-10LaD 23Sep90-Grade I	fst	1¼	:46^2	1:36^1	2:02	Super Dby	9	9	94¾	3^2	43½	23½	Velez J A Jr	L	126	*.90	102 —	HomeAtLst1263½Unbridled126^{nk}C'sTizzy126^1	6-wide into lane	9
3Sep90- 8AP 3Sep90-Grade I	fm	1¼ Ⓣ	:49^1	1:37^2	2:01^3	Secretariat	4	7	75½	63¼	3^{nk}	2¾	Fires E	L	126	*.50e	103-03	SuperAbound114¾Unbridled1261½SuperFan117¾	Brushed start	8
18Aug90- 3AP	fst	1	:45^1	1:09^2	1:34^2	3↑Alw 23500	1	4	4^2	2^1	1^3	1^{11}½	Fires E	L	112	*.30	99-12	Unbrdld112^{11}½LmpnCch116½Rmngtn'sPrd119^4	Much the best	8
9Jun90- 8Bel 9Jun90-Grade I	gd	1½	:48	2:01^4	2:27^1	Belmont	5	6	63¾	44½	4^6	412¾	Perret C		126	*1.10	81-13	GoAndGo1268¼ThirtySixRd126^{2}BrondVux1262½	Bid wide,tired	9
19May90-10Pim 19May90-Grade I	fst	1$\frac{3}{16}$	:47	1:10^4	1:53^3	Preakness	6	9	87¼	5^4	2^{hd}	22¼	Perret C		126	*1.70	95-12	SummrSquil1262¼Unbridld126^{9}MistrFrisky126½	Best of others	9
5May90- 8CD 5May90-Grade I	gd	1¼	:46	1:37^3	2:02	Ky Derby	8	11	12^{14}	2½	1^1	13½	Perret C		126	10.80	101 —	Unbridled1263½SummerSqull126^{6}PlesntTp126^3	In tight, clear	15
14Apr90- 8Kee 14Apr90-Grade II	my	1⅛	:47^4	1:12^1	1:48^3	Blue Grass	4	5	5^2	41¾	31½	33¾	Perret C		121	4.10	87-10	SummerSquali1211¾LndRush121^{2}Unbridled121^3	Flattened out	5
17Mar90-10GP 17Mar90-Grade I	fst	1⅛	:48^2	1:12^3	1:52	Fla Derby	4	5	4^2	41¾	3^1	1^4	Day P		122	2.50	77-22	Unbridled122^4 Slavic122^{nk} Run Turn122^1	Brushed	9
3Mar90-10GP 3Mar90-Grade II	fst	1$\frac{1}{16}$	:47^3	1:12^2	1:44^3	Ftn Youth	5	10	12^7	99¼	51¾	3½	Day P		117	7.60e	87-24	Shot Gun Scott122½ Smelly119^{no} Unbridled117¾	Lacked room	13
14Jan90-10Crc 14Jan90-Grade III	fst	1⅛	:48^3	1:13^1	1:52^2	Trop Pk Dby	4	3	3^2	32½	43½	55¾	Perret C		119	*1.30	91-11	Run Turn1174¼ Country Day112^{hd} Shot Gun Scott119½	Tired	8

The horse above was a longshot winner of the 1990 Kentucky Derby and Breeders' Cup Classic. In both instances, trainer Carl Nafzger used seemingly important stakes as true prep races to prepare this top horse for his ultimate goals. A classic piece of horsemanship by a man who demonstrated considerable calm while focusing on the two toughest races in America.

Chris Evert is another example of a well-managed, top-grade race-horse at a seasonal peak. Notice the way trainer Joe Trovato established a solid foundation in 1973 and stretched Chris out in distance with each succeeding start in 1974. A fine piece of work by a man who knew how to get a horse to produce and keep producing.

These were the past performances of Chris Evert prior to her fifty-length "upset" victory over the speedy Miss Musket on July 20, 1974, in one of the richest match races of all time. Although the key to her winning performance was in the workout line, it was not possible to know

1¼ MILES—$350,000 PURSE, HOLLYWOOD PARK, JULY 20, 1974

Chris Evert **121** Ch. f (1971), by Swoon's Son—Miss Carmie, by T. V. Lark.
Breeder, Echo Valley Horse Farm (Ky.). 1974 4 3 0 1 $159,789
Owner, C. Rosen. Trainer, J. A. Trovato. 1973 5 4 1 0 $93,012

Jun22-74^{8}Bel	1 1-2	2:28⅘ ft	4-5	▲121	2^{h}	1^{h}	$1^{1\frac{1}{2}}$	$1^{3\frac{1}{2}}$	Vel'q'zJ^{1}	ScwS 76	Ⓕ ChrisEvert121 F'staLibre M'dM'll'r	10
Jun 1-74^{8}Bel	1 1-8	1:48⅗ sy	2¾	121	3^{2}	$2^{1\frac{1}{2}}$	1^{h}	1½	Vel'ezJ^{14}	ScwS 84	Ⓕ ChrisEvert121 M'dMuller QuazeQ'lt	14
May11-74^{8}Aqu	1	1:36 ft	9-5	▲121	2^{1}	4^{3}	$3^{1\frac{1}{2}}$	1¾	Vel'q'zJ^{1}	ScwS 87	Ⓕ ChrisEvert121 ClearC'py FiestaLibre	9
May 1-74^{8}Aqu	7 f	1:24⅖ ft	2	▲118	$7^{4\frac{3}{4}}$	$6^{6\frac{1}{4}}$	$6^{7\frac{1}{2}}$	$3^{4\frac{1}{2}}$	Vel'q'zJ^{10}	AlwS 74	Ⓕ ClearCopy113 ShyDawn ChrisEvert	10
Nov14-73^{8}Aqu	1	1:36⅖ ft	4-5	▲121	2^{h}	2^{h}	1^{1}	$1^{1\frac{1}{4}}$	Pi'yLJr^{11}	AlwS 85	Ⓕ ChrisEvert121 Amb'lero Kh'd'sK'er	11
Nov 3-73^{8}CD	7 f	1:25⅕ ft	6-5	▲116	9^{11}	9^{13}	$4^{3\frac{1}{2}}$	$1^{1\frac{1}{4}}$	Pin'yLJr^{2}	AlwS 81	Ⓕ ChrisEvert116 B'ndl'r KissMeD'rlin	13
Oct 6-73^{7}Bel	1	1:36⅖ ft	6¼	121	9^{4}	$3^{1\frac{1}{2}}$	4^{1}	2½	Cas'aM^{11}	ScwS 85	Ⓕ Bundler121 ChrisEvert I'm a Pl's're	14
Oct 2-73^{6}Bel	6 f	1:10⅘ ft	3	120	$5^{2\frac{1}{2}}$	$4^{4\frac{1}{2}}$	3½	$1^{2\frac{3}{4}}$	Pinc'yLJr^{10}	Alw 92	Ⓕ ChrisEv'rt120 Symp'th'tic F'h'gL'dy	10
Sep14-73^{3}Bel	6 f	1:11 ft	3¾	120	$3^{1\frac{1}{2}}$	3^{2}	2½	$1^{1\frac{3}{4}}$	Pin'yLJr^{10}	Mdn 88	Ⓕ ChrisEvert120 M'dMuller MamaKali	13

July 18 Hol 4f ft :46⅖h July 14 Hol 1m ft 1:38⅖h July 9 Hol 6f ft 1:15b

that without searching for other clues published in that day's edition of the *Form*.

Deep within the pages of the July 20, 1974, edition of the *Form*, California correspondent Pat Rogerson reported on the fractional times for the latest workouts of both horses. Although he was most impressed with Miss Musket's blazing one-mile training trial in 1:35⅕, the astute player might have noted that Chris's first quarter-mile fraction in her one-mile workout was noticeably faster. On July 17 Miss Musket worked a half-mile in 48 seconds, a relatively slow move compared with Chris' final workout on July 18. "I told Velasquez to break Chris sharply from the starting gate and not to be worried about getting her tired," said Trovato in Rogerson's report. The significance of Trovato's instructions could hardly be lost on the player who knew that 85 percent of all match races have been won wire to wire.

For Saturday stakes races and championship caliber events, *Daily Racing Form*'s reportage often is excellent. For the Kentucky Derby, for instance, executive columnist Joe Hirsch logs the daily doings of the key eligibles for more than two months. In addition, the *Form* publishes a weekly recap of the latest Derby news and training regimens plus updated Las Vegas odds. Similar coverage is provided for the Breeders' Cup and, on a smaller scale, for other major events.

In some contemporary editions, the *Form* supplements past-performance profiles with a "Closer Look," a 20–50 word handicapper's perspective on the overall credentials of each horse. At its best Closer Look provides valuable breeding hints on first-time starters, offtrack and turf performers, plus some trainer information and track-bias notes. But *caveat emptor*. At its worst, Closer Look may contain subtle inaccuracies, or press forward weak, personal handicapping prejudices of the Closer Look author.

The following p.p. shows us that sometimes there are hidden factors in this game that can never be assessed or underestimated.

Can't Trick Me — Ch. g. 3(Jan), by Phone Trick—For Love Alone, by L'Enjoleur

JUDICE J C (61 9 4 7 .15) — $10,000 — Br.—Richard Poulson (Ky) — 117

Own.—Egide James A — Tr.—Poulson Richard (—)

Lifetime							
14 4 0 0	1992	12	3	0	0	$18,558
$22,158	1991	2	1	0	0	$3,600
	Turf	3	0	0	0	$918

22Nov92- 6BM	fst	1	:47	1:122	1:371	3↑Clm 16000	62	7	7	76½	95¾	98	99½	Judice J C	L	116	45.60	74-22	PlsntlyRnd1143FlshyEncr1153PcOfNsk117	Broke in air	9
31Oct92- 2LaD	gd	7f	:221	:452	1:254	Clm 25000	44	1	6	52¾	67	814	716½	Frazier R L	L	116	11.90	65-19	ThreeTimesAround1212MistyWgon1151½IcJws113	Tired	8
26Sep92-10LaD	fm	1 1/16	Ⓣ:49	1:124	1:434	3↑Clm 25000	69	1	8	811	814	711	712	Frazier D L	L	114	5.40	75-13	LstEghtClb113nkStonMll-GB1163DstySssfrs116	Outrun	8
19Sep92- 1LaD	fst	170	:481	1:123	1:42	3↑Clm 20000	50	2	6	711	713	713	720	Frazier R L	L	114	7.40	72-08	Tylor'sPlsur1081MmbointhPrk1134OvrthAplch114	Tired	7
1Aug92-10LaD	fst	6½f	:221	:451	1:181	Alw 20000	60	1	5	51¾	57	49	410¾	Holland M A	L	117	16.20	80-15	FreshKicks1192½CstlliMountin122nkFightingK117	Tired	6
2Jly92- 1LaD	fst	6f	:221	:461	1:114	Clm 25000	77	5	2	32	2hd	2hd	1hd	Holland M A	L	116	7.90	89-10	Cn'tTrickMe116hdRedStrk1196MovingColors108	Driving	6
24May92-11LaD	fm	*1	Ⓣ:46	1:113	1:364	Spur H	59	3	9	96½	86¼	58½	512¾	Holland M A	L	114	31.20	72-15	TrTxsTstr1134½RghTghDncr1192BMyRply113	No threat	9
24May92-Run in Divisions																					
4Apr92-10RP	fm	1	Ⓣ:47	1:121	1:371	Midwest City	50	1	4	41	62¼	95¾	913¼	Holland M A		117	11.40	78-15	TmlssDsn119nkDnbrGld115½RhThDncr117	Saved ground	10
15Mar92-10RP	fst	1 1/16	:463	1:112	1:433	R P Derby	61	7	8	1013	910	914	615¾	Pettinger D R		118	16.70	92 —	VngVctr1221¾EcsttcRd1226¾CptImprvmnt122	No threat	10
5Mar92- 9RP	fst	1 1/16	:481	1:132	1:461	Alw 10332	68	2	1	1hd	1hd	1hd	11¼	Pettinger D R		116	4.90	95-10	Cn'tTrckM1161¼RdyEffort1164½DnbrGold116	Game win	7

LATEST WORKOUTS Nov 29 BM 4f fst :474 H Nov 16 BM 4f fst :484 H Oct 27 LaD 4f fst :521 B Oct 20 LaD Tr. 5f fst 1:003 Hg

This horse won a $10,000 claiming race at Bay Meadows as if he was a solid $25,000 horse. Guess what? He was. After racing in the rear of the pack in four straight races, including one over the track and three in Louisiana, Can't Trick Me suddenly sprang to life with solid betting action and blew away the field from gate to wire by seven lengths. Although the past performances say he was trained by his breeder, Richard Paulson, the listed trainer in the track program was Steve Specht, a reputable horseman on the northern California circuit. The owner, James Egide, also had no negative marks on his record and apparently was only on the receiving end of an interesting score orchestrated out of state.

While in Oklahoma, Can't Trick Me was trained by Bobby Speck, whose brother Steve Speck cannot get a racing license in Arkansas or California, among other states. The horse was shipped to California, had one race around the track in which he broke awkwardly from the starting gate, then won for fun over a better than average $10,000 field that included a very fast front-running type. He was sold and shipped to Arkansas very soon after the winning race. The winning and losing races were investigated by the California Horse Racing Board and the Thoroughbred Racing Protective Bureau; jockeys Ricky Frazier and Joe Judice were interviewed by Louisiana and California stewards, respectively. El Zippo. Race over. On to the next race. The silver lining is that someone in the stewards' stand actually was watching.

All players know that worse goes on, not only at small tracks where purses are low, but on the major racing circuits as well. Some of the best players in New York have complained regularly for years that the game is being turned upside down by trainers who win races with illegal, undetectable drugs.

Racing in the 1990s remains the most compelling game on the planet and I have no trouble recommending it as a legitimate pursuit to you, your sister, your mother, your brother, your son, your daughter, your husband, or your wife. But I look for more activism from players to help solve the sport's problems because that has been the most vital development in the sport during my lifetime. Certainly it has fostered the handicapping information explosion. In the meantime, some of us with an endless desire to share the glories of the game will keep punching.

The Key Race Method Revisited

In late October 1972 I was faced with a unique problem. I had just moved to Columbia, Maryland, and was going to conduct a daily five-minute seminar on handicapping over WLMD radio in the Washington-Baltimore area.

Based on my private results, I thought that I could pick 50 percent winners, show a flat bet profit in the thirteen-week test period, and explain handicapping in the process.

The format was simple. I would handicap races at Laurel racetrack and explain the theories behind the best betting opportunities of the day.

There was one catch. I had been to Laurel racetrack only once, on opening day, October 2. And because I had just joined the staff of *Turf and Sport Digest*, I knew I would not be able to go out to the track more than once a week. I had some familiarity with the leading trainers and their patterns, but I didn't know the horses, the track, or very much else about the local conditions. And I only had a week to prepare myself. In desperation, I did further trainer research, studied post positions, pulled out past-performance records and workout listings, and studied the result charts as if I were preparing for an examination before the bar.

A brand-new racing surface complicated the problem. Wild upsets were taking place every day as the maintenance crew fought to stabilize conditions. Horses with late speed seemed to have a built-in edge during this period, but it was not easy to tell from the past-performance records which horses would be able to produce that late speed. I solved the problem by using a simple research tool I had developed a few years earlier, one that investigates the relationship between a race over the track and future winning performance.

Strange as it may seem, almost every stretch-running Laurel winner with a prior race over the track had displayed one major characteristic: a sign of increased speed on the turn in the previous Laurel race. The implications were too powerful to ignore. The turn was the roughest piece of real estate in Maryland. Any horse in good enough shape to make a move on it was a horse worth tabbing for improvement next time out.

Admittedly, as form settled down and the track stabilized, I was forced to handicap races more thoroughly than that. But I got past the first four weeks with 45 percent winners, including some outrageous longshots. And I was on the air to stay.

It is also true that this was a particularly unusual set of conditions,

THIRD RACE											

THIRD RACE — 1⅛ MILES. (Turf)(1.43⁴) ALLOWANCE. Purse $60,000. 4-year-olds and upward which are non-winners of $22,500 other than closed or claiming at one mile or over since October 1. Weights: 4-year-olds, 120 lbs. Older, 121 lbs. Non-winners of such a race since August 1, allowed 2 lbs. Of such a race since June 1, allowed 4 lb. Of such a race since April 1, 6 lbs.

Santa Anita
JANUARY 15, 1994

Value of Race: $60,000 Winner $33,000; second $12,000; third $9,000; fourth $4,500; fifth $1,500. Mutuel Pool $439,640.00 Exacta Pool $349,708.00 Quinella Pool $43,740.00 Minus Show Pool $22,254.20

Last Raced	Horse	M/Eqt.	A.Wt	PP	St	¼	½	¾	Str	Fin	Jockey	Odds $1
1Jan94 8SA2	Fanmore	B	6 116	1	2	1^1	1^1	$1\frac{1}{2}$	$1\frac{1}{2}$	1^1	Desormeaux K J	0.40
30Dec93 8SA2	Myrakalu-Fr	LB	6 115	4	3	$3\frac{1}{2}$	3^{hd}	$2^{1}\frac{1}{2}$	2^7	2^6	Stevens G L	3.40
5Dec93 7Hol5	Dick Tracy-Fr	LB	5 115	3	1	2^2	2^2	3^1	3^2	$3^3\frac{1}{2}$	Black C A	13.30
5Dec93 7Hol6	Peter Davies	L	6 115	5	4	4^{10}	4^{10}	4^8	$4^3\frac{1}{2}$	$4\frac{3}{4}$	Solis A	10.00
7Sep93 Lch4	Navire-Fr	LB	5 117	2	5	5	5	5	5	5	McCarron C J	8.30

OFF AT 1:31 Start Good For All But NAVIRE. Won handily. Time, :24⁴, :48², 1:12, 1:35⁴, 1:48² Course firm.

$2 Mutuel Prices:				
	1–FANMORE	2.80	2.20	2.10
	4–MYRAKALU–FR		2.40	2.10
	3–DICK TRACY–FR			2.10

$2 EXACTA 1–4 PAID $5.60 $2 QUINELLA 1–4 PAID $4.00

B. g, by Lear Fan–Lady Blackfoot, by Prince Tenderfoot. Trainer Frankel Robert. Bred by Johnson Don & Trimble Ann M (Ky).

FANMORE quickly sprinted to a short lead inside DICK TRACY, responded gamely when challenged by MYRAKALU leaving the backstretch, repulsed that rival's bid in midstretch while in hand and continued in hand to the wire. MYRAKALU outside PETER DAVIES early, moved up alongside the winner approaching the second turn but could not get by. DICK TRACY prompted the early pace outside the winner while appearing rank, then was not a factor after six furlongs. PETER DAVIES saved ground to no avail. NAVIRE dwelt at the start to be off far behind and was not a factor.

Owners— 1, Juddmonte Farms; 2, Recachina Dion A; 3, Taub Stephen M; 4, Lucayan Stud Ltd; 5, Cohen & Red Baron's Barn
Trainers— 1, Frankel Robert; 2, Lukas D Wayne; 3, Hendricks Dan L; 4, McAnally Ronald; 5, Vienna Darrell
Scratched— Alzarina (25Jly93 DLB3)

yet the investigative tool has served me well for many purposes, as it might well serve you. Here is how to set it up. Again you will need to work with a set of chronologically dated result charts.

First, with the most recent race on top, check the index date and race number of the winner's last race: These index dates are displayed to the left of each horse who competed in the race, except for first-time starters who have no index date. In the result chart on the previous page, the index date for the winner Fanmore is 1 Jan. 94, which means that Fanmore last raced on January 1 at Santa Anita, in the eighth race, finishing second. Second-place finisher Myrakalu-Fr. last raced on December 30, in the eighth race, finishing second.

Using the index date for the race winner, thumb back to the date and race number indicated to see what the winner did in his last race. Whatever he did, *circle his name.* That circle forever will mean that Fanmore won his *next* start.

EIGHTH RACE

Santa Anita
JANUARY 1, 1994

1⅛ MILES. (Turf)(1.43⁴) 47th Running of THE SAN GABRIEL HANDICAP. $100,000 Added. Grade III. 4-year-olds and upward. By subscription of $100 each to accompany the nomination, $1,000 additional to start, with $100,000 added, of which $20,000 to second, $15,000 to third, $7,500 to fourth and $2,500 to fifth. Weights Tuesday, December 28. High weights preferred. Starters to be named through the entry box by the closing time of entries. A trophy will be presented to the owner of the winner. Closed Wednesday, December 22, 1993 with 23 nominations.

Value of Race: $110,300 Winner $65,300; second $20,000; third $15,000; fourth $7,500; fifth $2,500. Mutuel Pool $569,996.00 Exacta Pool $527,625.00 Quinella Pool $71,183.00

Last Raced	Horse	M/Eqt. A.Wt	PP	St	¼	½	¾	Str	Fin	Jockey	Odds $1
20Nov93 6Hol³	Earl Of Barking-Ir	LB	4 118	8	8	7½	6hd	4hd	2¹	1no	McCarron C J	3.70
28Nov93 5Hol⁴	Fanmore	B	6 116	3	4	6¹½	4hd	3²	1hd	2⁵	Desormeaux K J	2.50
5Dec93 7Hol²	Navarone	LB	6 119	6	7	8	8	7⁴	5²	3½	Stevens G L	1.90
20Nov93 4Hol⁴	D'arros-Ir	LBb	5 114	7	6	2½	2³	2²	3½	4²	Nakatani C S	14.10
20Nov93 6Hol¹³	Eastern Memories-Ir	LB	4 116	2	1	1¹	1¹	1hd	4⁴	5¹½	Delahoussaye E	12.20
19Dec93 7Hol²	Bossanova	LBb	5 114	1	3	3hd	3¹	5¹½	6²	6²½	Solis A	9.50
12Dec93 4BM¹	Ranger-Fr	LB	4 115	5	2	4¹½	5²	6²	7¹²	7¹⁸	Boulanger G	11.10
12Dec93 8Hol⁶	Square Cut	LB	5 115	4	5	5½	7³½	8	8	8	Antley C W	33.40

OFF AT 4:13 Start Good. Won driving. Time, :24, :47², 1:11, 1:36, 1:48³ Course firm.

$2 Mutuel Prices:

9–EARL OF BARKING–IR	9.40	4.40	2.80
3–FANMORE		3.80	2.60
7–NAVARONE			2.60

$2 EXACTA 9–3 PAID $40.80 $2 QUINELLA 3–9 PAID $17.60

B. c, by Common Grounds–The Saltings, by Morston. Trainer Cross Richard J. Bred by O'Callaghan Gay (Ire).

EARL OF BARKING settled off the early pace slightly off the rail after angling inward into the first turn, moved up inside into the second turn, swung four wide into the lane and just bested FANMORE under urging in a long drive. FANMORE saved ground down the backstretch, moved up inside on the second turn, swung out for the drive to gain the lead in midstretch and battled gamely inside the winner to just miss. NAVARONE unhurried to the second turn, moved up outside on that bend and into the stretch but could not make up the needed ground. D'ARROS prompted the pace outside EASTERN MEMORIES to midstretch and weakened. EASTERN MEMORIES sped to the early lead inside, held the advantage to midstretch and weakened. BOSSANOVA was not far back a bit off the rail down the backstretch, then weakened. RANGER, outside FANMORE early, angled in for the second turn and did not rally. SQUARE CUT, a bit wide on the first turn, raced outside the winner early on the backstretch, gave way readily and was not persevered with in the stretch.

Owners— 1, Pabst Henry; 2, Juddmonte Farms; 3, Hibbert R E; 4, Wall Peter; 5, Team Valor & Amerman & Stibor; 6, Kenis & 3 Plus U Stable; 7, Lonergan Frank; 8, E W Racing Stable

Trainers—1, Cross Richard J; 2, Frankel Robert; 3, Rash Rodney; 4, Frankel Robert; 5, Hennig Mark; 6, Van Berg Jack C; 7, Bonde Jeff; 8, Devereux Joseph A

If you repeat this simple exercise for every new result at your favorite track, you will be adding exceedingly valuable information to your result charts. The added data may help you distinguish patterns not otherwise detectable.

Maybe you will discover as I did, back in the early 1970s, that a very high percentage of maiden-claiming winners prep in higher-class maiden events, including a significant proportion who turn in relatively weak performances in Maiden Special Weight (non-claiming maiden) races. Perhaps you will observe the winning tendency of California shippers in New York stakes, or Charles Town shippers in lower-class claiming races on the Maryland circuit, and the apparent edge Longacres horses had shipping to northern California during the 1980s, or the inordinate amount of maiden sprinters who successfully stretched out in distance at the Laurel Racecourse in the early 1990s. Other specific relationships between previous performances at one distance will become apparent with performances at another.

The possibilities are without limit and without really trying, you also will be laying the foundation for the *Key Race Method*, a powerful handicapping tool that isolates well-run races at every class level.

For example, the three horses circled in the following result chart,

FIRST RACE
Aqu
July 15, 1976

1⅛ MILES. (1:47). CLAIMING. Purse $7,500. For 3-year-olds and upward. 3-year-olds, 116 lbs.; older, 122 lbs. Non-winners of a race at a mile and a furlong or over since July 1 allowed 3 lbs.; of such a race since June 15, 5 lbs. Claiming price $8,500; if for less, 2 lbs. allowed for each $250 to $8,000. (Races when entered to be claimed for $7,000 or less not considered.)

Value to winner, $4,500; second, $1,650; third, $900; fourth, $450. Track Mutuel Pool, $106,946. OTB Pool, $87,971.

Last Raced	Horses	Eqt A	Wt	PP	St	¼	½	¾	Str	Fin	Jockeys	Owners	Odds to $1
25Jun76 ^{6}Bel^3	Charms Hope	b5	113	1	2	4^4	4^3	4^7	$3^{\frac{1}{2}}$	1^{nk}	MVenezia	J J Stippel	2.50
7Jly 76 ^{1}Aqu^1	Finney Finster	b4	117	3	7	6^8	5^2	$3^{1\frac{1}{2}}$	2^h	$2^{1\frac{1}{4}}$	ASantiago	Camijo Stable	5.60
9Jly 76 ^{1}Aqu^1	Good and Bold	5	110	4	1	1^4	1^6	1^6	1^3	$3^{1\frac{3}{4}}$	BDiNicola^5	Emmarr Stable	3.00
9Jly 76 ^{1}Aqu^6	Just Like Pa	b3	109	2	4	$3^{\frac{1}{2}}$	$3^{1\frac{1}{2}}$	2^h	4^8	4^9	DMontoya†	Audley Farm Stable	8.50
8Jly 76 ^{1}Aqu^1	Wave the Flag	6	115	5	6	7	7	7	5^6	$5^{4\frac{1}{2}}$	RHernandez	O S Barrera	3.40
1Jly 76 ^{2}Aqu^1	Jolly Mister	b4	113	6	5	5^1	6^7	$6^{\frac{1}{2}}$	6^{12}	6^{22}	PDay	Stan-Mar Stable	7.30
9Jly 76 ^{3}Aqu^5	Acosado II.	4	117	7	3	2^5	2^3	5^1	7	7	JVasquez	Bellrose Farm	11.90

†Five pounds apprentice allowance waived.

OFF AT 10:30 PDT. START GOOD. WON DRIVING. Time, :24; :47⅕, 1:12⅗, 1:39⅗, 1:53⅖. Track fast.

$2 Mutuel Prices				
	1-CHARMS HOPE	7.00	4.00	2.60
	3-FINNEY FINSTER		6.20	3.60
	4-GOOD AND BOLD			2.80

B. h, by Abe's Hope—Cold Dead, by Dead Ahead. Trainer, F. J. Horan. Bred by Criterion Farms (Fla.).

CHARMS HOPE, unhurried early, rallied approaching the stretch and outfinished FINNEY FINSTER. The latter, off slowly, advanced steadily to loom a threat near midstretch and continued on with good courage. GOOD AND BOLD tired from his early efforts. JUST LIKE PA rallied leaving the far turn but lacked the needed late response. WAVE THE FLAG was never close. JOLLY MISTER was always outrun. ACOSADO II tired badly.

Charms Hope claimed by M. Garren, trainer G. Puentes; Good and Bold claimed by S. Sommer, trainer F. Martin.

Claiming Prices (in order of finish)—$8000, 8500, 8250, 8250, 8250, 8000, 8500.

taken from the original *Betting Thoroughbreds*, came out of the race to win their very next starts. *A Key Race.*

Wave the Flag won a $5,000 claimer on July 21. Charms Hope won an allowance race on July 23. Good and Bold won a $10,000–$12,000 claimer on July 31. In addition, Just Like Pa ran fourth on July 29, encountering traffic problems, and won a $9,000 claimer on August 18.

Coincidence might dilute the impact of the added information, but nine out of ten times there is a better explanation. Either this race was superior to the designated class or else it contained an unusually fit group of horses. In either case, that's important information.

Indeed, after Wave the Flag's easy score at $5,000 claiming and Charms Hope's five-length victory in allowance company, the Key Race method would have certainly pointed out the merits of Good and Bold at 9–1 in a six-furlong race on July 31 (note the running line of Good and Bold in the Key Race chart). Observant race watchers and chart readers might similarly have made a strong case for Just Like Pa when he went to the post at 6–1 on August 18.

The Key Race method has many applications, but it is simply sensational in pointing out above-average fields in maiden races and turf events.

Maiden races are a mixed bag. Very few horses entered in such races have established their true class level. Some maidens will turn out to be useful racehorses; others will be little more than walking feed bills. Sooner or later, most often sooner, the best of the maidens wind up in the winner's circle. With deadly precision the Key Race method points out those maiden races that contained the fastest nonwinners on the grounds.

Maybe the winner of a maiden race returns to win a stakes race. Maybe the fifth horse in the maiden race comes back to graduate in its next start. If so, I would begin looking for the second, third, and fourth horses to come out of that maiden race. There could be little question that they had raced against above-average stock. Naturally, I would not suspend the handicapping process. I would still want to know what the rest of the field looked like, whether there was a prevailing track bias, what type it was, what if any trainer patterns were present, and so on. I would, however, surely upgrade the chances of any horse coming out of such a strong field.

Similar logic explains the effectiveness of the Key Race method in classifying turf races. Regardless of a horse's record on dirt, its ability to compete on grass is never established until it has raced on grass. In effect, the horse is a maiden on the turf until it wins on the turf. Again, the Key Race method will isolate the stronger fields.

SIXTH RACE	1 MILE 70 YARDS. (1.39¹) CLAIMING. Purse $15,000. 3-year-olds and upward. Weights: 3-year-olds,
Meadowlands	116 lbs. Older, 122 lbs. Non-winners of three races at a mile or over since July 25, allowed 3 lbs. Two such races, 5 lbs. One such race, 7 lbs. Claiming price $20,000; for each $1,000 to $16,000, allowed 1 lb. (Races
SEPTEMBER 5, 1994	where entered for $15,000 or less not considered).

Value of Race: $15,000 Winner $9,000; second $3,000; third $1,800; fourth $750; fifth $150; sixth $150; seventh $150. Mutuel Pool $143,167.00 Exacta Pool $196,246.00

Last Raced	Horse	M/Eqt.	A.Wt	PP	St	¼	½	¾	Str	Fin	Jockey	Cl'g Pr	Odds $1
24Aug94 5Mth¹ ~	Perfect Star	Lbf	7 115	6	6	5³	4²	2½	2⁵	1³	Lopez C C	20000	1.40
26Aug94 7Mth¹	Three Dreams ~	Lb	5 115	2	3	1½	11½	1³	1¹	2³	Santagata N	20000	6.90
28Aug94 4Mth⁴	Nauset Flash	Lf	7 114	1	2	6²	6hd	7	4hd	33½	Chavez J F	19000	6.00
26Aug94 7Mth²	Smart Time	Lf	6 115	5	1	4³	5 2½	4hd	3hd	43½	Marquez C H Jr	20000	4.40
19Aug94 10Mth¹	Sabinal	Lb	4 117	7	7	7	7	5¹	6 10	5½	Torres C A	18000	4.70
23Aug94 6Mth⁷	Dancing Chas	Lb	5 115	3	5	3½	3³	3²	5½	6	Castillo R E	20000	30.80
21Aug94 1Mth⁵	Funinthesun	Lbf	8 115	4	4	2⁵	23½	6hd	7	—	McCauley W H	20000	6.40

Funinthesun:Eased

OFF AT 3:06 Start Good. Won driving. Time, :21⁴, :45, 1:10, 1:35², 1:39¹ Track fast. **"KR"**
(Equals Track Record)

$2 Mutuel Prices:

7–PERFECT STAR	4.80	3.20	2.60
2–THREE DREAMS		6.60	5.00
1–NAUSET FLASH			4.20

$2 EXACTA 7–2 PAID $32.80

Dk. b. or br. g, by Morning Bob–Faneuil Lady, by Diplomat Way. Trainer Lotti Gene A Jr. Bred by Farnsworth Farm (Fla).

PERFECT STAR began moving to contention three wide through the far turn, moved to equal terms with THREE DREAMS a sixteenth out, then was going away to the finish. THREE DREAMS made all the pace, then was no match for the winner late while clear for the place. NAUSET FLASH rallied mildly to gain a share. SMART TIME went fairly evenly. SABINAL failed to reach serious contention. DANCING CHAS tired from his early efforts. FUNINTHESUN was used early and was being eased in the stretch.

Owners— 1, Team Stable Inc; 2, Jones Anderson Farm; 3, Pierce Sheila; 4, Conover Stable; 5, Golden Key Racing Stable; 6, Mamone Raymond; 7, Picciolo Frank J

Trainers—1, Lotti Gene A Jr; 2, Cash Russell J; 3, Pierce Joseph H Jr; 4, Tammaro John J III; 5, Brown Steven R; 6, Vincitore Michael J; 7, Durso Robert J

Three Dreams was claimed by Angelo Frank; trainer, Iwinski Allen.

Scratched— Will To Reign (23Aug94 6MTH⁵)

KEY RACE SYMBOLS

↑   indicates a jump up in class

↓   indicates a drop in class

~   indicates no class change

Ⓣ   indicates a turf race

⊗   indicates a wet track race

Sp   indicates a switch to a sprint

Rt   indicates a switch to a route

"KR"   indicates a *very fast race* for the class and distance, a potential Key Race. As a rule of thumb, I insist on clockings ⅗ of a second faster than normal to qualify

Over the years I have been pleased to see many professional handicappers and authors utilize the Key Race method and attempt to increase its potency. I too have tinkered with it while incorporating some of northern California professional Ron Cox's ideas along with author Mark Cramer's and a few wrinkles of my own. For instance, the result chart below includes several *fictional* notations to illustrate a variety of situations in one compact result chart. Always, circled horses indicate next out winners, but the added notations show whether or not these future winners went *up*, or *down* in class, or if the winning race was at a different *distance* and/or *track condition.* Today's winner also has a class notation to the left of his name to indicate if he was stepping up or dropping in class for *this race.* Other notations concerning distance or racing surface are indicated in available spaces on the same line as the circled horse.

Some players label key races in questionable ways. Some water down the power of the concept beyond recognition by labeling any race with an extremely high speed or pace figure as a Key Race. While it is true that fast races tend to produce winners, many times the only horses of value are those who earned the speed and/or pace figures. In such situations, I make a "KR" notation in the corner of the chart to indicate a *potential* Key Race in the making and may give the first horse who races back from these races some extra credit for an above-average performance. When a horse other than the winner does return with a superior performance, I certainly will gain confidence in the "KR" label and drop the quotation marks.

A true Key Race produces above-par performances that may not be wholly explainable via normal means. For this reason I now include all horses who emerge from a given race to finish second in their next outings, as suggested by Cox. The underline in the chart is the logical counterpart to the circle; this means that the horse in question finished *second* in its next outing. This, along with the appropriate symbols, some of which also are used by Cramer, invariably adds considerable depth to my result charts by providing important insights not published in *Daily Racing Form* past performances.

Once in a while you will encounter the phenomenon of a result chart with six, seven, or more circled *and* underlined horses—a Key Race in the ultimate sense of the word. Recent research says this occurs about once every 750 races. By the time four horses come out of the same field to win or run second in their next starts, you should get the message.

The Key Race at Saratoga on August 5, 1972, is my personal favorite. The circles are not included. They aren't necessary. Every last horse provided a winning effort.

EIGHTH RACE
Saratoga
AUGUST 5, 1972

1 $\frac{1}{16}$ MILES.(turf). (1.39 2/5) ALLOWANCES. Purse $15,000. 3-year-olds and upward which have not won three races other than maiden, claiming or starter. Weights, 3-year-olds, 117 lbs. Older, 122 lbs. Non-winners of $7,200 at a mile or over since July 1, allowed 2 lbs. $6,600 at a mile or over since June 17, 4 lbs. $6,000 at a mile or over since May 15, 6 lbs. (Maidens, claiming and starter races not considered inallowances.)
Value of race $15,000, value to winner $9,000, second $3,300, third $1,800, fourth $900. Mutuel pool $128,695, OTB pool $70,388.

Last Raced	Horse	Eqt.A.Wt	PP	St	¼	½	¾	Str	Fin	Jockey	Odds $1
23Jly72 ^{8}Del^{2}	Scrimshaw	4 116	2	2	7^{1}	$7\frac{1}{2}$	4^{1}	1^{3}	1^{4}	Marquez C H	2.40
20Jly72 ^{6}Aqu^{4}	Gay Gambler	3 108	8	8	$9^{1\frac{1}{2}}$	9^{5}	9^{8}	$8^{1\frac{1}{2}}$	$2^{1\frac{1}{2}}$	Patterson G	5.60
22Jly72 ^{6}Aqu^{3}	Fast Judge	b 3 111	7	7	6^{2}	6^{1}	$6\frac{1}{2}$	4^{hd}	3^{hd}	Velasquez J	10.00
28Jly72 ^{6}Aqu^{1}	Straight To Paris	3 115	9	3	$2\frac{1}{2}$	$2^{1\frac{1}{2}}$	$2\frac{1}{2}$	$2\frac{1}{2}$	4no	Vasquez J	2.70
25Jly72 ^{9}Aqu^{1}	Search the Farm	b 4 116	3	9	$8^{1\frac{1}{2}}$	$8^{1\frac{1}{2}}$	8^{1}	6^{hd}	5no	Guadalupe J	11.20
23Jly72 ^{8}Del^{3}	Chrisaway	4 116	4	6	$5^{1\frac{1}{2}}$	4^{hd}	$7\frac{1}{2}$	$7\frac{1}{2}$	6^{2}	Howard R	25.30
25Jly72 ^{9}Aqu^{5}	Navy Lieutenant	b 4 116	1	1	$3\frac{1}{2}$	5^{1}	$3\frac{1}{2}$	$5\frac{1}{2}$	7^{4}	Belmonte E	10.90
25Jly72 ^{7}Aqu^{4}	Head Table	b 3 113	10	5	4^{1}	3^{1}	$5\frac{1}{2}$	9^{10}	8^{2}	Baeza B	7.50
17Jly72 ^{8}Del^{3}	Mongo's Image	3 111	5	4	$1^{1\frac{1}{2}}$	$1\frac{1}{2}$	1^{1}	3^{hd}	9^{10}	Nelson E	28.70
21Jly72 ^{7}Aqu^{5}	Chartered Course	b 4 116	6	10	10	10	10	10	10	Arellano J	16.70

Time, :23⅕, :46⅖, 1:09⅘, 1:34⅗, 1:40⅘ (Against Wind in Backstretch). Course firm.

$2 Mutuel Prices:				
	2-(B)- SCRIMSHAW	6.80	3.60	3.20
	8-(H)- GAY GAMBLER		7.00	4.80
	7-(G)- FAST JUDGE			5.60

B. g, by Jaipur—Ivory Tower, by Hill Prince. Trainer Lake R P. Bred by Vanderbilt A G (Md).
IN GATE AT 5.23; OFF AT 5.23 EASTERN DAYLIGHT TIME. Start Good Won Handily

SCRIMSHAW, taken back after breaking alertly, swung out to go after the leaders on the far turn, quickly drew off and was never seriously threatened. GAY GAMBLER, void of early foot, was unable to split horses entering the stretch, altered course to the extreme outside and finished strongly. FAST JUDGE, reserved behind the leaders, split horses leaving the far turn but was not match for the top pair. STRAIGHT TO PARIS prompted the pace much of the way and weakened during the drive. SEARCH THE FARM failed to menace. CHRISAWAY raced within easy striking distance while outside horses much of the way but lacked a late response. NAVY LIEUTENANT, a factor to the stretch while saving ground, gave way. HEAD TABLE was finished leaving the far turn. MONGO'S IMAGE stopped badly after showing to midstretch.

Owners— 1, Vanderbilt A G; 2, Whitney C V; 3, Wygod M J; 4, Rokeby Stable; 5, Nadler Evelyn; 6, Steinman Beverly R; 7, Sommer S; 8, Happy Hill Farm; 9, Reynolds J A; 10, Camijo Stable.

Trainers— 1, Lake R P; 2, Poole G T; 3, Nickerson V J; 4, Burch Elliott; 5, Nadler H; 6, Fout P R; 7, Martin F; 8, Wright F I; 9, Reynolds J A; 10, King W P.

Overweight: Head Table 2 pounds.

On August 12 Scrimshaw won the first division of the Bernard Baruch Handicap. One half-hour later Chrisaway took the second division at 50–1. A few days later Chartered Course won a daily double race paying $25. On the same card Gay Gambler—probably the best bet of the year—took the sixth race. Straight to Paris shipped to Monmouth for his win; Fast Judge, Search the Farm, and Navy Lieutenant raced out of the money in their next starts at Saratoga but won on the rebound at Belmont in September. Mongo's Image won a high-class allowance race at the end of the Saratoga meeting at 8–1.

The only horse that didn't race back during this period was Head Table. For weeks I hunted through the *Racing Form* hoping to find his name among the entries. I was prepared to fly anywhere. But he never showed up.

Believe it or not, Head Table returned to the races on April 21, 1973, nine months after the Key Race. Yes, you guessed it: Head Table won by six. That's weird.

An Edge in Class

At Charles Town racetrack in West Virginia, where the racing is cheap and the betting action takes exotic forms, the horseplayer seldom has a chance to see a top-drawer horse in action. Nevertheless, the player would be making a serious mistake if he or she failed to incorporate notions about class into handicapping.

On a typical racing program at a minor-league track like Charles Town, the majority of races are for $2,500 claiming horses—just a cut above the lowest level of horsedom. These are horses who have seen better days or just are not fast enough to compete in the higher class-claiming events found at the major one-mile tracks.

Actually, that is not quite true. A respectable number of Charles Town horses can run fast—and a select few can run very fast—but they are too short-winded or too battle-scarred to be able to sustain their speed in three-quarter-mile races at the majors. After all, there are no four-furlong races for three-year-olds and up at Arlington Park, and there are no six-furlong races for $2,500 horses either.

For all the wrong reasons, major-track handicappers tend to have a snobbish attitude toward their compatriots at the minors, thinking perhaps that the cheaper racing is less formful, less predictable. I can assure you, however, that there are more winning players per capita at "bull ring" tracks like Charles Town than there are at Aqueduct or Hollywood Park.

Far from being the indecipherable mess that it seems on the surface, minor-track racing offers some of the most attractive betting opportunities in all of racing. Examining the class factor will show exactly why this is so, and for the astute player the applications extend to a large body of races at the major tracks as well.

The first step toward success at Charles Town is to use the result charts to construct a record of the eligibility conditions of all the cheapest races. About 90 percent of Charles Town claiming events have restrictive clauses that resemble the eligibility conditions found in allowance (nonclaiming) races at the major one-mile tracks.

For example, the first, fifth, sixth, seventh and eighth races at Charles Town on January 21, 1993, were $2,500 claiming races, but any bettor who assumed that all of those races involved the same class of horse was doomed to a disastrous evening of betting.

The first $2,500 race was for nonwinners of two races in six months, the second was for nonwinners of a single race during that time frame; the third and fourth were for nonwinners of three races lifetime and the fifth for nonwinners of two.

The next evening there were four more $2,500 claiming races including two races for nonwinners of two and a pair for nonwinners of three. Confusing? Perhaps. But it turns out that there is a measurable difference between each of the restricted $2,500 races. This difference not only is reflected in the average winning times for each separate restricted class but is greater than the average difference between $2,500 and $3,000 races. In other words, it can be more difficult to advance within the same $2,500 claiming class than to step up to the $3,000 level.

This is because the next step up within the same $2,500 claiming class is for horses who already have won at the lower level. In other words, there are more horses with better records at the next level, which makes for intense, tougher competition.

Indeed, most $2,500 Charles Town claimers have a hard time scoring two wins back to back. Even when they repeat a similar effort they probably will not advance until all the better $2,500 horses win their way out of the same class within the class. In a very real sense, the slower horses are hopelessly trapped by their own mediocrity, and some will remain at the same level for months.

To single out horses who subtly move up and down within these lower-class claiming races, I used to rely on a self-constructed classification system that provided a shorthand marker for each restrictive eligibility clause. But by the end of 1993, *Daily Racing Form* was supplementing its improved past performances with sufficient symbols that substitute nicely for the most important restrictive eligibility conditions at every class level, including the lowest levels.

ABBREVIATIONS FOR TYPES OF RACES

Alw 15000	**ALLOWANCE RACE WITH NO RESTRICTIONS (Purse of $15,000)**
Alw 15000N1x	Allowance race for non-winners of a race other than maiden, claiming, or starter (Also used for non-winners of up to 5 races)
Alw 15000N1y	Allowance race for non-winners of a race (or more, depending on number after N) in, or since, a specified time period
Alw 15000N2L	Allowance race for non-winners of two (or more) races lifetime
Alw 15000N$y	Allowance race for non-winners of a specific amount of money one (or more) times in a specified time period
Alw 15000N1m	Allowance race for non-winners of one (or more) races at a mile or over in a specified time period
Alw 15000N1s	Allowance race for non-winners of one (or more) stakes lifetime
Alw 15000N1t	Allowance race for non-winners of one (or more) turf races
Clm 10000	**CLAIMING RACE (Entered to be claimed for $10,000)**
Clm 10000N2L	Claiming race for non-winners of two (or more) races lifetime
Clm 10000N1y	Claiming race for non-winners of a race (or more, depending on number after N) in, or since, a specified time period
Clm 10000N1my	Claiming race for non-winners of a race (or more) at a mile or over in a specified time period
OTHER CONDITIONS	
Md Sp Wt	Maiden Special Weight race (for horses that have never won)
Md 32000	Maiden Claiming race (entered to be claimed for $32,000
Handicap 40k	**OVERNIGHT HANDICAP RACE (Purse of $40,000)**
OC 10000N	Optional Claiming race (entered NOT to be claimed)
OC 10000	Optional Claiming race (entered to be claimed)
Alw 8000s	Starter Allowance race (number indicates minimum claiming price horse must have started for to be eligible)
Hcp 8000s	Starter Handicap race (number indicates minimum claiming price horse must have started for to be eligible)
Ky Derby–G1	Graded Stakes race, with name of race (North American races are graded in order of status, with G1 being the best)
PrincetonH 40k	Ungraded, but named Stakes race (H indicates handicap) Purse value is $40,000

In the 1990s, restricted claiming races no longer are the exclusive province of West Virginia tracks like Charles Town or Mountaineer Park, or Finger Lakes in upstate New York, or Penn National Racecourse in Grantville, Pennsylvania. In today's racing world we see several levels of class within the bottom-price claiming races at all but a few American racetracks. The patterns exhibited at Charles Town in the 1970s are just as potent now at Golden Gate Fields, or Thistledown, or Ak-Sar-Ben.

Because some tracks subdivide their cheapest races into several categories not represented by *DRF*'s improved past performances, it still pays to rank these races in a format that resembles the original classification code outlined in the 1978 edition of *Betting Thoroughbreds*. The chart below also includes the approximate *DRF* classification symbols.

REVISED CLASSIFICATION CODE FOR ($2,500) CLAIMING RACES

CLASSIFICATION CODES	DRF SYMBOLS
A—Open race, unrestricted eligibility (top class)	clm2500
B—Nonwinners of two races in six months (usually strong)	clm2500n2y
C—Nonwinners of a race in six months	clm2500n1y
D—Nonwinners of two races lifetime, other than a lower claiming price	clm2500n2x
E—Nonwinners of three races lifetime	clm2500n3L
F—Nonwinners of two races lifetime, or in two years	clm2500n2L
M—Nonwinners (maidens)	Mdn2500

Beyond the above subdivisions, races restricted to three-year-olds tend to be weaker than the same class race for four-year-olds and/or three-year-olds and up. For instance, an E class $2,500 claiming race for three-year-olds in July probably will be run about 2/5 seconds slower than the identical class race for three-year-olds and up. That is a significant difference worth about three notches on the classification code.

Increments between each class level within the $2,500 claiming class at Charles Town are relatively steep. The same is true for bottom-claiming races at other tracks where restrictive clauses subdivide the competition. In all cases, however, the easiest class jump is the M (maiden) to F class, because F-class horses tend to have very little ability and most have failed to win their way out of the category after several attempts. For several weeks in succession, groups of F-class horses may be so weak that they become easy prey for a series of recent maiden graduates who have the added edge gained from their recent victories. Yet M winners who skip a step and go immediately to D-, C- or B-class claiming races are very poor risks. The edge gained from a recent win over nonwinners is lost when facing multiple winners.

The player should also note that maiden-claiming graduates rarely repeat at tracks where there is no F class at the bottom level, or whenever the F-class category temporarily includes an abundance of lightly raced horses with only one or two starts since graduation day. (Periodic spot checks of these phenomena at Charles Town since 1977 reveal more than 30 percent repeaters in Maiden to F-class situations. A collateral check of A horses dropping to C reveals similar percentages, at an average mutuel of better than $7. These results virtually replicate those obtained in the 1970s for the original edition of *Betting Thoroughbreds*.)

Not every racetrack has the same approach to bottom-level claiming races. For instance, at Bay Meadows, which has a rich $140,000 daily purse structure yet cards a surprisingly large number of cheap claiming races, there are three distinct bottoms: $12,500 for maidens, $6,250 for limited winners and $4,000 for open company, mostly veteran campaigners.

Where $12,500 maiden graduates may compete for $12,500 nonwinners of two, they also may compete for $6,250 against nonwinners in six months and/or nonwinners of two races lifetime in which victories at $5,000 or less do not count. The absurdity of having so many complicated subdivisions is lost on racing officials who wonder why newcomers have a hard time understanding this game, but they can be resolved by consulting Beyer speed figures or by working with a streamlined classification code for a few weeks until you can get a handle on the true balance between each internal class level. The following is a simulated Bay Meadows classification code for its lower-level claiming races.

BAY MEADOWS CLASSIFICATION CODE		DRF SYMBOLS
A +	Unrestricted $12,500 claiming race	clm12,500
A	Unrestricted $10,000 claiming race	clm10,000
B +	Unrestricted $8,000 claiming race	clm 8,000
B −	Nonwinners of two, $8,000, in which maiden and $6,250 races do not count	clm8000n2x
C +	Nonwinners of two, $6,250, in which maiden and $5,000 races do not count	clm6250n2x
C	Unrestricted $6,250 claiming race	clm 6,250
C −	$6,250 nonwinners in six months	clm 6250n1y
D	Unrestricted $4,000 claiming	clm4000
E +	Nonwinners of two lifetime, $12,500	clm12500n2L
M	$12,500 maiden claiming	mdn12500

It is not an illusion to note that $6,250 races for nonwinners in six months are more difficult than $12,500 races for nonwinners of two, or that the cheapest claiming races (open $4,000 at Bay Meadows) usually are stronger than more expensive, restricted races. Failing to win two races in a career is a form flaw that invites a probable thrashing by a well-prepared multiple winner, or by a multiple winner who may have been absent from competition for several months. Using the above, or any other class ladder, the player may spot many meaningful class maneuvers that lead to sensible race results. The nuts and bolts of all of this can be stated simply: Multiple winners have a built-in edge when meeting habitual losers or horses with only one victory. Bay Meadows horses moving down from A+ to D are taking huge drops without any change in claiming price; Bay Meadows horses moving up from E+ to B, or F to C, can expect challenges as difficult as the move from B to A+, while the move from M to F (with a drop of 50 percent in claiming price) is only slightly more difficult than the move from M to F at Charles Town.

With or without classification codes, I cannot stress enough the value of building your game around result charts supplemented with added data such as Key Race notations and reminders about the restrictive eligibility conditions. Such designations do not pick winners by themselves, but they improve the player's ability to spot internal-class maneuvers. Alert players will find many ways to integrate knowledge of such maneuvers into a broader handicapping approach, but the two most powerful angles are listed below:

- Very often a bottom-rock claimer will be entered in a multiple winners race when it is still eligible for a race with a restricted eligibility clause. In all but a few instances these horses can be safely eliminated. Such overmatched horses are out for the exercise, or the trainer is seeking to darken their form, preparing for a future drop into a more realistic spot at the same claiming level. If the horse really is good enough to skip conditions and defeat multiple winners, the trainer probably will choose a higher-priced claiming race where purses are appropriately scaled higher.
- Horses who have shown signs of life in races against multiple winners are excellent wagers when properly placed in less demanding, restricted events, even if there is an artificial increase in the claiming price for today's race.

For example, at defunct Green Mountain Park in Vermont, where I enjoyed many an evening during the 1960s while working as a counselor at nearby Camp Watitoh, one of the most satisfying bets of my entire career came in the first week after putting my first minor-track classification code to work.

Amazingly, I spotted a 14—1 shot in a $2,000 D-class race who had recently flashed high early speed in an A-class $1,500 race. The hidden class maneuver led me to conclude that this horse was dropping down sharply in company despite the increase in claiming price. An examination of the rest of the field added to my confidence. There was no major rival for the early lead, no other hidden class dropdown to worry about. I had uncovered a horse with a powerful edge, and he won by nine lengths!

11

The Mystery of Allowance Races

Allowance races probably are the most difficult races for the novice and intermediate player to handicap. Yet they offer fertile ground for players willing to dig a little deeper into factors not readily seen in the past performances.

In order to handicap allowance races successfully, the player should learn something about breeding as it relates to distance potential and get a fix on the local pecking order of different horse groups.

Who are the best sprinters on the grounds? Who are the best routers, the best turf horses, the best three-year-old fillies and the best colts?

The player also must be familiar with the purse structure at his or her favorite track, as well as the approximate stops on the claiming scale when claiming races are equal to, or superior to specific allowance conditions.

Deputy Fife — Ch. g. 4, by Deputy Minister—Proud Halo, by Halo
Br.—Kingsbrook Farm (Can)
Tr.—Duniavy Terrance W (8 3 0 1 .38)
114
MCKNIGHT J (8 2 0 2 .25)
Own.—Double R Farms

Lifetime							
22 4 4 7	1992	13	3	1	5	$42,042
$60,780	1991	7	0	3	2	$11,105
	Turf	1	0	0	0	
	Wet	3	1	0	2	$14,880

17Oct92- 3Kee	gd	1⅛		:50^{2}	1:15	1:51^{2}	3↑Clm 30000	84	1	4	2^{1}	2^{hd}	1^{hd}	1no	Smith M E	LB	117	4.90	78-23 DeputyFife117^{no}CattleBron117^{nk}Cocoboy114	Lost whip 6
8Oct92- 8TP	sly	1$\frac{1}{16}$		:47	1:11^{4}	1:44^{2}	3↑Alw 24300	84	3	4	3^{8}	3^{5½}	4^{7½}	3^{9}	McKnight J	LB	113	5.20	76-20 BountyHunt107^{2}Scrto'sHidwy114^{7}DputyFif113	No rally 5
18Sep92- 6TP	my	1		:46^{2}	1:11	1:36^{4}	3↑Clm 25000	87	7	5	5^{13}	6^{8}	4^{9½}	3^{4}	McKnight J	LB	119	2.70	89-18 CttlBron113^{1½}AnthonyRmbo116^{2½}DputyFif119	Mld gain 7
4Sep92- 9EIP	fst	1		:46^{4}	1:11^{2}	1:37^{3}	3↑Clm 25000	77	2	8	8^{6¼}	5^{3½}	4^{2}	2^{2½}	McKnight J	LB	118	*1.70	86-18 MbNtW112^{2½}DptFf118^{nk}StllBllsh112	Wide turn bumped 8
19Aug92- 8EIP	fst	1		:47^{2}	1:13	1:39^{1}	3↑Clm 25000	70	2	7	7^{7¼}	5^{2½}	3^{1½}	3^{2¼}	Bartram B E	LB	121	*1.90	79-19 Cool Corbett112^{nk}StillBullish112^{2}DeputyFife121	Up rail 8
6Aug92- 7AP	gd	*1	Ⓣ	:48^{3}	1:13	1:36^{4}	3↑Clm 40000	70	1	9	9^{6}	11^{9¾}	12^{14}	12^{13¾}	Clark K D	L	115	28.10	76-17 TutTobgo117^{1½}SokngSmokng117^{1¼}AlDnt117	Shwd little 12
25Jly92- 7AP	sly	1		:46^{4}	1:12^{4}	1:39^{2}	3↑Alw 20500	97	7	7	7^{9}	6^{6¼}	3^{½}	1^{hd}	Stevens G L		116	5.60	69-41 DeputyFif116^{hd}JustLikPrfct111^{6}FritzBrthold116	All out 9
9Jly92- 6EIP	fst	1		:46^{1}	1:11	1:37	3↑Clm 25000	89	3	7	7^{5¼}	6^{2¼}	1^{½}	1^{1½}	Bartram B E	LB	115	2.90	92-19 DputyFf115^{1½}CountV.J.115^{2¼}LocoRmbo115	In hand late 7
26Jun92- 5CD	fst	6½f		:22^{4}	:46	1:17^{3}	3↑Clm 25000	72	5	8	9^{5½}	7^{3¾}	3^{4}	3^{2¾}	Day P	LB	118	*1.60	89-11 PlcEcho112^{nk}AliGzib118^{2½}DputyFf118	No late response 10
2May92-10CD	fst	1$\frac{1}{16}$		:49	1:13^{2}	1:44^{4}	3↑Alw 29650	88	9	8	7^{2¾}	6^{1¾}	3^{½}	4^{¾}	Arguello F A Jr	LB	115	9.90	89-06 Rngfort115^{½}DscontBrkr117^{nk}BllShls117	Bid flatten out 9

LATEST WORKOUTS Oct 3 CD 5f fst 1:03 B Sep 1 CD 3f fst :38 B

Bright Ways
Own: Golden Eagle Farm
STEVENS G L (108 25 14 10 .23) — $95,000
Dk. b or br f. 4
Sire: Procida (Mr. Prospector)
Dam: Incredible Idea (Youth)
Br: Mabee Mr–Mrs John C (Cal)
Tr: Hess R B Jr (43 7 9 7 .16)
L 114

Lifetime Record:	14	5	3	2	$134,800						
1993	5	1	2	1	$53,300	Turf	6	2	1	1	$57,650
1992	9	4	1	1	$81,500	Wet	1	0	1	0	$9,200
Hol Ⓣ	2	1	0	0	$22,100	Dist Ⓣ	2	1	0	1	$25,850

14May93-7Hol	fm	1⅛	Ⓣ	:482	1:114	1:35	1:472		ⒻCnvnience H 60k	89	3	4	55	54½	44	44	Delahoussaye E	LB 116 b	2.50	83-12	Miss Turkana1171¾ Gumpher114no Certam De May1142¼	No late bid	6
1Apr93-3SA	fm	1	Ⓣ	:234	:471	1:111	1:354		ⒻClm 100000	94	1	2	1hd	1½	12½	31	Stevens G L	LB 119 b	*2.30	85-14	Misterioso115½ Paula Revere115½ Bright Ways1192¾	Overtaken late	8
24Feb93-5SA	gd	1⅛	⊗	:474	1:13	1:373	1:502		ⒻAlw 44000N3X	96	3	1	11	12	14	15	Stevens G L	LB 116 b	3.40	78-28	Bright Ways1165 Changed Tune118¾ Secretly1142	Ridden out	8
4Feb93-8SA	fm	1⅛	Ⓣ	:464	1:102	1:352	1:473		ⒻAlw 44000N3X	87	3	3	32½	31½	2hd	23	Stevens G L	LB 116 b	5.60	78-19	Sun And Shade1183 Bright Ways116½ Changed Tune1181¼	Jostled start	8
6Jan93-8SA	sly	1 1/16	⊗	:232	:464	1:11	1:422		ⒻAlw 46000N3X	82	1	4	41¾	3½	11	21¾	Stevens G L	LB 118 b	2.70	90-05	Potrichal1171¾ Bright Ways1185 Cafe West115hd	Overtaken late	5
10Dec92-8Hol	fst	1 1/16	⊗	:233	:47	1:114	1:434	3↑	ⒻAlw 37000N2X	87	5	3	41½	21	2½	11¼	Desormeaux K J	LB 116 b	3.40	82-19	Bright Ways1161¼ Colours1181¾ Lyin To The Moon1141	Wide, ridden out	6
25Nov92-5Hol	fm	1 1/16	Ⓣ	:234	:482	1:131	1:43		ⒻClm 57500	84	9	5	54	53¾	32	1hd	Desormeaux K J	LB 116 b	*2.10	80-16	Bright Ways116hd Chabeli1131¼ Gettin' Air116	Strong finish	10
27Aug92-8Dmr	fm	1	Ⓣ	:233	:473	1:123	1:373	3↑	Ⓕ[S]Alw 35000	83	4	4	52¼	52	1½	11½	Desormeaux K J	LB 115 b	*1.90	83-17	BrightWys1151½ Gloriousness118no MountinsOfLune117	Boxed in 3/8-1/4	9
6Aug92-7Dmr	fm	1 1/16	Ⓣ	:243	:484	1:131	1:432	3↑	ⒻAlw 36000	79	5	5	66	64½	63	53½	Desormeaux K J	LB 114 b	7.30	85-11	BllCntn-NZ119nk [DH]LynToThMon116 [DH]RvrPtrl-GB122	Broke slowly	7
24Jun92-8Hol	fst	1 1/16		:232	:47	1:112	1:432		ⒻAlw 34000	77	3	4	53½	52½	42½	42	Desormeaux K J	LB 115 b	*.80e	82-16	Omjii I119nk Terre Haute117nk Sovereign Liz119	No mishap	7

WORKOUTS: May 11 Hol 4f fst :484 H 9/26 May 5 Hol 4f fst :494 H 26/44 Apr 30 Hol 4f fst :532 B 27/27 Apr 18 Hol 4f fst :502 H 29/36 Apr 12 SA 4f fst :473 H 7/41 Mar 20 SA 5f fst 1:05 H 59/59

At the major tracks, eligibility conditions for allowance races include some of the same restrictive clauses found in minor-track claiming races. And as illustrated in the previous chapter, *DRF*'s past performances now include several allowance-race and claiming-class designations, most of which were borrowed from the short-lived *Racing Times*. Nearly all are relatively easy to interpret on first glance.

The following are full allowance race conditions for two different allowance races in different regions of the country.

NINTH RACE
Suffolk
NOVEMBER 23, 1992

1 MILE 70 YARDS. (1.40) ALLOWANCE. Purse $10,000. 3-year-olds and upward which have never won two races. Weights, 3-year-olds 119 lbs. Older 122 lbs. Non-winners of a race at one mile or over since October 23 allowed 3 lbs. One such race since September 23, 6 lbs. (Races where entered for $10,000 or less not considered in estimating allowances).
Value of race $10,000; value to winner $6,000; second $2,000; third $1,000; fourth $500; balance of starters $100 each.

FOURTH RACE
Hawthorne
DECEMBER 17, 1993

1 MILE 70 YARDS. (1.391) ALLOWANCE. Purse $21,780 (includes $1,980 IBF). 3-year-olds and upward, non-winners of three races other than maiden, claiming or starter. Illinois registered, conceived and/or foaled. Weights: 3-year-olds, 120 lbs. Older, 122 lbs. Non-winners of two races since October 30, allowed 3 lbs. A race, 5 lbs. Two races in 1993, 7 lbs. A race, 9 lbs. (Claiming races not considered.)

NOTE: *The term* allowance *derives from weight allowances subtracted from the maximum assigned weights as spelled out in each race's eligibility conditions. Yet the term is senseless because the same basic weight allowances are used to adjust assigned weights in claiming races.*

In many cases trainers who have skill with allowance-class stock do the same thing that Charles Town trainers do with bottom-rock claimers. They frequently race them against more experienced multiple winners before subtly dropping them into restricted, easier allowance races where they may dominate. Sometimes the tougher race is an allowance race against older runners, or against multiple-allowance or stakes winners, or perhaps it is a high-priced claiming race featuring several horses with numerous victories. Indeed, the move from a rugged claiming race to a relatively restricted allowance race can be the key to many solid allowance-race plays—some at generous prices—because it goes against an erroneous assumption often made by the betting public. Horses going from claiming races to allowance conditions are always going up in class. Many times over the opposite is true.

Tip's Terror   Dk. b. or br. f. 4, by Singular—Tip and Run, by Crafty Admiral
Br.—Andrewskiewicz Lee (Fla)
Tr.—Dubuc Charles E Jr (—)
Own.—Andrewskiewicz Lee A
116

Lifetime							
20 6 2 2	1992	14	5	2	2	$28,927
$32,599	1991	6	1	0	0	$3,672
	Turf	6	2	2	0	$15,607
	Wet	1	0	0	0	

4Sep92- 9Mth	fm	1$\frac{1}{16}$	Ⓣ:46^4	1:11^3	1:44^1	+ 3↑ⒻAlw 20000	81	3	5	5^7	7$^{3\frac{1}{4}}$	6$^{1\frac{1}{4}}$	4$^{4\frac{1}{4}}$	Diaz L F	Lb 116	21.40	75-19 HotTmsArHr116^{3}FshonModl116^{1}AlwysNtt113	6 wd lane	8
25Aug92- 8Atl	fm	*1$\frac{1}{16}$	Ⓣ:47^3	1:12^1	1:45^3	3↑ⒻAlw 9200	86	1	6	6^{10}	3^4	1$^{1\frac{1}{2}}$	1^3	Diaz L F	Lb 122	11.10	90-07 Tip's Terror122^3 Currently Safe116$^{\frac{3}{4}}$Sallyana116	Driving	8
13Aug92- 8Atl	gd	1⅛	Ⓣ:49^1	1:13^4	1:53^1	3↑ⒻClm 30000	74	7	3	3$^{2\frac{1}{2}}$	3^1	1^{hd}	6^2	Diaz L F	Lb 119	9.50	73-25 SemiL'Enjoleur113$^{\frac{1}{2}}$Rgllino115^{no}B.J.Brnnr108	Bid, tired	8
6Aug92- 8Atl	fst	5½f	:21^4	:46^3	1:05	3↑ⒻAlw 12500s	60	7	1	5$^{5\frac{3}{4}}$	4^5	5$^{5\frac{3}{4}}$	7$^{4\frac{1}{4}}$	Diaz L F	Lb 122	9.90	88-17 Rchel'sTurn117$^{2\frac{1}{4}}$HorriblGift122$^{\frac{3}{4}}$FourPunch114	No rally	7
28Jly92- 6Atl	fm	*1	Ⓣ:48^1	1:14^2	1:41^4	3↑ⒻAlw 10000s	74	5	6	3^3	1$^{1\frac{1}{2}}$	1^4	1$^{3\frac{3}{4}}$	Diaz L F	Lb 117	2.80	85-22 Tip's Terror117$^{3\frac{3}{4}}$ ClassicIndex117^{1}AtlasAxis117	Driving	9
21Jly92- 9Mth	fst	6f	:22	:45^2	1:11^1	3↑ⒻAlw 17000	58	4	6	6$^{6\frac{1}{2}}$	6^8	6^9	6$^{8\frac{1}{2}}$	Diaz L F	Lb 116	21.20	76-18 CherokeVil107$^{1\frac{1}{4}}$YouthfulSis110$^{1\frac{1}{2}}$CoolNumbr112	No bid	8
12Jly92-12Del	fst	6f	:22^3	:47	1:13^1	3↑ⒻAlw 5000s	57	3	3	5$^{2\frac{1}{2}}$	5^5	4^5	4^6	Diaz L F	Lb 122	1.50	75-26 Dixie Card119^5 StormDoctor114$^{\frac{1}{2}}$GoldPicker114	Outrun	5
24Jun92- 9Atl	fm	*5½f	Ⓣ:22^2	:46^3	1:05^1	3↑ⒻAlw 12500s	79	5	3	4$^{2\frac{1}{4}}$	3^4	2^3	2^{hd}	Diaz L F	Lb 122	2.90	92-10 PrincssFiddld122^{hd}Tp'sTrror122$^{4\frac{1}{2}}$CshTwnty112	Gamely	7
18Jun92- 5Atl	fst	5f	:22	:45^3	:58^1	3↑ⒻAlw 6500s	70	6	3	4$^{2\frac{1}{4}}$	3$^{\frac{1}{2}}$	1$^{\frac{1}{2}}$	1$^{3\frac{1}{4}}$	Diaz L F	Lb 119	*.70	93-09 Tip'sTerror119$^{3\frac{1}{4}}$SimplyGoldn119^{no}RickyTim117	Driving	6
10Jun92- 8Atl	fst	5½f	:22	:46^1	1:05^1	3↑ⒻAlw 8200	68	5	1	4^2	1^{hd}	1$^{2\frac{1}{2}}$	1$^{1\frac{3}{4}}$	Diaz L F	Lb 116	2.00	91-13 Tp'sTrror116$^{1\frac{3}{4}}$Intnwththtms116$^{1\frac{1}{4}}$IslofBchs116	Driving	5

LATEST WORKOUTS   Nov 16 Pha   5f fst 1:06^3 Bg

Just as trainer Charles Dubuc, Jr., knew in the example above that a $30,000 claiming race is roughly equivalent to a medium-grade allowance race at Atlantic City, most of the better players at Santa Anita know that a fit $80,000-claiming horse can compete against all but the best-stakes horses on the grounds.

At the Meadowlands in New Jersey, a solid $40,000 claimer is going to be a rough customer in most allowance races; at Louisiana Downs a solid $25,000 claimer will tower over most medium-grade allowance fields, while a hard-hitting $35,000 claimer shipping in from Monmouth Park or Belmont will deserve serious consideration against all but the fastest horses at Philadelphia Park.

Every track in the country has similar relationships between claiming and allowance horses. While these relationships may differ slightly from season to season, due to competitive factors between different racing circuits, they are invaluable reference points missed by most casual horseplayers.

At Calder Racecourse in Florida, a sharp $20,000–$30,000 claimer should be given a careful look in allowance races restricted to nonwinners of one or two races other than maiden or claiming. At Arlington International Racecourse, a $35,000 claimer fits right in with nonwinners of two races other than maiden or claiming.

Players who take the time to investigate and update these subtle relationships will surprise themselves with dozens of extra winners. Indeed, it is exceedingly useful to know if subtle differences in quality exist between similar class races at neighboring tracks, even if they employ the same purse structure. And there are two crucial points to be made about this type of research:

These ideas pay extra dividends at the mutuel windows because they rely on insights not found in the past performances. As Chicago-based professional Scott McMannis likes to point out in his daily seminars at Arlington International Racecourse, this is the "X Factor" in racing. The X Factor is what the winning player must find to beat the general betting public, which consistently picks about 30–33 percent winning favorites while driving the odds down on horses with obvious credentials.

On the other hand, horses with obvious form credentials usually are overbet by the majority of bettors. (The recent inclusion of Beyer speed figures in the past performances only intensifies that betting phenomenon.)

In northern California, for instance, a $27,000 unrestricted allowance race at Golden Gate Fields is odds-on to contain a substantially better group of horses than a $34,000 allowance race at Santa Anita, even though the northern California purse is lower and the overall quality of racing is much higher in the south.

A $27,000 allowance race at Golden Gate is likely to attract stakes-quality shippers from southern California. In fact, if purses were assigned strictly according to merit, the typical $27,000 allowance race at Golden Gate Fields probably would deserve $41,000 based on Santa Anita standards.

In the Northeast we find similar anomalies. Some of Monmouth Park's $20,000–$30,000 allowance races are stronger than New York races with slightly higher purses, and every state in the region offers dozens of races and stakes that carry inflated purses to promote local or regional breeding.

At Finger Lakes Racetrack in upstate New York, for example, the following allowance races were presented for fillies and mares on November 1, 1992.

- Allowance purse $7,000; *nonwinners of four races lifetime.*
- Allowance purse $11,700; *New York-bred; nonwinners of two races other than maiden or claiming, or state-bred.*

Interestingly, the actual winners of the above two races ran identical clockings in their respective victories, but both were slightly slower than the fastest race of the day turned in by a six-year-old New York-bred mare who was scoring her 11th career win in an *unrestricted $10,000 claiming race*. And I suggest you read that again to grasp the point.

While purse values offer clues to the relative strength of allowance races at one track, the player will be tossing away considerable insight if no attempt is made to identify the point at which claiming races are equal or superior to specific allowance races. Similarly, a careful comparison of allowance-race eligibility restrictions will prove equally useful when comparing horses shipping from one track to another.

Whether it be in stakes, allowances or claiming races, there is something to be gleaned from knowing the severity of an increase or decrease in class. When such shifts occur in claiming races, questions must be asked about the logic of the situation. Is the trainer trying to unload the horse at a discounted price because the horse is going sour, or is today's drop an attempt to sneak a fit runner into a soft spot where the competition will not be able to cope? Is the trainer willing to lose the horse for the sake of the purse, or merely hoping to lose it via the claim box to save feed and vet bills?

BAY MEADOWS, MARCH 4, 1993. 6 FURLONGS, $16,000 CLAIMING, 3-YEAR-OLD FILLIES

Preview Point	Ch. f. 3(Mar), by Pencil Point–IR—Martial Lady, by Eager Eagle		Lifetime	1993 1 0 0 0	$1,125
DOOCY T T (52 9 12 14 .18)	$16,000 Br.—Duffel Joseph A (Cal)		3 1 0 0	1992 2 1 0 0	$10,450
Own.—G C Stable	Tr.—Walsh Kathy (12 3 1 2 .25)	116	$11,575	Wet 2 0 0 0	$1,125

7Jan93- 1BM sly 1	:454 1:11 1:38	⑥Clm 25000	52 4 3 3⁶ 3³ 43½ 48¾ Baze R A	B 116	4.90	71-17 BrStlBb117⁴⅓WngMChms115¾JnBrs116	Stumbled start 5
2Dec92- 7P M sly 6f	:214 :443 1:122	⑥Alw 16000	22 6 6 65½ 71³ 61⁴ 616½ Baze R A	B 116	3.40	57-24 Coltn'sBttrfly114¾TknghtMyLdy118²⅓SyhJl117	No rally 8
18Jun92- 6GG fst 5f	:204 :444 :573	⑥Md Sp Wt	62 1 7 43½ 4⁴ 21½ 1½ Baze R A	B 117	12.50	94-10 PrvwPont117½LostBllt117⁴SyhSptRn117	Closed gamely 11
LATEST WORKOUTS	Mar 1BM 3f fst :354 H		Feb 24 BM 5f my 1:01⁴ H	●Feb 16 BM 5f fst :59³ H		Feb 10 BM 3f gd :36 H	

In the case of Preview Point, the move from allowance to $25,000 claiming on January 7 was an obvious attempt to improve this filly's winning chances. But the subsequent absence from competition, noted by the thin black line above the January 7, 1993 racing date, indicates that something went wrong—again. Sharp recent workouts and another drop in class are aimed in a dual direction. Trainer Kathy Walsh is trying to win with a fresh and fit horse, and $16,000 seems a fair selling price, with acceptable risk of losing this filly to another trainer via the claim box.

When a move up or down occurs in allowance races or stakes, the risk of a claim is nonexistent and the talent of the horse for that particular situation must be evaluated in light of the horse's overall potential.

Where cheap horses may be overmatched a few times or sent an inappropriate distance to darken form for a betting score, the effect of such manipulations on a horse with stakes potential can be disastrous. As repeatedly pointed out in earlier chapters, good trainers select races that will help promising horses reach their potential. If the horse is rushed, or overmatched a few times, it will get discouraged or lose focus and slide down the ladder. Good horses are like top pitching prospects in baseball. Rush them and you will ruin their arms. Overmatch them too often and you will ruin their confidence. Many prospective good horses are ruined exactly that way.

Below is the past-performance profile of Lukas' 1986 Juvenile Champion, Capote, who went from a maiden victory to win a Graded stakes at Santa Anita followed by victory in the Breeders' Cup Juvenile. Despite his obvious talent and early accomplishments, Capote never improved on his top two-year-old races and was a complete failure at three.

Capote — Dk. b. or br. c. 3, by Seattle Slew—Too Bald, by Bald Eagle
Own.—French, Beal & Klein **126** — Br.—North Ridge Farm (Ky) — 1987 2 0 0 0 $54,450
Tr.—Lukas D Wayne — 1986 4 3 0 0 $654,680
Lifetime 6 3 0 0 $709,130

18Apr87-8Aqu 1 1/8 :47 1:113 1:49 m *6-5 126 11 11 1/2 34 47 3/4 CrdrAJr5 Wood Mem 82-15 Gulch, Gone West, Shawklit Won 8
18Apr87—Grade I
4Apr87-8Aqu 1 :442 1:081 1:343sy *7-5 123 2hd 22 35 1/2 49 1/2 Day P5 Gotham 83-21 Gone West, Shawklit Won, Gulch 9
4Apr87—Grade II
1Nov86-1SA 1 1/16 :454 1:102 1:434ft *2 1/2 122 11 1/2 11 12 1/2 11 1/4 PincyLJr3 Br Cp Juv 82-13 Capote, Qualify, Alysheba 13
1Nov86—Grade I
11Oct86-8SA 1 1/16 :461 1:11 1:451ft 3 3/4 118 11 1/2 1 1/2 11 1/2 11 3/4 PincayLJr3 Norfolk 75-17 Capote, Gulch, Gold On Green 6
11Oct86—Grade I
3Oct86-6SA 6f :214 :443 1:092ft *3 118 12 1/2 15 17 111 Pincay L Jr1 Mdn 91-17 Cpot,WndwoodLn,BooBoo'sBckro 12
1Sep86-6Dmr 6f :22 :444 1:094ft 4 118 3 1/2 35 1116 1121 3/4 Shoemaker W8 Mdn 67-13 SpecilTrick,SwordChrger,ChrlieZe 12
1Sep86—Green backstretch; wide 3/8 turn
Apr 27 Bel 6f ft 1:142 b ●Apr 11 Bel 6f ft 1:123 h ●Mar 29 Hol 5f ft :592 h ●Mar 24 Hol 6f ft 1:15 h

I would not like to leave the impression that all winners in allowance races come from dropdown maneuvers, or have precocious Capote-type records. The truth is neither factor may come into play in many allowance races. Such races cannot be handicapped successfully without considering track bias, trainer patterns, trips and other relevant data. Nevertheless, the player who appreciates the subtle power of the hidden class dropdown and incorporates purse values, eligibility conditions and Key Race studies into the handicapping process will move many lengths ahead of the crowd. Players also will benefit if they remain in touch with dramatic changes occurring within the industry.

Certainly, we expect to see fewer tracks, fewer live races and more intertrack simulcasting in the 1990s to compensate for the declines in horse population that have resulted from a worldwide contraction of the breeding marketplace. From 1985 to 1989 there were about 50,000 Thoroughbred foals per year in America, while in 1991–92, there were about 35,000. Otherwise, well-managed simulcasting between tracks may boost purses sharply in some regions, especially where oversaturation of racing is weakening the quality of the live product.

When purses go up or down sharply, trainers must rethink their entire 12-month game plan. Some will ship selected horses out of town to take advantage of perceived weaknesses in competition or inflated purses; others will move out completely, or point for specific meetings, laying low for months. These changes will force inevitable shifts in the balance between various claiming and allowance levels and will require different handicapping interpretations.

Meanwhile, it is imperative to realize that allowance races and stakes cover a wide spectrum of class levels and each internal subdivision tends to be dominated by horses with relatively identifiable profiles.

ALLOWANCE- AND STAKES-WINNING PROFILES

Allowance races for nonwinners of two races lifetime may be easy prey for a fast recent maiden grad, or the horse who has performed well in limited starts against similar or better allowance rivals, or a horse who ran credibly in a recent open-claiming race against multiple winners.

Allowance races for nonwinners of a race other than maiden or claiming can be deceptively strong races in which multiple-claiming winners deserve preference over horses who have lost a few similar allowance races. Multiple-claiming winners have one thing their rivals do not: considerable experience defeating winners.

Allowance races for nonwinners of two races other than maiden or claiming may also be won by high-priced claiming winners, but they will have no special edge over recent allowance winners who seem to have stakes potential or lightly raced horses who have one or two good races at this level.

Higher-grade allowance races rarely are won by claiming horses, unless we are talking about the very top level of claiming, i.e., $80–$100,000 at Santa Anita. Most top-of-the-line allowance races—called "classified" allowance races in some regions—will be won by proven stakes horses, or by multiple-allowance winners who have already competed well at this level. Again, at tracks such as Santa Anita and Belmont Park, $100,000 claiming races are close to Grade 3 stakes races with claiming tags attached.

Stakes for older Grade 1 runners at 1⅛ miles and longer tend to be won by previous Grade 1 winners or solid Grade 2 types in peak form. Yet Grade 3 races are for horses with varying credentials, from Grade 1 and 2 dropdowns to improving allowance types.

Graded stakes for three-year-olds deserve special treatment according to the time of the year. In the late winter and early spring, they are dominated by horses with Triple Crown potential. Yet beyond the Triple Crown chase the majority of three-year-olds stakes at all grades on major track circuits are won by:

- Horses who previously competed against the best in Triple Crown races and preps
- Top two-year-olds of the previous year who were forced to miss the Triple Crown season
- Developing summer stars who have won a few allowance races and/or low-level stakes while earning above-average speed figures and/or style points

Slew O' Gold
B. c. 4, by Seattle Slew—Alluvial, by Buckpasser
Own.—Equusequity Stable 126
Br.—Claiborne Farm (Ky) 1984 5 5 0 0 $1,952,944
Tr.—Hertler John O 1983 12 5 4 1 $883,390
Lifetime 20 12 4 1 $2,858,534

20Oct84-8Bel	1½	:49^3	2:03^4	2:28^{4}ft	*1-9	126	2^2	12½	14½	19¾	CordrAJr^5	J C Gld Cp	76-17	SlwO'Gold,HlBoldKng,BoundngBsq	5
20Oct84—Grade I															
29Sep84-8Bel	1¼	:47^4	1:36^4	2:02^{2}ft	*4-5	129	3½	11½	11½	11¾	CrdrAJr^6	Mrlbro Cp H	86-19	SlewO'Gold,CarrDeNskr,CndinFctor	9
29Sep84—Grade I															
15Sep84-8Bel	1⅛	:45^1	1:09^2	1:47^{4}sy	*2-3	126	3½	21½	2^1	1½	CrdrAJr^6	Woodward	88-18	Slew O' Gold, Shifty Sheik, Bet Big	6
15Sep84—Grade I															
4Aug84-8Sar	1⅛	:46^4	1:10	1:48^{3}ft	*2-5	126	2^{hd}	2^{hd}	1^{hd}	11¾	CrdrAJr^1	Whitney H	92-13	SlewO'Gold,TrckBrron,Thumbsuckr	3
4Aug84—Grade I															
2Jly84-1Bel	1	:44^4	1:09^2	1:34^{2}gd	*2-5	115	2^4	1^{hd}	1^3	17½	Cordero AJr^1	Aw36000	93-15	SlewO'Gold,CnnonShell,NorthernIc	5
15Oct83-8Bel	1½	:48	2:01	2:26^{1}ft	3e	121	63¼	2½	1^2	1^3	CrdrAJr^3	J C GoldCup	89-14	SlwO'Gold,HghlndBld,BondngBsq	11
24Sep83-8Bel	1¼	:47^2	1:36^1	2:01^{1}ft	4½	119	1^{hd}	1^3	1½	2^{nk}	CrdrAJr^2	Mrlbro Cp H	92-17	HighlndBlde,SlewO'Gold,BtesMotel	9
24Sep83—Wide															
3Sep83-8Bel	1⅛	:45^4	1:09^2	1:46^{3}ft	4e	118	4^2	2^1	1^{hd}	1no	CordrAJr^6	Woodward	94-13	Slew O' Gold,BatesMotel,SingSing	10
13Aug83-8Sar	1¼	:46^4	1:35^2	2:01 gd	*2½	126	2½	2^{hd}	2^{hd}	21¾	Cordero A Jr^1	Travers	93-11	PlayFellow,SlewO'Gold,Hyperboren	7
30Jly83-9Mth	1⅛	:46^3	1:10^2	1:49^{1}ft	*1	124	8^7	4^4	51¾	6^4	CordroAJr^5	Haskell H	85-17	DeputedTestmony,BtBig,Prfitmnt	10
30Jly83—Lacked room final 1/8															

Nov 4 Bel 6f ft 1:14^2 b   Oct 31 Bel 5f ft 1:03^1 b   Oct 18 Bel 3f ft :37^2 b   ●Oct 14 Bel 6f ft 1:14^3 b

While good players know that three-year-olds tend to be at a disadvantage against experienced older rivals, there is money to be made in the exceptions, especially during the late summer and fall. In fact, the most dangerous horse in all of racing is the improving three-year-old who successfully moves from allowance races into stakes and seems to be thriving on an active training regimen. Many of these improving types will go on important winning streaks at generous prices.

None of this will tax many minds, but players who hope to win consistently must come to grips with such subtleties or lose sight of a crucial truth at the heart of the game: Racing is a living entity; changes occur regularly. Amid all this flux the player's best chance to stay on even keel is to use his or her own observation powers and plain old common sense.

Below is a linked example of a few races that illustrates how great bets may be made by having a fix on some of the subtle class comparisons we have been detailing. It also demonstrates how the relative class of previous competition may not always be evident to the casual player.

Dusty Screen — Ch. g. 4, by Silent Screen—Azulejos, by Buckfinder
Br.—Riversmere Inc (Pa)
Own.—Ljoka Daniel J — Tr.—Pregman John S Jr (12 0 3 1 .00) — **120**
Lifetime 19 6 1 3 $110,463 — 1992 9 2 0 3 $39,245 — 1991 10 4 1 0 $71,218 — Turf 3 0 0 0 $260 — Wet 3 1 0 1 $20.940

21Oct92- 7Aqu fm 1 (T):47^2 1:12^2 1:36 3↑Alw 47000 82 1 1 1½ 1^{hd} 6 3½ 6^{10} Madrid A Jr b 115 19.50 86-13 Kr'sClown112^{3}TrkyPont115^{nk}SoStrlng117 Used in pace 6
6Sep92- 9Pen sly 1 1/16 :46^1 1:10^4 1:43^3 3↑[S]Capital City 99 4 1 1^1 1^3 1^7 1^9 Lopez C C Lb 119 1.50 92-28 DustyScren119^{9}MnilHmp110^{1}CouldBGood119 Drew off 6
6Sep92-Originally scheduled for turf
21Aug92- 9Mth fst 1 :47 1:11 1:37^2 3↑Alw 20000 95 2 3 3^{nk} 1^{hd} 2½ 1no King E L Jr Lb 116 20.90 85-20 DustyScren116^{no}ColonlHill116^{10}Edbrt116 Stead 1st trn 6
11Aug92- 8Mth gd 1 (T):47 1:12 1:38^1 3↑Alw 26000 66 7 3 38½ 6^{10} 7^{10} 615½ Gryder A T Lb 115 13.10 59-17 RocktFul1221¼MgicIntrlud115^{3}ArForsGun115 Gave way 7
24Jly92- 7Bel my 6f :22^2 :45 1:09 3↑Alw 34000 72 3 4 5^2 52½ 6^6 69½ Antley C W b 117 31.50 85-15 San Romano114^2 SolidSunny117½Nucleon117 No factor 6
12Jly92- 8Mth fst 6f :21^3 :44 1:09^1 3↑Alw 26000 86 6 1 62¾ 65¾ 54¼ 34¼ Grabowski J A Lb 115 37.30 90-15 [D]FriendlyLovr117½BigJwl115^{4}DustyScrn115 Some gain 7
21Jun92- 8Pha fst 6f :22^1 :45^2 1:10 3↑Alw 23833 69 6 4 42½ 43½ 57½ 512¾ Lloyd J S Lb 116 5.40 78-19 BornToShop1195½RckbyJsh1162½DkfSxny119 Came out 7
7Jun92- 6Mth fst 6f :21^2 :44^1 1:09^4 3↑Alw 19000 80 4 3 3^2 41¼ 3½ 3^3 Bravo J Lb 116 7.10 89-09 BlzingFire1161¾NusetFlsh1161¼DustyScrn116 Weakened 6
16May92- 9GS sly 6f :22 :45^1 1:09^2 3↑Alw 15000 84 3 6 5^2 43½ 57¼ 37½ Bravo J Lb 117 17.60 87-17 HtthMhgony117^{5}BornTShp1172½DstyScrn117 Mild rally 10
26Dec91- 8GS fst 6f :22^1 :45^1 1:10^3 3↑Holly 52 3 7 5^5 68¼ 7^{12} 716¾ Molina V H 115 11.10 73-18 Dontcloseyoureys119^{nk}FroznDw117^{no}Dlmtic110 Outrun 7
LATEST WORKOUTS Nov 2 Med 4f fst :47^3 H — Oct 4 Med 5f fst :59 H

Lord Cardinal — B. c. 4, by Deputy Minister—Katie Cochran, by Roberto
Br.—Ledyard Lewis C (Pa)
Own.—Barge Marc — Tr.—Reid Mark J (320 53 38 42 .17) — **113**
Lifetime 13 2 0 1 $36,180 — 1992 6 1 0 1 $15,840 — 1991 7 1 0 0 $20,340 — Turf 9 1 0 1 $22,980 — Wet 1 0 0 0

15Oct92- 5Bel fst 7f :23^1 :46 1:22^4 3↑Clm 32500 85 9 2 3^1 3½ 21½ 1no Davis R G b 115 60.10 90-15 LrdCrdnl115^{no}ThGrtCrl117^{nk}EstrnBrv114 Wide, driving 9
28Sep92- 5Bel sly 1 1/16 :46^4 1:11 1:43^2 3↑Clm c-25000 13 6 6 9^{14} 9^{22} 9^{29} 943¾ Antley C W 117 14.60 41-22 QckCommndr117^{hd}[D]HdOrphn108^{4}PcktStrkr119 Outrun 9
28Sep92-Claimed from Peace John H, Arnold George R II Trainer
21Sep92- 3Bel fm 1 1/16 [T]:47 1:10^1 1:40^2 3↑Clm 35000 81 6 6 84¼ 84¼ 56½ 66¾ Antley C W 117 5.90 89-11 Shs1173¾TurtleBech117¾CommissionerBrt117 No threat 10
4Sep92- 9Bel yl 1 (T):46^1 1:11 1:36^2 3↑Clm 35000 74 11 7 94¼ 83¼ 44½ 4^7 Antley C W 117 11.40 73-20 SthrnSl117^2[D]Dr.Brtl117^{2}TrnngFrHm119 Took up 1/2 pl 12
4Sep92-Placed third through disqualification
21Aug92- 5Sar fm 1⅛ [T]:47^4 1:12 1:49 3↑Clm 35000 70 12 9 6^4 85¼ 10^8 10^{11} Davis R G 117 8.50 83-09 GldnExplsv117^{nk}Prnc'sCv1173¾A.M.Swngr117 Wide trip 12
9Aug92- 1Sar gd 6f :22^2 :45 1:09^2 3↑Clm 35000 77 5 7 74¼ 66½ 46½ 47¼ Davis R G 117 29.50 90-06 LuckyTent115¾SunnyndPlesnt117^{6}ShinPls113 No threat 7
13Oct91- 7Bel fm 1⅜ [T]:46^4 1:36^3 2:14^2 3↑Alw 29000 83 8 5 6^5 42½ 3^1 51¾ Smith M E 114 *1.50 77-20 Jill'sTank114^{1}ExplosiveRule114^{nk}CrownSalute107 Tired 8
8Sep91- 8Pim fm 1 1/16 (T):46^2 1:10^3 1:43 Marylnd Turf 82 13 11 12^{10} 8^{12} 6^8 58¾ Krone J A 117 7.40 81-10 Scottsvll1171½SbtlStp1221½BmbthBrdg117 Pas'd faders 13
25Aug91- 6Sar fm 1 1/16 [T]:48^1 1:12^2 1:43^1 3↑Alw 29000 82 4 5 6^7 76¼ 5^3 4^2 Day P 112 5.40 90-13 GoldnExplosv112^{nk}Pnchpssr1171½MdvlClssc117 Lt rally 9
14Aug91- 7Sar fm 1 1/16 (T):45^3 1:10 1:42^1 3↑Alw 29000 83 1 4 5^{13} 7^6 6^4 5^3 Smith M E 112 10.70 82-09 Wtmotl1121DoblDngr114^{nk}GldnExplsv113 Saved ground 10
LATEST WORKOUTS Nov 2 Bel 4f fst :47^4 H — Oct 26 Bel 4f fst :48 B — Oct 8 Bel 4f fst :48^1 H

We are at Philadelphia Park for the running of the $35,000 Pennsylvania Championship stakes, at seven furlongs, on November 7, 1992. Dusty Screen and Lord Cardinal are four-year-old Pennsylvania breds who have been racing in open company in New York.

Two races back, Dusty Screen shipped to Penn National racecourse to soundly trounce a field of Pennsylvania breds in a 1 1/16-mile restricted stakes. And before that he won a hard-fought $20,000 allowance race at Monmouth Park by a nose at 20–1.

Lord Cardinal was claimed from a terrible $25,000 claiming performance by very successful Mark Reid, who has won 53 of 320 starters at Philadelphia Park during the current season, an enviable record. Lord Cardinal promptly rewarded Reid with a narrow victory over $32,000 claimers at, get this, $60.10–$1 odds!

Today is Lord Cardinal's debut against Pennsylvania breds, and his effort is going to be a good one, but, as the chart below suggests, not good enough to handle Dusty Screen.

EIGHTH RACE		7 FURLONGS. (1.212) 10th Running PENNSYLVANIA SPRINT CHAMPIONSHIP HANDI-CAP. Purse $35,000 Added. 3-year-olds and upward, registered Pennsylvania Breds. By subscription of $50 each, which should accompany the nomination, $100 to pass the entry box, $200 additional to start. Weights, Monday, November 2. Starters to be named through the entry box by the usual time of closing. Trophy will be presented to the winning owner. Closed		
Phila Park				
NOVEMBER 7, 1992				

with 22 nominations.

Value of race $38,550; value to winner $23,130; second $7,710; third $4,241; fourth $2,313; fifth $1,156. Mutuel pool $63,715. Exacta Pool $81,334

Last Raced	Horse	M/Eqt.A.Wt	PP St	¼	½	Str	Fin	Jockey	Odds $1
21Oct92 7Aqu6	Dusty Screen	Lb 4 120	3 3	1hd	1½	15	16	Molina V H	2.70
15Oct92 5Bel1	Lord Cardinal	b 4 114	5 8	8	71	52	2no	Black A S	a-3.50
22Aug92 9Mth11	Ligature	Lb 6 122	1 6	62	66	41½	3nk	Saumell L	3.60
26Sep92 5Bel2	Gate to Success	Lb 3 112	8 5	52½	5½	2hd	4no	Jocson G J	a-3.50
29Oct92 8Pha7	Rob Gelb	Lb 3 113	2 1	41	41	31	55½	Cruz C	13.60
17Oct92 8Lrl2	Charlie You Know	Lb 4 117	4 4	3hd	3hd	61	66	Ryan K	2.10
25Oct92 9Del2	Duke of Saxony	L 5 115	7 2	2hd	2hd	76	72	Salvaggio M V	10.80
26Oct92 8Pha1	Privilegio	L 3 112	6 7	71½	8	8	8	Vigliotti M J	28.80

a–Coupled: Lord Cardinal and Gate to Success.

OFF AT 3:31 Start Good, Won handily. Time, :222, :452, 1:103, 1:234 Track fast.

$2 Mutuel Prices:

5–DUSTY SCREEN	7.40	4.80	3.00
1–LORD CARDINAL (a–entry)		4.00	2.60
3–LIGATURE			3.20

$2 EXACTA 5–1 PAID $34.20

Ch. g, by Silent Screen—Azulejos, by Buckfinder. Trainer Pregman John S Jr. Bred by Riversmere Inc (Pa).

DUSTY SCREEN dueled for command while racing two wide, quickly shook loose to open a clear lead entering the stretch, was roused in midstretch and then was taken in hand through the final sixteenth. LORD CARDINAL was outrun early racing out from the rail, continued outside and while no threat to winner, gained place. LIGATURE saved ground just off the pace, lacked a strong finish. ROB GELB dueled for command inside, drifted off the rail near the quarter pole crossing in front of DUKE OF SAXONY and bumping gate to success. GATE TO SUCCESS raced wide and just off the pace, was bumped entering the lane and lacked a rally. CHARLIE YOU KNOW dueled for command three wide and tired. DUKE OF SAXONY vied for command four wide, steadied briefly when ROB GELB came out and tired.

Owners— 1, Ljoka Daniel J; 2, Barge Marc; 3, Marcus Mark I; 4, Caruso Michael J; 5, Garcia Efrain T; 6, Perry Joseph C; 7, Keystone Stable; 8, Shoemaker Janet L.

Trainers— 1, Pregman John S Jr; 2, Reid Mark J; 3, Benshoff Ronald L; 4, Reid Mark J; 5, Garcia Efrain T; 6, Neilson Wallace C; 7, Ritchey Tim F; 8, Sroka Douglas J.

Overweight: Lord Cardinal 1 pound; Privilegio 5.

While I am not sure if it was easy to pick Dusty Screen to win the Pennsylvania Championship, because there were other shippers of reasonable quality in the field, Lord Cardinal was an excellent wager at 6–1 the next time he competed in a limited-allowance race back at Aqueduct on November 25. Here was a horse who had defeated multiple winners in a $32,500 claiming race at Belmont, who confirmed his improved form for trainer Reid with a good second placing in a stakes that included several other multiple winners, including stakes winners from New York, New Jersey, Maryland and Delaware. Now he was dropping down sharply in class to meet nonwinners of a race other than maiden or claiming at one mile around one turn at Aqueduct—a situation and distance tailor-made for his talents.

SEVENTH RACE — 1 MILE. (1.32²) ALLOWANCE. Purse $29,000. 3-year-olds and upward which have never won a race other than maiden, claiming or starter. Weight: 3-year-olds 120 lbs. Older 122 lbs.

Aqueduct — Non-winners of a race other than claiming at a mile or over since November 15 allowed 3 lbs. Of such a race since November 1, 5 lbs.

NOVEMBER 25, 1992

Value of race $29,000; value to winner $17,400; second $6,380; third $3,480; fourth $1,740. Mutuel pool $173,982. Exacta Pool $369,400

Last Raced	Horse	M/Eqt.A.Wt	PP	St	¼	½	¾	Str	Fin	Jockey	Odds $1
7Nov92 8Pha²	Lord Cardinal	b 4 117	3	4	5$2\frac{1}{2}$	6	2¹	1½	1¹	Davis R G	6.90
11Nov92 4Aqu²	Scudbuster	b 3 115	6	1	2½	2²	1¹	2$2\frac{1}{2}$	2$4\frac{1}{2}$	Migliore R	3.80
8Nov92 1Aqu¹	Danzig's Dance	b 3 115	5	3	4¹	3²	3$1\frac{1}{2}$	3⁴	3⁷	Romero R P	a-.80
16Feb92 7Aqu³	Filch	3 115	2	6	6	5¹	4¹	4$1\frac{1}{2}$	4$4\frac{1}{2}$	Smith M E	a-.80
6Nov92 7Aqu³	Saratoga Fever	3 115	4	2	3½	4^{hd}	5$2\frac{1}{2}$	5⁷	5$13\frac{1}{2}$	Madrid A Jr	3.40
5Nov92 5Med¹	Bludan	3 117	1	5	1½	1^{hd}	6	6	6	Ferrer J C	9.10

a-Coupled: Danzig's Dance and Filch.

OFF AT 3:06 Start good, Won driving. Time, :23², :46², 1:11³, 1:37³ Track muddy.

$2 Mutuel Prices:

3-(C)-LORD CARDINAL	....	15.80	6.20	2.20
6-(G)-SCUDBUSTER	....		5.20	2.20
1-(F)-DANZIG'S DANCE (a-entry)	....			2.10

$2 EXACTA 3–6 PAID $71.00

B. c, by Deputy Minister—Katie Cochran, by Roberto. Trainer Reid Mark J. Bred by Ledyard Lewis C (Pa).

LORD CARDINAL, far back early, rapidly gained between horses on the turn, surged to the front in midstretch then edged clear under pressure. SCUDBUSTER, forced the early pace from outside, opened a clear advantage midway on the turn, relinquished the lead to the winner in midstretch then continued on well to best the others. DANZIG'S DANCE, rated just behind the early leaders while three wide, angled in entering the stretch and lacked a strong closing response. FILCH was never a serious threat. SARATOGA FEVER showed only brief speed. BLUDAN dueled along the rail for five furlongs and gave way.

Owners— 1, Barge Marc; 2, Joques Farm; 3, Green Beverly; 4, Perry William Haggin; 5, Jundt James R; 6, Bertolino Frank.

Trainers— 1, Reid Mark J; 2, Moschera Gasper S; 3, Mott William I; 4, Mott William I; 5, Lewis Lisa L; 6, Daniels Edward J Jr.

Trainer Reid was not discouraged by the wet track conditions because he had turned this horse around with the addition of blinkers for the October 15 winning race. Furthermore, the colt's breeding line clearly suggests a probable preference for wet footing. (More on breeding to come in Chapter 21.) This example illustrates some of the subtle relationships between claiming, allowance and restricted stakes in the Northeast, but the result also confirms that trainer Mark J. Reid has intimate expertise with the subtleties of racing in his region, where there are several tracks open simultaneously. To bet thoroughbreds for profit in the 1990s—not just for fun—horseplayers need be just as sharp, just as knowledgeable.

Speed Handicapping 101

In previous chapters I made a point of introducing the importance of time as it relates to class. At Charles Town, the cheapest $2,500 claiming race usually is run slower than the next step up the classification code. At Finger Lakes, open $10,000 claimers tend to run faster than lower-level allowance winners and the same is true for $30,000 claimers at Philadelphia Park. With minor variations, such orderly relationships between class and final race clockings tend to exist at every track in the country. Nevertheless, it is just as true that the official time of a race is worthless information by itself.

In order to make sense out of time, in order to make it a meaningful piece of information, the player must be able to answer four intriguing questions:

1. What is a good time or slow time for that distance and that class at that track?
2. How fast or slow was the racetrack the day the race was run? That is, to what extent must the time of the race be adjusted to compensate for the speed of the track itself?
3. To what extent, if any, is final time influenced by track bias, by fractional times, or by unusual pace tactics? And to what extent is it possible to detect a fluky time?
4. When is it most useful to know how fast the horse ran and under what conditions is time a waste of time?

Too many fans still fail to take these questions seriously. It's an understandable failing. Many well-respected trainers continue to regard time suspiciously. Some dismiss it completely and the same is true for numerous public handicappers who are too lazy to take the time to study time. Many rely strictly on the ready-made answers provided by track condition labels (fast, sloppy, wet-fast, good, muddy, heavy, or slow) or *DRF* speed ratings and Beyer figures that were first introduced in past performances by *The Racing Times* in April 1991. Some official track programs, i.e., *Post Parade*, the official track program at New York and Kentucky tracks, use Equibase-generated past performances and provide their own high-quality speed figures.

Convenient track condition labels, such as "fast" or "good," are not much help to players seeking to know the relative speed of the racing surface. A "fast" track, for instance, can have a wide range of speed conduciveness—from lightning fast to not very fast at all. A "good" track, which implies a drying-out racing surface, may be quite glib in spots and very tiring in others. While *DRF* speed ratings and track variants have been improved a bit for the 1990s, they still are based on serious inconsistencies that severely corrupt their utility.

Modern *DRF* speed ratings are based on comparisons with the best times recorded during the past three years instead of track records, which formerly were used as the basis for *DRF* speed ratings. Today, a horse earns 100 *DRF* speed-rating points by equaling the time standard

SANTA ANITA

	3-YEAR-TIME STANDARD	TRACK RECORDS
5½ furlongs	: 1:02	1:02
6 furlongs	: 1:07⅖	1:07⅕
6½ furlongs	: 1:14⅕	1:14
7 furlongs	: 1:20⅗	1:20
1 mile	: 1:34	1:33⅖
1¹⁄₁₆ miles	: 1:40⅘	1:39
1⅛ miles	: 1:46	1:45⅘
1¼ miles	: 1:59	1:57⅘
1½ miles	: 2:28⅗	2:27⅕

for the distance and one point is deducted for each ⅕ second slower than the time standard. Thus all horses racing at Santa Anita in 1993 earned their *DRF* speed ratings by comparisons to the standards listed on the chart. There are several things wrong with this method.

First, some time standards invariably are set on extremely fast racing days by moderately fast horses, others by exceptionally fast horses on "normal" fast tracks, and still others by the fastest horses in training on exceedingly glib tracks that may produce world-record clockings. Under such shifting circumstances, it will be more difficult for a horse to approach the time standard at one distance than another, which nullifies the value in using time standards as yardsticks to compare clockings at different distances.

The *DRF* method also insists that one length equals ⅕ second at all distances, at all rates of speed. Mathematically speaking, however, a length should equal ⅕ second only when a horse travels a furlong in 15 seconds. The only horses who go that slow charge 10 cents a ride. (According to several studies, including one performed by author Steve Carroll and another by Dr. John Fisher, a veterinarian in Pennsylvania, one length equals approximately 8.5–9 feet. A better adjustment might be six *DRF* points for every five lengths.)

While inconsistencies between time standards can be shown to exist at most racetracks, the error is compounded by *DRF track variants*, which purport to measure the relative speed of the racetrack.

These variants are computed separately by averaging the winning speed ratings earned for sprints, routes or different track conditions as they occur on a single day. If weather remains constant and all races are

Tabasco Cat
Own: Overbrook Farm & Reynolds D P

Ch. c. 3 (Apr)
Sire: Storm Cat (Storm Bird)
Dam: Barbicue Sauce (Sauce Boat)
Br: Overbrook Farm & Reynolds David (Ky)
Tr: Lukas D Wayne (13 1 0 2 .08)

Lifetime Record :	10	5	1	1	$483,037						
1994	4	2	1	0	$299,700	Turf	0	0	0	0	
1993	6	3	0	1	$183,337	Wet	2	1	0	0	$18,000
CD	1	0	0	0		Dist	1	1	0	0	$14,100

7May94-8CD	sly	$1\frac{1}{4}$	$:47^1$	$1:11^4$	$1:37^3$	$2:03^3$	Ky Derby-G1	99	9	4	$4^{2\frac{1}{2}}$	$5^{4\frac{1}{2}}$	$7^{6\frac{1}{4}}$	6^9	Day P	L	126 b	6.10	85–06	Go For Gin126^2 Strodes Creek$126^{2\frac{1}{2}}$ Blumin Affair$126^{\frac{3}{4}}$		14
Bothered start, gave way																						
9Apr94-5SA	fst	$1\frac{1}{8}$	$:45^2$	$1:10^2$	$1:35^3$	$1:48^1$	SA Derby-G1	104	1	2	$2^{4\frac{1}{2}}$	2^1	1^{hd}	$2^{\frac{3}{4}}$	Day P	LB	122 b	2.50	91–16	Brocco$122^{\frac{3}{4}}$ Tabasco Cat122^1 Strodes Creek122^5	Game try	6
6Mar94-4SA	fst	1	$:22^3$	$:45^4$	$1:10^4$	$1:36^1$	San Rafael-G2	102	1	1	1^{hd}	1^{hd}	$1^{\frac{1}{2}}$	1^1	Day P	LB	121 b	1.90	88–18	Tabasco Cat121^1 Powis Castle115^{18} Shepherd's Field121^3	Game inside	5
22Jan94-3BM	fst	$1\frac{1}{16}$	$:23^1$	:47	$1:11^3$	$1:42^3$	El Cm Rl Dy-G3	90	7	3	$3^{1\frac{1}{2}}$	3^1	1^{hd}	1^1	Day P	LB	113 b	2.30	90–13	Tabasco Cat113^1 Flying Sensation115^6 Robannier115^{nk}	Wide, hard drive	7
6Nov93-6SA	fst	$1\frac{1}{16}$	$:22^3$	$:46^2$	$1:10^4$	$1:42^4$	B C Juvnle-G1	86	4	3	3^3	$4^{3\frac{1}{2}}$	$6^{4\frac{1}{4}}$	$3^{6\frac{1}{2}}$	Day P	LB	122 b	33.30	83–10	Brocco122^5 Blumin Affair$122^{1\frac{1}{2}}$ Tabasco Cat122^3	Best of rest	11
15Oct93-8Kee	fst	7f	$:22^2$	$:45^1$	$1:09^4$	$1:21^4$	Ft Sprngs47k	84	3	3	2^{hd}	1^{hd}	2^{hd}	1^{nk}	Day P	L	118 b	*.80	92–04	Tabasco Cat118^{nk} Golden Gear116^7 Sir Cognac110^1	Driving, gamely	6
19Sep93-7Bel	my	1	$:22^3$	:46	$1:11^1$	$1:37^3$	Alw 30000N1X	78	4	3	3^2	$2^{1\frac{1}{2}}$	$1^{\frac{1}{2}}$	1^{nk}	Migliore R		117 b	*2.30	80–16	Tabasco Cat117^{nk} Amathos117^4 Linkatariat117^3	Driving	7
28Aug93-5Sar	fst	6f	$:22^2$	$:45^3$	$:58^1$	$1:10^4$	Md Sp Wt	79	5	3	$2^{1\frac{1}{2}}$	3^{nk}	2^1	$1^{1\frac{1}{2}}$	Migliore R		118 b	4.10	88–14	Tabasco Cat$118^{1\frac{1}{2}}$ Magic Caver$118^{2\frac{1}{2}}$ Pauliano$118^{2\frac{1}{2}}$	Checked 1/4, driving	9
7Aug93-5Sar	gd	5f	$:21^3$	:45		$:57^3$	Md Sp Wt	69	8	8	5^7	$4^{4\frac{1}{2}}$	$5^{3\frac{1}{2}}$	$4^{2\frac{3}{4}}$	Migliore R		118	19.30	92–08	Upping The Ante$118^{\frac{1}{2}}$ Youthful Legs118^{nk} Frisco Gold118^2		10
Stumbled, checked break, wide																						
19Jly93-3Bel	gd	$5\frac{1}{2}$f	$:22^1$	$:45^4$	$:58^1$	$1:04^3$	Md Sp Wt	42	8	8	5^5	$5^{4\frac{1}{2}}$	8^9	$7^{15\frac{1}{4}}$	Bailey J D		118	12.90	77–13	Whitney Tower$118^{3\frac{1}{2}}$ End Sweep$118^{\frac{3}{4}}$ Gold Tower118^3	Broke slowly	8

WORKOUTS: May 2 CD 6f fst 1:15 B *4/6*

sprints, there will be only one track variant. If there are three route races, three sprints plus three turf races, there will be three separate variants assigned to that day. If the track turns sloppy midday, there will be two sets of *DRF* track variants.

For a simple example, the average winning-speed ratings for all route races run at Churchill Downs on Kentucky Derby Day, 1994, was only 1⅕ seconds, or six variant points slower than the appropriate time standards. So Tabasco Cat, who ran three seconds or 15 points slower than Sea Hero's 2:02⅖ time standard set in 1993, earned a *DRF* speed rating of 85 and a track variant of 06, which is represented in the form as 85–06. (Using the old method of *DRF* speed ratings, Tabasco Cat's clocking of 2:05⅖ would have been compared to Secretariat's track record clocking of 1:59⅖, for a *DRF* speed rating of 70, while the variant for the day would have been significantly larger.)

Sea Hero's time standard of	2:02⅖	=	100 *DRF* speed rating
Tabasco Cat's clocking of	2:05⅖	=	85 *DRF* speed rating

I do wish to discourage horseplayers from using *DRF* track variants in conjunction with *DRF* speed figures for horse-by-horse comparisons. In Tabasco Cat's case, the 85–06 produced a combined Derby number of 91, which supposedly was a better rating than a horse who earned a combined 90 or lower on another day. Sorry, but if you insist on believing that, you might as well give your money away before entering the track.

DRF track variants fail because Saturday, Sunday and holiday racing cards tend to offer generally faster competition than weekday racing cards. This automatically gives the illusion of a faster racing strip when faster horses probably are responsible for the smaller track variant.

Derby Day 1994 at Churchill Downs was such a day, when several stakes races produced a small *DRF* track variant. On a similar strip the following Thursday, the *DRF* variant was 13, or 1⅖ seconds slower than Derby Day, when the only substantive difference was the quality of the races being run. Thus any horse who earned a raw *DRF* speed rating on Thursday was destined to receive an inflated, combined *DRF* speed rating-track variant of 104, compared to Tabasco Cat's 101.

For 20 years these flaws have muted the value of *DRF* track variants, yet they show up in the majority of computer handicapping programs and in the works of several otherwise reputable pace handicappers who, despite their desire for accurate pace and speed numbers, are willing to accept a built-in error factor that is beyond any rational defense.

DRF track variants do have one redeeming value—they offer a sliver of insight to players seeking an inexact, quick read while casually visiting strange, unfamiliar racetracks. Consider the following:

- Except for days featuring several stakes, any variant under 10 implies a very fast racing surface, including frozen strips during the winter, or rain-soaked "sealed" strips that play lightning fast. Imagine a packed-down beach near the ocean's edge, or a paved highway with a thin water covering.
- Variants in the midteens-to-low 20s represent the majority of track conditions, including tracks frequently mislabeled as good. Unfortunately, the range of speed conduciveness is too wide for practical use.
- Variants of 30 and above suggest relatively slow tracks, regardless of their official track condition labels.
- Variants in the high 30s and 40s hint at very slow, very deep tracks, perhaps deep, sticky mud, or hazardous conditions.

As many players realize, it is possible to win at the races without paying attention to time; there are other windows to look through, other methods to determine which horse is most likely to prevail. But the availability of Beyer speed figures in contemporary *DRF* past performances gives players a powerful tool to evaluate every performance in each horse's career. Beyer figures, which are the inspired creation of my good friend Andy Beyer, facilitate horse-by-horse comparisons between different distances and different tracks.

E = MC²

Beyer speed figures actually were the original creation of Sheldon Kovitz, a math wiz at Harvard in the 1960s who divided his time between classes, trips to the track, and the nearest IBM computer. I never met Kovitz, but my good friend Andy Beyer learned the method firsthand and refined it for practical use ten years later.

In their present form, Beyer speed figures have evolved past the stage where players have to bury themselves in reems of result charts to determine the logical relationship between clockings at all distances for every type of race at one or more tracks. The work already is done for players who consult Beyer figures in *Daily Racing Form*, or have access to other competent figures via the Bloodstock Research Information Services computer system, or various weekly newsletters such as Ron Cox's excellent *Northern California Track Record*, Bob Selvin and Jeff Siegel's *Handicapper's Report in Southern California*, the West Coast's popular *Racing Digest*, *Post Parade* in the East, or the Len Ragozin "*Sheets*" and Jerry Brown's *Thorograph* numbers, which are sold at several tracks. All provide useful figures for players willing to spend the extra money *and* learn how to interpret them. Yet the player who chooses to develop figures privately will gain deep insights into the races being run at his or her track, and will have a significant "insider's edge" over those who rely on the work of others. At the very least, learning how to create good speed figures is as useful as learning how to perform basic mathematical calculations before deferring all multiplication to a calculator.

Making speed figures begins with a two-step research project that will do a great deal to broaden your understanding of the how's and why's of racing in your area. And if you're as crazy about handicapping as I am you might even love the work involved. Otherwise the following material is offered to provide insight into the mechanics behind the Beyer figures and how they are lined up for different distances and different tracks.

STEP 1: Using a complete set of result charts from the previous meeting, compile a list of all final times recorded on "fast" racetracks at every class level and distance. If back copies of the *Form* are unavailable, or too expensive to consider, a trip to the nearest library file of daily local newspapers will suffice. *Daily Racing Form* chart books, available in microfiche, are another alternative.

For the purpose of this research project you are not concerned with anything but age, sex, class of race, distance, and fast-track final times. But for dependable results you should study a minimum of fifteen races at each class and distance. Obviously, the more races you use to work up the data, the more reliable the data will be.

STEP 2: Obtain the *average* winning time for each class and distance.

Logically, to determine a good time for a six-furlong, $20,000 claiming race, you must determine the *average* time for that class and distance. These averages then will serve as the par, or standard, for each class and distance. The following is a sample of six-furlong average times for New York tracks.

3-YEAR-OLDS AND UP	
Grade 1 stakes	1:09⅗
Grade 3 stakes	1:10
Top class allowance races	1:10⅕
Allowance nonwinners of a race other than maiden or claiming	1:10⅘
$40,000 claiming	1:10⅘
$25,000 claiming	1:11
Maiden special weights	1:11⅕
$15,000 claiming	1:11⅕

Here are representative clockings for $10,000 claimers at Calder racetrack in Florida and Turf Paradise in Arizona. Calder is a relatively slow track, while Turf Paradise is one of the fastest tracks in the country.

$10,000 CLAIMERS AT CALDER AND TURF PARADISE		
	6 FURLS.	1 MI.
Turf Paradise:	1:08⅘	1:35⅕
Calder:	1:12⅖	1:40⅘

While such (class par) research is the first step toward developing a workable time chart to compare clockings at all distances, such a chart must reflect two fundamental realities:

1. There is a mathematical relationship between one distance and another.
2. It takes more effort for a horse to sustain a rate of speed at longer distances. In other words, horses slow down naturally as distances lengthen.

These two principles are fundamental to all computations involving the overall speed of a race and to the pace of the race as well. Consider this:

Horses who travel six furlongs in 1:12.00 on a fast, neutral racing surface probably could compete against $8,000 claiming company. But horses capable of tacking on another 24-second quarter mile to go a full mile in 1:36 would fit in nicely with allowance or stakes horses, and horses who could add a fifth quarter at the same 24-second rate would reach 1¼ miles in 2:00 flat. That clocking would win the majority of the Grade 1 stakes run at that distance every season. Adding another 24 seconds would merely equal Secretariat's 2:24 clocking for 1½ miles, which broke Gallant Man's 16-year-old track mark by an amazing 2⅗ seconds and established a world record for a dirt performance that has remained on the books for two decades.

Several top-notch speed-figure handicappers, including Steve Crist, former editor of the *Racing Times,* use Secretariat's Belmont as the top-of-the-line number in their speed-figure charts. On Beyer's chart it ranks as a 138, the highest figure of his handicapping career. As stated in Chapter 1, Secretariat remains a standard to measure the rest of the horse kingdom against.

While pace will be discussed in some detail, a chart purporting to measure speed at different distances must be pegged at clockings that take into account the natural rate of deceleration for racehorses attempting longer distances. This can only be accomplished by comparing extensive tabulations of clockings at each distance. For example, below are average winning times at several distances for $25,000 claimers at Santa Anita Park.

$25,000 CLAIMING AT SANTA ANITA PARK

6 FURLS.	6½ FURLS.	7 FURLS.	1 MI.	1⅛ MI.
1:10	1:16⅖	1:22⅖	1:37	1:50⅖

NOTE: *As a concession to recent improvements in teletiming equipment, all clockings in this book will be expressed in hundredths of a second from this point forward. The equivalent in familiar ⅕ths is obvious, i.e., ⅕ second = .20 seconds; ⅖ = .40; ⅗ = .60 seconds and so on. Players seeking greater accuracy may round off clockings to the nearest .10 where clockings in hundredths are provided, or where interpolation serves a useful purpose.*

After computing speed figures for dozens of tracks through 2½ decades, Andy Beyer developed a parallel time chart that serves as a basic model for many American racetracks. Andy graciously has made available much of his research through the years, including his theoretical time charts for one-turn and two-turn distances.

To the best of my knowledge, Kovitz and Beyer were the first to insist on a truly parallel time chart, one in which the value of each ⅕ second is proportionately greater at shorter distances. All previous charts, including those published by revered authors and legendary experts included fundamental mathematical errors that no doubt contributed to the widespread skepticism about time as a valid handicapping tool.

The theoretical charts in this book also serve as correct parallel time charts for Aqueduct's main dirt oval, which features a one-turn mile

SAMPLE THEORETICAL TIME CHART FOR ONE-TURN RACES

BASIC BEYER FIG.	5 FURLS.	5½	6 FURLS.	6½	7 FURLS.	1 MILE
127:	56.20	1:02.40	1:08.60	1:14.80	1:21.00	1:33.80
124:	56.40	1:02.60	1:08.80	1:15.00	1:21.40	1:34.00
117:	56.80	1:03.00	1:09.40	1:15.60	1:22.00	1:34.60
113:	57.00	1:03.40	1:09.60	1:15.80	1:22.20	1:35.00
110:	57.20	1:03.40	1:09.80	1:16.20	1:22.40	1:35.40
109:	57.20	1:03.40	1:09.80	1:16.20	1:22.50	1:35.50
108:	57.30	1:03.60	1:09.90	1:16.30	1:22.60	1:35.60
107:	57.40	1:03.70	1:10.00	1:16.40	1:22.70	1:35.70
106:	57.40	1:03.80	1:10:00	1:16.40	1:22.80	1:35.80
96:	58.00	1:04.40	1:10.80	1:17.20	1:23.60	1:36.60
79:	59.00	1:05.40	1:12.00	1:18.60	1:25.20	1:38.40
62:	1:00.00	1:06.60	1:13.20	1:19.80	1:26.60	1:40.00
45:	1:01.00	1:07.80	1:14.40	1:21.20	1:28.00	1:41.60

NOTE: *An example of using ¹⁄₁₀ths is given for 106–110 Beyer speed-figure points on the one-turn chart above and the two-turn chart on page 121. More extensive one- and two-turn time charts are in Appendix B.*

race plus two-turn races at 1⅛ miles and longer. Interpolation can be used to expand any chart in this book for all clockings.

Beyer suggests using the above chart for all tracks unless there are peculiarities that must be accommodated. I agree. Tampa Bay Downs, for instance, features a seven-furlong race that begins from an angled chute on the clubhouse turn. On my parallel time chart for Tampa, I add about .60 (³⁄₅) seconds to the seven-furlong clockings on the parallel time chart to keep it in line with the six-furlong clockings.

When figures are being made for a faster track such as Santa Anita, the relationships between distances essentially remain intact, but the extra speed of the racing surface will show up in the daily track variants. In Santa Anita's case the average variant will be about 14 points faster than Aqueduct for one-turn races when each track is playing relatively normal.

For two-turn races, Beyer also uses a theoretical chart, and some minor internal adjustments may be more common between distances due to the variations in size, or the position of the starting gate relative to the first turn and other technical factors.

SAMPLE THEORETICAL TIME CHART FOR TWO-TURN RACES

BASIC BEYER FIG.	1 MILE	1 MI, 70 YDS	1¹⁄₁₆MI	1⅛	1³⁄₁₆	1¼
133:	1:34.00	1:38.20	1:40.40	1:46.80	1:53.20	1:59.80
126:	1:34.60	1:38.80	1:41.20	1:47.60	1:54.00	2:00.60
122:	1:35.00	1:39.20	1:41.60	1:48.00	1:54.40	2:01.00
112:	1:36.00	1:40.20	1:42.60	1:49.20	1:55.60	2:02.20
108:	1:36.40	1:40.60	1:43.00	1:49.60	1:56.00	2:02.60
107:	1:36.50	1:40.70	1:43.10	1:49.70	1:56.20	2:02.80
106:	1:36.60	1:40.80	1:43.20	1:49.80	1:56.40	2:03.00
101:	1:37.00	1:41.40	1:43.80	1:50.40	1:57.00	2.03.80
92:	1:38.00	1:42.20	1:44.00	1:51.40	1:58.20	2:05.00
86:	1:38.60	1:42.80	1:45.20	1:52.00	1:58.80	2:05.60
85:	1:38.60	1:43.00	1:45.40	1:52.20	1:59.00	2:05.80
71:	1:40.00	1:44.40	1:46.80	1:53.60	2:00.40	2:07.40
51:	1:42.00	1:46.40	1:49.00	1:56.00	2:03.20	2:10.40

Most often the only adjustment needed will be to align the point values of the two-turn races with the point values on the one-turn chart. Santa Anita, for instance, requires a two-turn adjustment of plus five points to each clocking on the two-turn chart. (The Aqueduct inner track requires a six-point adjustment.) Making this adjustment will ensure that a raw rating of 100 will mean the same thing at any distance at Santa Anita.

The chart below carries out a time comparison between one- and two-turn distances at Santa Anita, Aqueduct and Belmont Park. The 1⅛-mile distance at Belmont is a one-turn race (Belmont is 1½ miles in circumference). Point values for this 1⅛-mile race were generated by class par research and by proportionately extending the theoretical one-turn chart an extra furlong. All clockings on the chart below are roughly equal to a net Beyer-style fig of 92 on a track with a zero track variant.

92 BEYER-STYLE FIGURES—AQUEDUCT AND SANTA ANITA

	SIX FURLS.	ONE-TURN MILE	TWO-TURN MILE	ONE-TURN 1⅛ MILE (BELMONT)	TWO-TURN 1⅛ MILE
S.A.	1.10.00		1:37.00		1:50.40
N.Y.	1:11.00	1:37.00		1:50.20	1:51.40

While it may be necessary to compile average clockings for at least three of the most popular race classes to set up an accurate parallel time chart for a difficult track, it is entirely possible to invoke a shortcut method for tracks that do not feature unusual configurations. Indeed, it is quite possible to make an accurate parallel time chart on the basis of a *single day's* worth of races.

At Canterbury Downs in 1985, for instance, I was able to use the first race on the inaugural racing card in June 1985 to set up a perfectly workable parallel time chart. The process may prove instructive:

The race winner, Faiz, completed a $6,250 claiming race at one mile in 1:39.00, yet seemed a perfectly representative $10,000 horse, so I assigned the race a Beyer figure of 80, my rating for $10,000 midwestern claimers at the time. From this "par," a logic-based two-turn chart was possible using 1:39.00 as a starting point. While monitoring the effectiveness of this chart, several horses, including Faiz, came back from that first race to run representative races at $10,000. This substantiated Faiz's original figure *and* my original assumptions.

SHORTCUT METHOD TO CONSTRUCT A PARALLEL TIME CHART

The shortcut method insists on finding a race that seems truly representative of a popular class and distance. This is not as difficult as it may seem, given stable weather and a few good races from which to choose. Once the par race is selected, plug in a numerical point value from the Beyer scale and begin extrapolating the point values and clockings up and down the theoretical time chart presented in this book. To line up the chart between one- and two-turn distances, at least one representative race must be chosen for one-turn sprints and two-turn routes at the same class level. (To double-check the legitimacy of this chart, repeat the same steps with one or two other "representative races" at other class levels.) Except for practical adjustments forced by unusual track geometry or other quirks, the shortcut time chart should require very little tinkering.

For the *DRF*, Beyer and associates compare figures on one circuit with figures on another to determine the matching points between specific classes, if any. In fact, Beyer's research in 1992 and 1993 led him to conclude that a fundamental tenet of speed-figure handicapping requires rethinking.

"Every major authority on speed figures, including myself, has asserted that the secret to making reasonable comparisons between figures on different circuits is to focus on the $10,000 claimer. The assumption has been that a $10,000 horse at Laurel is a $10,000 horse at Hollywood Park is a $10,000 horse at Arapahoe Park (in Colorado). But this is just not the case," he said. "Many tracks do match up, but to make really good comparisons between tracks you have to know where the $10,000 races are not equal to each other."

A computer program has been developed to track all shippers who race at selected tracks during the season. Additional computer programs analyze Beyer figures earned by each shipper at the new and former track. From these comparisons come adjustments to the data base.

"In 1993, a $10,000 claimer at Aqueduct earned about an 85 rating on our scale," Beyer said, "but an average $10,000 claimer at Detroit was getting a 73" (about five lengths slower).

On the following page are the class pars for New York and southern California tracks.

Due to maturation factors, it is important to adjust class pars for fillies and/or younger horses. A $32,000 claiming race for three-year-olds at six furlongs in February invariably is a much weaker race than a $32,000 claimer for four-year-olds and up on the same day. By mid-December the differences between these two races will narrow considerably.

NEW YORK CLASS PARS

109 = Grade 1 stakes

106 = Grade 2 stakes

103 = Grade 3 stakes

101 = Allowance nonwinners of three races other than maiden or claiming

 99 = Allowance nonwinners of two races other than maiden or claiming

 98 = $60,000 claiming

 96 = $50,000 claiming

 95 = Allowance nonwinners of a race other than maiden or claiming

 94 = $35,000 claiming

 92 = $25,000 claiming

 90 = Maiden special weight; June–October

 88 = Maiden special weight; April, May, November and December

 87 = $15,000 claiming

 85 = $10,000 claiming

 80 = Maiden special weight; winter racing on inner track

 75 = New York-bred maiden special weight

 69 = $30,000 maiden claiming

SOUTHERN CALIFORNIA CLASS PARS

109 = Grade 1 (123 theoretical figure, less 14 points for one-turn sprints)
        (118 theoretical figure, less 9 points for two-turn routes)

107 = Grade 2 stakes

104 = Grade 3 stakes

102 = Allowance nonwinners of three races other than maiden or claiming

100 = Allowance nonwinners of two other than maiden or claiming

100 = $80,000 claiming

 97 = Allowance nonwinners other than maiden or claiming

 96 = $50,000 claiming

 95 = $35,000 claiming

 91 = $25,000 claiming

 90 = Maiden special weight

 88 = $15,000 claiming

 85 = $10,000 claiming

 79 = $50,000 maiden claiming

 72 = $32,000 maiden claiming

By my calculations, races for fillies generally are about eight points slower on the Beyer scale compared to male races at the same class, except for Graded stakes, which only get a 5-point adjustment.

All speed-figure handicappers seem to have slight variations in the adjustments they make for age and sex; the adjustments I use are displayed below.

- Races for fillies and mares deduct:
    8 points from par, 5 for Graded stakes
- Races for two-year-olds, no pars until June
- Races for two-year-old maiden special weights (nonclaiming), deduct:
    12 for June
    10 for July
    8 for August in sprints, 10 at 1-mile or longer (routes)
    5 for September in sprints, 8 for routes
    2 for October–December in sprints, 4 for routes

For all other maiden special weight races deduct for fillies, not age. (Some allowance races for two-year-olds in the summer and fall and some allowance races for three-year-olds in the spring will have lower pars than maiden special weight races, which attract the best-bred youngsters on the grounds.)

For claimers, allowances and stakes, deduct according to the charts below.

SPRINTS

AGE	JAN	FEB	MAR	APR	MAY	JUN	JUL	AUG	SEPT	OCT	NOV	DEC
2	—	—	—	—	—	(22)	(18)	(14)	(12)	(12)	(10)	(10)
3	(8)	(8)	(8)	(6)	(6)	(6)	(4)	(4)	(4)	(3)	(3)	(3)
4	(2)	(2)	(2)	(2)								

ROUTES

AGE	JAN	FEB	MAR	APR	MAY	JUN	JUL	AUG	SEPT	OCT	NOV	DEC
2	—	—	—	—	—	(22)	(18)	(18)	(14)	(14)	(12)	(12)
3	(10)	(10)	(10)	(8)	(8)	(8)	(6)	(6)	(6)	(4)	(4)	(4)
4	(2)	(2)	(2)	(2)								

For convenience, the Kovitz-Beyer rating system also assigns the appropriate number of points for each ⅕th second at every distance and each beaten length.

Logically, ⅕ of a second is going to be worth relatively more in a five-furlong race than a 1⅛-mile race. To illustrate, consider that a human athlete who regularly runs one second slower than the world record for 100 meters might struggle to win a college track meet, while another, running one or two seconds slower than the world record for 1,500 meters, would be a serious gold medal threat in the Olympic games. In these cases, the identical one-second differential was far more meaningful at 100 meters than 1,500. Thus, ⅕ second is more meaningful at shorter distances. The following table portrays the average numerical values for ⅕ second at common thoroughbred distances.

⅕ SECONDS: ONE-TURN RACES

5 FURLS.	5½	6 FURLS.	6½	7 FURLS.	1 MI
3.4	3.2	2.75	2.5	2.3	2.0

⅕ SECONDS: TWO-TURN RACES

1 MI	1 MI, 70 YDS	1¹⁄₁₆ MI	1⅕	1³⁄₁₆	1¼
2.0	2.0	1.8	1.6	1.6	1.5

As previously stated, the value of *one length* is incorrectly assumed to be ⅕ second in the *Daily Racing Form* and by most horsemen and horseplayers. Why some veteran speed handicappers who know better continue to use the *DRF* variants and old formulas for beaten lengths and ⅕ths of a second is beyond explanation. At the very least, a beaten-lengths chart similar to the one used for adjusting Beyer figures will improve all calculations.

In making figures for turf races, the theoretical time chart will be of little use due to the practice of moving the inner rail to protect the grass from overuse. Wide variations in the downhill pitch used for infield chutes to accommodate 1¹⁄₁₆- and 1⅛-mile races and variations in tighter, steeper-banked turns also affect relationships between clockings. Another problem is the wide range of "run up" distances from starting gate to the electronic starting beam used for each different distance on the same turf course. I commend fellow author Jim Quinn for

BEATEN LENGTHS	5F	5½F	6F	6½F	7F	7½F	1 MILE	1¹⁄₁₆M	1⅛M	1¼M	1½M
NS	1	1	1	1	1	1	0	0	0	0	0
NK	1	1	1	1	1	1	0	0	0	0	0
HD	1	1	1	1	1	1	0	0	0	0	0
¼	1	1	1	1	1	1	0	0	0	0	0
½	1	1	1	1	1	1	1	1	1	1	1
¾	2	2	2	2	2	2	1	1	1	1	1
1	3	3	2	2	2	2	2	2	2	2	1
1¼	4	4	3	3	3	3	2	2	2	2	1
1½	4	4	4	4	3	3	3	3	2	2	2
1¾	5	5	4	4	4	4	3	3	3	3	2
2	6	6	5	5	4	4	4	3	3	3	2
2¼	7	7	6	6	5	5	4	4	4	4	3
2½	7	7	6	6	5	5	4	4	4	4	3
2¾	8	8	7	7	6	6	5	5	5	4	3
3	9	8	7	7	6	6	5	5	5	4	3
3¼	9	9	8	8	7	7	6	5	5	5	4
3½	10	10	9	8	7	7	6	6	6	5	4
3¾	11	10	9	9	8	8	7	6	6	5	4
4	12	11	10	9	8	8	7	7	6	6	5
4¼	12	11	10	10	9	9	8	7	7	6	5
4½	13	12	11	10	9	9	8	8	7	6	5
4¾	14	13	11	11	10	10	9	8	8	7	5
5	15	14	12	11	10	10	9	8	8	7	6
5¼	15	14	12	11	10	10	9	8	8	7	6
5½	16	15	13	12	11	11	10	9	9	8	6
5¾	17	16	14	13	11	11	10	9	9	8	6
6	18	17	15	14	12	12	11	10	9	8	7
6¼	18	17	15	14	12	12	11	10	9	8	7
6½	19	18	16	15	13	13	12	11	10	9	8
6¾	19	18	16	15	13	13	12	11	10	9	8
7	20	19	17	16	14	14	13	12	11	10	8
7¼	21	19	17	16	14	14	13	12	11	10	8
7½	22	20	18	17	15	14	13	13	12	11	9
7¾	22	21	19	18	16	15	13	13	12	11	9
8	23	22	20	19	17	16	14	13	13	12	10
9	26	24	22	21	19	18	16	15	14	13	11
10	29	27	24	22	20	19	18	17	17	15	12
11	32	30	27	25	23	22	20	18	18	16	13
12	35	32	29	27	25	23	21	20	20	17	14
13	38	35	32	30	27	25	23	22	22	19	15
14	41	38	34	32	29	27	25	23	23	20	16
15	44	41	37	34	31	29	27	25	25	21	17
16	47	43	39	36	33	31	29	27	27	23	18

laboriously working through the steps in his *Figure Handicapping*, published in 1993 to establish basic relationships between sprints and two-turn distances at 28 different turf courses, but I am not sure all the relationships are the same when the rails are moved from one day to the next.

I have done similar research for only a handful of tracks and concluded that different relationships do exist for *every* position of the inner rail *and* for different conditions of the course. Severe time differences may occur between firm and soft footing not adequately factored out by loosely configured course variants. Errors are inevitable unless you are on the scene to note all nuances. For these reasons, Beyer's *DRF* speed figures on turf seem necessarily weaker than his main track figures. Certainly they seem a bit lower than reasonable for top-grade stakes horses and a bit high for very cheap races and slow horses at tracks where I have computed my own turf figures. With this background it is gratifying to note that Andy's own research forced him to switch in mid-1993 to a slightly different parallel time chart for turf routes, as well as slightly altered values for beaten lengths to accommodate the different pace structure of these races.* In other words, independent research by Quinn, Beyer and myself leads to an inescapable conclusion: Each turf course must be mapped according to the specific design characteristics of each layout, and further adjustments must be made to deal with pace issues peculiar to turf routes.

Facing reality, handicappers attempting turf speed figures will be forced to deal with a high percentage of inaccurate clockings. Some players will resort to their own clockings via hand-held timing devices that may solve some problems while introducing more human error. All time-based rating systems for turf races are further hampered by so few races to compare on a single racing card. (Some players use two or three days lumped together if conditions remain the same.)

Another inescapable conclusion: Turf figures are less reliable on grass; they may help isolate probable contenders, but are often too im-

---

*In an interesting concession to the need to adjust his turf-racing figures, Beyer announced through his partner Mark Hopkins' *DRF* column in July 1993 that the 6½-furlong beaten-length adjustment is now being used for all turf races at one mile or longer. This adjustment approximates my own approach to turf routes, which always has been to regard a ½-length margin at the finish to be as significant as a full length on dirt, and five lengths to be the signature of a complete breakdown in the pace mechanics of the race or the stamp of a total runaway. More on turf racing to follow in Chapters 20, 21, and Appendix C.

precise to be trusted for fine-line separation of contenders. Even speed-figure handicapping's staunchest devotees have begun to conclude that other tools will prove more useful, including rough use of final fractional splits to determine the strongest finisher—an important consideration in most turf races. A sampling of turf courses relationships and turf racing pars at selected tracks can be found in Appendix B, where approximate standards for final fractional splits are offered along with many facets of pace calculations for all racing surfaces.

Back on dirt, any player may begin making reasonably accurate speed figures and track variants with a set of class pars, parallel time charts and a beaten-length chart. While many might simply prefer to use Beyer's excellent *DRF* numbers, I strongly urge interested players to compute their own figures from scratch for one full racing season before relying strictly on Beyer's—if ever. I assure you the effort will pay for itself in a cartload of exciting insights into racing at your track, as well as improve your ability to construct and implement various pace numbers, as will be detailed in later chapters. It also will lead directly to several lucrative plays each year when your private observations indicate subtle differences of opinion or mistakes by Beyer's team of experts.

Interested players are referred to Appendix B for step-by-step development of Beyer-style speed figures and additional support material. I strongly recommend Andy's beautifully written book, *Picking Winners*, which has been a fountainhead for speed-figure research for two decades. And if you wonder about the utility of speed figures in the handicapping equation, the next chapter should set your mind straight.

The Race Is to the Swift

When is time important? How potent is speed-figure handicapping? What about fractional times? Does "pace make the race," as so many handicappers believe?

It is rare that a horseplayer gets a chance to confront a major mystery of the racetrack puzzle. Being naturally bent toward such mysteries helps. I confess. I am always willing to put my most effective handicapping methods aside and experiment with new tools and test out new ideas.

It was in that spirit that I incorporated Andy Beyer's speed figures in my handicapping in 1972, and it was in the same spirit that I stopped using them in the second year of my handicapping broadcasts in 1974.

In the first season with the Beyer figures I had picked 176 spot-play winners from 310 picks (including 13 in a row and 20 out of 22 during one stretch) for a very satisfying 53 percent.

I had relied on an integrated handicapping approach, but as long as Andy's speed figures were available on a daily basis, I was never sure how much they contributed. I designed an informal test to find out.

For the first three months of the new season I continued using figures and made note of when they seemed to be the major reason for a selection. For the next three months I operated without using them at all. Andy thought I was nuts, but there was no question that the absence of speed figures forced a deeper review of trainer patterns and result charts to compensate. Fortunately, I managed to sustain my 50 percent win ratio at similar profit levels, which gave me enormous confidence, but after reviewing the data closely, I went back to using speed figures when results of previous use suggested their relevance.

While more scientific surveys still need to be conducted, my 1972 test under fire was so illuminating that I have used much of the guidance they provided ever since. Here are my current thoughts on this subject.

1. Speed figures, by definition, tell how fast the horse ran at a given racetrack at a given distance on a given day. They do not automatically tell how fast a horse *will* run, especially at a different distance. But the top speed-figure horse in the race does win approximately 30 percent of the time at a slight loss for every $2 wager. With no handicapping at all, speed figures produce as many winners as public favorites and at slightly better prices.

2. By computing the *par times* for each distance and class at your favorite track(s), the player will instantly know which claiming horses have been meeting better stock than allowance horses. For instance, the player will know at a glance whether a $20,000 or $30,000 claiming race is better than a restricted allowance race without having to consult any other fact. The player also will know what class of fillies is faster than colts and what class group is outperforming the established pars, which can lead to extraordinary play.

   At Golden Gate Fields in 1992–93, for example, the typical $25,000 claiming race for fillies and mares earned figures slightly slower than $12,500 male sprinters. Even more interesting and more lucrative, $10,000 claiming sprinters were a faster group than the horses competing at the $12,500 level. Anomalies like this regularly occur, yet the only way to detect them is by doing class par research and updating various categories periodically. I am sure you can imagine how many good bets at square prices were made when horses in good form stepped up from $10,000 to $12,500 at Golden Gate Fields in 1992.

3. When a horse is stepping up in claiming price, prior speed figures can be an important clue to its winning potential. If it has run fast enough in the past, the class raise probably is an illusion.

Big Quake — B. g. 4, by Be a Native—Velvet Champagne, by Prince of Reason
MEZA R Q (44 11 8 8 .25) — Br.—Smith James E (Cal)
Own.—Doyle Casey & Smith James E — Tr.—Doyle Casey (3 2 0 0 .67) — 115
Lifetime 15 4 1 4 $34,247 — 1993 1 1 0 0 $9,900 — 1992 12 3 1 4 $24,110 — Turf 3 0 1 0 $3,525 — Wet 1 1 0 0 $9,900

10Feb93- 4GG my 1 1/16 :474 1:122 1:442 Clm 20000 79 5 5 59 42 11 11 Belvoir V T LB 117 3.30 75–32 BigQuake1171TurkishLord115½GlIntGuy117 Rallied wide 6
26Dec92- 7BM fm 1 3/8 Ⓣ:471 1:382 2:18 3↑Hcp 12500s 77 3 8 818 85½ 46½ 23½ Meza R Q LB 114 15.50 95–01 Baltistan1163½ Big Quake1141 SaberSix118 Rallied wide 9
2Dec92- 2Hol fst 1 1/16 :47 1:111 1:43 Clm 12500 77 2 11 1110 75½ 52¼ 1no Solis A LB 115 6.50 86–15 BigQuke115noKingsridgeDrive1142½Frbet108 Wide rally 11
1Nov92- 1BM gd 1 1/8 :472 1:122 1:51 Hcp 12500s 77 2 6 616 68 35½ 32¼ Belvoir V T LB 115 4.90 79–19 Jon'sPrnc116nkCrprtPrft1142BgQk115 Rallied for wide 6
23Oct92-10BM fst 1 1/16 :461 1:112 1:432 Clm 8000 78 3 9 917 97¾ 32 15 Belvoir V T LB 117 4.70 82–22 BigQuake1175OutsideInfo1172TpsNBts117 Rallied wide 9
10Oct92-10BM fm *1 1/8 Ⓣ:48 1:124 1:473 Hcp 12500s 68 11 9 98¾ 95¾ 812 711½ Tohill K S LB 112 15.50 82–06 DbnrAstr1164½UndrcrStn122½BttlsWhrf115 Raced wide 11
18Sep92- 3BM fm 1 1/16 Ⓣ:473 1:123 1:451 Hcp 12500s 72 11 11 118¾1110 1011 43½ Tohill K S LB 112 78.20 80–16 SpcyNtiv117hdRomo'sRoylty1181½CshLgcy115 Far wide 11
7Sep92- 7BM fst 1 1/16 :483 1:13 1:434 Clm 12500 70 8 8 84¾ 64¼ 77¾ 57 Kaenel J L LB 117 11.90 73–21 ValidTry1171½SpacyNtive117½GenerlDmges119 Far wide 9
23Aug92- 7Fer fst 1 5/8 :484 2:091 2:464 3↑Hmbldt Cty H 71 5 7 41½ 32 42½ 33½ Peterson T L Bb 114 5.00 105 — RcingDy1153ClshOfIds-Ir116½BigQuk114 Saved ground 8
31Jly92-10SR fst 1 1/16 :481 1:124 1:434 Hcp 12500s 72 2 8 811 87 76½ 64¼ Tohill K S LB 113 30.40 84–13 UndrcovrSting115nkJoni'sPrinc116noArvd117 No threat 9
LATEST WORKOUTS Feb 25 GG 6f gd 1:173 H — Feb 7 GG 3f fst :382 H — ●Jan 29 GG 6f fst 1:133 H — Jan 11 GG 4f gd :501 H

Big Quake earned par figures for $15,000 three-year-olds in October, defeated Hollywood Park's $12,500 types in December, then took advantage of a weak group of $20,000 four-year-olds when he earned a similar speed figure at Golden Gate Fields in February.

4. When the average figures for one claiming class are competitive with the figures earned by allowance races for nonwinners of one or two races, winning plays may be made when multiple winning claimers "drop in class" to allowance races that do not contain any clearly superior stakes-type performers.

Fizzarene — Ch. f. 3(Mar), by Hold Your Peace—Lisa's Exploding, by Explodent
Br.—Hidden Point Farm Inc (Fla)
Own.—Rustlewood Farm Inc — Tr.—Alter Happy (4 1 1 0 .25) — 115
Lifetime 15 5 1 2 $51,170 — 1992 13 5 1 2 $51,170 — 1991 2 M 0 0 — Turf 5 0 0 1 $3,060 — Wet 2 2 0 0 $15,400

6Nov92- 9Crc gd 1 1/16 :482 1:134 1:482 3↑ⒻAlw 20300 69 3 7 611 48½ 46 46 Moore B G 115 *2.00 79–19 Althos112½HghstNt1173½AlwysNtt114 Failed to menace 7
6Nov92-Originally scheduled on turf
10Oct92- 8Crc fm 1 1/16 Ⓣ:484 1:12 1:423 ⒻHandicap 67 8 6 67 67 69¼ 414 Moore B G 110 7.70 73–13 Silent Greatness1163 TimelyKris1148Iowa110 Late rally 8
12Sep92- 7Crc fst 1 1/16 :484 1:141 1:48 3↑ⒻClm 37500 77 3 6 65 43¼ 21½ 11 Moore B G 110 *1.40 87–11 Fizzrene1101IronndSilvr1121BlnchBMin114 Drvg 7-wide 7
12Sep92-Originally scheduled on turf
9Aug92- 9Crc fst 1 1/16 :473 1:13 1:471 3↑ⒻAlw 16600 74 6 7 614 46½ 32 12 Moore B G 113 2.60 91–10 Fizzarene1132 Acty1132½ One Sea Miss111 Driving 6 wd 8
23Jly92-10Crc fst 1 1/8 :491 1:143 1:544 ⒻClm 25000 79 1 6 52¼ 21½ 11 11½ Moore B G 116 1.50 89–13 Fizzrene1161½Slew'sDel1161BlusningAuntiR.111 Driving 8
23Jly92-Originally scheduled on turf
3Jly92- 8Crc fm *1 1/16 Ⓣ 1:463 ⒻClm 40000 70 1 8 813 85 84¾ 55¼ Moore B G 116 7.10 74–18 TllGt116hdSssy'nProud1123½TwoStppinGrl105 No threat 8
5Jun92-10Crc sly 1 1/8 :483 1:134 1:552 ⒻClm 30000 78 9 8 87¼ 611 43½ 1¾ Moore B G 112 4.10 86–18 Fizzarene112¾Sendbrod116nkTeilGte116 Drvg, drifted in 9
5Jun92-Originally scheduled on turf
LATEST WORKOUTS Nov 20 Crc 4f sly :51 B (d) — ●Oct 28 Crc 5f fst 1:012 H — Oct 19 Crc 5f fst 1:014 H — Oct 1 Crc 5f fst 1:023 B

While the availability of Beyer speed figures in the *DRF* of the 1990s makes it more difficult to get generous payoffs on speed-figure standouts, I conducted a repeat test of the 1974 speed-figure experiment in 1992–93, while providing daily handicapping analysis at Bay Meadows for National Turf Phone Seminars in California. Results resolutely confirmed that a variety of hidden class dropdown maneuvers that rely on speed-figure support still produce flat bet profits. Here are two examples from other tracks.

Sauvage Isn't Home
Own: Poujol Al

Dk. b or br g. 2 (Mar)
Sire: Ariva (Riva Ridge)
Dam: Sauvage At Holme (Sauvage)
Br: Poujol Al (Tex)
Tr: Richard Earnest (38 2 1 1 .05)

112

Lifetime Record :	6	2	0	2	$12,260					
1994	6	2	0	2	$12,260	Turf	0	0	0	0
1993	0	M	0	0		Wet	0	0	0	0
TrM	2	1	0	0	$4,680	Dist	0	0	0	0

31Jly94- 2TrM	fst	5f	:223	:471		1:001	Alw 7500N2L	49	6	1	21	2hd	11	1½	White J R	117	5.40	86-20	Sauvage Isn't Home117½ Gemma's Top1151 FlyToRome115hd	Drove clear	6
26Jun94- 8TrM	fst	5½f	:222	:461	:591	1:06	Clm 20000N2L	48	2	5	52¾	54	43	52½	Acevedo D A	117 f	3.90	87-12	Doc's Buck117½ Lester Polyester120nk Borders Jewel117nk	Even try	7
15Jun94- 9Hou	fst	5f	:214	:461		:593	[S]Md 20000	49	6	1	11½	1hd	15	18½	Castillo F	118 f	5.10	— —	SauvageIsn'tHome1188½ Bobbi'sCndyMn118no TexsUprising1152½	Driving	11
4Jun94- 3Hou	fst	5f	:222	:463		1:00	[S]Md Sp Wt	35	2	1	1hd	21½	21½	34¼	Castillo F	118 f	3.80	— —	Loud Record1203¾ Glazed Over118½ Sauvage Isn't Home1182¾	Faded	9
24May94- 4Hou	fst	5f	:22	:454		:584	[S]Md Sp Wt	37	8	6	34½	33½	37½	310¾	Castillo F	118 f	28.20	— —	ThickWsted11510 SirKeystone118nk SuvgeIsn'tHome1181¾	Lacked late bid	8
30Apr94- 3Hou	gd	4½f	:223	:462		:523	[S]Md Sp Wt	32	6	3	54½		611	613½	Harris B B	118	21.70	— —	Martha's Pride1182½ Triple Elegance1181 Oliver And Company1184	Tired	12

WORKOUTS: Aug 17 TrM 3f fst :361 H 4/29 Aug 10 TrM 3f fst :414 H 34/35 Jly 26 TrM 3f fst :383 H 1/1 Jly 9 TrM 4f fst :513 Bg25/38 Jun 11 Hou 5f my 1:023 Hg2/9

Amberfax
JOCSON G J (—)
Own.—Ardboe Stable

B. g. 4, by Topsider—Amber News, by Ambernash
Br.—Moseley Mr-Mrs J B (Ky)
Tr.—McCarthy William E (—)

117

Lifetime 25 4 3 4 $54,477

1992	9	1	1	3	$21,115
1991	14	3	2	1	$33,362
Turf	15	3	1	3	$37,315
Wet	3	0	1	1	$5,572

24Oct92- 3Med	gd	170	[T]:452	1:101	1:411	3↑Alw 19000	86	1	6	67½	53	41¼	21	Jocson G J	Lb	116	9.00	89-10	Maston1111 Amberfax1161½ River Wolf116	Saved grd	8
14Oct92- 9Med	fm	1$\frac{1}{16}$	[T]:462	1:104	1:42	3↑Alw 19000	86	8	4	69½	55	4¾	33½	Jocson G J	Lb	116	25.10	89-15	Be Nimble1162¾ Rega116¾ Amberfax116	Fin well	8
4Oct92- 8Pha	yl	1$\frac{1}{16}$	(T):482	1:131	1:451	3↑Alw 19795	84	2	8	74¾	62¼	32	45¼	Jocson G J	Lb	118	8.30	80-22	FrozenReef1144½RobRoy116½RivrWolf116	Flattened out	11
5Sep92- 7Pha	fm	1$\frac{1}{16}$	(T):473	1:122	1:441	3↑Alw 16500	85	8	10	106½	42	2hd	1¾	Jocson G J	Lb	116	11.50	90-17	Amberfax116¾ SuperModest119¾FrozenReef113	Driving	10
28Aug92- 2Sar	fm	1⅜	[T]:481	1:384	2:171	3↑Clm 35000	85	6	8	63½	52¼	73	56	Nelson D	b	117	54.70	78-08	Pulrus1174½Venturist117hdImprsontor117	Flattened out	10
8Aug92- 2Sar	fm	1⅛	[T]:473	1:113	1:473	3↑Clm 45000	73	8	11	1111	119¼	119¾	1110¾	Nelson D	b	113	55.50	90 —	HighlndDvotion113½WildCtrct113nkIntllgntly117	Outrun	12
28Jun92- 3Pha	fm	1$\frac{1}{16}$	(T):472	1:121	1:44	3↑Alw 16500	77	1	2	23½	22	1hd	34	Jocson G J	Lb	116	6.80	87-10	Sunseth1223HerculePoirot-Fr1161Amberfx116	Steadied	8
10Jun92- 8Mth	gd	*1$\frac{1}{16}$	(T):492	1:134	1:46	+ 3↑Alw 18000	76	6	6	75¼	65	47	36	Jocson G J	Lb	117	16.60	72-19	ValFleuri-Fr1173Bartt-En1173Amberfx117	Fanned wide	8
29May92- 6Pha	fm	1⅛	(T):48	1:124	1:493	3↑Clm 25000	76	1	8	84	55	56½	56½	Jocson G J	Lb	116	6.40	89-04	Corinto-Ge1124½ Still Bullish112nk Wiz Jim116	Wide	12
24Nov91-10Pha	fst	1$\frac{1}{16}$	:484	1:134	1:453	3↑Alw 15500	50	4	9	94½	814	813	718½	Ryan K	Lb	112	12.80	62-29	ArlngtnHghts116¾Imprprt112noSptmbrStr112	No factor	9

LATEST WORKOUTS Nov 14 Pha 4f fst :493 B Nov 7 Pha 4f fst :51 B Sep 30 Pha 4f fst :51 B Sep 22 Pha 3f fst :371 B

5. When maiden graduates are entered in races against winners, their maiden winning speed figure often will indicate their suitability to the new class. Young, well-bred maiden grads are always eligible for significant improvement, but the best strategy is to downgrade maiden grads with subpar figures unless there is strong workout evidence to support significant improvement, or the trainer is a known ace with similar types. An important exception to this is when none of the winners in the allowance race have earned figures approaching par for the class themselves. Even so, play on a subpar maiden grad must be supported by a strong track bias or trainer data. Conversely, maiden grads who earned seemingly superior speed figures with a track bias-aided performance, or were able to coast on the lead in modest fractional splits, are unlikely to repeat their figure when stepped up to a race with proven winners.

It also is wise to discount figures earned by bottom-rock maiden claiming grads in their first outings with claiming winners *unless* they are facing horses who have repeatedly failed in the same class. An exception to this guideline is a bottom-rock maiden claiming winner from another, classier circuit, or one that recently earned his maiden claiming victory in his first start after shipping in from a classier circuit. With the victory behind them, these recent arrivals are likely to improve another notch, and many are simply better than the modest local winners they face in their second or third local races.

Crafty Johnny
Own: McVey & Morrison & Olivier
BAZE R A (595 146 100 80 .25) $25,000

Ch. g. 3 (May)
Sire: Crafty Prospector (Mr. Prospector)
Dam: Village Jazz (Stage Door Johnny)
Br: LaGrange-Chance Partnership (Ky)
Tr: Arterburn Lonnie (96 28 22 8 .29)

L 117

Lifetime Record:	3 2 0 0	$12,250			
1993	3 2 0 0	$12,250	Turf	0 0 0 0	
1992	0 M 0 0		Wet	1 1 0 0	$8,250
BM	2 2 0 0	$11,825	Dist	3 2 0 0	$12,250

12Dec93-3BM	my	6f	:22^1	:45^1	:57^2	1:10^2	Clm 20000	78	2	6	$1^{1\frac{1}{2}}$	$1^{1\frac{1}{2}}$	1^2	$1^{\frac{3}{4}}$	Baze R A	LB 115 b	4.00	84-20	Crafty Johnny115$^{\frac{3}{4}}$ Imua Keoki109^3 He Wanted More114^{hd}	Steady drive	8
19Nov93-2BM	fst	6f	:22^1	:45^2	:58	1:10^4	Md 12500	69	1	6	1^{hd}	1^{hd}	1^2	1^{hd}	Belvoir V T	B 118 b	*.90	82-13	Crafty Johnny118^{hd} Zoroastro118^6 Some Trooper118$^{3\frac{1}{2}}$	Hard drive	8
30Oct93-2SA	fst	6f	:21^1	:44^4	:58^1	1:11^2	Md 32000	48	5	5	1^{hd}	1^{hd}	$3^{\frac{1}{2}}$	$5^{7\frac{1}{4}}$	Stevens G L	B 118 b	7.20	73-12	Water Garden118^{no} Decidedly Friendly118$^{2\frac{3}{4}}$ Cajero118$^{2\frac{1}{2}}$	Inside duel	12

WORKOUTS: Jan 6 BM 3f fst :37^4 H *13/18* Dec 31 BM 6f fst 1:13^4 H *3/5* Dec 23 BM 6f fst 1:15^4 H *7/10* Dec 5 BM 6f fst 1:14^1 H *12/17* Nov 28 BM 4f fst :50 H *27/44* Nov 14 BM 3f fst :36^3 H *10/29*

6. Special attention should be given to horses who do improve sharply from a respectable maiden race victory to produce a significantly higher Beyer figure in their next outing. Such horses are likely to be the best horses on the grounds, if not Graded stakes winners.

Wekiva Springs
Own: Dizney Donald R

Gr. c. 3 (Mar)
Sire: Runaway Groom (Blushing Groom)
Dam: Jetting Angel (Tri Jet)
Br: Dizney Donald R (Fla)
Tr: Hess R B Jr (—)

0

Lifetime Record:	4 3 0 0	$84,400		
1994	2 2 0 0	$67,900	Turf	0 0 0 0
1993	2 1 0 0	$16,500	Wet	0 0 0 0
Sar	0 0 0 0		Dist	0 0 0 0

22Jan94-3SA	fst	$1\frac{1}{16}$	:23^4	:47^3	1:11	1:41^4	[R]S Catalina75k	94	5	4	$3^{1\frac{1}{2}}$	$2^{\frac{1}{2}}$	1^1	1^4	Desormeaux K J	LB 121	*.70	86-12	Wekiva Springs121^4 GraciousGhost116$^{\frac{3}{4}}$ DreamTrapp117$^{1\frac{1}{4}}$	Clear, driving	5
2Jan94-4SA	fst	$1\frac{1}{16}$	:23^3	:47^2	1:10^4	1:41	Alw 40000N1X	98	1	2	$2^{1\frac{1}{2}}$	2^1	1^{hd}	1^3	Desormeaux K J	LB 118	*1.70	90-10	Wekiva Springs118^3 Ferrara115$^{3\frac{1}{2}}$ Crowning Decision118^6	Rail trip	6
31Oct93-6SA	fst	$1\frac{1}{16}$	:22^3	:46^1	1:11^1	1:43^2	Md Sp Wt	90	5	5	$5^{2\frac{3}{4}}$	3^1	1^2	1^{11}	Desormeaux K J	LB 117	*1.00	87-15	WekivaSprings117^{11} CollectbleWine117$^{2\frac{3}{4}}$ Let'sBeCurious117^2	Much best	9
4Sep93-6Dmr	fst	6f	:22^1	:45^2	:57^2	1:09^4	Md Sp Wt	78	2	5	$6^{3\frac{1}{4}}$	6^5	$6^{4\frac{1}{4}}$	6^4	Desormeaux K J	LB 118	5.80	86-10	Shephrd'sFild118$^{\frac{1}{2}}$ [D]DrouillyRivr118^2 SmoothRunnr118^{nk}	5 Wide stretch	10

WORKOUTS: ●Jan 18 Hol 4f fst :48 H *1/21* Jan 12 Hol 5f fst 1:00^1 H *8/28* Dec 29 Hol 4f fst :50^2 H *14/20* ●Dec 23 Hol 7f fst 1:26^2 H *1/5* Dec 17 Hol 5f fst 1:00^1 H *2/44* Dec 11 Hol 5f fst 1:01^1 H *28/51*

7. The two-year-old graduate who earns a superior speed figure may not be overmatched in any company.

You And I
Own: Triumviri Stable

Dk. b or br c. 3 (Feb)
Sire: Kris S. (Roberto)
Dam: La Chaposa (Ups)
Br: Fabry W A & Johnson Jeffrey E (Fla)
Tr: Hough Stanley M (—)

0

Lifetime Record:	3 3 0 0	$101,280			
1994	1 1 0 0	$16,800	Turf	0 0 0 0	
1993	2 2 0 0	$84,480	Wet	2 2 0 0	$86,280
Sar	0 0 0 0		Dist	0 0 0 0	

11Jan94-6GP	sly	7f	:22^3	:46	1:10^4	1:23^3	Alw 24000N2X	94	5	1	2^{hd}	$2^{\frac{1}{2}}$	2^{hd}	1^{nk}	Bailey J D	117	*.40	85-20	You And I117^{nk} Pren De Ville110^{13} Crary117^2	Fully extended	6
20Oct93-8Aqu	sly	7f	:22^2	:45^2	1:09^4	1:22^3	Cowdin-G2	99	3	3	$1^{\frac{1}{2}}$	2^{hd}	$1^{1\frac{1}{2}}$	1^5	Perret C	122	*1.80	91-13	You And I122^5 Bermuda Cedar122^{11} Gulliviegold122^{hd}	Drew off	7
13Sep93-5Bel	fst	6f	:22^1	:45^4	:58^2	1:11	Md Sp Wt	93	11	2	2^{hd}	1^{hd}	1^1	$1^{1\frac{1}{2}}$	Perret C	118	1.60	85-23	You And I118$^{1\frac{1}{2}}$ Palance118$^{1\frac{1}{4}}$ Hussonet118$^{2\frac{3}{4}}$	Driving	11

WORKOUTS: ●Jan 25 GP 5f fst :59 H *1/14* Jan 20 GP 4f fst :48^2 H *11/67* ●Jan 3 GP 5f gd :59 H *1/29* Dec 28 GP 5f fst 1:01 H *4/46* Dec 16 GP 3f fst :36^2 B *6/26*

8. When a field of maidens is mixed between horses with minimum racing experience and first-time starters, the figures for the horses who have raced will point out the difficulty of the task for the first-timers. If the horses with racing experience have been producing above-par figures for the class, the first-timer has to be a tiger to compete. If the figures are subpar, the player would be wise to review the first-timers carefully. A nicely bred, fast-

working firster could be an excellent wager against a field of subpar figure maidens. The same is true for a first-timer with Lasix and/or blinkers who has modest workouts, but is bred for the task and is handled by a known ace with firsters.

This, incidentally, is one of those ideas that a good teacher would feel failed in his or her task if he or she did not stop to stress its inordinate value. So I am stopping. Please read this slowly: Measuring the vulnerability of a group of maidens by their speed figures versus the class par is one of the most reliable handicapping concepts to apply to maiden races anywhere in the country. In the straightforward example below, Fondly Remembered had already established her ability to produce very good maiden-class speed figures, and it would have taken an exceptional first-time starter to deny her victory on February 20, 1992, at Santa Anita Park.

9. Ever since 1971, when Andy excitedly met me in a motel room outside Washington, D.C., to show me his initial experiments with speed figures, the following has produced a running stream of winning plays.

When a horse has consistently produced superior speed figures—when his *lowest* figure is better than the *best* figure of the competition—it will win at least 80 percent of the time! In the 1970s this occurred about once in 250 races; in the 1990s, it occurs less frequently, but it still shows a significant flat-bet profit. (More horses seem to go through wilder form-cycle swings due to longer racing seasons, more shipping, more drugs—legal and illegal.)

10. As an adjunct to the above, any horse whose last two speed figures are higher than the best previous figure earned by any other horse in the field can be expected to win about 40 percent of the

time, also at a flat-bet profit, this despite the availability of Beyer figures in the *DRF* past performances.

11. According to my own private research during the 1980s at Bay Meadows, Golden Gate Fields, Oaklawn Park, Churchill Downs, Canterbury Downs and Saratoga, whenever comparisons are restricted between the top speed figures earned under *the same conditions as today's race* (same track condition and distance, give or take 1/16 miles) the horse with the top figure by at least two full points in sprints and three points in routes wins about 35 percent of all starts at a slight flat-bet profit. (The outstanding public handicapper Randy Moss supplied Beyer figures for Oaklawn Park and Churchill Downs in 1988, 1989 and 1990 and Paul Deblinger, a former student who is the top public handicapper in Oklahoma, computed separate Beyer figures for 1987 and 1988 at Canterbury Downs for these studies.)

12. Speed figures are excellent tools to evaluate the legitimacy of the betting favorite.

Favorites who do not rank among the top three speed-figure horses in the field are eminently beatable. Indeed, if the figures are low for the class or the competition, the player must have well-thought-out reasons to accept such horses at shorter odds for anything more than a place on the bottom of exactas and trifecta tickets, if at all. Such reasons may include a powerful trainer pattern, visual evidence, vastly improved workouts, and so on. This is not to discount the win play value of longshots who may lack speed-figure support but have solid trainer patterns. In such instances, higher odds provide ample compensation for the higher risks.

NOTE: *If you compute your own speed figures, you will occasionally have important differences of opinion between your numbers and Beyer's. Instead of automatically leaning to Beyer, I strongly urge you to trust or confirm your own. Yours are based on close personal contact with local racing, and Beyer is working with an associate in the region who is covering two to six tracks simultaneously.*

Beyer's *DRF* contract also calls for him to provide a figure for every race, and that automatically introduces a few erroneous figures because some races and days may be impossible to rate accurately. Other Beyer figure errors tend to be purely typographical, but during my test period in October–December 1992, I found several that were not in concert with midday shifts in the track bias, which pushed his numbers around a slightly wider range than mine. These differences were confirmed by fellow handicappers Ron Cox and Dan Montilion, two excellent professional players who make their own figures and track variants in northern California.

13. Aside from the above caution, it is indisputable that Beyer's *DRF* numbers are very very good and serve to greatly improve the player's ability to compare horses shipping from track to track.

Cherokee Run
Own: Robinson Jill E

Dk. b or br c. 3 (Mar)
Sire: Runaway Groom (Blushing Groom–Fr)
Dam: Cherokee Dame (Silver Saber)
Br: Onett George L (Fla)
Tr: Alexander Frank A (—)

122

Lifetime Record:	14 9 2 1	$477,615			
1993	7 4 1 1	$408,875	Turf	0 0 0 0	
1992	7 5 1 0	$68,740	Wet	4 3 0 1	$195,367
Mth	0 0 0 0		Dist	1 1 0 0	$120,000

3Jly93- 8Bel	my	1⅛	:454	1:093	1:344	1:473	Dwyer-G2	102	6	2	2½	1½	12	16	Day P		123	1.70	91-11	Cherokee Run1236 Miner's Mark1231¼ Silver Of Silver123¾	Ridden out	6
5Jun93- 9Bel	gd	1½	:484	1:132	2:024	2:294	Belmont-G1	88	1	2	2hd	1½	68	613	Antley C W		126	4.20	68-15	Colonial Affair1262¼ Kissin Kris126¾ Wild Gale1262	Nothing left	13
15May93-10Pim	fst	1 3/16	:464	1:111	1:37	1:563	Preakness-G1	97	12	3	41¼	42	1hd	2½	Day P		126	9.40	78-18	Prairie Bayou126½ Cherokee Run1267 El Bakan126nk	Stubbornly	12
24Apr93- 9CD	sly	1	:23	:462	1:113	1:372	Derby Trial-G3	103	2	2	1hd	11	13	13	Day P	L	122	*.70	92-27	CherokeRun1223 DrinDcon1149 GroundForc1172	Ridden out,much best	9
6Apr93- 8Kee	fst	7f	:222	:45	1:091	1:211	Lafayette-G3	103	5	1	2½	2½	1½	13½	Day P	L	118	*1.50	103-07	CherokeeRun1183½ PovertySlew1123 Willimstown1211	Sharp, ridden out	8
20Mar93- 8GP	sly	7f	:223	:453	1:101	1:231	Swale-G3	99	7	4	42	41¼	21½	3½	Bailey J D		114	*.90	87-12	PrmrExploson114hd DmlootDmshoot113nk ChrokRn1142¼	Closed willingly	8
5Mar93- 7GP	fst	7f	:234	:473	1:112	1:231	Alw 31000NC	99	3	2	2½	1½	15	15	Vasquez J		117	*.90	87-16	Cherokee Run1175 Wild Gale1176 Ziao112	Ridden out	4
26Dec92-10Crc	fst	1 1/16	:241	:483	1:141	1:481	What a Plsr-G3	85	6	4	51¼	21	2½	2½	Vasquez J		115	*.60	85-15	Virgil Cain115½ Cherokee Run1152¼ Kassec1122		7
Bumped near far turn, gamely																						
16Dec92- 9Crc	fst	170	:241	:483	1:13	1:451	Alw 19000NC	89	3	4	42	31½	11½	11½	Vasquez J		120	*.40	87-20	Cherokee Run1201½ Ziao1121¼ Game Red112nk	Driving	7
22Nov92- 9Crc	gd	7f	:223	:461	1:11	1:234	Alw 22500	91	2	4	35½	32½	11½	12¾	Vasquez J		114	*.40	96-10	Cherokee Run1142¾ Virgil Cain1144 Dr. Roses Hope112	Strong handling	5

WORKOUTS: ●Jly 17 Bel 5f fst :583 H 1/35 Jun 26 Bel 5f fst 1:013 B 9/18 Jun 19 Bel 5f fst 1:002 B 3/24 Jun 1 Bel 4f gd :492 B 12/19 May 26 Bel 6f fst 1:141 B 4/4 May 12 Bel 3f fst :373 B 12/18

14. If a horse is likely to get a clear early lead for the first time in its recent racing record, the player should expect a minimum of two-lengths improvement over the horse's customary speed figures. In many cases the improvement is so substantial that no mathematical scale can be used to represent it. In fact, a horse

Sandy Looks Good
Own.—Cook Tim

B. f. 3(Feb), by Sandy Steve—Looks Good, by King of the Castle
$6,000 Br.—Hirst R E (Okla)
Tr.—Dickey Charles L (1 0 0 0 .00)

112

Lifetime	1992	14	3	1	3	$8,645
14 3 1 3	1991	0	M	0	0	
$8,645	Wet	2	0	0	1	$396

5Aug92- 1Aks	fst	6f	:222	:46	1:12		ⒻClm 5000	60	2	2	11½	11½	13	12½	Corbett G W	B	120	14.90	84-21	SndyLoksGd1202½SvntyTwAbv1171RgtmStr115	Driving	8
22Jly92- 9Aks	fst	6f	:224	:461	1:12		ⒻClm 5000	26	6	3	31	66	614	612¾	Corbett G W	B	120	6.30	71-17	BuyMeTime1204LadyBdri115nkBostonNtive120	Outside	9
16Jly92- 4Aks	fst	6f	:224	:464	1:131		ⒻClm 6500	50	10	1	21	2hd	12	14½	Corbett G W	B	116	5.80	78-12	SndyLooksGood1164½Hnylps1184PnnyPrspct115	Driving	11
5Jly92- 7Aks	my	6f	:223	:462	1:14		ⒻClm 9000	0	10	5	51¾	67	819	820	Murray K C	B	116	5.90	54-19	BostonNtive116noCherinIc1202PnnyProspct115	Outside	10
24Jun92- 7Aks	fst	6f	:222	:454	1:121		ⒻClm 9000	53	9	6	41½	3nk	65¼	33½	Murray K C	B	116	10.50	79-16	ShdownthWnd1161½Imshb1162SndyLoksGd116	Outside	9
15Jun92- 5Aks	fst	6f	:222	:454	1:123	3↑	ⒻMd 10000	42	2	3	32½	31	21	11	Corbett G W	B	115	3.60	81-12	SndyLooksGood1151LLKrr115hdShowPoppr115	Driving	12
31May92- 1Aks	fst	6f	:223	:461	1:13	3↑	ⒻMd 10000	40	5	3	3½	63	32	31¾	Corbett G W	B	114	9.00	77-13	PdiJoGo114nkR!Dplomcy1151½SndyLooksGood114	Hung	9
22May92- 5Aks	my	6f	:23	:471	1:152	3↑	ⒻMd 10000	40	5	3	1½	1hd	21½	31¼	Corbett G W	B	114	17.80	66-22	Honornss114½DntStr110¾SndyLooksGod114	Hung drive	12
24Apr92- 6RP	fst	6f	:231	:48	1:13		ⒻⓈMd 14000	22	8	5	65	74¾	68	512	Bickel R		118	14.20	63-19	GntlRctl1187¾CdllcStl1182RprtnAhrr118	Wide into lane	12
8Apr92- 3RP	fst	6f	:223	:46	1:123		ⒻⓈMd 14000	34	2	10	96¾	97¾	69½	58¼	Steinberg P W		118	4.90	69-08	RvrAngl113hdLorlynS1181½MssMrvlos118	Off slow, wide	11

LATEST WORKOUTS Sep 18 RP 6f fst 1:154 H

who is likely to get a clear early lead for the first time usually is difficult to beat, especially in maiden claiming races.

15. If a horse with the top figure in his most recent race also is the horse most likely to get a clear early lead, it deserves a solid edge, providing it is not racing against a stretch-running track bias or clearly performing beyond its distance capabilities. To make this assessment it may be necessary to use a form of pace numbers, or fractional time comparisons, or author Bill Quirin's rudimentary but very effective "speed-point" approach, which focuses on the early position calls in the running line, (See chapters 15–18). Despite repeated speed-figure edges, Henderson Bay below had been tiring in all starts at six furlongs, but did score two successive victories over tracks decidedly biased toward front-running types (April 23 and May 29).

Henderson Bay
Own: Burke Gary W
PATTERSON A (16 2 3 2 .13)

B. g. 4
Sire: Gumboy (Gummo)
Dam: Hunter Seven (Disdainful)
Br: Zeren Mr-Mrs E (Wash)
Tr: Wingfield Robert E (—)

116

Lifetime Record: 17 5 1 5 $67,780

1993	5	2	1	2	$35,100	Turf	0 0 0 0		
1992	10	2	0	2	$25,110	Wet	1 1 0 0	$2,530	
Stk	0	0	0	0		Dist	13 4 1 4	$59,935	

29May93-4GG	fst	6f	:22	:443	:563	1:092	Clm 40000	92	4	2	1½	12	12	11½	Boulanger G	LB 119 f	*2.20	93-08	Henderson Bay1191½ Express Me115nk Icy Kevin117nk	Steady drive	7
23Apr93-8GG	fst	6f	:214	:441	:563	1:092	Alw 25000N2X	88	3	2	1hd	11	11½	11½	Boulanger G	LB 119 f	7.00	93-13	Henderson Bay1191½ Regional1191½ Sir Gilley122nk	Steady urging	6
31Mar93-7GG	fst	6f	:213	:433	:554	1:084	Clm 32000	87	1	4	11	1½	11	21¼	Boulanger G	LB 117 f	12.10	95-06	MoonlightDream1171¼ HendersonBy117no BobbRobb117½	Weakened late	8
15Feb93-6GG	fst	6f	:214	:441	:562	1:093	Clm 12500	78	5	2	12	13	11½	3¾	Castaneda M	LB 117 b	7.40	91-10	DH Dunant Easy117 DH Sir Fatih117¾ HendersonBay1173	Weakened late	9
30Jan93-1GG	fst	6f	:212	:441	:562	1:091	Clm 10000	74	3	2	11½	11½	11½	31¾	Baze R A	LB 117 b	4.40	92-09	Dunant Easy116nk Persico1171½ Henderson Bay1174½	Weakened late	6
13Dec92-12LA	fst	870-QH		:44.95		:45.54	3↑ Clm 20000		5			75	76¼	53¾	McReynolds C	120	29.20	73	Nicotine 1988122½ Trucklin Six122½ Raise An Impudent122	Faded Late	8
29Nov92-11LA	fst	870-QH		:44.71		:46.12	3↑ Clm 20000		8			811	710	78¾	Garcia E	LB 122 b	11.90	58	Sables Select1222 Trucklin Six1221 Shake Six122	No Factor	8
11Nov92-9Hol	fst	6f	:214	:443	:571	1:094	Clm 12500	57	1	7	32½	22	41½	107¾	Gulas L L5	LB 110 b	33.50	83-09	Orphan Monk116no Darryl's Choice117nk Akin For Racin'118	Gave way	11
25Oct92-2Hol	fst	870-QH		:44.82		:45.38	Clm 20000		6			66	64¼	33½	Lewis J	LB 122 b	6.20	106	Mac Mackin1222 Rebs Sign Off1221½ Henderson Bay Tb122	Well-placed	6
3Oct92-3Fpx	fst	870-QH		:46.83		:46.86	3↑ Alw 7840		6			53¾		2nk	Gulas L	116	6.10	68	Easy Blurr119nk Henderson Bay Tb1161¾ Ramblin Rod119	Second Best	6

WORKOUTS: Jun 22 GG 5f fst 1:04 H 13/17 Jun 16 GG 5f fst 1:004 H 2/26 Jun 8 GG 4f fst :472 H 2/29 ●May 23 GG 6f fst 1:124 H 1/13 May 16 GG 5f fst 1:011 H 13/64 May 8 GG 5f fst :592 H 2/44

16. Given the lower pari-mutuel prices for speed-figure standouts in the modern era, it is comforting to note that speed figures remain one of the best tools to isolate solid horses in multi-race exotics. Turning a pick six into a pick five with a solid speed figure winner can reduce the overall cost of betting into these jackpots. Relying on top figure horses for an otherwise wide-open trifecta is another excellent use of sound speed-figure handicapping. In exotic wagering, price-getting power occasionally is secondary to (a) reducing the cost of play, (b) isolating probable contenders and (c) increasing the prospects for crushing a race by concentrating the bet on just a few combinations.

17. The presence of a powerful, one-dimensional track bias of any kind can make speed figures almost as irrelevant as the times

they are based on. In such instances the name of the game is running style, post position and fitness.

When a front-running type encounters a particularly slow-breaking field—or has a track bias in his favor—no other horse in the race can safely be played with confidence. In fact, such a horse may be the best bet on the card. Once again Henderson Bay serves as a fine example of this, winning for fun on an extremely biased racing surface at Golden Gate on May 29. Under the circumstances, the payoff was a generous $6.40, as were the $8.00 and $6.20 payoffs on Scarlet Friendship, who outperformed her previous distance limitations when stretched out to one mile on the severely biased Golden Gate strips.

Scarlet Friendship			

Scarlet Friendship
Own: Buckley R E & Enbom Del

CHAPMAN T M (16 1 2 4 .06)

B. f. 4
Sire: Falamoun (Kalamoun)
Dam: Bishops Scarlet (King's Bishop)
Br: Bradyleigh Farms, Inc. & Ron McAnal (Ky)
Tr: Jenda Charles J (9 1 2 2 .11)

116

									Lifetime Record:	14 3 4 2	$52,475	
1993	6 2 2 0	$26,475	Turf	1 0 0 0	
1992	8 1 2 2	$26,000	Wet	2 0 1 0	$3,875
Pln	0 0 0 0		Dist	1 1 0 0	$9,900

29May93-10GG fst 1 :22 :45² 1:09⁴ 1:35⁴ (F)Clm 25000 83 4 1 11½ 11 13 15 Chapman T M LB 116 b *2.10 91-07 Scarlet Friendship116⁵ Heartsaflying114ʰᵈ Pleasant Day114½ Ridden out 6
6May93- 8GG fst 1 :23 :45⁴ 1:10³ 1:36³ (F)Clm 16000 81 3 2 12 12 12 15 Chapman T M LB 116 b 3.00 87-20 Scarlet Friendship116⁵ Pleasant Day118½ Hat Girl116½ Steady urging 8
16Apr93- 8GG fst 6f :21⁴ :45¹ :58¹ 1:11 (F)Clm 20000 61 5 9 74 97¾ 97½ 46 Chapman T M LB 116 b 5.70 79-15 Tolder116½ Labiblica116²½ Dragonetta116³ Lacked room into str 9
4Apr93- 7GG fst 6f :22 :45 :57² 1:09⁴ (F)Clm 16000 80 4 6 53 23 21 2½ Chapman T M LB 116 b 10.60 90-14 NorthernCloud116² ScarletFriendship116⁵ FstSqueeze114² Closed well 9
13Feb93- 4GG fst 1 :22² :45³ :57⁴ 1:10³ (F)Alw 22000N1x 61 1 4 42½ 42½ 67½ 77 Hansen R D LB 118 b 9.50 80-12 Whothruslew118² Chile Missouri118² Serenity Stream118½ Gave way 7
1Jan93- 9BM my 1 :22³ :46 1:11 1:37 (F)Clm c-20000 75 3 5 32 22 21 2ⁿᵒ Hansen R D L 116 b 3.80 85-14 Speak Halory116ⁿ Scarlet Friendship116³¾ Red Jewel116½ Game try 7
Claimed from Halo Farms, Hollendorfer Jerry Trainer
18Dec92- 7BM my 1 :22³ 1:12¹ 1:38² 3+(F)Alw 17000N1x 60 4 3 31½ 42 64¾ 49½ Baze R A L 115 b 2.50 68-28 Hishi Dahar115⁴ Later On116³½ Serenity Stream115² 7
Bobbled sharply midstretch
29Nov92- 7BM fm 1¹⁄₁₆ ① :22⁴ :46² 1:11³ 1:45 3+(F)Alw 19000N1x 71 4 2 21 53½ 45 98 Baze R A L 115 b 4.00 77-11 Queenmaker116ⁿᵒ Petite Sonnerie115³½ Later On116² Stopped 12
12Nov92- 8BM fst 1 :23³ 1:11¹ 1:37² 3+(F)Alw 19000 73 4 3 31½ 32½ 21 2½ Baze R A L 115 b *.80 82-21 Got The Look117½ Scarlet Friendship115½ Later On116 Wide trip 6
24Oct92- 3BM fst 1 :22⁴ :46¹ 1:11¹ 1:37² 3+(F)Alw 21000 73 4 2 2ʰᵈ 2½ 33 2² Baze R A L 115 b 2.30 81-20 Miss Bereta117² Scarlet Friendship115ⁿᵏ Later On116 2nd best 5

WORKOUTS: Jly 1 GG 7f fst 1:27² H 1/1 Jun 22 GG 5f fst 1:01² H 2/17 ●Jun 15 GG 5f fst :59³ H 1/20 Jun 6 GG 4f fst :47⁴ H 10/31 ●May 23 GG 6f fst 1:12⁴ H 1/13 May 15 GG 4f fst :48⁴ H 9/41

On a front-running track bias, a fast-breaking horse with a speed-figure edge is capable of outrunning its apparent distance limitations and can be a wonderful wager at substantial odds. Again, on such tracks, the early position calls in the running line and the early fractional splits are the most important clues to the cashier's window. If the bias also is to the inside part of the track, post position is the player's best means to separate closely matched contenders.

On a stretch runner's track, the final quarter-mile time is useful and the turn time (middle quarter in sprints, third quarter in routes) is important, but the dominant handicapping considerations are *sustainable speed* or true stamina, class, condition and post position.

As detailed in earlier chapters, every racetrack in America periodically offers aberrant conditions like the ones described above. Clearly, the player who recognizes these tendencies and adjusts his or her handicapping accordingly will have a substantial handicapping advantage and the best shot at the equivalent of pitching a perfect game. It is possible to sweep the card on days like that.

NOTE: *The early speed in the Schuylerville Stakes—the sample race exhibited in Chapter 4—was Our Dancing Girl. This determination was made by noting the first call position of Our Dancing Girl in her race with the great Ruffian, perhaps the fastest filly who ever lived. Post position number 2 didn't hurt either. The next best speed in the race seemed to be Secret's Out, and the top closer was But Exclusive. This was the result:*

SEVENTH RACE
Saratoga
JULY 29, 1974

6 FURLONGS. (1.08) 57TH RUNNING THE SCHUYLERVILLE. $25,000 Added. 1st Division. Fillies, 2-year-olds. By subscription of $50 each, which shall accompany the nomination; $125 to pass the entry box; $125 to start, with $25,000 added. The added money and all fees to be divided 60% to the winner, 22% to second, 12% to third and 6% to fourth. Weights, 119 lbs. Non-winners of a sweepstakes allowed 3 lbs.; maidens, 7 lbs. Starters to be named at the closing time of entries. A trophy will be presented to the owner of the winner. Closed Monday, July 15 with 30 Nominations. Value of race $27,625, value to winner $16,575, second $6,077, third $3,315, fourth $1,658. Mutuel pool $108,621, OTB pool $46,764. Exacta Pool $79,247. OTB Exacta Pool $98,708.

Last Raced	Horse	Eqt.	A.	Wt	PP	St	¼	½	Str	Fin	Jockey	Odds $1
10Jly74 ^{8}Aqu^3	Our Dancing Girl	b	2	116	2	1	1^2	$1^{2\frac{1}{2}}$	1^2	1no	Bracciale V Jr	10.20
19Jun74 ^{8}Mth^5	Secret's Out		2	119	5	3	2^1	2^2	2^3	$2^{2\frac{1}{2}}$	Vasquez J	4.70
12Jly74 ^{4}Aqu^2	But Exclusive		2	116	7	7	$6^{\frac{1}{2}}$	5^4	5^5	3^1	Cordero A Jr	3.60
8Jly74 ^{6}Crc^1	Some Swinger	b	2	116	4	4	5^2	$4^{1\frac{1}{2}}$	$3^{\frac{1}{2}}$	$4^{1\frac{1}{4}}$	Velasquez J	6.00
20Jly74 ^{3}Mth^1	My Compliments		2	116	1	5	3^2	$3^{\frac{1}{2}}$	4^{hd}	5^6	Venezia M	1.60
14Jly74 ^{6}WO^2	La Bourrasque	b	2	116	3	6	7	6^5	6^5	$6^{7\frac{1}{2}}$	Turcotte R	5.90
15Jly74 ^{3}Aqu^2	Precious Elaine	b	2	112	6	2	4^{hd}	7	7	7	Santiago A	15.60

OFF AT 4:42 1/2 EDT. Start Good, Won driving. Time, :22⅕, :45⅕, 1:11⅕ Track fast.

$2 Mutuel Prices:				
	2-(B)-OUR DANCING GIRL	22.40	7.00	4.60
	5-(E)-SECRET'S OUT		5.00	4.00
	7-(H)-BUT EXCLUSIVE			3.20

$2 EXACTA 2-5 PAID $80.40.

B. f, by Solo Landing—Amber Dancer, by Native Dancer. Trainer Rigione J. Bred by Elcee H Stable (Fla).

OUR DANCING GIRL quickly sprinted clear, saved ground while making the pace and, after settling into the stretch with a clear lead, lasted over SECRET'S OUT. The latter prompted the pace throughought, lugged in slightly nearing midstretch and finished strongly, just missing. BUT EXCLUSIVE, off slowly, finished well while racing wide. SOME SWINGER rallied along the inside leaving the turn, eased out for the drive but lacked the needed late response. MY COMPLIMENTS had no excuse. LA BOURRASQUE was always outrun after breaking slowly. PRECIOUS ELAINE broke through before the start and was finished early.

Owners— 1, Elcee-H Stable; 2, Schott Marcia W; 3, Levin W A; 4, Mangurian H T Jr; 5, Reineman R L; 6, Levesque J L; 7, Brodsky A J.

Trainers— 1, Rigione J; 2, Picou J E; 3, Imperio D A; 4, Root T Jr; 5, Freeman W C; 6, Starr J; 7, Conway J P.

Scratched—Elsie Marley (30Apr74 ^{4}Aqu^1).

Pace: The New-Old Frontier

While the old handicapping bromide "pace makes the race," is an over-simplification of racing's complexities, pace analysis is a formidable approach to handicapping and one of the few handicapping tools yet to be fully exploited. Adventurous players willing to revisit old notions of pace and redefine them for modern, practical use are sure to be among the best equipped handicappers of the 1990s.

A few basic points:

- In sprints, moderate or slow fractional clockings rarely influence the ultimate speed figure earned by the race winner, but they may help promote a front-running or pace-pressing type to a winning position.
- An ultra-quick or hotly contested pace between two or more rivals can cost the contending horses on the pace their energy for the stretch drive. Even so, it is dangerous to accent late movers over pace-pressing types or mid-pack closers on most American tracks naturally tilted toward early speed.
- Some horses may become discouraged merely chasing an ultra-quick early pace, but a few actually may respond to competitive pace struggles by running harder. The player should have no trouble spotting such game creatures in the past-performance profiles.

Aloma's Ruler
Own.—Scherr N

126

Dk. b. or br. c. 3, by Iron Ruler—Aloma, by Native Charger
Br.—Silk Willoughby Farm (Fla) 1982 4 3 1 0 $269,894
Tr.—Lenzini John J Jr 1981 4 3 1 0 $30,135
Lifetime 8 6 2 0 $300,029

15May82-8Pim	1 $\frac{3}{16}$	:48	1:12	1:55^{2}ft	7	126	1^{1}	1^{1}	1$^{1\frac{1}{2}}$	1$^{\frac{1}{2}}$	Kaenel J L^{7}	Preakness	93	Aloma's Ruler, Linkage, Cut Away	7
8May82-8Aqu	1	:46	1:10^{1}	1:35^{2}ft	7	126	2^{1}	1$^{\frac{1}{2}}$	1$^{\frac{1}{2}}$	1^{nk}	Kaenel J L^{5}	Withers	89	Alom'sRulr,SpnshDrms,John'sGold	6
29Apr82-8Pim	6f	:22^{4}	:45^{3}	1:10^{4}ft	*1-3	115	1^{hd}	1^{hd}	1^{1}	2no	BraccialeVJr^{6}	Aw16200	92	HppyHoolign,Alom'sRuler,St.Chrisb	6
27Jan82-9Hia	7f	:22^{3}	:45^{1}	1:22^{1}ft	3½	117	3$^{2\frac{1}{2}}$	4^{3}	3$^{1\frac{1}{2}}$	1^{hd}	CorderoAJr^{3}	Bahamas	92	Alom'sRlr,DstnctvPro,LtsDontFght	9
17Oct81-5Med	6f	:22	:45^{1}	1:10 ft	2½	117	2$^{1\frac{1}{2}}$	2^{hd}	1^{1}	1$^{2\frac{1}{4}}$	Cordero A Jr^{3}	Nutley	93	Aloma's Ruler, Obgyn, Sleek Gold	7
28Sep81-5Med	6f	:22^{2}	:46^{1}	1:11^{2}ft	*6-5	120	1^{hd}	1^{hd}	1^{hd}	1$^{2\frac{1}{4}}$	Cordero AJr^{5}	Aw12000	86	Alom'sRuler,Rjb'sSon,JettingPlsur	8
14Sep81-5Med	6f	:22^{3}	:46^{1}	1:12^{1}ft	*6-5	118	3$^{1\frac{1}{2}}$	3$^{1\frac{1}{2}}$	1^{2}	1$^{1\frac{1}{2}}$	Cordero A Jr^{7}	Mdn	82	Alom'sRuler,Mythology,I'mPurGold	9
29Aug81-4Mth	6f	:22^{3}	:46^{1}	1:11^{2}ft	11	118	2^{hd}	2^{hd}	2^{1}	2^{4}	Kurtz J^{9}	Mdn	79	CrftyProspctor,Alm'sRlr,WtAMnt	12

●May 30 Bel 1 ft 1:39^{4} b May 25 Lrl 5f ft 1:01^{4} b May 7 Aqu 3f ft :37^{3} b ●Apr 27 Lrl 3f m :37^{1} b (d)

- In routes, a slow early pace can have a dramatic impact on the final speed figure as well as the race result, depending on the action that follows. Certainly it may help a front-running type reach the stretch with more gas in the tank. But just as interesting, the final speed figure may not always represent the true abilities of horses who finish behind a slow-down winner.
- A very fast or highly competitive pace frequently will tax a front runner and lead to an abysmal defeat—far below the horse's speed-figure potential—while the identical pace conditions will offer stretch runners maximum conditions to run their best races. Actually, the best horses, especially those able to stalk the leaders and fire sustained moves, are prone to use exceptionally fast fractions as springboards toward track records.

EIGHTH RACE
AP 35688
August 24, 1968

1 MILE (chute). (Buckpasser, June 25, 1966, 1:32⅗, 3, 125.)
Forty-first running WASHINGTON PARK HANDICAP. $100,000 added. 3-year-olds and upward. By subscription of $100 each, which shall accompany the nomination, $250 to pass the entry box and $750 additional to start, with $100,000 added, of which $20,000 to second, $15,000 to third and $10,000 to fourth. The winning owner to receive a trophy. Closed with 27 nominations.
Value of race $112,700. Value to winner $67,700; second, $20,000; third, $15,000; fourth, $10,000.
Mutuel Pool, $282,271.

Index	Horses	Eq't	A	Wt	PP	St	¼	½	¾	Str	Fin	Jockeys	Cl'g Pr.	Owners	Odds to $1
35524Sar^{1}	—Dr. Fager		4	134	9	1	6^{1}	2^{h}	1$^{\frac{1}{2}}$	1^{3}	1^{10}	B Baeza		Tartan Stable	.30
35415AP^{1}	—Racing Room		4	116	2	7	4$^{\frac{1}{2}}$	3^{2}	2^{3}	2$^{1\frac{1}{2}}$	2$^{1\frac{1}{2}}$	J Sellers		Llangollen Farm	10.40
35553AP^{4}	—Info		4	112	3	6	8^{2}	6^{2}	3^{1}	3^{3}	3^{1}	E Fires		Mrs E J Brisbine	37.00
35580AP^{1}	—Out the Window	b	4	115	5	8	9^{6}	9^{7}	7^{2}	5$^{\frac{1}{2}}$	4^{nk}	H Moreno		J R Chapman	13.90
35625AP^{3}	—R. Thomas	b	7	118	1	9	5^{1}	1^{h}	4^{2}	4^{2}	5^{6}	J Nichols		Wilson-McDermott	24.80
35553AP^{6}	—Cabildo		5	114	8	10	10	10	10	10	6no	M Sol'mone		Mrs J W Brown	a-13.60
35625AP^{2}	—Angelico		5	111	6	5	1^{h}	4$^{\frac{1}{2}}$	5$^{\frac{1}{2}}$	7^{3}	7^{nk}	L Pincay Jr		Foxcatcher Farm	16.00
35606Atl^{2}	—Hedevar		6	112	10	2	3$^{\frac{1}{2}}$	8^{h}	6^{h}	6^{2}	8$^{1\frac{1}{4}}$	T Lee		Mrs Edith W Bancroft	47.60
35625AP^{1}	—High Tribute	b	4	112	7	3	7$^{\frac{1}{2}}$	7$^{1\frac{1}{2}}$	9^{5}	9^{2}	9$^{1\frac{3}{4}}$	D Brumfield		Elmendorf	18.40
35433AP^{3}	—Kentucky Sherry		3	112	4	4	2$^{\frac{1}{2}}$	5$^{\frac{1}{2}}$	8^{1}	8^{h}	10	J Combest		Mrs J W Brown	a-13.60

a-Coupled, Cabildo and Kentucky Sherry.

Time, :22⅘, :44, 1:07⅗, 1:32⅕ (new track and world record). Track fast.

$2 Mutuel Prices:			
8-DR. FAGER	2.60	2.20	2.20
3-RACING ROOM		3.80	3.20
4-INFO			5.20

B. c, by Rough'n Tumble—Aspidistra, by Better Self. Trainer, J. A. Nerud. Bred by Tartan Farms (Fla.).
IN GATE—5:36. OFF AT 5:36½ CENTRAL DAYLIGHT TIME. Start good. Won easily.
DR. FAGER, away alertly but hard held to be reserved just off the lead, moved with a rush while still under restraint to take command leaving the backstretch, continued slightly wide to shake off RACING ROOM on the final turn, commenced lugging in while drawing off through the stretch run and won with something left.

- Pace and speed figures may be applied in tandem to get a fix on the overall speed potential of any horse, but the reliability of speed figures as a handicapping tool is severely limited whenever the pace is likely to be super fast or super slow.

The example from the original *Betting Thoroughbreds* below includes two of the top three-year-old fillies of 1976 whose speed figures were significantly faster than the opposition. While I could insert hundreds of subsequent examples, this race remains a classic reminder of pace theory 101, or the power of pace to nullify speed figures in super-fast pace situations. The exceedingly fast-paced duel between Dearly Precious and Optimistic Gal canceled out their relative advantages over the field and made them extremely vulnerable. Actually, they practically gave the race away to Girl in Love, who came from more than 16 lengths back to win going away—while pulling up lame.

EIGHTH RACE
Bel
June 4, 1976

1⅛ MILES (chute). (1:45⅗). Twentieth running MOTHER GOOSE. SCALE WEIGHTS. $75,000 added. Fillies. 3-year-olds. Weight, 121 lbs. By subscription of $150 each, which shall accompany the nomination; $375 to pass the entry box; $375 to start, with $75,000 added. The added money and all fees to be divided: 60% to the winner, 22% to second, 12% to third and 6% to fourth. Trophies will be presented to the winning owner, trainer and jockey. Closed with 14 nominations.

Value of race $80,850. Value to winner $48,510; second, $17,787; third, $9,702; fourth, $4,851. Mutuel Pool, $328,981. Off-track betting, $129,405.

Last Raced	Horse	EqtAWt	PP	St	¼	½	¾	Str	Fin	Jockeys	Owners	Odds to $1
22 May76 ^{8}Bel^{4}	Girl in Love	3 121	4	5	5	5	5	2^{7}	$1^{1\frac{1}{4}}$	JCruguet	Elmendorf	4.00
22 May76 ^{8}Bel^{2}	Optimistic Gal	3 121	2	2	2^{5}	2^{5}	1^{2}	1^{2}	2^{11}	BBaeza	Mrs R B Firestone	1.00
29 May76 ^{8}GS^{1}	Ancient Fables	b3 121	5	1	4^{10}	4^{8}	4^{2}	$3^{\frac{1}{2}}$	$3^{6\frac{3}{4}}$	ACorderoJr	Brazil Stable	18.50
22 May76 ^{8}Bel^{5}	Artfully	b3 121	3	4	3^{2}	3^{4}	3^{3}	4^{2}	$4^{3\frac{1}{4}}$	GPIntels'noJr	R N Webster	30.40
22 May76 ^{8}Bel^{1}	Dearly Precious	3 121	1	3	$1^{\frac{1}{2}}$	$1^{\frac{1}{2}}$	2^{3}	5	5	JVelasquez	R E Bailey	1.20

OFF AT 5:02½ EDT. Start good. Won driving. Time, :22⅕, :44⅖, 1:08⅘, 1:35⅕, 1:48⅘. Track fast.

$2 Mutuel Prices:			
4-GIRL IN LOVE	10.00	4.00	4.40
2-OPTIMISTIC GAL		2.60	2.20
5-ANCIENT FABLES			3.80

Ch. f, by Lucky Debonair—Lover's Quarrel, by Battle Joined. Trainer, John P. Campo. Bred by Elmendorf Farm (Ky.).

GIRL IN LOVE, badly outrun on the backstretch, commenced to rally after going five furlongs, raced wide into the stretch, continued to advance under left-handed pressure and proved clearly best after catching OPTIMISTIC GAL. GIRL IN LOVE pulled up lame. OPTIMISTIC GAL, bothered by DEARLY PRECIOUS while racing outside that rival on the backstretch, took over while racing well out in the track on the turn, quickly opened a clear lead but wasn't able to withstand the winner. ANCIENT FABLES failed to be a serious factor. ARTFULLY raced within striking distance to the stretch and flattened out. DEARLY PRECIOUS ducked out into OPTIMISTIC GAL after the start, made the pace while bearing out into that rival throughout the run down the backstretch and was finished soon after going six furlongs.

The most passionate students of pace who have surfaced in recent years have been based mostly in California, where the tracks are glib and the riders very aggressive. While this hardly means that pace has no place in eastern racing, it does mean that the mathematics of pace must be interpreted differently on tracks where speed does not carry as well, or the jockey colony is not hellbent to win the battle for an early striking position. No doubt this is why the best eastern-based handicappers I know have used numerically based pace handicapping mostly in the context of visualizing the way a race might be run, while in the West the best players have accented selections based on their numerical comparisons. In the 1990s however, through the influence of Dr. Howard Sartin and one of his disciples, author Tom Brohamer, eastern handicappers have begun to put their calculators and computers to work.

Steven Crist, one of the finest pick six players in the nation, has begun using pace calculations in New York. "At the very least, they help me make more accurate speed figures," Crist said at the fourth Handicapping Expo in Las Vegas in April 1993. "Pace numbers add another component to the speed-figure picture," Crist concluded.

My own intersectional handicapping experience includes early exposures to Beyer and his speed figures, Bill Quirin and his "speed points" and "race shapes," plus practical playing time alongside Ron Cox in northern California. Cox, a solid professional player who publishes weekly trip notes and pace figures in the *Northern California Track Record*, is a devout believer in Quirin's race-shape approach and the power of his own pace figures. But he admits that his highly specialized pace numbers are tailor-made for the northern California tracks, where there are no sprints beyond six furlongs. Indeed, Cox has found his pace numbers to be more reliable as predictive tools at six furlongs than any other distance, although they do provide insights into some route race situations. Interestingly, Cox is totally unprepared to state that his numbers would work anywhere else.

"The relationship between quarter-mile and half-mile fractional splits at six furlongs is different than the splits you might use for 6½ furlongs and seven furlongs, which are common sprint distances at other tracks, but not here in northern California," he explained. "I have no way of knowing what the splits should be for those distances or if my formula for making figures for six furlongs would work for six-furlong fractional splits at slower eastern tracks."

I have played with Cox-style speed and pace numbers and been impressed with their potential in such a closed set of races over such few racetracks and distances. But I also believe the power of pace as a predictive tool will be reliable only when a rock-solid computer program is developed to adjust for all fractional splits at all distances at all tracks. Practical experience convinces me that this is possible, but not achievable until such a program is infused with *accurate* pace pars for every fractional split. These pars would have to take into account many subtleties, including the relatively long run from the gate to the starting beam for one-mile races at Santa Anita, to the relatively slower fractional splits for the seven-furlong distance at the same track, to the nonexistent run up to the starting beam for six-furlong races at Pimlico, to the way wind changes pace pars for several distances during some weather cycles in New York.

At this point, no one has produced a satisfying table or par times covering all tracks that will work on their own, although California-based Gordon Pine annually publishes a useful set of par times for all tracks and others sell less imposing par charts for $10,000 claimers. In all such instances, the clockings are good starting points for serious students of pace to build accurate par charts, but they are based on sparse results at some distances and/or rigidly tied to long-term averages that seem to miss seasonal shifts in wind or radical track maintenance.

Even under the best of circumstances, pace handicapping can be severely undermined by gross inaccuracies in clockings of horses who race behind the leader at the various points of call, because such clockings must be deduced from estimates recorded by *Daily Racing Form* and *Equibase* trackmen.

When a horse is listed as six lengths behind the leader at the ½-mile call, is he really six lengths behind, or 5½, or seven lengths? If a horse really is fifth, six lengths behind the leader, should that be worth ⅗ths of a second or one full second or 1.30 seconds? Or do we really know?

In a game in which necks, heads and noses decide thousands of races, it is difficult to understand why the sport does not install electronic sensing devices in all saddle cloths to eliminate clocking errors in result charts. The technology has been available since the mid-1960s.

In the mid-1990s, the state of the art of pace handicapping is incomplete. At some tracks the commercially sold pace par listings may prove to be a perfect fit, while at others they may work with minor adjustments in the spring but be out of synch in the fall, or require severe adjustments at some distances and not at others.

Regardless, the maximum value of pace analysis may be in broader terms: to help predict the flow of a race, to make selections with it only when it clearly points out a solo front runner in a paceless field—or the logical, mid-race mover or late kicker in a field doomed to duel—or when the track is tilted strongly toward a running-style bias that makes it imperative to know which horses are going to be helped or hindered by a relatively severe pace issue. Pace is one component of the way a race may play out, one issue contributing to the probable trip each horse may have. At its best, it can help the player assess the merits and demerits of individual horse performance in races already run and provide insights into the prospective pattern(s) of today's race.

I want to know when the pace has been too fast or too slow for a given race so I can upgrade horses who overcame unfavorable pace scenarios. I want to know which horses failed to take advantage of a favorable pace and which ones deserve to be excused for poor performances because the pace was against them. In other words, my instinct tells me to treat pace analysis as a method to detect a *single-race pace bias*.

If the pace was (or will be) stacked against a horse, the predicament is as difficult as any prevailing bias in the racing surface. If the pace was (or will be) red-hot, any horse on or near the lead will deserve careful consideration in a less competitive situation.

Similarly, any horse who rallies after a solo front runner gets away with a soft, uncontested pace may deserve additional credit, as will any horse who makes a mid-race move into a fast pace—before the front runners spit out the bit. Stretch runners who fail to make any impact after a soft pace probably had little chance to win, and many will deserve ready-made excuses. With these powerful analytical concepts in mind, I pay close attention to the following pace-related scenarios.

- The pace was competitive and/or fast enough to hurt the chances of *most* front runners or pace-pressing types.
- The pace was too slow or uncontested for most stretch runners. (This does not apply in turf races at 1¹⁄₁₆ miles or longer, where final bursts of speed can be very effective even if the pace is very slow. Such extreme slow-down-tactics emulate the pattern of most European races, where many horses are allowed to creep into contending positions before they are asked to match late bursts of speed.)
- A horse displays an unusual burst of speed to indicate sharpness, or pending improvement not necessarily revealed in his speed or pace figures. My criteria for such bursts depend on a few interre-

lated issues, including the context in which they occur. For instance, there is a greater correlation of likely improvement if the burst of speed occurs in a sprint than if it occurs in a two-turn route.

Here are some useful combinations to look for:

For a burst during the first ¼ mile to be noteworthy, it must be *slightly uncharacteristic of the horse's usual running style* and be sustained long enough for the horse to be within two lengths of the leader at the first ¼-mile call. About .60 (⅗ seconds) faster than par for the class and distance would be about right, but lacking pace par information, which will be discussed in Chapter 17, the burst should be as fast or faster than any other opening ¼ mile on the horse's past-performance profile. Below are two classic examples:

Alan K. is not a pure front-running type, but he took the lead and flashed his best fractions on May 9 to signal advancing condition. In his next outing Alan K. took the next step forward to score a dead-heat win from slightly off the pace against better at 6.80–1. On June 12, he dueled for the lead through a half at above-par clockings that were reasonably close to his previous tip-off try. Seven days later he scored another win over $4,000 rivals at 5–1 odds.

Summer Playmate graduated with an off-the-pace effort in early April and tackled much, much better on April 29 when she flashed even more speed en route to a ninth-place finish. Down in class three weeks later at a slightly shorter sprint distance, and this logical contender won by four lengths at *thirty-eight to one!*

The importance of early speed in American racing has been substantiated by numerous computer studies, including some performed by Frederick S. Davis, whose work was cited by Tom Ainslie in a few publications and Bill Quirin in *Winning at the Races*, a 1979 work based on computer studies. Quirin found that more than five out of every nine races on dirt are won by horses who rank 1-2-3 through the first ¼-mile call in sprints and ½-mile call in routes. While more recent pace studies have concluded that the half-mile call in sprints and ¾ mile in routes provide more predictive power, the first-position call still is the most reliable indicator to the crucial pace question facing any handicapper:

Which horse is going to set and how fast will the pace be?

While pace numbers may be used to identify when a possible lone front runner or an extremely contentious pace is involved, my research clearly states that they are less reliable when applied to route races, distance switches and to horses moving from one track or racing surface to another.

Fear not. Despite the technical direction of modern pace theory, I seriously doubt that a more useful instrument yet exists to indicate the severity of the early pace than a rudimentary tool Bill Quirin created a decade ago. Quirin called this tool "the speed-point method" and with a few minor changes based on practical usage, it remains a streamlined, intuitive tool to assess the prospects for a hot or soft pace.

Don't laugh! After a few weeks of using this simple calculation, I am sure you will be stunned by its persistent effectiveness. My gratitude to Bill Quirin for allowing me to resuscitate it in a slightly altered form for contemporary use.

FIGURING BILL QUIRIN'S SPEED POINTS

FOR A SPRINT RACE TODAY. Using the three most recent races of each horse, assign 1 point for any sprint in which the horse was 1-2-3 at the first call in past performances, excluding the start itself.

Also assign one point for that sprint, or any other sprint in the three most recent races in which the horse was within two lengths of the leader at the first call in the past performances. Here I prefer to score the point within three lengths of the leader if the sprint was at least a furlong shorter than today's sprint, i.e., a 5½-furlong race when today's sprint is 6½ furlongs.

No points for any other sprint performance.

No points for any route performance (for speed points, 1 mile around one turn is considered a route).

Give a bye to any horse who competed in a route and led or was within one length of the leader at the first call. If a horse qualifies for a bye, go down one more race in his past-performance profile for a ratable sprint or give a second bye if another qualified route performance is encountered.

Award one bonus point to any horse who has led or raced within a neck of the leader at the first position call in *all three* rated races.

Never accept more than two qualified byes to develop a speed point profile.

Horses with less than three ratable races receive their earned speed points in their ratable races and an alternate projected rating to indicate what they might have earned if there had been three ratable races, i.e., four points in two races = "4/6" speed points.

Although turf races and wet track races count equally in Quirin speed points, I suggest substituting the most recent wet track or turf race for the third ratable race if today's race is on turf or a wet track. If today's race is on a fast track and all three ratable races were on turf or wet tracks, I will substitute the most recent fast track race for the third ratable race.

Each horse starts with one rating point, but gets that taken away if it fails to beat half the field to the first call in all three ratable races.

Examples will follow the speed-point method for routes below:

FOR RACES ONE MILE OR LONGER. Using the three most recent races, assign one point for any route in which the horse was *1-2-3* at the first call in the past-performance profile.

Also assign one point for any route in which the horse ran within *three lengths* of the leader at the first call. Here I give the point only if the route was *not* ¼ mile longer than today's race. In such longer races the horse must have led at the first call to get the extra point (i.e., the last race was 1½ miles and today it is 1⅛ miles).

No points for any other route in the last three races.

Assign one point for any sprint in which the horse raced within *six lengths* of the leader at the first call.

Also assign one point for any sprint in which the horse was within three lengths, or *1-2-3* at the first call.

Although I do not give any byes in calculating speed points for route races, I subjectively will seek a substitute wet track or turf race if today's race is on either surface; or a fast track race if the last three ratable races were on turf or wet tracks.

All horses start with one point, which can be taken away if they do not beat half the field to the first ¼-mile call in all three rated races.

USING THE SPEED-POINT METHOD. Cox reintroduced this method to me in 1991, and I have found that it has worked wonderfully predicting hot and soft pace structures, particularly in routes where pace figures can be so elusive. Here are recommended guidelines for using my version of modified Quirin speed points.

Any horse with eight speed points probably is a front runner or a strong candidate to bid for the lead. Only in the face of a much faster rival will such a horse be kept out of the early pace equation.

Any horse with seven points is nearly as likely to be on the pace or very close to it.

When three horses in a given race combine for 21–24 speed points, or four have a combined total of 27+, the pace is very likely to be hot, and late movers will have a much better chance than usual. On a stretch runner's track these criteria should be lowered to 18 and 23 points, respectively.

On a front runner's track bias, top contenders regularly can be isolated among the top speed-point earners. Factor in fractional splits and/ or pace numbers, and you will be making regular trips to the cashier's window.

When any horse has a four-point edge over all rivals, he should be examined for a probable lone front-running trip.

When any horse has at least five speed points *and* a two-point edge over his rivals, a potential pace advantage exists and must be considered, pending analysis of post positions, jockey tendencies, and so on. Any support from fractional splits and/or pace numbers would reinforce the possibility.

When the top speed-point horse in the field has four points, the pace probably will be slower than par for the class. This too can lead to a lone front runner's race, or a chaotic race in which different horses may show more "speed" than they have previously demonstrated.

Here are three post-performance profiles to assist in making accurate speed-point profiles. After a little practice, completing an entire card will take less than 20 minutes.

```
Win Man          B. g. 7, by Con Man—Winnie's Double, by Double Edge Sword     Lifetime      1992 18  6  5  2   $64,112
                 Br.—Brandt Louise & R L (Pa)                                  126 26 28 19  1991 20  3  4  4   $43,229
Own.—Our Farm Inc Tr.—Iwinski Allen (200 31 43 21 .16)               125       $210,766      Turf  3  0  0  0
                                                                                             Wet  17  5  6  1   $43,688
1Nov92- 5Pha fst 1 3/16 :49 2 1:14 2:00 2 3+Hcp 5000s 76 5 2 1 2 1 2 1 6 1 4 3/4 Black A S Lb 123 *.90 88-26 WinMn123 4 3/4 AsinStr112 no RflctNutrlity109 Under wraps 5
18Oct92- 5Pha fst 1 1/4 :48 1:39 2:05 4 3+Hcp 5000s 78 4 3 3 1 1/2 1hd 1 2 1/2 1 2 1/2 Black A S Lb 120 *.70 92-19 Win Man120 2 1/2 Zakhir113 1 Gliding Eagle112 Driving 7
28Sep92- 8Pha my 170 :46 1 1:11 4 1:42 3 3+Alw 16585 79 1 2 2 4 2 1 1/2 1hd 2 1 Black A S Lb 116 *1.80 82-20 GrnvilleGold116 1 WinMn116 4 1/2 Perdition'sGt122 2nd best 6
7Sep92- 9Pha gd 7f :21 4 :44 2 1:24 2 3+Alw 19575 75 5 8 7 7 7 7 1/2 3 4 1/2 2 1/2 Mucciolo J Lb 116 2.90 84-20 Requiem116 1/2 WinMan116 3/4 BattlingBldes111 Outfinished 10
22Aug92- 4Pha fst 1 1/16 :47 1 1:11 4 1:43 3 3+Alw 16585 79 1 3 3 1 1/2 1hd 2 2 2 4 1/2 Mucciolo J Lb 119 4.30 86-09 PipingHot111 4 1/2 WinMn119 5 1/2 BrssMonky116 Second best 8
24Jly92- 9Pha my 7f :23 :46 1:25 3+[S]Alw 19575 66 4 5 7 6 1/4 6 4 1/2 3 1 2 2 Mucciolo J Lb 122 5.10 80-18 RomeoMyRomeo116 2 WinMan122 no Requiem116 Fin well 12
3Jly92- 1Pha fst 170 :46 3 1:11 3 1:43 1 3+Clm 11000 76 3 6 6 7 1/4 6 3 1/2 4 3 3 4 1/4 Mucciolo J Lb 119 5.40 76-21 VitBoy114 nk RustyAttitude119 4 WinMn119 Flattened out 6
14Jun92- 7Pha fst 1 1/2 :49 3 2:06 2 2:32 4 3+Hcp 5000s 85 5 3 4 5 1/2 3nk 3 1 1/2 2 4 1/2 Mucciolo J Lb 119 *3.20 91-20 FireNorth114 4 1/2 WinMan119 3/4 BoldN.A.A.117 Gained place 8
31May92- 6Pha sly 1 1/4 :51 1 1:40 3 2:06 2 3+Hcp 5000s 82 3 1 1hd 1 2 1/2 1 5 1 9 1/2 D'Agusto J G Lb 115 *1.20 89-27 Win Man115 9 1/2 Cloudcroft115 10 1/2 Deltaic112 Driving 6
16May92- 6Pha sly 170 :47 2 1:12 3 1:43 4 3+Clm 6500 74 5 3 3 2 1/2 1hd 1 1 1 2 1/2 D'Agusto J G Lb 119 3.30 77-23 Win Man119 2 1/2 CreightonHall116 5 1/2 AsianStar119 Driving 7
```

Win Man is entered in a 1¼-mile starter handicap on dirt and gets six speed points including the one point given to all horses. Nov. 1 = 2 points; Oct. 18 = 2 points; Sept. 28 = 1 point.

If the same horse were to be entered in a $1\frac{1}{16}$-mile race, the revised speed-point total would be 5, including the base one point. Nov. 1 = 2 points; Oct. 18 = 1 point; Sept. 28 = 1 point.

If Muddy Rudder is entered at $1\frac{1}{16}$ miles on dirt, he earns seven speed points, including the base one. Nov. 6 = 2 points; skip the Oct. 24 turf race; Oct. 13 = 2 points; Oct. 4 = 2 points.

```
Muddy Rudder     B. g. 7, by Double Zeus—Steamboat Annie, by Potomac           Lifetime      1992 11  1  3  1   $19,695
         $14,500 Br.—Barnesville Thoroughbred Farm (Md)                        70 9 20 15    1991 20  1  6  4   $79,190
Own.—Stonefield Andrew J Tr.—Devereux Joseph A (26 6 2 2 .23)        117       $249,215      Turf 16  0  5  4   $55,425
                                                                                             Wet   6  1  2  1   $24,235
6Nov92- 2Lrl fst 1 1/16 :48 2 1:13 1 1:45 1 3+Clm 8500 72 7 1 1 1 1/2 1 2 1 2 1/2 1 3 1/2 Hutton G W Lb 117 *3.10 87-10 MddyRddr117 3 1/2 Ronok'sImg117 3 1/4 LnImprssn117 Driving 8
24Oct92- 3Lrl fm 1 1/16 (T):47 2 1:11 2 1:41 3+Clm 11500 67 3 9 10 10 10 11 9 15 9 14 1/2 Hutton G W Lb 117 9.30 82-03 DixieDncer117 5 1/4 RighteousMn118 1 3/4 BestLord117 Outrun 10
13Oct92- 6Lrl fst 1 1/16 :48 1:12 4 1:44 2 3+Clm 18500 67 4 4 2 1/2 1hd 3 2 1/2 5 6 3/4 Hutton G W Lb 117 5.60 84-08 SptmbrStr117 no HvYTstfd117 3 1/2 DctrIchbd112 Weakened 7
4Oct92- 9Pim fst 1 1/16 :49 1:13 4 1:45 4 3+Clm 20000 70 7 2 1hd 2hd 2 1 4 1 1/2 Luzzi M J Lb 117 *1.20 73-23 WolfTon115 1 BrothrRobrts113 1/2 DctrIchbd117 Weakened 7
5Sep92-11Mth fm 1 1/16 (T):47 1:10 1 1:42 4 3+Clm 25000 70 8 7 7 3 3/4 8 4 8 6 1/4 7 8 1/2 Luzzi M J Lb 115 7.50 81-19 Anglus115 1 1/4 ThirdndMorris113 nk WildrThnEvr118 No bid 10
7Aug92-10Lrl fst 1 1/16 :48 1:13 1:44 3 3+Clm 25000 82 1 3 4 4 4 2 1/2 3 3 2 6 1/4 Prado E S Lb 117 *1.80 84-17 LttlBldJhn117 6 1/4 MddyRddr117 1 3/4 PrttyAmsng117 Rallied 8
26Jly92- 4Lrl fst 1 1/8 :47 4 1:12 2 1:51 3+Clm 35000 87 1 1 2hd 1hd 1hd 2 1 Prado E S Lb 117 *.70 84-28 ArcticOcen115 1 MuddyRudder117 1 1/4 LerndJk117 Gamely 3
   26Jly92-Originally scheduled on turf
12Jly92- 8Lrl fst 1 1/16 :48 1 1:12 4 1:43 1 3+Clm 35000 87 3 2 2hd 1hd 2 1 2 3 1/2 Prado E S Lb 117 7.90 90-13 Dess'sCherokee112 3 1/2 MuddyRudder117 nk Lnc117 Gamely 6
4Jly92- 8Lrl fst 6 1/2f :22 3 :45 2 1:15 4 3+Clm 35000 69 2 7 6 5 5 6 3/4 6 7 1/4 5 8 Guerra W A Lb 117 25.30 90-08 Dss'sChrok112 1 Jwlr'sChoic117 3/4 ColonlHill117 No factor 8
15Feb92-12Lrl sly 1 1/16 :46 1:10 3 1:43 2 Alw 23000 77 2 4 3 4 1/2 3 6 3 9 3 12 Luzzi M J Lb 114 4.10 84-23 HeIsRisen117 5 FruglDoc119 7 MuddyRuddr114 No mishap 5
LATEST WORKOUTS  Nov 21 Lrl 5f fst 1:01 1 H
```

If Muddy Rudder is entered in a 1 1/16-mile race on turf, his speed point total is five points, including the base one. Nov. 6 = 2 points; Oct. 24 = 0 points; Oct. 13 = 2 points.

If Glaring, below, were entered in a six-furlong sprint, he would earn five speed points via two byes for his recent route races, two points for his front-running 4½-furlong try on June 4, zero points for his January 31 sprint and two points for his six-furlong race on February 15, plus the base point awarded to all horses.

Glaring				Dk. b. or br. c. 3(Apr), by Known Fact—Great Finesse, by Bold Bidder				Lifetime		1993	4	1	2	0	$28,000
				Br.—Pin Oak Stud (Ky)				5 2 2 0		1992	1	1	0	0	$9,500
Own.—Pine Oak Stable				Tr.—Von Hemel Donnie K (—)			126			Wet	1	1	0	0	$6,000
3Apr93- 8RP	fst 1¹ₜₑ	:46³ 1:11² 1:43⁴	Rem Dby	73 3 2 2½ 2¹½ 4² 7¹³½	Pettinger D R	b 118	4.00	84 — MrkedTr122ⁿᵏBrothrBrown122²½RgtimRbl122						Gave way	9
13Mar93- 9RP	fst 1⁷⁰	:45³ 1:10³ 1:39³	Great West	104 11 1 1¹½ 1² 1¹½ 2ʰᵈ	Pettinger D R	b 111	20.10	103-10 MrkedTree117ʰᵈGlring118¹½BrotherBrown117						Game try	11
15Feb93- 2RP	sly 6½f	:22 :45¹ 1:18¹	Alw 10000	84 4 3 2½ 1½ 12½ 15½	Pettinger D R	b 116	2.20	84-29 Glrng116⁵½KnocknDrs122²SkpDwnBrdwy122						Much best	5
31Jan93- 2RP	fst 5½f	:21⁴ :45³ 1:05⁴	Alw 10000	63 2 5 4³ 44½ 32½ 2ⁿᵏ	Pettinger D R	116	*.50	87-14 Lesson116ⁿᵏ Glaring116¹ Cornish Brush116						Too late	8
4Jun92- 1AP	fst 4½f	:22³ :46 :52³	Md Sp Wt	70 6 6 1ʰᵈ 1ʰᵈ 12½	Fires E	118	8.60	98-17 Glaring118²½ⓓTaylorsRock118²½TabascoCid118						Driving	7
LATEST WORKOUTS		Mar 28 RP	5f fst 1:01 H		Mar 22 RP 5f my 1:04³ B			●Mar 8 RP 6f fst 1:12⁴ H			●Mar 2 RP 7f my 1:33² H (d)				

If Glaring were entered in a 1⅛-mile route, he would earn seven speed points, two for each of the three most recent races plus the base point.

Beyond speed points and sharp bursts of early speed, I am careful to note horses who fired an acceleration bullet elsewhere during the race. A final 1/16 mile in 6.00 in a 1 1/16-mile stakes or allowance race can be a significant hint of physical fitness or pending improvement, regardless of what transpired previously. The same may be true for a $5,000 claiming race in which the final ¼ mile is 25.00 seconds or ⅛ mile in 12.60. These standards are not cast in stone; they can be reset to reflect a meaningful late burst at any class level, any racetrack, any track condition.

Here are my standards for sharp bursts of late speed at Saratoga and Penn National. A brief study of your own track will help you construct similar charts.

Actually, I pay little attention to such late moves unless the horse also gained ground during the middle portion of the race, or was within five lengths of the leader at the ½-mile call. Improved stretch punch may be wasted on horses who cannot get into gear before the top of the stretch. The same is true if today's racing surface favors early speed, or if the pace is likely to be dominated by a lone front-running type. But

SARATOGA		
	GRADE 1 STAKES	$20,000 CLAIMING
Final ¼	24.20	24.60
Final ⅛	12.20	12.40
Final ¹⁄₁₆	6.00	6.20
PENN NATIONAL		
	$10,000 CLAIMING	$3,200 CLAIMING
Final ¼	25.40	26.00
Final ⅛	12.60	13.00
Final ¹⁄₁₆	6.40	6.40

there is one situation when no such proviso need be considered: route races on the turf.

As suggested earlier and to be covered in more detail later, turf races are frequently dominated by the horses with the strongest late moves. Even well-tooled front runners on grass tend to have some reserve power and do not win too often by merely getting away with soft splits. Indeed, a serious late mover is seldom a throwout on turf regardless of pace issues—although a closely cropped, tight-turning course, where the inner rails have been moved out to the middle of the course to preserve fragile grass, can be severely biased toward early speed.

These are my standards for noteworthy late moves at the New York–southern California $35,000 claiming level, which also approximates a decent allowance race at most other "major" tracks. Let me assure you these little buggers are powerful weapons that should be added to your turf-racing arsenal. Slower standards will work just as well in cheaper turf races or soft courses, and slightly faster ones may be needed on extremely glib courses that resemble billiard tables.

POSITIVE TURF MOVES
37.00 for the final ⅜ mile in 1⅛-mile races
30.60 for the final ⁵⁄₁₆ mile in 1¹⁄₁₆-mile races
24.40 for the final ¼ mile in 1-mile–1¼-mile races
18.40 for the final ³⁄₁₆ mile in 1³⁄₁₆-mile races

Extra credit for the above when the following also occurs:
12.20 for the final ⅛ mile
 6.20 for the final ¹⁄₁₆ mile

On dirt or turf, a move in the middle of the race can be very significant in a sprint on dirt or turf. Such horses are firing hard into the teeth of the pace and have shown the ability to take control of the contest at the point when most races are being decided.

Worth noting are mid-race moves equal to or faster than the opening ¼-mile split posted by the race leader and moves clocked in 22.60 (22.40 at a western track). Generally speaking, I ignore any such move clocked slower than 23.60, but significant lengths gained will loosen this standard in slower races.

Surprisingly, the strongest mid-race move to take seriously is by the horse who set the pace or is racing head and head for the lead. Here I give extra credit to horses who race on the pace and match their opening pace, or slow down only slightly depending on how fast the opening ¼ mile was run. This type deserves more flexibility because more energy is being expended for a longer portion of the race.

It is worth keeping in mind that a well-placed horse with a front-running or pace-pressing style capable of unleashing a sharp middle move is eligible to blow a race wide open entering the stretch. This angle applies powerfully to horses who seem likely to face reduced early pressure in today's race.

The horse below, Six Thirty Two, offers a wonderful illustration of these issues linked together. Note how he flashed a sharp middle move in 22⅖ seconds on the straightaway run of a seven-furlong sprint on March 4 after competing in five consecutive moderately paced routes at Calder and Gulfstream. Note his subsequent middle move in 23 seconds around the turn in a six-furlong sprint on March 16. The result of the March 27 route speaks for itself.

Six Thirty Two B. c. 3(May), by Tunerup—Esplanade, by Explodent
ANTLEY C W (143 24 31 23 .17) Br.—Casse N E & Valley Stream Farm (Fla)
Own.—Our Junco Stable Tr.—Monaci David (13 1 1 2 .08) **110**

Lifetime 16 3 0 2 $49,170 | 1993 7 2 0 2 $39,270 | 1992 9 1 0 0 $9,900 | Wet 2 1 0 0 $8,700

17Apr93- 8Aqu	fst	1⅛	:46^{4}	1:10^{1}	1:48	Cahill Road	30	6	5	$5^{5\frac{1}{2}}$	4^{7}	7^{19}	$7^{43\frac{1}{2}}$	Migliore R		113	10.60	52-05	KolctooJmmyAl116$^{6\frac{1}{2}}$TooWld113^{2}BondngDsy116	Faded	8
27Mar93- 7GP	fst	1$\frac{1}{16}$	:48	1:12^{4}	1:46^{1}	Clm 40000	96	9	2	2^{1}	$1^{\frac{1}{2}}$	$1^{2\frac{1}{2}}$	1^{8}	Castillo H Jr		113	8.00	79-30	SixThirtyTwo113^{8}KnightWaltz116^{no}Barbada120	Driving	9
16Mar93- 5GP	fst	6f	:22	:45^{1}	1:11	Clm 50000	74	1	4	$2^{3\frac{1}{2}}$	2^{2}	3^{nk}	3^{3}	Castillo H Jr	b	113	*2.20	83-13	Syndicte'sPl113^{3}ProBrite116^{no}SixThirtyTwo113	Gamely	7
4Mar93- 3GP	fst	7f	:23	:45^{2}	1:25^{2}	Clm 45000	69	4	2	1^{hd}	1^{1}	1^{hd}	3^{1}	Ferrer J C	b	114	*2.90	75-20	Trthsk112^{no}AnothrAnton116^{1}SxThrtyTw114	Weakened	8
23Feb93- 7GP	sly	1$\frac{1}{16}$	:48	1:14	1:47^{1}	Clm 50000	63	3	4	$3^{1\frac{1}{2}}$	2^{2}	2^{3}	$4^{4\frac{3}{4}}$	Nunez E O		116	*2.10	69-29	JohnRyder112$^{\frac{3}{4}}$VangurdKnight116$^{1\frac{1}{2}}$Brbd116	Weakened	9
7Feb93- 5GP	fst	1$\frac{1}{16}$	:48^{4}	1:13^{3}	1:46^{4}	Clm c-35000	78	5	2	$2^{1\frac{1}{2}}$	$2^{1\frac{1}{2}}$	2^{hd}	1no	Nunez E O		116	5.90	76-25	Six Thirty Two116^{no} Sea School112$^{1\frac{1}{2}}$ Coyote Sam116		8
7Feb93-Fully extended, forced wide; Claimed from Cobble View Stable, Olivares Luis Trainer																					
12Jan93- 5GP	fst	1$\frac{1}{16}$	:48^{4}	1:13^{4}	1:44^{4}	Alw 19000	70	7	1	$1^{\frac{1}{2}}$	$1^{\frac{1}{2}}$	3^{nk}	4^{5}	Nunez E O		112	33.90	81-13	AmbushAlley115$^{2\frac{3}{4}}$Rndi'sPlesure113$^{1\frac{1}{2}}$SSchool107	Faded	8
15Dec92- 7Crc	fst	1$\frac{1}{16}$	:48^{3}	1:13^{3}	1:48^{1}	Alw 16600	64	2	2	$4^{1\frac{3}{4}}$	5^{6}	$5^{9\frac{1}{2}}$	$5^{10\frac{1}{2}}$	Madrid S O		112	41.10	75-13	Kassec110^{no} Duc d'Sligovil115^{1} Itaka115	Tried badly	5
5Dec92- 8Crc	fst	1^{70}	:47	1:13^{1}	1:45	Alw 15000	66	1	1	$1^{\frac{1}{2}}$	$2^{1\frac{1}{2}}$	4^{6}	$4^{8\frac{1}{4}}$	Madrid S O		113	23.30	80-12	SummrSt112^{3}PrmirCommndr114$^{\frac{3}{4}}$SnImgintion117	Tired	7
28Nov92- 7Crc	fst	6f	:22	:45^{2}	1:11^{2}	Alw 15500	70	2	4	$4^{2\frac{1}{2}}$	$5^{6\frac{1}{2}}$	5^{8}	$5^{4\frac{1}{4}}$	Madrid S O		113	51.50	90-10	TrdeBill109^{1}SuprWorld114$^{2\frac{1}{2}}$PridOfBurkn112	No excuse	7

LATEST WORKOUTS Apr 25 Bel 4f fst :49 B Mar 2 GP 5f fst 1:01 Hg

Unfortunately, it is exceedingly difficult to evaluate middle moves in routes. Middle moves may occur between several different points of call and/or be tied to sustained runs at slightly slower rates of speed for ⅜ths or ½ miles. Class also plays a tricky role. Stakes horses routinely throw in one or more middle quarter-mile runs in 23 and change while $5,000 claimers can produce similar interior fractions under ideal circumstances. For these reasons, I measure mid-race moves in routes in the context of lengths gained and/or visual terms rather than via strict teletimer clockings or numerical ratings. The horse below, for instance, made two moves in her July 10 race at Belmont Park, the first of which was not reflected by anything noteworthy in the fractional splits. The past performances are provided by *Post Parade*, the official track program for New York racing.

Sidney L. Port — **Thomas J. Skiffington** (42-11-7-5)

Green, Pink Sash, Pink Sleeves, Two Gray Hoops, Green and Pink Cap

Garendare (GB) **117** **Julie Krone** (308-54-51-43)

Dk.B./Br.f.4 Vacarme Girouette by Nodouble

1993:	7	1	2	3	$38,705	Turf :	14	3	3	4	$104,650
1992:	6	2	0	1	$58,688	Wet :	0	0	0	0	$0
Life :	14	3	3	4	$104,650	Course :	1	0	0	0	$0

10Jul93	Bel1	fm	3uf	Alw36500	T $1\frac{1}{16}$	:47 78	1:11 90	1:40.94	81	6/6	4^{3}	$4^{2\frac{1}{2}}$	$3^{\frac{1}{2}}$	$3^{1\frac{1}{2}}$	2^{hd}	Bailey	117		2.50	Heed ^{hd}, Garendare $1\frac{1}{2}$, FrenchSteal $\frac{1}{2}$	gaining
19Jun93	Bel8	fm	3uf	2New YorkH	T $1\frac{1}{4}$	:47 38	1:35.13	1:59.05	80	2/11	$7^{6\frac{1}{2}}$	$9^{7\frac{3}{4}}$	$10^{5\frac{1}{2}}$	$7^{3\frac{3}{4}}$	$7^{4\frac{3}{4}}$	Velazquez	113		22.80	Aqlegia ^{ns}, VBorghese $\frac{3}{4}$, GnyDre 3	angled out, bid 3w
23May93	Bel7	fm	3uf	Hcp46000	T $1\frac{1}{16}$	:47 15	1:11 16	1:41 20	80	5/8	$6^{6\frac{1}{2}}$	6^{7}	$7^{4\frac{1}{4}}$	$4^{1\frac{3}{4}}$	$3^{1\frac{3}{4}}$	Bailey	119		4.50	LaPiaf 1, BuckSomeBelle $\frac{3}{4}$, Garendare ^{hd}	closed fast
28Apr93	CD8	fm	3uf	Alw43950	T $1\frac{1}{16}$	:48 86	1:13 05	1:43 26	78	5/10	$6^{4\frac{1}{4}}$	5^{3}	3^{1}	$3^{\frac{1}{2}}$	3^{1}	Bailey	117	L	*1.30	Wassila $\frac{3}{4}$, JolieBand ^{nk}, Garendare ^{hd}	4 wide, hung
08Apr93	Kee9	fm	4uf	Alw27600	T $1\frac{1}{16}$	46 98	1:12 01	1:42 88	79	5/9	$6^{7\frac{1}{2}}$	$5^{6\frac{1}{2}}$	$3^{4\frac{1}{2}}$	2^{hd}	$1^{1\frac{3}{4}}$	Bailey	121	L	*2.10	Garendare $1\frac{3}{4}$, MusicalDelight ^{ns}, MisakoTogo $\frac{3}{4}$	driving
17Mar93	GP8	fm	4uf	Alw35000	T a $1\frac{1}{8}$			1:52 60	76	7/10	$9^{5\frac{1}{2}}$	$9^{3\frac{1}{2}}$	$8^{3\frac{3}{4}}$	$5^{1\frac{3}{4}}$	$2^{1\frac{1}{2}}$	Bailey	117		*1.30	MissLenora $1\frac{1}{2}$, Garendare $2\frac{1}{2}$, MysticHawk ^{nk}	late rally
14Feb93	GP9	fm	4uf	Alw28000	T $1\frac{1}{16}$	:47.09	1:11.57	1:42 28	76	2/12	$8^{8\frac{1}{2}}$	8^{8}	$6^{3\frac{1}{2}}$	$5^{2\frac{3}{4}}$	$3^{3\frac{1}{4}}$	Bailey	117		3.70	PinkTurtle $\frac{1}{2}$, FoolishLine $2\frac{3}{4}$, Garendare $3\frac{1}{2}$	mild rally
04Oct92	Lch*	sf	3uf	2l'Opera	T a $1\frac{1}{8}$			2:02 50		12	---	---	---	---	12	Boeuf	121			Hatoof $\frac{1}{2}$, LaFavorita 1, RubyTiger ^{ns}	
14Jun92	Chy*	gd	3f	1D Hermes	T a $1\frac{5}{16}$			2:09 50		12	---	---	---	---	12	Mongil	128			Jolypha 1, ShebaDancer ^{hd}, Verveine 1	
08May92	StC*	gd	3f	3Cleopatre	T a $1\frac{5}{16}$			2:16.40		7	---	---	---	---	1^{hd}	Boeuf	121			Garendare ^{hd}, PaixBlanche ^{hd}, TripleTiara ^{hd}	

Workouts: **21Jul BEL 4f ft :49.21 b** **07Jul BEL 4f ft :48.77 b** **02Jul BEL 4f ft :48.43 b** **16Jun BEL 4f ft :51.06 b**

All this brings to mind an anecdote involving Andy Beyer and Triple Crown winner Seattle Slew, which he is man enough to recall with a laugh.

During the spring of 1977, Andy was convinced that Seattle Slew was overrated based on a critical examination of Slew's runaway performance in the Flamingo stakes at Hialeah. "The track was very fast for the Flamingo," Andy said. "The move he made to open up a huge lead on the turn was an illusion. The other horses were just slowing down rapidly, and he wasn't doing as much running as it seemed." While that may have been partially supported by Andy's adjusted speed figures and intuitive pace analysis, the numbers were hiding quite a bit. Seattle Slew was overpowering his opposition, and the visual impression he made on those tuned in to the power of his huge athletic body were in for a treat during the 1977 Triple Crown. In other words, pure numbers can lie, and visual evidence, even in the teeth of numerical contradictions, is valid evidence.

The trick is to be certain that you have developed the ability to judge the racehorse in athletic terms before discounting numerical values. Consider the remarks of Jeff Siegel, the extremely talented horse owner-buyer-handicapper based in southern California, who puts out the *Handicapper's Report* with Bob Selvin, among other contributions to the game.

"I use numbers all the time," Siegel said at a symposium on speed figures at the Handicapping Expo III in 1990. "But when my eyes tell me that a horse is traveling well, or showing me more energy than he is delivering, I've learned to trust that above all other things."

Me too. That is why I must state here, amidst all the numerical aspects of handicapping, not to get lost in a search for the magic number. It does not exist. These numbers—all of them—are clues to interpret, part of the picture. They help identify important characteristics of the improving, or declining, horse. The thoroughbred is a living, breathing flesh-and-blood creature who cannot be reduced to a piece on a chessboard, no matter how hard you try.

Pace as Science and Pseudoscience

According to the way pace is being portrayed in the current handicapping literature, one might think an advanced degree in mathematics is required to study the subject. Indeed, there are several complex formulas for pace analysis gaining in popularity, including some with their own obtuse language seemingly designed to raise the level of inquiry to Newtonian physics. Dr. Howard Sartin, a clinical psychologist-horseplayer, is perhaps the chief proponent of numerically based pace analysis. Sartin, the story goes, began his horseracing adventures when he decided to lead a group of addicted gamblers through their therapy sessions with the following wonderful precept:

"The cure for losing is winning."

You can't argue with that, and perhaps to prove the point, Sartin has gone on to bigger and better things with his "Sartin Methodology," including a lucrative career of promoting computer-driven handicapping aids and a long-running series of lectures and newsletters that feed his growing list of clients.

Sartin seems well intentioned, but not opposed to superimposing his terminology on the work of others. (In early 1993, he made a concerted effort to convince his followers that "track valence" should be substituted for "track bias," in an attempt to place his own stamp of identity on the concept.) In response, I have no plans to substitute my own terms for "incremental velocity" or "energy distribution," but prefer to point out that the good Doctor of Pace and his disciples have raised some interesting handicapping issues to be delved into more deeply.

At its core, the Sartin methodology is serious work, focusing on feet-per-second calculations of speed between the various points of call and a multitude of comparisons between segments of a given race. All comparisons get some play in the approach, most particularly the first ½-mile call with the final ¼ mile in sprints and the ¾-mile call with the final ¼ in routes, among other ratios.

On the next page is a Sartin-style chart representing all reasonable fractional clockings in a feet-per-second format as they were derived through the application of a rudimentary physics formula kept in mothballs since high school.

Surely, there is considerable merit to breaking down a race into segments and to establishing how fast a horse comparatively displayed his speed during each segment. But for a method that employs feet-per-second velocity formulas in its attempt at greater accuracy, it always seemed strange to find a few mathematical dinosaurs employed by pace handicappers until corrections were acknowledged in advanced Sartin programs in 1993.

For instance, the value of ⅕ second at all distances and all rates of speed does not equal one length, as has been stated so often by many others, and neither does the traditional one-horse length equal about 10 feet. Research has clearly shown that six lengths per second is a lot closer to reality and that the average length of the racehorse is about 8.5–9.0 feet.

These discrepancies may seem innocent variations from reality, but they are at odds with a method taking pains to express mathematical relationships in precise feet-per-second formulations and they underscore an absolutely ironic, essential point:

Given the indisputable success many pace handicappers enjoy—despite having such errors imbedded in their calculations—*there is ample evidence that numerical pace handicapping does not require as much accuracy as the feet-per-second calculations pretend to provide.* Indeed, pace calculations may be off by as much as 20 percent in cases where beaten lengths are involved. This does not include the normal range of errors found in result charts in which beaten lengths are

DISTANCE COVERED BY THE HORSE IN FEET

TIME EXPIRED, IN SECONDS, DURING THE FRACTIONAL SPLIT

Example: ¼ mile clocked in 22.40 seconds

$$\frac{¼ \text{ mile} = 1{,}320 \text{ feet}}{22.40 \text{ seconds}} = 58.93 \text{ per second}$$

FEET PER SECOND TIME CHART

³⁄₁₆ MILE	¼ MILE	⁵⁄₁₆ MILE	⅜ MILE	½ MILE	6 FURLONGS
16.00–61.87	21.00–62.86	28.00–58.92	34.00–58.25	43.00–61.39	1:08.00–58.23
.20–61.11	.20–62.26	.20–58.51	.20–59.89	.20–61.11	.20–58.06
.40–60.36	.40–61.68	.40–58.09	.40–59.56	.40–60.82	.40–57.89
.60–59.63	.60–61.12	.60–57.69	.60–57.23	.60–60.55	.60–57.72
.80–58.92					
17.00–58.23	22.00–60.00	29.00–56.89	35.00–56.57	44.00–60.00	1:09.00–57.39
.20–57.55	.20–59.45	.20–56.50	.20–56.25	.20–59.72	.20–57.23
.40–56.89	.40–58.93	.40–56.12	.40–55.93	.40–59.45	.40–57.06
.60–56.25	.60–58.40	.60–56.74	.60–55.61	.60–59.19	.60–56.89
.80–55.62	.80–57.89	.80–55.37	.80–55.30	.80–58.92	.80–56.73
18.00–55.00	23.00–57.39	30.00–55.00	36.00–55.00	45.00–58.65	1:10.00–56.57
.20–54.38	.20–56.89	.20–54.63	.20–54.69	.20–58.40	.20–56.41
.40–53.67	.40–56.41	.40–54.27	.40–54.39	.40–58.14	.40–56.25
.60–53.09	.60–55.93	.60–53.22	.60–54.09	.60–57.89	.60–56.09
.80–52.64	.80–55.46	.80–53.57	.80–53.80	.80–57.64	.80–55.93
19.00–52.10	24.00–55.00	31.00–53.22	37.00–53.51	46.00–57.39	1:11.00–55.77
.20–51.56	.20–54.54	.20–52.88	.20–53.22	.20–57.14	.20–55.61
.40–51.03	.40–54.09	.40–52.54	.40–52.94	.40–56.89	.40–55.46
.60–50.51	.60–53.65	.60–52.22	.60–52.65	.60–56.65	.60–55.30
.80–50.00	.80–53.22	.80–51.88	.80–52.37	.80–56.41	.80–55.15
20.00–19.51	25.00–52.80	32.00–51.56	38.00–52.10	47.00–56.17	1:12.00–55.00
.20–19.00	.20–52.38	.20–51.25	.20–51.83	.20–55.93	.20–54.84
.40–48.52	.40–51.96	.40–50.92	.40–51.56	.40–55.69	.40–54.69
.60–48.05	.60–51.56	.60–50.61	.60–51.29	.60–55.46	.60–54.54
.80–47.59	.80–51.16	.80–50.30	.80–51.03	.80–55.23	.80–54.41
21.00–47.14	26.00–50.76	33.00–50.00	39.00–50.76	48.00–55.00	1:13.00–54.24
.20–46.69	.20–50.38	.20–49.69	.20–50.51	.20–54.77	.20–54.09
.40–46.26	.40–50.00	.40–49.41	.40–50.25	.40–54.54	.40–53.95
.60–45.83	.60–49.62	.60–49.10	.60–50.00	.60–54.32	.60–53.80
.80–45.41	.80–49.25	.80–48.81	.80–49.74	.80–54.00	.80–53.65
22.00–45.00	27.00–48.88	34.00–48.52	40.00–59.50	49.00–53.88	1:14.00–53.51
22.20–48.59	.20–48.52	.20–48.24	.20–49.25	.20–53.65	.20–53.36
22.40–44.19	.40–48.17	.40–47.94	.40–49.00	.40–53.44	.40–53.22

roughly approximated by the trackmen on the scene. (See Appendix C for mathematical computations on the beaten-length error factor.)

Most pace handicappers tend to overlook such built-in errors, yet nearly all will admit that their numbers are most effective comparing front-running or near-the-pace types in sprints, probably because these races can be dissected into three equal or nearly equal segments and the substantive portion occurs around a single turn.

Accurate pace numbers may prove useful in routes—particularly to locate the probable pacesetter(s) or determine how fast the maximum pace may be—but my experience suggests that pace handicapping must deal with a wide range of middle moves that are not easily scored by any present mathematical method. Indeed, route races tend to defy precise mathematical comparisons because they invite more flexible pace scenarios than sprints. Add to this the extra difficulty of rating horses who lag inertly far behind the pace and we have a quagmire of elusive calculations that just do not fit any reliable method, at least not yet.

By necessity, pace handicappers must fudge true mathematical values for beaten lengths and develop artificial measuring tools to resolve other inconsistencies. This is nothing to be ashamed of; from such efforts inevitably will come the next phase in pace handicapping. In the meantime, forgive me for hoping that pace handicappers will discard pseudoscientific jargon and make fewer claims for the universal applications of their methods.

Among other things, I have seen enough evidence to believe that the power of pace handicapping in two-turn races seems to rest with running-style comparisons and bursts of speed of varying length.

An important exception occurs when the player confronts a severely biased racetrack. In such instances some use of numerical pace ratings can prove helpful in conjunction with speed points or fractional splits to identify horses who fit the prevailing bias in routes as well as in sprints. In this regard I recommend *Modern Pace Handicapping*, a 1991 book authored by Sartin disciple Tom Brohamer.

Brohamer, a versatile handicapper with a facile mind, has designed a fine research tool to quantify track bias in the context of pace profiles. Brohamer's track profile relies on comprehensive use of Sartin-style measurements and is the single best argument I have seen for learning them.

Otherwise, my research into pace suggests it is a losing move to emphasize any form of pace calculations over speed figures in races where fractional splits are within a wide range of normalcy. Starting with that handicapping nugget, here are the most prominent conclusions gleaned from three years of experimentation and testing of pace measurements at several tracks:

- If the pace of a given race is within .60 (³⁄₅) seconds of normal for the class, pace is a distinctly weak handicapping tool.
- If the internal fractions are within .60 range of normalcy for the class and distance, speed figures pick slightly more winners than top pace figures and the overall win percentage does not improve to any reliable degree when the speed-figure horse has an added marginal pace advantage.
- When the pace is .60 faster, or slower than par for the class, the top speed-figure horse wins slightly less often than the normal range cited above.
- When the pace is .60 faster, pace figures pick slightly more winners than speed figures.
- When the pace is .60 slower, pace-figure standouts win a higher percentage compared to speed figures. (In such slow-pace scenarios a pace-figure standout is any horse with an edge of .40 seconds or better to the half-mile marker.)

The most dominant winning situations confirmed results presented independently by authors James Quinn and Tom Brohamer.

Any horse with a *two-length edge* to the ½-mile call in sprints, or three lengths to the ¾-mile call in routes, wins as often as any horse with a two-three length speed-figure edge. In sprints, horses who have a minimum two-length edge in both categories win substantially more often than horses with the edge in only one of the categories. No such added advantage was found in routes, however.

In bottom-level claiming sprints at minor tracks and maiden-claiming sprints everywhere, a marginal pace advantage translates to a win more often than a marginal speed-figure edge. Better still, if the pace advantage is not marginal, but a clear two lengths, these horses win as often as public favorites—about 30 percent of the time—sometimes at outrageous prices. A 20 percent flat-bet profit was generated from a spot sampling of this angle in 250 maiden claiming races run at 18 different tracks in 1992–1993.

As suggested by Quinn and Brohamer and tentatively supported by my own research, a different game may exist for two-year-olds in claiming races at one mile or more. In a random sample of 260 such races on fast tracks in 1990, 1991 and 1992, more than 40 percent were won by horses who reached the six-furlong split in the lead or within one length of the lead.

While these pet research nuggets do not describe the complete utility of pace calculations in modern handicapping, I remain troubled by the flaws built into virtually all pace-handicapping regimens, including those being sold en masse to the public via computer programs. For one thing, too much reliance is placed on existing past races for a representative "pace line" to base serious comparisons. Too many interactive realities are ignored when the player relies strictly on the last race, or any one race for such important comparisons.

A better approach would emulate speed-figure handicappers by plugging in an *estimated pace line* based on a total reading of the horse's past performances. In the hands of a potentially good player, this subjective choice will prove far superior to any mechanical method. For a clearcut example, consider the automatic error factor in the following setup:

A horse is entered in a $10,000 claiming sprint today, but his last race was a 1 1/16-mile route 10 days ago in which he finished fourth after stalking the pace. Ten days earlier, the same horse raced in third position throughout another $10,000 sprint, while beaten three lengths.

According to one of Sartin's computer programs and most pace handicappers, the player would be encouraged to skip over the 1 1/16-mile race to plug in the pace line for the prior $10,000 race, selecting that six-furlong race for a better fit.

The intervening 1 1/16-mile race is certain to have a residual impact on this horse's sprint pace potential today. Such races tend to dull a horse's early zip, while improving its stamina. Clearly, then, it will be necessary for the player to adjust the pace line for the sprint to reflect the impact of the intervening route.

It says here that a perfect fit taken from a previous running line is not often possible from the past performances; it makes better sense to use your own intuitive estimate of what this horse is now capable of producing. Similar estimates, or *projections*, will be necessary to establish probable pace lines for horses attempting new distances or changing tracks, none of which is adequately dealt with by any computer-generated program I have seen, including Sartin's.

Again, Sartin and his disciple Tom Brohamer's astute conceptualization of a race into segmented parts deserves serious attention, but at present there is little to be gained favoring their equations over fractional splits or other numerical approaches.

Converting Beyer Figures for Pace Analysis

I believe there are three logical pace issues that have significant power in the handicapping equation and each can be stated in the form of a question:

1. Was the pace of the race an important factor in promoting or eliminating any horse in a race already run?
2. Is the pace of today's race likely to produce a lone front-running standout and/or a favorable or unfavorable trip for specific horses?
3. Which horse or horses have demonstrated extraordinary acceleration or staying power that could place them in favorable positions or seriously alter the way any race may be run?

Fractional clockings coupled to a sensible track-variant adjustment are sufficient to answer any of the above questions, but there is little doubt that regular use of *pace numbers* will provide greater insights. Knowledge of a given track's peculiarities at different distances is required along with an accurate track variant for the day, which is not published in *DRF* with the Beyer numbers. This is another reason to do your own Beyer-style speed figures.

Short of purchasing par charts sold through the mail, we will need to develop pace par clockings for key points of call at each distance. Here we are indebted to Ray Talbot of the 1950s and contemporary pace authors Bill Quirin, James Quinn, Tom Brohamer and Howard Sartin, too, for confirming the relatively minor role of ¼-mile splits in sprints and ½-mile fractions in routes.

WORKING WITH PACE PARS

Pace pars should represent the "normal" fractions for each clocking regardless of track conditions. They are obtained by cataloging the fractional splits for specific final time clockings. To develop the pace pars for six furlongs in 1:11.00 or any other final time, we need to know the midpoint of a representative range of fractional clockings for this final clocking at this track. As per the following:

When a horse travels 1:08.80 for six furlongs, the fractional par clockings for that six-furlong clocking will be proportionately expressed on the chart.

¼ MI.	½ MI.	6-FURLS.
(22.00)	44.80	1:08.80

If the same horse encounters a very slow racing surface and runs 1:12.20, the appropriate pace par clockings will be proportionately slower.

¼ MI.	½ MI.	6 FURLS.
(22.60)	46.50	1:12.20

To spare all of us from unnecessary technical detail, all further steps in this procedure along with extensive illustrations and examples can be found in Appendix C.

For convenience, I have developed a pace par chart based on a tighter numerical rating scale, because Beyer speed figures tend to lose meaning when applied to ¼-mile and ½-mile clockings due to the increased numerical value of ⅕ second at the shorter distances on the Beyer scale. To strictly use Beyer figures for pace calculations would be as cumbersome as paying for a meal with Italian lira in a Mexico City restaurant.

As a starting point, my converted pace-speed numbers are pegged to a 100 Beyer speed figure. All fractional clockings on the 100 Beyer pace line will equal a 100 converted pace-speed number. From that starting point, I configure pace lines for each .20 difference in final time, adjusting one point on the converted pace-speed number scale for each increment up or down the chart.

For example:

¼ MI.		½ MI.		6 FURLS.		BEYER FIG.		CONVERTED PACE-SPEED #
22.30	=	45.50	=	1:10.40	=	100	=	100
22.30	=	45.60		1:10.60		(98)	=	99

The portion of the six-furlong pace par chart (see following page), which includes Beyer speed figures for the final time clocking and a tighter pace-rating scale for convenience, is a product of those steps. To adapt the chart for your own track, simply slide the ¼-mile and ½-mile splits up or down—independently—according to the results of your own class par research for a few popular final clockings. There is nothing wrong with using interpolation to extrapolate a complete set of pace pars from a sampling of the most popular final clockings.

Although the above chart serves equally well for 6½ furlongs and needs only minor adjustments for seven furlongs, each distance at every track must be computed separately due to chute length or angle, starting gate position relative to the first turn, banking of the first turn and/or the different "run-up" distances from starting gate to initial teletimer beam, which trips the electronic clock for the race several strides after the horses have began to run.

At Pimlico and Laurel racecourses in Maryland, for instance, fractional clockings tend to be somewhat slower than Aqueduct, and run-up distances also come into play. At Pimlico, the starting gate for six-furlong races is very close to the electronic starting beam, so the ½-mile

AQUEDUCT SIX-FURLONG PACE PARS

¼ MI.		½ MI.		6 FURLS.		BEYER FIG.		CONVERTED PACE-SPEED #
21.80	=	44.40	=	1:08.20	=	131	=	112
22.00	=	44.50	=	1:08.40	=	129	=	111
22.10	=	44.80	=	1:09.00	=	120	=	108
22.10	=	45.00	=	1:09.40	=	115	=	106
22.20	=	45.20	=	1:09.80	=	109	=	104
22.20	=	45.30	=	1:10.00	=	106	=	103
22.20	=	45.40	=	1:10.20	=	103	=	101
22.30	=	45.50	=	1:10.40	=	100	=	100
22.30	=	45.60	=	1:10.60	=	98	=	99
22.30	=	45.70	=	1:10.80	=	95	=	98
22.40	=	45.80	=	1:11.00	=	92	=	97
22.40	=	46.00	=	1:11.40	=	86	=	95
22.50	=	46.20	=	1:11.70	=	82	=	93
22.50	=	46.40	=	1:12.00	=	79	=	92
22.50	=	46.50	=	1:12.20	=	76	=	91
22.60	=	46.60	=	1:12.40	=	73	=	90
22.70	=	46.90	=	1:13.00	=	64	=	87
22.70	=	47.00	=	1:13.20	=	62	=	86
22.90	=	47.40	=	1:14.00	=	51	=	82
23.10	=	47.90	=	1:15.00	=	37	=	77
23.40	=	48.40	=	1:16.00	=	25	=	72

fractional split tends to be about .80 (⅘) seconds slower than the same distance at Laurel, where the run-up distance is about 15 yards longer.

Similarly, the one-mile distance around two turns at Santa Anita features a relatively long run-up distance, especially when compared to the 1-1¹⁄₁₆-mile distance. This speeds up the first ¼-call fractional split for one-mile races as much as the tendency for Santa Anita jockeys to gun their horses out of the gate to get good position going into the first turn. On the other hand, seven furlongs at Santa Anita produces slower early fractions than six-furlong races, due to a shorter run-up distance to the starting beam *and* a slightly slower backstretch starting chute.

Otherwise, run-up distances have their greatest impact on early fractional splits, while their effect on final clockings may hardly be noticeable.

Clockings are timed in traditional ⅕-second intervals at most tracks and in hundredths of a second in New York, California and a few other states. I encourage serious students of pace to interpolate and/or round off pace clockings to .10 seconds or use actual data where available.

If a horse wins a stakes race in 1:08.80, the pace par would be: (22.10)   44.70   1:08.80.

If he actually goes 22.00 and 44.60 he would earn a pace rating based on the ½-mile clocking of 126 on the Beyer scale, which I convert to 110 on my scale.

NOTE: *When an individual fractional clocking is represented on two or more lines with different point values, choose the median point value, or the lower of two median pace numbers to break ties. Thus, on a day when there is no track variant to consider, the interpolated pace-line numbers for the example above would be (107)   110   109 on my converted pace-speed number scale.*

Beyer style figures listed are for each final time clocking and references to "Beyer pace line numbers" in the text are strictly for convenience. In his most recent and very intriguing book, *Beyer on Speed*, Andy gives his own version of pace numbers based on *DRF* Beyer speed figures.

Most pace-figure handicappers concentrate on ½-mile clockings in sprints and ¾-mile clockings in routes; I suggest adjusting for beaten lengths at all fractional clockings to get a better feel for the true speed potential of each horse and to set up the possibility for measuring mid-race, or turn-time moves (first-call fractional split subtracted from second-call fractional split). All this work can be done by hand, of course, but in the age of the computer, it makes much more sense to incorporate these and other ideas into a sound computer program to pare down the necessary computations to minutes per day.

BEATEN-LENGTHS ADJUSTMENTS

According to the mathematically sound beaten-lengths chart displayed in Chapter 15, ten beaten lengths at one mile is equal to 18 points, while at six furlongs it is 24 points, five furlongs it is 29 and for ½ mile it would be 33, or as below:

VALUE OF ONE BEATEN LENGTH ON THE BEYER SCALE

2 FURLS.	4 FURLS.	6 FURLS.
3.5	3.3 points	2.4 points

Thus, according to the above, the value of one length at the ½-mile call is *greater* than it is at the finish of a six-furlong race. But wait a minute. This might be mathematically true for comparing horses after the finish of a race, but it is exactly the opposite while a race is in progress. Consider the following.

A horse traveling at 22 seconds for the first ¼ mile is moving faster than he is when completing a six-furlong race, even when he is throwing in a terrific final ¼ mile in 24 seconds to complete a near track record performance of 1:08 flat. Consider that it takes the horse *less time* to make up the one length at the first ¼ mile clocked in 22 than it does to make up the one length in the final quarter when being clocked in 24. Thus, if we are adjusting clockings based on lengths behind the leader at the ¼- or ½-mile call, we must deduct proportionately *less per length* to reflect the reality that a horse will cover the same gap in faster time. This may contradict widely accepted formulas for adjusting beaten lengths at the pace call, but it is right.

Another reality affects beaten-length-point values although it is not possible to assess how much. Consider that a horse two lengths behind the leader at the ¼- or ½-mile call is very much involved in the race, while a horse four lengths behind is on the fringe of the pace and a horse six lengths behind is not involved in the pace at all. Obviously, this subtle, practical reality is never reflected in strict mathematical relationships, much as Beyer came to realize when he subjectively substituted his 6½-furlong beaten-lengths chart for the turf routes in 1993. It is my view that astute players may be justified in subjectively adjusting beaten lengths via an "impact value," although this may require constant tinkering and is dangerous territory for the inexperienced. In the meantime, I cannot accept the standard point values suggested by the majority of pace authors (1 length = .20 (⅕) seconds = 1 point at the finish and one length = .10 (¹⁄₁₀) seconds = 1 point at the pace call) and I suggest you don't either.

While rounding off is almost inevitable and does force us closer to these erroneous standards, important differences can be plugged into our pace charts and computer programs.

I suggest Beyer figures for pure speed figures and a converted point scale to make pace calculations based on Beyer figures. After considerable experimentation, I have settled on the beaten-lengths adjustments below:

BEATEN LENGTHS AT FRACTIONAL CALLS

¼ MI	½ MI	¾ MI (ROUTES)	
.10 seconds	.10	.20	for ¾ to 1 length
.10	.10	.20	for 1¼ to 1¾ lengths
.20	.20	.30	for 2 lengths
.20	.30	.40	2¼ to 2¾ lengths
.30	.40	.50	3 lengths
.30	.50	.60	3¼ to 3¾ lengths
.40	.60	.70	4 lengths
.50	.70	.80	4¼ to 4¾ lengths
.60	.80	.90	5 lengths
.70	.90	1.00	5¼ to 5¾ lengths
.80	1.00	1.10	6 lengths
.90	1.10	1.20	6¼ to 6¾
1.00	1.20	1.30	7 lengths
1.10	1.30	1.40	7¼ to 7¾ lengths
1.20	1.40	1.50	8 lengths
1.30	1.50	1.60	8¼ to 8¾ lengths
1.40	1.60	1.70	9 lengths
1.50	1.60	1.80	9¼ to 9¾ lengths
1.40	1.70	1.90	10 lengths
1.60	1.80	2.00	11 lengths
1.80	2.00	2.20	12 lengths
2.00	2.20	2.40	13 lengths
2.20	2.40	2.60	14 lengths
2.40	2.70	2.80 seconds	15 lengths

As a rule, separately computed track variants for fractional clockings are a waste of time because they are virtually impossible to compute without accepting unexplainable distortions. At a windy track, the only successful, separate track variants for pace will be made by those meticulous enough to chart every shift in the wind during the card. It will not be enough to rely on time differences themselves to hint at the shifts.

Distortions in pace numbers also will occur if full credit is given to the pace call for any track variant based on final time. Thus, as a working compromise, I distribute a proportionate fraction of the Beyer style variant to the fractional call I am seeking to adjust.

TRACK-VARIANT ADJUSTMENTS FOR PACE CALLS

¼ mile is ⅓ of a six-furlong sprint.

½ mile is ⅔ of a six-furlong sprint.

½ mile is ½ of a one-turn mile.

¾ mile call is ¾ of a two-turn mile, or 1¹⁄₁₆ miles.

¾ mile is ⅔ of 1⅛ miles (six of nine furlongs).

EXAMPLE: A six-furlong race for $17,500 claimers has been clocked in 46.20 and 1:11.20 to earn a Beyer speed figure of 92 in the *DRF* or via your own calculations. Since 1:11.20 equals a raw 89 on the Beyer scale for six furlongs, we can deduce this 92 was scored on a track playing +3 Beyer points slow (or about .20 seconds). Before we convert to the tighter pace number scale, we should jot down the raw Beyer pace number associated with 46.20, which is 81.

We will adjust this pace line number by ⅔ of the +3 Beyer variant, which is 2 points.

The raw Beyer pace line numbers are:

½ MI	6 FURLS.
81	89

The adjusted Beyer pace line numbers are:

½ MI	6 FURLS.
83	92

Using the tighter number scale the converted pace-speed figures are:

½ MI	FINAL
94	97

The converted pace-line number represents the race as it was run. A representative pace, with a steady finish slightly above par for the clocking. The next example will be more dramatic.

EXAMPLE: A wire-to-wire winner at Aqueduct is clocked in (22.20), 46.00 and 1:12.40 and is given a Beyer figure of 67 in her past-performance line, which was below average for the class of race, a $35,000 claiming race for filly New York breds. Because a 1:12.40 clocking is a 72 Beyer figure on the time chart, we can conclude that Beyer made this day five points fast (about .40 seconds fast).

We should then adjust the fractional pace numbers as follows:

46.00 = 86 on the Beyer pace line.

Variant adjustment = about −3 points (⅔ of −5 points) = 83 adjusted Beyer pace line number.

The adjusted Beyer pace line is:

83, 67, an unwieldly spread that distorts the relationship between the clockings.

The conversion to my scale:

83 Beyer pace line = 94 converted pace number.

67 Beyer speed figure = 89 converted speed number.

The converted pace numbers are: 94, 89.

Regardless of which scale is used, the flow of pace in the example race above suggested a winner who blitzed the field early and was tiring steadily in the drive. More evidence of this can be gleaned from the first ¼-mile split of 22.20, which after an adjustment of a Beyer point remains proportionately faster than the ½-mile split that already earned a 94 pace number. This in turn was five points faster than the final number, a par clocking for the class. As author Bill Quirin suggested in 1984, labeling the shape of the race is a great way to catalog important pace information.

Pace and the Single Race Bias

The only argument I have with Bill Quirin and his invaluable contribution to pace analysis is his use of the word *average* to describe the par range of clockings that often implies a very good performance. Frequently an *average* pace-*average* final clocking is the hallmark of a horse who can step up in class, or stretch out in distance, while any horse who sets a very fast pace *and* finishes in reasonable time for the class also is worth extra attention.

Independent of this minor quibble, the real value of Quirin's "race shapes" is in using them to diagnose *a single race pace bias* as powerful as any caused by weather or track geometry.

QUIRIN'S RACE SHAPES

1. Fast-Fast
2. Fast-Average
3. Fast-Slow
4. Average-Fast
5. Average-Average
6. Average-Slow
7. Slow-Fast
8. Slow-Average
9. Slow-Slow

Quirin suggests two lengths above or below par for his race shapes, but I find it depends on the level of class under consideration.

For races at or above $25,000 claiming, three lengths at the pace call is a preferable standard, or about four points on my tighter point scale at the ½-mile call. For cheaper races, a small difference may be more important than usual and two lengths is perfectly adequate. I also believe in labeling extreme pace scenarios.

For instance, the example race in Chapter 17, that featured a New York-bred filly claimer earning 94–89 converted pace-speed numbers, the race shape was *average early-slow late*. This is a shape in which front runners scored well, but closers who failed to gain significant ground in the stretch deserve to be downgraded.

A fit stretch runner should make more impact into such a pace scenario. Indeed, the winner was lucky to maintain her advantage while slowing down so noticeably. Next time against faster rivals who sport higher pace or speed figures, she would be a poor risk to repeat her victory.

Experience has shown that horses forced to expend more energy during the early stages of their races will lose energy in the final drive. How much they lose cannot be reduced to simple formulas as many pace authors suggest, but a loss of energy does occur. It can be a proportionate loss of a length or two to a dramatic retreat to the rear of the pack. Pace analysis may be overplayed as precise mathematics, but it does give us insight into the way races have been run and a tool to measure the approximate fit of individual horses to potential pace dilemmas.

For a twist to the previous example, consider if the same New York-bred filly had run the identical race while dueling with two or more horses. In that instance, I would put serious negative marks on the result chart next to the name of each stretch-running horse who failed to make a solid run at her. The shape and dynamics of the race would clearly indicate that the pace setters were vulnerable to late attack.

It is extremely important to realize that any horse who closed ground for second or third in this race was helped by the race shape. Such horses are worth betting against next time out unless they closed furiously after traffic problems.

Players who understand the implications of a weak or mediocre performance against a favorable pace or track bias may find cause to play this race's defeated stretch runners on the bottom of exactas and trifectas, but there is more money to be made betting against such horses who rally weakly when the pace was in their favor.

Using the pace-speed numbers described in the previous chapter, consider the following example all the way through the process.

Senor Rex	Dk. b. or br. g. 3(May), by Rexson—Flor de Luna, by Cutlass		Lifetime	1993	1 M	1	0	$5,170

MIGLIORE R (110 29 22 6 .26)   Br.—Samuels & Hushion (Fla)   1 0 1 0   1992   0 M   0   0
Own.—Hausman Eugene E   Tr.—Hushion Michael E (59 23 11 6 .39)   **122** $5,170
18Apr93- 5Aqu fst 6f   :22³   :46¹ 1:10   3 ↑ Md Sp Wt   91 2 4 42½ 2ʰᵈ 2¹ 21¼ Migliore R   115   2.90   91-15 Boundary115½ Senor Rex115¹¼ Bo Bo Star124 Gamely 6
LATEST WORKOUTS   Apr 25 Bel 4f fst :47² B   ● Apr 13 Bel tr.t 5f fst 1:00¹ H   Apr 5 Bel tr.t 5f fst 1:03   B   Mar 31 Bel tr.t 6f fst 1:19   B

First ¼-mile call: Senor Rex was 2½ lengths behind the leader at the first quarter call clocked in 22.60 (22⅗).

Senor Rex went the ¼ in 22.90. Yes, I round upward 2½ lengths to 3 lengths.

The ½-mile call: Senor Rex is a head behind the ½-mile clocked in 46.20 (46⅕) and no beaten-length adjustment is needed.

Senor Rex's raw pace line is: (22.90)   46.20   1:10.20

Using Beyer-style figures his raw pace line is: 82   103

Estimated Beyer variant for this race equals 12 points fast.

EXPLANATION: Senor Rex was credited in *Daily Racing Form* with a net Beyer speed figure of 91 for running 1:10.20. Because 1:10.20 actually is a 103 Beyer figure on the Aqueduct time chart, Beyer adjusted the raw figure downward to reflect the track variant of 12 points fast for the race $(103 - 12 = 91)$.

Also, we should note that the winner's adjusted Beyer figure was 93, five points (about two lengths) faster than par for maiden special weight races during April in New York.

Adjustments to the pace line: −8 points for ⅔ of the 12-point variant.

Senor Rex's adjusted Beyer paceline is:

½	6 FURLS.
74	91
(82−8)	(103−12)

On the converted number scale:

74 Beyer pace line = 90 converted pace number

91 Beyer figure   = 97 converted final fig

Senor Rex's converted pace-speed numbers are:

½	6 FURLS.
90	97

These numbers do not tell us if the race was slow early–average late, because race-shape designations apply to the clockings of the leader at each call. But we do know from the shape of the pace numbers that Senor Rex made a good run to the finish. We know this because even though he slowed down as measured by raw time, he slowed down less than horses generally do while running six furlongs in 1:10.20. This of course, relates to the optical illusion of stretch-running horses who rarely run faster at the end of their races. They merely slow down less than the rest of the field.

In raw fractional splits, Senor Rex went the first ¼ mile in 23.20, the second ¼ in 23.00 and the final ¼ in 23.80. The running line suggests he actually turned in a very solid performance, making a sharp move on the turn and sustaining it at above average speed through the lane. This is a horse who should win a maiden race very soon, and because he sustained a good middle move all the way to the wire, he is likely to handle longer distances.

Although reasonably close to the lead throughout, Senor Rex earns a slow early–average late race shape, but when we include his first ¼-mile fractional split and stop to visualize his move on the turn, we should give him extra credit for an above-average, sustained final ½-mile run.

Here are some more pace-related handicapping ideas and guidelines.

In sprints, if the Beyer speed figure was more than five points higher than the class par, I give significant extra credit to any horse who closed ground against a pace that was *slow early* for the time posted. Such a race usually favors front-running horses who also must be examined for possible versatility in future starts.

If a race was dominated by closers and the Beyer speed figure is more than five points slower than the class, I designate the race *slow late* and downgrade all horses in the field, including the winner. If, however, the pace at the half-mile call was aberrantly faster—at least .60 (³/₅) seconds faster—I will look hard for the *fast early* horses to return in races where less early pressure is likely. Closers who took down the money positions in such a *fast early–slow late* race were helped by the race shape and failed to run a good speed figure. Horses who faded out of contention were running terrific for a good portion of the race and deserve to be evaluated carefully next time out. Ron Cox and the fine West Coast handicapper Lee Rousso are two other handicappers I know who are especially fond of this angle, having employed it several times a season with their own pace ratings.

"I look for horses who survived a hot-pace duel to finish third or fourth, with a final speed figure close to average for the class," Cox says. "I get especially interested if the horse was caught four or five wide, or made his run while stuck inside when the rail was dead."

The race below produced just such a play. Note that Skipion made a

EIGHTH RACE — 6 FURLONGS. (1.07¹) ALLOWANCE. Purse $22,000. Fillies and mares 3-year-olds and upward which have not won a race other than maiden, claiming, starter, classified handicap or state bred. Weights: 3-year-olds, 119 lbs. Older, 121 lbs. Non-winners of a race other than claiming, starter or classified handicap since November 1, allowed 3 lbs. Such a race since October 1, 5 lbs.

Bay Meadows
DECEMBER 31, 1993

Value of Race: $22,000 Winner $12,100; second $4,400; third $3,300; fourth $1,650; fifth $550. Mutuel Pool $247,360.00 Exacta Pool $308,470.00

Last Raced	Horse	M/Eqt. A.Wt	PP	St	¼	½	Str	Fin	Jockey	Odds $1
9Dec93 8BM¹	Red Chimes	L 4 115	2	6	7²	6²	3hd	1¹	Baze R A	2.70
19Dec93 6BM⁶	Inyala Rouge	LB 4 109	1	8	8	8	5¹½	2½	Beckner D⁵	27.60
1Dec93 1BM²	Vive Le Torch	LB 6 116	7	3	3²	4²	4½	3nk	Meza R Q	10.70
2Dec93 3Hol³	Alydenann	LB 5 118	4	1	2hd	1hd	1¹	4nk	Kaenel J L	1.80
12Nov93 8BM⁴	Skipion	L 5 116	5	4	4¹½	2hd	2¹½	5⁴½	Belvoir V T	12.10
1Dec93 4BM²	Poetry Writer	LB 4 114	3	2	1½	3¹½	6³	6¹	Boulanger G	11.50
10Dec93 6BM²	Born to Be Queen	LB 5 116	6	5	5²	5½	7²	7⁴	Warren R J Jr	2.90
26Nov93 6BM⁴	Truly Fascinating	B 4 114	8	7	6¹	7¹	8	8	Jauregui L H	28.10

OFF AT 5:06 Start Good. Won driving. Time, :22², :45, :57², 1:10¹ Track fast.

$2 Mutuel Prices:

2-RED CHIMES	7.40	4.60	3.60
1-INYALA ROUGE		15.80	8.80
7-VIVE LE TORCH			5.80

$2 EXACTA 2-1 PAID $117.40

Ch. f, (Mar), by Siyah Kalem–Chocolate Chimes, by Forceten. Trainer Hollendorfer Jerry. Bred by Abruzzo Fred (Cal).

RED CHIMES reserved early, moved up inside on the turn, angled out for room in upper stretch and closed full of run to be along in time. INYALA ROUGE outrun to the stretch, rallied inside into the stretch, came through tight quarters in deep stretch and closed willingly. VIVE LE TORCH prompted the early pace, fell back lightly on the turn, responded into the stretch and had a mild late bid. ALYDENANN dueled for the early lead, drifted wide on the turn, remained wide in the drive while holding a short lead and weakened in the late stages. SKIPION just off the early pace, moved to challenge on the turn, remained a threat to midstretch and weakened late. POETRY WRITER dueled for the lead to the stretch and faltered. BORN TO BE QUEEN showed little. TRULY FASCINATING raced wide.

Owners— 1, Hansen Naomi & Hollendorfer Jerry; 2, Lanning Curt & Lila; 3, Lamonica Anthony; 4, Abrams & Karim & Perez; 5, Green Valley Ranch & Santucci G; 6, Roffe Sam; 7, Ossa Enterprises Inc; 8, Golden Eagle Farm

Trainers— 1, Hollendorfer Jerry; 2, Moger Ed Jr; 3, Brown Guy; 4, Jeanotte Bob; 5, Arterburn Lonnie; 6, Ross Larry; 7, Fierce Fordell; 8, Severinsen Allen

22.30 middle move from only two lengths off the pace into the teeth of a brisk 45.00 half mile. Note also that she was beaten by only ½ length and two necks for second in a race dominated by closers who finished 1-2-3. Fourth-place finisher Alydenann went back to southern California only to be forced into another hot-speed duel, but Skipion dropped a notch in class, turned back to 5½ furlongs and won for fun.

Whenever the Beyer figure is within normal limits for the class, then I apply the following pace guidelines:

If the pace for the ½-mile call is at least .60 (⅗) seconds faster than the par fractional clocking, I conclude the early pace was very fast and quite favorable to a mid-pack closer or deep closer depending upon the severity of the early pace. Front runners who outlast the competition have run strongly.

If a fast pace has been set by one horse, I may anticipate this horse setting the pace against similar or higher-class rivals in future starts. Any horse who exhibits superior speed during the early stages of a race is a serious threat to wire a similar field, even at a longer distance.

If the fast pace was the consequence of a hot duel, I will take a close look at the horses who were involved in the duel next time out. If no track bias was involved, I will conclude that a *single-race pace bias* favoring closers was a dominant issue in the race. All such closers who failed to contend ran poorly. Any of the dueling horses are likely to wire a similar field with less early pressure.

If the winner's speed figure is at or above par for the class, any horse who races at or above par throughout the race deserves credit for a sustained, positive run. Quirin's labels might label this horse: average–average/average–fast/fast–average/fast–fast/, but the individual horse who sustained a good pace deserves an extra mark for a *solid-pace* rating.

Frequently, a solid-pace pattern tips off stretch-out winners and horses who are improving. (When we look at Senor Rex's complete race, he becomes an example of this solid-pace pattern.)

A solid-pace pattern also points out the type of speed horse who may compete successfully against confirmed stretch runners on a track biased toward stalkers and closers. The higher the converted pace-speed numbers, the classier the horse.

If a duel pushes the pace *one full second faster* than par through the key fractional call, I will conclude a powerful pace strong enough to affect the performances of all horses in the race. As you might expect, a slow or average finish would be a serious indictment against the closers in the field, while the front runner would deserve extra credit for sticking around at the finish. If the finishing portion of the race shape was fast, any horse in contention at any stage of the race would deserve some credit while horses in the hunt at the end would score highly in any evaluation system.

Even when front runner(s) retreat to the rear of the pack, it is important to watch for pace setters coming out of fast-paced races, hoping they are matched against softer competition for the early lead.

Except for turf routes, whenever the pace is .60 (⅗) seconds slower at the second call, I conclude it was favorable to front-running and/or near-pace types. This is a slow—early pace scenario. If the second portion of the race shape is average or fast, the race will need to be looked at more closely. If a front runner took advantage of the slow-early pace to win the contest, his fast final fractions suggest fitness and versatility, not necessarily a horse who got away with a soft pace, although that too may be the case. In any case, there is no mistaking the positive effort of a stretch runner who overcomes a slow pace to finish boldly.

If the pace is *one second slower*, I will conclude a single race bias strongly tilted toward the front runner in the race. I label this scenario *very slow pace*, and very few stretch runners win against the bias of this race shape.

If either of the above slow-early scenarios also produce slow-late races, I will conclude that no horse in the field ran well enough to merit a good mark for the race.

Be mindful of horses who improve their ½-mile fractional clockings (or pace numbers) by more than .60 (⅗) seconds *from one race to the next*. Such horses may be tipping off pending improvement.

Any horse who throws in a single burst of speed .60 (⅗) seconds *faster than par* for the ½-mile call after running a modest or slow first ¼ mile has shown good acceleration on the turn and deserves a close look in subsequent starts.

Sometimes these horses are merely firing a short burst without any positive implications, while on other occasions, it may tip off a sustained run of significant quality. Again, Senor Rex is a good example of this later positive performance. As a lightly raced runner, he probably was not yet at his peak to sustain his burst, but he was running fast into the teeth of the pace. We would be wise to assess this horse carefully as he progresses through maiden and allowance competition. Perhaps he needed the outing, or a few more workouts, or Lasix, or an equipment change to harness or sustain his speed for a maiden win. Surely the numbers and the race shape give us valuable clues to appreciate his performance, but they do not tell the whole story. With some fine-tuning such horses frequently come back with a winning stroke, some at surprisingly generous odds.

PACE HANDICAPPING IN TWO-TURN ROUTES

To use any of the handicapping ideas cited in sprints, demand *one full second* thresholds instead of .60 (⅗) seconds and 1.60 seconds instead of one-second thresholds. I further suggest that Graded route stakes and other route races with Beyer figures higher than 105 may be unaffected by variations in pace under two seconds to the ¾-mile call. Many high-class route stakes defy sensible pace analysis as much as they may contradict a given track bias. Class is at work here and hard to quantify.

Pace par charts and procedures for two-turn routes and other sprint distances also can be found in Appendix C.

Another quirk worth noting: In claiming or allowance races, which feature extremely fast preliminary fractions, it is wise to score that race toward a fast-early race shape, even if neutral fractions persist in the traditional ¾-mile pace lines. If for example, the pace for a $25,000 claiming route at Santa Anita is 21.80 for the first ¼ mile and/or 45.40 for the ½ mile, that alone could explain a mid-race or late-race slowdown.

Too fast preliminary fractional pars for 25 North American racetracks are listed in Appendix C. They were derived from personal playing experience, and I am quite sure you will find them very helpful in your pace analysis.

At the bottom line, pace handicapping is a valued tool to spot situations when a horse can be expected to dominate the running or get an easy trip. If he has the early speed to control the pace—or a track bias in his favor—the implications should be obvious. If he has a middle move in a race with fainthearted contenders, such as you often see in lower-level claiming races—especially maiden claiming races—that too is powerful information, as is the knowledge that a horse with sufficient pace ability is likely to get a good position in a complex race.

If severe competition for the lead is anticipated, the strength of the track bias should dictate inclusion or exclusion of horses on the pace, while late movers deserve preference on a stamina-favoring strip. But here it must be pointed out that running style, stamina preparation and Beyer figures take precedence over pace numbers when a true late-speed bias presents itself, and the best form to look for in such races is a horse who has been racing on or near the lead in longer races, or a stretch-running type who tends to get rolling before the final ¼ mile.

Horses who lack the sufficient pace to get a safe position from a tricky post also may be severely compromised on any racing surface at any distance. Otherwise, I remain convinced that pace analysis is at its best in analyzing races already run. There is one more point to be reiterated: No matter what method of making pace numbers you employ, there is a guaranteed error factor that cannot be weeded out until fractional clockings are registered by electronic means for each horse.

The trackman's visual approximation of the horses' relative positions at each ¼-mile call will contain errors regardless of the trackman's skill. Try calling a 12-horse field going five furlongs at 11:00 P.M. at Penn National Racecourse some time if you doubt my word on this, or double check the pre-stretch call of any race anywhere where several horses are bunched together, or the race occurs in poor weather. At some tracks I estimate the error factor for beaten lengths at the pre-stretch call to be as much as three lengths on horses behind the top few. Put that into your pace line computer-handicapping system and smell the smoke. It's just your money burning.

Theory Versus Experience

For each and every piece of information in the past-performance profile, there is a popular theory purporting to measure its exact significance. The interesting thing about that is I know of no winning player who subscribes to any such rigid approach to any aspect of the game.

WEIGHT

The old saying that "weight will stop a freight train" is true enough. But except for a few special cases, it is pure conjecture that a fit racehorse can be stopped or slowed by the addition of a few pounds. Weight is simply the most overrated factor in handicapping.

Perhaps 105 pounds will help a horse run a fifth of a second faster than 110 pounds and two-fifths of a second faster than 115. But there is no proof to demonstrate the validity of such a rigid relationship. Indeed between 105 and 115 pounds the amount of weight carried by the horse is demonstrably unimportant.

Beyond 115 pounds, the effect of added weight on performance is an individual thing.

Some horses can't handle 120 pounds; others are able to run just as fast and as far with considerably more. Past-performance profiles usually provide sufficient clues to make such determinations; but because the betting public tends to automatically downgrade the chances of a top-weighted horse, the reward for a more flexible attitude is generally generous mutuel prices.

```
Gallant Bob                      126  Dk. b. or br. g (1972), by Gallant Romeo—Wisp O'Will, by New Policy.
                                       Breeder, J. L. Homan (Ky.).        1975  16 12  1  2   $229,213
Owner, R. Horton.  Trainer, J. D. Morquette.                             1974  10  3  4  0    $58,118
22 Nov75 8Key    6 f :221 :4511:094gd 3-5 ^119   2½  1½  1½  11¼ GalltnoG3  AlwS 93 GallantBob119    BearerBond  8
 4 Oct75 8Key   6½ f :22  :4441:163ft 2-5 ^119   3½  2¹  11½ 1²  GalltnoG3  AlwS 94 Gallant Bob 119        Talc  6
 6 Sep75 8Key    7 f :214 :4411:24 ft 6-5 ^129   3¹  3²  2h  1³  GalltnoG7  HcpO 89 Gallant Bob 129        Talc  9
13 Aug75 8Mth    6 f :204 :4341:092ft   2 ^129   27  23½ 2½  11½ GalltnoG5  HcpO 93 Gallant Bob 129        Talc  7
 5 Jly 75 8Bow   6 f :223 :4541:102ft 2-5 ^127   2h  11½ 1³  13½ GalltnoG5  HcpO 91 GallantBob127 FrchWhistler  6
21 Jun75 8AP     7 f :22  :4431:232ft  4½  124   1h  1½  1²  1¹  GallitnoG5 AlwS 85 Gallant Bob 124        Doug 11
 1 Jun75 8Del  1¹⁄₁₆ :4621:12 1:461ft 3-2 ^117   1h  1h  56  512 GallitnoG5 AlwS 66 GreyBeret111 Dr'sEnjyDollrs 10
24 May75 8Del    6 f :214 :45 1:111ft 4-5 ^124   2h  2h  2h  1½  GallitnoG4 AlwS 89 Gallant Bob 124     Bold Gun  7
22 Mar75 8Pim    6 f :224 :4611:111ft   1 ^122   3½  2h  1¹  2h  GallitnoG8 AlwS 90 BombayDuck122 GallantBob  9
15 Mar75 8Aqu    7 f :223 :4531:234sy 2¾ ^119   2h  2h  1½  3¾  GallitnoG8 AlwS 81 Lefty 113            Tass  8
 1 Mar75 8Aqu    6 f :214 :4521:094ft   3  117   1h  11  2½  331½ GalltinoG9 AlwS 90 Singh 114     Laramie Trail 10
22Feb75 8GS      7 f :221 :45 1:253ft 2-5 ^119   13  16  18  110 GallitnoG1 AlwS 81 GallantBob119    WickedPark 11
15 Feb75 8GS     6 f :221 :4541:11 gd 2-5 ^122   1h  13  15  19  GallitnoG6 AlwS 88 GallantBob122    LuckeyLeaf  7
 1 Feb75 8Bow    6 f :224 :4631:12 gd 4-5 ^124   13  15  15  14½ GallitnoG6 AlwS 83 GallantBob124  PendulmSam  6
25 Jan75 8Key    6 f :222 :4611:132sy 4-5 ^119   1½  1h  1½  1²  GallitnoG6 AlwS 75 Gallant Bob 119    Sgt. Hunt  7
    Nov 29 Key 4f ft :48⅘b
```

Give me an obviously sharp horse with a proven superiority over the contenders and I'll gladly support him carrying 120, 125, or 128 pounds, especially if he has successfully carried that kind of weight before. Give me a horse that is not in shape and I don't care what weight he carries.

Several years ago I remember getting 6—1 on a horse that had beaten the same field of starter handicap horses five straight times. The betting crowd was so afraid of the horse's 134-pound weight assignment that it failed to accept him at face value.

If the fans had bothered to look up his record, they might not have been so apprehensive. The season before the horse won a similar-class event under 136 pounds. To a certain extent the same kind of situation occurs several times a season at every racetrack in America.

Of course, common sense dictates paying some attention to large weight shifts or to heavy weight assignments, especially when two or more closely matched contenders are involved.

Two honest, hard-hitting horses were among the top handicap horses of the 1970s. Forego in fact, finished fourth in Secretariat's Kentucky Derby and later won three straight Horse of the Year titles, including one at the direct expense of his arch rival, True Knight. The difference between them never was more than a length or two.

In Florida, during the winter of 1974, Forego won three straight races over True Knight, each by a narrow margin. In May and June,

1¼ MILES—SUBURBAN HANDICAP, AQUEDUCT, JULY 20, 1974

True Knight * **127** Dk. b. or br. h (1969), by Chateaugay—Stealaway, by Olympia.
Breeder, J. W. Galbreath (Ky.). 1974 . . 8 3 3 0 $283,638
Owner, Darby Dan Farm. Trainer, T. L. Rondinello. 1973 . . 12 3 2 2 $200,858

Jly 13-74^{8}Mth	1 1-4	2:02 ft	8-5	▲124	9^{13}	4^{3}	$1^{1\frac{1}{2}}$	$1^{3\frac{3}{4}}$	Riv'aMA^{5}	HcpS 92	TrueKnight124	EcoleEtage HeyRube	9
Jun16-74^{9}Suf	1 1-8	1:48⅗ft	3-5	▲121	7^{18}	7^{19}	$5^{8\frac{1}{2}}$	4^{3}	C'd'oAJr^{6}	HcpS 95	BillyComeLately109	Forage NorthSea	7
May27-74^{8}Bel	1	1:34⅖ft	7	125	8^{22}	8^{13}	$7^{9\frac{3}{4}}$	$6^{8\frac{1}{4}}$	Riv'aMA^{5}	HcpS 88	ArbeesBoy112	Forego Timel'ssMom'nt	8
Apr 6-74^{8}GS	1 1-4	2:06 sl	6-5	125	$6^{8\frac{3}{4}}$	4^{3}	$2^{1\frac{1}{2}}$	$1^{\frac{3}{4}}$	C'd'oAJr4	HcpS 70	TrueKnight125	ProveO't PlayTheF'ld	6
Mar23-74^{9}Hia	1 1-4	2:01⅕ft	9-5	124	7^{19}	$7^{7\frac{1}{2}}$	$3^{2\frac{1}{2}}$	2^{1}	C'd'oAJr^{3}	HcpS 91	Forego 129	True Knight Play the Field	7
Mar 9-74^{8}Bow	1 1-4	2:05⅖ft	3-5	▲123	14^{15}	10^{10}	$5^{4\frac{3}{4}}$	$1^{\frac{1}{2}}$	C'd'oAJr^{4}	HcpS 96	True Knight 123	Delay Ecole Etage	14
Feb23-74^{9}GP	1 1-4	1:59⅘ft	1	▲123	6^{16}	$4^{5\frac{1}{2}}$	2^{h}	$2^{\frac{1}{2}}$	C'd'oAJr^{4}	HcpS 97	Forego127	TrueKnight GoldenDon	6
Feb 9-74^{9}GP	1 1-8	1:48⅗ft	2¼	123	5^{16}	5^{16}	4^{6}	2no	C'd'oAJr^{3}	HcpS 91	Forego125	TrueKnight Proud andBold	5
Nov22-73^{8}Aqu	1 3/16	1:55 ft	4½	126	$11^{9\frac{1}{4}}$	$9^{7\frac{1}{2}}$	$3^{\frac{1}{2}}$	1^{2}	C'd'oAJr^{9}	HcpS 87	TrueKnight126	Triangular NorthSea	12
Oct27-73^{7}Aqu	2	3:20 ft	4½	124	5^{12}	3^{8}	3^{17}	4^{18}	C'd'oAJr^{2}	WfaS 78	Prove Out 124	Loud Twice A Prince	6
Oct15-73^{8}Aqu	1 1-8	1:47 ft	4	122	8^{11}	$5^{5\frac{1}{2}}$	3^{6}	$3^{4\frac{3}{4}}$	Cast'daM^{7}	HcpS 96	Riva Ridge 130	Forage True Knight	9
Sep22-73^{8}Bow	1 1-8	1:49⅘ft	5½	120	9^{14}	8^{10}	1^{1}	1^{4}	C't'daM^{5}	HcpS 102	TrueKnight 120	Delay BurningOn	12

July 19 Bel 3f ft :39b July 12 Bel 4f ft :50b July 8 Bel 6f ft 1:16b

Forego **131** B. g (1970), by Forli—Lady Golconda, by Hasty Road.
Breeder, Lazy F Ranch (Ky.). 1974 7 5 2 0 $322,378
Owner, Mrs. Edward F. Gerry. Trainer, S. W. Ward. 1973 18 8 3 3 $188,909

Jly 4-74^{8}Aqu	1 3/16	1:54⅘ft	2-5	▲129	6^{15}	4^{8}	2^{h}	$1^{\frac{3}{4}}$	Gust'sH^{6}	HcpS 88	Forego129	BillyComeLately ArbeesBoy	7
Jun26-74^{8}Aqu	7 f	1:21⅕ft	2-3	▲132	6^{12}	6^{12}	$5^{6\frac{1}{2}}$	$2^{\frac{1}{2}}$	G'tinesH^{2}	HcpS 94	Timel'ssM'm'nt112	Forego N'rthSea	6
May27-74^{8}Bel	1	1:34⅖ft	6-5	▲134	6^{11}	2^{h}	$1^{1\frac{1}{2}}$	2^{2}	G'tinesH^{2}	HcpS 94	ArbeesBoy112	Forego Timel'ssMom'nt	8
May18-74^{8}Bel	7 f	1:22⅕ft	7-5	▲129	8^{9}	$6^{3\frac{1}{2}}$	$1^{1\frac{1}{2}}$	$1^{2\frac{1}{4}}$	Gust'sH^{7}	HcpS 91	F'r'go129	Mr.Pr'sp'ct'r Tim'l'sM'm'nt	8
Mar23-74^{9}Hia	1 1-4	2:01⅕ft	4-5	▲120	5^{10}	$1^{\frac{1}{2}}$	$1^{1\frac{1}{2}}$	1^{1}	G'tinesH^{5}	HcpS 92	Forego 129	True Knight Play the Field	7
Feb23-74^{9}GP	1 1-4	1:59⅘ft	7-5	127	4^{8}	2^{2}	1^{h}	$1^{\frac{1}{2}}$	G'stinesH^{2}	HcpS 98	Forego127	TrueKnight GoldenDon	6
Feb 9-74^{9}GP	1 1-8	1:48⅗ft	2-3	▲125	4^{6}	$3^{2\frac{1}{2}}$	2^{1}	1no	G'tinesH^{2}	HcpS 91	Forego125	TrueKnight Proud andBold	5
Dec 8-73^{8}Aqu	1 1-8	1:47⅕ft	3-5	▲127	5^{6}	3^{4}	$1^{1\frac{1}{2}}$	$1^{\frac{3}{4}}$	G'tinesH^{6}	HcpS 99	For'go127	MyG'll'nt Key to theK'gd'm	7
Nov24-73^{8}Aqu	1 3/16	1:54⅗ft	2	▲123	4^{5}	$3^{2\frac{1}{2}}$	1^{3}	1^{5}	Gust'esH^{9}	HcpS 89	Forego123	MyGallant Twice aPrince	10
Nov10-73^{6}Aqu	7 f	1:22⅗ft	4-5	▲122	$3^{5\frac{1}{2}}$	3^{6}	3^{4}	3^{4}	GustinesH^{2}	Alw 84	North Sea 115	Tap The Tree Forego	5

July 19 Bel 3f ft :35⅕b July 15 Bel 7f ft 1:24h July 13 Bel 3f ft :36⅘b

Forego was unsuccessful in two attempts to carry 130 pounds and had been life and death to defeat weaker rivals in his latest under 129 pounds at 2–5 odds. Either he had lost his sharp edge in physical condition, or as a four-year-old was inhibited slightly by such heavy weight loads. True Knight, on the other hand, was razor sharp for the Suburban, having turned in his best race to date, winning a stakes at Monmouth Park on July 13, only one week before the Suburban. (In those days it was relatively common for top older horses to run back so quickly—in fact, it was a positive sign of fitness. In the 1990s, only cheap claimers are wheeled back within a week of a previous start.)

True Knight's clear-cut edge in condition, the spread in the Suburban weights and Forego's previous inability to win under 130 pounds or more were factors that deserved to be taken into account. Somehow, and I don't believe it yet, True Knight paid $10.60.

Aside from very large weight shifts and seemingly clear-cut weight barriers (that eventually fall), there is one special circumstance in which a rigid approach to the weight factor is supported by fact. Few players know about it.

Before the turn of the century the Jockey Club Scale of Weights was created as a concession to the natural maturation rate of horses. It is a common fact that a horse is not as well developed at age three as it is likely to be at age four.

Racing secretaries use the scale of age-linked weight concessions as a guide when carding races for horses of mixed age groups.

THE JOCKEY CLUB SCALE OF WEIGHTS

DISTANCE	AGE	JAN. & FEB.	MAR. & APR.	MAY	JUNE	JULY	AUG.	SEP.	OCT.	NOV. & DEC.
½ Mile	2	. . .	. . .	. . .	. . .	. . .	105	108	111	114
	3	117	119	121	123	125	126	127	128	129
	4	130	130	130	130	130	130	130	130	130
	5 & up	130	130	130	130	130	130	137	130	130
6 Furlongs	2	. . .	. . .	. . .	. . .	. . .	102	105	108	111
	3	114	117	119	121	123	125	126	127	128
	4	129	130	130	130	130	130	130	130	130
	5 & up	130	130	130	130	130	130	130	130	130
1 Mile	2	. . .	. . .	. . .	. . .	. . .	. . .	96	99	102
	3	107	111	113	115	117	119	121	122	123
	4	127	128	127	126	126	126	126	126	126
	5 & up	128	128	127	126	126	126	126	126	126
1¼ Miles	2	. . .	. . .	. . .	. . .	. . .	. . .	. . .	. . .	. . .
	3	101	107	111	113	116	118	120	121	122
	4	125	127	127	126	126	126	126	126	126
	5 & up	127	127	127	126	126	126	126	126	126
1½ Miles	2	. . .	. . .	. . .	. . .	. . .	. . .	. . .	. . .	. . .
	3	98	104	108	111	114	117	119	121	122
	4	124	126	126	126	126	126	126	126	126
	5 & up	126	126	126	126	126	126	126	126	126
2 Miles	3	96	102	106	109	112	114	117	119	120
	4	124	126	126	126	126	125	125	124	124
	5 & up	126	126	126	126	126	125	125	124	124

NOTE: *Fillies are entitled to a five-pound sex allowance in races against colts.*

For reasons I cannot fathom, there is a great deal of controversy in racing circles about the legitimacy of age-linked weight concessions. Every season there is talk of abolishing or amending the scale of weights. Most say that three-year-olds should not get automatic weight concessions in the late summer or fall. Nonsense. It seems to me the old-timers had a pretty good idea. The effectiveness of the scale and the need for the concessions are made abundantly clear in the following remarkable statement, checked out in a research project that included several thousand races.

When a three-year-old is assigned actual top weight in a race for horses three years and up, the three-year-old has little or no chance of winning. I suggest you read that again.

In all stakes and allowance races run at seven of the nation's major tracks during the 1970s, there were only 10 documented exceptions to this rule. In 1982, at three eastern tracks there were only two. And in the late 1980s and early 1990s, I was able to find only five top-weighted three-year-old winners from more than 100 who tried. One was Belmont stakes winner Easy Goer. Easy Goer may not have been as versatile as his nemesis Sunday Silence, but he was a powerful runner whose success under actual top weight in the 1989 Woodward Stakes proved his quality as much as anything he accomplished.

Incidentally, all 10 horses in the original study who defied the age-linked weight concessions "bounced" or showed a decline in their form in subsequent starts. This bounce phenomenon afflicted the vast majority of winners who defied the scale of weights in other sample studies. In all, I have chartered more than 600 top-weighted three-year-olds since the first study in the mid-1970s. Fewer than 35 winners in 20 years is pretty convincing evidence that 3-year-olds should get weight concessions when meeting older rivals.

SEX

In Europe fillies race against colts and win with absolute impunity. In America most trainers are reluctant to match the so-called weaker sex against males. Ruffian's tragic demise in the match race against Foolish Pleasure didn't help reverse the trend. But to his credit, it didn't change Frank Whiteley, Jr.'s commitment to the experiment. Only two of Honorable Miss's races shown in the p.p.'s below were against members of her own sex.

Honorable Miss 120 B. m (1970). by Damascus—Court Circuit, by Royal Vale.
Breeder, Mrs. T. Bancroft (Ky.). 1976 8 3 2 1 $100,148
Owner, Pen-Y-Bryn Farm. Trainer, F. J. Whiteley, Jr. 1975 13 7 2 0 $183,857

30 Aug76 ^{8}Bel	6 f	:22^3	:45^4	1:10 ft	7-5	▲130	9$^{7\frac{1}{2}}$	5$^{3\frac{1}{2}}$	1^h	1$^{4\frac{1}{4}}$	ShmrW^{10}	HcpS	92	HonorableMiss130	Lachesis 10
25 Jly 76 ^{8}Aqu	7 f	:23^2	:47	1:24^{2}ft	1	▲118	6^{12}	6^9	4^2	3$^{1\frac{1}{4}}$	VsquezJ^2	HcpS	78	El Fitirre 114	Nalee'sKnight 6
12 Jly 76 ^{4}Atl	6 f	:22^1	:44^4	1:09 ft	1	▲119	10^{10}	10^{12}	9^{10}	5^6	VasqzJ^{10}	HcpS	91	North Call 115	Our Hero 10
4 Jly 76 ^{8}Aqu	6 f	:22	:44^4	1:09^{2}ft	1	▲125	5^{14}	4^{11}	4^7	5$^{1\frac{1}{4}}$	VsquezJ^5	HcpS	95	Red Cross 118	Shy Dawn 5
27 May76 ^{8}Bel	6 f	:22^3	:45^4	1:10^{2}ft	2-5e	▲123	6^{11}	6^5	2^1	1$^{3\frac{3}{4}}$	VasquezJ^1	Alw	90	Honorable Miss 123	Lachesis 6
15 May76 ^{8}Bel	7 f	:22^2	:44^2	1:21 ft	9-5	▲121	9^{12}	9$^{9\frac{1}{4}}$	5$^{7\frac{1}{4}}$	2$^{6\frac{1}{4}}$	VsquezJ^1	HcpS	91	LordRebeau115	HonorbleMiss 9
1 May76 ^{8}Aqu	7 f	:22^1	:44^2	1:22^{2}sy	4$\frac{3}{4}$	122	8^{11}	8^{13}	5^7	2$^{\frac{3}{4}}$	VasquezJ^5	HcpS	88	DueDiligence111	HnrbleMiss 8
23 Apr76 ^{8}Aqu	6 f	:22^2	:45^4	1:10^{3}gd	1	▲123	6^{14}	6^{10}	3^3	1$^{\frac{3}{4}}$	VasquezJ^3	Alw	90	ⒻHonrbleMiss123	FltVictrss 6
1 Nov75 ^{8}Bel	7 f	:22	:44^3	1:22^{4}ft	7-5e	▲125	11^{17}	10^{12}	5$^{8\frac{1}{2}}$	4$^{5\frac{1}{2}}$	VasqezJ^9	HcpS	82	No Bias 116	Step Nicely 11
13 Oct75 ^{8}Bel	6 f	:22^3	:45^3	1:09^{4}ft	9-5e	▲133	14^{11}	11$^{6\frac{1}{2}}$	5$^{:\frac{1}{2}}$	1^2	VasqzJ^{15}	HcpS	93	Honorable Miss 133	No Bias 15
25 Sep75 ^{8}Bel	7 f	:22^4	:45^3	1:23^{1}sy	1-2	▲119	4$^{8\frac{1}{2}}$	4^6	3$^{\frac{1}{2}}$	2$^{2\frac{3}{4}}$	VasquezJ^1	Alw	83	ⒻFltVictress112	HnrbleMiss 4

Sept 14 Bel 4f ft :46⅗h Sept 10 Bel 4f ft :46⅘h Sept 5 Bel 4f ft :48b

Of course in 1980 the filly Genuine Risk changed a lot of people's minds. Not since 1915 had a filly won the Kentucky Derby; not since 1959 had any owner or trainer elected to make the attempt. But through her gritty performances in all three Triple Crown races, Genuine Risk served notice to all chauvinistic types that the times are achanging.

Genuine Risk Ch. f. 3, by Exclusive Native—Virtuous, by Gallant Man
Br.—Humphrey Mrs G W Jr (Ky) 1980 8 4 3 1 $503,742
Own.—Firestone Mrs B R Tr.—Jolley Leroy 1979 4 4 0 0 $100,245

27Sep80-8Bel	1⅛	:48	1:12^2	1:49^{1}ft	*1-2	118	3$^{\frac{1}{2}}$	3^1	2^{hd}	1no	VsquezJ^1	ⒻRuffian H	81	GenuineRisk,MistyGllor,It'sInthAir	6
10Sep80-8Bel	1	:46^1	1:10^4	1:35^{2}ft	*6-5	118	4^5	3^1	1^{hd}	2no	VsquezJ^2	ⒻMaskette	91	Bold'NDtrmind,GnuinRisk,LovSign	5
7Jun80-8Bel	1½	:50^1	2:04	2:29^{4}m	5	121	5^3	2$^{\frac{1}{2}}$	1^{hd}	2^2	Vasquez J^1	Belmont	69	TmprncHill,GnuinRisk,RockhillNtv	10
17May80-9Pim	1$\frac{3}{16}$	:47^4	1:11^1	1:54^{1}ft	*2	121	4^4	4$^{3\frac{1}{4}}$	2^1	2$^{4\frac{3}{4}}$	Vasquez J^5	Preakness	94	Codex, Genuine Risk,ColonelMoran	8
3May80-8CD	1¼	:48	1:37^3	2:02 ft	13	121	7$^{4\frac{1}{4}}$	1$^{1\frac{1}{2}}$	1^2	1^1	VasquezJ^{10}	Ky Derby	87	GenuineRisk,Rumbo,JaklinKlugmn	13
19Apr80-8Aqu	1⅛	:47^2	1:11^3	1:50^{4}ft	8$\frac{1}{4}$	121	3^2	3$^{1\frac{1}{2}}$	3^2	3$^{1\frac{1}{2}}$	VsquezJ^3	Wood Mem	79	PluggdNickl,ColonlMorn,GnunRsk	11
5Apr80-7Aqu	1	:46^4	1:12	1:38^{3}gd	*1-5	124	3^2	1$^{1\frac{1}{2}}$	1^1	1$^{2\frac{1}{4}}$	Vasquez J^4	ⒻHcp0	73	GenuineRisk,TellASecret,SprucePin	4
19Mar80-7GP	7f	:22	:44^4	1:22^{3}ft	*2-5	113	4^4	3$^{2\frac{1}{2}}$	1$^{\frac{1}{2}}$	1$^{2\frac{1}{2}}$	Vasquez J^3	ⒻAlw	91	Genuine Risk, Sober Jig,PeaceBells	6

Genuine Risk's victory was not simply a triumph of one rugged female over ordinary colts, but a portent of things to come.

In 1986, Horse of the Year Lady's Secret defeated males in the Whitney at Saratoga before toying with her own division in the $1 million Breeders' Cup Distaff that year. In 1988, Winning Colors ended trainer D. Wayne Lukas' Kentucky Derby drought with a wire-to-wire win over Forty Niner in the Run for the Roses. In August, unbeaten Personal Ensign followed Lady's Secret's program by beating male handicap horses in the 1988 Whitney. Two months later at Churchill Downs, Personal Ensign caught Winning Colors in the final stride of the Distaff in one of the most thrilling races of modern times to retire undefeated. Within another 40 minutes, however, the French-based filly Miesque did Personal Ensign one better, soundly defeating male rivals for the second year in succession in the $1 million Breeders' Cup Mile.

1988 BREEDERS' CUP DISTAFF AND UNBEATEN PERSONAL ENSIGN

```
Personal Ensign *            B. f. 4, by Private Account—Grecian Banner, by Hoist the Flag
                             Br.—Phipps O (Ky)                     1988  6  6  0  0   $752,640
Own.—Phipps O                Tr.—McGaughey Claude III              1987  4  4  0  0   $302,640
                         Lifetime   12 12  0  0 $1,229,880
16Oct88-8Bel   1¼ :48^1 1:36^2 2:01^1ft  *1-9 123  2^2 2^hd 1^2 1^5½  RmrRP^1 (F)Beldame  92-16 PersonlEnsign,ClssicCrown,ShmSy 5
    16Oct88—Grade I
10Sep88-8Bel   1  :45^1 1:09 1:34^1ft  *1-3 123  3^6 2^2 2^hd 1¾  RmrRP^2 (F)Maskette  94-14 PrsonlEnsign,WinnngColors,ShmSy 4
    10Sep88—Grade I
6Aug88-8Sar   1⅛ :47^2 1:11^3 1:47^4sy  *4-5 117  3^3 2^1 1^hd 1^1½  RomrRP^3 Whitney H  96-12 Personal Ensign, Gulch,King'sSwan 3
    6Aug88—Grade I
4Jly88-10Mth   1 1/16 :47^2 1:10^4 1:41^4ft  *2-5 125  2^3 2½ 1^2½ 1^8  RrRP^5 (F)M Pitcher H  96-14 PrsonlEnsign,GrcinFlight,LL'Argnt 5
    4Jly88—Grade II; Bmpd, forced wide
11Jun88-7Bel   1⅛ :47^1 1:11^2 1:47^3ft  *2-5 123  3^1½ 3^1 1^4 1^7  RrRP^5 (F)Hempstead H  89-13 PrsonlEnsgn,HomtownQn,ClbbrGrl 5
    11Jun88—Grade I
15May88-8Bel   1 1/16 :45^3 1:10 1:41^3ft  *2-3 121  3^3 2^hd 1½ 1^1¾  RmrRP^5 (F)Shuvee H  94-15 PrsonlEnsgn,ClbbrGrl,Bshop'sDlght 6
    15May88—Grade I
18Oct87-8Bel   1¼ :49^3 1:38^2 2:04^2ft  6-5 118  2½ 1^3 1^4 1^2¼  RmrRP^8 (F)Beldame  76-23 PrsonlEnsign,CoupDFusl,SlntTurn 10
    18Oct87—Grade I
10Oct87-5Bel   1  :45^4 1:10^2 1:36^3ft  *4-5 115  1^1 1^5 1^5 1^4¾  RrRP^2 (F)Rare Prfme  82-22 PersonlEnsign,OneFromHvn,KyBid 9
    10Oct87—Grade II
24Sep87-5Bel   1  :46^4 1:11^3 1:36^1ft  *1-5 113  1^2½ 1^3 1^5 1^7¾  RomeroRP^5 (F)Aw33000  84-20 PersonalEnsign,WithATwist,RosMy 5
6Sep87-5Bel   7f  :23^2 :46^2 1:23^1ft  *2-3 113  4^3 1^hd 1^1½ 1^3¾  Bailey J D^3 (F)Aw31000  86-19 PrsonlEnsign,ChicShirin,WthATwst 6
13Oct86-8Bel   1  :46 1:10^1 1:36^2ft  *1-3 119  2½ 2^hd 1^hd 1^hd  RomrRP^2 (F)Frizette  83-16 PersonalEnsign,Collins,FlyingKtun 3
    13Oct86—Grade I
28Sep86-6Bel   7f  :23^1 :46^3 1:22^4m  *4-5 117  2^2½ 1^1½ 1^7 1^12¾  Romero R P^5 (F)Mdn  88-15 PersonlEnsign,GrcefulDrby,Nstique 7
    28Sep86—Hesitated st; clr
  Oct 15 Bel 3f ft :36^4 b     Oct 10 Bel 5f gd 1:01^1 b     Oct 6 Bel 4f ft :49^2 b     Oct 1 Bel 5f ft 1:02^1 b
```

1987 AND 1988 BREEDERS' CUP MILE WINNER MIESQUE

```
Miesque                       B. f. 4, by Nureyev—Pasadoble, by Prove Out
  HEAD F                      Br.—Flaxman Holdings Ltd (Ky)          1988  3  2  1  0    $228,774
                     123      Tr.—Boutin Francois                    1987  8  6  2  0  $1,198,158
Own.—Niarchos S           Lifetime  15 11  3  1 $1,537,514           Turf 15 11  3  1  $1,537,514
4Sep88♦4Longchamp(Fra) a1   1:40^1sf *1-5e 124  (T) 2^hd  Head F  Pr duMoulin(Gr1)  Soviet Star, Miesque, Gabina  7
14Aug88♦4Deauville(Fra) a1   1:38^3gd *3-5 124  (T) 1^1  HdF  PrJacquesLeMariois(Gr1)  Miesque, Warning, Gabrina  6
29May88♦3Longchamp(Fra) a1⅛ 1:55^1yl *1-5e 124  (T) 1^nk  Head F  Pr d'Ispahan(Gr1)  Miesque, St Andrews, Jalaajel  6
21Nov87-4Hol  1 (T):45^3 1:09 1:32^4fm 3½ 120  3^3½ 3^2 1^2 1^3½  Head F^4  Br Cp Mile 103 — Miesque, Show Dancer, SonicLady 14
    21Nov87—Grade I
26Sep87♦4Ascot(Eng) 1   1:40 gd *1-4 120  (T) 2^2½  CthS QueenElizabethIIStks(Gr1)  Milligram, Miesque, Sonic Lady  5
6Sep87♦3Longchamps(Fra) a1   1:37^2gd *1-9e 120  (T) 1^2½  Head F  Prix du Moulin(Gr1)  Miesque, Soviet Star, Grecian Urn  7
16Aug87♦3Deauville(Fra) a1   1:35 gd *2-3e 118  (T) 1^3  HdF  PrixJacquesLeMarios(Gr1)  Miesque, Nashmeel, Hadeer  9
14Jun87♦4Chantilly(Fra) a1 5/16   2:11^2sf  1e 128  (T) 2^4  Head F  (F)Prix de Diane(Gr1)  IndianSkimmer,Miesque,Masmoud  11
17May87♦5Longchamp(Fra) a1   1:38 yl *1-5e 128  (T) 1^2½  HdF  (F)PouleEssaiPouliches(Gr1  Miesque, Sakura Reiko, Libertine  8
30Apr87♦4Newmarket(Eng) 1   1:38^2gd *9-5 126  (T) 1^1½  HeadF  (F)1000 GuineasSks(Gr I)  Miesque, Milligram, Interval  14
```

Royal Heroine also defeated males in the first Breeders' Cup Mile in 1984, while Very Subtle and Safely Kept defeated males in the $1 million Breeders' Cup Sprint in 1987 and 1990, respectively, and Meafara finished a close second to different male rivals in the 1992 and 1993 Breeders' Cup Sprints.

In 1991, Canadian star Dance Smartly defeated colts in Canada's

Triple Crown races, but was kept out of the Breeders' Cup Classic in favor of a winning romp in the Distaff (see Running Style section of this chapter for Dance Smartly's p.p.'s).

Obviously, American trainers are beginning to see merit in the European approach, with very good results. Yet some of America's most astute trainers are convinced that caution is the wiser course.

"Why run a good filly against a top colt when there are so many opportunities to run fillies against their own kind?" asks Ron McAnally, who saw his Eclipse Award–winning mare, Paseana, soundly trounced by males in the 1992 Pacific Classic.

"Once in a while it can be a good idea, especially if the filly is built ruggedly," McAnally insists. "But if you make a mistake, or do it too often, you can wear a filly down in a hurry."

It is difficult to take a stand against McAnally on anything to do with fillies, considering his extraordinary success. But there is nothing in my research that says a fast filly will lose to slower colts. Of course, it is true that a $15,000 claiming filly usually will run about three-fifth seconds slower (about 6–8 Beyer speed-figure points) than the same price colt. But if the filly is intrinsically the fastest horse in the field, the European experience and private research suggests that nothing linked to sex differences will prevent her from showing it.

ONE CAUTION: During the late spring and early summer, female horses tend to go into heat. Occasionally that will bring out excessive kidney sweating and other nervous habits. A filly acting in that manner during the post parade is telling you she has other things besides racing on her mind. (This can happen in a race carded exclusively for fillies too.)

RUNNING STYLE AND THE DISTANCE FACTOR

While most racehorses tend to have a preferred racing distance and some horses are incapable of winning a race when out of their element, there is great power in the training regimen to alter the distance capability of the horse. In addition, there is a most intriguing and predictable relationship between each different distance and running style.

A good trainer can increase or decrease the distance potential of a horse through workouts, special equipment, and actual races at longer and shorter distances. Allen Jerkens does it all the time; so do hundreds of other trainers of lesser talent. The following two principles illustrate the manner in which the vast majority of horses react to distance manipulations:

1. A horse that has been sprinting will most often race closer to the lead or will even set the pace in a longer, slower-paced route event.
2. A horse that has been on the pace in a longer, slower route may be unable to cope with the faster pace of a sprint but is nevertheless likely to show improved stretch punch.

The partial past-performance profiles below demonstrate both principles at work.

Play For Play — Ch. m. 6, by Play Fellow—Golden Highlights, by Great Nephew
$12,500 Br.—Perrotto J (NY)
Own.—Vires George M — Tr.—Kopaj Paul (8 2 1 0 .25) — **115**

24Oct92- 6Med	sly	$1\frac{1}{16}$	:48	1:12^{2}	1:47	3↑ⒻClm 9000	**61**	6	1	1^{1}	1^{2}	1^{6}	$1^{5\frac{1}{4}}$	Marquez C H Jr	L	115	2.70	72-23 F.
10Oct92- 3Med	fst	$1\frac{1}{16}$	:47^{2}	1:12^{3}	1:46	3↑ⒻClm 8000	**59**	7	2	2^{3}	2^{hd}	1^{1}	1^{nk}	Marquez C H Jr	L	115	*2.30	77-18 Play
1Oct92- 7Med	fst	1 70	:47	1:12^{3}	1:42^{2}	3↑ⒻClm 10000	**57**	2	2	1^{hd}	1^{hd}	$2\frac{1}{2}$	$3^{7\frac{1}{2}}$	Martin C W	L	115	3.90	78-18 InitilA.
7Sep92- 4Rkm	fst	6f	:22	:46	1:13^{1}	3↑ⒻClm 16000	**59**	6	7	6^{7}	6^{8}	$5^{8\frac{1}{2}}$	$4^{4\frac{1}{4}}$	Vega H	LB	116	*2.20	75-24 QstforP
23Aug92- 8Rkm	fm	$1\frac{1}{16}$ Ⓣ	:47^{1}	1:13	1:46^{3}	3↑ⒻClm 16000	**38**	3	1	$1^{1\frac{1}{2}}$	2^{hd}	9^{12}	10^{24}	Vega H	LB	116	9.60	56-22 Physical L
15Aug92- 6Rkm	fst	6f	:22	:45^{3}	1:12^{1}	3↑ⒻClm 18000	**70**	7	2	6^{5}	4^{4}	$3^{2\frac{1}{2}}$	$2^{1\frac{3}{4}}$	Vega H	LB	112	9.80	82-13 Up116$1\frac{3}{4}$ Plav
24Jly92- 8Rkm	fm	1 Ⓣ	:47^{3}	1:12^{2}	1:38^{3}	3↑ⒻClm 16000	**61**	10	1	$1^{1\frac{1}{2}}$	2^{hd}	$3^{1\frac{1}{2}}$	$8^{8\frac{3}{4}}$	Martin C W	LB	116	4.00	84-18 SilverP
6Jly92- 8Rkm	yl	$1\frac{1}{16}$ Ⓣ	:48^{3}	1:13^{2}	1:48	3↑ⒻClm 16000	**61**	10	1	$1^{1\frac{1}{2}}$	$1^{1\frac{1}{2}}$	2^{hd}	9^{7}	Martin C W	LB	116	*3.10	66-25 Phy
22Jun92- 9Fox	fst	*$6\frac{1}{2}$f	:22^{4}	:47^{1}	1:20^{3}	3↑ⒻAlw 9000	**66**	3	5	5^{3}	$3^{2\frac{1}{2}}$	$3^{2\frac{1}{2}}$	$2^{3\frac{1}{2}}$	Martin C W	LB	115	*1.20	— —
3Jun92- 9Rkm	fm	1 Ⓣ	:46^{2}	1:11^{3}	1:39^{2}	3↑ⒻAlw 12500	**68**	5	2	2^{hd}	$2\frac{1}{2}$	$2^{2\frac{1}{2}}$	4^{6}	Martin C W	LB	116	5.60	

LATEST WORKOUTS Sep 29 Bel tr.t 4f gd :52 B Sep 25 Rkm 5f fst 1:03 B

J. and A. Hero — B. g. 6, by T V Commercial—Dadad's Grndauters, by Iron Ruler
Br.—Caputo Joseph (NJ)
Own.—Rosenborg Suzanne A — Tr.—Price Harry W Jr (33 4 4 4 .12) — **122**

18Oct92- 8Del	fst	$1\frac{1}{16}$	:47	1:11^{4}	1:46	3↑Alw 5000s	**75**	6	4	$3^{4\frac{1}{2}}$	2^{2}	2^{1}	$1^{1\frac{1}{4}}$	Cabrera S	Lb	116	19.40	82-
17Sep92- 6Pha	fst	7f	:22^{1}	:44^{4}	1:24^{3}	3↑Clm 10000	**53**	10	7	8^{10}	8^{15}	8^{9}	$8^{10\frac{1}{2}}$	Cabrera S	Lb	117	65.90	73-20
30Aug92-10Del	fm	*$1\frac{1}{16}$ Ⓣ	:47^{2}	1:12	1:44^{1}	3↑Alw 5000s	**61**	3	7	7^{6}	$6^{4\frac{1}{2}}$	$7^{9\frac{3}{4}}$	$7^{12\frac{1}{2}}$	Cabrera S	Lb	119	9.60	76-11 M.
16Aug92-12Del	sly	$1\frac{1}{8}$	:47^{2}	1:12	1:53^{1}	3↑Alw 5000s	**76**	5	3	$2^{2\frac{1}{2}}$	3^{3}	$4^{2\frac{1}{4}}$	2^{2}	Cabrera S	Lb	122	2.40	82-24 Scr.
16Aug92-Originally scheduled on turf																		
24Jly92- 9Del	sly	$1\frac{1}{16}$	:49	1:14	1:47^{2}	3↑Alw 10000s	**71**	5	4	$3^{1\frac{1}{2}}$	1^{hd}	1^{hd}	1^{nk}	Cabrera S	Lb	114	3.40	75-31 J.andA.H
24Jly92-Originally scheduled on turf																		
6Jly92- 8Del	fst	6f	:22^{2}	:46^{1}	1:12	3↑Alw 5000s	**63**	1	6	6^{6}	6^{6}	$6^{6\frac{1}{2}}$	$5^{6\frac{1}{4}}$	Cabrera S	Lb	119	10.90	81-23 M
19Jun92-10Del	my	1	:48	1:12^{4}	1:39^{2}	3↑Clm 9000	**70**	5	4	$4^{\frac{3}{4}}$	1^{hd}	2^{hd}	1^{nk}	Cabrera S	Lb	112	*2.20	85
8Jun92-11Del	sly	6f	:22	:45^{2}	1:11	3↑Clm 7500	**62**	6	5	$6^{6\frac{1}{2}}$	$7^{6\frac{3}{4}}$	6^{8}	$3^{2\frac{3}{4}}$	Cabrera S	Lb	114	10.90	
29May92- 2Pha	fst	7f	:23	:45^{4}	1:24	3↑Clm 9000	**65**	7	3	1^{hd}	4^{3}	$5^{5\frac{1}{2}}$	$6^{6\frac{1}{4}}$	Conner S E	Lb	112		
10May92-10Del	fst	6f	:22^{2}	:46^{1}	1:10^{4}	3↑Alw 8400	**60**	3	4	$5^{7\frac{1}{2}}$	$5^{6\frac{1}{2}}$	$5^{8\frac{1}{2}}$	$4^{8\frac{1}{4}}$	Carberry M O5	Lb			

Huckster Rose — **111** — **Mike Smith** (138-29-20-19) — 1992 Record: 12 — 1991 Record: 9 1
B.f.3 Huckster-Homeroad Rose by Super Concorde,TX

23Jul92	Bel5	sy	3f	Clm75000	$1\frac{1}{16}$	:46.02	1:11.03	1:44.83	**75**	4/4	$1^{1\frac{1}{2}}$	1^{2}	$1^{1\frac{1}{2}}$	$1^{3\frac{1}{2}}$	$1^{5\frac{1}{4}}$	Davis	111	f	1.80
09Jul92	Bel6	ft	3f	Alw27000	7f	:23.01	:46.13	1:24.18	**69**	3/5	3	3^{2}	$3^{1\frac{1}{2}}$	2^{1}	$1\frac{1}{2}$	Davis	116	f	*1.50 H.
26Jun92	Bel1	ft	3f	Clm47500	6f	:21.88	:45.36	1:10.26	**68**	3/8	6	7^{4}	5^{2}	$3^{1\frac{1}{2}}$	$2^{1\frac{1}{4}}$	Davis	114		*1.70 Gtn
10Jun92	Bel6	ft	3f	Clm35000c	6f	:22.64	:46.50	1:11.73	**62**	8/8	7	2^{1}	2^{1}	2^{2}	2^{4}	McCauley	118		*.90 BdyMk
06May92	Crc6	ft	3f	Clm32500c	7f	:22.84	:46.85	1:26.83		5/9	3	$3^{3\frac{1}{2}}$	$2\frac{1}{2}$	1^{2}	$1^{1\frac{1}{4}}$	Lee	114		*.90 HckstrRs
26Apr92	Crc4	ft	3f	Clm25000	7f	:23.04	:46.48	1:25.10		8/10	1	3^{nk}	3^{nk}	$1\frac{1}{2}$	1^{4}	Lee	118		*1.80 Hckst
10Apr92	Crc7	ft	3uf	Clm20000	7f	:22.94	:45.90	1:25.06		5/8	2	$3\frac{1}{2}$	$1\frac{1}{2}$	1^{2}	$1^{1\frac{1}{2}}$	Lee	110		6.30
26Mar92	Crc5	ft	3f	Clm25000	6f	:22.41	:46.32	1:12.42		3/7	5	$4^{2\frac{1}{2}}$	$5^{4\frac{1}{2}}$	$5^{3\frac{1}{4}}$	$4^{7\frac{1}{2}}$	Castillo Jr	116		14
10Mar92	GP6	ft	3f	Clm25000	6f	:21.99	:45.61	1:12.31		11/12	6	$7^{4\frac{1}{4}}$	$6^{2\frac{1}{4}}$	5^{4}	$5^{6\frac{3}{4}}$	Vasquez	116		
13Feb92	GP3	ft	3f	Clm25000	1 70	:48.53	1:13.55	1:44.03		6/7	4^{4}	2^{hd}	$2\frac{1}{2}$	3^{2}	4^{5}	Martinez	109		

Workouts: 20Aug SAR tr 4f ft :48.47 h 03Aug SAR 4f ft :47.22 h

While many distance switches may impact the horse's ability to race on or off the pace, it is incorrect to assume that a horse who lags behind early in a six-furlong sprint, but closes a dozen lengths or so in the stretch, will automatically improve his punch at seven furlongs. Nor is there any guarantee that a sprinter with a late kick will naturally prefer 1 1/16 miles or longer. If anything, the impact of the switch to a longer, two-turn race—which tends to put sprinters closer to a naturally slower pace—may flatten out the horse's late move. In many cases these late movers actually prefer one-turn races and are totally ineffective beyond one mile or around two turns. Here, breeding (see Chapter 21) and training patterns are extremely helpful.

As a general approach, I tend to play away from such one-turn Whirlaways unless the horse is a two-year-old maiden with only one career start who is bred for longer and in a barn that frequently wins with such maneuvers, or an older runner with two sprint preps—not one—and the stretchout also is supported by breeding and trainer clues.

Walking To Heaven	Ch. c. 3(Mar), by Thirty Eight Paces—Celestial Wings, by Winged T				
	Br.—Shannon Peter Jr (Md)			**119**	$10,
Own.—Eppler Mary E	Tr.—Eppler Mary E (9 1 1 0 .11)				
15Oct92- 2Lrl fst 1 1/16	:471 1:124 1:451 3↑Md Sp Wt	69 8 2 2hd 11½ 12½ 11½ Guerra W A	Lb 118	26.30	87-14 WlkingToH
4Oct92- 2Pim fst 6f	:234 :48 1:144 3↑Md 25000	37 5 5 31½ 2hd 2hd 32 Guerra W A	Lb 119	4.00	69-23 Fallston119½
15Sep92- 1Pim fst 6f	:234 :47 1:112 3↑Md Sp Wt	40 4 7 63 56 711 718½ Guerra W A	118	13.50	70-15 Land Grant119
12Apr92- 4Pim fst 6f	:233 :472 1:132 3↑Md Sp Wt	43 7 7 74½ 76½ 76½ 79½ Prado E S	112	6.60	68-19 Prosper
LATEST WORKOUTS	●Sep 29 Pim 3f gd :36 Hg				

Walking To Heaven had two sprint preps since his return to competition, including an improved try with the diuretic drug Lasix. With only one published workout we have no trouble realizing that owner-trainer Mary Eppler has to have access to a nearby training track. The win at 1 1/16 miles may not have been totally anticipated at 26–1, but it was logically possible. This horse's sire is Thirty Eight Paces, a middle-distance star on the Maryland circuit and son of Nodouble, a potent, versatile sire of milers, turf horses, and mud runners. (Breeding will be discussed in depth in Chapter 21.)

Any horse who has been racing on or near the lead for five, six, or seven furlongs of a route may be an excellent wager when turned back to a shorter distance. On any unbiased, or stretch-running track, this type of turn-back runner frequently benefits from the extra conditioning gained over the longer haul and may prove too strong for a typical field of pure sprinters. Players should examine turn-back runners very carefully, especially at seven furlongs, which is a perfect distance for the turn-back runner with good pace numbers or fractional clockings through six furlongs in routes. This type also does well at six furlongs and 6½ when the pace is extremely fast and deep, or when the running surface is bias-free or favorable to stamina types.

For example, the six-furlong Breeders' Cup Sprint is frequently won by a turn-back miler type, usually because the sustained pace is extraordinarily quick—as it should be—for the classiest six-furlong race of the year.

1988 BREEDERS' CUP SPRINT WINNER

Gulch ✻
B. c. 4, by Mr Prospector—Jameela, by Rambunctious
Br.—Brant P M (Ky)
Tr.—Lukas D Wayne
Own.—Brant P M

1988 10 4 4 2 $910,840
1987 14 3 3 2 $1,297,171
Lifetime 31 12 8 4 $2,645,521

9Oct88-7Bel	7f	:22^{3}	:45^{2}	1:22^{2}m	*1-2e	126	42½	32½	2^{2}	22¾	CordrAJr^{2}	Vosburgh	87-24	Mining, Gulch, High Brite	4
9Oct88—Grade I															
27Aug88-9Mth	1⅛	:46^{2}	1:09^{4}	1:47^{4}ft	2½	122	3^{1}	3^{1}	32½	34¾	CordroAJr^{2}	Iselin H	90-12	Alysheba, Bet Twice, Gulch	6
27Aug88—Grade I															
6Aug88-8Sar	1⅛	:47^{2}	1:11^{3}	1:47^{4}sy	9-5	124	11½	1^{1}	2^{hd}	21½	SntosJA^{2}	Whitney H	94-12	Personal Ensign, Gulch,King'sSwan	3
6Aug88—Grade I															
16Jly88-8Bel	7f	:23	:46^{1}	1:22^{2}ft	*2-5	128	2½	2^{hd}	2^{hd}	2¾	SntosJA^{1}	Tom Fool	89-22	King's Swan, Gulch, Abject	4
16Jly88—Grade II; Brushed late															
12Jun88-8Hol	1⅛	:47^{3}	1:10^{4}	1:47^{3}ft	4¼	126	3½	3^{1}	2^{1}	22¾	StevnsGL^{4}	Californian	96-09	CutlssRelity,Gulch,JudgeAngelucci	4
12Jun88—Grade I															
30May88-8Bel	1	:44^{4}	1:08^{4}	1:34^{3}ft	7-5e	125	2^{1}	2^{hd}	1½	1½	SntosJA^{4}	Metropltn H	92-19	Gulch, Afleet, Stacked Pack	8
30May88—Grade I															
7May88-8Aqu	7f	:22^{3}	:44^{4}	1:20^{2}ft	2¼	124	1½	1^{hd}	1½	11¼	SantosJA^{3}	Carter H	99-13	Gulch, Afleet, Its Acedemic	8
7May88—Grade I															
16Apr88-9OP	1⅛	:46^{3}	1:10^{3}	1:47 gd	5¾	120	4^{2}	42¼	2^{2}	33¾	DlhssyE^{7}	Oaklawn H	94-12	Lost Code, Cryptoclearance, Gulch	8
16Apr88—Grade I															
30Mar88-8SA	6½f	:21^{4}	:44^{2}	1:15 ft	6-5	123	1½	2^{1}	21½	11¼	DlhssyE^{3}	Ptro Grnd H	95-18	Gulch, Very Subtle, Gallant Sailor	3
18Mar88-8SA	6f	:22^{1}	:45	1:08^{4}ft	3	116	4^{1}	2^{hd}	1^{hd}	11¾	DelhoussyeE^{6}	Aw55000	94-18	Gulch, Sebrof, My Gallant Game	6
21Nov87-7Hol	1¼	:46^{2}	1:35^{2}	2:01^{2}ft	25	122	87¾	87½	9^{10}	915¼	SntosJA^{11}	Br Cp Clsc	70-12	Ferdinnd,Alysheb,JudgeAngelucci	12
21Nov87—Grade I															
21Oct87-8Aqu	1	:45^{2}	1:09^{2}	1:34^{4}ft	*4-5	123	7^{11}	65½	33½	2¾	SntosJA^{1}	Jamaica H	91-19	Stacked Pack, Gulch, Homebuilder	8
21Oct87—Grade III															

Sep 30 Bel 5f ft 1:02^{2} b **Sep 25 Bel 6f ft 1:15^{3} b** **●Sep 19 Bel 5f ft :58^{4} h** **Sep 7 Bel 4f ft :49^{4} b**

Gulch, Smile, Precisionist and Dancing Spree were all major stakes winners at 1⅛ miles who turned back to win the Breeders' Cup Sprint in the 1980s, and they surely will not be the last to do so.

It is a subtlety of the distance factor that often goes unnoticed, but routers who close ground at 1⅛ miles may be even more effective if dropped back to one mile, or 1¹⁄₁₆ miles, because the slightly shorter race may attract one or more sprinters stretching out in distance who may increase the tempo of the early pace. Also, some horses, regardless of their running style, may respond with a vastly improved race when returned to a favored distance. Good trainers tend to build training regimens around such narrow preferences. It is a big plus to find the horse's complete record at today's track and distance in *Racing Times*' style past-performance profiles adopted by *DRF* since May 1993.

Lifetime Record:	111	19	15	17	$249,539						
1993	8	0	1	4	$12,350	Turf	32	7	6	5	$87,143
1992	9	2	2	1	$29,150	Wet	7	0	3	2	$10,522
Hol	12	3	0	2	$43,350	Dist	8	2	0	1	$18,774

NOTE: The horse with the above lifetime record has won two of eight career starts at this distance—7½ furlongs on the main track. Only one other horse in the field of $10,000 claimers had a single win at this unusual distance. They ran 1–2.

Yaros B. c. 3(Feb), by Rare Brick—Lightning Mountain, by Cox's Ridge
KRONE J A (40 7 5 9 .18) **$85,000** Br.—Loblolly Stable (Ky)
Own.—Jewel E Stable Tr.—Ferriola Peter (34 11 6 4 .32) **116**

29Oct92- 7Aqu	fst	1⅛	:47^{2}	1:11	1:49^{4}	3↑ Alw 31000	94	8	1	2^{hd}	1½	1^{3}	1^{3}	Krone J A	b	114	1.50	87-ℒ.
11Oct92- 2Bel	gd	6f	:22^{1}	:45^{1}	1:10^{3}	Clm 50000	86	4	4	3^{1}	3^{nk}	3½	2^{nk}	Smith M E	b	117	*1.90	87-18 ı
6Sep92- 7Bel	fst	1$\frac{1}{16}$	:46^{3}	1:10^{4}	1:42^{2}	3↑ Alw 31000	85	1	1	1$^{1\frac{1}{2}}$	1^{1}	3$^{1\frac{1}{2}}$	3$^{6\frac{3}{4}}$	Migliore R	b	113	5.90	83-12 Po.
10Aug92- 1Sar	fst	1	:45^{4}	1:10^{2}	1:36^{2}	Clm 70000	80	1	2	1^{hd}	2½	5^{4}	5$^{3\frac{1}{4}}$	Smith M E	b	113	*.70	— — Bord
1Jly92- 6Bel	my	1	:44^{4}	1:09^{4}	1:34^{4}	Clm 50000	97	4	1	1$^{1\frac{1}{2}}$	1^{2}	1$^{3\frac{1}{2}}$	1$^{6\frac{1}{4}}$	Smith M E	b	117	2.20	96-04 Yaros1
12Jun92- 6Bel	fst	7f	:22^{4}	:45^{4}	1:23^{4}	3↑ Alw 28000	76	8	1	6^{3}	1^{hd}	6$^{3\frac{3}{4}}$	7$^{6\frac{1}{4}}$	Smith M E	b	114	5.10	79-14 Royal
18May92- 5Bel	fst	1⅛	:45^{4}	1:09^{4}	1:48^{1}	3↑ Alw 29000	90	5	2	2½	1½	1^{2}	1^{4}	Smith M E	b	112	2.10	88-13 Y-
2May92- 5Aqu	fst	6f	:22^{1}	:45^{1}	1:09^{3}	3↑ Alw 27000	94	3	1	3$^{1\frac{1}{2}}$	3^{1}	2$^{1\frac{1}{2}}$	2$^{1\frac{1}{2}}$	McCauley W H	b	113	4.10	91-0
17Apr92- 7Aqu	sly	1	:45^{2}	1:09^{3}	1:36	Alw 29000	84	5	1	2½	2^{hd}	1^{hd}	2no	Smith M E	b	117	*1.50	
2Apr92- 9Aqu	fst	7f	:22^{3}	:45^{3}	1:24	Clm c-35000	77	7	2	1$^{1\frac{1}{2}}$	1^{hd}	3$^{1\frac{1}{2}}$	3$^{8\frac{1}{2}}$	Santagata N	b	117	8.70	

LATEST WORKOUTS Oct 23 Aqu 4f fst :49^{1} B

The above horse has been perfectly positioned to win three races at one mile or longer following an intermediary sprint prep. He also began the pattern in April 1992 with a sharp second in his first outing for trainer Peter Ferriola, who, along with relative newcomer Mike Hushion

Bet On Bill Dk. b. or br. g. 4, by Secret Prince—Burn a Bet, by J P Brother
CARR D (64 4 4 7 .06) **$14,000** Br.—Terrill William (NY)
Own.—Stripp William H Tr.—Terrill William V (28 2 2 2 .07) **119**

23Nov92- 3Aqu	my	1	:46^{1}	1:12	1:39	3↑ Clm 15500	75	6	2	2½	2^{hd}	1$^{2\frac{1}{2}}$	1$^{4\frac{3}{4}}$	Carr D	b	113	9.10	67-
16Nov92- 9Aqu	fst	6f	:22^{1}	:45^{2}	1:10^{4}	3↑ Clm 12000	59	2	6	3$^{2\frac{1}{2}}$	3$^{2\frac{1}{2}}$	3$^{2\frac{1}{2}}$	4^{7}	Carr D	b	113	13.60	80-05
6Nov92- 4Aqu	my	7f	:22^{4}	:46^{1}	1:25^{1}	3↑ Clm 14000	53	5	1	4$^{1\frac{1}{2}}$	3$^{2\frac{1}{2}}$	4^{7}	5$^{10\frac{3}{4}}$	Bisono C V^{5}	b	112	8.90	68-18 U
28Oct92- 9Aqu	fst	6f	:22^{1}	:45	1:11	3↑ Clm 14000	51	10	11	8$^{6\frac{1}{4}}$	11^{13}	11^{14}	11$^{10\frac{1}{2}}$	Bisono C V^{5}	b	112	56.00	75-14 Mx.
28Mar92- 9Aqu	fst	6f	:22^{4}	:47	1:11^{3}	Clm 14000	35	10	11	11$^{8\frac{1}{4}}$	11^{10}	12^{13}	12$^{20\frac{1}{4}}$	BrocklbnkGV^{5}	b	112	23.00	63-16 Major
26Jan92- 9Aqu	fst	6f	[•]:23^{2}	:47^{1}	1:12^{1}	Clm 14000	55	7	9	9$^{6\frac{3}{4}}$	10$^{7\frac{1}{4}}$	11$^{9\frac{1}{4}}$	11$^{12\frac{3}{4}}$	Madrid A Jr	b	117	13.80	69-22 MjorM
29Dec91- 2Aqu	sly	1⅛	[•]:47^{4}	1:13^{3}	1:55^{2}	Clm 20000	8	9	4	7^{9}	10^{14}	10^{20}	10$^{36\frac{1}{4}}$	Carr D	b	113	6.80	29-23 Str
15Dec91- 2Aqu	fst	6f	[•]:22^{1}	:46	1:11^{2}	Clm 17500	63	5	4	3^{2}	3^{4}	5^{7}	5$^{10\frac{1}{2}}$	Carr D	b	119	3.50	75-19
22Nov91- 3Aqu	sly	1	:46^{1}	1:11^{2}	1:38^{4}	Clm 16500	71	2	6	2^{hd}	1^{hd}	1$^{3\frac{1}{2}}$	1$^{1\frac{1}{2}}$	Carr D	b	115	*1.20	68-
14Nov91- 3Aqu	fst	7f	:22^{3}	:45^{3}	1:23^{1}	Clm 17500	69	5	4	9$^{3\frac{3}{4}}$	5$^{2\frac{1}{2}}$	2$^{2\frac{1}{2}}$	2$^{3\frac{3}{4}}$	Carr D	b	119	3.40	

LATEST WORKOUTS Oct 21 Bel 5f fst 1:02^{2} H Oct 9 Med 4f fst :51^{2} B

and veteran Gaspar Moschera, are powerful forces in the New York claiming and allowance arena.

Bet On Bill handles wet footing very nicely, but he just loves one mile around one turn at Aqueduct following a decent sprint.

Lots of Laughter					Dk. b. or br. f. 3(Feb), by Rollicking—Lysine, by Majestic Light											
				$5,000	Br.—Myers Frances Hill (Md)											
Own.—Myers Frances Hill					Tr.—Myers Frances H (—)							107⁵				
16Oct92-10CT fst 6½f✓	:24	:48⁴	1:23¹	3↑ⓕClm 5000	59 10 3	3⁴	42½	33½	1¹ ✓	Barnett W A	Lb 117	6.40	72–2₂			
2Oct92- 5CT fst 7f	:24¹	:48²	1:29²	3↑ⓕClm 5000	45 7 7	4³	43½	43½	4⁵	Barnett W A	Lb 117	2.00	71–21 ₍			
5Sep92- 8Tim fst 1	:48¹	1:15	1:42⁴	ⓕClm 6500	45 1 7	7¹⁵	79½	6¹¹	47½	Moorefild WT⁵	Lb 109	2.40	65–27 Pr,			
29Aug92- 7Tim fst *6½f✓	:23¹	:48	1:21¹	3↑ⓕClm 5000	53 5 4	5⁵	5⁷	56¾	14½ ✓	Moorefild WT⁵	Lb 112	8.20	69–20 Lots.			
14Aug92- 2Lrl fst 6f	:23²	:48²	1:14⁴	ⓕClm 6500	40 1 4	6⁶	4³	67½	55½	Moorefild WT⁵	Lb 109	21.30	62–26 Summ,			
4Jun92-10Pim fst 6f	:23³	:47¹	1:12³	3↑ⓕClm 6500	24 4 1	5⁴	68½	8¹⁵	817¾	Moorefild WT⁵	Lb 108	4.50	64–17 Clvr⁻			
24May92- 3Pim fst 6f	:23¹	:46⁴	1:13⁴	3↑ⓕMd 8500	38 11 2	66½	57½	23½	12½	Moorefild WT⁵	Lb 107	10.80	76–18 I			
6Dec91- 5Lrl fst 6f	:22²	:46⁴	1:13²	ⓕMd 7500	10 7 10	65½	68½	6¹¹	614½	Perez J A⁵	Lb 112	5.10	59–?			
29Nov91- 3Lrl fst 6½f✓	:22⁴	:47¹	1:21³	ⓕMd 7500	24 4 2	1½	11½	21½	23½ ✓	Perez J A⁵	Lb 112	4.70	f⁻			
21Nov91- 5Lrl fst 6f	:22³	:47²	1:14	ⓕMd 7500	23 13 5	32½	2hd	32½	6⁷	Perez J A⁵	Lb 112	70.30				

If the Kentucky Derby were a 6½-furlong race for $5,000 claimers, Lots of Laughter would be world famous.

OPTIONAL EQUIPMENT

BLINKERS. There is nothing like a pair of blinkers (eye cups) to help keep a horse's mind on its business, particularly a young horse that has had a difficult time running a straight course. Blinkers also tend to improve a horse's gate-breaking ability or early speed; and as a tool of last resort blinkers sometimes help the quitter type—the kind that stops in its tracks the moment another horse challenges it for the lead. If the quitter can't see the competition, it just might hold on long enough to get a piece of the purse.

Although more than half of the 70,000 horses racing in America go to the post with blinkers, "blinkers on" for the first time is generally a very positive sign of trainer intention. "Blinkers off" is not so easy to interpret.

In the case of a speedball, or perhaps a quitter type, the removal of blinkers may help the horse relax a bit and conserve some of its energy for the stretch. A few horses also run better when they see the competition. For obvious reasons, some trainers remove blinkers when they send a sprinter into a longer race or, conversely, put them on when a router is seriously meant in a sprint.

The following are edited examples taken from three randomly selected days of *Daily Racing Form* past performances in November 1992. Each illustrates common circumstances when *blinkers on* usually translates into a much improved performance. You will note that each positive race with blinkers also was accompanied by another significant change in distance, or track condition. Most also occurred when the horse was dropped into softer company.

Virginia Rapids Ch. c. 2(Mar), by Riverman—Virginiana, by Sir Ivor
LIDBERG D W (15 1 0 4 .07) Br.—Stabola Joseph & William Inc (NJ)
Own.—Middletown Stables Tr.—Jerkens H Allen (28 2 6 2 .07) **117**

20Oct92- 8Bel fm 1 1/16 Ⓣ:464 1:111 1:423 Pilgrim **39** 9 8 4¾ 73½ 917 1024 Cruguet J b 113 10.80 59-15 Awa
20Oct92-Grade III
7Sep92- 2Bel fm 1 Ⓣ:463 1:101 1:362 Md Sp Wt **76** 3 3 11 1hd 12½ 1nk Cruguet J b 118 *2.00 80-19 VirginiRp
29Aug92- 4Sar fst 6f :214 :444 1:104 Md Sp Wt **54** 9 1 2½ 2½ 1hd 48½ Perret C 118 2.20 81-07 DncngHr
16Aug92- 4Sar my 6f :221 :461 1:12 Md Sp Wt **62** 6 6 63 41½ 52 51¾ Perret C 118 4.20e 82-14 Sara
LATEST WORKOUTS Nov 16 Bel tr.t 4f fst :481 H Nov 12 Bel tr.t 7f fst 1:34 B Oct 29 Bel tr.t 4f fst

---

What a Tack Gr. f. 2(Feb), by Red Attack—What a Shack, by Al Hattab
$35,000 Br.—D J Stable (Ky)
Own.—Tobio Manuel Tr.—Ramos Faustino F (19 1 6 1 .05) **115**

30Sep92- 1Bel fst 1 :481 1:131 1:393 ⒻAlw 29000 **10** 1 1 4¾ 44 317 327¾ Carle J D b 118 4.70 44-20 Stndr
21Sep92- 5Bel fm 1 Ⓣ:454 1:093 1:351 ⒻAlw 29000 **67** 5 2 21 21½ 34 46½ Carle J D b 116 3.80 79-11 CtchFlg
21Sep92-Placed third through disqualification
7Sep92- 8Pha gd 6f :214 :45 1:112 ⒻCriticalmiss **53** 3 4 43 32½ 37 48½ Carle J D b 116 3.20 75-20 Carnirainbow
20Aug92- 6Sar fst 7f :223 :453 1:243 ⒻMd Sp Wt **69** 9 1 12½ 15 14 16¾ Carle J D b 117 14.50 82-14 WhataTack
13Aug92- 8Sar fst 6f :214 :451 1:10 ⒻAdirondack **47** 4 6 67½ 67 67 619 Carle J D 112 64.10 75-13 SkyBu
13Aug92-Grade II
15Jly92- 1Bel fst 6f :23 :462 1:112 ⒻMd 70000 **47** 4 4 31½ 21½ 35½ 411¼ Carle J D 113 6.90 72-1
3Jly92- 5Bel fst 5f :22 :454 :59 ⒻMd Sp Wt **56** 6 6 66¼ 65¼ 43¼ 34¼ Carle J D 117 42.80
LATEST WORKOUTS Nov 14 Med 5f fst 1:013 H ●Nov 9 Med 3f fst :35 H Oct 30 Aq

---

Prevailed B. c. 4, by It's Freezing—Hail to the Queen, by Native Royalty
VELASQUEZ J (15 1 3 1 .07) Br.—Harbor View Farm (Ky)
Own.—Downturn Stable Tr.—Martin Carlos F (15 3 1 0 .20) **117**

5Nov92- 9Aqu sly 7f :223 :46 1:233 3↑Clm 35000 **95** 1 9 1hd 11 13 12¼ Velasquez J b 117 11.50 87-
4Oct92- 1Bel fst 7f :224 :46 1:233 3↑Clm c-50000 **57** 7 4 3½ 1½ 73½ 815 Maple E 117 5.30 71-15
4Oct92-Claimed from Harbor View Farm, Kelly Patrick J Trainer
25Sep92- 7Bel fm 1 1/16 [T]:47 1:103 1:411 3↑Alw 33000 **86** 7 2 2hd 2hd 41½ 65¾ Romero R P 117 7.70e 86-10 Shrt
14Sep92- 6Bel fm 1 1/16 Ⓣ:473 1:111 1:42 3↑Clm 75000 **87** 4 2 2½ 2hd 1hd 44 Romero R P 117 13.00 82-14 PowrBl
9Aug92- 7Sar gd 1 [T]:461 1:102 1:352 3↑Alw 33000 **79** 7 5 43½ 41¼ 64¾ 710½ Maple E 117 22.10 91-10 Up in Fro
31Jly92- 1Sar sly 1 :471 1:114 1:361 3↑Alw 33000 **87** 4 2 22 21½ 22 37¾ Maple E 117 3.70 — — Majesty's T
31Jly92-Originally scheduled on turf
19Jly92- 7Bel fst 7f :224 :454 1:22 3↑Alw 30000 **65** 7 3 31 42 710 617¼ Maple E 117 9.10 77-13 W
28Mar92- 8Crc fst 1 1/16 :473 1:122 1:452 Alw 20800 **96** 2 1 11 1½ 2hd 2½ Ramos W S L 112 *1.10 —
14Mar92- 8GP fst 7f :223 :454 1:234 3↑Sprint Chp H **94** 3 5 3½ 42½ 43½ 56 Duarte J C L 113 30.70
27Feb92- 8GP fst 7f :224 :461 1:242 Alw 20000 **95** 2 4 22 2½ 12 16 Duarte J C L 115 *1.9
LATEST WORKOUTS ●Oct 30 Bel tr.t 4f fst :48 H ●Oct 24 Bel tr.t 4f fst :473 H Sep 2

Another, more powerful handicapping idea to keep in mind is a change of equipment in tandem with the addition of the powerful diuretic drug Lasix, legal in all racing states except New York. (Washington bars Lasix for two-year-olds.)

Some trainers are expert at changing a horse's running style through workouts, or through a series of races. And some horses are so versatile they can do anything. Dance Smartly, below, is one of those horses. Note how she won a 5½-furlong race in a pace duel, finished second from off the pace at six furlongs, won going two turns on the lead, on the turf at one mile and after burning up in a pace duel in the Breeders' Cup Juvenile, returned as a 3-year-old to win a long series of races from the same basic mid-pack or stalking position regardless of distance, track surface or the level of competition.

Dance Smartly won at six furlongs, $1\frac{1}{16}$ miles, 1⅛ miles and four times against colts at 1¼ miles, $1\frac{3}{16}$ miles, 1½ miles on the turf and 1⅛, before completing her spectacular campaign by winning the $1 million Breeders' Cup Distaff with a similar run from mid-pack. I also had the distinct pleasure of cashing a future book bet on Dance Smartly at 50–1 to win and 20–1 to place at the Harveys' Hotel and Casino in Lake Tahoe—a rather comfortable spot to play the game. The bet was made in August 1992, after she already had won the Canadian Triple Crown for the biggest overlay of my life. Here are her *Racing Times*' p.p.'s.

Dance Smartly
3yo (Apr) filly, dk. bay/brown
Trainer: James E Day
Owner: Sam-Son Farms

Sire: **Danzig** ($225,000) by Northern Dancer
Dam: **Classy 'N Smart** by Smarten
Bred in CAN by Sam-Son Farms

Career: 12 10 1 1 $1,563,456

Wet:	1	0	1	0	$22,585	**1991:**	7 7 0 0	$1,356,821
Turf:	2	2	0	0	$232,270	**1990:**	5 3 1 1	$206,635
Dist:	5	4	0	1	$1,007,953	**CD:**	0 0 0 0	$0

120 LB **Pat Day**

15Sep91	9Wdb	ft	3	Stk1000000	1⅛	23.90	48.50	1:12.30	1:49.30	**108**	10/10	3	3½	2^{1}	2½	2^{hd}	1^{2}	P Day	116 f	1.65 Dance Smartly116^{2}Shudanz117^{6}Majesterian117^{1}
				Gr.2 Molson Export Million																*Away alertly, stalked leader, rallied qtr pole, drew off, handily*
13Aug91	8Wdb	yl	3	Ⓡ Stk303567	1½ Ⓣ	47.10	1:12.10	1:39.50	2:31.50	**102**	6/10	3	$3^{3\frac{1}{2}}$	$3^{4\frac{1}{2}}$	$1^{1\frac{1}{2}}$	1^{3}	1^{8}	P Day	121	**0.30***Dance Smartly121^{8}Shiny Key126^{hd}January Man126^{5}
				Breeders Stakes																*Stalked, nicely rated, rallied 3/8 pole, drew off, handily*
28Jly91	8FE	ft	3	Ⓢ Stk186067	$1\frac{3}{16}$	22.90	45.90	1:10.10	1:56.70	**102**	5/6	3	3^{1}	3^{2}	$3^{2\frac{1}{2}}$	$1^{1\frac{1}{2}}$	1^{2}	P Day	121	**0.10***Dance Smartly121^{2}Professor Rabbit$126^{2\frac{3}{4}}$Shudanz$126^{4\frac{3}{4}}$
				Prince Of Wales Stakes																*Unhurried early, saved grnd, crcled field, took command, drew off*
7Jly91	8Wdb	ft	3	Ⓢ Stk391400	1¼	23.70	47.50	1:37.30	2:03.50	**108**	3/9	4	4^{2}	3^{3}	$3^{1\frac{1}{2}}$	1^{2}	1^{8}	P Day	121	**0.55***Dance Smartly121^{8}Wilderness Song$121^{3\frac{1}{2}}$Shudanz$126^{\frac{1}{2}}$
				Queen's Plate																*Stalked pace for 3/4, took over upper stretch, drew off, driving*
16Jun91	8Wdb	ft	3F	Ⓢ Stk150000	1⅛	23.90	48.10	1:12.70	1:51.30	**102**	3/8	2	$2^{1\frac{1}{2}}$	$2^{1\frac{1}{2}}$	2½	1^{hd}	$1^{4\frac{1}{2}}$	P Day	121	**0.05** Dance Smartly$121^{4\frac{1}{2}}$Wilderness Song121^{10}Platinum Paws$121^{1\frac{1}{2}}$
				Canadian Oaks Stakes																*Stalked pace, rallied far turn, won driving*
1Jun91	9Wdb	ft	3F	Stk100000	$1\frac{1}{16}$	24.10	48.70	1:12.50	1:43.70	**100**	2/9	3	3^{2}	3^{2}	3^{2}	2^{hd}	$1^{3\frac{1}{4}}$	B Swatuk	120	**0.50** Dance Smartly$120^{3\frac{1}{4}}$Through Flight123^{nk}Areydne113^{hd}
				Selene Stakes																*Well rated, rallied at 1/4 pole, assumed command, won handily*
4May91	9Wdb	ft	3F	Stk60000	6f	22.50	45.70		1:10.70	**94**	2/7	6	$4^{2\frac{1}{4}}$	2^{1}		1½	$1^{2\frac{1}{2}}$	B Swatuk	120	**0.35** Dance Smartly$120^{2\frac{1}{2}}$Diamond Syl$116^{4\frac{1}{2}}$Areydne$114^{1\frac{1}{4}}$
				Star Shoot Stakes																*Never far back, rallied, gained command stretch, drew off,handily*
27Oct90	4Bel	ft	2F	Stk1000000	$1\frac{1}{16}$	22.74	45.94	1:11.09	1:44.01	**88**	7/13	3	1½	1^{hd}	2^{hd}	2^{2}	3^{6}	S Hawley	119 b	13.50*Meadow Star119^{5}Private Treasure119^{1}Dance Smartly$119^{4\frac{1}{2}}$
				Gr.1 Breeders' Cup Juvenile Fillies																*Set pace undr pressure, couldn't stay with winner, wknd 1/16 pole*
15Sep90	7Wdb	yl	2F	Stk83550	1m Ⓣ		46.90	1:11.90	1:39.50	**76**	3/8						1½	S Hawley	116 b	**1.10** Dance Smartly$116^{\frac{1}{2}}$Lady Be Great[D]$114^{4\frac{1}{2}}$Malbay$114^{1\frac{1}{2}}$
				Natalma Stakes																
13Aug90	8FE	sy	2F	Ⓢ Stk112920	6f	23.10	47.10		1:13.30	**69**	7/8						$2^{2\frac{1}{2}}$	S Hawley	116	**0.45** Regal Pennant$115^{2\frac{1}{2}}$Dance Smartly$116^{7\frac{1}{4}}$Unreal Affair$116^{1\frac{1}{2}}$
				Ontario Debutante Stakes																
1Aug90	8Wdb	ft	2F	Alw23200Nw2x	5½f	22.50	46.30		1:05.10	**78**	4/8						$1^{4\frac{3}{4}}$	S Hawley	116	**0.50** Dance Smartly$116^{4\frac{3}{4}}$Silent Battle^{4}Kaydanna^{nk}
7Jly90	3Wdb	ft	2F	MaidenSpWt	5½f	22.90	46.30		1:06.30	**75**	3/6						$1^{3\frac{1}{2}}$	I Driedger	114	**0.50** Dance Smartly$114^{3\frac{1}{2}}$Kaydanna$^{\frac{3}{4}}$Chili Lee$^{2\frac{1}{2}}$

Best 1990-91 Beyer Speed Figures - Dirt: 108 15Sep91 Wdb 1⅛ ft **Wet: 69** 13Aug90 FE 6f sy **Dist: 108** 15Sep91 Wdb 1⅛ ft

Workouts: 25Oct CD 6f gd 1:13.10 H 20Oct CD 4f ft 53.30 B 8Oct Wdb 4f ft 51.90 B 10Sep Wdb 5f ft 58.50 B 4Sep Wdb 6f sy 1:12.90 B

Private Access, below, won with blinkers on July 23, 1992, and won his second race of the year four starts later with first time Lasix in his first start for his new trainer Tim Ritchey. Don't let Ritchey's record at Philadelphia Park deceive; through the late 1980s and early 1990s, he won 25 percent of all starts at his home base, Penn National Racecourse, home of the fantastic World Series of Handicapping in October. (Drugs will be discussed in Chapter 22.)

Private Access — B. g. 4, by Private Account—Empress of Canada, by Accomplish
$14,000 Br.—Indian Creek & Tenney E W (Ky)
Own.—Burnside Charles F — Tr.—Ritchey Tim F (43 6 6 3 .14) — **117**

29Oct92- 6Pha	fst	$1\frac{1}{16}$	$:46^4$	$1:11^4$	$1:46^1$	3↑Clm 16000	**67**	2	4	5^5	4^6	6^7	5^6	Salvaggio M V	Lb	119	5.00	72–28
9Oct92- 8Pha	sly	$1\frac{1}{8}$	$:46^4$	$1:11^2$	$1:52^3$	3↑Alw 16616	**76**	1	3	2^3	2^3	$3^{1\frac{1}{2}}$	1^{nk}	Salvaggio M V	Lb	116	3.50	75–27 Pr
9Oct92-Originally scheduled on turf																		
20Sep92- 6Pha	fst	7f	$:22^1$	$:45^1$	1:24	3↑Clm c-13000	**63**	4	8	8^8	8^9	7^{12}	$6^{9\frac{1}{4}}$	Taylor K T	b	118	6.40	78–18 Roughh
20Sep92-Claimed from Augustin Stables, Sheppard Jonathan E Trainer																		
11Sep92- 2Med	fst	$1\frac{1}{16}$	$:48^4$	$1:12^2$	$1:43^4$	3↑Alw 17000	**76**	1	2	2^{hd}	2^{hd}	2^3	$2^{1\frac{1}{4}}$	Taylor K T	b	116	.90	87–07 ToYou$112^{1\frac{1}{4}}$
11Sep92-Originally scheduled on turf																		
25Aug92- 7Atl	fm	*1	Ⓣ$:47^1$	$1:12^2$	$1:38^1$	3↑Clm 20000	**78**	4	4	4^8	5^5	4^1	$2^{2\frac{1}{4}}$	Carberry M O	b	119	7.20	101–07 Dncno
23Jly92- 9Atl	sly	$1\frac{1}{16}$	$:46^4$	$1:12^1$	1:45	3↑Clm 12500	**71**	3	3	$3^{3\frac{1}{2}}$	4^2	2^{hd}	1no	Taylor K T	b	117	2.20	85–22 Pr
18Jun92-10Atl	fm	*$1\frac{1}{16}$	Ⓣ:49	$1:13^3$	$1:47^2$	3↑Clm 20000	**62**	3	5	$3^{3\frac{1}{2}}$	$5^{3\frac{3}{4}}$	$6^{3\frac{3}{4}}$	$4^{2\frac{1}{4}}$	Taylor K T		117	*.90	79–17
15May92- 7GS	fm	1	Ⓣ$:46^3$	$1:11^3$	$1:37^3$	3↑Clm 20000	**78**	8	9	9^9	$9^{6\frac{3}{4}}$	$4^{6\frac{1}{2}}$	$4^{3\frac{3}{4}}$	Castaneda K		115	5.10	10
8Jun91♦5Epsom(Eng)	gd	$1\frac{1}{16}$			$1:43^1$	Ⓣ Croydex Hcp							$10^{16\frac{3}{4}}$	O'Gorman S	b	107	25.00	

LATEST WORKOUTS ●Oct 4 Del 5f fst $1:00^4$ B

MUD CAULKS. If the track is muddy, heavy or slow, or if the turf is anything but firm or hard, the addition of mud caulks is a sign of trainer intent, and it may also be helpful to the horse's ability to negotiate the course with confidence.

Mud caulks are horseshoes with small, flattened prongs for better traction. On fast or hard racing surfaces these shoes can do damage to the horse's ankle or hoof, but on a soggy or sticky track, mud caulks are a distinct advantage.

Few tracks permit mud caulks on the turf, even though they would be a major advantage to any horse wearing them. The digging action of the cleats would rip up the course beyond repair. But a smaller version of caulks are permitted and very useful on courses with deep grass such as Golden Gate Fields and the Fair Grounds, and are worth noting on any rain-softened course anywhere else.

On sealed wet-fast tracks, in which the upper cushion has been rolled tight, mud caulks may be potentially dangerous or of hit or miss value, but the trainer is a cheapskate or a fool if he consistently avoids spending the extra few dollars for caulked shoes when conditions are bad enough to warrant them. And the player is taking a big risk if he or she fails to pay attention to this information when it is available.

STEEL SHOES AND BAR SHOES. The player takes a bigger risk investing money on horses equipped with steel shoes or bar shoes, unless the horse in question has won with that kind of equipment before. Both types are danger signals. The horse usually has foot problems, and the shoe is an attempt to give more secure footing at the cost of extra, unfamiliar weight.

NOTE: *In the early 1990s a new horseshoe, called a "turn down," was gaining acceptance on eastern sandy tracks. The turn-down shoe features a slightly different grip design than the conventional shoe and reportedly was responsible for several form reversals in dry racing conditions before it was banned for use in August 1993.*

Unfortunately, it saddens me to report that many racetracks still do not care about the fan sufficiently to provide a complete, working shoe board on the grounds. This is another example of the complete lack of understanding shown by racing officials and track operators about the needs of the racing fan.

BANDAGES. Many trainers apply bandages on the rear legs as a matter of course to keep a horse from hitting itself in close quarters. But the presence of front leg bandages may have distinctly negative implications: a minor injury or a weak ankle or a sore muscle. Ironically, as front-leg bandage information now is part of *DRF* past performances, its import has been muted as more trainers are using them as standard equipment for many horses in their care. And there always have been horses at the lowest end of the racing spectrum who have run their best races with front wraps and some on the highest levels as well—Forego, as an example. Until the 1990s I rarely wagered on a horse with front-leg bandages unless I knew it had won with them or passed a rigorous personal inspection in the paddock, post parade and pre-race warm-up. On muddy tracks I *never* wagered on a front-leg bandaged horse because of the extra weight that inevitably would adhere to these wrappings.

Things have changed: In the 1990s veterinarians and trainers may use lightweight wraps made out of space age material that repels foreign substances, including mud. No longer is it wise to automatically toss out horses with front wraps on wet tracks. Now the player must either trust the clues in the past-performance profile, or improve his or her observation skills to detect leg soreness in the post parade.

PHYSICAL APPEARANCE

It takes a trained eye and many years of experience to reach valid conclusions about physical fitness on sight. A few basics should help; but I caution you to pay close attention to the clues in the *Racing Form* until you have mastered the art.

NEGATIVE SIGNS. Excessive kidney sweat between the flanks. And on cool days, heavy sweating of any kind in the paddock or post parade. Fractious, uncontrollable behavior during the post parade and warm-up period. Unusual swelling at the knee joints. Stiff leggedness. A gimpy stride, favoring one leg, or a short stride in the walking ring or post parade in which the rear leg never reaches the hoofprint of the front leg. Cantankerous or listless behavior. A dull coat that fails to reflect light on a sunny day.

POSITIVE SIGNS. Aggressive but controllable behavior in the post parade and warm-up. A fluid transition from a walking gait to the gallop to the run. Attentive, alert behavior nearing the gate (watch the ears and head). A well-groomed, shiny coat.

NOTE: *Before author Bonnie Ledbetter died a few years ago, she made two worthwhile videos on judging physical condition in the paddock and post parade. In the 1990s, Philadelphia-based Joe Takach has done considerable work in this area, and his published material and videos, also are worth checking out. The titles and publishers are listed in Appendix D.*

JOCKEYS

Most trainers have alliances with one or more jockeys. Some jockeys ride every race for the trainer; others ride only when the trainer is serious. The player should learn who the top jockeys are, who rides for what stable, and who can't ride a merry-go-round.

Some trainers like to use apprentice jockeys because of the three-, five-, seven-, or ten-pound weight concession permitted during their apprenticeship.

My standards for jockeys may not be your standards, but I will play a well-qualified contender ridden by a hot apprentice, by an established veteran or star, by a rider who has won with the horse before, or by a stable favorite. Under no circumstances will I play a horse ridden by a ten-pound apprentice or a proven incompetent.

During the 1970s and early 1980s the only way to uncover pertinent jockey-trainer statistics was through private observations and research. While that still is required to fine-tune one's knowledge of these important relationships, today's players have access to reams of data from previously mentioned Bloodstock Research Information Services and Equiline, both based in Lexington, Kentucky, and from a scattering of daily and weekly newsletters and other handicapping supplements. One of the best of these is *Today's Racing Digest*, a popular daily handicapping aid published in northern and southern California.

When the original *Betting Thoroughbreds* was published in 1977 and updated five years later, there were only a handful of women jockeys who were capable of competing with the better male riders. Mary Alligood, Amy Rankin, Robyn Smith, Patty Cooksey, Patty Barton and a young Julie Krone were among the first to impress, and the list has grown appreciably every year.

In the 1990s, Julie Krone has emerged as the finest woman rider of all time, a sure-fire cinch for membership in the Hall of Fame. How else to recognize the achievements of a woman who won the 1993 Belmont Stakes, has led the jockey standings at every New Jersey track, and been among the top five jockeys in New York for several years? Otherwise, there are several dozen female riders now performing on equal ground with the better male riders at tracks throughout America, but I could not do justice to this fact without mentioning the three female riders who broke the sex barrier.

Kathy Kusner, the first to get a jockey license in 1968, Diane Krump the first to ride in a pari-mutuel race, February 7, 1969, at Hialeah Park in Florida, and Barbara Jo Rubin, the first to win, two weeks later at Charles Town Racetrack. All belong in the Hall of Fame alongside Julie Krone.

In handicapping, the jockey factor is not one that reduces itself to simple dos or don'ts. The player simply has to watch races very carefully to assess the strengths and weaknesses of the prominent riders on the local circuit.

Some of the best of them wind up boxed, blocked, or hopelessly out-foxed without rhyme or reason. And we have also seen prominent names dragged through court testimony about fixed or suspiciously run races. It is a tough, exacting life to be a 115-pound horserider and it is the rare jockey who makes a full career without arousing controversy.

All too many of them—like Ron Turcotte—wind up in wheelchairs. Others, like Alverdo Pineda and his brother Robert, have lost their lives on the job. That's no joke. The risks are enormous and the unwritten code of macho ethics that comes with the territory can exert an un-healthy influence on a slumping rider's judgment. And there are always a few trainers willing to play loose with the rules.

I have a lot of admiration and respect for jockeys who conduct them-selves honestly, trying to win as many races as possible.

All riders have their strengths, weaknesses and tendencies, and the player can make much better selections by knowing which riders fit which horses, which ones are risks to get into traffic trouble, or prone to swing widest, or likely to break especially well or poorly. And more than a few have working relationships with specific trainers who entrust them with their best runners.

Put western-based Eddie Delahoussaye aboard a classy router, and you can expect a patient, extremely well-timed move from behind horses. Eddie D. is smooth as silk, has first call on Neil Drysdale's horses and has other leading southern California trainers lining up for his services with stretch-running horses at all distances.

By contrast, Gary Stevens and Russell Baze are very quick out of the gate and have always used the inside rail path to best advantage.

Few can match Kent Desormeaux's versatility or Laffit Pincay's con-sistency, or Pat Day's extraordinary ability to get out of tight spots or Mike Smith's handling of turf horses or Chris Antley's ability to spot a track bias, especially on wet tracks.

Every racing circuit also has specialists or hidden jewels—Richard Migliore is one of New York's best-kept secrets, and the same is true for Kerwin Clark in the Midwest. Before he got hurt in a spill at Saratoga in 1978, no rider ever was more precocious than Steve Cauthen, who at 18 seemed as good as Bill Shoemaker, Eddie Arcaro or Bill Hartack at their best.

Cauthen's Triple Crown performances aboard Affirmed in 1978 were Hall of Fame material. But after a leg injury at Saratoga in August 1978, he returned to the saddle too soon, lost his timing and 110 consecutive races at Santa Anita. Practically booed out of southern California, Cauthen cut a sweetheart deal with wealthy British owner-breeder Robert Sangster and went to England to regain his confidence, which he did. Cauthen stayed 13 years until he retired in 1993, but it is a curious fact that this young master of the saddle never did win a Breeders' Cup, or a major stakes in any of his many return visits to America.

Which brings up one last point about jockeys. All jockeys hit slumps. Terrible slumps. Like zero for 35, or two for 60. Not only should the player avoid these jockeys when they are losing, but he or she should expect improvement from the horses they rode when a switch to another rider takes place.

Two decades ago, Johnny Rotz, a solid 20-year veteran, was riding so poorly that the "Rotz off" angle produced six longshot winners in two weeks and a dozen or more during the next two months. Mr. Rotz apparently got the message and retired gracefully the following winter.

Working With Workouts

Racing legend is filled with stories of horses who suddenly turned their careers around in an important training drill.

The Italian master trainer-breeder Frederico Tessio certainly set the standard for workout maneuvers with a brilliant relay-team drill involving three horses as he prepared Nearco for a smasher in the 1930 Italian Derby. Nearco, incidentally, through his sons Nearctic and Nasrullah, was destined to ensure Tessio's immortal impact on racing throughout the world.

Nearctic sired 1964 Kentucky Derby winner Northern Dancer, the most prolific sire of stakes winners on the international racing stage, and Nasrullah sired 1957 Preakness winner Bold Ruler, who ranks with Calumet Farm's Bull Lea as the most dominating sires of American stakes winners of the twentieth century. (I strongly recommend Tessio's rare book, *Breeding the Racehorse*, which is one of the most insightful books on *training* and breeding ever written.)

Racing history is filled with many other examples, including Secretariat's five-furlong work in 58.40 during Derby week to recover the form he seemed to have lost in the Wood Memorial 10 days earlier.

Nearly as many good horses have left their best races on the training track in miscalculated morning moves. Hall of Fame trainer James P. Conway regretted forever the ultra-fast one-mile drill he gave Kentucky

Tuesday, October 26, 1993

AQUEDUCT — Track Fast

Three Furlongs		Frisky's Finale	:48 H	Calibeau	1:05² B	Little Arturo	1:02² H
Mercy's Baby	:37 H	Return To Newport	:50² H	Get The Bags	1:02⁴ B	Ma Be Dit	1:02⁴ B
Four Furlongs		Vivano	:48³ B	Hair House	1:02³ B		
Cazzy B.	:52¹ B	Five Furlongs :57		Lite The Fuse	1:00³ H		

BELMONT PARK — Track Fast

Three Furlongs		Blazon Song	:49² H	Loam	:48² H	Five Furlongs :56¹	
Churkin	:37² B	Burdur(GB)	:49¹ H	Lure	:48² H	Adonara	1:03 B
Flaming Falcon	:37⁴ B	Camcorder	:51 B	Makadir	:48³ H	Alyjul	1:03¹ B
Heavenly Prize	:39³ B	Chou Chou Dancer	:50 B	Mcdee	:50⁴ B	**Bobbetta**	1:02 H
Icabod Rider	:38³ B	Confidente(Chi)	:50⁴ B	My Quincy	:49¹ B	Broad Grin	1:06 B
Magnetic Money	:37³ B	Dayflower	:47² H	Nikki's Rose	:49² H	**Damaskra**	1:02 H
Moskovskaya	:36² H	Dispute	:48² B	Preporant	:47¹ H	Doug Secret	1:05 B
Noble Niner	:39² B	Eloping	:49 H	Princess Haifa	:53 B	**Eaton Row**	1:02 B
Not For Love	:39² B	Excellent Tipper	:50 H	Private Session	:49² H	Royal Comorant	1:04⁴ B
Option Contract	:37 B	Exotic Slew	:53 B	Running Holme	:50¹ B	Sentimental Moi	1:02³ B
Perfect Fan	:38⁴ B	Flying American	:50² B	Schnappsy	:50³ B	Staple Queen	1:02⁴ B
Possibilities	:37 H	Footing	:49¹ B	Seattle Baby	:50 H	Sultan Of Java	1:03 B
Retirement Account	:37² B	Huckster Rose	:48³ H	ShimmringSnds(GB)	:47³ H	Wilton Place	1:04³ B
River Arly(Fr)	:36² H	Inagroove	:49⁴ B	Sluicing	:49² H	**Six Furlongs 1:07⁴**	
Share The Glory	:39² B	Inside Information	:48¹ H	Star Majesty	:51 B	Admirably(Uru)	1:19³ B
Sky Hero	:37² B	Jodi's The Best	:50 B	Syrian Princess	:50¹ B	Jesse F	1:16 H
Four Furlongs		Key Contender	:48⁴ H	There Goes Patsy	:52 B	Sixth Of May	1:18⁴ B
Amathos	:51 B	Khaleefa	:49 H	Wild Dame	:52 B		
Aztec Empire	:52 B	La Vie Dansant	:53 B	Winnetka	:49¹ B		
Baron De Vaux	:49 B	Lech	:49 B	**Zero To Sixty**	:46⁴ H		

HEAVENLY PRIZE (3f) looked good while just galloping. DISPUTE (4f) holds her form. LURE (4f) his last 1/4 in :24 flat and galloped out 5 furlongs in 1:00 3/5. EXCELLENT TIPPER (4f) went his last 1/8 in :12 flat.

EXPLANATION OF ABBREVIATIONS AND TERMS IN WORKOUTS

B-Breezing—Horse working at a moderate rate; not asked for top speed.

H-Handily—Horse working with increased effort, but not under pressure.

D-Driving—Horse working all-out under strong urging by rider.

g-Worked from the starting gate—Horse worked from a standing start in gate, simulating race conditions.

d-Around the dogs—Horse worked outside moveable barriers that protect the inner portion of the track.

Track records follow the distance, where applicable (for example: four furlongs—:45)

The day's best workout at each distance is listed in **bold face** type.

Derby winner Chateaugay for the 1963 Preakness to blow his chance for a Triple Crown Sweep. Shug McGaughey will not admit it publicly, but he was forced to second-guess himself for not pressing Easy Goer for more speed in training trials leading up to the 1989 Kentucky Derby and Breeders' Cup Classic.

Too many horseplayers fail to appreciate the subtle clues hidden in the workout line. Although the partial reason for this is genuine distrust of the accuracy of workout clockings, this still is a mistake. Workouts are windows into the trainer's mind. Even with some skepticism, an alert player can use workout information in tandem with distance switches, layoffs, changes in surface or circuits to make uncanny assessments of impending improvement or probable defeat. Interpreting workouts is part of the art of handicapping.

The racetrack is open for training in the early morning hours, and the official clockers for *Daily Racing Form*, various racetracks and private newsletters have a tough job. As many as 75 horses may be out on the track at the same time, and there are precious few names or numbers on the saddlecloths to help identify the horses. Having privately clocked virtually every Kentucky Derby, Preakness and Belmont starter for all but three years since 1977, I can attest to the degree of difficulty of the assignment. Nevertheless, if you are interested in fine-tuning your assessments of trainers and are looking for a catalog of longshot angles, the following hints on how to interpret workout information should prove very useful. Workouts can be powerful clues to probable performance.

Daily tabular listings in some *DRF* editions contain selected comments such as those on page 204 on the most noteworthy training drills of the day. I have repeatedly asked *DRF* management and racetrack officials to expand this valuable feature to all editions—to no avail. Maybe if players press the issue in their own interest, *DRF* management finally will follow through. Otherwise, keeping a private file of very good workouts at each distance in a special notebook will pay dividends when reviewing first-time starters and absentees. Spot checking the daily tabular listings for a few days before a new meet opens also may provide some clues as to the relative speed of the racing surface. Generally speaking, a tab of slow works will translate to a holding or stamina-favoring racing surface; a tab of *very* fast works not only will imply a speed-favoring

Thursday, July 22, 1993

HOLLYWOOD PARK — Track Fast

Three Furlongs			
A Treek For Roses	:37³ H	Highland Park Ms	:48 H
Bel Purdue	:37³ B	James Be Frank	:47³ Hg
Bobs Bikini	:36² H	Juliannus	:50⁴ H
Bridger Creek	:39³ H	Ladies Cruise	:48² B
Cutie Who	:35⁴ Hg	Littliest Charm	:49¹ H
Desert Stormette	:35² H	Maid's Day Off *	:49¹ B
Gotadawinda	:37² Hg	Majesty Son	:50² H
Imperial Kid	:37² H	Marfa's Joy	:49³ H
Magical Flash	:36 H	Mill Sham	:51³ H
Maria's Sport	:39³ H	Minidar	:51³ H
Mob Stage	:36³ H	Miss Checo Gray	:49¹ H
Playful Position	:36² H	Nossemblyrequird	:47² Hg
State Craft	:36² H	Prenup	:48 H
Tricky Code	:34³ Hg	Princess Of Money	:49 H
Wish Fulfilled	:39³ B	Saturnino	:48³ H
Four Furlongs		**Savona Belle**	:46³ H
Aldo Rose	:49² H	Sindina *	:51 H
Best Pal	:50² B	Southworth	:51³ H
Celona	:48³ H	Spiritual Fantasy *	:51 H
Centennial Axe	:50³ H	Striking Offer	:49⁴ H
Cloudy Line	:50² H	Tequila Rose	:49¹ B
Dive For Cover	:47² H	Tomorrow's Spirit	:48³ H
Dumping Ways *	:49² H	**Virtuous Regent**	:46³ H
Foxy Reb	:47³ H	West Coast Halo	:48³ H
Gold Conde	:48² H	White Heart	:48 H
Her Elegant Ways	:47² H	**Five Furlongs** :56²	
		Bon Oeuf	1:01² H

Brave Mi Mi *	1:01² H	Torole	:59¹ H
Captivant	1:01 H	Valenti-Ar	1:00¹ H
ConsciousDecision	1:01³ H	Wedding Ring-Ir	:59⁴ H
Danza Regio	1:02³ H	**Six Furlongs** 1:08	
Fernandazo	1:02 H	Ala Merced	1:13 H
First Instinct	1:00³ H	Belle Of Ack	1:15³ H
I'm So Clever	1:00¹ H	**Bolger's Lead**	1:12² H
Immobilize	1:01¹ H	Capital Raiser	1:17² H
King Coping	1:00³ Hg	Chief's Omega	1:13⁴ H
LarkInTheMeadow	1:04³ H	**Del Mar Dennis**	1:12² H
Luv N Tears	1:00² H	Der Rosenkavalier	1:13² H
Makinnhonestbuck	1:01¹ H	Dolce Amore	1:13¹ H
Miss Hapa Hoale *	1:01² H	Ez Turbo	1:16¹ H
Mountain Passage	1:01³ H	Fine Impression	1:13¹ H
Neversettleforless	1:02² H	Hidden Dark	1:15⁴ H
Portugese Starlet	1:00⁴ H	Little By Little	1:14¹ H
Prevasive Force	1:01² H	Potridee-Ar	1:13³ H
Private Persuasion	:59² H	Slick Surface	1:17¹ H
Roman Susan	1:00² Hg	Sunday's Sis	1:15² H
Sheezforkeeps	1:01² H	We Piddle Around	1:15¹ H
Slew Supreme	:59 H	**Seven Furlongs** 1:20⁴	
Smoothermover	1:00⁴ H	Runaway Dunaway	1:28² H
Stolen Loot	1:00¹ H	**1 Mile 1:32³**	
Stone Hedge	1:01³ H	Sir Beaufort	1:38 H
Super Trax	:59 H		
Tara's Secret	1:00⁴ H		
Tennis Racket	1:00¹ H		

WORKOUT AVERAGES

HOLLYWOOD PARK MAIN TRACK FAST—JULY 22

DISTANCE	NO. OF HORSES	FASTEST	SLOWEST	AVERAGE TIME
3 furlongs	15	:34 3/5	:39 3/5	:37
4 furlongs	35	:46 3/5	:51 3/5	:49
5 furlongs	31	:59	1:04 3/5	1:00 4/5
6 furlongs	16	1:12 2/5	1:17 2/5	1:14 2/5
7 furlongs	1	1:28 2/5	1:28 2/5	1:28 2/5

strip, but a possible inside speed bias because quick clockings are not likely while horses are forced to race on a dead rail or in the middle of the track.

The absence of workouts from any past-performance profile does not mean the absence of training. As stated, some works are missed, missing or misidentified, and many trainers have access to private training tracks. Until all states adopt a rule requiring at least two on-track workouts to qualify a horse to compete, the player simply is going to have to keep a record of trainers who like to sneak hot horses past the betting public.

For obvious reasons, this practice is most often attempted with first-time starters in cheap maiden claiming races and is particularly rampant in Maryland and Illinois, breeding states where supervision of workouts by each state racing commission is a farce and there are about fifty private training tracks within 100 miles of the Baltimore and Chicago area racetracks, respectively. Kentucky, Florida, Louisiana and Texas are other states where numerous off-course workouts occur on private farms and training centers.

The clockings reported are as accurate as the clockers are skillful and honest. Because the vast majority of clockers are skillful but not well paid, the player should expect some of the best workouts to be misrepresented.

ARLINGTON – Track Muddy

Three Furlongs					
Berry's Request	:38² B	Crafty Annie	:54 B	**Freezenly**	1:00 H
Charging Walk	:38¹ B	LightningBeatie	:51² B	Ginny's Big Boy	1:02⁴ Bg
Find One	:37² **B**	**Sister's K.**	:48² **Hg**	Her Lady Shipp	1:06³ B
Lear Fame	:38 B	Sportin Teresa	:50 B	Mayan King	1:03⁴ Bg
Powerful Punch	:39² B	Valrhona	:52¹ B	Randi'sPleasure	1:02⁴ B
Four Furlongs		Westering	:53² B	Three G's	1:06⁴ B
		Five Furlongs—	:57¹	Yankee Kisses	1:04² Bg

Six Furlongs—1:08

Hold Old Blue 1:15⁴ **Hg**
Writer's Honor 1:16 Bg
Your Ladyship 1:17⁴ B

HAWTHORNE – Track Sloppy

Three Furlongs		Four Furlongs		Pocket Vision	:53¹ B	**Five Furlongs—** :58¹
Pocket Choice	:42¹ B	Flash CanDance	:53¹ B	**Volumetric**	:51² **B**	Nodoubtaspy 1:02 B

FAIRMOUNT PARK – Track Fast

Three Furlongs		Four Furlongs—	:45⁴	Sister's Orphan	:53³ B	Six Furlongs—1:08³
Annimine	:41² B	Batoonie	:52¹ B	TurnpikeDancer	:50⁴ Bg	
Full Rine	:36³ **Hg**	Jessica Del Ray	:51¹ Bg	**Yesbwana**	:49² **H**	Hercomsthprinc 1:18⁴ B
Native Guy	:38¹ B	Licensed Denied	:50⁴ B	**Five Furlongs—** :56⁴		**Our Man Mez** 1:17⁴ **B**
Police Red	:38² B	LongDarkDaddy	:50² B	Billcapade	1:07 Bg	
Shiekslittle Sis	:38³ B	NorthernSundnc	:50⁴ B	**Blinker Signal**	1:04³ **Bg**	**1 Mile—1:37²**
Time Run Out	:38¹ B	Notice My Act	:51 B	Imo's Numbers	1:07 Bg	
TooFastforLove	:37¹ B	Polite Belle	:50⁴ B	Lin D Ruler	1:05³ B	Intriquing Song 1:48³ B

The most accurate clocking crews operate at the major tracks in California, where a positive workout identification system is backed up by the California Horse Racing Board and the clockers are employed by the individual racetracks. Relatively accurate clockings also are available in Florida during the classy winter meets and New York where the *DRF* and New York Racing Association clockers work independently under NYRA supervision. At all but a few racetracks, however, nearly all workouts for established stakes horses and 70–80 percent of the remaining workouts are as accurate as a hand-held stopwatch can make them. At the bottom line, racing has no excuse for its failure to implement accurate workout identification procedures at every track in the nation. Public money and confidence is at stake, and the flow of tax dollars is jeopardized as much as the integrity of the game.

The term *breezing* is used by clockers to mean radically different things in different locations. In California, for example, clockers rarely label a workout breezing (b) unless the horse was under heavy restraint throughout the move. In New York and most other eastern tracks the majority of workouts are labeled breezing and the term handily (h) is reserved for horses who are whipped at least semi-seriously through the stretch. (See charts on pages 206 and 207.)

Some tracks provide an auxiliary training track to handle the overflow of horses on the grounds. These training tracks tend to be considerably deeper and slower than the main track, and the following table of representative times should be adjusted accordingly.

MAJOR-TRACK TABLE OF NOTEWORTHY WORKOUT TIMES

DISTANCE	BREEZING (WITHOUT SERIOUS WHIPPING)	HANDILY	FROM GATE	MUD
3 furlongs	.35$\frac{4}{5}$b	.35$\frac{2}{5}$h	Add $\frac{2}{5}$ sec.	Add $\frac{4}{5}$ sec.
4 furlongs	.48b	.47$\frac{3}{5}$h	Add $\frac{2}{5}$	Add 1
5 furlongs	1:00$\frac{3}{5}$b	1:00$\frac{1}{5}$h	Add $\frac{2}{5}$	Add 1$\frac{1}{5}$
6 furlongs	1:13$\frac{3}{5}$b	1:13h	Add $\frac{2}{5}$	Add 1$\frac{2}{5}$
7 furlongs	1:27b	1:26$\frac{2}{5}$h	Add $\frac{2}{5}$	Add 1$\frac{3}{5}$
1 mile	1:41b	1:40$\frac{2}{5}$h	Add $\frac{2}{5}$	Add $\frac{4}{5}$
1$\frac{1}{8}$ miles	1:56b	1:55$\frac{2}{5}$h	Add $\frac{2}{5}$ sec.	Add 2 sec.

Admittedly, the value of the preceding chart is limited. It is only a guide. On lightning-fast racetracks the standards should be adjusted by at least one full second, and at minor tracks few horses will ever work fast enough to spark the player's attention.

The value of workouts is not restricted to speed. Indeed, a fast workout is not often conclusive evidence of improved physical condition; nor is a series of short, speedy drills of any special import to a horse that consistently shows high early speed in its races. Instead the player

Solid Truth B. g. 3(May), by Proud Truth—Kettle, by Levee Dancer
ALVARADO F J (—) Br.—Thornton Mr-Mrs C (Ky)
Own.—505 Farm Tr.—Rothblum Steve (—) **112**

Lifetime						
11 2 1 0	1992	9	2	1	0	$57,150
$57,850	1991	2	M	0	0	$700
	Turf	1	0	0	0	
	Wet	1	1	0	0	$16,500

23Oct92- 7SA	fst	$1\frac{1}{16}$	:46^3	1:10^4	1:43	Alw 32000	91	2	4	2^1	5$^{1\frac{3}{4}}$	3^3	1$^{1\frac{3}{4}}$	Desormeaux K J	LB	120	7.10	88–21	SldTrth120$^{1\frac{3}{4}}$SEvrClvr117^{hd}Cn'tBSlw120	4-wide stretch	9
13Sep92- 4Dmr	fst	1	:46^1	1:11	1:36^1	Clm c-50000	78	2	7	6^5	6$^{5\frac{1}{2}}$	5$^{6\frac{1}{2}}$	5$^{6\frac{3}{4}}$	Valenzuela P A	LB	116	5.50	79–11	Ciglino110^{3}LordOfMotion115^{no}Aurig115	4-wide stretch	9
13Sep92-Claimed from Arnold Florence or Jack H, Mulhall Richard W Trainer																					
29Aug92- 9Dmr	fst	$6\frac{1}{2}$f	:22	:44^4	1:16	Clm 50000	84	6	4	7$^{5\frac{3}{4}}$	7$^{5\frac{1}{2}}$	8^3	7$^{3\frac{1}{2}}$	Pincay L Jr	LB	117	22.60	89–12	CrsLdr116^{nk}StrOfMsc115$^{\frac{1}{2}}$KnsOTp115	Wide backstretch	6
4Jun92- 5Hol	fm	1	Ⓣ:46^1	1:09^2	1:33^4	Alw 34000	64	4	5	8$^{5\frac{1}{4}}$	9^{11}	9^{11}	8^{16}	Alvarado F J	LB	120	12.50	80–05	BlinkingLights117$^{\frac{3}{4}}$MjorImpct120$^{1\frac{1}{4}}$BienBin120	No rally	10
4Apr92- 5SA	fst	$1\frac{1}{8}$	:46^1	1:10^2	1:49^1	S A Derby	77	6	5	6$^{4\frac{3}{4}}$	7^{10}	6^9	6^{11}	Nakatani C S	LB	122	55.70	73–11	A.P.Indy122$^{1\frac{3}{4}}$Bertrando122^{nk}CasulLies122	Jostled start	7
4Apr92-Grade I																					
6Mar92- 8SA	fst	1	:44^2	1:08^4	1:34^1	Pirate Cove	83	3	6	5^7	4^3	3^4	2^5	Alvarado F J	LB	117	2.40	91–03	Bold Assert120^5 Solid Truth117$^{1\frac{1}{4}}$ Bossanova117		6
6Mar92-5-wide into stretch, lost whip 1/4; Originally scheduled on turf; Originally scheduled on turf																					
19Feb92- 8SA	fst	$1\frac{1}{8}$	:46^1	1:10^2	1:49^1	ⓇBradbury	87	3	7	7^7	7^9	5$^{4\frac{1}{2}}$	4$^{4\frac{1}{2}}$	Alvarado F J	LB	115	9.60	79–18	NaturalNine115^{hd}AlSabin117$^{2\frac{1}{2}}$ChainOfLife115	Came on	8
29Jan92- 8SA	fst	$1\frac{1}{16}$	:46^2	1:11^3	1:44^1	ⓇS Catalina	83	6	8	7^4	4^3	4^5	4^5	Alvarado F J	LB	114	10.90	77–20	VyingVictor115^{3}TurbulntKrs114$^{\frac{1}{2}}$AlSbn117	Jostled start	11
5Jan92- 9SA	sly	$1\frac{1}{16}$	:47^2	1:13^1	1:48^1	Md Sp Wt	84	12	7	6^8	3^5	2$^{1\frac{1}{2}}$	1^2	Alvarado F J	LB	117	6.50	62–31	SldTrth117^{2}LttryWnnr117^{15}RchDnsr117	4-wide 1st turn	12

LATEST WORKOUTS Oct 18 SA 7f fst 1:25^4 H Oct 13 SA 4f fst :47^3 H Oct 8 SA 5f fst 1:00^2 H Oct 2 SA 5f fst 1:01^2 H

should consider the value of workouts in the light of the following principles; they are the concepts many of the best trainers use, and the ones many of the best players use as well.

1. Pay special note to the frequency of workouts and give a horse extra credit for positive physical condition if it has several good workouts to its credit or has raced well recently and has worked four furlongs or longer at least once in the interim. This is especially true at minor racetracks and for horses that have been out of action sometime during the recent past. (See Solid Truth above.)

2. A recent fast workout at three or four furlongs is a positive sign if the horse has shown little speed in his recent races, or has been racing in a route and now is attempting a sprint. Conversely, if he has been showing high early speed, or is attempting a significantly longer distance, a longer, slower workout would suggest the trainer's attempt to build staying power. In the first example following, 1991 Kentucky Derby winner Strike The Gold showed unexpected high speed in his five-furlong training drill on May 1, 1992, and more speed than usual in his

Strike the Gold Ch. c. 4, by Alydar—Majestic Gold, by Hatchet Man
NO RIDER (—) Br.—Calumet Farm (Ky)
Own.—Condron W J & Cornacchia J Tr.—Zito Nicholas P (—) **114**
Lifetime 20 3 6 4 $1,554,426 | 1992 5 0 3 1 $93,176 | 1991 12 2 3 3 $1,443,850

4Apr92- 7Aqu	fst	1⅜	:481	1:12	1:553	3↑Thrty Six Rd	101	3	4	413	413	37	26	Antley C W		117	*.80	90-21 RedPine1196StriketheGold117hdAlyten117	Up for place	4
7Mar92-10GP	fst	1¼	:473	1:363	2:013	3↑Gulf Park H	110	6	5	518	511	48	27	Krone J A		115	2.00	86-14 SeCdet1197StrikthGold1152½SunnySunris114	4 wide str	6
7Mar92-Grade I																				
17Feb92-10GP	fst	1⅛	:472	1:112	1:492	3↑Broward H	107	3	6	614	58	44	31	Krone J A		117	*.80	89-21 HnstEnsgn109noPntBttrOnt1141StrkthGld117	4 wide str	7
17Feb92-Grade III																				
1Feb92- 9GP	fst	1⅛	:464	1:101	1:48	3↑Donn H	104	6	8	818	815	711	67	Antley C W		116	*1.30	90-12 SeCdet1153OutofPlc114nkSunnySunris115	Vry wide str	8
1Feb92-Grade I																				
8Jan92- 7GP	fst	7f	:234	:462	1:241	Alw 22900	99	11	9	1214	911	55	2¾	Antley C W		120	*.70	84-16 ByShrk112¾StriketheGold120½PerfctFit114	Wide bckstr	12
2Nov91- 8CD	fst	1¼	:482	1:38	2:024	3↑Br Cp Class	113	10	9	915	97¾	67	54½	Valenzuela P A	B	122	6.20	91-09 BlackTieAffir-Ir1261¼TwilightAgend1262¼Unbridled126		11
2Nov91-Grade I; 7-wide in stretch, late rally																				
5Oct91- 7Bel	fst	1¼	:473	1:36	2:003	3↑J C Gold Cp	112	4	5	58½	32½	2hd	31½	Valenzuela P A		121	2.80	92-07 Fstn-Ar1261¼ChfHonch126nkStrkthGld121	Inside, wknd	5
5Oct91-Grade I																				
15Sep91- 6Bel	fst	1⅛	:463	1:093	1:461	3↑Woodward	111	1	5	58	56	54½	43	Valenzuela P A		121	4.20	95-02 InExcess-Ir1261¾FrmWy1261½Festin-Ar126	Rallied wide	6
15Sep91-Grade I																				
17Aug91- 8Sar	fst	1¼	:472	1:36	2:011	Travers	100	5	6	614	42½	45	45¾	Cordero A Jr		126	*1.70	92-06 CorporteReport126nkHnsl1262½FlySoFr126	Lacked rally	6
17Aug91-Grade I																				
28Jly91- 8Sar	fst	1⅛	:462	1:103	1:484	Jim Dandy	99	3	7	819	810	53½	34½	Antley C W		128	*1.20	89-08 FlySoFr1261½UponMySoul1143StrkthGold128	Wide trip	8
28Jly91-Grade II																				

LATEST WORKOUTS May 6 Bel 4f fst :482 H | May 1 Bel 5f fst :581 H ✓ | Apr 24 Bel 5f fst 1:012 B | Apr 15 Bel 4f fst :512 B

deceptively modest four-furlong move five days later. A week later, Strike The Gold proceeded to break an extended losing streak with an upset victory in the $750,000 Pimlico Special.

Playing catch-up ball because of bad weather on the West Coast during February 1978, trainer Laz Barrera was fully tested to get Affirmed in peak condition for a memorable Triple Crown duel with Alydar. Barrera's genius is reflected in the workout line of Affirmed's Kentucky Derby past performances.

On the weekend before the 1¼-mile classic, Barrera supervised one of the most unusual and most effective pre-Derby workouts in Triple Crown history: 1⅛ miles around three turns, clocked in a deceptive 1:56⅕, on a tiring, drying-out track with successively faster splits from start to finish.

Affirmed **126** Ch. c (1975), by Exclusive Native—Won't Tell You, by Crafty Admiral.
Breeder, Harbor View Farm (Fla.). 1978 4 4 0 0 $356,650
Owner, Harbor View Farm. Trainer, Lazaro Barrera. 1977 9 7 2 0 $343,477

16 Apr78	8Hol	1⅛	:45	1:092	1:481ft	1-3	▴122	1h	11	12½	12	CauthnS2	SpwS 91	Affirmed 122		Think Snow	9
2 Apr78	8SA	1⅛	:454	1:094	1:48 ft	1-3	▴120	11	11½	13½	18	PincyLJr7	AlwS 92	Affirmed 120		Balzac	12
18 Mar78	8SA	1 1/16	:482	1:12	1:423ft	1-3	▴126	21	2h	1h	12	CauthnS4	HcpS 89	Affirmed 126		Chance Dancer	6
8 Mar78	6SA	6½ f	:213	:442	1:153ft	1-5	▴124	43½	11½	14	15	CauthenS1	Alw 92	Affirmed124		SpottedCharger	5
29 Oct77	8Lrl	1 1/16	:484	1:133	1:441ft	7-5	122	21	2h	1h	1nk	CauthenS3	AlwS 92	Affirmed 122		Alydar	4
15 Oct77	6Bel	1	:481	1:122	1:363m	6-5	▴122	32	1h	1½	21¼	CauthnS5	ScwS 84	Alydar 122		Affirmed	6
10 Sep77	8Bel	7 f	:233	:463	1:213gd	6-5	▴122	2½	1h	2h	1no	CauthnS2	ScwS 94	Affirmed 122		Alydar	5
27 Aug77	8Sar	6½ f	:224	:451	1:152ft	2¼	122	32	2h	1h	1½	CauthnS4	ScwS 98	Affirmed 122		Alydar	5
17 Aug77	8Sar	6 f	:214	:443	1:093ft	6-5	▴124	35½	43	2½	12¾	CauthnS3	AlwS 92	Affirmed 124		Tilt Up	6
23 Jly 77	5Hol	6 f	:214	:442	1:091ft	2-5	▴122	1h	1½	14	17	PincyLJr6	HcpS 93	Affirmed122		He'sDewan	8
6 Jly 77	8Bel	5½ f	:222	:454	1:033ft	4½	122	11	2h	21½	23½	CrdroAJr1	AlwS 93	Alydar 117		Affirmed	7
15 Jun77	8Bel	5½ f	:222	:453	1:05 ft	3½	119	2½	2½	1h	1nk	CrdroAJr1	AlwS 90	Affirmed 119		Wood Native	11
24 May77	4Bel	5½ f	:23	:472	1:06 ft	9½	1175	1½	11½	12	14½	GonzlzB10	Mdn 85	Affirmed '17		Innocuous	10

May 3 CD 5f ft :59h | Apr 29 CD 9f ft 1:56⅕b | Apr 12 Hol 5f ft 1:01⅘h

The three turns added difficulty to the workout, and the faster quarter-mile splits were even more impressive because Affirmed picked up the pace without serious urging to complete a fast final eighth-mile elbowing around the third and last turn.

"No horse other than Affirmed could have put in a workout like that so easily," Barrera said. And if Laz was exaggerating, I still want to bet on the next one who can duplicate the effort. Wednesday of Derby week—three days prior to the Run for the Roses—Barrera sent Affirmed out for still one more tuneup: five furlongs in a brisk 59 seconds, with a final quarter mile clocked in a sharp 23⅕.

In the case of Bold Forbes, whose past performances going into the 1976 Belmont stakes are seen below, Barrera employed several long, slow workouts to set this very fast colt for a maximum effort in the Kentucky Derby. His workout prior to the Preakness—a blazing half-mile drill—did nothing to advance the horse and may have put him too much on edge. For the demanding 1½-mile Belmont, Barrera readily admitted his mistake and changed strategies as reflected by the colt's two beautifully designed workouts at 1½ miles and 1⅛ miles, respectively. While Barrera probably earned a deserved place in the Hall of Fame with his work with Triple Crown winner Affirmed, his masterful handling of the speed-crazy Bold Forbes ranks among the finest training achievements of the twentieth century.

Bold Forbes **126** Dk. b. or br. c (1973), by Irish Castle—Comely Nell, by Commodore M.
Br., Eaton Farms & Red Bull Stable (Ky.). 1976 . . 7 4 1 2 $318,890
Owner, E. R. Tizol. Trainer, L. S. Barrera. 1975 . 8 7 0 1 $62,749

15 May76	8Pim	$1\frac{3}{16}$	:45 1:09 1:55	ft	1e	126	1^{2}	1^{2}	2^{h}	3^{4}	CoroAJr4	ScwS	91	Elocutionist126	Play theRed	6
1 May76	8CD	$1\frac{1}{4}$	:45^{4}1:10^{2}2:01^{3}	ft	3	126	1^{5}	$1^{1\frac{1}{2}}$	$1^{1\frac{1}{2}}$	1^{1}	CrdroAJr2	ScwS	89	BoldForbes126	HonestPlesre	9
17 Apr76	8Aqu	$1\frac{1}{8}$	:46 1:09^{4}1:47^{2}	ft	2-5	*126	1^{3}	$1^{1\frac{1}{2}}$	1^{4}	$1^{4\frac{3}{4}}$	CdroAJr5	ScwS	98	Bold Forbes 126	On The Sly	7
20 Mar76	8Aqu	7 f	:22^{1} :44 1:20^{4}	ft	8-5	119	2^{h}	1^{2}	1^{7}	$1^{7\frac{3}{4}}$	CdroAJr7	AlwS	97	Bold Forbes 119	Eustace	8
28 Feb76	8SA	1	:45^{3}1:09^{3}1:35	ft	2	117	1^{2}	2^{1}	1^{4}	1^{3}	PincyLJr5	AlwS	94	BoldForbes117	Grandaries	7
14 Feb76	8SA	7 f	:22 :44^{3}1:21^{4}	ft	8-5	*119	1^{h}	$2^{\frac{1}{2}}$	$1^{2\frac{1}{2}}$	$3^{\frac{3}{4}}$	PincyLJr7	AlwS	93	ThrmlEnrgy117	StaindGlass	7
24 Jan76	8SA	6 f	:22^{1} :45 1:09^{3}	ft	6-5	*120	$2^{\frac{1}{2}}$	2^{2}	$2^{\frac{1}{2}}$	2no	PincyLJr2	AlwS	91	Sure Fire 114	Bold Forbes	6
31 Dec75	4SA	$5\frac{1}{2}$ f	:21^{4} :44^{2}1:03	ft	1-3	*122	$1^{\frac{1}{2}}$	$2^{\frac{1}{2}}$	2^{h}	3^{5}	PincayLJr1	Alw	94	Sure Fire 114	Beau Talent	5
3 Aug75	8Sar	6 f	:21^{4} :44^{1}1:09^{4}	ft	1-10	*120	1^{2}	1^{8}	1^{10}	1^{8}	V'squezJ5	AlwS	91	BoldForbes120	FamilyDoct'r	5
23 Jly 75	8Bel	6 f	:22^{2} :45^{2}1:09^{2}	ft	8-5	120	$1^{1\frac{1}{2}}$	1^{2}	1^{4}	1^{5}	PincyLJr2	AlwS	96	Bold Forbes 120	Iron Bit	5
15 Jun75	7PR	6 f	:22^{2} :44^{3}1:10^{3}	ft	1-6	*118	1^{2}	1^{4}	1^{5}	1^{13}	HiraldoJ2	Stk	101	Bold Forbes 118	Lovely Jay	4
4 Jun75	4PR	6 f	:23 :45^{3}1:11^{2}	ft	1-4e	*114	1^{2}	$1^{3\frac{1}{2}}$	1^{5}	1^{8}	HiraldoJ3	Alw	97	Bold Forbes 114	Lovely Jay	10
25 Apr75	1PR	5 f	:22 :45^{3} :59^{1}	ft	1-6	*116	1^{4}	1^{5}	1^{6}	$1^{8\frac{1}{2}}$	HiraldoJ3	Alw	95	Bold Forbes 116	Lovely Jay	5
11 Apr75	1PR	5 f	:22 :45^{3} :58^{4}	ft	1-3	*115	1^{5}	1^{5}	1^{5}	1^{5}	HiraldoJ4	Alw	97	Bold Forbes 115	Lovely Jay	5
12 Mar75	1PR	5 f	:22 :45^{4} :59^{2}	ft	35	116	1^{5}	1^{6}	1^{8}	1^{17}	HiraldoJ2	Mdn	94	BoldForbes116	MyDad'sBrdy	8

June 1 Bel 1m ft 1:50⅗bg May 27 Bel 1½m ft 2:43⅘b May 13 Pim 4f ft :45⅘h

3. A workout of any distance at any reasonable speed one or two days before a race is a useful "blowout" and can be interpreted as a positive sign of trainer intention, yet it was considerably more popular in

Prairie Bayou — Ch. g. 3(Mar), by Little Missouri—Whiffling, by Wavering Monarch
Br.—Loblolly Stable (Ky)
Own.—Loblolly Stable — Tr.—Bohannan Thomas (—) — **126**
Lifetime 11 7 3 0 $1,450,621 — 1993 7 5 2 0 $1,405,521 — 1992 4 2 1 0 $45,100 — Wet 2 0 2 0 $21,616

15May93-10Pim	fst	$1\frac{3}{16}$	$:46^4$	$1:11^1$	$1:56^3$	Preakness	**98**	3	10	$9^{7\frac{1}{4}}$	$8^{5\frac{1}{2}}$	2^{hd}	$1^{\frac{1}{2}}$	Smith M E		126	*2.20	79-18	PrairieBayou$126^{\frac{1}{2}}$CherokeeRun126^7ElBakn126	Steadied	12
15May93-Grade I																					
1May93-8CD	fst	$1\frac{1}{4}$	$:46^3$	$1:36^4$	$2:02^2$	Ky Derby	**101**	5	16	16^{14}	$9^{4\frac{3}{4}}$	$6^{3\frac{1}{2}}$	$2^{2\frac{1}{2}}$	Smith M E		126	*4.40	95-07	SeHero$126^{2\frac{1}{2}}$PririeByou126^{hd}WildGle126	6 wide, gamely	19
1May93-Grade I																					
10Apr93-8Kee	fst	$1\frac{1}{8}$	$:48^1$	$1:12^1$	$1:49^3$	Blue Grass	**96**	8	8	$8^{7\frac{1}{2}}$	$8^{3\frac{1}{2}}$	1^{hd}	1^2	Smith M E		121	3.70	87-16	PririByou121^2WllInd121^{no}DixilndHt121	5 Wide rddn out	9
10Apr93-Grade II																					
27Mar93-11TP	fst	$1\frac{1}{8}$	$:47^2$	$1:11^3$	$1:50^4$	Jim Beam	**98**	1	8	$8^{7\frac{3}{4}}$	$7^{4\frac{3}{4}}$	$1^{1\frac{1}{2}}$	$1^{\frac{3}{4}}$	McCarron C J		121	*1.20	79-18	PrrByo$121^{\frac{3}{4}}$ProdstRom121^2Mnr'sMrk121	5 wide driving	9
27Mar93-Grade II																					
20Feb93-8Aqu	fst	$1\frac{1}{16}$ ⊡	$:48^3$	$1:13^1$	$1:45^1$	Whirlaway	**99**	4	5	$2^{\frac{1}{2}}$	$2^{\frac{1}{2}}$	1^{hd}	1^3	Smith M E		117	*.40	79-24	Prairie Bayou117^3 Rohwer114^3 Slews Gold114	Driving	5
24Jan93-8Aqu	fst	1^{70} ⊡	:48	$1:12^2$	$1:42^4$	Count Fleet	**93**	1	5	$4^{5\frac{1}{2}}$	$3^{1\frac{1}{2}}$	$1^{\frac{1}{2}}$	1^3	Smith M E		117	*.90	88-24	Prairie Bayou117^3 Slews Gold$117^{5\frac{1}{2}}$ Rohwer117	Driving	6
13Jan93-8Aqu	sly	1^{70} ⊡	$:49^3$	$1:14^2$	$1:43^3$	Pappa Riccio	**90**	2	4	4^5	4^4	$2^{1\frac{1}{2}}$	$2^{1\frac{1}{4}}$	Smith M E		117	*1.30	83-20	Brt'sBubbltor$117^{1\frac{1}{4}}$PrrByou117^1ClssEnvoy117	Mild rally	4
20Dec92-10Lrl	my	$1\frac{1}{8}$	$:48^4$	$1:13^4$	$1:52^4$	Inner Harbor	**84**	6	8	$8^{9\frac{3}{4}}$	$6^{5\frac{1}{2}}$	2^{hd}	2no	Velazquez J R		122	*1.50e	76-32	JorgofMxco113^{no}PrrByo$122^{3\frac{1}{2}}$Ozn113	Wide bmpd hung	9
18Nov92-7CD	fst	$1\frac{1}{16}$	$:47^4$	$1:13^2$	1:45	Alw 28700	**85**	9	9	10^{11}	$9^{6\frac{3}{4}}$	$1^{\frac{1}{2}}$	1^3	Bartram B E	B	121	*2.40	89-15	PrrByou121^3EnchntngFtr118^4ColonlMnr123	Ridden out	11
10Nov92-4CD	fst	$1\frac{1}{16}$	$:48^2$	$1:14^3$	$1:46^1$	Md Sp Wt	**79**	6	11	9^{12}	$6^{3\frac{1}{2}}$	$1^{1\frac{1}{2}}$	$1^{1\frac{1}{2}}$	Bartram B E	B	119	6.60	83-22	PririeByou$119^{1\frac{1}{2}}$UnionCity119^3Wxhchi119	Wide, driving	11
14Oct92-5Kee	fst	7f	$:22^2$	:46	$1:23^4$	Md Sp Wt	**61**	9	11	$6^{4\frac{1}{4}}$	8^5	$8^{9\frac{3}{4}}$	7^{10}	Miller D A Jr	B	119	8.10	80-14	TurnOffthLts119^4ContryEldr$119^{\frac{3}{4}}$ChrmdHlo119	No rally	12

LATEST WORKOUTS May 10 Bel 4f fst $:49^3$ B ●Apr 26 CD 5f sly 1:01 H ●Apr 21 CD 5f fst $1:00^1$ H Apr 6 CD 4f fst :51 B

the 1970s and 1980s. The "blowout" of the 1990s is a mid-week four- or five-furlong move, and the speed of the work rarely is important. Consider the works posted by Prairie Bayou, who certainly could have worked considerably faster, but was kept in tune with modest four-furlong moves a few days before the last two victories of his life.

To obtain yesterday's workouts, which are never included in the past performances due to publishing schedules, check the official track program and listings posted at information booths at most tracks. Some tracks announce such late workouts or other works missing from the official program or *DRF*. At some tracks, however, publicly announced workouts may be inaccurate and merely for public relations. In my view these horses should be scratched unless the missing works are caused by *DRF* error, and they should be ineligible to run until their local workouts are documented.

Super Tuned — B. c. 2(Mar), by Tunerup—Neat And Fast, by Wise Exchange
$16,000 Br.—Wheeler C L (Fla)
Own.—ContinentlRcersInc-McGovernD — Tr.—Pace Denise (35 2 2 3 .06) — **118**
Lifetime 11 1 2 2 $9,820 — 1992 11 1 2 2 $9,820 — Wet 2 0 0 1 $1,070

25Oct92-5Crc	fst	$1\frac{1}{16}$	:51	$1:16^2$	$1:49^2$	Clm 20000	**44**	3	6	$6^{6\frac{1}{2}}$	$7^{7\frac{1}{4}}$	$6^{8\frac{1}{4}}$	$6^{9\frac{1}{2}}$	Gonzalez M A		118	4.60	70-12	SSchol$114^{2\frac{1}{2}}$FlghtBfrDwn$114^{\frac{1}{2}}$WrldGm118	Showed little	7
14Oct92-2Crc	fst	$1\frac{1}{16}$	:49	$1:14^2$	$1:48^1$	Clm 16000	**56**	7	8	8^{11}	$7^{9\frac{1}{4}}$	$5^{8\frac{1}{2}}$	2^6	Suckie M C		118	13.80	80-18	Bck'snthbn114^6SprTnd118^{no}Trblnmdct109	Rallied 7-wd	8
2Oct92-6Crc	fst	1^{70}	:48	$1:15^4$	$1:48^3$	Md 18000	**48**	8	7	6^{10}	3^8	2^3	$1^{\frac{1}{2}}$	Suckie M C		113	3.70	70-24	SuprTund$113^{\frac{1}{2}}$NoblJstc$117^{6\frac{1}{2}}$RsrvGrd113	Fully extended	9
23Sep92-1Crc	sly	1	$:48^1$	$1:14^4$	$1:43^3$	Md 16000	**30**	3	8	8^{24}	6^{18}	4^{12}	3^9	De'Oliveira W G		116	*1.30	68-15	MyLittleBird111^7Uncnny109^2SuperTuned116	Late rally	9
19Sep92-6Crc	fst	1	$:48^4$	$1:13^4$	$1:40^2$	Md Sp Wt	**39**	9	9	$9^{8\frac{3}{4}}$	11^{16}	11^{20}	11^{23}	Bracho J A^5		111	30.00	70-04	SanImagination116^8TonyBlue$116^{1\frac{1}{2}}$SirTim116	No factor	12
6Sep92-1Crc	fst	7f	$:22^3$	$:46^1$	$1:26^1$	Md 25000	**43**	2	7	8^{11}	8^{13}	4^7	3^{10}	De'Oliveira W G		117	5.50	74-12	ElDom117^7MdnghtAssuit112^3SuprTnd117	Rally, 5 wide	8
28Aug92-1Crc	fst	7f	:23	:47	$1:29^2$	Md 16000	**32**	7	4	11^{13}	9^{13}	$6^{8\frac{1}{4}}$	2^1	De'Oliveira W G		116	5.80	67-20	DustyBlu116^1SuprTund116^2MyLittlBrd112	Rallied 8-wd	12
21Aug92-3Crc	fst	6f	$:22^2$	$:46^2$	1:13	Md 25000	**37**	1	12	11^{12}	10^{15}	9^{16}	5^{13}	De'Oliveira WG	b	116	30.40	73-15	Warthog$116^{3\frac{1}{2}}$Syndicte'sPl$116^{1\frac{1}{2}}$Huglug116	Rlld 10 wide	12
13Aug92-7Crc	fst	6f	$:21^4$	$:46^1$	$1:14^1$	Md 25000	**26**	8	10	12^{14}	12^{14}	11^{13}	$11^{11\frac{1}{4}}$	Squartino R A		116	6.50	69-17	ExuberantKing116^1Warthog116^{hd}BHead116	Never close	12
1Jly92-3Crc	fst	$5\frac{1}{2}$f	:23	$:47^1$	$1:07^4$	Md 25000	**33**	8	8	$10^{8\frac{3}{4}}$	10^8	6^8	$4^{5\frac{1}{2}}$	Nunez E O		116	11.10	— —	Troblnmdcty114^1HrtsforHny$116^{1\frac{1}{2}}$RlntlssStr116	Belated	11

LATEST WORKOUTS Oct 1 Crc 3f fst $:37^3$ B

4. Most stakes-class horses work fast, and with a well-trained horse every training drill has a purpose. The following past performance pro-

file shows the great Kelso preparing for the Washington, D.C., International, a 1½-mile classic run each fall on Laurel's grass course. In this particular case, Kelso, who was never 100 percent comfortable on the grass, lost by a narrow margin to Mongo, one of the top grass horses of the past thirty-five years. The defeat was surely no disgrace and certainly not the fault of trainer Carl Hanford, who made all the right moves.

Kelso X **126** Dk. b. or br. g (1957), by Your Host—Maid of Flight, by Count Fleet.
Breeder, Mrs. R. C. duPont. 1963 11 9 1 0 $544,762
Owner, Bohemia Stable. Trainer, C. H. Hanford. 1962 12 6 4 0 $289,685

Oct19-637Aqu	2	3:22	ft	1-6	▲124	41¾	12	16	14	Val'z'lal1	WfaS	87	Kelso 124	Guadalcanal 124	Garwol	7
Sep28-637Aqu	1 1-4	2:00⅘	sft	1-4	▲126	34	2½	1½	13½	Val'z'lal2	WfaS	96	Kelso126	NeverBend120	CrimsonSatan	5
Sep 2-637Aqu	1 1-8	1:49⅘	sft	2-3	▲134	32	31	12	15½	Val'z'lal7	AlwS	92	Kelso134	CrimsonSatan129	Garwol	8
Aug 3-636Sar	1 1-8	1:50⅖	sft	1-3	▲130	43	42½	11	12¼	Val'elal2	SpwS	93	Kelso130	Saidam111	SunriseCounty	7
Jly 4-637Aqu	1 1-4	2:01⅘	sft	2-5	▲133	32	31½	11½	11¼	Val'z'lal7	HcpS	91	Kelso 133	Saidam 111	Garwol	7
Jun19-637Aqu	1 1-8	1:48⅘	sft	1-3	▲132	33½	31	12	11½	Val'uelal3	AlwS	97	Kelso 132	Lanvin 114	Polylad	5
Mar23-638Bow	1 1/16	1:43	ft	4-5	▲131	55	33	21½	1¾	Val"z'lal5	HcpS	98	Kelso131	CrimsonSat'n124	G'sh'gWind	6
Mar16-638G.P	1 1-4	2:03⅕	sft	1-5	▲130	2h	12	12	13¼	Val'uelal2	HcpS	83	Kelso 130	Sensitivo 112	Jay Fox	6
Feb23-637Hia	1 1-4	2:01⅘	sft	2-5	▲131	31	42½	23	22¼	Val'z'lal5	HcpS	87	BeauPurple125	Kelso131	Heroshogala	9
Feb 9-637Hia	1 1-8	1:48⅘	sft	2¼	128	45	42	12	12¾	Val'z'lal1	HcpS	91	Kelso 128	Ridan 129	Sensitivo	6
Jan30-638Hia	7 f	1:22⅘	sft	2½	128	2h	32	43½	45½	Val'z'lal4	HcpS	89	Ridan 127	Jaipur 127	Merry Ruler	5
Dec 1-628G.S	1 1-2	2:30⅕	sft	2-5	▲129	1h	13	13	15	Val'z'lal2	AlwS	105	Kelso 129	Bass Clef 117	Polylad	5

Nov 5 Lrl tc 1 1-8m fm 1:50⅘h   Nov 4 Lrl tc 3f fm :37⅖b   Nov 1 Lrl 7f m 1:27⅖b

5. A horse that races regularly, particularly one in good form, does not necessarily need any workouts to stay in shape. A prior victory without workouts is sufficient proof of this. See Laura Who at the bottom of the page.

6. To properly determine the fitness of a first-time starter or an absentee, the player should study the winning patterns of trainers and review the daily tabular listings for comments and works in company for additional clues. In maiden special weight (nonclaiming) maiden races at the top-class tracks, very few first-timers win without showing very good speed in one or more training trials, or drawing at least one rave review from the clockers. Even fewer win without showing at least one very good workout at five furlongs or longer among other trials stretching back over four, six or eight weeks of preparation. A good workout from the starting gate also is reassuring. On the other hand, three or

Laura Who B. m. 5, by Deputed Testamony—Tiger Rep, by The Reprobate
$15,000 Br.—D A J Stable (NJ)
Own.—Garden State Thoroughbreds Tr.—Salzman Les (17 3 1 2 .18) **119**
Lifetime 46 8 6 8 $124,534 | 1992 16 2 3 1 $25,000 | 1991 12 3 2 1 $48,410 | Turf 2 0 0 0 | Wet 2 0 0 0

7Nov92- 5Pha	fst	6½f	:223	:462	1:183	3↑ⒻClm 15000	77	5	1	2hd	11	14	14¼	Jocson G J	L 119	3.60	85-21	LurWho1194¼Shrpy'sGirl-Ch116noLmbertLn116	Driving	8
25Oct92- 7Pha	fst	6f	:223	:46	1:12	3↑ⒻClm 15000	53	2	1	12½	15	14	33¼	Sousonis S	L 122	*1.90	78-23	CounslorTroy1161¼PrncssI.R.A.1192LurWho122	Faltered	8
10Oct92- 7Pha	my	6f	:214	:453	1:11	3↑ⒻClm 15000	54	11	2	42	31½	77	85¾	Sousonis S	L 122	4.40	80-17	Nicki1162 Basque Song1161¼ Sharpy's Girl-Ch116	Tired	12
17Sep92- 7Med	fst	6f	:221	:451	1:102	3↑ⒻClm 22500	42	2	5	1hd	52¼	57½	713	Santagata N	L 114	5.70	78-12	MornflMsc114noMnrNrth119nkFlwrfrlxndr116	Gave way	8
4Sep92- 2Mth	fst	6f	:221	:453	1:103	3↑ⒻClm 16000	90	4	3	1½	11½	15½	16	Santagata N	L 116	*1.90	88-17	LurWho1166JestingVixen1143MenMissy116	Ridden out	8
2Aug92- 2Mth	fst	6f	:213	:451	1:103	3↑ⒻClm 20000	34	4	6	33	67	714	719¼	Santagata N	L 116	5.10	69-12	MnorNorth11911¾FncyEqpmnt1162¼GLssG114	Gave way	8
12Jly92- 6Mth	fst	6f	:22	:444	1:11	3↑ⒻⓈClm 22500	78	4	3	11	11	1½	21	Santagata N	L 114	5.00	85-15	MnorNorth1161LurWho114¾CremeCountss116	Good try	6
28Jun92- 3Mth	fst	6f	:22	:453	1:112	3↑ⒻClm 16000	65	7	1	11½	1hd	1½	22¾	Santagata N	L 116	11.80	81-19	CrftyRen1162¾LurWho1163KoluctheMony114	2nd best	8
9Jun92- 2Mth	fst	6f	:22	:452	1:114	3↑ⒻClm 22500	14	8	1	2hd	35½	819	824¼	Saumell L	L 115	8.20	58-13	HorribleGift115nkValidDelta1161¾BradfordBy115	Faded	8
17May92- 8GS	fst	6f	:221	:451	1:094	3↑ⒻⓈHandicap	58	7	1	2½	21	42¼	89¼	Sousonis S	L 113	27.80	83-15	AllThVs1181¼CutAndCunning1172¼MdmPrsdnt116	Tired	9

LATEST WORKOUTS Oct 3 Med 4f fst :484 B *NO WORKOUTS SINCE OCT 3.*

four drills from the starting gate among the last six workouts would suggest possible starting gate problems.

In California, where the tracks are very fast and the purse structure is the highest in the nation, first-time starters in better-grade maiden races must show solid speed in at least two or more workouts to be seriously considered.

An ill-fated champion making a sharp impression:

Landaluce — Dk. b. or br. f. 2, by Seattle Slew—Strip Poker, by Bold Bidder
Br.—SpendthriftFm&KernnFrncis (Ky) 1982 1 1 0 0 $9,350
Own.—French & Beal **116** Tr.—Lukas D Wayne
Lifetime 1 1 0 0 $9,350
3Jly82-4Hol 6f :22 :443 1.081ft *4-5 117 11½ 13 16 17 Pincay L Jr6 ⒻMdn 96 Lncluc,MidnightRptur,MissBigWig 7
Jun 27 Hol 4f ft :464 h Jun 21 Hol 5f ft :594 h Jun 11 Hol 4f ft :473 h May 31 Hol 4f ft :53 h

A late season two-year-old winner in his debut at six furlongs:

Los Gatos — Ch. c. 2(Feb), by Cutlass Reality—Tomato Sauce, by Sauce Boat
Lifetime 0 0 0 0 1992 0 M 0 0
SIBILLE R (278 27 31 38 .10) Br.—Harris Farms Inc (Cal)
Own.—Harris Farms Inc Tr.—Gaines Carla (28 5 2 6 .18) **119**
LATEST WORKOUTS ●Dec 16 BM 4f fst :47 Hg Dec 5 BM 6f gd 1:142 Hg Nov 28 BM 6f fst 1:124 H Nov 20 BM 5f fst 1:01 H

An early season two-year-old winner in his five-furlong debut:

Flagship Commander — B. g. 2 (Feb)
Own: Kieckhefer Robert
Sire: Northern Flagship (Northern Dancer)
Dam: Voler (Vertex)
Br: Bruce Hundley & Doug Arnold (Ky)
NAKATANI C S (188 30 38 24 .16) Tr: Baffert Bob (20 6 0 2 .30) **117**
Lifetime Record: 0 M 0 0
1993 0 M 0 0 | Turf
1992 0 M 0 0 | Wet
Hol 0 0 0 0 | Dist
WORKOUTS: Jun 4 SA 5f fst 1:00 H 2/34 May 28 SA 5f fst 1:014 Hg 19/39 May 22 SA 5f fst 1:004 Hg 12/36 May 16 SA 3f fst :361 Hg 8/32 ●Apr 28 SA 3f fst :352 B 1/21 Apr 27 SA 3f fst :372 H 12/24

The workout line below contains some powerful clues that this horse was ready to fire a very good race in his first start in 17 months.

Note the five-furlong move in 1:00.60 on February 7, which simply means Navy Flag was close to racing shape more than a month before he was entered in a lowly $6,250 claiming race, on March 29, 1993. Note

Navy Flag — Dk. b. or br. h. 6, by Pirate's Bounty—Kell My Pet, by Petrone
SIBILLE R (62 1 6 9 .02) $6,250 Br.—Wygod M J (Cal)
Own.—Lanning C or Lila Tr.—Moger Ed Jr (34 2 8 3 .06) **119**
Lifetime 16 2 4 2 $78,025
1991 3 1 1 0 $6,300
1990 9 0 2 1 $25,425
Turf 2 0 0 0 $6,450

6Oct91- 9BM	fst	1	:452	1:092	1:351	3↑Clm 10000	90	7	5	55½	44¼	21½	2½	Judice J C	LB	117	*1.50	93-13 OffcrsChc117½NFl1174½MscSmmt117	Raced wide, game	7
15Sep91- 9BM	fst	1	:46	1:111	1:37	3↑Clm 8000	80	3	6	43	2½	11	12	Judice J C	LB	117	3.00	85-20 NavyFlag1172JimPrice117nkOurBrandX117	Rallied wide	10
6Sep91- 9BM	fst	6f	:221	:444	1:092	3↑Clm 30000	76	3	7	77¾	76¾	78¾	65½	Lovato A J5	LB	110	16.80	83-17 EgleLesh1171GoldFinl1173RdTrcton117	Stumbled start	7
25Oct90- 4SA	fst	6½f	:214	:443	1:161	3↑ⓈAlw 32000	71	1	5	64½	65¼	65	65½	Sorenson D	LB	118	7.10	83-15 Noble Boss1101 Snoozetime115nk PowerFull118	Trailed	6
25Aug90- 7Dmr	fm	1	Ⓣ:473	1:114	1:372	3↑Alw 36000	84	5	7	74¼	63¾	52	42	Baze R A	LB	117	2.10	85-13 PrBs114noMchl'sFlyr1191¾ExplsvWst114	Checked at 1/8	9
19Aug90- 1Dmr	fst	6½f	:213	:433	1:143	3↑Alw 33000	95	1	6	68¾	610	65	44½	Pincay L Jr	LB	117	11.90	90-07 Timbnk1174CndymnB117nkKingOfWill121	Broke slowly	7
29Jly90-11SR	fst	1⅛	:473	1:113	1:441	J F Lytl H	72	3	6	69	67½	412	49½	Martinez O A Jr	L	113	3.10	71-21 LittleRisin115noStying'sToughr1162½Mklh122	No punch	6
7Jly90-11Pln	fst	1⅛	:473	1:103	1:422	Pln H	90	5	4	34½	33	32	32½	Frazier R L	L	114	3.30	100-08 Makleh121noStying'sTougher1152½NvyFlg114	Even late	6
29Jun90-11Pln	fst	170	:50	1:131	1:413	Alw 23000	89	4	4	4¾	41	42½	2½	Frazier R L		114	2.20	88-18 AstrDimond122½NvyFlg114nkHvenDrive117	Rallied wide	5
17Jun90- 8GG	fm	1	Ⓣ:464	1:111	1:364	ⓇBenecia H	84	4	7	76½	63¾	73½	44½	Doocy T T		115	8.40	84-15 CapeLudtke118hdBarryChancy118nkMakleh121	Far wide	7

LATEST WORKOUTS Mar 5 GG 5f fst 1:002 H Feb 25 GG 4f gd :504 H Feb 13 GG 6f gd 1:163 H Feb 7 GG 5f fst 1:003 H

the two intermediary works followed by another crisp five-furlong move in 1:00.40 on March 5. This time trainer Ed Moger is putting Navy Flag in a suitable race, not just giving him a leisurely six-furlong workout, as he did on February 13. Moger's effort was rewarded by a nice score at 9–1 odds. The pattern embodied by this past-performance profile is worth careful study. There is little doubt it will occur many times over every year, at every track in the country. It can be summarized by the following:

Whenever a horse with "back class" and a history of layoffs returns from an extended absence at a substantially discounted claiming price, good trainers know they stand little risk of losing the horse via the claim box. But they also know they do not have time to waste any bullets. If the veteran is ready to fire, the good trainer will place him in the easiest race possible, and the workout line might provide one or two key clues to let you in on the score.

Seminole Canyon	Ch. c. 2(Apr), by Chief's Crown—My Maravilla, by Blushing Groom-Fr		Lifetime	1992 0 M 0 0
SMITH M E (117 24 15 17 .21)	$50,000	Br.—Alexander-Monade Thoroughbreds (Ky)	0 0 0 0	
Own.—Alexander Dorothy D		Tr.—Thompson J Willard (8 2 0 2 .25)	113	
LATEST WORKOUTS	●Nov 14 Aqu 6f fst 1:14² H	Nov 8 Aqu 5f fst 1:00⁴ Hg	Nov 2 Aqu 4f fst :48⁴ B	Oct 28 Med 4f fst :49 B

Icy Tactics	B. g. 3 (Feb)			Life
Own: Siemon Margaret T & William	Sire: It's Freezing (T. V. Commercial)		1992	0 M
	Dam: Syntactic (Forward Pass)		1991	0 M
	Br: Loch Lea Farm, Inc. (Ky)		Hol	0 0
FLORES D R (146 16 13 11 .11)	$32,000	Tr: Whitby Steve M (—)	116	
WORKOUTS:	Jun 3 SA 5f fst 1:00 H 2/28 May 24 SA 4f fst :48³ H 12/30 May 16 SA 5f fst 1:02⁴ Hg24/30 May 9 SA 5f fst 1:03¹ H 22/24 Apr 29 SA 5f fst 1:01¹ H 6/12			
	Apr 15 SA 4f fst :48¹ Hg 17 42 Mar 31 SA 4f fst :48³ Hg 32/56 Mar 20 SA 5f fst 1:02 H 39/59 Mar 7 SA 4f fst :48⁴ H 21/54 Mar 1 SA 4f fst :49⁴ H 33/51			

Listen In	B. f. 3(Apr), by Phone Trick—Queen's Revelry, by His Majesty		Lifetime	1991 0 M 0 0
CASTANEDA M (316 34 36 49 $$42,283)	$20,000	Br.—Whiting Mr-Mrs Peter J (Cal)	0 0 0 0	
Own.—The Anvil		Tr.—Sherman Art (96 12 16 20 $164,800)	117	
LATEST WORKOUTS	Apr 29 GG 6f fst 1:13³ Hg	Apr 22 GG 6f fst 1:15 H	Apr 15 GG 5f fst 1:03 Hg	Apr 6 GG 5f fst 1:01³ H

Rhea's Two Stepper	Dk. b or br f. 2 (Apr)			Lif
Own: James Greg	Sire: Go Step (Bold Reasoning)		1993	0 M
	Dam: Controlled Landing (First Landing)		1992	0 M
	Br: Ted Bates (Ky)		GG	0 0
GONZALEZ R M (365 55 28 45 .15)	$18,000	Tr: James Greg (37 3 1 3 .08)	L 115	
WORKOUTS:	Jun 4 BM 3f fst :37² H 11/18 May 29 BM 5f fst 1:01² H 14/31 May 21 BM 5f fst 1:01⁴ H 3/13 May 14 BM 4f fst :49 H 7/20 May 7 BM 4f fst :50 Hg2/8			
	●Apr 23 BM 3f fst :35⁴ H 1/11 Apr 16 BM 3f fst :38² Hg 15/20 Apr 10 BM 2f fst :23⁴ H 1/3			

Tisa Charmer	Dk. b. or br. f. 3(Mar), by In Tissar—Annie Greensprings, by Exalted Rullah		Lifetime	1992 0 M 0 0
TOHILL K S (281 25 24 38 .09)	$12,500	Br.—Stevens Mrs Merry C (Cal)	0 0 0 0	
Own.—G C Stable & Stevens Merry		Tr.—Stoker John (26 5 2 1 .19)	117	
LATEST WORKOUTS	●Jan 15 BM 6f sly 1:15¹ Hg(d)	Jan 8 BM 4f sly :49⁴ Hg(d)	Jan 3 BM 5f fst 1:02¹ Hg	Dec 28 BM 5f sly 1:03¹ H

The above five examples show the kind of training regimens that are representative of first-time starter winners at different maiden claiming levels. Keep in mind that Aqueduct is a slower track than Golden Gate Fields; two-year-olds are less mature than three-year-olds; and that workouts around temporary "dogs" (d) involve extra yardage than the posted distance. Note the subtle but real difference in workout times between these $50,000, $32,000, $20,000, $18,000 and $12,500 first-time-out winners. If any of these horses had been entered in top-class maiden company, faster workouts would have been required to accept them as contenders, unless they had been trained by known aces who used similarly slow or sparse workout patterns to score previous victories.

It may seem hard to believe but when Landaluce's daddy, the great Seattle Slew, made his debut at Belmont Park on September 20, 1976, he had no published workouts in the Western edition of the *Form*. A few mediocre works were listed in the Eastern *Form*, but they were no indication of his true ability. Only the heavy play he received on the tote board suggested he was ready for a solid performance. Trainer Billy Turner, who managed this incredible horse to a two-year-old Championship and a Triple Crown sweep, was nobody's fool.

Seattle Slew	122	Dk. b. or br. c (19794), by Bold Reasoning—My Charmer, by Poker.
		Breeder, B. S. Castleman (Ky.). 1976 0 M 0 0 (——)

Owner, Karen L. Taylor. Trainer, William H. Turner, Jr.

---

7. A workout on the turf course is an extremely valuable clue to trainer intention. A good drill on the turf is excellent evidence of the horse's ability to handle such footing. Sometimes the trainer will enter such a horse in a grass race immediately following a good turf work; sometimes he will wait until the workout is no longer listed in the past performances. As a rule, it makes good sense to keep a special record of all good turf works.

SARATOGA – (Turf) Course Firm

Three Furlongs		Puorro	:50 B	Patriot Strike	:59³ B	Runaway Royalty 1:15³ H
Danny'sLegIEgle	:36² B	StatelyMatrirch	:49² B	Regally Refined	1:05 H	**Seven Furlongs**
Slew of Dishes	:37 B	War Music	:49¹ H	Scott the Great	1:00² B	Over Loaded 1:26² H
Four Furlongs		**Five Furlongs**		Stagecraft	:59⁴ H	**1 Mile**
Basso	:48³ H	Easy Spender	1:00³ H	**Six Furlongs**		Jucjeveda 1:43² H
Chisholm Flight	:48³ H	Inexcelleis Deo	1:00 B	Native Hawaiian 1:17⁴ B		

PATRIOT STRIKE (5f) bested STAGECRAFT (5f) in company. SCOTT THE GREAT (5f) went the last quarter in :23.

Shug McGaughey's Lure, winner of the 1992 and 1993 Breeders' Cup Mile races, was a disappointment until late in his three-year-old season, but hinted at a special affinity for grass racing with three smart workouts prior to winning his turf debut on September 14, 1992. "The way he worked on grass, I had to believe he would turn himself around," McGaughey said. Nevertheless, there are times when the best laid plans simply do not pan out as expected.

Consider Mi Lucia, below, who prepped beautifully for her turf debut in the Lakes and Flowers Handicap at Golden Gate Fields in 1991. En route to an apparent victory, Mi Lucia decided to take the name of the race literally, so she tossed her rider, Roberto Gonzalez, jumped the infield fence and went straight to the flower bed by the infield lake.

Mi Lucia												
GONZALEZ R M		B. f. 3(May), by Icecapade—Not a Flaw, by T V Commerical							Lifetime	1991 2 2 0 0		$29,550
Own.—Yu Lucy W		Br.—Grousemont Farm (Ky)						**117**	5 4 0 1	1990 3 2 0 1		$45,950
		Tr.—Bonde Jeff								$75,500		
10May91- 8GG fst 6f	:22 :444 1:10	⑦Rs Yr Skrt H	2 1 1hd 11 2hd 1nk	Gonzalez R M	LB 120	*.60	88-17 MiLucia120nk BerryRod1151½FnTheBreeze116½				Came back on	5
26Apr91- 8GG fst 6f	:213 :443 1:092	⑦Alw 23000	5 1 1½ 11 11 11½	Gonzalez R M	LB 117	*1.10	91-17 Mi Lucia1171½ No Kayela1173FanTheBreeze1203				Strong drive	5
19Sep90-12Fpx fst 6½f	:214 :452 1:17	⑦⑧BarrettsDeb	7 2 2hd 11 34½	Baze R A	LB 117	2.90	87-07 BeyondPerfection1203½LadiesDontLie1151½MiLuci117nk				Tired	9
5Jly90-11Pln fst 5½f	:22 :443 1:041	⑦J Gnlz Mm	1 1 11 13 12 12½	Gonzalez R M	L 116	*.30	95-11 MiLuc1162½Stutously1141WomnOfMystry1161				Handy victress	8
22Jun90- 3GG fst 5f	:211 :443 :57	⑦Md Sp Wt	4 2 11 12 14 18	Gonzalez R M	117	*2.50	100-10 Mi Lucia1178 Eluding1171 MiamiVacation117½				Much the best	8
Speed Index:	Last Race: (—)		3-Race Avg.: (—)		12-Race Avg.: (—)				**Overall Avg.: +4.6**			
LATEST WORKOUTS	●Jun 5 GG ⑦ 4f fm :492 B (d) ✔		May 30 GG ⑦ 7f fm 1:321 H (d) ✔		May 22 GG ⑦ 5f fm 1:04 H ✔			May 7 GG 3f fst :383 H				

8. Improving workouts can contribute to or confirm improving physical condition. Consider carefully the workout line under lightly raced Ruthie's Relic, a New York-bred training at Delaware Park. While hardly the second coming of Ruffian, Ruthie clearly benefited from her lone start and is revving up for a sharper effort.

Ruthie's Relic											
BRUIN J E (55 1 1 2 .02)		Ch. f. 2(Mar), by Titanic—Ruthie's Move, by Ruthie's Native						Lifetime	1992 1 M 0 0		$1,440
Own.—Casey Francis J		Br.—Casey Francis S (NY)					**117**	1 0 0 0			
		Tr.—Walsh Michael P (1 0 0 0 .00)						$1,440			
24Oct92- 4Aqu fst 6f	:224 :464 1:13	⑧⑤Md Sp Wt	43 5 8 94½ 75¼ 43½ 43½	Bravo J	117 12.60	72-18 EmotionlWv1121MImyJsli117⅔DrkStrLn117				Rallied wide	13
LATEST WORKOUTS	●Nov 16 Del 5f fst 1:004 B ✔		Nov 9 Del 5f fst 1:04 B		Nov 2 Del 5f fst 1:013 B ✔			Oct 7 Del 5f fst 1:051 B			

9. A series of closely spaced workouts or workouts mixed with racing ordinarily points out a horse in sound physical health. Very often the average horseplayer eliminates an active horse with mediocre finishes in his past-performance profile without realizing how fit the horse really is. On the other hand, a horse in apparent good form cannot be expected to hold that form if the trainer insists on working the horse hard and fast every few days between starts. Studying the strengths and weak-

nesses of trainers is the only reliable way to make accurate judgments about this type of training regimen.

I have to admit to getting a special kick every time I look at the past performances for Sarimiento, below.

I was at Harvey's in Lake Tahoe with a $60 win bet on this horse when two young men from San Francisco sitting near me laughed after I told them Sarimiento was ready to run a very sharp race. They laughed louder when Sarimiento struggled home eighth, beaten 11¼ lengths and thought I was a complete wacko when I said: "If you look at this horse's racing and workout activity—together you will see a fit, need-the-lead-type horse who is going to get a field of cheapies he can outrun pretty soon. Today he had a slow start and was forced wide into the first turn and still was only 3½ lengths away from the leader turning into the stretch. Laugh all you want, but this is the kind of horse who leaves people shaking their heads when he wins and pays $100."

I hope my young friends from San Francisco got a piece of this when the bills came due. Do I really have to say what Sarimiento paid when he wired a similar field in his next outing May 16, 1992? Would you believe $103!

10. Consult the clocker's comments, where available, for special mention of noteworthy training drills, fractional times, workouts in company, and other important clues. Pay particular attention to the tone of the clocker's remarks. If the comment is a positive one, you might well expect improvement from the horse in the next race or two. A good "horses to watch" list can be compiled this way, depending of course on the reliability of the clocker in question.

SAMPLE CLOCKER COMMENTS, BELMONT PARK, SEPTEMBER 1976

SEATTLE SLEW is sharp. WARM FRONT had all his speed. DANCE SPELL acts good. HONORABLE MISS was full of run. ASHMORE AND MAITLAND II were in company. BOLD FORBES is doing well. FIGHTING BILL had Jockey Day up.

Most of the horses who drew the comments above were well-known stakes horses. There were, however, two strangers who worked in company on even terms, and the player might not have paid attention to the modest comment they received. But the moment Ashmore was exposed as a contender for the $350,000 Jockey Club Gold Cup, the value of Maitland II's stock increased.

Workouts in company are particularly useful to the trainer and the horseplayer. Very often a trainer will not know which of two lightly raced horses is the faster. A workout in company may provide a definitive answer. As you might imagine, one of the most reliable workout clues is a victory by the slower of two horses that worked in company. From that moment onward, the faster worker becomes a four-star entry in my "horses to watch" list. A young maiden working on even terms with a known stakes horse is another key clue provided by workouts in company.

FROZEN DEW and ROB GELB (3f) worked well in company. SPANISH HOLLOW (3f) continues to look sharp. DO YOU KNOW ME (5f) big effort, out (6f) 1:14 3/5. PREMIER DIPLOMAT (5f) starting to look very sharp. BLUSH‑ING JULIAN (6f) very impressive effort. Jockey Joe Peterson up.

Most of the above comments are quite helpful, but I would want to know how well each of these horses performed in their next races to help assess the reliability of this clocker's positive impressions. The same standards should be applied to professional clocking services, such as those provided by *Handicapper's Report* a weekly newsletter and com‑puter-linked database for southern California produced by Jeff Seigel, a sample of which is reproduced on the following page.

CLOCKER'S REPORT

RUN BOLDLY (5f, 1:03.2h)

Worked with NARADANCE (same time) and was going the easier of the two for Heap, finishing about 3/4 length in front at the finish while pretty much in hand. Probably worth a look in more serious drills, workmate had to be asked and didn't look like much.

SECRET SIGHT (5f, :59.3h)

Mild coaxing late after going off slowly, looking okay for Gonzalez, splits of :24 flat, :47.4 and 1:00.2, slower than given but a decent move nonetheless. Lost a toughie last time out, probably will be a short price to graduate next time out.

SIEBE (6f, 1:13.2h)

Went off slowly, was asked late and did okay for Olivares with splits of :24 flat and 1:13.2. Been in tough lately and probably should try expensive claimers now.

STAN'S NATTI (5f, :59.4h)

Splits of :35.1 and :59.4 in solid fashion for Jory while besting LIL ORPHAN MOONIE (same time) and GALLANT DEL SOL (5f, 1:01h). Looks good, should have a productive Del Mar meeting.

STOP THE CROQUET (5f, 1:01.4h)

Breezing early, then finished out okay for Jones, splits of :36.1 and 1:01.4. In good hands and is worth following in more serious drills. Pointing for Del Mar.

STREET RODDER (5f, 1:01.3h)

Splits of :36.3 and 1:01.3 in moderate fashion under smooth pressure late. May be fair type, getting fit.

SUN AND SHADE (6f, 1:14.4h)

Splits of 1:02.2 and 1:14.4 for Drysdale while in company with CHANGING TIMES (same time), both finishing well in hand. Both look good and should surface soon.

THREE PEAT (4f, :48.1b)

Certainly wasn't breezing as official clockers called it, as Sadler-trained sprinter was pushed pretty hard late after going off slowly, splits of :12.2, :36.1 and :48 flat. A cut or two below the real good sprinters around here now.

21

It's in the Blood

I am not an expert on the history of thoroughbred pedigrees, or breeding niches, although practical necessity has helped me realize that breeding is one of the great pathways toward long shot winners. While an older horse's racing record takes precedence over his bloodlines, I strongly recommend paying attention to bloodlines to predict the way a young horse will respond to new situations. Breeding, it seems, is invaluable in predicting precocity, distance potential, suitability to the turf and off tracks.

Good selections can be made with knowledge of the top two-year-old sires, the top mud sires and, of course, the top turf sires, leaving additional room to cope with a theory of breeding known as "Dosage," as it applies to distance limitations rather than its advertised ability to pick Kentucky Derby winners.

While the importance of turf breeding has been muted slightly in recent years because so many horses now are bred to handle it, the following list of potent turf-course sires and grandsires still remains one of the best tools in evaluating first- or second-time turf runners. Double asterisks (**) denote extraordinary potency and single asterisks (*) indicate young sires from turf families who are expected to pass on the trait during the next several years.

POTENT TURF-COURSE SIRES

THE NEARCO FAMILY
Assert
Be My Guest
Blushing Groom
Caereleon
Caro
Caucasus
**Caveat
Compliance
Cox's Ridge
**Cozzene
Cure The Blues
Dancing Champ
Danzig
Diplomat Way
Explodent
Fred Astaire
Green Dancer
Halo
*Hawkster
Icecapade
**Irish River
**Kris S.
**Lyphard
Lyphard's Wish
Manila
Mari's Book
**Mill Reef
Mr. Leader
Naskra
**Northern Dancer
Northern Jove
Nureyev
One For All

*Opening Verse
*Prized
*Riverman
**Roberto
**Royal Charger
**Sadler Wells
Seattle Slew
**Secretariat
Secreto
**Silver Hawk
Sir Ivor
**Sovereign Dancer
Stop The Music
Storm Bird
Strawberry Road
*Summer Squall
**The Minstrel
Tsunami Slew
**Vice Regent
Ziggy's Boy
*Zilzal

THE RIBOT FAMILY
**Aferd
**Alleged
Arts and Letters
Grustark
**His Majesty
Pleasant Colony
Ribocco
Sir Ribot
**Tom Rolfe

THE HYPERION FAMILY
Forli

Interco
Vaguely Noble

THE PRINCEQUILLO FAMILY
Advocator
Just The Time
**Speak John
**Stagedoor Johnny
Wolf Power

OTHER DOMINANT TURF
SIRES FROM ASSORTED
FAMILIES
Acaroid
**Affirmed
*Alysheba
Big Spruce
Court Trial
**Dr. Fager
Exclusive Native
Grey Dawn II
*Hansel
Herberger
Le Fabuleux
Little Current
Majestic Light
Mill Native
Mr. Prospector
Raise A Native
Sea Bird
The Axe II
**Vigors
Wavering Monarch
Woodman

HANDCAPPING HINT: It is wise to respect proven turf form over inexperienced turfers, unless the proven turf form is below par for the class, or the "proven" horse is a front-running type on a course not strongly biased toward early speed. Speed-biased turf courses tend to occur when the inner rail has been moved out 10–30 feet to refurbish well-worn grass, or when banking on turns is virtually nonexistent, or the course has been cut very low to the ground.

Otherwise, most turf races are won from off the pace, even though the overall pace of the race usually is relatively slow. Here, Beyer figures in the *DRF* (or your own) help to isolate probable contenders, but class comparisons, finishing speed, trainer patterns, trips, breeding and jockey skills tend to be the most powerful factors. Also, with the growing popularity of American turf racing, European and South American imports have a distinct advantage in many situations, including the premier turf events on the Breeders' Cup card and numerous stakes and allowance races on both coasts. (American-based turf horses tend to be extremely tough, however, on the tight-turning, moderately banked course at Gulfstream Park.)

The trick is to identify imports who faced superior opposition in Group (Graded) or Listed stakes at first-class racetracks in Europe, such as Epsom, Newmarket, Ascot, Doncaster, Goodwood in England; Longchamps, Chantilly, Deauville, Saint Cloud, Every in France; and the Curragh in Ireland, while downgrading those who ship in from Italy and Germany in all but a few cases. Many good European runners win "right off the plane," but have a difficult time adjusting to American conditions over a longer time frame. Exceptions, however, do show up every year trained by Robert Frankel, Billy Mott, Gary Jones and other known aces.

These include Richard Mandella (trainer of Kotashaan, 1993 Breeders' Cup champion), Neil Drysdale (takes his time with his imports) and of course Charles Whittingham and Ron McAnally. McAnally in particular has a very strong connection to South American racing, having developed numerous top performers, including Paseana and Bayakoa. But when any of these expert horsemen sets a horse up for an American campaign, the player should anticipate sharp performances in their first or second local starts, with possibly more down the road.

Some European trainers, most notably Francois Boutin, Alain De-Royer-Dupre, Clive Brittain, Luca Camani, Robert Collet, Dermet Weld, Paul Cole, Andre Fabre, Christiane Head and Michael Stoute have fine records with transatlantic shippers in U.S. stakes. In general, European horses fresh off the plane can be expected to run at or above their most recent form, provided they do not flash excessively nervous traits in the paddock or have not had a seriously troubled trip from Europe through American quarantine as documented by the sporting press. For instance, the British miler Warning was a nervous wreck in the paddock for the 1989 Mile and favored Indian Skimmer was unmanageable for the 1988 Turf.

Great ballyhoo also is to be avoided, as the odds seldom are worth the risk even for European champions such as the highly touted Dancing Brave, who seemed listless in his Breeders' Cup training drills at Santa Anita in 1986. The following chart belongs to Arazi, the wonder horse turned to bust between his scintillating win in the 1991 Breeders' Cup Juvenile and 1992 Kentucky Derby. Everyone who had seen his first race in America had reason to be impressed.

Arazi		Ch. c. 3(Mar), by Blushing Groom—Danseur Fabuleux, by Northern Dancer Br.—Wilson Ralph C Jr (Ky)					Lifetime 14 9 1 1 $1,208,475	1992 6 2 0 1 $112,673 1991 8 7 1 0 $1,095,802 Turf 12 8 1 1 $688,475
Own.—PulsonAE - MktomShkMohmnd		Tr.- Boutin Francois (—)						
31Oct92- 7GP fm 1 ① :45⁴ 1.09 1:32¹ 3↑Br Cp Mile	95 3 4 4³ 5²¹¹⁰¹⁰¹¹⁹ Valenzuela P A	122	*1.50	100	– – Lure123³PrdiseCreek122ⁿᵏBriefTruc122 Svd grnd, tired 14			
31Oct92-Grade I								
4Oct92- 2Longchamp(Fra) sf*1	1.44 ① Prix duRondPont(Gr2)	1⁴	Cauthen S	123	*1.20	– – Arazi123⁴ CllingCollect123ʰᵈ Alhijz130 Bid, drew away 11		
20Sep92- 4Longchamp(Fra) gd*1¼	2.07² ① Prix Prince d'Orange(Gr3)	3⁶	Cauthen S	121	*.40	– – Arcangues 126⁶ Prince Polino121ʰᵏ Arazi121 Bid, wknd 5		
16Jun92- 3Ascot(Eng) gd 1	1.39¹ ① St.James'sPalaceStks(Gr1)	5²¹	Cauthen S	126	*.90	– – Brief Truce 126ⁿᵒ Zaahi 126¹ Ezzoud 126 No late rally 8		
2May92- 8CD fst 1¼ :46⁴ 1.36³ 2.03 Ky Derby	95 17 17 17¹³ 31¹ 4³ 8⁸¹ Valenzuela P A B 126		*.90	87-06 LilE.Tee126¹CsulLies126³¹DncFloor126 Bid 8 wide,tired 18				
2May92-Grade I								
7Apr92- 3StCloud(Fra) sf*1	1.48 ① Prix Omnium II(L)	1⁵	Cauthen S	128	*.20e	– – Arzi128⁵ Supermec128²¹ RiverMjesty128 Unchallenged 8		
2Nov91- 6CD fst 1¹⁄₁₆ :46³ 1:12 1:44³ Br Cp Juv	101 14 13 8⁵¹ 2ʰᵈ 1⁵ Valenzuela P A B 122		*2.10	92-09 Arazi122⁵ Bertrando122³¹ Snappy Landing122 14				
2Nov91-Grade I. Drifted out into stretch, taken in hand last 70 yards								
5Oct91- 4Longchamp(Fra) yl*1	1.41² ① Grand Criterium(Gr1)	1³	Mosse G	124	*.20	– – Arzi124³ RinbowCorner123ʰᵏ SettlRhym123 Bid, easily 6		
8Sep91- 3Longchamp(Fra) gd*7f	1.20⁴ ① Prix Salamandre(Gr1)	1⁵	Mosse G	123	*.20	– – Arazi 123⁵ Made of Gold123ⁿᵏ SilverKite123 Cantering 8		
18Aug91- 4Deauville(Fra) gd*6f	1.13¹ ① Prix Morny(Gr1)	1³	Mosse G	123	*.50	– – Arazi 123³ Kenbu 120³ Lion Cavern 123 Gving away 4		
21Jly91- 2MLaffitte(Fra) gd*5½f	1.05² ① Prix Robert Papin(Gr2)	11¹	Mosse G	123	*.80	– – Arazi123¹¹ Showbrook 123³ Steinbeck123 B ', handily 6		
3Jly91- 4Longchamp(Fra) gd*5f	58³ ① Prix du Bois(Gr3)	1³	Mosse G	124	1.40	– – Arazi 123³ Steinbeck 123¹ Woldwide 121 Well up, drvg 4		
12Jun91- 4Evry(Fra) gd*6f	1.14¹ ① Prix la FLeche	1³	Head F	121	1.90	– – Arazi 121³ Tabac 126² Valley Road 121 Well pl, clear 7		
30May91- 2Chantilly(Fra) gd*5f	59 ① Prix d'Orgemont(Mdn)	22¹	Head F	123	*1.50	–⁃ – Steinbeck 123²¹ Arazi 123ⁿᵏ Gramatique 118 Led 4f 6		
LATEST WORKOUTS	Apr 30 CD 5f fst 1:03¹ B							

I wrote the Breeders' Cup result charts for the *Racing Times* and can still see Arazi making a Secretariat-like move through traffic, under a stranglehold before Patrick Valenzuela eased him to the outside of Bertrando at the top of the stretch. Seeing Arazi put on that spectacular show where Secretariat had made one of his most memorable runs was a touch of déjà vu. Unfortunately, Arazi did not grow very much between his two- and three-year-old seasons and had little time to prepare for the Derby following minor knee surgery a few days after the Breeders' Cup. All he could muster in the 1992 Derby was the first half of his run on the extreme outside before fizzling to an ignominious eighth. From there to the Breeders' Cup at Gulfstream six months later, it was catch-up ball for another ill-timed trip to America and early retirement. The moral of the story once again was: horses do not walk on water, especially talented ones who seek to cross the Atlantic.

OFF-TRACK BREEDING

Previous form in the mud is the single most important handicapping factor on wet tracks, yet it is possible to anticipate good off-track performances by examining the pedigree, especially the sire. A few sires and sire families tend to transmit the trait to nearly all their offspring. The most prominent of these are Mr. Prospector and his sons, including Conquistador Cielo, whose past performances are in Chapter 8, and the entire Bold Ruler line, especially What A Pleasure and the Bold Commander–Dust Commander wing of that line.

Cinteelo, a son of Jacinto, who in turn was a son of Bold Ruler, is a case in point. In the original *Betting Thoroughbreds* I wrote that he was the best mud runner I had ever seen. Almost 20 years later the statement still applies. Except for Spanish Riddle's track record victory in a Saratoga stakes on a wet track in the 1970s and Secretariat's amazing facility to run at unprecedented speeds on any racing surface, no horse has approached Cinteelo's off-track prowess.

Cinteelo		119	B. c (1973), by Jacinto—Teela, by Cockrullah.										
Owner, J. M. Schiff. Trainer, T. J. Kelly.			Breeder, J. M. Schiff (Ky.).					1976	6 2 0 2	$24,60			
								1975	7 2 0 1	$13,26			
19 May76 8Bel	1¹ₜ :46²1:113 1:43	sy	2-3 ▲106⁵	12	11½	15	17½	VelezRI3	Alw 86	Cinteelo106	BabyFaceBeau
1 May76 6Aqu	1 :45 1:09 1:34³	sy	6-5e▲104⁵	2ʰ	11	15	18½	VelezRI4	Alw 93	Cinteelo 104	El Portugues
17 Apr76 6Aqu	1 :45²1:094 1:35¹	ft	2 ▲104⁵	2ʰ	2ʰ	1½	32½	VelezRI1	Alw 87	RoughPunch112	BrownCat
27 Mar76 6Aqu	1 :46 1:094 1:35²	ft	14 112⁵	1ʰ	1ʰ	2ʰ	34	VelezRI4	Alw 85	MountSterling119	NwCollctn
3 Mar76 6Aqu	7 f :23¹ :463 1:234	ft	3 115	32½	33	711	814	VelasquzJ5	Alw 68	GabeBenzur117	PlayTheRed
24 Jan76 5Hia	ⓣ 1¹ₜ	1:43²fm	4½ 119	42	34	35½	57½	CruguetJ1	Alw 74	Controllerlke122	GrstarkLad
21 Nov75 7Aqu	1 :444 1:084 1:34	sy	12 117	13	15	14	16	CruguetJ4	Alw 92	Cinteelo 117	Play the Red
15 Nov75 5Aqu	7 f :23 :46 1:23²	ft	37 115	41½	51½	3ⁿᵏ	42½	CruguetJ2	Alw 81	JumpOvr theMn122	Wn'tYld
28 Aug75 4Bel	7 f :23¹ :47 1:25¹	ft	3-2 ▲120	53½	2½	11½	11	CrugtJ6	M35000 76	Cinteelo 120	Ahoy John

June 3 Bel 3f ft :35b   May 30 Bel trt 5f ft 1:01¾h   May 26 Bel trt 4f ft :52b

The following is a potent list of off-track sires as gleaned from personal research and from the records of Bloodstock Information Services of Lexington, Kentucky, which provides computer access to voluminous handicapping data, including trainer profiles and breeding tendencies. To make this list, a sire had to produce several superior off-track performers or offspring that have won 14 percent or more of all wet track racing attempts, which is almost double the national average.

POTENT OFF-TRACK SIRES

Ack Ack	Far Out East	Oh Say
Affirmed	Fatih	Pirates Bounty
Air Forbes Won	Fifty Six Ina Row	Play Fellow
Al Nasr	Fighting Fit	Pleasant Colony
Alydar	Fit to Fight	Princely Native
At The Threshold	Flying Paster	Private Account
Badger Land	Foolish Pleasure	Prospect North
Bagdad	Gallant Best	Proud Birdie
Big Spruce	Great Above	Quack
Bob's Dusty	Gulch	Quadrangle
Bold Commander	Gummo	Raised Socially
Bold Ruler	Hold Your Peace	Raja Baba
Bolger	Illustrious	Relaunch
Broad Brush	In Reality	Riva Ridge
Buckaroo	Island Whirl	Rock Talk
Buckfinder	It's Freezing	Romeo
Buckpasser	Jade Hunter	Run of Luck
Bucksplasher	Jaklin Klugman	Ruritania
Chief's Crown	Jig Time	Saros
Chisos	Kennedy Road	Sauce Boat
Cinteelo	Key To The Mint	Seattle Slew
Clever Trick	Knight In Savannah	Secretariat
Coastal	Knight's Choice	Siyah Kalem
Conquistador Cielo	Little Current	Skywalker
Crafty Prospector	Majestic Prince	Slew o' Gold
Cure The Blues	Marfa	Sovereign Dancer
Cutlass Reality	Moscow Ballet	Staff Writer
Damascus	Mastery Derby	Stalwart
Danzig	Miswaki	Star De Naskra
Danzig Connection	Mr. Leader	Stop The Music
Darby Creek Road	Mr. Prospector	Storm Bird
Deputy Minister	Mt. Livermore	Tough Knight
Desert Wine	Naskra	Traffic Cop
Dewan	Nasty And Bold	Tri Jet
Dimaggio	Never Tabled	Truce Maker
Dixieland Band	Night Mover	Unreal Zeal
Drouilly	Nodouble	Wavering Monarch
Duck Dance	Northern Baby	What A Pleasure
Dust Commander	Nostalgia	

NOTE: *The most interesting horses on the mud sire list are Tri Jet and Riva Ridge. Tri Jet hated wet tracks and won the Whitney Handicap at Saratoga like a scared jackrabbit, when lightning and rain began to fall five minutes before post time. Riva Ridge did win one race on a wet-fast track in his career but failed to handle mud in two important races because he didn't like the goo. In these cases, like father,* not *like son.*

SPEED SIRES

In early season 2-year-old races at three, four and five furlongs, the emphasis is on speed and precocious physical development. This gives players with access to statistics that show the precocity of "early win" sires, a built-in edge spotting potential contenders in fields that contain little information, including sparse workouts. Such early-win sire statistics are a regular feature of Bloodstock Research Information Services' handicapper's database. BRIS also publishes similar breeding stats once yearly in "Maiden Stats," at $99 retail. But it is far cheaper to compile a list of sires on your own circuit which have strong early-win and early-speed tendencies.

If the get of Semi-Pro, Master Ego, Eldorado Kid, Coup De Kas and other one-dimensional speed specialists are going to win any stakes or allowance races, they will usually do so in early-season abbreviated dashes. Many win at first asking. Few hold their form beyond six furlongs.

On page 228 is a list of potent speed sires, who also tend to be precocious early-win types. Some, including Mr. Prospector, can be found on the turf-racing and off-track sire's list because of their exceptional versatility. Others lack such potency in other categories but are nevertheless capable of siring horses who hold their form beyond early season sprints.

STAMINA SIRES

During the 1970s and 1980s, Leon Rasmussen, the former breeding columnist for the *Daily Racing Form,* wrote extensively about "Chef-de-Race Sires," an attempt to group pre-potent sires by their distance preferences and limitations. The idea, first proposed by renowned French breeding expert J. J. Vuilier, was refined in the 1930s by Italian breeding authority Dr. Franco Varola and again by America's Dr. Steven A. Roman in the late 1970s.

Before discussing the utility of the Chef-de-Race list, I should first point out that Conquistador Cielo's 14-length victory in the Belmont Stakes was a bit of a shock to the breeding community. Nevertheless, it did not take long for the same gentry to take advantage of their mistake.

POTENT SPEED SIRES

Air Forbes Won	Geiger Counter	Relaunch
Allen's Prospect	Gold Stage	Rollicking
Ali Oop	Groton	Saratoga Six
Apalachee	Gone West	Seattle Slew
An Eldorado	Gulch	Secreto
Ascot Knight	Hawkin's Special	Shimatoree
Barrera	It's Freezing	Silver Deputy
Be A Prospect	Jade Hunter	Siyah Kalem
Beau's Eagle	Jim J.	Shanekite
Big Burn	Known Fact	Smile
Bold Ego	Knights Choice	Staff Writer
Bold Play	Loom	Staunch Avenger
Bold Ruckus	Lost Code	Storm Cat
Brazen Brother	Mito	Strike Gold
Broad Brush	Mr. Kaskaskia	Stutz Blackhawk
Christopher R.	Moscow's Ballet	Sovereign Dancer
Clever Trick	Northern Prospect	Sunny Clime
Capote	North Prospect	Three Martinis
Charming Turn	Ogygian	Tilt Up
Cherokee Fellow	Our Michael	Timeless Moment
Copelan	Pappa Riccio	Tri Jet
Crafty Prospector	Pirate's Bounty	Triple Bend
Cutlass	Pac Mania	Triple Sec
Danzig	Premiership	Tyrant
Deputy Minister	Proud Appeal	Unpredictable
Dixieland Band	Meadowlake	Unreal Zeal
Distinctive Pro	Megaturn	Valid Appeal
Duck Dance	Mr. Prospector	Wayne's Crane
Expressman	Mt. Livermore	Well Decorated
Fappiano	Quip	What A Pleasure
Fire Dancer	Raised Socially	World Appeal
Fortunate Prospect	Rajab	Woodman
Forty Niner	Rambunctious	Ziggy's Boy
Full Pocket	Rare Brick	Zuppardo's Prince

In August 1982 Cielo was syndicated for a staggering $36.4 million to usher in a promiscuous era of wild syndications and exorbitant yearling prices which reached a dizzying $13.1 million for a single untried thoroughbred prospect at the Keeneland Summer Yearling Sales in 1985.

The breeding business still is the biggest crapshoot in racing, with many top-class horses emerging with modest price tags. But the Chef-de-Race list may have import to handicappers with a penchant for breeding research, especially those who dabble in the "Dosage Index" formula created by Roman, a former professional confidant to Rassmussen.

CHEFS-DE-RACE BY APTITUDINAL GROUP

BRILLIANT

Abernant
Apalachee
Baldski*
Black Toney*
Blushing Groom*
Bold Ruler*
British Empire
Bull Dog
Cicero
Court Martial
Double Jay
Fair Trial
Fairway
Gallant Man*
Grey Dawn II*
Grey Sovereign
Habitat
Halo*
Heliopolis
Hoist the Flag*
Hyperion*
Icecapade*
In Reality*
Intentionally*
Key to the Mint*
King's Bishop*
Mr. Prospector*
My Babu
Nasrullah
Nearco*
Never Bend*
Noholme II*
Northern Dancer*
Olympia
Orby
Panorama
Phalaris
Pharis II
Pompey
Raise a Native
Reviewer*
Roman*
Royal Charger
Seattle Slew*
Sharpen Up*
Sir Cosmo
Speak John*
Spy Song
Tudor Minstrel
Turn-to*
Ultimus
What a Pleasure

INTERMEDIATE

Ack Ack*
Baldski*
Ben Brush
Big Game
Black Toney*
Bold Bidder*
Bold Ruler*
Broomstick
Caro*
Colorado
Congreve
Damascus*
Danzig*
Djebel
Eight Thirty
Equipoise*
Full Sail
Gallant Man*
Grey Dawn II*
Havresac II
Hoist the Flag*
Intentionally*
Khaled
King Salmon
King's Bishop*
Mahmoud*
Nashua*
Native Dancer*
Never Bend*
Petition
Pharos
Polynesian
Princequillo*
Riverman*
Roman*
Sir Gaylord*
Sir Ivor*
Speak John*
Star Kingdom*
Star Shoot
Sweep
The Tetrarch
Tom Fool*
Traghetto
Turn-to*
T. V. Lark

CLASSIC

Ack Ack*
Alibhai
Alydar
Aureole
Bahram
Best Turn
Blandford
Blenheim II*
Blue Larkspur
Blushing Groom*
Bold Bidder*
Brantome
Buckpasser
Bull Lea
Caro*
Clarissimus
Count Fleet
Creme dela Creme*
Damascus*
Danzig*
Equipoise*
Exclusive Native
Forli
Gainsborough
Graustark*
Gundomar
Hail to Reason
Halo*
Herbager*

High Top
His Majesty
Hyperion*
Icecapade*
In Reality*
Key to the Mint*
Luthier
Lyphard
Mahmoud*
Midstream
Mill Reef*
Mossborough
Mr. Prospector*
Nashua*
Native Dancer*
Navarro
Nearco*

Never Say Die
Nijinsky II*
Noholme II*
Northern Dancer*
Nureyev
Persian Gulf
Pilate
Pretense
Prince Bio
Prince Chevalier
Prince John
Prince Rose
Reviewer*
Ribot*
Riverman*
Roberto
Rock Sand*

Seattle Slew*
Sharpen Up*
Sicambre
Sideral
Sir Gallahad III
Sir Gaylord*
Sir Ivor*
Star Kingdom*
Swynford
Ticino*
Tom Fool*
Tom Rolfe*
Tourbillon*
Tracery
Vaguely Noble*
Vieux Manoir
War Admiral

SOLID

Asterus
Bachelor's Double
Ballymoss
Blenheim II*
Bois Roussel
Chaucer
Creme dela Creme*
Discovery
Fair Play*

Graustark*
Herbager*
Man o' War
Mill Reef*
Nijinsky II*
Oleander
Pia Star
Princequillo*
Relko
Right Royal

Rock Sand*
Round Table
Sea-Bird
Stage Door Johnny*
Sunstar
Tantieme
Teddy
Ticino*
Vatout
Worden

PROFESSIONAL

Admiral Drake
Alcantara II
Alizier
Alycidon
Bayardo
Bruleur
Chateau Bouscaut
Crepello
Dark Ronald
Donatello II
Fair Play*

Foxbridge
Hurry On
La Farina
Le Fabuleux
Massine
Mieuxce
Ortello
Precipitation
Rabelais
Ribot*
Run the Gantlet
Sardanapale

Solario
Son-in-Law
Spearmint
Stage Door Johnny*
Sunny Boy
Tom Rolfe*
Tourbillon*
Vaguely Noble*
Vandale
Vatellor
Wild Risk

Brilliant: speed potency of the highest order, with most stakes winners up to one mile.

Intermediate and **Classic:** *potency up to and including the true Derby distance of 1½ miles, by European standards.*

Solid and **Professional:** sire lines for stayers and marathon runners.

NOTE: *An asterisk following a sire's name indicates he has been placed in two separate classes. Therefore, his influence in any generation is likely to be divided equally between those two classes.*

According to Roman, horses with Dosage Indexes of 4.00 or more likely to win two-year-old races in the spring and summer and less likely to have the stamina to win classic races in the spring of their three-year-old season. While Dosage may seem like hocus-pocus, it is backed up by substantial research.

Roman's explains his formula: *"There are five aptitudinal categories of breeding tendencies—brilliant, intermediate, classic, solid, professional—and each Chef-de-Race sire is assigned to one or possibly two of these five groups to best reflect the trait he predictably and consistently transmits to his offspring."*

For bookkeeping purposes Roman allows 16 points to be assigned to each of the first four generations in any horse's pedigree. Roman also incorporates the idea that each generation's influence diminishes proportionately the further back in the pedigree that we go.

Since there are twice as many sires in the pedigree each generation back from the starting point, a "Chef-de Race" appearing in the first generation will contribute 16 points, while each of the two Chefs in the second generation will earn eight points and third-generation Chefs will get four points each and fourth-generation chefs, two.

Points are distributed to the five aptitudinal categories to form the Dosage Profile.

On the following page is the extended pedigree of Diazo, a multiple-stakes winner trained by Bill Shoemaker, who has some of the most potent sires of the twentieth century in his pedigree.

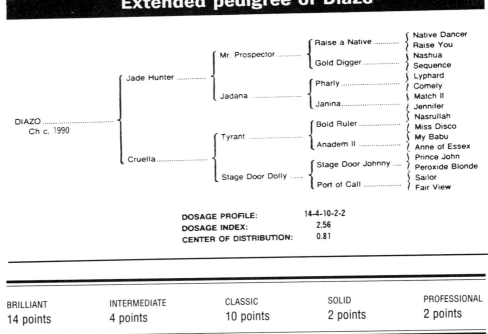

Extended pedigree of Diazo

				Native Dancer
		Raise a Native		Raise You
	Mr. Prospector			Nashua
		Gold Digger		Sequence
Jade Hunter				Lyphard
		Pharly		Comely
	Jadana			Match II
		Janina		Jennifer
DIAZO					Nasrullah
Ch c. 1990			Bold Ruler		Miss Disco
	Tyrant			My Babu
		Anadem II		Anne of Essex
Cruella				Prince John
		Stage Door Johnny		Peroxide Blonde
	Stage Door Dolly			Sailor
		Port of Call		Fair View

DOSAGE PROFILE: 14-4-10-2-2
DOSAGE INDEX: 2.56
CENTER OF DISTRIBUTION: 0.81

BRILLIANT	INTERMEDIATE	CLASSIC	SOLID	PROFESSIONAL
14 points	4 points	10 points	2 points	2 points

Note that Mr. Prospector is listed as both a Brilliant and Classic sire. Thus, the eight points in the second generation are split between the Brilliant and Classic columns. The Dosage Index (DI) is computed as a ratio between all the points in the speed wing of the pedigree divided by the points in the stamina wing, via the formula below:

$$\frac{\text{Brilliant pts.} + \text{Intermediate pts.} + \frac{1}{2}\text{Classic pts.}}{\frac{1}{2}\text{Classic pts.} + \text{solid pts.} + \text{professional pts.}} = \text{D.I.}$$

In Diazo's case, the D.I. would compute as follows:

$$\frac{14 + 4 + 5}{5 + 2 + 2} = \frac{23}{9} = 2.56 \text{ D.I.}$$

To refine the distance potential of the pedigree further, Roman suggests another computation, the center of distribution, which helps to determine the balance of dosage points on the stamina and speed wings of the pedigree. The weighted model for this exercise can be seen below, followed by the formula to compute Roman's C.D.

COMPUTING THE CENTER OF DISTRIBUTION:

$$\frac{(2 \times \text{Brill. pts}) + \text{Intermed. pts.} - \text{Solid pts} + (2 \times \text{prof. pts})}{\text{Total points in the Dosage profile}} = \text{C.D.}$$

Anything in excess of $+1.25$ C.D. is deemed to be skewered toward the speed wing, while true stayers usually register under $+1.0$, or 0, or even minus numbers.

Diazo's Center of Distribution:

$$\frac{\left[\begin{array}{c}2 \times (14) \\ (\text{Brill.})\end{array}\right] + \left[\begin{array}{c}(4) \\ (\text{Int.})\end{array}\right] - \left[\begin{array}{c}2 \\ (\text{Solid})\end{array}\right] + \left[\begin{array}{c}2 \times (2) \\ (\text{Prof.})\end{array}\right] = 34}{\underset{(\text{Brill.})}{14} + \underset{(\text{Int.})}{4} + \underset{(\text{Classic})}{10} + \underset{(\text{Solid})}{2} + \underset{(\text{Prof.})}{2} = 32} = 1.06 \text{ C.D.}$$

Few handicappers actually take advantage of these formulas, but they should. Just as turf breeding is a potent indicator for first- or second-timers on grass, so too may Dosage offer clues to the first-time miler or the two-year-old first-time starter going five furlongs. Yet it is Roman's use of Dosage with respect to predicting the outcome of the Kentucky Derby and Belmont Stakes that has caused the most controversy.

According to Roman: "No winner of the Derby since 1940 other than Strike the Gold, and only three winners of the Belmont over the same time frame, have had a D.I. over 4.00 and only two have exceeded C.D.'s of 1.25. This is in direct contrast with stakes winners in general, of which 35 percent have a D.I. over 4.00 and the average D.I. for all horses is between 4.00 and 4.50." (As an example, 1986 Kentucky Derby winner Ferdinand qualified as a longshot with excellent Dosage numbers, while the race favorite, Snow Chief, did not.)

Many Derby handicappers swear by the D.I. and C.D. to eliminate contenders. Yet the validity of the proposition remains suspect in the light of other results. For instance, Snow Chief promptly debunked his lack of classic stamina by winning the Preakness Stakes at 1³⁄₁₆ miles and the Jersey Derby at 1¼ miles within one month of his Derby debacle. (The ill-fated Prairie Bayou also won the Preakness in 1993, two weeks after he was second in the Derby with high Dosage numbers.)

Critics had a field day following Strike the Gold's victory in the 1991 Derby with a D.I. of 9.00 that would have suited a five-furlong winner at Blue Ribbon Downs. A few months later controversy erupted when Roman added Strike the Gold's sire Alydar to the Classic Chef-de-Race list to comfortably lower Strike the Gold's D.I. below the 4.00 maximum.

YEAR	WINNER	PAYOFF	DI	CD	PROFILE	FAVORITE	FINISH	DI	CD	PROFILE
1992	Lil E. Tee	$35.60	3.00	0.88	6-2-8-0-0	ARAZI	8th	1.74	0.52	22-1-15-0-10
1991	Strike the Gold*	11.60	9.00	1.30	10-6-4-0-0	HANSEL	10th	2.29	0.75	10-3-13-2-0
1990	UNBRIDLED	23.60	1.12	0.03	11-3-10-0-12	MISTER FRISKY	8th	1.29	0.25	2-5-4-5-0
1989	Sunday Silence	8.20	2.56	0.69	4-3-9-0-0	EASY GOER	2nd	3.29	0.87	10-6-14-0-0
1988	Winning Colors	8.80	3.50	0.72	10-14-8-0-4	Private Terms	9th	3.75	0.87	11-13-12-2-0
1987	ALYSHEBA	18.80	3.80	1.08	12-4-6-2-0	DEMONS BEGONE	DNF	3.00	0.81	5-3-8-0-0
1986	FERDINAND	37.40	1.50	0.55	14-2-16-8-0	Snow Chief	11th	5.00	0.67	0-4-2-0-0
1985	SPEND A BUCK	10.20	1.40	0.25	2-3-18-1-0	Chief's Crown*	3rd	5.00	1.04	9-8-6-1-0
1984	SWALE	8.80	1.93	0.68	8-1-11-2-0	Althea*	19th	5.55	1.22	19-8-7-2-0
1983	SUNNY'S HALO	7.00	1.82	0.46	4-5-13-2-0	Marfa	5th	5.50	1.19	14-5-6-0-1

*Dosage numbers shown are those at the time of the race. Since then, sires added to the chefs-de-race list have changed some of the listed dosage figures.

In my view, it was as absurd to fix Strike the Gold's Dosage numbers after the fact as it was to explain Alydar's absence from the Chef-de-Race list in the first place. Yet the debacle pointed out two weaknesses in the Derby Dosage system.

1. Some important pedigree influences remain unrepresented in Dosage.
2. Any rote approach to handicapping is sure to endure a serious losing streak as soon as everyone believes in its infalibility.

"I do not propose Dosage as an iron-clad Kentucky Derby handicapping system," Roman insists. "I use it in conjunction with the top-rated two-year-olds of the prior year to narrow down Derby contenders, and the results surely speak for themselves. Dosage is best used as a guide toward distance capabilities and limitations."

I agree and suggest to those who do not wish to compute their own D.P.'s, D.I.'s and C.D.'s by hand to investigate an impressive, nine-megabyte, 10-disk computer program designed to do all the Dosage formulations at $595 (ouch!) per copy. Not many may choose to spend so much for such an esoteric piece of the racetrack puzzle, but networking among fellow handicappers can lower the cost. See Appendix D for further details. Breeding is one area of handicapping not likely to be corrupted on the tote board through widespread usage.

The Drug Factor

SEVENTH RACE
CD 34634
May 4. 1968

1 1-4 MILES. (Northern Dancer, May 2, 1964, 2:00, 3, 126.)
Ninety-fourth running KENTUCKY DERBY. Scale weights. $125,000 added. 3-year-olds. By subscription of $100 each in cash which covers nomination for both the Kentucky Derby and Derby Trial. All nomination fees to Derby winner, $500 to pass the entry box, $1,000 additional to start, $125,000 added of which $25,000 to second, $12,500 to third, $5,000 to fourth. $100,000 guaranteed to winner (to be divided equally in event of a dead heat). Weight, 126 lbs. The owner of the winner to receive a gold trophy. A nomination may be withdrawn before time of closing nominations. Closed Thursday, Feb. 15, 1968, with 191 nominations.
Value of race $165,100. Value to winner $122,600; second, $25,000; third, $12,500; fourth, $5,000.
Mutuel Pool, $2,350,470.

Inde.	Horses	Eq't A Wt	PP	$\frac{1}{4}$	$\frac{1}{2}$	$\frac{3}{4}$	1	Str	Fin	Jockeys	Owners	Odds to $1
34451Aqu[1]	—Dancer's Image	3 126	12	14	14	10$\frac{1}{2}$	8h	1 1	1 1$\frac{1}{2}$	R Ussery	Peter Fuller	3.60
34402Kee[1]	—Forward Pass	b 3 126	13	3^2	4^4	3^4	2^2	2$\frac{1}{2}$	2nk	I Valenz'ela	Calumet Farm	2.20
34402Kee[3]	—Francie's Hat	3 126	10	11^{3}11^2	7^2	7^2	4^2	3$^{2}\frac{1}{2}$	E Fires	Saddle Rock Farm	23.50
34402Kee[2]	—T. V. C'mercial	b 3 126	2	9$\frac{1}{2}$	8^1	9^1	6$\frac{1}{2}$	5h	4^1	H Grant	Bwamazon Farm	24.00
34307CD[4]	—Kentucky Sherry	3 126	4	1$\frac{1}{2}$	1^2	1^2	1h	3^2	5^1	J Combest	Mrs Joe W Brown	f-14.70
34325CD[2]	—Jig Time	b 3 126	3	7^{1}16$\frac{1}{2}$	6$\frac{1}{2}$	4h	6h	6$\frac{1}{2}$	R Brouss'rd	Cragwood Stable	36.30
34425GG[2]	—Don B.	3 126	7	5^2	5^2	5^1	5$^1\frac{1}{2}$	7^4	7^5	D Pierce	D B Wood	35.50
34307CD[2]	—Trouble Brewing	3 126	5	12$\frac{1}{2}$	9^1	11^2	13^4	12^4	8nk	B Thornb'rg	Coventry Rock Farm	f-14.70
34325CD[1]	—Proper Proof	3 126	11	13^{3}12^1	12^2	11^2	8$^1\frac{1}{2}$	9^4	J Sellers	Mrs Montgomery Fisher	9.90
34325CD[4]	—Te Vega	b 3 126	6	8^{h}13^{2h}	13^1	12^2	9^2	10$\frac{3}{4}$	M Mang'llo	F C Sullivan	f-14.70
34307CD[1]	—Captain's Gig	3 126	9	2^h	2^h	2^1	3^2	10^2	11$^1\frac{1}{2}$	M Ycaza	Cain Hoy Stable	6.10
34451Aqu[2]	—Iron Ruler	3 126	1	10$\frac{1}{2}$	7$\frac{1}{2}$	8$\frac{1}{2}$	9h	11^1	12^3	B Baeza	October House Farm	5.70
34325CD[3]	—Verbatim	b 3 126	8	6^{h}10^h	14	14	14	13no	A Cord'o Jr	Elmendorf	37.40
34402Kee[5]	—Gl'ming Sword	b 3 126	14	4$\frac{1}{2}$	3$\frac{1}{2}$	4h	10^2	13^1	14	E Belmonte	C V Whitney	31.20

f-Mutuel field.

Time, :22$\frac{1}{5}$, :45$\frac{4}{5}$, 1:09$\frac{4}{5}$, 1:36$\frac{1}{5}$, 2:02$\frac{1}{5}$. Track fast.

$2 Mutuel Prices:

9-DANCER'S IMAGE	9.20	4.40	4.00
10-FORWARD PASS		4.20	3.20
7-FRANCIE'S HAT			6.40

Gr. c, by Native Dancer—Noors Image, by Noor. Trainer, L. C. Cavalaris, Jr. Bred by P. Fuller (Md.).

IN GATE—4:40. OFF AT 4:40$\frac{1}{2}$ EASTERN DAYLIGHT TIME. Start good. Won driving.

DANCER'S IMAGE, void of speed through the early stages after being bumped at the start, commenced a rally after three-quarters to advance between horses on the second turn, cut back to the inside when clear entering the stretch at which point his rider dropped his whip. Responding to a vigorous hand ride the colt continued to save ground to take command nearing the furlong marker and was hard pressed to edge FORWARD PASS. The latter broke alertly only to be bumped and knocked into the winner, continued gamely while maintaining a forward position along the outside, moved boldly to take command between calls in the upper stretch and held on stubbornly in a prolonged drive. FRANCIE'S HAT, allowed to settle in stride, commenced a rally after three-quarters and finished full of run. T. V. COMMERCIAL closed some ground in his late rally but could not seriously menace. KENTUCKY SHERRY broke in stride to make the pace under good rating, saved ground to the stretch where he drifted out while tiring. JIG TIME faltered after making a menacing bid on the second turn. PROPER PROOF was always outrun. CAPTAIN'S GIG tired badly after prompting the issue for three-quarters. IRON RULER failed to enter contention. GLEAMING SWORD broke alertly but sharply to the inside to bump with FORWARD PASS, continued in a forward position for five furlongs and commenced dropping back steadily

NOTE: DANCER'S IMAGE DISQUALIFIED FROM PURSE MONEY BY ORDER OF CHURCHILL DOWNS STEWARDS, MAY 15, 1968 AND RULING SUSTAINED BY THE KENTUCKY STATE RACING COMMISSION

On the first Sunday in May 1968 the ninety-fourth running of the Kentucky Derby was decided in the laboratory of the state chemist. A small trace of the prohibited painkilling drug phenylbutazone was found in the urine sample of Dancer's Image, the winner of the world's most famous horserace. Thoroughbred racing in America hasn't been the same since.

Today it is impossible to handicap most races in any state without taking into account the drug factor. Three decades after Dancer's Image shocked the racing world, the integrity of the game is under deep suspicion. Not surprisingly, the only people who seem oblivious to this insidious development are the trainers, veterinarians and track officials who blindly insist they need access to a select group of legalized drugs to keep their horses in running condition through a 12-month, wall-to-wall, coast-to-coast racing season.

Bute and Lasix may seem innocent enough—Bute tends to reduce swelling in inflamed joints and Lasix curbs capillary bleeding in the nasal passages. While no one knows exactly why Lasix works this way, top veterinarians guess that draining excess fluid from the body lowers blood pressure, which may limit bleeding through the thin membranes in the pulmonary system.

The widespread use of these and other drugs, detectable and undetectable, continue to undermine the essence of handicapping. So long as racing commissioners and track owners refuse to join together in a nationwide program to fund research for sophisticated drug detection, the sport faces the prospect of more scandals during the coming decade.

In the 1990s, the following clearly is true about drugs in racing:

1. Because drugs interfere with the horse's warning system (pain), more horses are breaking down in the era of legalized drugs than without them.
2. Administering Lasix for the first time can and often does create a wake-up effect.
3. Regular use of Bute is so widespread it is impossible to assess its impact as a handicapping factor.
4. While drug detection has improved in recent years, both Lasix and Bute still may screen the presence of other drugs in a few jurisdictions.
5. The testing procedures used to protect against drug abuse are not sufficient to cope with the variety of sophisticated drugs currently

on the market. A multimillion dollar, nationwide, industry-run testing laboratory is the only realistic answer to this problem, but there is presently little interest in that proposal.

6. It is not possible to tell whether trainers who persistently put over dramatic form reversals are in fact training their horses from the bottle. But the player should keep a record of all such horsemen for future reference.

7. If the player is so suspicious of the drug factor that he is unable to handicap races successfully, he probably has lost touch with other aspects of his game. Nevertheless, he could do a tremendous service to racing by saving past-performance profiles of the most suspicious form reversals and forward copies to a competent steward or racing writer at his favorite track, or write to me, in care of the publisher.

Otherwise, evidence has been introduced by reputable veterinary researchers at the University of Pennsylvania to suggest that horses do run faster with Lasix. This finding, first released in 1989, has provoked plenty of controversy among veterinarians and trainers while confirming the impressions of thousands of handicappers. Whether this improvement is directly traceable to Lasix, or to its cleansing effects on the horse's breathing apparatus—or as a screen to illegal drugs—no one can state unequivocally. Yet no handicapper in the game can ignore the potency of first-time Lasix use when the horse flashed some speed in his most recent start before tiring abruptly.

Since such horses may have stopped because of difficulty getting their air, first-time Lasix might do as advertised—clear the nasal passages.

Many handicappers insist that second-time Lasix is nearly as effective as first-time use. I disagree and so does Andy Beyer. Both of us have found independently that dramatic improvement with second-time Lasix usually is accompanied by mitigating factors. These may include the wrong distance, wrong track condition, lack of training, or a difficult pace scenario, or severe track bias in the first Lasix race. Of course, exceptions do occasionally achieve top form with unadulterated second usage to fuel the argument. Perhaps the first race with Lasix was a confidence builder?

Absentees with first-time Lasix are very dangerous, especially in maiden claiming races, or when accompanied by a sharp drop in class, a series of credible workouts, or the horse's training regimen or racing pattern conforms to one of the trainer's preferred winning strategies. Similarly, when any good trainer on any racing circuit employs Lasix in conjunction with a significant change of situation, such as a class drop or a distance switch or a change of racing surface, the player should upgrade the horse's chances for a maximum effort.

Among these Lasix-linked combinations, one of the most effective is the drop to the bottom level of maiden claiming for the first time coupled with the addition of first-time Lasix, and as Ron Cox likes to point out, one of the trickiest is the first time on the bottom *since* Lasix was added. I strongly urge players to study the past performances included on the next few pages. Each contains nuances of Lasix angles in various combinations that resemble many others at tracks from coast to coast. While I am not crazy about legalized drugs in racing—I have strong opinions about their widespread use and abuse—handicapping in the 1990s requires players to identify every situation in which drugs are linked to pending improvement.

The first set of examples on the next few pages includes first-time Lasix use in several different contexts. Set number two includes a pair of second-time Lasix users who displayed a significant change of situation between first- and second-time use. The third set includes horses shipping in and out of New York, where Lasix is barred.

While some regular Lasix users will run just as well without the drug, there is almost no way to predict it except for one basic situation: A true bleeder—one who receives Lasix after stopping badly in the pre-Lasix race (or one in which bleeding from the nostrils was officially reported in result charts and/or the sporting press)—is most likely to produce a subpar race on a muggy, hot day.

Unbridled, for instance, whose 1990 *DRF* past performancs did not include Lasix notations, failed miserably without the drug in the 1990 Belmont Stakes, but won the Breeders' Cup Classic at Belmont five months later on a windy, cold autumn day. For this reason it pays to observe the demeanor of "Lasix-off" horses in the paddock and post parade for signs of listlessness, extreme sweating, or even dehydration.

Horses who repeatedly go from non-Lasix states (or countries) to Lasix states and back again should be monitored for possible betting scores.

NOTE: *While it remains true that astute handicappers can make serious money cataloging trainers who are most effective with Lasix, it is nevertheless tragic that the sport's credibility has been seriously damaged, perhaps forever.*

FIRST-TIME LASIX USE

Sentimentaldiamond
Dk. b. or br. f. 2(Mar), by Maudlin—Beautiful Diamond, by Fappiano
Br.—Frazier D W (Fla)
Own.—Arc B Stable
Tr.—Barr Donald H (21 1 1 3 .05)
113
Lifetime 3 1 0 0 $7,165
1992 3 1 0 0 $7,165
Wet 1 0 0 0 $310
19Nov92- 5Lrl fst 6f :23 :472 1:114 ⒻMd 25000 69 4 3 32 32½ 1½ 16¼ Johnston M T Lb 119 3.10 82-20 Sntmntldmnd1196¼RnglRd1192½SmbdEls119 Ridden out 11
1Nov92- 5Lrl my 6f :23 :474 1:134 ⒻMd Sp Wt 29 10 1 2hd 2hd 55½ 611½ Johnston M T b 119 27.80 60-24 PerkinsStr1192½LeCrtr119noWildsBstTurn119 Gave way 13
17Oct92- 3Lrl fst 6f :224 :472 1:131 ⒻMd Sp Wt 10 8 5 46½ 78½ 716 720½ Rocco J b 119 14.60 54-18 ChinofFlowers1193½Abovehwii1142½Distnz119 Bore in st 9
LATEST WORKOUTS Oct 27 Bow 5f fst 1:024 B ●Oct 8 Bow 3f fst :362 Hg Oct 1 Bow 5f fst 1:02 B

Issaquah Knight
Dk. b. or br. g. 3(May), by Knights Choice—Kristi Anniti, by Winds of Thought
SIBILLE R (426 48 66 61 .11) $12,500 Br.—Carrigan Andrew J&Barbara J (Wash)
Own.—Carragan Andy & Barbara
Tr.—Ross Larry (124 16 21 18 .13)
119
Lifetime 3 1 0 0 $3,300
1992 3 1 0 0 $3,300
1991 0 M 0 0
29May92- 1GG fst 6f :214 :451 1:112 Md 12500 62 4 1 14 13 14 13 Baze R A LBb 118 2.40 81-16 IsshKnght1183Hdn'sMystr1182ScffldMn118 Drew clear 8
17May92- 5GG fst 6f :22 :451 1:11 Md 20000 34 9 7 33 33½ 47½ 713 Baze R A LBb 118 5.30 70-18 SnshnSprmn1181½Rom'sRylty1186CllnJms118 Gave way 12
18Apr92- 6GG fst 6f :221 :451 1:092 Md Sp Wt 39 4 8 65½ 79 816 919½ Baze R A LB 118 8.40 71-13 CrftyDd1184GllntG1182RndThEdgs118 Steadied stretch 9
LATEST WORKOUTS May 10 GG 5f fst :594 H May 3 GG 5f fst 1:011 Hg Apr 26 GG 4f fst :47 H Apr 12 GG 5f gd 1:064 Hg(d)

Single Cut
Ch. f. 3(Feb), by Singular—Delicious Cut, by Blade
Br.—Hatfill Norm (Fla)
Own.—Ballou Frances W
Tr.—Hurtak Daniel C (4 1 0 0 .25)
112
Lifetime 4 2 0 0 $9,710
1992 1 1 0 0 $5,400
1991 3 1 0 0 $4,310
Wet 1 1 0 0 $5,400
5Nov92- 7Crc sly 6f :214 :454 1:123 3↑ⒻClm 18000 81 2 3 13 11 14 11 Nunez E O Lb 111 17.30 88-18 SingleCut1111DruidWoman1204TriGranMaw112 Driving 6
19Oct91- 5Crc fst 6f :22 :46 1:131 ⒻClm 45000 16 5 3 52½ 57½ 613 617¾ Velez J A Jr 113 5.50 66-15 VldMssZnd118hdRssurus1142½Copln'sCcht114 No factor 6
26Sep91- 4Crc fst 6f :221 :462 1:133 ⒻClm 40000 55 6 7 77 76¾ 73¾ 74¾ Hernandez R 114 5.50 77-16 SpnnnOut116½SngulrlySnny118½Rssrs116 Bumped start 8
3Jly91- 5Crc fst 5½f :224 :473 1:074 ⒻMd c-20000 55 5 2 22½ 21½ 15 13¼ Lee M A 116 4.00 87-13 Single Cut1163¼ LividLass1163¾MyMinkCoat116 Driving 12
LATEST WORKOUTS Nov 4 Crc 3f sly :363 Hg(d) Oct 27 Crc 5f fst 1:01 H Oct 20 Crc 5f fst 1:03 B ●Oct 13 Crc 5f fst 1:011 H

Screamin Emma
Dk. b. or br. f. 4, by Wild Again—Miss Royal Kret, by Royal Note
$10,000 Br.—Agnew Dan J (Ky)
Own.—Stox N Box Stable
Tr.—Serey Juan (68 18 8 9 .26)
115
Lifetime 26 5 2 0 $44,235
1992 17 4 0 0 $28,195
1991 9 1 2 0 $16,040
Turf 1 0 0 0
Wet 5 1 0 0 $4,255
3Nov92- 5Med sly 170 :464 1:122 1:423 3↑ⒻClm 7500 65 1 1 11 12 13½ 14 Tejeira J L 116 2.40 85-13 ScreminEmm1164GlowingWild1159NrlySpnt115 Driving 6
22Oct92- 3Med fst 1 1/16 :481 1:132 1:47 3↑ⒻClm 6250 59 4 2 1½ 1hd 12½ 12 Tejeira J L 115 2.60 72-21 ScreminEmm1152Shecnmove1133DivineGlxy115 Driving 6
26Sep92- 2Med sly 6f :221 :454 1:114 3↑ⒻClm 5000 48 4 9 86¾ 67½ 64¾ 55¾ Santagata N 116 17.00 78-11 GldCshmr116hdRnnngDl1161½Incrdbbbl116 No solid bid 9
16Sep92- 1Bel fst 7f :23 :464 1:244 3↑ⒻClm 12000 22 6 4 42½ 73¾ 79¾ 622 Davis R G 113 8.50 58-18 SprklngHnnh1174½RodBlck106nkWhrIsM113 Done early 7
27Jly92- 4Bel yl 1 Ⓣ:463 1:113 1:374 ⒻClm 35000 42 6 8 913 98½ 813 820½ Chavez J F b 117 42.50 53-29 Slsflower1171LifeOntheFrm1192½GrtRviw117 No factor 9
19Jly92- 3Bel fst 7f :224 :461 1:244 ⒻClm 12000 39 2 6 21 23½ 57 413½ Chavez J F b 113 4.90 66-13 RthrBScl1136½TrkAlBrr1132ATmThtWs113 Forced pace 7
8Jly92- 3Bel fst 6f :22 :451 1:103 ⒻClm 13000 43 5 6 57 79½ 712 713¾ Pezua J M 115 15.10 73-16 TownCreek113¾MileHighGlory1172½BrvGrcin113 Outrun 8
24Jun92- 1Bel sly 6½f :222 :453 1:172 ⒻClm 16500 29 2 2 57 59 612 621½ Migliore R 115 10.30 65-09 Crli'sCommnd117¾MissThiti11712¼WhereIsM113 Outrun 6
28May92- 5Bel fst 6f :221 :452 1:104 ⒻClm c-12000 61 7 8 97½ 97 65½ 65¾ Smith M E 113 2.30 80-14 Plythbgbs1101½BrdfrdB1133Chtt'sDrm113 Broke slowly 9
28May92-Claimed from Schwartz Barry K, Alexander Frank A Trainer
7May92- 9Bel fst 6f :221 :451 1:10 ⒻClm 13000 67 10 7 85½ 63¾ 43½ 45½ Smith M E 115 6.80 84-13 EpicVilla1172¾DualThreat117½RoylSummit117 Wide trip 12

Whoever
Dk. b. or br. f. 3(Mar), by Well Decorated—Friendly Gesture-Ir, by Sallust
$5,000 Br.—O'Farrell J M Jr (Fla)
Own.—Venezia Robert J
Tr.—Lowe Ernest A Jr (49 6 6 7 .12)
120
Lifetime 4 1 1 1 $6,240
1992 4 1 1 1 $6,240
1991 0 M 0 0
Wet 1 0 0 0 $450
13Nov92- 3Suf fst 6f :222 :474 1:151 3↑ⒻMd 10000 36 4 5 45 35 25 1no Ma H C H LB 120 2.30 71-17 Whoever120noRidThBounds115½Puppy'sDrm116 Driving 8
11Apr92- 3Suf sly 1 :49 1:152 1:441 ⒻMd Sp Wt 22 7 3 33 35½ 47 411¾ Baez R B 120 *1.20 62-13 PureConcorde1202¾Bileys1201½DefndMyHonor120 Tired 8
3Apr92- 6Suf fst 6f :224 :48 1:163 ⒻMd Sp Wt 44 1 2 42 35½ 35½ 35½ Baez R B 120 4.00 58-34 Daisy Buck1203¾ Safe Shelter1201¾ Whoever120 Evenly 8
23Mar92- 5Suf gd 6f :24 :491 1:163 ⒻMd Sp Wt 53 3 3 3½ 32 24½ 21 Baez R B 112 8.00 63-33 CrimsonBrbi1221Whoever1124½Chowder122 Came again 7
LATEST WORKOUTS Nov 20 Suf 4f fst :512 B Nov 8 Suf 3f fst :373 B Oct 24 Suf 6f fst 1:17 Hg

Miniaturist B. f. 3(Feb), by Lines of Power—Madam Schu, by Nureyev

Br.—Sharp Sharp (Md)

Own.—Crigler William H Tr.—Gruwell Bessie S (103 21 23 17 .20) 1115

Lifetime 11 3 1 1 $19,470 | 1992 10 2 1 1 $14,070 | 1991 1 1 0 0 $5,400 | Turf 1 0 0 0 | Wet 2 1 1 0 $8,880

31Oct92- 5Del my 5½f :213 :462 1:06 3↑ⒻAlw 9300 65 11 4 44½ 45½ 34 12 Umana J L5 Lb 106 *1.70 85-19 Miniturist1062Friend'sOpinion1192¼MissFpp116 Driving 12

27Sep92- 6Pim sly 6f :223 :462 1:12 3↑ⒻAlw 16800 68 4 3 11½ 1½ 21 26¼ Guerra W A b 113 39.40 79-18 CraftyNEger1146¼Miniturist1133¾UThree114 Weakened 7

9Sep92- 8Del yl *5f Ⓣ:222 :472 :593 3↑ⒻAlw 9300 24 8 7 77½ 812 812 912¾ Reynolds R L 116 9.40 71-16 SistrCorrin115¾Z.ShySpirit1142¾Pryform110 Used early 10

29Aug92-12Pha fst 7f :223 :453 1:252 3↑ⒻAlw 15000 40 6 3 53 65½ 412 412¼ Molina V H 110 8.70 68-19 LdyAprl110hdAprl'sSlw1168¾KtchnGossp119 Came in st. 7

13Aug92- 9Pha fst 6½f :214 :45 1:183 3↑ⒻAlw 18150 37 6 6 84¾109 911 1014 Reynolds R L 116 11.70 71-18 MeetHuncMunc116½LdyApril1102April'sSlew116 Outrun 10

26Jly92- 9Pha fst 6½f :214 :444 1:174 ⒻClm 15000 66 1 3 1½ 1hd 3½ 32½ Reynolds R L 116 5.00 86-18 Ctln'sWrror112nkCndyWood1162¼Mntrst116 Weakened 8

4Jly92- 4Pha gd 6f :222 :461 1:113 ⒻClm 7500 64 4 2 2hd 1½ 13 17¾ Colton R E L 116 3.40 83-11 Miniaturist1167¾ Spicy Tale122½ Palarca116 Handily 8

28Jun92- 1Pim fst 6f :234 :473 1:132 ⒻClm 6500 42 2 3 2hd 32½ 32½ 63¾ Luzzi M J 114 4.10 74-17 HrrysShrew114¾FliciD.1142DncingWinwrd114 Gave way 7

20Jun92- 4Pim fst 6f :23 :471 1:132 ⒻClm 10000 34 6 4 33 42½ 66 69¼ Guerra W A L 112 7.10 69-23 Fbrry'sLss1143¼Jzm1191Un'sSnBnny114 Dropped back 6

11Jun92- 7Pim fst 6f :231 :461 1:111 ⒻAlw 16000 21 2 7 77¾ 819 715 625¼ Luzzi M J 112 16.50 64-13 Singing Ring1121½ Mz.ZillBear1129Kimonina117 Outrun 8

LATEST WORKOUTS Oct 4 Del 4f fst :521 B

Campo Marzio (Chi) Dk. b or br h. 5

Own: Harrington & Horton & K C Stable

Sire: Roy (Fappiano)

Dam: Memsahib (Musketeer)

Br: Haras Figuron (Chi)

STEVENS G L (221 51 34 29 .23) $100,000 Tr: Mitchell Mike (103 33 16 13 .32) L 116

Lifetime Record: 24 9 5 1 $165,136 | 1993 8 3 1 0 $94,876 | 1992 6 0 0 1 $12,375 | Hol Ⓣ 5 1 0 0 $34,375 | Turf 17 8 1 1 $123,954 | Wet 1 0 1 0 $8,000 | Dist Ⓣ 4 1 1 0 $27,501

3Jly93- 3Hol fst 1¼ :462 1:101 1:35 2:00 3↑ Hol Gld Cp HG1 89 3 9 1010 910 915 718¾ Garcia J A LB 109 29.00 78-05 Best Pal1212½ Bertrando1185½ Major Impact114nk 5 Wide stretch 10

23Jun93- 3Hol fm 1 1/16 Ⓣ :242 :48 1:111 1:41 Alw 55000N$mY 81 2 5 58½ 57 67 66 Delahoussaye E LB 118 *1.00 85-11 Portoferraio114no Have Fun118½ Silver Ending1162½ No threat 7

13May93- 8Hol gd 1 1/16 Ⓣ :23 :462 1:10 1:401 Clm 100000 99 3 5 56½ 54½ 31 11½ Stevens G L LB 119 2.50 95-05 Campo Marzio1191½ River Rhythm1161½ Seahawk Gold112½ 5 Wide 1/4 7

25Apr93- 7Hol fst 1 1/16 :23 :454 1:092 1:412 Alw 55000N$mY 103 3 7 79½ 45½ 35 11 Stevens G L LB 114 7.10 94-10 Campo Marzio1141 J. F. Williams1172¾ Tertian1161½ Wide, late surge 7

18Apr93- 8SA fm 1⅛ Ⓣ :461 1:094 1:343 1:471 Clm c-80000 90 3 2 32 31½ 22 43¼ Valenzuela P A B 119 5.40 80-12 River Rhythm1161 Scheimer1151¾ Lanner115½ Always close 8

Claimed from Paulson Allen E, Whittingham Charles Trainer

24Mar93- 5SA gd 1 Ⓣ :234 :48 1:12 1:363 Clm 80000 96 8 3 21½ 22 21½ 1no Atkinson P B 115 6.50 82-15 Campo Marzio115no River Rhythm116½ Scottish Castle117½ Gamely 9

18Feb93- 2SA sly 1 ⊗ :224 :454 1:10 1:354 Clm 80000 98 2 1 11 1½ 2hd 2½ Valenzuela P A 116 6.50 90-15 Saratoga Gambler116½ Campo Marzio1163 Total Tempo1133 Good try 5

31Jan93- 3SA fm 1 Ⓣ :233 :471 1:112 1:352 Alw 55000N$Y 92 2 6 63½ 63½ 64½ 54½ Valenzuela P A B 117 30.20 84-12 LuthierEnchnteur117nk Gogrty119hd DH TheTendrTrck116 5 Wide stretch 7

18Dec92- 8Hol gd 1⅛ Ⓣ :483 1:13 1:371 1:492 3↑ ⓇHandicap55K 80 1 5 63½ 64½ 65½ 612 Valenzuela P A B 117 25.50 65-23 Star Of Cozzene1213½ Gogarty1174 Super May119nk 4 Wide stretch 6

9Nov92- 2SA fm 1⅛ Ⓣ :491 1:13 1:364 1:49 3↑ Alw 55000 85 3 4 44½ 43½ 36 37½ Valenzuela P A B 117 28.20 66-21 Barraq-Fr1153½ Gogarty-Ir1194 Campo Marzio-Ch117 Not enough late 6

WORKOUTS: Jly 17 Hol 4f fst :482 H *15/45* Jly 12 Hol 4f fst :484 B *15/32* Jun 14 Hol 6f fst 1:123 H *2/26* Jun 7 Hol 4f fst :482 H *13/60* May 31 Hol 4f fst :484 H *17/36* May 26 Hol 3f fst :362 H *14/23*

The Great M. B. Ch. c. 3(Mar), by Medieval Man—Saisonic, by Saidam

DAVIS R G (130 22 14 17 .17) $75,000 Br.—Zellen Larry (Fla)

Own.—Denker Jerry Tr.—Margotta Anthony Jr (9 1 1 0 .11) 117

Lifetime 7 3 0 1 $33,960 | 1992 4 1 0 1 $13,560 | 1991 3 2 0 0 $20,400

12Nov92- 7Aqu fst 6f :222 :45 1:10 3↑ Alw 30000 77 1 3 65½ 65¼ 66 67¾ Samyn J L 117 6.20 83-16 Vermont1171¼ Curbex1121½ Prevailed117 No threat 8

20Oct92- 9Med fst 6f :221 :45 1:094 3↑ Alw 17000 88 4 4 3nk 11½ 13 1¾ Samyn J L L 113 4.60 94-08 TheGreatM.B.113¾OneBigHug1135WildDante113 Driving 6

30Aug92- 4Sar fst 6f :221 :45 1:09 3↑ Alw 28000 73 3 5 62¼ 42½ 33½ 310 Samyn J L 112 10.80 89-08 BorderCat1129CseStudy1121TheGretM.B.112 Lckd rally 7

7Aug92- 9Sar fst 6f :214 :443 1:10 3↑ Alw 28000 73 6 7 108½106 95 76 Samyn J L 112 41.50 88-10 RnsGrmsn1121¼RchrdOfEnlnd112hdMnRn112 No factor 11

22Sep91-10Crc fst 7f :221 :451 1:244 ⓇFla Stallion 75 3 7 31½ 52½ 56 56¼ Velazquez J R L 118 7.50 85-06 NkedGreed1181MjsticSwp118nkLittlBrothr118 Faltered 11

22Sep91-Run in Divisions-Affirmed Division

23Aug91- 3Mth fst 6f :214 :444 1:103 Alw 17000 73 3 3 2hd 2½ 11 11¾ Rivera L Jr L 113 3.90 88-12 ThGrtM.B.1131¾SprkyDunC1172BddngProud117 Driving 6

14Aug91-10Mth fst 6f :213 :451 1:113 Md 25000 62 5 4 1hd 12½ 13 18 Rivera L Jr L 118 13.90 83-13 TheGrtM.B.1188Bigtdo118hdVinni'sPlsur114 Ridden out 11

LATEST WORKOUTS Nov 7 Bel 6f gd 1:153 B Oct 29 Bel 4f fst :52 B Oct 7 Bel 5f fst 1:03 B Oct 2 Bel 4f fst :492 H

Summer Playmate Ch. f. 3 (Feb)

Own: Cavanagh Thomas M & Marguerite F

Sire: Captain Nick-GB (Sharpen Up-GB)

Dam: Easelette (Painted Wagon)

Br: Mr. & Mrs. Thomas M. Cavanagh (Cal)

MCCARRON C J (231 37 48 40 .16) $25,000 Tr: Peterson Douglas R (37 5 7 3 .14) L 116

Lifetime Record: 8 2 0 0 $25,700 | 1993 8 2 0 0 $25,700 | 1992 0 M 0 0 | Hol 3 1 0 0 $9,900 | Turf 2 0 0 0 $3,900 | Wet 1 0 0 0 $1,275 | Dist 2 0 0 0 $2,550

7Jly93- 7Hol fst 7f :221 :45 1:093 1:22 ⒻClm 40000 66 9 7 75½ 74¾ 76 89½ Castaneda M LB 116 8.50 84-09 Jan's Turn1162¾ Numberthirtyfive116nk Decidedly Natalie116nk Wide trip 9

17Jun93- 8Hol fm 1 Ⓣ :232 :464 1:104 1:344 ⒻAlw 39000N1X 73 4 6 52½ 42 42½ 45½ Castaneda M LB 115 43.10 85-05 Shuggleswon1172 Tansaui1161½ Short Temper1101¾ Not enough late 7

4Jun93- 8Hol fm 1 1/16 Ⓣ :234 :472 1:11 1:414 ⒻAlw 39000N1X 73 5 6 75½ 64 63½ 55¾ Castaneda M LB 115 62.20 81-09 FondlyRemmbrd119½ Shugglswon1173½ BoundlssColony119½ No mishap 8

19May93- 9Hol fst 6½f :214 :444 1:104 1:172 ⒻClm 20000 73 8 5 42 32 2½ 14 Black C A LB 119 38.70 82-13 Summer Playmate1194 Buy A Bride1161½ Snow Vest1162½ Ridden out 10

29Apr93- 7Hol fst 7f :22 :444 1:093 1:232 ⒻClm 40000 42 3 5 1½ 1hd 89 915 Black C A LB 116 44.90 72-10 C. C. Overdrive116½ Jan's Turn1161½ Eurythmic116hd Faltered 9

11Apr93- 9SA fst 6½f :22 :451 1:104 1:172 ⒻⓈMd 32000 69 5 6 41¾ 31½ 2hd 1hd Black C A LB 117 5.10 84-13 SummerPlaymate117hd DecidedlyNatlie117¾ IrishMccool1183½ Hard drive 12

26Mar93- 2SA my 6f :212 :444 :571 1:10 ⒻⓈMd 32000 48 3 11 99½ 78 66½ 46½ Black C A B 117 12.20 80-09 Flying Vicki1175 Irish Maccool117¾ Wild Vickie117¾ Dwelt start, wide 11

26Feb93- 9SA gd 6f :213 :442 :571 1:104 ⒻⓈMd 32000 50 3 6 65½ 69¾ 68½ 46½ Pincay L Jr B 117 4.20 76-11 Snow Vest117no Carefree Colleen1176 FlyingVicki117½ Wide backstretch 8

WORKOUTS: Jun 7 Hol 3f fst :364 H *23/51* Mar 22 SA 4f fst :502 H *19/25* Mar 15 SA 5f fst 1:021 H *34/47* Feb 22 SA 4f gd :484 Hg*26/71* Feb 16 Hol 5f fst 1:031 H *27/33* Feb 11 Hol 5f fst 1:011 H *15/30*

SECOND-TIME LASIX USE

Stormy Ernie Ch. g. 4, by Erins Isle-Ir—Storm's Honor, by Storm Bird
$4,000 Br.—Combs James E (Ky) 119
Own.—Monarch Stable Inc Tr.—Meade Sherryl F (39 9 5 0 .23)
Lifetime 23 4 2 1 $20,368 | 1992 8 2 0 0 $5,350 | 1991 14 2 2 1 $14,981 | Turf 10 1 2 1 $11,610 | Wet 1 0 0 0

13Nov92- 10Suf fst 1⅛ :471 1:123 1:534 3↑Clm 4000 73 2 1 14 14 16 12 Molinari E LBb 119 *1.40 78-21 StormyErnie1192NoseClippr1161ErlyAct119 Ridden out 12
24Oct92- 8Suf gd *1 1/16 Ⓣ 1:50 3↑Alw 5000s 56 4 4 3½ 33 89¾1014½ Molinari E LBb 116 7.10 61-24 SpunGlass1161¾BallyBunion1163½G.I'mNice116 Stopped 10
18Oct92- 12Suf fst 5f :221 :463 :593 3↑Alw 5000s 62 4 8 65 48 45½ 46 Molinari E LBb 116 7.40 94-14 SrgnCp1161¼RbsRbsRbs1192¾BlcJcRlph116 No late resp 10
18Oct92-Originally scheduled on turf
7Oct92- 3Suf fst 170 :462 1:113 1:431 3↑Clm 5000 82 5 1 13½ 14 16 18 Molinari E LBb 116 19.80 97-07 Stormy Ernie1168 Kedge1154¾ T.Terrific114 Ridden out 10
27Jly92- 9Rkmfst 6f :221 :454 1:12 3↑Clm 5000 50 8 2 74¾ 44½ 45½ 610½ Vargas J L LBb 116 10.80 74-18 StonwllWill1162½Dr.Mlrky1121½DndyDllon119 Wide turn 8
17Jly92- 11Rkmfst 6f :221 :46 1:123 3↑Clm 5000 28 8 4 31½ 43 811 915 Vargas J L Bb 116 11.50 67-17 JetWorld1154¾WinforChrli113noAirForc116 Wide, stppd 9
6Mar92- 7FG fst 6f :22 :454 1:113 Clm 10000 34 3 7 46½ 58 714 716 Ardoin R Lb 117 27.60 70-16 RedyinnHour1224PC'sGlory1192MgusProv117 Gave way 7
7Feb92- 5DeD fst 7f :234 :482 1:283 Clm 7500 26 1 1 54½ 43½ 58½ 622½ Theriot B J Lb 121 6.90 67-14 BigFootDevil1197¾GrotonRos116½TxsHonor117 Faltered 7

Track Announcer Dk. b. or br. f. 4, by Track Barron—Squawker, by Bold Lad
$4,000 Br.—International Thbrd Breeders Inc (Ky) 119
Own.—Daffodill Hill Farm Tr.—Sienkewicz William M (6 0 0 1 .00)
Lifetime 26 4 2 4 $27,776 | 1992 17 4 1 1 $19,846 | 1991 9 M 1 3 $7,930 | Turf 1 0 0 0 | Wet 3 0 0 1 $2,025

1Nov92- 2Suf fst 1 :49 1:152 1:424 3↑ⒻClm 4000 15 10 5 3½ 55 919 929 Baez R LBb 119 6.90 52-20 SnuggleBr1166¾BGrt1178½Rinbowgm116 Drftd, stopped 10
4Oct92- 4Rkmfst 6f :223 :463 1:133 3↑ⒻClm 5000 18 6 5 54 56½ 611 716¼ Cotrone F Jr LBb 116 5.40 61-22 GoodGracious116nkFarra116½SpiritedRacer116 Stopped 7
20Sep92- 3Rkmfst 6f :214 :463 1:14 3↑ⒻClm 3500 52 1 8 614 48 21½ 11 Cotrone F Jr LBb 116 2.30 75-24 TrckAnnncr1161Dncltlsdstp1162¼MchlsEprss116 Driving 9
28Aug92- 9Rkmfst 6f :214 :452 1:12 3↑ⒻClm 10000 38 3 7 66 58 68 913½ Cotrone F Jr LBb 116 22.30 71-20 Slem'sSndy1124¾Dr.Jolyn1161½CrftyFbl116 Brshed early 10
21Aug92- 3Mth fst 6f :214 :46 1:123 3↑ⒻClm 9000 47 5 4 34 42½ 35 47¼ Wilson R Lb 114 10.50 71-19 Luvinherisluv'113¾ Go Lassie Go1173½ Couloir112 Tired 7
9Aug92- 4Mth sly 6f :212 :443 1:104 3↑ⒻClm 10000 36 6 2 52½ 45 510 511¼ Ferrer J C Lb 116 6.50 76-10 Timber Ghost1162½KolucttheMoney1164¾Ange112 Tired 8
2Aug92- 2Mth fst 6f :213 :451 1:103 3↑ⒻClm 20000 40 7 2 63½ 56 612 617 Wilson R Lb 116 12.10 71-12 MnrNrth11911¾FncEpmnt1162¼GLssG114 Tried to gt ot 8
29May92- 7Mth fm 1 Ⓣ:473 1:111 1:362 3↑ⒻClm 28000 14 7 2 1hd 1214 1223 1237½ Saumell L Lb 114 25.00 46-16 NrthAn112hdMrlnsMdnss117noMstSc113 Chckd far turn 12

ON-AGAIN, OFF-AGAIN LASIX USE

Media Luna B. m. 5, by Cutlass—Majestic Tudor, by Majestic Prince
$10,000 Br.—El Batey Bloodstock (Fla) 114
Own.—Doe Run Farm Tr.—Blom Linda (51 9 6 5 .18)
Lifetime 42 12 7 2 $46,243 | 1992 18 6 3 0 $23,533 | 1991 4 2 0 0 $6,445 | Wet 3 0 0 0 $372

1Oct92- 5Pha fst 6f :221 :46 1:132 3↑ⒻClm c-11000 27 6 1 48½ 614 617 614 Rohena J A L 119 7.10 60-24 OrWsh1111½TrnngBlossom1162½Undrnsrd116 No factor 7
1Oct92-Claimed from Ygual Angel, Rosado Raphael Trainer
20Sep92- 11Pha fst 6f :22 :452 1:114 3↑ⒻClm 11000 68 6 2 41¾ 41½ 31½ 21¾ Salinas P L L 119 13.50 80-18 Ri'sRondzvous1191¾MdLun1192¾Sntor'sLdy115 2nd best 8
31Aug92- 5Pha fst 5½f :221 :461 1:053 3↑ⒻClm 14000 51 5 2 43½ 43 55½ 55 Salinas P L L 116 7.80 81-21 CrftyRen1162½ChnsonDeRolnd119½TendrGorgi119 Tired 6
7Aug92- 6Pha fst 7f :222 :453 1:244 3↑ⒻClm 9000 67 1 2 3½ 33 21 11¾ Brennan M J L 112 11.20 83-19 MdiLun1121¾StolnSkts1167½StrkMGntly112 Stead, drvg 7
21Jly92- 11FL gd 6f :221 :462 1:134 3↑ⒻClm 25500 30 2 4 43½ 66 613 616¾ Salinas P L 114 14.30 60-28 MjstcAnr1131½MstcWll1153¾LttlAbrAnn112 Thru early 6
16Jun92- 9FL fst 6f :222 :462 1:123 3↑ⒻClm 7500 73 6 2 21 1hd 14½ 17½ Salinas P L 119 6.80e 83-21 MdiLun1197½FoolishEmbrc1153RgThAnswr108 Drew off 9
22May92- 5FL fst 5½f :223 :464 1:061 3↑ⒻClm 9000 65 5 1 2½ 2hd 1½ 1½ Salinas P L 116 *1.70 83-20 MediaLun116½DretoDrem1135Gibeon116 Drifted str, drv 6
16May92- 7FL fst 6f :222 :471 1:14 3↑ⒻClm 9000 44 1 1 1hd 3½ 33½ 67 Salinas P L 114 3.30 69-23 MarksOutrge119½TringleLdy1143LdyTriAnn117 Used up 6
10May92- 6FL fst 6f :22 :462 1:131 3↑ⒻClm 9000 56 1 6 32 1hd 2hd 24 Salinas P L 116 4.10 76-20 RomanRuins1164MediLun116noTlcumDee116 Weakened 9
29Apr92- 5FL fst 6f :221 :453 1:124 3↑ⒻClm 9000 41 2 7 3½ 41 45½ 76¾ Salinas P L 119 2.60e 75-18 RoseofIron113noVikingMistress1165Esprit113 Gave way 9
LATEST WORKOUTS Oct 30 Pha 6f fst 1:174 B Oct 24 Pha 4f fst :501 B

Old Madrid Ch. f. 3(May), by Villamor—Skeptic Lady, by Olden Times
$12,500 Br.—Rancho Jonata (Cal) 118
Own.—Bethlehem Stables Tr.—Reid Mark J (55 14 11 9 .25)
Lifetime 11 4 2 0 $18,995 | 1992 11 4 2 0 $18,995 | 1991 0 M 0 0 | Turf 1 0 0 0 $130

13Oct92- 5Med fst 6f :222 :453 1:111 ⒻClm 10500 62 4 1 1½ 11 12½ 14¾ Bravo J Lb 111 *1.50 87-14 Old Madrid1114¾StormFlag116nkBurstingUp111 Driving 6
20Sep92- 9Bel fst 1 :452 1:11 1:381 ⒻClm 15500 47 7 3 33 31½ 64¾ 613¼ Antley C W b 114 7.30 66-15 MissIronQuill1122¼FshionDsignr1165½ScPrncss116 Tired 9
11Sep92- 5Med fst 1 1/16 :472 1:12 1:45 ⒻClm 12500 59 5 1 12 12 2hd 24¼ HomistrRBJr5 Lb 111 *1.70 78-07 StutzsCrw1144¼OldMdrid1112¾FlyHighLdy114 No match 7
29Aug92- 1Mth fst 170 :47 1:132 1:46 ⒻClm 10000 63 3 1 12½ 14 14½ 14¼ HomistrRBJr5 Lb 109 4.90 66-24 OldMdrid1094½Bev'sMiss1121SummrSign114 Well clear 7
7Aug92- 3Mth fst 170 :453 1:101 1:423 ⒻClm 10000 47 8 4 33 45½ 88½ 87¾ HomistrRBJr5 b 111 4.00 75-10 CtyTrdtn1141¾Bv'sMss112hdCrystlCnscnc114 Gave way 10
14Jly92- 2Mth fst 170 :461 1:13 1:462 ⒻClm 10000 59 6 1 18 15 13 12½ HomistrRBJr5 b 109 2.90 64-30 OldMadrid1092½Bev'sMiss1121½JeanMcWard112 Driving 8
28Jun92- 8Mth fm 1 1/16 Ⓣ:461 1:103 1:44 + ⒻClm 22500 15 7 3 32½ 109 1019 1031¼ Verge M E b 112 20.20 50-10 SrfGld1161¾NrthrnMrn109noPrrPrspct106 Thru after 1/2 10
13Jun92- 2Mth fst 6f :22 :46 1:133 ⒻClm c-8500 45 8 5 41½ 43 43 53¾ HomistrRBJr5 b 107 *2.20 69-15 FshnLst1062Cstl'sCrss1151½ChkRcktt115 Lunged break 9
13Jun92-Claimed from Lotti Gene A Jr, Lotti Gene A Jr Trainer
30May92- 3GS gd 6f :221 :454 1:123 ⒻClm 8000 47 7 1 3nk 31½ 23 21¼ Vega A 116 *1.90 78-14 NhtNmbrs1181¼OldMdrd1161½DndsOnMnd121 2nd best 7
29Mar92- 9Tam fst 6f :221 :453 1:112 ⒻAlw 5500 59 10 9 65¾ 76½ 510 510 Algarin E 116 36.00 79-14 LoylScrtry1227LdyDmnsns1161IrshSssy122 No response 10

At the Gate Ch. f. 4, by Hero's Honor—Hobby, by Falcon
SANTIAGO A (14 1 0 2 .07) $35,000 Br.—Singer Craig B (Ky) 117
Own.—Zapczynski Eugene R Tr.—O'Brien Leo (17 1 2 2 .06)
Lifetime 31 3 6 5 $58,813 | 1992 7 0 1 0 $5,999 | 1991 18 2 3 4 $43,956 | Turf 14 1 3 3 $39,302 | Wet 7 1 0 0 $7,767

18Oct92- 2Bel gd 1¼ Ⓣ:50 1:392 2:043 3↑ⒻClm 45000 66 4 10 94¼ 83¼ 108¾ 1015¼ Chavez J F b 113 5.30 52-22 MyLdy'sWm1132BgBgAffr1151QnOfSvns117 Wide tired 10
25Sep92- 6Bel fm 1 1/16 Ⓣ:472 1:111 1:414 3↑ⒻClm 35000 79 7 9 96 62½ 32 21¾ Bravo J b 117 7.90 85-10 Q.E.Slew1191¾AttheGate117nkAShakyQueen117 Fin well 10
9Sep92- 8Med fm 1 1/16 Ⓣ:473 1:111 1:413 3↑ⒻClm 35000 77 2 4 45½ 31½ 22½ 42 Bravo J Lb 115 4.60 88-15 RidetoGlory1142MrflousMm115hdCremiest115 Willingly 6
7Aug92- 8AP fm *1 1/16 Ⓣ:491 1:134 1:444 3↑ⒻAlw 23000 75 10 11 1112 118¼ 119½ 75¾ Meier R Lb 116 51.70 68-31 TcsWd-Ir119nkPrPrc1191½SrchthShds116 Late wide bid 11
4Jly92- 8Det fst 1 :464 1:133 1:411 3↑ⒻAlw 8700 35 5 5 56½ 511 615 618 Gonzalez L A Lb 116 8.80 63-22 JcklynSld116½DoblLnk1104½TwStpTll111 Saved ground 6
18Jun92- 9Det sly 1 :492 1:151 1:423 3↑ⒻAlw 8700 39 7 2 2½ 55½ 69 715¾ Martinez Luis Lb 116 7.10 58-30 Jg'sDoubl119hdJcklynSld1167RllyJnny116 Tired outside 7
28May92- 3Det fst 6f :222 :453 1:112 3↑ⒻAlw 8500 40 5 1 610 611 614 611½ Martinez Luis Lb 116 6.10 80-11 ImpPowr1131½ShmrockSu1165Rck'sBty116 Outside trip 6
16Nov91- 5Aqu fm 1 Ⓣ:484 1:141 1:39 ⒻClm 75000 79 2 9 86¾ 62¾ 64½ 32½ Chavez J F b 111 4.60 79-16 AShkyQueen1171½Loufdm115½AtthGt111 Finished wrell 9
27Oct91- 3Aqu fm 1⅛ Ⓣ:474 1:121 1:522 ⒻClm 45000 79 8 7 710 77¼ 63 11½ Chavez J F b 112 30.70 84-15 AttheGte1121½SyYou'llSty1161½SpyLdrLdy112 Wide drv 10
12Oct91- 5Bel gd 1 1/16 Ⓣ:49 1:123 1:432 ⒻClm 70000 78 1 8 83¾ 83¾ 74 74¾ Lidberg D W b 113 29.20 76-18 MadameJumel114hdStrswhirl1122PlesntReef116 Outrun 8
LATEST WORKOUTS Sep 22 Bel 4f fst :493 B

In New York, most professional horseplayers believe that serious drug abuse has been rampant for decades. The late Oscar Barrera's ability to move horses up sharply after he claimed them remains the legend of "juice" training. In contemporary New York racing, several trainers are accused frequently of using similar magic potions, with no formal proof on the table. Cynicism flourishes because nature alone will not do what some trainers seem capable of doing with too many horses in New York. Similar suspicions are voiced about a handful of trainers on Lasix-legal circuits, who dramatically improve newly acquired horses overnight.

Meanwhile, the argument rages whether Lasix and or Bute have curative or preventative benefits to the running horse with no long-term side effects. If they do, the solution is obvious. Everyone in racing should be working his or her tail off to get public approval to allow all horses to be treated with these drugs in every race. But if they are being used insidiously, everyone should be fighting for their permanent removal from the game.

To Bet or Not to Bet . . . and How Much

When a gambler goes to Las Vegas for a weekend of roulette, craps, or blackjack, he should know in advance that the percentages constantly favor the house. Before the payoff odds are calculated, approximately 3 to 6 cents is raked off the top of every dollar wagered and the payoff odds are always lower than the actual mathematical odds.

This of course is the house take, and except for the one-in-a-million blackjack memory expert, no amount of skill will change the odds to the player's favor. I'm sorry folks, but the only way to beat the house is through unabashed luck—the longer one plays craps or roulette, the greater the probability for a wipeout.

A good casino gambler, then, is simply one who knows to quit if he's lucky enough to be ahead.

In betting on pro football and other team sports, the point spread theoretically balances out the action between supporters of two competing teams, and the player usually pays a 10 percent charge, or "vigorish," on all winning plays for the privilege of betting with a bookie. I won't go into the theories of proper football betting strategy in this book other than to say that racetrack bettors should only have it so easy. Consider the following:

By flipping a coin to determine which team should be played, anyone can expect approximately 50 percent winners. With some degree of skill

55 to 65 percent spot-play winners is well within the grasp of serious players.

At the racetrack the average field has nine horses, most of whom never have faced each other before and never will again. The best horse in the race may get into trouble, step on a pebble, lose its jockey, jump a puddle, or decide to go for a swim in the infield lake. The jockey may have a toothache or commit a terrible mistake, or the stewards may have or do the same.

Meanwhile, for all his trouble in researching the complexities of racing, the horseplayer is told that the state and the track will take away some 20 cents per dollar on straight win bets and that much and more on most combination bets like the exacta or big triple. That's a tough nut to overcome. Good handicapping and thorough research help, but sound money management is just as important (see Appendix A for pari-mutuel takeout percentages).

Whether you are a four-time-a-year novice or a once-a-week regular, the way you play your money at the track will determine whether you win or lose and how much you win or lose. Through skill, the odds can be turned to the player's favor, but it takes intelligent handling of betting capital to be in a position to take advantage. At 20 cents on the dollar, you can get wiped out pretty fast if you do not have a healthy respect for your money.

If you know something about two-year-old sprint racing but lack an understanding of stakes, claimers, or routes, it would be smart to concentrate your strongest bets on your specialty. If you use speed figures and know how to recognize a speed-figure standout, it would be foolish to bet the same amounts on races when you have no reason to be so confident. And if you do not know *what* you know, you should spend some time finding out.

Keep a record of your bets. Be honest with yourself.

Do you know how to spot a track bias when you see one? Do you have a feel for turf racing or stakes? Are claiming-class sprints easier than allowance-class routes? Do you have special insights about the winning and losing tendencies of the top trainers in your area? Perhaps you find it easy to narrow the field to live contenders but very difficult to separate the winner from the second- or the third-best horse. Can you pass up a race or an entire card, or must you have a bet every half-hour?

Asking questions like those above will do wonders for your profit-

and-loss statement. They will also bring to light the strengths and weaknesses in your game.

When I go unprepared to a strange racetrack, I do not bring very much money. Without the necessary insights about the track, the trainers, and all the other fundamentals that influence results, I am no more likely to win than thousands of other players in the crowd. I have my winning days at such racetracks—I do pay attention—but I have to be lucky and extremely cautious with my money.

When I prepare for a serious assault on a track, I do the research necessary to uncover any prevailing track bias and learn as much as I can about the trainers, jockeys, and horses I will be asked to compare. At most racetracks that kind of preparation takes about thirty to fifty hours of advance work, requires two hours of daily follow-up, and yields approximately one to three good bets a day; but that is not enough action for me and I know it.

Most racing fans, myself included, like something to root for in almost every race. It's tough to sit through a whole card waiting around for the ninth-race goodie. So most of the time I don't.

Instead, and as a concession to my personality, I separate my money into four different categories of wagers: Action Bets, Prime Bets, Reasonable Longshots and Promising Exotic Plays.

ACTION BETS. These bets exist because nothing would upset my concentration more than a $40 winner or a $300 exacta that I liked well enough to think about but didn't bet a dime. These bets rarely get more than a token play, and sometimes I will play one-way exactas keying my selection with two longshots, or my longshot with two favorites, or put up $36–$40 for the whole card and punch out a place nine ticket where that is offered, or commit to a series of three or four $5–$10 parlays involving horses I lightly prefer, but on which I do not wish to risk serious capital. I expect to lose some money on action bets, but they keep me in the race and provide peace of mind.

PRIME BETS. I have two very stiff requirements for a serious Prime Bet. When I think a horse deserves a 50 percent or better chance to win the race, I expect to be right at least 50 percent of the time. That's my first requirement. The second is a minimum payoff price of 8–5 ($1.60–$1.00 odds) or higher.

Fifty percent may seem to be an outrageously high win percentage, but with the tools and insights I have been detailing in this book, it is a reasonable goal in spot-play situations.

Clear-cut front-running types who seem likely to get to the rail on a severely biased, inside speed-favoring track will win at least 50 percent, as will horses in paceless fields who figure to get uncontested leads for the first time.

Jack Van Berg repeaters going up in class; fit Allen Jerkens—trained horses right back or stretching out in distance; Charlie Whittingham—trained Grade 1 horses with four or more weeks of impressive workouts; Billy Mott and Ron McAnally shippers and repeaters in Grade 1 and 2 stakes; Robert Frankel's imported turf runners dropping into high-class allowance races; Jerry Hollendorfer's first-timers with slow six-furlong works in northern California; and Richard Matlow's first timers in southern California generally win about 50 percent of the time with very little handicapping.

With the help of minor track classification codes, hidden class drop-downs in allowance races, Key Race notations, trainer patterns, clocker's comments, pace and race shape analysis, class pars, speed figures and track bias, anyone willing to put in the necessary research time can approach 50 percent spot-play winners. But if 35 percent is your upper limit, then you must adjust your minimum odds requirement to 3–1 or better.

The key to successful Prime Betting is to reserve serious play for situations when confidence is high *and* the payoff odds are greater than they should be—greater than the horse's chance to win the race *and* greater than your own average win percentage.

Yet beyond prime betting, which was the cornerstone to my own conservative gameplan for many years, I now focus much more attention on lucrative exactas, daily doubles, triples and trifectas, to be covered in the next chapter on *promising exotic plays*. Also I have begun to feel comfortable playing joint tickets with other good players in the Pick Six. In fact, about half of my serious wagering action now goes in the exotic pools, whereas it used to be less than 20 percent.

REASONABLE LONGSHOTS. In races where I have no Prime Bet, a reasonable longshot rates a serious winning chance, or embodies a compelling handicapping angle and goes to post at substantial odds. These horses may display positive breeding clues for distance racing or turf or off tracks, or give hints of dramatic improvement. They also may be logical, undervalued contenders in contentious races.

Maybe the horse flashed improved early speed or a mid-race move in a recent race and now is scheduled for an important equipment change, or a change of distance, or is switching to a new and stronger trainer or jockey. If so, a moderate win play or exacta combination may be in order.

I win money playing my reasonable longshots, because the angles are well researched and the odds are generally much higher than they should be. But, in good conscience, I cannot play them to the hilt for an important reason that goes to the heart of this game.

No bankroll should be put in the position of having to regularly cope with a long series of losses. While it is possible to win three, four, or five longshot plays in a row, you may lose 15–20 in succession just as easily.

To ferret out good plays, I try to make a pre-race estimate—or odds line on my preferred contenders—and will take into account late scratches and track bias information to formulate or adjust these probabilities. My intent is to know what odds to accept as a minimum wagering price.

For example, when Riva Ridge, winner of the 1972 Kentucky Derby, went to Pimlico two weeks later for the Preakness Stakes, it was a foregone conclusion that his overall record and TV popularity would make him a prohibitive odds-on favorite. A good morning line surely would have pegged him at 1–2. A good value line might have been willing to accept 4–5 as a fair estimate of his winning chances—that is, until the rains began to fall on the eve of the Preakness.

Riva Ridge was no mud runner, by any stretch of the term. He had already been beaten in the Everglades Stakes by a common sort named Head of the River and had always worked below par on sloppy tracks. A professional handicapper who knew that about Riva Ridge could hardly have made him anything but third choice in the Preakness to No Le Hace and Key to the Mint, two horses that eventually did finish in front of him (Bee Bee Bee won).

Three weeks later Riva Ridge tackled most of these horses again on a fast racetrack in the 1½-mile Belmont Stakes. A good value line on the race would have established the horse at even money or 4–5. There was nothing wrong with Riva Ridge. He was still in top form, far and away the best three-year-old in America. And he had trained brilliantly for the race. The only potential danger was Key to the Mint, who was on the comeback trail. With or without some fine-line handicapping of Key to the Mint's credentials (he worked much too fast for the race and, in a rare mistake for Elliot Burch, was somewhat short on distance preparation), the 8–5 post-time odds on Riva Ridge were a gift presented by national TV coverage of the Derby winner's horrible Preakness performance. Although horses are not robots, and it is dangerous to think that every race on paper will be run exactly to specifications in the flesh, there is money to be made betting the best horse in the race at generous odds. That is, in fact, the heart and soul of the game.

"If they ran this race 100 times, how many times would Riva Ridge win?" That's the kind of question that helps to establish the vaiue line. On Belmont's fast racetrack Riva Ridge seemed strong enough and fit enough to have at least 50 percent of the race all to himself. That's the kind of answer that sets up prime betting possibilities, and it happens every day.

On the other hand, the morning line—the odds posted on the tote board before the betting begins—is supposed to provide an estimate of the probable post-time odds for each horse in the race. In the days before pari-mutuel betting, the morning line was a matter of professional pride. If an operating bookmaker in the track's betting ring didn't make a first-class morning line, the best bettors in the crowd would pounce on his mistakes. In those days a good morning line had to have value. It had to reflect a balanced book of percentages and reflect the realities of the race at hand. Frankly, I envy the players who had a chance to play the game in the age of the trackside bookmaker. It must have been great fun.

Today at the racetrack, in the age of simulcasting and off-track betting, the morning line exerts an influence on the betting habits of uninformed bettors. Almost automatically the average horseplayer will include the top two or three morning-line choices in his double and exacta combinations. This has three predictable effects: (1) it tends to create lower double and exacta payoffs on morning-line choices regardless of their merits; (2) it forces higher payoffs on overlooked longshots; and (3) it sometimes helps to single out a betting stable's serious intentions with an otherwise lightly regarded horse.

Considering the reliability of depressed payoff possibilities for all morning-line choices in daily doubles and exactas the player can conclude with reasonable certainty that a longshot getting substantially greater play than his morning-line odds in these "blind" betting pools is getting play from informed sources. I know several professional handicappers who pay careful attention to the flow of money in daily doubles and exactas, and all of them say that the morning-line angle is fundamental to their calculations. Naturally, these players put their own money on the line only when a stable with a good winning history is involved.

Aside from such tote-board readings, most professional players assign their own realistic odds to each horse in the race. This has nothing to do with post-time odds.

At the bottom line, I am more interested in what I think the horses deserve to be and whether the odds offered are sufficiently higher than they should be. Author Barry Meadow in his instructive *Money Secrets at the Racetrack* recommends a minimum 50 percent overlay for each odds level for serious wagers, which is a good guideline to consider. My table of acceptable win pool odds for prime bets and reasonable long shots is very similar:

MY ESTIMATE OF TRUE ODDS			MINIMUM ACCEPTABLE PRICE
50 PERCENT ESTIMATED CHANCE (EVEN MONEY) A PRIME WIN BET SITUATION		=	$8–5 OR BETTER
45 percent	chance (6–5 proposition)	=	$ 9–5
42 percent	(7–5)	=	$ 2–1
40 percent	(3–2)	=	$ 5–2
38–36 percent	(8–5 and 9–5)	=	$ 3–1
33 percent	(2–1)	=	$ 7–2
28 percent	(5–2)	=	$ 4–1
25 percent	(3–1)	=	$ 9–2
22 percent	(7–2)	=	$ 5–1
20 percent	(4–1)	=	$ 6–1
18 percent	(9–2)	=	$ 8–1
16–14 percent	(5–1 and 6–1)	=	$10–1
12 percent	(8–1)	=	$12–1
10–09 percent	(10–1)	=	$20–1

To make a tight morning line, or value line, consult the partial list of percentages on the left column of the above betting chart, or see Appendix D for a complete list.

Morning lines are constructed with 117–125 total percentage points to provide a fudge factor for the takeout removed from each dollar wagered, but a "value line" should be made with 100 percentage points to reflect the mathematical possibilities in the race. As a general rule, I only make odds lines on races in which I have a confident or semi-serious handicapping opinion.

In some cases it will be impossible to assign a reasonable odds rating. A field of first-timers certainly presents more than a few question marks, as does a field of foreign grass runners competing on a dirt track. For each question-mark horse I tend to insist on slightly higher prices than the acceptable minimum for a playable selection and will consider using question-mark horses at fair odds in exacta combinations with a preferred choice if the option presents itself.

To refine these skills, I suggest periodic checking of your odds lines to the following criteria.

1. How often does your top percentage horse win versus your second top percentage horse, versus your third top percentage horse?
2. How often do your 50 percent horses win?
3. How often do your top three percentage horses go off at a price in excess of the wagering minimums, and would you show a theoretical profit or loss on them?

Making odds lines and comparing results is one of the best experimental designs to improve handicapping and wagering. At the same time, by keeping accurate wagering records you will be amazed how quickly you can reverse negative trends and gain a foothold on a winning season.

Overlays, incidentally, are not always desirable. Every once in a while I will accept a price lower than the recommended minimums, because the tote board is giving me reasons to revise my original handicapping estimate.

For instance, a well-bred, fast-working first-time starter from a good barn who attracts solid betting action may be a sharp contender in a field where the experienced horses have raced below par. On the other hand, the absence of betting activity would warn that the stable is not confident today. This clue is even more potent when a known betting stable is involved. Conversely, when the pedigree, stable and/or workouts are not exceptional, serious wagering activity takes on greater significance, as does the lack of betting activity in the following highly reliable tote board situation, which has been dubbed "dead on the board, dead on the track."

THE SITUATION: An obvious betting favorite has a few recent wins or generally excellent form and is entered in a seemingly easy spot. He towers over the opposition, but instead of getting bet down to 4–5 odds, or $1–1, he flirts with 2–1, or 5–2 odds. The player would do well to examine the rest of the field closely. Tepidly played standouts seldom win.

Promising Exotic Plays

During my formative years as a handicapper I learned to rank all contenders and keep an eye out for horses who hinted at potential improvement. I liked wagering on such horses, but soon realized that you can't play a steady diet of upset types into the teeth of solid contenders without paying a heavy toll. But you don't have to. Not when there are daily doubles, exactas, trifectas, pick threes and pick sixes in the betting mix.

The ability to recognize a promising exotic play is inseparable from learning how to distribute the wager properly. On one hand, it is necessary to recognize when prospects for success are reasonable. On the other, it is vital to know how best to take full advantage of the possibilities without getting too greedy or losing one's perspective. Sometimes I forget this and get overly aggressive, only to suffer the consequences, but the following guidelines are useful for regaining my equilibrium.

DAILY DOUBLES. While most players are willing to bet a few daily doubles as an opening ritual to the betting day, significant money can be made when there is:

- A very questionable morning line favorite in either race, accompanied by two, three or four promising contenders in both races
- A Prime Betting horse in either race
- A track bias favoring one specific running style, or cluster of post positions

- A clear-cut pace scenario in which the win contenders are readily identifiable and likely to benefit
- One or two legitimate longshot threats deserving more than action bet consideration in either race

To upgrade a daily double wager to Prime Bet status I still require an estimated 50 percent winning chance at better than 8–5 payoff odds as I measure the total wager in the double. Otherwise, when prospects are good for a large payoff with two or three reasonable contenders in each race, I might upgrade the total play to half of a prime betting unit.

Several preferred methods of distributing daily double wagers (and other exotic bets) are presented in Appendix D, including crisscross combinations, single-key, double-key and weighted plays.

EXACTAS. While much of what applies to daily doubles also applies to exactas, most players—including 20-year veterans—tend to misplay one of the most lucrative wagering options on the betting menu. The problem is easily corrected, but requires careful perception of the bet's main mission. Specifically, *to pick the winner and second-place finisher on the same pari-mutuel ticket.*

Please note that this does not mean picking the two best horses or the two most likely winners. Quite the contrary; the second-best horse or the second most likely winner is not always a good bet to finish second.

Consider, for instance, the scenario that involves two dueling rivals, both with the highest speed figures in the field. By mid-stretch one may assert superiority, while the other spits out the bit in defeat and fades to fifth. Moreover, the betting public almost is certain to overbet these two horses with similar win credentials in the exactas. It also is likely to overbet any exacta combination involving the top two morning line favorites.

Below is a restatement of the above exacta situation, along with several others to keep in mind.

- When a top-rated win candidate is a front runner, the most likely second-place horse is not the horse he has to defeat in a pace duel. It is more often the horse who can close ground late to pick up the pieces.

- In a race involving a solid, lone front-running type, the horse who figures to coast along in second for most of the journey is a poor threat to win, but a useful exacta companion. If the pace is soft, the stalker could be just as hard to catch.
- Horses with a high proportion of second- and/or third-place finishes are excellent candidates for the bottom slot in exactas (and trifectas). See Chapter 26 for several examples of the chronic second- and third-place finisher.
- Horses with competitive speed figures prepared by weak trainers or ridden by weak jockeys usually offer better value underneath, not on the top end of exactas. Ron Cox calls this a "bottom only" play.
- Similarly, a very sharp stretch runner on a track biased toward front-running speed or an extremely quick front runner on a stretch-running track are poor win risks, but they do offer occasional value in the second slot of exactas and trifectas.
- On any biased track and/or when the probable pace seems to favor a particular running style, the predominant exacta threats are modestly divided between top-rated horses running against the bias and talented, weak-win types who fit the bias or race shape.
- Playing three or four horses in an exacta box at equal strength is reasonable only when nearly equal contention runs that deep, or a prevailing bias or pace scenario is favoring one type of running style or post position cluster. Instead of trying to separate these "contenders," it might be best to use them all, or choose one and use it as a top and bottom exacta key with the others.
- Reasonable longshots, as described previously, invariably offer value in exactas, especially as companions top and bottom with a confident win selection. Good exacta players also know that the win pool sometimes offers more value than any combination of exacta plays.

  For instance, if you like the number one horse at 3–1 odds in the third race and believe there are three logical candidates to finish second—numbers two, three and four—then a series of three $2 exacta plays on the 1–2, 1–3, 1–4 combinations would cost $6. But why would you make this bet if each of the exacta payoffs were $25, $32 and $33, respectively, when a simple $6 win wager would return $24?

On the other hand, if the 1–2, 1–3, 1–4 exactas are $25, $47 and $51, respectively, it would make perfect sense to bet the 1–2 combination twice along with the 1–3, 1–4. This would set up minimum payoffs of $50, $47 and $51, respectively, against an $8 win bet that would return $32 at the stated 3–1 odds.

Various exacta wagering strategies, including some involving "double win keys" and others made in tandem with win plays, are in Appendix D, which also explains how to construct a morning line and how to compute approximate place and show payoffs.

TRIFECTAS. Most of the above daily double and exacta strategies should be applied to trifectas with a few provisos.

Trifectas can be dangerous to your health. They are more difficult to hit and generally more expensive to play than exactas. Yet they can offer huge bonus profits when played in tandem with exactas or win bets, especially when a betting principle I call "garbage time" is at work.

In professional basketball, garbage time occurs in the final minutes—after the game seems decided. This is when serious pro basketball bettors have heart attacks watching the "scrubs" screw up the outcome of a wager against the betting spread.

In horseracing, garbage time occurs when the race has been decided and second or third money is going to be won by default. This happens in many races, especially bottom-rock maiden claiming races and other wide-open affairs. Sometimes the chaos even determines the race winner. Of course, there is one benefit to be gleaned from this uncertainty: better trifecta payoffs.

If I find a race has narrow contention and favorable payoff possibilities, I will use any pool, including the trifecta, to get the most value out of the situation. But if I am deep into the exacta already, I will use the trifecta as an action-bet vehicle for a moon shot, or as a saver hedge against a wild upset, or I will play into the trifecta's tendency to offer inflated payoffs when chaos seems likely to determine the minor finishing positions. Among other things, I may spread out in the third position to include some longshot bombs with suspect credentials. By accepting the increased role of luck in the trifecta—especially in the minor finishing positions—I may not increase my win percentage, but I will increase my long-term profits.

The trick is to use trifectas strictly as profit boosters with minimum cash outlay, unless there is substantial reason to believe the race will be dominated by very few horses. Such races may be crushed by well-bankrolled players willing to buy multiple tickets on a few select combinations. Again, I refer you to Appendix D for more trifecta wagering strategies.

THE PICK THREE. Known also as the "daily triple," the pick three is an extended daily double involving three consecutive races. Logically it is more difficult to hit, but tends to offer increased payoffs compared to the added risk. This is partly due to the fact that the pari-mutuel takeout, which ranges from 17 to 25 percent in different states, is removed just once, not three times.

Certainly, inflated triple payoffs are likely when compared against most win parlays involving the same three winners. Nevertheless, it is imperative to consider the following simple points about playing the triple.

- Triple betting is an expensive waste of time if there is no added value to be gleaned from the total investment.
- If there is a Prime Bet possibility in one of the three races, it pays to reserve at least half of the Prime Bet for straight-win play *unless* confidence is so high and the likely triple payoffs are so inflated that no other choice seems reasonable.
- The best triple value occurs when there is a vulnerable odds-on betting favorite in one of the three aces, or two vulnerable morning line favorites in the three events.
- When no Prime Betting type is involved, the player should restrict triple betting to the same limits and expectations applied to any other promising exotic possibility or action bet.

PICK SIX. This six-race wager requires substantial capital to play correctly, and long losing streaks are inevitable. These are some other basic pick six realities:

- Except for a single $2 play on the luckiest day of your life, there is no reasonable chance of hitting a pick six with less than $48 invested.

- If you wager $48 on the pick six you may hit it when favorites win four, five or six races, or on the second luckiest day of your life.
- If you wager $48 on 100 pick sixes this year, you might cash a few consolation tickets and maybe you will catch one or two small fry, but you should expect to lose in excess of $2,400 for your efforts.
- You can increase your chances of cashing the pick six by investing your small sum as a token part of a pick six syndicate with your friends. This plays to the old adage that two percent of something is better than 100 percent of nothing.
- If you have shown success at daily doubles and daily triples, you might consider forming a pick six syndicate of your own.
- The one who forms the syndicate, or is designated in control, should make all final selections on the pick six ticket(s).
- No one who participates in a pick six syndicate should make a separate pick six play, simply because you do not want to be murdered in the parking lot by your friend who invested $1,000 and kindly let you in for $20. Or worse, you both hit the pick six to split the entire pool, which costs your friendly syndicate head $100,000, or so. The exception occurs when your friend does not object and you offer him in advance a sizable chunk of your winnings should you hit with your paltry bet.

Generally speaking, it takes about $30,000 to be properly capitalized for a sustained run at the pick six, and in many cases more than double that sum would make better sense. The reason is demonstrated by the escalating cost of pick six tickets for simple coverage of two, three, or four horses in each of the six races. Consider the cost of the following basic pick six tickets.

$$2 \times 2 \times 2 \times 2 \times 2 \times 2 = \quad 64 \quad \text{combinations @ \$2} = \$\ 128$$
$$3 \times 3 \times 3 \times 3 \times 3 \times 3 = \quad 729 \quad \text{combinations @ \$2} = \$1558$$
$$4 \times 4 \times 4 \times 4 \times 4 \times 4 = 4{,}096 \quad \text{combinations @ \$2} = \$8192$$

Okay, I have an experiment for you. Handicap the races at your favorite track for the next four days and make out hypothetical pick six tickets using four horses in each race. My guess is that you will not hit it once unless four or five favorites win, in which case you probably will not get back your $8,192—unless there is a gigantic carryover.

I also would guess that only a small percentage of players would hit it more than once in every five tries with this 4 × 4 format at a cost of $40,000+. When you are dealing with six consecutive races of all sizes and shapes, you will be shocked to see how many fifth-, sixth- and seventh-rated choices knock you out of the game.

Still, the bet does offer tremendous possibilities for serious players who understand how a pick six with carryover can be a gift from the racing game to the sharp, bankrolled player.

Steve Crist, who consistently hits 15+ percent of his pick six plays, offers these personal guidelines.

Said Crist: "When there is no carryover, I wager less than $500 on my pick six tickets. When there is a carryover of $50,000, I may increase my play to $1,000. When there is $100,000 or more I may increase my total investment to $2,500 and with a monster, $300,000 carryover to $1 million or more, I *might* go as high as $5,000, but that would be a stretch. I see no reason ever to play more. There's no rationale to pursue any pot if I can't hit it with a sensible sum."

My sensible sums stop at about $1,200 regardless of the situation, and I reach that level only rarely each year.

I want to play the pick six aggressively in only two clear-cut situations: I have capital to spare and believe I have 50 percent of the race covered by one or two horses in at least three races.

- No one hit the pick six yesterday, and there is a carryover of at least $50,000 going into today's pick six—preferably higher. On such days pick six players will be playing for the money on the table and the money left there from yesterday's pick six pool. While consolation payoffs are awarded for pick fives and/or pick fours in some locations, carryovers can nullify the takeout percentages completely.

  For example, a $50,000 carryover may produce another $50,000 in play today. The total net pool after takeout would be about $87,000. Thus today's players who did not feed the pool yesterday will be playing for more money than they bet. (In New York a $50,000 carryover would attract about $105,000 in play; in southern California, closer to $150,000.)

- In playing pick sixes, I strongly urge multiple tickets to cover top-rated selections and backups in three or four races, plus greater depth of coverage in the most wide-open races.

Distributing the bet among top-level contenders and backup selections is an art that requires practice. In the case of using "only $512," a pick six play involving two singles and several backups may include as many as 24 logical companion tickets to complete the play properly. A few sample pick six formats are included in Appendix D.

Otherwise, I strongly urge interested players who have pick six fever to master first the pick three and consult the recommended reading list, also in Appendix D. I assure you that is precisely the approach I have been taking toward my own pick six play.

As for managing your whole bankroll, it makes sense to wager according to your confidence in success. These are my guidelines:

PRIME BETS. A maximum of 5 to 8 percent of total betting capital for the meet per play; 8 percent reserved for superconfident plays in the midst of winning streaks; a maximum of three Prime Bets allowed per day at about (3–5 percent apiece), unless the first two Prime Bets win.

PROMISING EXOTIC PLAYS. A maximum of half the available Prime Betting unit, whether a separate win bet is made with the other half or not. These also include aggressive pick six plays made when there is a substantial carryover ($100,000 or more).

ACTION BETS. A maximum of 3 percent of total betting capital for the meet per day.

REASONABLE LONGSHOTS. Somewhere between an action bet and a Prime Bet. I generally allocate about one Prime Betting unit per day for possible play in this category.

Betting tends to be dangerous territory for most players, because it is easy to be seduced into thinking there is a reasonable longshot or a cinch favorite in five or six races per day, or certainly in the last race after eight straight losers.

Without keeping records, without understanding your own

strengths, and weaknesses, without making a private odds line, or setting up a balanced betting approach, a winning season is almost impossible.

For example, if my total available betting capital for the meet is $2,500, a Prime Bet would be $125–$175, depending on how well I have been doing at the meet and how much more than a 50 percent edge the horse or race situation offers. On that scale I would freely play the rest of the card with $75 on sensible longshots and contenders lacking Prime Betting qualifications, or on wild stabs, loose daily doubles and exactas, parlays to win, place, or show. As capital increases, or decreases, the amount of the bet changes but not the percentages.

I realize, of course, that not many racing fans can afford to put aside $2,500 to bet on horseraces. Not many should either. But the truth is many horseplayers lose that much and more in a season, and if you go to the racetrack regularly and want to improve your chances of success, you must take care to plan your betting activity along similar guidelines.

Whether your typical daily capital is $100 or you bring considerably more to the track, the point is to consolidate the power of your money on the races in which you have some insight.

Betting odds-on favorites is taking the worst of it. Betting a large percentage of your capital in the daily double or triple is a sure-fire way to put yourself in the hole to stay. Betting a disproportionate amount on any one race places too much emphasis on the luck factor. Doubling up your bet to "get even" on the last race is a way to triple your losses in track record time.

Every horseplayer has losing streaks. But there is no reason why a player should lose serious money during such streaks.

Losing three or four Prime Bets in a row is a warning sign, a sign to cut down all serious play until the problem is solved. Maybe you have lost touch with the track or have failed to note the presence of a hot trainer. Maybe you are bothered by personal problems, or a tough defeat has upset you more than you thought.

Take a day or two off. Go to a ballgame. Rediscover your family and friends. Watch TV, and if that doesn't work, try a few exercises in fundamentals.

Rather than trying to pick the race winner, try instead to pick the worst horse in the race or the horse most likely to be in front ten strides out of the gate. Check the past three days of racing. Has there been a subtle change in the bias? Has the bias disappeared? It happens.

These exercises can be fun, and like a baseball player who needs to take extra batting practice, you will find they help straighten out many a weakness. Try some of them, or invent others to suit your fancy. Lighten up. It's only a game.

La Prevoyante to Win, My Wife to Place

With the pick six, pick three, trifectas and other forms of exotic wagering, very few racing fans have been schooled in the finer points of place and show betting. While no argument will be presented here to suggest an emphasis on the minor payoff spots, there are times at the track when it pays handsomely to think second best.

In the early 1960s I remember being at a New York racetrack when so much money was bet on the mighty Kelso to win and so little was bet on him to place that he paid $2.40–$3.60–$2.40 across the board. By thinking win, and win only, the crowd in attendance that day offered one of the safest bets of modern times, an overlay of gigantic proportions. If Kelso was worth 20 cents on the dollar to win the race, which I will not debate, he was surely worth 80 cents on the dollar to finish second or better. It's doubtful Lloyds of London could have offered a better deal.

Of course, most racetrack crowds do not let such absurd situations occur every day, but I've seen enough $3.60 win, $4.00 place payoffs in my lifetime to give the tote board a close look before parting with my money. And if in truth I wasn't always careful to do that, my ex-wife, Laurie, gave me ample cause to do so a few years ago.

At Saratoga during the 1972 racing season Laurie thought it would be a good idea if she came out to the track to see Robyn Smith, a pretty tough cookie and one of the best female jockeys in America. My friend Andy Beyer and I traded in our two reserved seats plus a dollar for three seats together. Andy and I were enjoying a spectacular meeting but didn't know we were about to miss out on the easiest bet of the year.

During the first six races on the card Robyn won one and lost one; so did Laurie. Andy and I had won the one Robyn and Laurie lost and had lost the one they both had won. Not that we were prejudiced against female jockeys or anything; we just figured one race *right* and one race *wrong*. So the day went. Andy and I had shoved almost half a thousand through the windows to be plus $40 apiece. Laurie had bet maybe $8 and was ahead $50.

I wasn't depressed, far from it. I was glad to see her winning; maybe she would get hooked or something. After all, it would be nice to talk about horses with someone besides Andy. In any case, the point of this setting was the race on deck: the $50,000-added Spinaway Stakes.

La Prevoyante, undefeated and on her way to a two-year-old championship, was the odds-on favorite. Yet in spite of her unblemished record, neither of us thought she was very much horse. She had never run a truly fast race, and she had been beating up on the worst bunch of stakes-class juvenile fillies we had ever seen. She had beaten them pretty badly, though, and she figured to do so again; but there was a new challenger in the field—Princess Doubleday—a shipper from Chicago.

Although Princess Doubleday had finished last in her most recent race in the slop, she had raced strongly in Chicago throughout the summer, winning two races and finishing a close third in a stakes. After checking some out-of-town result charts to determine the quality of the Midwestern juvenile fillies and after one last review of the *Form*, Andy and I concluded independently that Princess Doubleday had a great chance to win the Spinaway at 40–1.

Now it isn't too often that a sound piece of handicapping turns up a 40–1 shot that should really be a solid second choice in the betting, and naturally we were excited. We didn't want to go overboard; we still knew that we had to beat an undefeated 1–5 shot. We each decided to make a maximum-limit action bet—$60—and with just five minutes to post Laurie returned from the saddling area to share in the good news. I was surprised by her response. "It all sounds great," she said, "but shouldn't you bet your money to place?" Almost instinctively my stomach grumbled its reply to this heresy. I agreed that it would certainly be safer to bet to place but patiently explained to her that since the money bet to place on a heavy favorite like La Prevoyante would be returned to her supporters in the place pool, she would deflate the place prices on every other horse in the race. I argued that the value of this longshot was only in the win pool.

"As it is," I said, "we have to beat a filly that has slaughtered her opposition half a dozen times just to win our bet. For us to get a big place price on Princess Doubleday, La Prevoyante would have to run third or worse. Besides," I added, "40–1 on this filly is a tremendous overlay." Convinced by my own logic, my stomach relaxed. Laurie said she understood my position but insisted we would be better off if we followed her advice.

By that time I began to feel that Laurie should have stayed out by the trees or gone to talk to Robyn. Shaking our heads in unison, Andy and I gave up on the talking and headed for the win windows. He went upstairs and I went downstairs.

At the windows, after I had traded serious money for pasteboard, a sudden impulse crossed by brain. I ran as fast as I could to the place line and just did get in a small bet before the bell rang. "And they're off," the PA system said. But I knew exactly what was going to happen.

La Prevoyante breezed to victory as Princess Doubleday rallied to get second money.

Back at the seats, we watched the prices go up on the board. La Prevoyante paid $2.80 to win, $3.00 to place, $2.60 to show. Princess Doubleday paid $15.20 in the middle—at least $6 more than an early reading of the tote board had indicated. Laurie didn't say a word, but just counted her money and smiled. Andy, I found out, had made the same play I had, and our impulsive saver wagers to place gave us each a slight profit on the race. But some fifteen minutes later, while scooping some of Saratoga's great homemade ice cream, I nearly choked on the reality of what had happened.

"We're both idiots," I screamed abruptly, causing Andy to spill his sundae on the floor. "Supposing we had been told La Prevoyante was a late scratch and wouldn't be in the Spinaway. What price would we then have made Princess Doubleday to beat the rest of that weak field? Even money? Seven to five? Well, by ignoring the place pool, by being so long-shot conscious, we just passed up the sweetest 6–1 prime bet of the year." We could have made an action bet on her to win and quadrupled the place bet with absolute confidence.

Strangely, my stomach never bothered me any longer while talking horses with Laurie even after we divorced 10 years later. And ever since that eye-opening experience I have had no trouble remembering to check the place and show pools very carefully. You just never know when the track is going to give it away.

Betting Myths and Longshot Angles

Sometimes the act of wagering on a horse is more than a simple process of translating one's own opinion into cash. At times it becomes a test of willpower. Tipsters, touts and the blinking lights on the tote board can exert an amazing influence on the rational decision-making process, and any player who doesn't have a basic knowledge of the reliability of these enticing sources of information will be busted out of the game every time.

There is such a thing as smart money, but it is not likely to be aligned with anyone who claims to know where it is going to be spent. Nor is it likely to be represented by the wildest bettors in the crowd. Although most players get caught up in the tidal wave of enthusiasm generated by strong late play on the tote, very few moves of that kind are worth any consideration. The major exceptions are:

1. A shipper
2. A first-time starter or absentee, especially one with modest workouts
3. A stable that has a history of such doings

Generally speaking, the winning potential of a horse that gets excessive play is logically limited to the winning capacity of the people behind it. Most often there will be ample clues in the past-performance profile to suggest an all-out performance. Certain trainers, however, such as Bennie Raub in southern California and J. P. Bernadini in New England, who generally have low profiles, rarely win a race unless the tote board says tilt.

Ivoreto
Own: S T D Racing Stable
FLORES D R (69 6 10 8 .09)

B. g. 4
Sire: Roberto (Hail to Reason)
Dam: Northeastern (Northern Dancer)
Br: Owens P T & N D (Ky)
Tr: Raub Bennie H (1 0 0 0 .00)

L 119

Lifetime Record :	5	1	0	1	$12,750					
1993	3	1	0	0	$8,250	Turf	0	0	0	0
1991	2	M	0	1	$4,500	Wet	0	0	0	0
Dmr Ⓣ	0	0	0	0		Dist Ⓣ	0	0	0	0

28Jly93-9Dmr	fst	1	$:22^3$	$:46^3$	$1:11^2$	$1:35^3$	3↑ Alw 36000N1X	61	5	7	8^5	$10^{6\frac{3}{4}}$	10^{14}	$10^{23\frac{3}{4}}$	Flores D R	LB 119	26.30	65-18	Sahara King119^5 Dixie Venture$119^{1\frac{1}{4}}$ Postponethedance$117^{\frac{1}{2}}$		10
Saddle slipped early																					
27Jun93-2Hol	fst	$7\frac{1}{2}$f	$:22^4$	$:45^1$	1:10	$1:29^1$	3↑ Alw 36000N1X	82	3	8	$4^{1\frac{1}{2}}$	$6^{2\frac{1}{2}}$	$6^{3\frac{3}{4}}$	$6^{3\frac{1}{4}}$	Flores D R	LB 119	27.40	85-13	Golden Slewpy115^{nk} Whata Boom$116^{2\frac{1}{2}}$ Skylaunch$119^{\frac{1}{2}}$	Off slowly, wide	8
12May93-6Hol	fst	7f	$:22^2$	$:45^2$	$1:10^4$	1:24	3↑ Md 25000	67	12	6	$6^{3\frac{1}{2}}$	$3^{2\frac{1}{2}}$	1^1	$1^{1\frac{3}{4}}$	Flores D R	L 122	2.90	84-08	Ivoreto$122^{1\frac{3}{4}}$ Allen's Hunter115^{no} Chocolate Kite115^5	Wide early	12
24Jly91-6Dmr	fst	$5\frac{1}{2}$f	$:21^2$	$:45^2$	:58	$1:04^4$	Md Sp Wt	71	7	11	$8^{6\frac{3}{4}}$	$7^{3\frac{3}{4}}$	$4^{2\frac{1}{2}}$	$3^{2\frac{3}{4}}$	Nakatani C S	LB 117	16.60	87-14	Roan Shark$117^{\frac{3}{4}}$ Mistery Kid117^2 Ivoreto117	Came on	11
22Jun91-7GG	fst	$5\frac{1}{2}$f	:21	$:43^3$	$:56^1$	$1:02^3$	Ladbroke Fut	30	2	7	7^{14}	7^{14}	7^{17}	$7^{21\frac{1}{2}}$	Gonzalez R M	LB 115	10.60e	78-10	Burnished Bronze117^3 Scherando117^6 Bigger Issues117	Off slowly	7

WORKOUTS: ●Aug 13 SLR tr.t 4f fst $:49^4$ H 1/7 Jly 22 SLR tr.t 6f fst $1:14^2$ H 5/7 Jly 10 SLR tr.t 5f fst $1:01^3$ H 2/12 ●Jun 22 SLR tr.t 4f fst $:48^2$ H 1/7 Jun 16 SLR tr.t 5f fst $1:03^3$ H 6/6 May 26 SLR tr.t 4f fst $:47^3$ H 2/8

Except for two specific situations, one described in the previous chapter and the other involving an insanely wild play by someone else in the crowd, it usually is a mistake to bet longshots in the place or show pool due to the compression of place and show prices when the betting favorite finishes in the money—which occurs about two out of three

EIGHTH RACE
Hollywood
JUNE 19, 1993

$1\frac{1}{16}$ MILES. (1.40) 28th Running of THE PRINCESS STAKES. Grade II. Purse $100,000 Added. Fillies, 3-year-olds. By subscription of $100 each which shall accompany the nomination, $1,000 additional to start with $100,000 added, of which $20,000 to second, $15,000 to third, $7,500 to fourth and $2,500 to fifth. Weight, 121 lbs. Non-winners of $30,000 twice at one mile or over since December 25, allowed 2 lbs. One such race in 1993 or $50,000 at a mile or over at any time, 4 lbs. $35,000 at any distance in 1993, 6 lbs. Starters to be named through the entry box by closing time of entries. Hollywood Park reserves the right not to divide this race. Should this race not be divided and the number of entries exceed the starting gate capacity; preference will be given to high weights based upon weight assigned as prescribed in the above conditions and an also eligible list will be drawn. Total earnings in 1993 will be used in determining the order of preference horses assigned equal weight. Failure to draw into this at scratch time cancels all fees. Trophies will be presentes to the winning owner, trainer and jockey. Closed Wednesday, June 9, with 10 nominations.

Value of Race: $106,000 Winner $61,000; second $20,000; third $15,000; fourth $7,500; fifth $2,500. Mutuel Pool $458,233.00 Exacta Pool $343,702.00

Last Raced	Horse	M/Eqt.	A.	Wt	PP	St	¼	½	¾	Str	Fin	Jockey	Odds $1
29May93 ^{8}Hol^2	Fit To Lead	LB	3	117	3	3	2^{hd}	2^2	2^6	1^1	1^{hd}	Delahoussaye E	4.20
29May93 ^{8}Hol^5	Swazi's Moment	B	3	115	5	4	4^{10}	4^8	$3^{2\frac{1}{2}}$	3^{hd}	2^{hd}	Stevens G L	5.00
5Jun93 ^{8}Hol^5	Passing Vice	LB	3	119	4	5	5	5	5	4^{25}	3^8	Desormeaux K J	15.30
30Apr93 ^{9}CD^2	Eliza	LB	3	119	1	1	1^1	$1^{1\frac{1}{2}}$	1^2	$2^{3\frac{1}{2}}$	4^{31}	Valenzuela P A	0.30
29May93 ^{8}Hol^8	Zoonaqua	LB	3	119	2	2	$3^{3\frac{1}{2}}$	3^4	4^2	5	5	McCarron C J	19.10

OFF AT 5:19 Start Good. Won driving. Time, $:22^3$, $:45^2$, $1:09^2$, $1:35^4$, $1:42^2$ Track fast.

$2 Mutuel Prices:

3-FIT TO LEAD	10.40	4.60	30.40
5-SWAZI'S MOMENT		5.20	31.80
4-PASSING VICE			51.40

$2 EXACTA 3-5 PAID $44.40

Dk. b. or br. f, (May), by Fit to Fight–Islands, by Forli. Trainer Mandella Richard. Bred by Laura Leigh Stable (Ky).

FIT TO LEAD, near the early pace, responded on the far turn when asked to go after the leading ELIZA, was under steady left handed pressure all the way down the stretch, took the lead approaching the furlong marker, drew well clear between calls nearing the sixteenth marker, then held on to narrowly prevail. SWAZI'S MOMENT, outrun early, propped to break stride approaching the half mile pole, closed strongly in the stretch but could not quite get up. PASSING VICE lagged far back early, raced along the inner rail through the final quarter, also closed strongly in the stretch but also could not quite get up. ELIZA, away alertly, established the early pace, was keen to go on around the clubhouse turn, could not put away FIT TO LEAD on the far turn, relinquished the lead to that opponent approaching the furlong marker and faltered in the final furlong. ZOONAQUA, near the early pace, stopped badly, lost contact aftear going six furlongs, entered the stretch four wide and was not persevered with in the stretch when hopelessly beaten.

Owners— 1, Colbert & Hubbard & Sczesny; 2, Gordy Berry; 3, Iron County Farms Inc; 4, Paulson Allen E; 5, Moss Mr & Mrs J S

Trainers—1, Mandella Richard; 2, Rash Rodney; 3, Lewis Craig A; 4, Hassinger Alex L Jr; 5, Mayberry Brian A

times. An example of a rare but lucrative exception occurred at Hollywood Park in June 1993 when a sizable sum was dumped on Juvenile champion Eliza in the show pool to cause completely wacko show payoffs when Eliza ran fourth.

I have made a few winning plays into more modest situations, where the payoffs on 3–1 shots in the win pool eventually paid $10–$15.00 to show, but I once made a play into a pool that promised to top the Eliza payoffs and lived to tell about it. The situation involved the great filly Ruffian, whom we met in Chapter 1. The occasion was the 1974 Spinaway Stakes, and I bet $200 to place on Laughing Bridge, who was clearly the second-best filly in the field. Why? Because a "bridge jumper" bet about $90,000 to place on Ruffian to distort the pools and Ruffian came out on the racetrack dripping with sweat, acting completely nuts.

Her behavior led me to believe she might go off form, and if this proved the case, the place payoffs would be astronomical. So, with the bet in, I watched Ruffian every step of the way through my 7 × 50s and was blown away by what I saw when she saw the starting gate moments before the race.

Jockey Jacinto Vasquez merely pointed her toward her starting stall, and Ruffian's ears went straight up in the air as if they had been coiled by a hot iron. Into the gate she went smooth as silk.

Bang, the gates opened and Ruffian jumped out of there like the proverbial bat out of you know where. She was gone before the first dozen strides, the easiest kind of winner, and I was forced to settle for an embarrassing $2.10 place on the ever present Laughing Bridge, who finished 13 lengths behind. But it was the right play then, as it would be today if given another inflated place or show pool.

There are other nuances to the game that crop up from time to time, many lessons to be learned, many traps awaiting the reckless or overly conservative player. What follows are several facts of racetrack life that every handicapper should find profitable to think through and recognize.

For instance, the average racetrack crowd can be counted on to seriously overbet horses whose past performances resemble those below. Experienced horseplayers have a pet name for such horses. They call them "sucker" horses, and the term applies equally to the players who bet on them.

It is important not to be a sucker twice with horses like the ones on the following pages. While they may be terrible win-bet risks, you should

Rumored Affair
Own: Semer Tamara G
JENKINS D C (379 59 49 60 .16) $1,500

B. g. 4
Sire: Elocutionist (Gallant Romeo)
Dam: Dangerous Damsel (Irish Castle)
Br: Jones Brereton C (Ky)
Tr: Semer John R (216 34 26 30 .16)

LB 118

Lifetime Record: 30 1 4 8 $6,474
1993 12 0 3 3 $1,970 | Turf 0 0 0 0
1992 18 1 1 5 $4,504 | Wet 10 0 1 1 $1,360
Mnr Ⓣ 0 0 0 0 | Dist Ⓣ 0 0 0 0

11Jly93-3Mnr fst 140 :231 :463 1:131 1:443 3+ Clm 1500N2L 27 6 6 611 510 52¾ 46¾ Jenkins D C LB 118 f 7.40 74-13 Taxatana118¾ Joey's Courage1212 Whipsnade1184 Wide trip 8
13Jun93-7Mnr fst 140 :24 :48 1:131 1:431 3+ Clm 1500N2L 24 4 7 86¾ 69 54½ 59¼ Bender P H LB 120 f 3.00 78-06 Percy114¾ Shotgun Shane118nk Dayton Trip1181½ No factor 9
5Jun93-3Mnr fst 170 :231 :47 1:133 1:45 3+ Clm 1500N2L 33 8 9 89¾ 74¼ 51½ 36½ Bender P H LB 120 f *2.70 81-10 Bronson Buck1195 Feisty Noble1151½ Rumored Affair1201 Too late 10
20May93-10Mnr fst 140 :232 :47 1:122 1:421 3+ Clm 1500N2L 37 2 6 610 68 37 212 Bender P H LB 119 f 5.10 81-18 ShrpenOrnmnt11812 RumordAffir1193½ EclipsTwo1182½ Swung wide drive 9
2May93-2Mnr fst 140 :244 :462 1:133 1:432 3+ Clm 1500N2L 30 3 4 44½ 43 2½ 24 Bender P H LB 119 f 2.40 83-09 ProvocativeBidder1214 RumoredAffir1192½ PrtyHuntr1212 Loomed,hung 6
24Apr93-3Mnr fst 170 :252 :492 1:15 1:463 3+ Clm 1500N2L 37 2 5 55 23 2hd 21 Gordon D J LB 118 f 11.20 79-24 Real Plastic1181 RumoredAffair1182 ComancheTribe118hd Sharp,missed 10
4Apr93-7Mnr gd 1 :261 :52 1:172 1:452 3+ Clm 1500N2L 14 3 5 53 56½ 57 411 Gordon D J LB 118 f 4.90 48-36 Big Tom1198 E. J.'s Fun1181 After Ralph1182 No factor 8
21Feb93-10Mnr my 1 :243 :483 1:133 1:41 3+ Clm 1500N2L 19 2 6 65¾ 45½ 57 513 Markham R L Jr LB 119 *2.80 68-11 Cheval's Cinteelo1211 Ott's Pride1182 E. J.'s Fun1182 No mishap 9
8Feb93-5Mnr gd 6f :234 :482 1:013 1:16 3+ Clm 1500N2L 16 10 6 106 913 910 810 Markham R L Jr LB 120 *2.70 57-28 Kid Sizzle118½ Canes Romance1182 Kirkenriola118hd Dull form 10
22Jan93-3Mnr sly 140 :252 :504 1:17 1:483 Clm 1500N2L 38 7 3 43½ 34 21½ 31½ Markham R L Jr LB 118 4.40 59-38 Lin's Troublemaker121hd Playhall1181½ Rumored Affair1181 Hung, drive 8

Bad Boy Willy
Own: Collins William G
ROCCO J (173 24 33 29 .14)

Ch. c. 3 (Mar)
Sire: Contare (Naskra)
Dam: Knight's Gold (Gold and Myrrh)
Br: Collins & Cox (Md)
Tr: Bailes W Robert (28 4 4 6 .14)

L 115

Lifetime Record: 12 M 7 1 $27,115
1993 12 M 7 1 $27,115 | Turf 1 0 0 0 $300
1992 0 M 0 0 | Wet 1 0 1 0 $3,465
Lrl 7 0 5 0 $17,250 | Dist 2 0 2 0 $6,510

16Jly93-7Lrl fst 6f :224 :463 :591 1:114 3+ Md Sp Wt 62 1 10 1010 98½ 75 42¾ Rocco J 115 f *2.30 78-17 Lord Gordon1151 Oliver Witha Twist1151½ Penalty Time115no Wide 11
27Jun93-11Lrl fst 7f :232 :472 1:131 1:254 3+ Md Sp Wt 57 1 7 13 12½ 21 25 Delgado A L 113 *3.30 75-13 Laughteristhekey1145 Bad Boy Willy113no Arab General1222 Weakened 9
10Jun93-5Lrl fm 1⅛ Ⓣ :454 1:101 1:354 1:483 3+ Md Sp Wt -0 2 1 21 710 730 850¾ Delgado A L 113 2.70 36-17 Geewhillikins1233½ Hamr It1134¾ Judge Connelly11417 Faltered 9
29May93-6Pha fst 170 :223 :472 1:14 1:453 Md Sp Wt 56 8 2 22 21½ 21½ 31½ Delgado A L 122 *2.90 66-26 Northern Sur122½ Dancing Douglas1221 BadBoyWilly1224 Flattened out 10
6May93-7Pim fst 6f :232 :464 :584 1:112 3+ Md Sp Wt 58 4 4 53¾ 32 45 47¾ Delgado A L 113 f *1.20 80-13 Thaumaturge1122 DancingDougls1121½ KingBishopQuest1084½ Weakened 8
16Apr93-10Pim sly 1 1/16 :233 :481 1:141 1:483 3+ Md Sp Wt 66 9 4 44 31 1hd 2½ Delgado A L 113 fb 2.40e 61-35 Primary Space114½ Bad Boy Willy113nk Busy Me1123 Wide 9
3Apr93-5Pim fst 1 1/16 :23 :463 1:124 1:464 3+ Md Sp Wt 71 8 3 32½ 1½ 2hd 2½ Delgado A L 113 fb *1.30 70-23 Age Group Jogger124½ Bad Boy Willy1134 Basque's Ad124nk Gamely 10
11Mar93-6Lrl fst 1 1/16 :233 :47 1:131 1:462 Md Sp Wt 62 4 1 1½ 13 13 23½ Delgado A L 120 b *.80 74-26 Smarten Up Dummy1203½ Bad Boy Willy1205½ Shwing1203 Erratic stretch 7
25Feb93-4Lrl fst 1 1/16 :244 :492 1:142 1:46 Md Sp Wt 75 6 2 2hd 1hd 2hd 2½ Delgado A L 120 b 6.90 79-18 ModernTroubadour120½ BdBoyWilly1208½ GoldenFlcon120hd Drifted wide 7
11Feb93-7Lrl fst 6f :231 :463 :582 1:104 Md Sp Wt 58 4 8 53 56½ 610 515¼ Delgado A L 120 b 4.60 71-23 Montbrook12013 The Joker's Parade120hd Crumpton1201½ Drifted stretch 13

WORKOUTS: Jly 12 Bow 4f fst :491 B 1/3 ● Jly 5 Bow 3f fst :344 H 1/6 ● Jun 23 Bow 3f fst :35 H 1/4 Jun 18 Bow 3f fst :372 B 2/10 Jun 5 Bow 4f my :49 B 4/22 May 26 Bow 3f fst :38 B 2/5

Azul Cielo
Own: Grum Janelle
BOREL C H (192 42 29 24 .22)

B. c. 4
Sire: Conquistador Cielo (Mr. Prospector)
Dam: Bullet Bonnet (Gallant Romeo)
Br: John Coates & Kennelot Stables Ltd. (Ky)
Tr: Borel Cecil P (34 3 7 5 .09)

L 116

Lifetime Record: 17 1 7 3 $37,986
1993 8 0 4 1 $16,080 | Turf 2 0 0 1 $1,608
1992 9 1 3 2 $21,906 | Wet 1 0 1 0 $2,800
LaD 9 0 6 2 $20,458 | Dist 2 0 2 0 $5,560

10Jly93-9LaD sly 6f :22 :453 :584 1:114 3+ Alw 14000N2L 81 1 6 612 69 52½ 2hd Borel C H L 116 *2.00 89-13 South's Rising111hd Azul Cielo1163 Papa Secreto1164 Wide 6
2Jly93-7LaD fm *1 1/16 Ⓣ :23 :473 1:114 1:43 Alw 14000N1X 60 10 10 1018 1014 610 56½ Borel C H L 115 *2.40 83-10 Amzi1152½ Dancey Dan115½ Twic Chairman1152½ Belated rally 10
9Jun93-1LaD fst 1 1/16 :232 :464 1:12 1:47 3+ Alw 14000N2L 60 6 6 616 69½ 23 21 Guillory D L 118 4.00 79-20 Fair American1181 Azul Cielo1182 Prince Reality118nk Rallied 7
26May93-9LaD fst 170 :241 :491 1:142 1:441 Alw 14000N2L 66 6 5 52½ 41 32 31½ Guillory D L 112 3.30 80-17 Kritso115nk Prince Reality1151 Azul Cielo112½ Rallied 7
25Apr93-1LaD fst 6½f :232 :471 1:121 1:184 Alw 14000N2L 60 3 5 64¾ 67 44½ 24 Borel C H L 115 *1.00 84-17 Fight For Peace1154 Azul Cielo115nk Drozdowski1151 4 Wide 5/16 7
7Mar93-6OP fst 1 1/16 :233 :47 1:122 1:45 Alw 23000N1X 66 7 9 911 108¾ 1010 1011 Borel C H L 114 6.00 65-17 Halo Tune1141 Annihili1141 Brite Speculation1174 Forced in 12
20Feb93-6OP fst 6f :213 :452 :574 1:102 Alw 22000N2L 70 6 8 86¾ 86¼ 63½ 43¼ Borel C H L 116 3.20 84-12 Come On Tater1161½ Bold Investor1161½ NeverSpeaking116nk Five wide 1/4 9
6Feb93-5OP fst 6f :22 :46 :583 1:103 Alw 22000N2L 78 3 5 78½ 78 53½ 23½ Borel C H L 115 *2.80 82-16 Chris'theatrical1153½ Azul Cielo1151 Come On Tater115½ Four wide 1/4 8
11Oct92-7LaD fm *1 1/16 Ⓣ :232 :481 1:13 1:44 3+ Alw 10800 71 8 4 41 1hd 2½ 32½ Borel C H L 113 5.30 77-19 Temperence Classic1121½ Happy Birthday Dad1071 Azul Cielo113 4 wide 10
27Sep92-7LaD fst 6f :221 :452 :58 1:111 3+ Alw 13800 74 7 8 1013 1014 616 22 Lovelace A K L 118 *1.10 90-09 Cicle Pod1072 Azul Cielo1182 Detroit Steel112 5 wide 1/4 10

WORKOUTS: Jun 5 LaD 4f fst :493 B 7/28 May 21 LaD 5f fst 1:022 B 13/24 May 8 LaD 4f fst :483 H 7/29 Apr 22 LaD 4f fst :502 B 10/14 Apr 12 OP 6f fst 1:151 H 3/4 Apr 3 OP 6f fst 1:18 B 11/11

Howeasyis
Own: Haller Jeffrey
VIVES J C (435 46 73 55 .11) $2,500

B. g. 4
Sire: Quick Painter (Speed Syndrome)
Dam: Della Dear (Delaware Chief)
Br: Haller Ralph F Jr (Pa)
Tr: Minnich Clarence H (260 27 35 35 .10)

117

Lifetime Record: 23 1 5 3 $8,528
1993 9 0 2 3 $3,583 | Turf 0 0 0 0
1992 12 1 3 0 $4,945 | Wet 3 0 0 0
Pen 23 1 5 3 $8,528 | Dist 14 1 3 2 $6,294

16Jly93-7Pen fst 6f :223 :47 1:004 1:133 3+ Clm 2500N2L 40 2 9 74½ 54½ 31½ 34½ Vives J C 117 b 4.60 73-18 Caveat's Tune1173¾ Reef112¾ Howeasyis1172 No excuse 10
9Jly93-10Pen fst 5½f :223 :47 :594 1:061 3+ Clm 4000N2L 35 2 5 61¾ 67½ 56½ 67 Vives J C 117 b 9.20 79-13 Keeperoftheflame113½ Choice Prize1172½ Mikerusscope114no No factor 8
21Jun93-8Pen sly 170 :234 :481 1:133 1:454 3+ Clm 3500N2L 23 3 2 22 57 511 615¾ Vives J C 115 b 10.90 61-23 Jungly1161 Track Buff1171 Fortunate Chief1176 Gave way 8
6Jun93-1Pen fst 6f :223 :464 1:002 1:142 3+ Clm 4000N2L 37 6 1 23 23½ 35 43¼ Vives J C 117 b 11.30 71-21 Summer Concerto114nk Trap Jaw116¾ Track Buff1172½ Weakened 8
26May93-6Pen fst 6f :222 :462 :59 1:12 3+ Clm 4000N2L 21 8 9 86¾ 98¾ 911 514¼ Vives J C 117 b *2.80 71-15 R. D.'s Magic1173 Dotsa's Dancer1148 Track Buff1143½ Outrun 10
10May93-1Pen fst 6f :224 :464 :593 1:13 3+ Clm 6000N2L 41 3 3 2hd 3nk 32 23¾ Vives J C 117 b 4.70 77-15 Mariachi1173¾ Howeasyis1172 Hal O. Weenie1142 Second best 6
24Apr93-4Pen fst 5½f :221 :471 1:004 1:072 3+ Clm 4000N2L 33 6 2 35 34½ 31½ 2no Vives J C 117 b 1.90 80-17 Burning Sensation114no Howeasyis117hd Springhouse1165½ No excuse 6
14Apr93-1Pen fst 6f :223 :47 :594 1:132 3+ Clm 4000N2L 36 5 1 56 41¾ 44 36 Vives J C 117 b 11.80 73-18 Kerzan1175 R. D.'s Magic1171 Howeasyis1172¾ Weakened 6
3Apr93-4Pen gd 5½f :23 :471 :594 1:07 Clm 4000N2L 23 1 3 42½ 45½ 410 312½ Vives J C 117 b 6.50 69-24 Trackable1162½ R. D.'s Magic11710 Howeasyis1173 No menace 5
1Jly92-1Pen fst 5½f :223 :463 :592 1:06 Clm 6500 20 4 8 710 812 811 712½ Deibler C E III 116 b 28.30 78-16 Mokele1224 Dominicks No No No116hd Power Lord109 No factor 8

Granite Island
Own: Flying Zee Stable

NO RIDER (—)

Ch. f. 3 (Apr)
Sire: Say I'm Smart (Clev Er Tell)
Dam: Reality Island (In Reality)
Br: Flying Zee Stables (NY)
Tr: Zemp Elizabeth M (—)

111

Lifetime Record : 11 M 9 1 $15,512

1993	11	M	9	1	$15,512	Turf	0	0	0	0	
1992	0	M	0	0		Wet	3	0	3	0	$3,724
Dmr	0	0	0	0		Dist	5	0	4	1	$9,548

27Jly93-9FL	fst	$5\frac{1}{2}$f	$:22^4$	$:47^2$	$1:01^1$	$1:07^3$	3↑ ⒻMd Sp Wt	50	4	2	$3^{2\frac{1}{2}}$	3^3	$3^{1\frac{1}{2}}$	2^1	Davila J R Jr	115	*2.80	76-23	Zephyr's Promise122^1 Granite Island$115^{6\frac{3}{4}}$ Timed Approach$122^{1\frac{1}{2}}$	Gaining	9
17Jly93-11FL	fst	6f	$:23^2$	:48	$1:01^3$	$1:14^3$	3↑ ⒻⓈMd Sp Wt	44	2	3	$3^{\frac{1}{2}}$	2^2	2^4	2^6	Davila J R Jr	115	3.50	67-25	Carruler115^6 Granite Island$115^{2\frac{1}{2}}$ Timed Approach122^{nk}	No match	8
3Jly93-10FL	fst	6f	$:22^3$	$:46^3$	$1:00^4$	$1:14^2$	3↑ ⒻⓈMd Sp Wt	28	1	4	$5^{5\frac{1}{2}}$	$6^{6\frac{1}{4}}$	3^8	2^7	Salinas P L	115	*2.10	67-22	MkinMelody115^7 [D]GrniteIslnd115^5 ChlsCov122^{hd}	Bumped rival 1/4 pole	10
Disqualified and placed third																					
19Jun93-7FL	fst	6f	:23	$:47^4$	$1:01^2$	$1:15^2$	3↑ ⒻⓈMd Sp Wt	36	5	6	$7^{6\frac{1}{2}}$	$4^{2\frac{1}{4}}$	$2^{2\frac{1}{2}}$	2^2	Salinas P L	114	2.50e	67-28	Lojakono114^2 Granite Island114^{nk} Carruler114^4	Good energy	9
5Jun93-6FL	sly	6f	$:23^2$	$:48^2$	1:03	$1:15^2$	ⒻⓈMd Sp Wt	44	7	2	3^2	$4^{4\frac{1}{2}}$	2^3	$2^{\frac{3}{4}}$	Salinas P L	120	3.10	68-29	Purple Mist$120^{\frac{3}{4}}$ Granite Island120^2 A. M. Arrival$120^{2\frac{1}{2}}$	4 Wide trip	11
30May93-1FL	fst	1	$:25^2$	$:50^1$	$1:17^3$	1:47	3↑ ⒻMd Sp Wt	36	6	3	3^1	$2^{1\frac{1}{2}}$	2^3	$2^{3\frac{3}{4}}$	Nicol P A Jr	113	*1.10	48-37	Wolf Tree$114^{3\frac{3}{4}}$ Granite Island113^1 Lacka Reason113^5	No match	6
16May93-9FL	fst	6f	$:23^1$	$:47^4$	$1:00^2$	1:13	ⒻⓈAlw 13000N$Y	40	1	5	4^3	$4^{4\frac{1}{2}}$	$3^{7\frac{1}{2}}$	$2^{11\frac{1}{2}}$	Nicol P A Jr	112	14.90	69-24	OurShoppingSpree111^{11} GraniteIslnd112^3 Cssie'sHome$113^{2\frac{3}{4}}$	Second best	5
12May93-7FL	fst	1	$:25^2$	$:49^4$	$1:15^3$	$1:44^1$	3↑ ⒻⓈMd Sp Wt	24	6	6	5^5	$5^{5\frac{1}{4}}$	$5^{6\frac{1}{2}}$	$5^{11\frac{1}{2}}$	Rohena J M	113	2.90	54-39	It's A Lulu122^1 Carra Mia$122^{7\frac{1}{2}}$ Corporate Crime122^{hd}	No threat	6
1May93-8FL	fst	1	$:24^1$	$:48^2$	$1:14^1$	$1:41^4$	3↑ ⒻⓈMd Sp Wt	34	6	5	3^3	$3^{4\frac{1}{2}}$	$2^{5\frac{1}{2}}$	2^7	Rohena J M	113	3.90	71-20	Queen Of The Waves114^7 Granite Island$113^{1\frac{1}{2}}$ Carra Mia$122^{2\frac{1}{2}}$	No match	7
17Apr93-6FL	sly	$4\frac{1}{2}$f	:23	$:48^2$		:55	3↑ ⒻⓈMd 15000	29	6	4	4^5		4^7	2^7	Rohena J M	112	3.60	76-15	ZiptoTheNorth112^7 GrniteIslnd112^{nk} [D]EndO'Innocenc112^1	Up for place	8

not be suckered into ignoring them in the second and third positions in exactas and trifectas.

Another sucker play is to expect a horse who closes ground in a sprint to do even better when stretched out to a two-turn route. As discussed in the section on running style and the distance factor, most late-moving sprinters will be closer to the pace in slower, longer-paced routes, and only true routers will show anything approaching their previous punch when stretched out. True routers usually are bred to go longer, or have proven talent at similar distances. Moreover, the most reliable sprint-to-route type will get two sprint preps for his route try, not one.

It also is a big mistake to assume that all horses who have flashed early zip only to fade out of contention are "quitters," or incapable of carrying their speed longer distances. Actually, such horses are likely to have an easier time taking control of the slower pace normally associated with a longer route, which can lead to longshot mutuels. Yet, as we saw in the Desert Boots illustration in Chapter 9, horses who consistently fail to hold their speed under optimium conditions are notorious money burners.

The player should appreciate that such money burners have physical or mental problems and will quit even at perfect distances, unless the trainer finds the new key in Lasix, or blinkers, or perhaps even surgery. (Although hardly a quitter, Tank's Prospect had an operation to remove a loose flap of skin from his throat in April 1985, and the difference in the horse's breathing helped him win the Arkansas Derby and Preakness Stakes. In 1987, Alysheba had the same operation to remove a "trapped epiglottis" and suddenly became a wonder horse.)

Keep in mind that a severe front runner's track bias can promote even a stone-cold "quitter" into the winner's circle practically against his will. I love playing horses who have stopped badly in prior races who now figure to get a ride on a track playing like a conveyor belt.

While good players rightfully downgrade horses trained by low-percentage trainers, it is important to note the exceptions:

- Research performed by Ron Cox in northern California and Clem Florio in Maryland has shown that horses with off-track pedigrees and/or positive wet-track racing records frequently outperform weak trainer stats on their favorite racing surface.
- Trainers who have poor win percentages overall yet have good form with a particular horse deserve no demerits with the horse they know how to handle. Trainer Arlene Blake below has a win, two seconds and a third in seven tries with Patchin Lil; she is zip for eight with no seconds and one third with the rest of her stable.

Patchin Lil
Own: Blake Arlene
FAINE C (173 8 14 11 .05) $3,000

Ch. m. 5
Sire: Not Surprised (His Majesty)
Dam: Prissis Pebble (Precision)
Br: Huber Mrs T (NY)
Tr: Blake Arlene (15 1 2 2 .07)

122

Lifetime Record:	30	4	5	3	$16,851						
1993	7	1	2	1	$3,516	Turf	0	0	0	0	
1992	15	2	3	2	$7,033	Wet	5	1	2	0	$3,676
FL	30	4	5	3	$16,851	Dist	7	1	3	0	$4,143

10Jly93- 5FL	fst	1	:242	:49	1:151	1:43	3↑ ⒻClm 3000N2Y	44	4	7	67½	56¼	48	38¾	Faine C	122 f	6.10	63-26	Dead Ender1166 Shrill Delight1192¾ Patchin Lil122½	Mild gain	7
22Jun93- 6FL	fst	1	:243	:491	1:162	1:444	3↑ ⒻClm 3000N1Y	41	2	6	47½	56	22	11	Faine C	120 f	*2.30	63-28	Patchin Lil1201 Papa's Peanut1201 Heres A Hug Cindy1204	Driving	10
12Jun93- 3FL	fst	170	:241	:493	1:16	1:50	3↑ ⒻClm 3000N1Y	45	5	6	64¼	65¼	24	2nk	Faine C	120 f	6.10	59-36	Jan's Jamel120nk Patchin Lil1204 Papa's Peanut1203	Rallied	10
4Jun93- 9FL	fst	1	:244	:494	1:174	1:454	3↑ ⒻClm 3000N1Y	45	1	9	88¼	44½	24	24½	Faine C	120 f	23.20	53-41	Alice Arden1204½ Patchin Lil1209 Fruit Cocktail1205	Best of rest	10
19May93- 4FL	fst	170	:243	:492	1:153	1:492	3↑ ⒻClm 3000N2Y	34	3	6	78½	68¼	67½	412	Faine C	116 f	16.00	50-40	Kite1163 Twenty Flags1224 Fruit Cocktail1165	No threat	8
5May93- 7FL	fst	1	:234	:471	1:131	1:411	3↑ ⒻⓈClm 8000N1Y	-0	3	5	68½	617	618	635¼	Faine C	116 f	14.80	46-19	Vivacite1161¾ Who's Sue Z. Q.1163½ Kite1162½	Showed little	6
16Apr93- 6FL	sly	4½f	:222	:47		:532	3↑ ⒻClm 5000N1Y	26	3	6	67¾		510	610	Faine C	116 f	32.90	81-09	Steve's Lucky Lady1161 Lace Of Love1165 Anguilla Miss116no	Outrun	7
29Nov92- 8FL	my	170	:234	:484	1:15	1:473	3↑ ⒻClm 3000N3L	46	-3	8	66½	2hd	2hd	13	Faine C	116	3.40	69-31	Patchin Lil1163 Heroic Thunder1141 Big Book12012	Drew off	10
17Nov92- 6FL	fst	1	:234	:48	1:134	1:394	3↑ ⒻClm 3000	44	6	10	65¾	47	36	39¼	Faine C	116	6.00	76-17	Bad Debt1166 Parisian Breeze1193¼ Patchin Lil116	Finished well	10
6Nov92-10FL	sly	170	:232	:483	1:142	1:50	3↑ ⒻClm 3000	42	5	7	45	36	22½	21	Faine C	116	3.40	56-33	Fast One1161 Patchin Lil1165 Summerset Miss116	Good energy	8

WORKOUTS: Apr 25 FL 4f fst :50 B 6/30 Apr 7 FL 3f fst :382 B 33/67

- There is no percentage in playing horses in good form who go from a winning to a losing trainer. Very few of these horses retain their sharpness for more than a few days or a week. The vast majority of these negative barn-switch types follow Murphy's most important law of ineptitude: If something can go wrong you can bet it will.

Al Torche, a New York-based professional player with a harness racing background, tells this story about a presently retired thoroughbred trainer who embodied the above point for more than two decades.

After watching this trainer claim about a dozen decent horses without getting a single win in three months, Torche approached him in a Soho bar, bought him a few drinks and turned the conversation to what had been on his mind all season.

"Let me ask you something," Torche began.

"What's that?" the trainer replied.

"When you get all those new horses in your barn, what do you do, stand by their stalls and hit them in the head with a hammer?"

If you look at the dismal records posted by some trainers it will make you wonder.

Beyond the above subtleties, which have considerable power in everyday play, the most egregious error committed by horseplayers from coast to coast is hard to overcome because it goes against the most natural tendency in handicapping: Too many players, even good ones, pay far too much attention to the results of the horse's most recent race.

While the most recent performance certainly must be incorporated into the conditioning picture and may well prove to contain the decisive clues, the player must develop the discipline to see beyond it, or to view it mostly as a stepping-stone toward something more significant: *today's race.*

Last week's race—regardless of the result—took place under its own set of conditions which will not be duplicated in the vast majority of situations, even if the distance, track and level of competition is the same. Post positions have changed, form cycles have changed and the opposition has changed in all but a few cases. All this puts new values into play, and it is equally imperative to assess the impact of last week's performance on today's potential.

Too many players fail to appreciate the continuum involved. Using last week's race without taking into account the progression of starts that preceded it is to miss your best chance to understand when everything may be falling into place, or beginning to fall apart. (That is why I have always stressed comparing a given trainer's past-performance profiles over straight statistical summaries or tendencies. Statistical tendencies provide general clues, while the past performances show precisely how the trainer executes those tendencies or veers away from them.)

Last week's race is not a statement of today's probable performance, no matter how many handicapping gurus or authors tell you it is. All last week's race can do is supply the most recent piece of the puzzle. It can tell you how fast a horse ran and/or how he managed to run so fast. It can tell you if he was overmatched, or not yet ready to run at that distance, or if everything fell into his lap and he took advantage, or let the race slip away. It can tell you if he was ridden poorly or well, but it will not tell you how he is going to run today. That is your decision, your moment on the stage. That is the essence of handicapping—to interpret last week and the preceding weeks' performances in the context of today's assignment, not to merely plug in the numbers or the apparent recent form and expect the matchups to reveal the race winners.

Sometimes this does happen, but if you want to win serious money at this game, you must allow your powers of observation and common sense to spot more than the obvious. A solid victory may be a good or a bad thing. A weak finish may be a signal of worse or better to come. All of which brings up the famous "Bounce Theory" of form cycle movement.

It is the esteemed New York handicapper Len Ragozin's contention that horses tend to bounce or drop off in their form as a consequence of two interrelated factors: when they have exerted "an effort" that taxes the horse's physical limitations and/or when the horse is brought back to the races too soon for full recovery to occur.

While Ragozin repeatedly stresses that each horse is an individual case, he expects the majority of mature, older horses to bounce when they reach a "new top" in their recent performance history, and he also expects younger fillies to regress after a serious effort.

"Older horses have established levels of peak form, and when they reach or exceed it, they don't recover as well or as fast," Ragozin explained at Handicapping Expo 1990. "Younger fillies just seem to react sharper to the extra exertion," he said.

There are other bounce patterns that are less straightforward and are quite controversial. Indeed, Andy Beyer has had so little confidence in the bounce theory that he frequently has labeled Ragozin and his former disciple Jerry Brown "sheet whackos" without really intending any malice. But this is too harsh. Bounce patterns do exist, but strangely enough, some of the most reliable bounces occur not after a "strenuous" effort but after the easiest winning trip imaginable.

For instance, a horse is likely to decline in form when it wins wire to wire on a speed-favoring track. Bounce may not be the technically correct term to apply here, but the effect is the same. Such horses almost never fire the same level of performance. As illustrated repeatedly, any horse who wins with a perfect trip, or a bias, or pace-aided setup should be avoided unless clear improvement in overall ability is in progress and/or the same favorable pace or track bias scenario is going to be repeated.

According to my own research conducted at Canterbury Downs in 1989 and in random samples at New York and California tracks, a true bounce seems to occur more than 50 percent of the time in few circumstances.

For instance, horses who ship across the country or across oceans may run powerfully in their first outing off the plane, but probably will bounce in the next outing, especially if it occurs within two or three weeks. This, however, is not automatic, as Bold Arrangement's performances in the 1986 Blue Grass Stakes and Kentucky Derby suggest, and as countless horses trained by Charlie Whittingham, Ron McAnally, Robert Frankel and others familiar with foreign horses and long-distance shipping have demonstrated. The picture on this issue is muddled, not definite, although a bounce does occur often enough to worry about. My advice is to believe that a hard-to-gauge horse is going to bounce if the odds are low and not to believe it if the odds are high.

The most reliable bounce pattern of them all involves the horse who runs an uncharacteristically high Beyer figure. Such horses rarely repeat the number, unless the big move forward was the result of a major change in training regimen or racing surface and the horse is "brand-new" as a result of these changes. Even so, the move forward may not be a straight line, but a step or two forward, or back or to the side followed by another surge to peak form. Interpreting these form cycle patterns is part of the art of handicapping, but there are too many exceptions for anyone to buy into a neat theory that will predict which horses will bounce off a new top and which ones will not, based strictly on numerical performance patterns. All things must be integrated, including the horse's age, the distance, the trainer, the breeding, the travel or time between races, the workout line, and previous cycles of forward and back movement. Ragozin and (former disciple Jerry) Brown call for flexibility here, especially with young horses as they rapidly mature from a modest or lackluster juvenile campaign into the spring, summer and fall of their three-year-old seasons.

When a newly turned three-year-old returns after a freshening to run a higher or faster number than his or her best as a 2-year-old, we are looking at a horse who is a serious candidate to improve a bunch.

I am including a few past-performance profiles of horses who typify possible bounce patterns. Certainly their speed figures fell off after a terrific performance. Your own interpretation is suggested and inevitably required.

Wild Gale

Own: My Littlefish Farm
NO RIDER (—)

Dk. b or br c. 3 (Mar)
Sire: Wild Again (Icecapade)
Dam: Meander (Little Current)
Br: Calumet Farm Inc-Runnymede Farm Inc (Ky)
Tr: Doyle Michael J (4 0 0 0 .00)

126

Lifetime Record:	15 3 3 4	$392,697			
1993	7 0 1 2	$187,328	Turf	0 0 0 0	
1992	8 3 2 2	$205,369	Wet	1 1 0 0	$16,080
Sar	1 0 0 0		Dist	2 0 0 1	$70,000

1Aug93-8Sar	fst	1⅛	:472 1:114 1:362 1:49	Jim Dandy-G2	88	3	4	57½	63½	56½	510½	Sellers S J	114	7.00	80-09	Miner's Mark117nk Virginia Rapids1214½ ColonialAffair1262¾	Bumped start	6
5Jun93-9Bel	gd	1½	:484 1:132 2:024 2:294	Belmont-G1	100	13	4	42½	32	23	33	Sellers S J	126	51.50	78-15	Colonial Affair1262¼ Kissin Kris126¾ Wild Gale1262	Lck needed response	13
15May93-10Pim	fst	1 3/16	:464 1:111 1:37 1:563	Preakness-G1	80	10	12	1114	108¾	97½	811½	Sellers S J	126	22.80	67-18	Prairie Bayou126½ Cherokee Run1267 El Bakan126nk	Sluggish start, wide	12
1May93-8CD	fst	1¼	:463 1:111 1:364 2:022	Ky Derby-G1	101	13	12	1311	63	32½	32½	Sellers S J	126	8.50f	95-07	Sea Hero1262½ Prairie Bayou126hd Wild Gale126nk	Good try	19
18Apr93-8Kee	fst	1 1/16	:24 :492 1:132 1:433	Lexington-G2	86	9	4	54½	53	53¼	52¾	Sellers S J	118	7.40	83-24	Grand Jewel118½ El Bakan1131 Truth Of It All118no	No rally	9
27Mar93-11TP	fst	1⅛	:472 1:113 1:372 1:504	Jim Beam-G2	83	6	9	99¾	98½	66	59¼	Sellers S J	121	3.90	70-18	Prairie Bayou121¾ Proudest Romeo1212 Miner's Mark1215		9
Fractious gate, always wide, passed tired horses																		
5Mar93-7GP	fst	7f	:234 :473 1:112 1:231	Alw 31000NC	88	1	3	3½	2½	25	25	Sellers S J	117	2.30	82-16	Cherokee Run1175 Wild Gale1176 Ziao112S	Best of others	4
28Nov92-10CD	fst	1 1/16	:233 :473 1:124 1:453	B&W Ky J C-G3	87	10	9	105½	94¾	3nk	1nk	Sellers S J	B 116	8.50	86-16	Wild Gale116nk Mi Cielo1165 Shoal Creek121nk	8-wide, driving	11
14Nov92-8Aqu	fst	1⅛	:47 1:114 1:372 1:501	Remsen-G2	86	11	8	64½	31	43½	36¼	Smith M E	115	9.30	79-23	Silver Of Silver122½ Dalhart115 Wild Gale115	Four wide	11
21Oct92-9WO	sl	170	:233 :474 1:134 1:44	Alw 26800	75	2	6	53½	42	12	18	Seymour D J	122	*.35	81-25	Wild Gale1228 CorporateRevenue117 ArcticGrail122	Boxed in, handily	6
11Oct92-9WO	fst	1 1/16	:231 :471 1:121 1:461	Grey-G3	77	4	9	95¾	42¾	13½	21½	Seymour D J	115	8.55	81-20	Truth of It All1151½ Wild Gale1154½ Reach theGold117	Weakened stretch	13
25Sep92-8WO	fst	6f	:223 :462 1:114	Alw 24400	72	3	5	54¼	59½	49	24½	Penna D	122	4.25	81-22	DemalootDemashoot1174½ WildGale122½ HrveyTheRbbit116	Closed well	7

WORKOUTS: Aug 16 Sar 7f fst 1:282 B *1/1* ●Aug 10 Sar 6f fst 1:122 H *1/10* ●Aug 6 Sar tr.t(T) 4f fm :472 H (d) *1/14* Jly 29 Sar 4f fst :48 B *3/36* Jly 15 Bel 7f fst 1:271 B *1/2* Jly 7 Bel 5f fst 1:002 B *6/33*

Impressions

Own: Hild Sharon L
NO RIDER (—) $5,000

Dk. b or br g. 5
Sire: Hurricane Ed (Intervener)
Dam: Miss S J (Turn Right)
Br: Hild Sharon L (Ark)
Tr: Hild Glenn L (149 10 26 22 .07)

119

Lifetime Record:	71 4 17 9	$50,091			
1993	13 2 3 2	$13,770	Turf	1 0 0 0	$70
1992	23 1 4 2	$10,611	Wet	11 1 4 0	$9,750
Pha	12 1 3 1	$8,670	Dist	1 0 1 0	$1,000

11Jly93-10Pha	fst	170	:231 :471 1:122 1:441 3↑	Clm 5000	41	7	6	710	710	611	615½	Black A S	119 b	3.70	59-25	Cojaks Or Bettor1161½ Case The Ace1191 Dancer's Light116½	Dull try	7
26Jun93-5Pha	fst	1 1/16	:232 :471 1:123 1:46 3↑	Clm 6500	56	5	7	74½	76½	79	712¼	Centeno V R	116 b	28.40	66-25	Captain Cash1158 Billy Ala Mode1152¼ Power Circle116nk	Took up	7
11Jun93-1Pha	fst	1 1/16	:233 :471 1:123 1:452 3↑	Clm 5000	59	6	4	416	415	313	316	Black A S	119 b	3.90	66-29	Summon Thee11611 Keen Marine1165 Impressions1195½	Evenly	6
28May93-1Pha	fst	170	:231 :472 1:131 1:444 3↑	Clm 5000	72	5	4	44½	36½	32	1hd	Black A S	116 b	8.00	72-31	Impressions116hd Par The Course1192 Minne Chiefs'11610	Driving	7
3May93-6Pha	fst	1 1/16	:242 :491 1:141 1:472 3↑	Clm 7500N2Y	51	2	7	87¾	810	611	511½	Somsanith N	119 b	16.80	60-30	Captain Cash1161½ Quoddy116hd Contare's Boy1163¾	No factor	8
10Apr93-2OP	fst	6f	:213 :452 :581 1:102	Clm 5000	53	12	1	107¼	1011	910	713¼	Kutz D	112 b	9.50	73-15	Holiday Pleasure1146 Her Prospect1143 Rob's Freeze1171	No factor	12
1Apr93-10OP	fst	1	:231 :471 1:123 1:391	[S]Clm 6250	73	4	4	54	46	44	23	Guillory D	114 b	1.60e	78-22	Excellent Bo1143 Impressions1142 Noble Accord1141	Up for place	8
20Mar93-1OP	my	1 1/16	:23 :47 1:122 1:453	Clm 5000	63	7	9	87¾	911	68½	49	Guillory D	114 b	10.30	64-18	Excellent Bo1172¼ Con Coraje1162¼ Spinnacle1194	Lacked rally	12
11Mar93-2OP	fst	6f	:223 :472 1:00 1:122	Clm 5000	63	11	2	31½	42¼	53	31¾	Guillory D	120 b	2.50e	75-23	Noble Accord1141½ Excellent Bo120nk Impressions1201	Lacked late bid	11
28Feb93-1OP	fst	1	:232 :47 1:121 1:393	[S]Clm 5000	63	9	4	55½	24	23	23	Guillory D	114 b	3.30	76-23	Excellent Bo1143 Impressions1143½ O. B. Dixie114hd	Second best	11

Lykatill Hil

Own: Zellerbach W J
DAY P (10 2 2 1 .20)

B. g. 3 (Apr)
Sire: Pilgrim (Northern Dancer)
Dam: Seven Arts (Arts and Letters)
Br: Downing C Gibson III (Ky)
Tr: Sherman Art (—)

L 123

Lifetime Record:	10 4 4 1	$222,400			
1993	6 2 2 1	$175,000	Turf	2 0 2 0	$35,000
1992	4 2 2 0	$47,400	Wet	3 2 0 1	$99,700
AP (T)	0 0 0 0		Dist (T)	0 0 0 0	

22May93-8Hol	fm	1 1/16 (T)	:224 :46 1:092 1:40	W Rogers H-G3	93	5	9	63¾	21	21½	2½	Black C A	LB 119	4.60	95-04	Future Storm116½ Lykatill Hil119hd Earl Of Barking1224	In tight 3/4	12
1May93-7Hol	fm	1 (T)	:232 :464 1:101 1:334	Sptlght BC HG3	89	9	8	93½	73¼	72¾	22¾	Black C A	LB 119	6.50	93-04	Earl Of Barking1202¾ Lykatill Hil1191 Elkhart114hd	Troubled trip	10
10Apr93-8Kee	fst	1⅛	:481 1:121 1:37 1:493	Blue Grass-G2	76	2	2	21	3nk	75	812¼	Baze R A	L 121	8.70	75-16	Prairie Bayou1212 Wallenda121no Dixieland Heat121¾	Tired	9
7Mar93-8GG	fst	1 1/16	:222 :461 1:102 1:42	Sausalito 100k	97	1	5	53½	32	21	1hd	Baze R A	LB 122	*1.90	87-18	Lykatill Hil122hd El Atroz1227 Monogamous1153	Closed gamely	7
23Jan93-3BM	my	1 1/16	:232 :471 1:121 1:433	Cmno Rl Dby-G3	77	8	8	86	31½	2hd	34½	Baze R A	LB 119	*.80	80-14	El Atroz1171 Offshore Pirate1173½ Lykatill Hil119nk		9
Forced far wide 2nd turn																		
1Jan93-8BM	my	1	:222 :453 1:101 1:353	Cal JuvenileG3	90	8	5	56	43	2½	1½	Baze R A	LB 115	*.50	92-14	Lykatill Hil115½ Gary Go Go1153 Brinkstone1152	Closed gamely	6
13Dec92-8BM	my	1	:224 :463 1:114 1:37	Cardff Std 25k	86	8	7	77½	53½	1hd	15	Baze R A	LB 120	*.70	85-24	Lykatill Hil1205 R. Payday1201¼ Imperial Ridge1165	Rallied well wide	10
14Nov92-8BM	fst	1	:23 :47 1:113 1:371	L Stanford 54k	85	5	6	1½	1hd	2hd	2nk	Baze R A	LB 118	*1.10e	84-20	Yappy116nk Lykatill Hil1182 [DH]Gary Go Go114	Drifted out 3/8	8
3Oct92-7BM	fst	1	:221 :46 1:111 1:362	Blmg Hills 30k	91	3	4	44½	21½	11	11	Baze R A	LB 115	2.30	88-14	Lykatill Hil1151 Corby115 Gary Go Go114	Bobbled start	9
13Sep92-6Dmr	fst	6f	:221 :452 :574 1:102	Md Sp Wt	80	5	4	31½	2hd	21½	2½	McCarron C J	LB 118	*2.20	86-14	Concept Win118½ Lykatill Hil118 Lakotay118	Wide backstretch	11

WORKOUTS: Jly 7 AP (T) 5f tf 1:002 H *2/6* Jun 27 BM 1 fst 1:382 H *1/1* Jun 21 BM 7f fst 1:241 H *1/1* Jun 15 BM 6f fst 1:123 H *1/2* Jun 9 BM 5f fst 1:014 H *11/18* May 20 Hol (T) 4f fm :512 H (d) *4/4*

AUGUST 22, 1992, SARATOGA, $1 MILLION STAKES, 1¼ MILES

Thunder Rumble Dk. b. or br. c. 3(Mar), by Thunder Puddles—Lyphette, by Lyphard
MCCAULEY W H (41 6 6 5 .15) Br.—Widmer Konrad (NY)
Own.—Braeburn Farm Tr.—O'Connell Richard (9 1 0 3 .11) 126
Lifetime 8 5 0 1 $265,302 | 1992 6 4 0 1 $250,902 | 1991 2 1 0 0 $14,400 | Turf 2 0 0 0

2Aug92- 8Sar fst 1⅛ :461 1:092 1:472 Jim Dandy 110 3 2 21 21 21 1½ McCauley W H 117 24.90 100 — ThundrRumbl117½DxBrss1267½DvlHsD126 Bmp brk drvg 8
2Aug92-Grade II
11Jly92- 7Bel fm 1 1/16 (T):48 1:111 1:41 3↑Alw 37000 86 7 2 21 32 66¼ 77¼ McCauley W H 112 3.70 84-12 Now Listen1171½ Ogle1171 Sir Salima117 Tired 8
13Mar92- 8Aqu fst 1⅛ :463 1:114 1:512 Gate Dancer 98 4 4 36½ 33 11½ 15 McCauley W H 119 *.80 79-32 ThndrRmbl1195StpOtFrnt117nkJcksnprt117 Ridden out 8
15Feb92- 8Aqu fst 1 1/16 [•]:481 1:13 1:441 Whirlaway 84 5 2 1½ 2hd 35 39 McCauley W H 126 *.90 78-26 DrUnrht1195½TnsNmbr1173½ThndrRbl126 Dueled, tired 10
26Jan92- 8Aqu fst 170 [•]:471 1:13 1:43 Count Fleet 91 2 1 1hd 1hd 12 12 McCauley W H 123 *2.50 90-17 ThunderRumble1232Dr.Unright1193PlceLine119 Driving 7
12Jan92- 8Aqu fst 1 1/16 [•]:481 1:131 1:464 [S]Montauk 91 7 4 32 21 11½ 14 McCauley W H 117 *2.30e 74-24 Thunder Rumble1174Prioritizer1172JayGee123 Drew off 10
23Dec91- 6Aqu fst 6f [•]:232 :47 1:113 Md Sp Wt 94 4 5 11½ 11 17 112¾ McCauley W H 118 4.30 85-18 ThundrRumbl11812¾Dlfild1182CllHmNtty118 Ridden out 12
24Oct91- 4Aqu fm 1 (T):49 1:143 1:402 [S]Md Sp Wt 30 1 2 86 97 815 720 Smith M E 118 *1.50 54-17 PowdrCp1182½A.J.Wrbcks1181StrtYorHrt118 Bolted trn 9
LATEST WORKOUTS ●Aug 17 Sar 5f gd :591 H ●Aug 11 Sar 5f fst :584 H ●Jly 26 Bel 6f fst 1:11 H Jly 19 Bel 4f fst :481 B

AUGUST 15, 1993, 1⅜-MILE, $75,000 STAKES ON THE TURF AT DEL MAR RACECOURSE

Slew of Damascus Ch. g. 5
Own: Harbeston & Losh & Naccaroto Sire: Slewacide (Seattle Slew)
Dam: Damascus Isle (Accipiter)
Br: Fulmer Farms (Tenn)
NAKATANI C S (70 12 4 5 .17) Tr: Roberts Craig (7 1 1 1 .14) L 117
Lifetime Record: 21 8 4 2 $180,125
1993 9 5 2 1 $158,920 | Turf 3 2 1 0 $71,760
1992 8 2 2 0 $16,755 | Wet 1 0 1 0 $5,000
Dmr (T) 1 1 0 0 $34,900 | Dist (T) 1 0 1 0 $20,000

29Jly93–8Dmr fm 1 (T) :23 :464 1:101 1:34 3↑Wickerr H 60k 109 5 1 11½ 11½ 13 13½ Nakatani C S LB 115 b 9.40 101 — Slew Of Damascus1153½ Myrakalu1171¼ Alnasr Alwasheek120hd Ridden out 7
3Jly93–8Hol fst 7f :213 :434 1:081 1:204 3↑Triple Bnd HG3 101 8 1 5¾ 52 42½ 44¼ Nakatani C S LB 113 b 16.40 96-09 Now Listen116¾ Cardmania116½ Star Of The Crop1203 Wide trip 10
12Jun93–7GG fm 1⅜ (T) :472 1:121 1:364 2:151 3↑Rlng Grn H-G3 100 4 2 22 1hd 1½ 22 Baze G LB 114 b 3.80 91-10 Emerald Jig1132 Slew Of Damascus1141½ Party Cited1151 Held gamely 6
29May93–8GG fst 1 1/16 :23 :462 1:093 1:403 3↑[R]Kensington H 40k 101 4 1 11 1½ 12 13 Baze G LB 116 b *1.30 94-07 Slew Of Damascus1163 AtheniaGreen1161½ MilitaryHawk1164 Ridden out 7
14May93–8GG fst 1 :222 :451 1:093 1:362 Pss the Glss 30k 96 6 5 610 56½ 53½ 3¾ Baze G LB 118 b *.80 87-22 MilitaryHwk116½ ASimpleWord117nk SlewOfDmscus1181½ Late bid inside 6
25Apr93–8GG fm 1 1/16 (T) :224 :464 1:102 1:411+ Gr Commnctr 30k 98 2 1 11½ 1hd 11½ 12 Baze G LB 116 b 4.30 100-08 Slew Of Damascus1162 Sekondi112½ Rolandthemonarch117nk Ridden out 8
28Mar93–10YM fst 1 :23 :453 1:083 1:33 Ykma Mile H 50k 100 2 1 13 13 15 17¼ Baze G LB 117 b *1.30 114-03 SlewOfDamascus1177¼ SneakinJake1203 TotalTempo122¾ Much the best 5
7Mar93–7GG fst 1 :22 :452 1:093 1:35 Clm 32000 100 6 4 31½ 14 18 17 Baze G LB 117 b 12.20 95-18 SlewOfDamscus1177 BobsBrotherChip1195 NiceBlloon1173 Ridden out 8
11Feb93–8GG sl 6f :214 :443 :57 1:102 Alw 25000N2X 91 4 5 56½ 57 35½ 21 Baze G LB 119 b 9.70 87-20 FiveDayForcast1191 SlewOfDamscus1196 PowerFull119½ Rallied inside 6
10Oct92–6BM fst 6f :221 :444 :571 1:093 3↑Clm 20000 91 2 3 1½ 11½ 11½ 1½ Doocy T T LB 117 b 30.80 88-17 SlewOfDamascus117½ SharpEvent1191½ Hrlen'sAgency117 Steady drive 9
WORKOUTS: Aug 12 Dmr (T) 4f fm :494 H (d) 3/8 Jly 23 BM 4f fst :491 H 6/11 Jly 15 BM 7f fst 1:25 H 1/2 Jun 27 BM 5f fst 1:034 H 9/10 ●Jun 9 BM 4f fst :464 H 1/13 May 23 BM 5f fst 1:011 H 5/18

JULY 25, 1993, SIX-FURLONG STAKES AT PIMLICO RACECOURSE

Secret Odds B. c. 3 (Apr)
Own: Bender Sondra D Sire: Secreto (Northern Dancer)
Dam: Clever Miss (Kaskaskia)
Br: Bender Howard M & Sondra (Md)
LUZZI M J (159 24 17 20 .15) Tr: Murray Lawrence E (12 2 2 3 .17) L 107
Lifetime Record: 11 5 2 1 $261,805
1993 2 1 0 1 $33,010 | Turf 1 0 1 0 $11,515
1992 9 4 2 0 $228,795 | Wet 0 0 0 0
Lrl 4 3 0 1 $73,150 | Dist 3 3 0 0 $91,140

27Jun93–8Bel fst 6f :221 :453 :574 1:103 Sewickely 45k 108 1 1 11½ 1½ 14 111 Luzzi M J 122 f *1.60 87-20 Secret Odds12211 Strikany1196 Chief Master119¾ Mild drive 5
10Jun93–8Lrl fst 7f :224 :451 1:102 1:241 Greek Money 35k 84 1 1 1½ 1hd 2hd 3nk Luzzi M J L 122 *.80 88-11 My Impression122no Bold Anthony122nk Secret Odds1222½ Hung 5
4Dec92–9Med fst 6f :214 :443 :572 1:104 Morven B C 60k 83 1 2 11½ 12 13 11 Saumell L L 122 *.40 89-13 Secret Odds1221 Inagroove1191½ Siews Gold1131½ Driving 8
15Nov92–10Lrl fst 7f :223 :46 1:11 1:233 [S]Devls Bag 60k 97 1 3 11½ 12½ 12 11¼ Prado E S L 119 *1.20 89-16 Secret Odds1191¼ Woods Of Windsor1149½ Olney115 Ridden out 6
31Oct92–8GP fst 1 1/16 :223 :46 1:102 1:432 Br Cp Juv-G1 66 8 1 1½ 41 42¼ 1012 Stevens G L L 122 28.90f 83-03 Gilded Time122¾ It'sali'lknownfact122½ River Special122 Used on pace 13
10Oct92–7Bel gd 1 :22 :443 1:09 1:344 Champagne-G1 88 4 1 1½ 1hd 2½ 25¾ Desormeaux K J 122 31.70 90-04 Sea Hero1225¾ Secret Odds1225¾ Press Card122 Gamely 10
13Sep92–11Pim fm 1 (T) :23 :47 1:114 1:38 Vnlndghm 57k 72 8 1 13 1½ 21½ 28 Reynolds L C 111 2.60 70-27 Storm Flight1108 Secret Odds1112¼ Qizilbash115 2nd best 11
30Aug92–8Sar fst 6½f :222 :45 1:091 1:153 Hopeful-G1 59 2 6 42 31½ 87½ 816½ Migliore R 122 17.10 80-08 GretNvigtor1223¾ StrollingAlong122¾ EnglndExpects122 Chkd brk, sted 8
2Aug92–9Lrl fst 6f :221 :454 :581 1:111 [S]Rollckng 40k 87 2 1 11 14 13½ 17½ Reynolds L C 113 *.30 85-19 Secret Odds1137½ Taking Risks11315 Buckeystown Pike113 Handily 6
17Jly92–8Lrl fst 5½f :222 :46 :581 1:042 Md Sp Wt 93 6 1 12 12 14 19 Reynolds L C 120 2.20 97-15 Secret Odds1209 Wild About Harry1208½ Taking Risks120 Easily 8
WORKOUTS: ●Jly 19 Lrl 4f fst :47 H 1/16 Jly 13 Lrl 4f fst :483 H 11/36 Jun 22 Lrl 4f fst :492 B 17/28 ●Jun 4 Lrl 5f fst :57 H 1/4 ●May 27 Lrl 5f fst :583 H 1/17 ●May 21 Lrl 4f fst :48 B 1/14

JULY 26, 1993, BELMONT PARK, FOURTH RACE, 1 1/16 MILES ON THE TURF, $45,000 CLAIMING

Ogalgyn
Own: David Barbara J
KRONE J A (306 54 51 42 .18) $45,000

B. f. 3 (May)
Sire: Ogygian (Damascus)
Dam: Skim (Nijinsky II)
Br: Indian Creek & Moran J Jr & W (Ky)
Tr: Moschera Gasper S (114 29 13 14 .25)

112

Lifetime Record:	16	2	1	4	$29,660						
1993	8	2	1	2	$26,780	Turf	3	0	1	0	$6,020
1992	8	M	0	2	$2,880	Wet	2	0	0	1	$2,400
Bel Ⓣ	3	0	1	0	$6,020	Dist Ⓣ	2	0	1	0	$4,730

5Jly93-6Bel	gd	$1\frac{1}{16}$	T	$:23^{4}$	$:47^{1}$	$1:11^{2}$	$1:42^{2}$	ⒻClm 35000	74	4	8	6^{5}	$6^{2\frac{3}{4}}$	$2^{1\frac{1}{2}}$	2^{5}	Krone J A	116 b	13.30	79–16	Five West118^{5} Ogalgyn116^{1} Smarten Up Kris116$^{2\frac{1}{2}}$	Rallied wide	10
26Jun93-2Bel	fm	$1\frac{1}{16}$	T	$:24^{3}$	$:47^{4}$	$1:11^{3}$	$1:43^{1}$	ⒻClm 35000	50	6	4	$4^{1\frac{1}{4}}$	3^{1}	$7^{7\frac{3}{4}}$	$7^{13\frac{1}{2}}$	Smith M E	116 b	*2.40	66–14	Butterfly Chaser116$^{1\frac{1}{4}}$ [DH]No Atoll At All118 [DH]Kim's Image116^{nk}	Tired	8
4Jun93-4Bel	fm	$1\frac{1}{4}$	T	$:48^{1}$	$1:13$	$1:37^{3}$	$2:02^{4}$	ⒻClm 35000	59	3	2	3^{1}	$1^{2\frac{1}{2}}$	2^{hd}	$4^{7\frac{1}{4}}$	Cruguet J	116 b	5.30	69–18	My Bride116$^{2\frac{3}{4}}$ In Full Color116$^{\frac{1}{2}}$ Wonder Wave116^{4}	Bid, weakened	7
31Mar93-4Aqu	fst	6f		$:22^{2}$	$:45^{2}$	$:58$	$1:11^{1}$	ⒻClm 32500	42	6	1	2^{hd}	2^{1}	$5^{4\frac{1}{4}}$	$6^{10\frac{3}{4}}$	Davis R G	114 b	3.30	75–16	Dolly'sBck113^{3} Notimelost116$^{\frac{1}{2}}$ Jessic'sTwoStep111^{1}	Forced pace,tired	6
20Mar93-2Aqu	fst	6f	⊡	$:23$	$:46^{4}$	$:59^{4}$	$1:12^{4}$	ⒻClm c-22500	52	2	3	3^{3}	$1^{\frac{1}{2}}$	$1^{\frac{1}{2}}$	$3^{4\frac{3}{4}}$	Laboccetta F Jr	114 b	2.30	74–14	Abby Dear116$^{1\frac{3}{4}}$ Jessica's Two Step112^{3} Ogalgyn114$^{1\frac{1}{4}}$	Bid tired	7
Claimed from Anchel Judith, Laboccetta Frank Trainer																						
5Mar93-6Aqu	sly	6f	⊡	$:23^{1}$	$:47^{1}$	$:59^{3}$	$1:12^{3}$	ⒻClm 30000	54	6	4	$7^{5\frac{3}{4}}$	$6^{6\frac{1}{2}}$	$5^{5\frac{1}{2}}$	$3^{5\frac{3}{4}}$	Laboccetta F Jr	112 b	5.20	74–20	Dolly's Back116$^{1\frac{3}{4}}$ Real Zeal116^{4} Ogalgyn112^{2}	Late gain	7
22Feb93-1Aqu	fst	6f	⊡	$:22^{4}$	$:46^{4}$	$:59^{1}$	$1:12^{2}$	ⒻClm 17500	57	3	3	3^{2}	$3^{\frac{1}{2}}$	$1^{1\frac{1}{2}}$	$1^{3\frac{1}{2}}$	Laboccetta F Jr	118 b	6.90	81–16	Ogalgyn118$^{3\frac{1}{2}}$ Current Crown116^{1} Familiar Green107^{nk}	Drew away	8
25Jan93-3Aqu	fst	6f	⊡	$:23^{4}$	$:48^{2}$	$1:01^{1}$	$1:14^{2}$	ⒻMd 30000	51	10	2	4^{3}	1^{1}	1^{2}	$1^{4\frac{3}{4}}$	Laboccetta F Jr	117 b	5.20	71–21	Ogalgyn117$^{4\frac{3}{4}}$ Lojakono116$^{1\frac{1}{2}}$ Hurry Up Marya117$^{\frac{1}{2}}$	Drew off	12
29Nov92-4Aqu	fst	6f		$:22^{2}$	$:46^{1}$	$:58^{1}$	$1:11^{2}$	ⒻMd 30000	52	8	7	4^{2}	$2^{\frac{1}{2}}$	1^{hd}	$3^{3\frac{1}{4}}$	Laboccetta F Jr	113 b	22.90	81–11	Tanks For Lunch113$^{1\frac{1}{2}}$ Eastern Tune117$^{1\frac{3}{4}}$ Ogalgyn113^{2}	Tired	11
14Nov92-4Aqu	fst	6f		$:22^{2}$	$:46^{4}$	$1:00$	$1:14$	ⒻMd 30000	30	4	4	2^{hd}	$1^{\frac{1}{2}}$	3^{2}	$6^{7\frac{1}{2}}$	Rodriguez R R^{7}	106 b	11.00	63–18	Mining Secret117$^{2\frac{1}{4}}$ Candle Of Life117$^{1\frac{1}{2}}$ GallantressAck117	Used in pace	13

WORKOUTS: Jun 17 Bel T 4f fm $:50^{1}$ B (d) *8/14* May 23 Bel 5f fst 1:01 H *9/30* May 13 Bel T 4f fm :50 B (d) *5/9* Apr 11 Bel tr.t 4f fst $:51^{4}$ B *14/15*

Here are a few horses who reached new "tops" in their latest race. Did they bounce? Good question. Maybe you can figure it out. The results are contained in the footnote below.*

The popularity of any theory should be viewed as a warning sign to alert players to look deeper into the handicapping equation. This is as true for bounce theory as it is for the excessive use made of speed figures, or the inevitable overplaying of pace computations and for those who rush to judgment on track bias as well. In fact, one of the most important traps to avoid in your handicapping education is to believe in any theory too strongly, especially a theory held dearly by a lot of people.

When I was first beginning my handicapping adventures at Rutgers in the early 1960s, I was appalled at how many popular handicapping bromides turned out to be nonsense. I am still shocked how many of them still remain in the basic language of the modern horseplayer. In fact, one of the earliest lessons I learned was to invert any such handicapping principle to achieve better results. Author Mark Cramer calls this "contrarian" handicapping. I call it plain old common sense. Here

***To bounce or not to bounce:* Thunder Rumble won the 1¼-mile Travers stakes at Saratoga, August 22, 1992, by 4½ lengths. Slew Of Damascus finished fourth in the 1⅜-mile Escondido stakes at Del Mar on August 14, 1993, and third in the San Francisco handicap at Bay Meadows on September 6, then regained top form with three straight stakes wins at Bay Meadows and Hollywood Park. Secret Odds "bounced" to the moon with a seventh-place finish in the Frank DeFrancis stakes at Pimlico in July and was sixth and ninth in two more stakes in September and October before he won the Paumonok handicap at Aqueduct on January 12, 1993, following a badly needed four-month layoff. Ogalgyn raced to a dead-heat win in a $45,000 claimer on July 26, but then threw in a dismal 10th-place performance in similar company on July 16 which knocked him out for the year.

are a few precepts still being shoved down the throats of horseplayers which deserve to be turned upside down:

"You can beat the race but not the races."

The truth is the reverse, always has been the reverse and always will be the reverse. A given bet may be won or lost by the jockeys, the unforeseen, or the stewards in the booth, but if you are wagering on horses who reflect winning patterns or trends, there is no reason in the world why you cannot beat the races *long-term*. No reason except your own need to know what the winning patterns are and when they are effective. Luck may well determine today's results, but you determine your ultimate success of failure.

"Throw out horses who have been away from the races for six months or longer."

As pointed out, you will do far better taking a very close look at all such absentees. If they have been placed in races that conform to their best previous levels, or are dropping sharply for a money run first out with workout support, or have been shipped in from better tracks, you'll be amazed at how often these horses deliver fine performances at generous prices.

Another piece of poor advice is to "never bet a horse to do what he or she has not done before."

As Dana Carvey would say, *"Not!"*

The irony of this is reflected in most of the concepts in this book and is one of the fundamental secrets to successful horseplay. Unless you plan to build your handicapping game around a succession of 6–5 favorites, the key word to keep firmly in mind is C-H-A-N-G-E.

Horses trying a distance of ground today after two or three sprints should be studied as carefully as horses who had three routes and now will attempt a sprint. Remember the question in Chapter 10: What is he doing in today's race? It is vitally important to develop a reasonable answer.

Horses stepping up or dropping down or changing equipment—or jockeys or racing surfaces or legalized drugs—are all deserving of close inspection. Some of these changes may be cosmetic or desperate or just what the doctor ordered. The past-performance illustrations below and in every chapter have been chosen to provide many lingering examples of this principle, even where traditional training regimens were being applied by Hall of Fame trainers to top-flight horses.

Today's change might be the missing link to put the horse in the best possible circumstance, or the single most valuable clue to a winning trainer's most productive pattern. Here is a horse who is set to blow away a $6,250 claiming field on the turf. In fact, he will win two straight, including this one at 9–1 odds and another against virtually the same field at 7–2. The prep race on dirt, the very strong workouts and a return to his best surface are all the doctor ordered.

Poupon		Gr. g. 8										
Own: Belvoir Howard		Sire: Linkage (Hoist the Flag)					Lifetime Record:	29 4 2 2	$79,825			
		Dam: Lost Virtue (Cloudy Dawn)					1993	1 0 0 0		Turf	6 2 0 0	$22,975
CHAPMAN T M (325 40 41 33 .12)	$6,250	Br: Nato (Ky)					1991	14 2 0 1	$22,995	Wet	2 0 0 0	$1,800
		Tr: Belvoir Howard (127 13 23 13 .10)				L 117	GG ⑦	1 0 0 0		Dist⑦	3 0 0 0	$1,800
15May93–3GG fst 1¹⁄₁₆ :23⁴ :48¹ 1:13 1:46	Clm 6250N1Y	40 8 3 4⁴ 7⁸¹ 10¹⁷10¹⁹¹	Belvoir V T	LB 119 f	*3.60 48–26	Mr. Inovator119ʰᵈ Bubastrelli119¹ Zin119⁷					Brief speed 10
22Sep91–10B M fm 1¹⁄₁₆ ⑦ :23¹ :47¹ 1:12³ 1:44² 3↑ Hcp 12500		78 2 2 2¹ 2ʰᵈ 3⁵ 6⁹¹	Campbell B C	LB 118	20.10 74–18	Falling Star118⁶ Hermelin–Ge115ʰᵈ Cannon Bar120					Weakened 12
5Sep91–8Lga fst 1¹⁄₁₆ :23² :47 1:11³ 1:44 3↑ Clm 12500		79 3 5 53¹ 3¹¹ 45 33¹	Maelfeyt B J	LB 120	*2.30 81–22	Ja Ro De117ⁿᵏ Monterrey John109³ Poupon120					Finished evenly 7
18Aug91–8Lga fst 1¹⁄₁₆ :24 :48 1:12³ 1:45²	Clm 25000	74 4 2 3¹¹ 44 57¹ 6¹⁰	Maelfeyt B J	LB 117	3.80 67–26	Our Man Ollie114⁴¹ Buffalo Runner114¹ Castabell114					Stopped 6
4Aug91–7Lga fst 1¹⁄₁₆ :23¹ :47¹ 1:12 1:45	Clm 25000	86 6 5 5⁴ 45¹ 5⁸ 43¹	Maelfeyt B J	LB 117	9.00 76–30	Safe To Say114ʰᵈ Castabell114¹ Our Man Ollie114					Evenly 8
27Jly91–7Lga fst 1¹⁄₁₆ :23³ :47 1:12¹ 1:44³	Clm 20000	83 6 4 32¹ 2¹ 2¹ 1ⁿᵒ	Maelfeyt B J	LB 117	12.50 81–25	Poupon117ⁿᵒ Our Man Ollie114³ Allaire Dancer115					Driving 9
14Jly91–5Lga fst 1¹⁄₁₆ :23⁴ :47³ 1:12⁴ 1:45	Clm 50000	70 2 6 6⁸¹ 6⁷ 6⁸¹ 6¹⁵	Steiner J J	LB 114	22.90 64–28	Erin's Lord117³ Big Paz117² Safe To Say116					Trailed 6
30Jun91–8Lga fst 6¹⁄₂f :21⁴ :45 1:10³ 1:17	Clm 40000	71 5 5 6⁸¹ 6⁷ 5⁴ 57¹	Steiner J J	LB 114	8.90 79–19	Forgotten Days114² Second Legend114²¹ Gallant Sailor116					Lacked rally 7
3Apr91–6GG fm 1¹⁄₁₆ ⑦ :47⁴ 1:12¹ 1:37³ 1:50⁴	Alw 24000	86 2 2 2¹¹ 2¹ 4² 8⁴¹	Martinez O A Jr	LB 119	5.90 89–05	LoftyPromise119¹ BeguiledAgin119¹ MightyDetermined116					Gave way 10
23Mar91–6GG sly 1¹⁄₁₆ :24 :48 1:11⁴ 1:43	Clm 50000	58 5 8 8⁹¹ 7⁹¹ 7¹⁶ 7¹⁸¹	Steiner J J	LB 117	8.00 64–22	Lot's Curiosity115⁷ Strung Up117ⁿᵏ Fairly Affirmed117					Outrun 8
WORKOUTS: Jun 9 GG 5f fst 1:00 H 7/57 Jun 2 GG 6f fst 1:12 H 1/3 ●May 11 GG 5f fst :59¹ H 1/23 May 5 GG 4f fst :47³ H 3/36 Apr 28 GG 6f fst 1:14¹ H 3/16 ●Apr 22 GG 6f fst 1:13⁴ H 1/5											

Yes, we are back at the last race, looking at it as the linchpin to the whole picture. Was it the end to a pattern, part of one in progress, or the beginning of something new? Or, as in the case of the absentees, is this the start and the end all at once?

Maybe today's change is just another in a long line of changes that have failed to help, or the last of a series of changes that have been designed to turn a horse around. The horse below is an extreme example that should alert us that some trainers may pull rabbits out of their hats when few sane people think they have any chance to win. Given the horse below, if Gary Contessa tries to walk across the Hudson River I'm not so sure he would sink.

Codys Key		Ro. c. 4										
Own: Sheerin Raymond T		Sire: Corridor Key (Danzig)					Lifetime Record:	16 5 2 3	$150,448			
		Dam: Go Thither (Cabin)					1993	4 2 0 1	$89,124	Turf	1 0 0 0	$400
CHAVEZ J F (315 57 33 31 .18)		Br: Wilkinson Jon (NJ)				122	1992	6 1 1 1	$20,922	Wet	1 0 0 0	
		Tr: Contessa Gary C (45 5 5 3 .11)					Bel	4 2 0 1	$89,124	Dist	12 5 2 2	$143,798
4Jly93–5Bel fst 6f :22³ :45² :57¹ 1:09¹ 3↑ Alw 40000N$Y		100 5 2 21¹ 3² 2ʰᵈ 1¹	Chavez J F	122	3.80 94–11	Codys Key122¹ Curbex117¹¹ Boom Towner117⁴¹					Driving 6
20Jun93–9Bel fst 6f :22 :45 :57² 1:10¹ 3↑ True North HG2		97 2 1 3¹ 3¹¹ 2¹ 3³	Chavez J F	111	17.00 86–20	Lion Cavern116¹ Arrowtown115² Codys Key111²					Bid, weakened 7
29May93–8Bel fst 6f :22⁴ :45³ :57³ 1:09⁴ 3↑ Roseben H–G3		95 5 1 1¹ 2¹ 2¹ 1ʰᵈ	Chavez J F	108	32.10 91–10	Codys Key108ʰᵈ Sunnybutcold111ⁿᵒ Slerp118²¹					Gamely 6
15May93–8Bel fst 6f :22² :45³ :57⁴ 1:10¹ 3↑ Handicap40K		50 3 7 62¹ 72³ 72⁰ 72⁰¹	Bravo J	110	18.20 69–17	Friendly Lover112¹¹ Curbex114²³ Drummond Lane120ⁿᵏ					No factor 7
15Sep92–3Med fst 6f :22 :45 :57 1:092	Clm 40000	71 6 1 12 1ʰᵈ 2⁴ 47¹	Bravo J	L 116	*.90 88–07	Mac's Clyde116⁴¹ Major Danger109¹ Royale Derby116					Tired 6
22Aug92–8Atl fst 6f :22 :44⁴ 1:09¹	⑤Mckee Cy H 22k	89 4 2 2¹ 2¹ 22¹ 23¹	Gryder A T	L 119	2.30 96–06	Dr. Louis A.116³¹ Codys Key119¹ Munch n' Nosh118					2nd best 4
2Jun92–5Mth gd 1¹⁄₁₆ ⑦ :24¹ :48 1:12² 1:43⁴	Restoratn 40k	70 9 5 45¹ 54¹ 5¹⁰ 6¹⁵²	Bravo J	L 115	14.90 69–21	Bidding Proud122⁹¹ Cobblestone Road117³¹ Coax Stardust114					Gave way 9
18Jly92–11Lrl fst 7f :23¹ :46² 1:11⁴ 1:24⁴	Cavalier 40k	72 4 5 54¹ 66 55 44¹	Chavez J F	L 119	6.10 78–17	Apparitiontofollow117¹³ Majesty's Turn119¹¹ Wood Fox114					Mild rally 8
3Jly92–6Mth fst 6f :21⁴ :44⁴ :57² 1:10⁴ 3↑ Alw 17000		89 1 6 1ʰᵈ 12 1¹ 12	Bravo J	L 110	8.50 87–17	Codys Key110² Majic Fountain113³ Bandit Corsair116					Drftd out, drvg 6
10Jun92–7Mth fst 6f :21⁴ :44² :57 1:10 3↑ ⑤Alw 22500		73 1 8 52³ 44¹ 35¹ 37¹	Collazo L	L 109	8.80 83–18	Shady Shadow116³¹ Crafty Goldena116³¹ Codys Key109					Saved ground 9
WORKOUTS: ●Jly 21 Bel 5f fst :57⁴ H 1/29 Jly 17 Bel tr.t 5f fst 1:05³ B 9/9 Jun 30 Bel 4f fst :49³ B 22/53 Jun 17 Bel ⑦ 3f fm :36⁴ H (d) 1/2 Jun 11 Bel 5f fst 1:01² H 16/46 May 22 Bel 3f fst :37⁴ B 22/34											

Shirl's Lad below is entered in a $12,500 claiming race for nonwinners of two races at Bay Meadows, January 8, 1993. Is trainer Jerry Hollendorfer trying to unload damaged goods, or is this gelding ready to fire a solid race?

Shirl's Lad	B. g. 3 (Feb)		Lifetime Record: 3 1 0 1 $6,075	
Own: St Francis Stable & Hollendorfer J	Sire: Saros–GB (Sassafras) Dam: Adelphal (Full Pocket) Br: Green Thumb Farm (Cal)		1993 3 1 0 1 $6,075 Turf 0 0 0 0	
KAENEL J L (368 53 43 44 .14)	$12,500	Tr: Hollendorfer Jerry (277 53 48 41 .19)	L 117	1992 0 M 0 0 Wet 1 0 0 0
				BM 3 1 0 1 $6,075 Dist 1 1 0 0 $4,950

8Dec93– 8BM my 1	:23¹ :46⁴ 1:11² 1:37¹	Alw 20000N1x	— 2 5 67½ 7¹² — —	Judice J C	L 116	3.00e — 19	Saratoga Bandit114² Night Letter119nk Veracity115½	Eased 7
24Sep93– 5BM fst 6f	:22¹ :44⁴ :57³ 1:11⁴	Md 20000	50 3 4 67¼ 6⁹ 77¾ 1½	Baze R A	L 118	*3.30 77–14	Shirl's Lad118½ Le Fabuleux Fort118hd Night Letter118¹	10
Steadied briefly upper stretch								
29Aug93– 4BM fst 5½f	:22¹ :46³ :59³ 1:06¹	Md 16000	45 6 4 64¼ 65¼ 64½ 3¼	Baze R A	L 118	3.00 78–17	Casiri118hd Just For Dino118¹½ Shirl's Lad118nk	7

WORKOUTS: Jan 1 BM 5f fst 1:03 H *11/15*   Dec 23 BM 5f fst 1:01¹ H *16/42*   Dec 2 BM 4f gd :50⁴ H *28/41*   Nov 24 BM 6f fst 1:15 H *5/11*   Nov 16 BM 6f fst 1:17² H *4/5*   Nov 10 BM 5f fst 1:01 H *10/24*

If you guessed that Hollendorfer is firing hard, you cash. Shirl's Lad embodies a wonderful pattern I call "a license to steal." The most recent race is so horrible, no trainer would spend $12,500 to claim him away today, right?

But, as the two recent workouts suggest, nothing is physically out of sorts here. Shirl's Lad returned to work a good five furlongs on December 23 and went comfortably again on January 1. The move back to a sprint and the drop to $12,500 by Hollendorfer are realistic changes designed to give this horse its best competitive shot. The move down in class is virtually risk-free and probably sets up an easy score at a better mutuel payoff than usual.

Change by itself does not guarantee anything, but taking things strictly at face value is as much a losing strategy as believing in the poppycock that has been spread around the track for decades. Racing is more complex, more subtle than it is casually represented. Fundamental handicapping approaches still must be employed for comparative analysis, but change is a signal to the modern, attentive player to stop in his or her tracks for closer inspection.

Learning to identify potentially positive changes—including the simple return to a previous winning formula—will boost your average payoff possibilities significantly. That is more than an exercise in how to play a few well-meant longshots. In this age of quasi-legal drug-altered performances, year-round racing and multi-race and multi-bet exotic wagers, it is the guiding pathway toward a winning horseplayer's edge.

The Best Handicapping
Tool Ever Invented

At the top of the stretch, Alydar was racing on the outside and gaining a razor-thin advantage over his nemisis, Affirmed, who had won the first two legs of the 1978 Triple Crown. Now, finally, Alydar seemed ready to gain his revenge.

Jockey Steve Cauthen, cramped by the inside rail, nevertheless managed to switch his whip to the left flank for one last surge of reserve power. Victory was in doubt all the way to the wire, but it did come—by a head—as Cauthen packed the whip away in the final yards and blended his body movement to the rhythm of Affirmed's extended stride. Many call this Belmont the finest race in American racing history, but from a handicapping perspective it provided a climax to one of the most instructive series of races anyone has had the chance to write about or study.

My exposures to Triple Crown racing always have been a crucial part of a sustained learning experience. Indeed, while hardened professional players such as the aforementioned Ron Cox and Scott McMannis tend to disclaim any wagering interest in these highly publicized races, I have found them—and their attendent prep races—to offer some of the most lucrative wagering opportunities on the national calendar. A cold Avatar–Foolish Pleasure exacta at 50–1 in the 1975 Belmont, for instance;

Riva Ridge at 8–5 in the 1972 Belmont, Affirmed over Alydar at 2–1 in the 1978 Derby, Jolly Johu at maximum strength and 4–1 to place in the 1974 Belmont; Sunday Silence over Easy Goer one way in the 1989 Preakness (whew, that was close!); Strike the Gold and Best Pal back and forth in the 1991 Derby exacta at 37–1, and an empty-my-pockets show play on the Easy Goer-Awe Inspiring entry in the 1989 Derby, to name only a few.

Ask Andy Beyer if he likes Triple Crown racing for major betting purposes, and Andy is likely to smile and say Swale to Pine Circle, at better than $100 grand. I can still see the expression on his face as our eyes met in the middle of the Belmont press box a few fifths of a second *before* Pine Circle completed that score for one of the top players of the twentieth century. At that precise moment I felt proud to have contributed something to Andy's education.

Apart from pointing out the relative power of track bias in the handicapping equation, the first handicapping ideas I passed along to Andy were to focus—line by line—on the complete past performances of good horses aimed at major stakes. The Triple Crown races in particular continue to provide amazing educational opportunities for beginners and players who have reached a dead end in their game. These races offer rare peeks into the minds of trainers—to see the consequences of their choices, as well as to measure the relative skills and weaknesses of dozens of jockeys. Simultaneously, they provide a rare proving ground for the role of pace (diminished) and breeding (enhanced) in distance races for top horses. The ups and downs of the form cycle also can be studied, as some horses will respond to accelerated training regimens in the face of longer races with stiffer competition, while others will expose their deficiencies under slightly rushed or tentative handling.

Indeed, in the 90s, the Triple Crown remains a powerful learning tool and betting opportunity, while dozens of other stakes have been added to the national television menu to broaden the possibilities. All of these races can be studied in great detail with the aid of the most underappreciated, most valuable handicapping tool ever invented. *The home video recorder.*

Repeated VCR viewings of a few days' worth of races at any racetrack will help you spot horses in traffic trouble not picked up in result charts. Using taped replays in tandem with the official track program or the result chart, the player can catalog extremely important trip information that will breathe life into the hieroglyphic symbols of the past-performance profiles.

The VCR is invaluable in identifying the fastest-breaking jockeys, the ones with the best finishing technique as well as those who insist on going around horses instead of hugging the inside rail. The VCR can confirm a track bias or help you realize that there was nothing in the track to cause three straight wire-to-wire winners other than each horse's inherent ability to outrun their rivals. The VCR puts professional players into the position of confirming or discovering subtle tidbits that will lead to solid wagers and it helps recreational players move their games sharply forward by directly acquiring real knowledge.

In 1978, my first VCR helped explain what Laz Barrera meant when he stated that Affirmed was a gifted athlete, one who could shift gears and respond to any challenge with great ability and power. Barerra was right. Affirmed did have a hidden dimension not fully exposed by the winning result or the teletimer. When Alydar came alongside him at the top of the stretch in the Preakness, the slow-mo replay showed Affirmed responding to the challenge without jockey Steve Cauthen doing anything at all. Affirmed's ears twirled back as Alydar approached. His head shifted to the right as if he saw Alydar coming. A split second later these two horses took off in full flight on the fastest run to the wire in Preakness history. After a few viewings there was no way you could play Alydar to reverse the verdict, not after Affirmed looked like he had an answer for every new gear Alydar reached. Not when Affirmed could have stayed in front of Alydar—by the slimmest of margins—all the way from Baltimore to New York.

A few years later, some of these same traits were seen in the immature Slew o' Gold, while he was losing two minor stakes early in his three-year-old campaign at Tampa Bay Downs. After a few VCR viewings of the Tampa Bay Derby, I was struck enough by the similarities between Slew o' Gold and Affirmed to believe the son of Seatle Slew might develop into the eventual divisional champion, and I put my opinions on the line in print in the March 29 issue of the *St. Petersburg Times.* I cashed a few nice tickets betting on that opinion along the way.

Last Tycoon scored a $73.80 win for me and former Oaklawn Park track announcer Terry Wallace in the 1986 Breeders' Cup Mile on the basis of a few taped replays of his gritty European sprint races. The same was true for the powerful impression Irish import Ibn Bay made winning the 1990 St. Leger Stakes prior to a remarkable second in the $3 million Breeders' Cup Classic at Belmont Park. The videotape of that race showed Ibn Bay getting passed in the upper stretch only to kick it in again—while going uphill—to surge ahead comfortably at the wire. Hard not to bet a horse off that kind of performance, even if he was going to run on dirt for the first time. I confess, however, that I did not bet a dime on Ibn Bay in the Classic. I succumbed to the feeling shared by many people that afternoon covering the Breeders' Cup for the *Minneapolis Star Tribune*. I turned back $200 win-place tickets on Ibn Bay, a half hour after Go For Wand died on the Belmont Park racetrack, to take the heart out of the seventh Breeders' Cup. That was the quietest press box in racing history.

The VCR review did not improve the feeling incurred by that incident. It has remained difficult to watch, but it did show what happened; inevitably the VCR will do that. Just as it singled out jockey Julie Krone's extraordinary skill on the Atlantic City turf course when she was beginning her career in the early 1980s, and as it pointed out the way Sunday Silence shied away from Pat Valenzuela's whip in the stretch run of the 1989 Kentucky Derby to provide solid evidence he was physically sound, with so much room to improve.

Given the opportunity to study top-class racehorses on VCR, I am convinced the player will improve his or her standards of judgment beyond anything previously possible. It used to take years to develop finely tuned visual skills. Now much can be accomplished with careful review of six months of videotapes. Serious-minded students and professionals know to develop a library of locally run races for review at least once weekly, or each racing day. Cataloging these races for easy access is just as important as saving chronologically dated result charts and *Racing Forms*. Cox, Siegel, Rousso, McMannis and Beyer put their VCR notes on their track programs. I put them on result charts photocopied on oversized sheets of paper chosen specifically for the extra room they allow in the margins for trip notations. I use VCR replays extensively to spot hidden abilities or potential not visible in live performances. Alydar, for instance, probably would have won the 1978 Triple Crown without the presence of Affirmed and was the victim of his own fatal flaw, as seen only with repeated viewings of videotape: He consistenly failed to change leads while trying to outfinish Affirmed in the stretch.

Changing leads is an interesting subtlety of racing. The four-legged racehorse runs with either his left or right front foot hitting the ground first and tends to shift his lead to the opposite leg coming off turns to limit leg weariness or to reach another running gear. Alydar never mastered the concept.

In the 1990s, when New York OTB outhandles the live gate, and satellite wagering dominates the racing scene in every region of the country, the VCR is your best link to hundreds of races you never will see in person. Does anyone doubt we are looking at a future that includes telephone wagering from one's living room on several tracks at once? (In Hong Kong, via all forms of OTB, satellite and telephone wagering, the *daily* handle approaches $300 million!)

It is long past debating that players should tape stakes race recap TV shows for simulcast wagering opportunities, including the Breeders' Cup and Triple Crown chase. Yet to reinforce the point, I firmly believe I could handicap a race meet without *Daily Racing Form* or any other handicapping aid as long as I have a VCR and a well-produced nightly replay show to tape. With *DRF* result charts, these replays go a long way toward bridging the gap between being there or not. Any TV homework you do on these out-of-town races could lead to a significant edge in several races each season.

On the other hand, until inter-track television coverage improves to provide longer views of the horses in the paddock and pre-race warm-up, and better access to wagering pools and payoff possibilities, it is important to acknowledge the disadvantages of playing the game via satellite.

You can only see so much on two-dimensional TV. Many nightly TV replay shows fail to give an adequate look at horses deep in the pack who may be halted from making a good move or stuck on a dead rail out of camera view. At any venue—on or off-track—it pays to be vigilant in watching the head-on replays when presented immediately after the race. Usually that is the only head-on view you will ever get.

The Winning Horseplayer

Ideally, the most instructive way to illustrate the practical applications of the material in this book would be to present thousands of actual races, playable and nonplayable.

We would select several different racetracks, do post-position studies for each, save and read result charts, compare the past-performance records of all the important trainers, and be careful to note and measure the relative power of the racing surface as it influences the action on the track.

To get a fix on the local horses we could do class par and pace par research to develop speed and pace figures which would help us establish criteria for race shapes and the breaking points between claiming prices and various allowance conditions. We could take notes on the daily work tab, review result charts for possible biases in the racing surface, hunt for Key Races and middle moves that would strengthen our opinion of specific horses, study trainer patterns, possibly subscribe to a reputable newsletter for trip notes and clocker info, or link up to Bloodstock Research Information Services for specialized data, and watch whatever races we are privileged to see to spot the unusual as it happens.

If the track provides videotape replays of races on a nightly TV program, we definitely should plan to tape all races during the season and if possible start watching at least two weeks in advance to get a better line on the performances of the horses *and* jockeys involved. (Some tracks now offer patrons easy access to their videotape library of recent races on the circuit.)

Not all professional players prepare so diligently or cover so many bases. Some rely strictly on speed figures or generally broad insights to uncover sound betting propositions. Some watch races with such skill they are able to build a catalog of live horses for future play. Some concentrate their serious play on one type of race over all others, i.e., turf events, claiming races, sprints, routes, maidens or stakes.

Frankly, I have no argument with players who are able to solve sufficient racetrack riddles through a single window or two. Specialization according to individual strength makes excellent sense. Different strokes for different folks. On one level, that is exactly what this book has been about. On another, it is not the case at all.

I have been very fortunate. During my years around the racetrack, I have been exposed continuously to the varied menu only an extensive itinerary can bring. Five years at Rutgers University—Garden State Park Division. Two years of handicapping fifty races a day at five or more tracks for *Daily Racing Form.* Triple Crown coverage for Mutual Broadcasting and several major newspapers, including the *Philadelphia Inquirer, St. Petersburg Times* and *Minneapolis Star Tribune;* Breeders' Cup and Triple Crown clocker reports for the *Star Tribune* and the *Racing Times,* the editorship of *Turf and Sport Digest Magazine,* columns and articles for all the above and almost 20 years of public handicapping at tracks in every region of the country, including several complete sessions at Atlantic City Racecourse, Delaware Park, Keystone–Philadelphia Park, Garden State Park, Saratoga, Del Mar, Bay Meadows, Golden Gate Fields, Sam Houston Race Park, Canterbury Downs, Tampa Bay Downs, Laurel Racecourse, Pimlico and a few tracks that have become parking lots. I have taken trips and had playing experience at 58 different racetracks, dozens of symposiums and handicapping seminars throughout the country, plus conversations with some of the best thinkers and players in the game. People like Andy Beyer and Clem Florio in Maryland; Jules Schanzer and the late, great Saul Rosen of *Daily Racing Form,* who tried to begin the handicapping revolution in 1970 but was stopped by former *DRF* management; John Pricci and Mark Berner of *Newsday* in Long Island; Scott McMannis in Chicago;

Ron Cox and Dan Montilion in northern California; Jeff Siegel, Lee Rousso and James Quinn in southern California; Randy Moss in Arkansas; Bill Stevenson and Craig Donnelly in New Jersey and Pennsylvania; Al Torche in New York; and Tom Ainslie, who first encouraged me to commit to print all the handicapping insights I have thus far gained. It has taken me nearly three hundred pages to do that. But I think it would help your focus if I reduced the essence of it all to a few key principles and a few key examples.

There are only two kinds of playable prime betting situations; easy ones and hard ones. The easy ones practically leap off the pages of *Daily Racing Form;* the hard ones require a bit of digging. To students of track bias, an easy one may come any time the bias is strong enough to prejudice the outcome of the race. To students of class, easy ones come in many forms. A hidden class dropdown like Lord Cardinal on page 108. A Laplander or Secretariat when he was only the second betting choice in the Sanford Stakes as a two-year-old at Saratoga, and/or any horse with significantly faster speed figures. Yes, that too is an edge in class.

Speed-figure handicappers realize that the days of $20 top-figure winners which regularly occurred before Beyer figures were included in past performances are gone forever. But we all should be comforted by the realization that there are ways to link top-figure horses in multi-race exotics for major scores, while simultaneously eliminating numerous horses because they simply are not fast enough.

Pace handicappers, those who work with numbers and those who do not, are comforted to know that many races—especially maiden claiming races—often are decided before the field turns for home. Pace handicappers also may be best equipped to identify which horse in what field will slip off to a clear, early lead and control the race.

For those who pay attention to trainers and their methods, there is nothing complicated about spotting a stakes-winning Charlie Whittngham—trained absentee in an important 1¼-mile stakes, or a Mack Miller first-timer on the grass, or a Shug McGaughey two-year-old in his first allowance race at Belmont or Saratoga. But for more power at the mutuel windows, trainer analysts should be more alert for horses generally overlooked by the betting public who have equally solid credentials.

Joe H. Pierce, Jr., shipping in from New Jersey to New York with a fit maiden has been a high-percentage play that frequently turns over a

$20 mutuel. Indeed, there are several trainers on every circuit who know how to score with a pet longshot pattern that can be uncovered by a diligent player.

For instance, a small group of trainers who gained their foundation in horsemanship on the Maryland hunt scene have perfected the art of putting over grass horses with specious-looking credentials. These trainers are deadly with absesntee turf pros returning to the major tracks after a layoff, or following a prep on the Maryland hunt circuit, where purses are small and pari-mutuel wagering is sparsely conducted. Many were personally schooled by Burley Cocks, a legendary developer of trainers who perfected the fine art of winning races off workouts and gallops, often at outrageous prices.

Johnathan Sheppard, known more for his steeplechase successes, Vinnie Blengs, Barclay Tagg, Katherine Voss and Seattle Slew's innovative trainer Billy Turner, Jr., are still clicking with fresh and fit underrated turfers up and down the eastern seaboard. Horseplayers could do worse than focus on trainers who regularly set up their stock for scores in repeat situations.

At Penn National Racecourse in the mid-1980s, I played in the annual World Series of Handicapping five straight years and finished sixth, second, third, twelfth and sixteenth, among the best combined finishes in the history of the tournament and the two best finishes for any "public handicapper."

One horse, an absentee grass horse named Another Ripple, was the key to my fortunes each year. Essentially a $10,000 claiming horse, Another Ripple was trained by John P. O'Conner, a Delaware Park-based horseman from the old school who seemed to relish putting over this horse on contest weekend in late October, the final weekend of the Penn National turf-racing season.

Every year, Another Ripple had a prep race, usually in a five-furlong turf sprint, before he was entered in a $1\frac{1}{16}$-mile claiming event, or starter allowance on the Penn National grass. The first year I doped him out, he won, but I did not bet enough on him to finish in the top five money positions, while the only other player to bet Another Ripple in the tournament won the contest.

The following year I bet enough to win $30,000 in prize money while the previous year's contest winner let him go without a dime, and the third year I bet enough to win $20,000 more. In year four, I was positioned to do at least as well and was salivating when I saw the seven-year-old Another Ripple listed in the final day's turf race. It rained; the race came off the grass; Another Ripple was scratched; I was out of the money.

In year five, we both were back, but I was knocked out of the contest before the eight-year-old Another Ripple race, so I bet him with enough real money and shared the proceeds of an amazing $10.40 mutuel with my contest assistant, Paul Deblinger, as we both paid our expenses to the best-run handicapping contest in America. I could not find a clean sample of Another Ripple's past performances to share with you, but if anyone out there has a set, I'd love to frame it.

Tough defeats? Completely wacky results? Of course. They happen every day. Horses and the humans who handle them are always capable of throwing in a clunker or improving beyond previous limitations. Mistakes? Certainly. The player is governed by the same laws of nature. But to win at the racetrack, the player must learn from his or her own mistakes and avoid the trap of punishing oneself too hard or too long for having made them. Self-doubt is sure to seep into your thinking after a series of bad selections or mismanaged plays. But the good player knows that his equilibrium will return as soon as he appreciates the fundamental truth that tomorrow is another day. The game is not going to go away. There will be other opportunities soon enough.

Usually such deep-rooted confidence comes only from many years of success, but it also can come from terrific preparation and a generally balanced disposition. At least the holes you punch in the wall of your favorite press box after a tough disqualification (see Andy Beyer) will not leave you with thoughts of jumping off the roof.

With no hesitation I can assure you that the concepts and research techniques contained in this book will prove successful to anyone willing to set up a reasonable work regimen. There are tools in here that were useful 20 years ago that will be useful 20 years from now. There are tools that I have never given away before and others I have personally taught to dozens of players who have gone on to bigger and better things. There is no magic formula to win at this game, but there is an edge to be gleaned through diligence, patience and the willingness to check things out for yourself. The patterns and ideas I have shared will isolate probable race winners in hundreds of races each season, but you must give yourself a chance to recognize them. Two of the most frequently encountered betting situations will bear a striking resemblance to the following examples:

ONE MILE—SOLANO RACETRACK—JULY 22, 1993 3-YEAR-OLD FILLIES, MAIDEN CLAIMING $12,500

Hilly's Empire

Own: Scott & Digango & Cypher
HANNA M A (24 2 4 3 .08) $12,500
B. f. 3 (Mar)
Sire: Empire Glory (Nijinsky II)
Dam: Zoom Up (Tilt Up)
Br: Harry Oda (Cal)
Tr: Scott Ronald (2 0 0 0 .00)
117

Lifetime Record:	4 M 0 0	$2,325		
1993	4 M 0 0	$2,325	Turf	0 0 0 0
1992	0 M 0 0		Wet	0 0 0 0
Sol	0 0 0 0		Dist	0 0 0 0

10Jly93-3Pln	fst	1 1/16	:234 :474 1:121 1:453	ⒻⓈMd 12500	57	7	9	710	58	55	44	Hanna M A	LB 117	19.70	76-11	Our Fast Ball117½ Miss Ice1173 O'let It Snow117½	Far wide drive 9
2Jly93-9Pln	fst	6f	:223 :451 :574 1:102	ⒻMd 14000	46	3	5	89½	79	610	49	Hanna M A	B 115	16.90	77-10	InyalaRouge1172 NativeSinsation1176 Herecomesthethrill1151	Even try 10
20Jun93-6Hol	fst	7f	:222 :45 1:102 1:24	3↑ⒻⓈMd 32000	40	3	12	911	912	912	912	Torres H	B 116	24.70	72-08	Empress Molly1161¼ DivineInspiration1162 PaneEVino114hd	Broke slowly 12
30May93-6Hol	fst	6f	:221 :454 :582 1:114	3↑ⒻⓈMd 32000	47	3	9	1010	911	610	46¼	Torres H	B 115	43.90	75-12	Brndy'sStrlet1153½ Bud'sNumberOn115¼ BluEydMiss1202¼	6 Wide stretch 10

WORKOUTS: Jun 28 Pln 4f fst :482 H 3/9 Jun 18 Fpx 3f fst :37 Hg 3/4 Jun 14 Fpx 5f fst 1:023 H 2/2 Jun 7 Fpx 4f fst :483 H 2/6 ●May 25 Fpx 4f fst :501 H 1/6 May 19 Fpx 6f fst 1:172 Hg 2/2

Ghost Lady

Own: Cipponeri Bill & Souza Richard
NOGUEZ A M (22 2 3 3 .09) $12,500
Dk. b or br f. 3 (May)
Sire: Under Tack (Crozier)
Dam: Baby Don't Lie (Forecast)
Br: Wayne Sharp & Jeffrey G. Monroe (Cal)
Tr: Souza Richard (6 0 0 1 .00)
117

Lifetime Record:	7 M 1 1	$3,050			
1993	7 M 1 1	$3,050	Turf	0 0 0 0	
1992	0 M 0 0		Wet	0 0 0 0	
Sol	1 0 0 0	$455	Dist	2 0 0 1	$1,365

13Jly93-7Sol	fst	1	:24 :49 1:143 1:42	ⒻMd 12500	40	1	3	2½	2hd	1hd	44¼	Noguez A M	LB 117 b	8.40	68-19	Saddles1172½ Thyra T1171¼ Kiss Me Regal117nk	Weakened 10
27Jun93-7Stk	fst	1	:221 :462 1:114 1:374	ⒻMd 12500	43	2	3	41½	2½	2hd	34½	Noguez A M	LB 118 b	7.80	79-06	Kirkezda118½ Kiss Me Regal1184 Ghost Lady1185	Inside bid 7
20Jun93-6Stk	fst	5f	:22 :452 :571	ⒻClm 12500N2L	37	5	6	67½	66¼	67	69¼	Miranda V	LB 115 b	20.90	87-08	Deadly Darling117¼ Sky Captive1172½ Foot Loose Girl1173¼	Outrun 6
13May93-3GG	fst	6f	:22 :45 :574 1:112	ⒻMd 12500	33	4	10	1010	811	711	711¾	Noguez A M	LB 117 b	49.90	71-15	Ifevrwizrdtherws1172½ ChosenJourney1173 TimlyScrt117½	Showed little 11
23Apr93-5GG	fst	6f	:22 :453 :582 1:112	ⒻMd 12500	38	10	9	99½	76¼	69	67¾	Doocy T T	LB 117 b	5.70	75-13	Miss Wardo117¾ Hoedown's Gone1173½ Tanfabulous1171	Wide trip 11
15Apr93-3GG	fst	6f	:222 :46 :584 1:122	ⒻMd 12500	51	8	4	53	33	24	24½	Noguez A M	LB 117 b	29.80	73-15	Political Reality1174½ Ghost Lady1171¼ Vale Of Honey1172½	Wide trip 11
1Apr93-3GG	gd	6f	:221 :462 :591 1:122	ⒻⓈMd 12500	35	8	8	65¼	42½	55	58½	Noguez A M	B 117 b	82.80	69-16	Ky's Ride1172 Agitatin' Luck1171½ Vale Of Honey1172	Even late 12

WORKOUTS: Jly 3 Sol 1 fst 1:442 H 1/2 Jun 4 Stk 6f fst 1:16 H 19/22 May 21 Stk 5f fst 1:031 H 12/25 May 8 BM 3f fst :384 H 7/20 Apr 9 BM 5f fst 1:024 H 5/16 Mar 27 BM 6f fst 1:172 H 11/16

Pebble Dancer

Own: Key Verlyne S
MERCADO P (35 5 3 5 .14) $12,500
Ro. f. 3 (May)
Sire: Northern Jove (Northern Dancer)
Dam: Pebbles (Prince Alert)
Br: Pollock Farms (Ala)
Tr: Campiotti George (6 0 0 0 .00)
117

Lifetime Record:	12 M 1 2	$6,155			
1993	7 M 0 0	$530	Turf	0 0 0 0	
1992	5 M 1 2	$5,625	Wet	1 0 0 0	$150
Sol	0 0 0 0		Dist	0 0 0 0	

30Jun93-8Pln	fst	5½f	:22 :46 :573 1:034	ⒻMd 12500	23	7	7	85¾	65¼	68	713¾	Lozoya D A	LB 117 fb	34.70	80-10	Daily Devil1175 Go Kathy Go1172½ Fractious Actress1172½	Showed little 10
20Jun93-8Stk	fst	5½f	:222 :461 :58 1:041	Md 8000	21	5	3	54½	47½	49½	411¼	Garcia M5	L 108 fb	5.50e	79-08	Dual Spirit1187 Kissability118½ Hay Bob1184	No rally 8
23Apr93-5GG	fst	6f	:22 :453 :582 1:112	ⒻMd 12500	16	1	8	55½	66	712	816¾	Ochoa A	LB 117 b	103.60	66-13	Miss Wardo117¾ Hoedown's Gone1173½ Tanfabulous1171	No threat 11
17Mar93-2GG	gd	6f	:22 :452 :584 1:122	ⒻMd 12500	13	5	4	55½	78½	811	618¼	Meza R Q	LB 117 b	21.70	59-20	Alibhai Island1172½ Mean Evil Woman1174½ Pure Mackee1172	Even try 10
24Feb93-3GG	gd	6f	:221 :46 :583 1:112	ⒻMd 12500	22	10	4	88½	97½	811	814¼	Belmonte J F	LB 117 b	25.30	68-13	Libation117no Sioux Sue1174½ Pleas Move Aside1173½	No threat 11
23Jan93-2BM	my	5f	:223 :461 :584	ⒻMd 12500	23	4	4	53¾	36½	46	59½	Boulanger G	LB 117 b	3.20	80-14	Hail Bold Lady1176 Island Bolger1171½ Pocket Numbers117hd	No rally 6
3Jan93-5BM	fst	6f	:223 :454 :584 1:12	ⒻMd 12500	10	9	2	42½	42½	610	917¼	Kaenel J L	LB 117 b	3.10	59-17	Ackful117hd Palace Madame117hd Miss Butterworth1124	Wide, faltered 12
16Dec92-2BM	fst	6f	:224 :46 :581 1:13	ⒻMd 12500	42	7	1	41¼	42½	42½	53	Baze R A	LB 118 b	*.70	68-22	Flying Queen118no Attractiveprospect118¾ Irish Victor118hd	Wide trip 11
27Nov92-3BM	fst	6f	:224 :461 :584 1:12	ⒻMd 20000	51	9	2	54	52¼	34	24¼	Baze R A	LB 117 b	2.50	72-19	Coastal Majesty1174 DH Misshollygolightly117 DH Pebble Dancer117½	9
Lacked room into stretch Placed second through disqualification.																	
30May92-1GG	fst	4½f	:221 :462 :524	ⒻMd 25000	45	9	5	44		32	3¾	Hansen R D	LB 117 b	6.50	92-11	D. Truce115½ Glittering Jessi117nk Pebble Dancer117	Wide late bid 10

WORKOUTS: Jun 14 Pln 3f fst :354 H 6/12 Jun 7 Pln 6f fst 1:133 H 7/12 Jun 1 Pln 5f fst 1:034 H 30/33 May 24 Pln 4f fst :493 H 10/21 Feb 16 Pln 5f fst 1:02 H 12/26

Starry Farrari

Own: Meeker Gary & Janet
GOMEZ E A (16 0 2 2 .00) $12,500
B. f. 3 (Apr)
Sire: Inherent Star (Pia Star)
Dam: Snow Boat (The Axe II)
Br: Russel Betker (Cal)
Tr: McDonald Melanie W (1 0 0 1 .00)
117

Lifetime Record:	6 M 0 1	$611			
1993	5 M 0 1	$611	Turf	0 0 0 0	
1992	1 M 0 0		Wet	0 0 0 0	
Sol	1 0 0 0	$65	Dist	1 0 0 0	$65

13Jly93-7Sol	fst	1	:24 :49 1:143 1:42	ⒻMd 12500	37	2	9	910	89¾	85	86½	Gomez E A	LB 117	58.20	66-19	Saddles1172½ Thyra T1171¼ Kiss Me Regal117nk	Outrun 10
22Jun93-5Stk	fst	6f	:223 :461 :59 1:113	ⒻMd 12500	31	2	8	87½	89¾	88	69	Gomez E A	LB 119	27.00	77-12	D Tyson's Folly1141 Intensly Bold1196½ Misty Lady119hd	No threat 9
Placed 5th through disqualification.																	
23May93-8TuP	fst	6f	:223 :454 :591 1:121	ⒻMd 8000	37	9	2	106¾	106½	62¼	34	Higuera A R	118	20.00	71-15	Shu Julie1132 French Cafe1182 Starry Farrari118nk	Finished well 11
14May93-9TuP	fst	6f	:222 :452 :574 1:111	ⒻMd 8000	34	4	11	108¾	910	611	59½	Drexler H A	118	9.20	70-17	Minute Star1182½ Shu Julie1134 French Cafe1183	Bumped early 12
28Apr93-1TuP	fst	6f	:214 :442 :57 1:102	ⒻMd 12500	22	10	1	95¾	99	913	911	Drexler H A	118	16.70	73-13	Sh'sSwGrcful1181 SongOfThSprt1181 VdvllLdy1181½	Fractious pre-race 10
28Oct92-9TuP	fst	6f	:22 :451 :573 1:103	ⒻStks Trl	19	9	2	72¾	86¾	912	814¼	Ortiz M F Jr	118	48.40	69-13	Peak At The Moon117hd Cabanal117½ Merits Misty117	Drifted out 1/16 9

WORKOUTS: Jly 6 SR 4f fst :482 H 3/5 ●Jun 19 SR 5f fst 1:001 H 1/10 Jun 12 SR 4f fst :513 H 3/5 May 9 TuP 5f fst :582 H 3/10 Apr 25 TuP 4f fst :461 H 3/22 Apr 19 TuP 6f fst 1:13 H 2/2

Kiss Me Regal

Own: Harralson Dan
CRUZ J B (7 0 2 1 .00) $12,500
Dk. b or br f. 3 (Mar)
Sire: Regalberto (Roberto)
Dam: Sensational Kiss (Figonero)
Br: Myron Johnson & Jane Johnson (Cal)
Tr: Castellanos Rito (4 0 2 1 .00)
117

Lifetime Record:	5 M 1 1	$2,735			
1993	4 M 1 1	$2,735	Turf	0 0 0 0	
1992	1 M 0 0		Wet	1 0 0 0	
Sol	1 0 0 1	$910	Dist	3 0 1 1	$2,735

13Jly93-7Sol	fst	1	:24 :49 1:143 1:42	ⒻMd 12500	41	5	5	43	41¾	5¾	34	Cruz J B	B 117 b	3.10	68-19	Saddles1172½ Thyra T1171½ Kiss Me Regal117nk	10
Steadied early stages, wide																	
27Jun93-7Stk	fst	1	:221 :462 1:114 1:374	ⒻMd 12500	50	6	2	1½	1½	1hd	2½	Cruz J B	B 118 b	5.70	83-06	Kirkezda118½ Kiss Me Regal1184 Ghost Lady1185	Game try 7
20Jun93-13Stk	fst	1	:223 :463 1:121 1:391	ⒻMd 12500	38	5	4	43¾	54	43½	44	Cruz J B	B 118	5.30	73-12	E. Z. Winner1182½ P. J.'s Hardhead1181½ Vaudeville Lady113hd	No rally 7
26May93-3GG	sl	6f	:224 :472 1:012 1:16	ⒻⓈMd 12500	42	5	11	1012	1014	913	812	Jauregui L H	B 117	111.70	48-39	Marella1172½ Round Is Funny1171 O'let It Snow1175	No threat 11
6Sep92-6Sac	fst	6f	:221 :462 :592 1:122	ⒻⓈMd 12500	11	2	10	97½	98	98	812	Allardyce R	B 118	24.40	65-14	Janskite1181 Bodanelli1185 Deadly Darling118	Off slowly 10

WORKOUTS: Jun 15 Stk 3f fst :36 Hg 2/7 May 14 Stk 6f fst 1:143 H 6/10 May 7 Stk 6f fst 1:163 H 6/7 Apr 30 Stk 5f fst 1:012 H 4/17

First Leap
Own: Sota Richard

Ch. f. 3 (Apr)
Sire: Lightning Leap (Nijinsky II)
Dam: Burayda (Vaguely Noble)
Br: Double R L Co. (Colo)
Tr: Pavan Eugene (1 0 0 0 .00)

117

	Lifetime Record:	4 M 0 0	$80		
1993	4 M 0 0	$80	Turf	0 0 0 0
1992	0 M 0 0		Wet	0 0 0 0
Sol	0 0 0 0		Dist	1 0 0 0

OCHOA A (15 1 1 0 .07) $12,500

2Jly93–9Pln fst 6f :223 :451 :574 1:102 ⑤Md 16000   33 4 2 2½ 32 59 814 Mercado P   LB 117 18.20   72–10 InyalaRouge117³ NativeSinsation117½ Herecomesthethrill115¹   Stopped 10
16May93–4GG fst 6f :214 :443 :572 1:103 3↑ⓈMd Sp Wt   21 4 8 76 711 821 821½ Ochoa A   LB 116 57.50   65–13 Sweet Savanna1154½ Kind And Gentle1152 Country Cruise1151½   Outrun 9
11Apr93–1GG fst 1 :231 :474 1:13 1:40 3↑ⓂMd Sp Wt   48 9 2 2½ 33 67½ 810 Ochoa A   LB 117 84.00   60–28 Fax Me117² Miz Interco117½ Stylish Accent117½   Stopped 9
7Mar93–2GG fst 6f :221 :452 :58 1:104 ⑤Md Sp Wt   26 2 6 3½ 44 610 618 Felton J E   B 117 26.50   68–13 Poetry Writer117½ Vedra117½ Financially Fit117³   Off slowly 6

WORKOUTS: ● Jun 28 Pln 4f fst :46² H 1/9   Jun 14 Pln 5f fst 1:01¹ H 10/23   Jun 7 Pln 5f fst 1:01¹ H 24/44   Jun 1 Pln 4f fst :47¹ H 3/20   ●May 24 Pln 4f fst :48 H 1/21   May 10 Pln 4f fst :49¹ H 10/19

Perky Partner
Own: Enlow Mark

Dk. b or br f. 3 (Apr)
Sire: Tsunami Slew (Seattle Slew)
Dam: General Partner (Understanding)
Br: North Ridge Farm (Ky)
Tr: Mastrangelo William (3 0 0 2 .00)

117

	Lifetime Record:	3 M 0 0	$240		
1993	3 M 0 0	$240	Turf	0 0 0 0
1992	0 M 0 0		Wet	0 0 0 0
Sol	0 0 0 0		Dist	0 0 0 0

PATTERSON A (8 1 0 0 .13) $12,500

30Jun93–8Pln fst 5½f :22 :46 :573 1:034 ⑥Md 12500   24 2 3 96½ 88½ 710 6¹0 Patterson A   LB 117 b 9.90   81–10 Daily Devil117⁵ Go Kathy Go117²½ Fractious Actress117²½   No threat 10
18Jun93–9GG fst 6f :213 :442 :564 1:10 ⑥Md 12500   37 9 12 1115 1016 819 516½ Warren R J Jr   LB 117 b 10.30   74–12 Miss Cuchillada117¹⁴ Real Gossip117ⁿᵏ Prominent Dancer117²   12
   Bobbled, steadied start
6Jun93–3GG fst 5½f :221 :451 :574 1:042 ⑥Md 12500   39 5 9 1010 109½ 811 68 Patterson A   LB 117 7.80   83–09 Retsina Dance117¹ Temper Me117²½ Fractious Actress117¹   Showed little 12

WORKOUTS: Jly 15 BM 7f fst 1:29⁴ H 2/2   Jly 7 BM 4f fst :48⁴ H 7/19   ● Jun 25 BM 4f fst :47¹ Hg 1/17   Jun 5 BM 4f gd :48³ H 2/6   May 27 BM 6f gd 1:14² H 2/2   May 23 BM 6f fst 1:15 H 6/11

Empire Pro
Own: Lang Austin

Dk. b or br f. 3 (Mar)
Sire: Empire Glory (Nijinsky II)
Dam: Prodigal Protege (Pirate's Bounty)
Br: Austin Lang (Cal)
Tr: Trinchard Barry (—)

117

	Lifetime Record:	2 M 0 0	$0		
1993	2 M 0 0		Turf	0 0 0 0
1992	0 M 0 0		Wet	0 0 0 0
Sol	0 0 0 0		Dist	0 0 0 0

CAMPBELL J G (1 0 0 0 .00) $12,500

   Entered 20Jly93– 7 SOL
9Apr93–4SA 6½f :214 :45 1:104 1:172 ⑤ⓈMd 32000   24 11 9 117½ 1016 916 819½ Pedroza M A   LB 117 61.00   65–13 Nskrnomicl117²½ Lucky'sBby117²½ Numbrthirtyfiv117³   Wide backstretch 12
13Mar93–9SA 6f :214 :451 :573 1:102 ⑤ⓈMd Sp Wt   27 2 11 118½ 109½ 1114 1121½ Pedroza M A   B 117 46.70   63–12 Francie's Fancy117¹ January Jeanie117¹½ Malojen117²½   Broke slowly 12

WORKOUTS: Jly 18 GG 3f fst :39² H 16/21   Jly 10 GG 3f fst :34⁴ H 2/11   Jly 1 GG 5f fst 1:01¹ Hg 5/18   ● Jun 24 GG 5f fst 1:00⁴ Hg 1/18   Jun 17 GG 5f fst 1:01³ H 9/27   Jun 10 GG 5f fst 1:02⁴ H 25/35

A Good Run
Own: Christiano John R

B. f. 3 (Feb)
Sire: A Run (Empery)
Dam: Good Times Ahead (Crack Ahead)
Br: John J. Christiano & Susan E. Chris (Cal)
Tr: Brewster Larry (5 0 1 0 .00)

117

	Lifetime Record:	1 M 0 0	$60		
1993	1 M 0 0	$60	Turf	0 0 0 0
1992	0 M 0 0		Wet	0 0 0 0
Sol	0 0 0 0		Dist	0 0 0 0

MIRANDA V (33 3 5 4 .09) $12,500

26Jun93–10Stk 5f :222 :461 :591 ⑥Md 12500   –0 10 7 87½ 810 811 712 Uribe S   118 78.90   75–08 Exclusive Taboo118½ Derousi Treat118¹ Capetic113³   No rally 9

WORKOUTS: Jly 18 Sol 4f fst :51⁴ H 7/8   Jly 12 Sol 7f fst 1:30³ H 1/1   Jly 6 Sol 5f fst 1:04⁴ H 10/10   Jun 4 Stk 5f fst 1:05¹ Hg 43/48   May 18 Stk 5f fst 1:05⁴ H 8/8   May 11 Stk 5f fst 1:04⁴ H 6/6

Florentine Angel
Own: David & Gilliam & Mann & Wynne

Dk. b or br f. 3 (Jan)
Sire: Greinton–GB (Green Dancer)
Dam: Barbsie (T V Lark)
Br: New Horizon Partnership XIV & Howel (Cal)
Tr: Stoker John (2 0 0 0 .00)

117

	Lifetime Record:	1 M 0 0	$100		
1993	1 M 0 0	$100	Turf	0 0 0 0
1992	0 M 0 0		Wet	0 0 0 0
Sol	0 0 0 0		Dist	0 0 0 0

HUMMEL C R (14 2 2 3 .14) $12,500

7Jly93–7Pln fst 6f :223 :46 :584 1:113 3↑ⓂMd 20000   16 5 8 9¹² 9¹⁷ 9¹⁵ 8¹⁵ Tohill K S   B 115 b 39.90   65–16 Miss Minnelli1155 A Glass Act115ʰᵈ Round Is Funny1154   No threat 9

WORKOUTS: Jly 17 BM 5f fst 1:03¹ H 14/26   Jly 3 BM 5f fst 1:01 H 3/13   Jun 27 BM 4f fst :49 Hg 2/12   Jun 19 GG 4f fst :49⁴ Hg 16/23   Jun 14 GG 6f fst 1:18¹ H 3/3   Jun 10 GG 5f fst 1:02³ H 23/35

We are at one of the tracks on the northern California Fair circuit, where purses for each claiming level match the major tracks in the region and the daily betting handle is upward of $1.8 million on the satellite network. Nevertheless, few players would see any merit in this race without taking a close look. It is not a very promising group, with only three second-place finishes from a combined 44 lifetime starts.

When we realize that it collectively costs about $180,000 to keep these horses in training for one year, we should have some sympathy for the owners who are taking a bath with these walking feed bills. Yet there is a standout, maximum-limit prime bet play in this race—First Leap, who has won a paltry $80 from four trips to the post and yet embodies a classic winning pattern.

In three of her four prior races, First Leap has hinted at more early speed than any of her nine rivals have ever had to face. Ghost Lady's best speed showing to date was her pace-pressing effort clocked in 24 and 49 seconds on a slow track. In her prior outing she was close to the realistic pace set by Kiss Me Regal clocked in 22.20 and 46.40, but there is nothing in the performances of either horse that looks strong enough to keep First Leap from putting herself into clear control of today's pace.

For this one-mile distance, we should be encouraged that First Leap was sired by a son of stoutly bred European champion Nijinsky and is out of a stoutly bred daughter of Vaguely Noble, winner of the European classic, L'Prix d'L'Arc deTriomphe. We should be encouraged that First Leap has never raced at this reduced level, which means she is a candidate for improvement, while Kiss Me Regal and Ghost Lady have been defeated in 11 combined starts at $12,500 maiden claiming, a terribly inept portfolio for the two most dangerous rivals.

At this level of competition, horses who control the pace tend to win a high percentage of races, and we should be encouraged by First Leap's last race, a sprint in which she was within two lengths of a realistic pace with identical 22.60 clockings for each ¼-mile split. No horse in this lineup with the exception of First Leap has ever run as fast or faster through the first ½ mile. Even her worst performance, in May at Golden Gate Fields against nonclaiming maidens, when she was six lengths behind the leader in 21.80 and 11 lengths behind the leader in 44.60, equals or surpasses Kiss Me Regal and Ghost Lady's best efforts!

Given that evidence, I am sure you can visualize the ease by which this filly will be able to sail to the front at will in this contest. And therein lies the heart and power of the pattern.

Except on a stretch-running, biased track, whenever a horse figures to get a clear, uncontested lead on the field for the first time, the player should expect dramatic improvement over recent performances. If the horse already rates close to the competition, as First Leap surely does, the expected improvement is odds-on to result in victory. Odds-on is what I said and odds-on is what I meant. Give a horse like that a slow-breaking field or a front-running racetrack, and the only thing that will defeat it is an act of God or war.

While this filly's edge was not quite that dramatic, it certainly was convincing enough to invite a strong play at $7.90—1 odds.

If speed points had been employed to dissect the probable pace, First Leap would be entitled to seven, while only one rival in the field, Ghost Lady would have as many as 5.

If pace numbers had been employed, First Leap would have scored very highly as a probable threat or possible winner. If middle moves were considered, First Leap would have looked dominating.

No matter how we slice this pie, there was a terrific play to be made in this corner of the racing world on July 22, 1993.

In the actual race, First Leap broke alertly, was restrained into a stalking position outside Ghost Lady for the first ½ mile, moved to a two-length lead with no undue urging on the backstretch, remained in safe control of the pace thereafter as Empire Pro rallied late to take second.

The other classic winning pattern I want to reinforce is contained in the past performances for the 9th Churchill Downs race taken from the original *Betting Thoroughbreds.* I submit it again precisely because it does not have speed figures, or any of the other past-performance improvements we could use to help us see the logical winner. Sometimes we need to have a pattern indelibly imprinted in our mind's eyes, to avoid missing it in the cloud of so much conflicting data.

As explained in Chapter 4, the position of the starting gate relative to the first turn is very important in middle-distance races at many racetracks. Churchill Downs is one of those tracks.

The favorite in this race for three-year-olds—the Twin Spires Purse, which used to be an annual fixture on the Derby Day program—is Greek Answer at 3—5. There are several reasons why this price is outrageously out of line with reality.

One of those reasons is Ruggles Ferry, who has run one subpar race (March 22), while meeting some of the better three-year-old-routers in America, including eventual Preakness winner Master Derby and other multi-stakes winners Circle Home, Honey Mark and Colonel Power. (On the date of this race, Honey Mark and Master Derby were among the listed starters for the Kentucky Derby.) Ruggles Ferry has shown enough speed in several of his races to suggest that he can secure a good placement behind the pace from his inner post position.

The other reasons lie with Greek Answer himself. This is a colt that has shown a tendency to tire in the late stages at 6½ furlongs and beyond; a colt whose lone win around two turns was scored on Gulfstream Park's notorious front-running track; a colt that will have to use much of his early speed to get clear of this field in the short run to the first turn. These are serious problems for a 3–5 shot to overcome. I made him 6–1.

The crowd made Ruggles Ferry 5–2; I made him even money, a 250 percent overlay.

9th Churchill Downs

MAY 3, 1975

1 1/16 MILES. (1:41⅗). ALLOWANCES. Purse $25,000. 3-year-olds. Weight, 122 lbs. Non-winners of a race of $9,775 at a mile or over allowed 3 lbs.; a race of $6,000 at any distance, 5 lbs.; a race of $4,875 at any distance, 7 lbs.; a race of $3,900 at a mile or over in 1975, 9 lbs. (Maiden, claiming and starter races not considered.)

Jim Dan Bob 113 B. c (1972), by Wa-Wa Cy—Legayle, by Bar Le Duc.
Breeder, G. Begley (Ky.).
Owner, G. Begley. Trainer, A. Montano.
1975 10 0 3 3 $7,754
1974 11 4 2 2 $9,265
26 Apr75 7CD 7 f :234 :4711:25 ft 52 117 77¼ 714 615 512 ArroyoH1 Alw 70 Greek Answer122 Gatch 7
17 Apr75 7Kee 7 f :23 :46 1:234ft 92 1075 913 99¾ 910 96¾ TrsclairAJ7 Alw 80 HoneyMark114 Brent'sPrnce 11
3 Apr75 7Lat 1 :4711:1241:402ft 8-5e 114 78¾ 410 210 37½ McKnghtJ9 Alw 69 Some Dude 115 Count Paco 9
29 Mar75 7Lat 1 :48 1:1321:40 gd 7½ 112 52½ 34½ 34½ 38 McKnhtJ2 AlwS 71 NaughtyJke119 PromndeLft 8
18 Mar75 8Lat 1 :4831:1441:433gd 3¾ 113 35 44½ 37 22 McKnghtJ6 Alw 59 ClarenceHenry120 JimDan 9
7 Mar75 7Lat 6 f :24 :4811:151gd 8-5 ▲116 2h 15 11½ 2no VasqzG1 A—— 72 MowingJoe113 JimDanBob 5
21 Feb75 7Lat 1 1/16 :4841:1441:494ft 2½ 113 33 2h 21 21½ VasquezG3 Alw 59 ClarenceHnry116 JmDanBob 6
1 Feb75 6Key 170 :4711:1441:47 gd 11 119 59 412 58½ 511 OrtizI3 Alw 54 Go Go Treniers 119 Prfct Gn 6
25 Jan75 8Key 6 f :222 :4611:132sy 11 112 58½ 48 511 619 OrtizI4 AlwS 56 Gallant Bob 119 Sgt. Hunt 7
17 Jan75 8Key 6 f :222 :4611:12 ft 17 117 66½ 51¾ 31½ 3¾ OrtizI3 Alw 81 SneakyWin 117 Dr.FrankB. 8
Dec28-747Cwl 6½ f 1:23⅘sy 1 ▲119 12 12 11 11 VasquezG2 Alw 79 JimDanBob119 Clar'nceH'ry B.J.King 6
April 24 CD 4f sy :52b March 27 Lat 3f ft :39b March 5 Lat 3f ft :37h

Ruggles Ferry 117 Gr. c (1972), by Drone—Trotta Sue, by Promised Land.
Breeder, F. Preston (Ky.).
Owner, Mrs. F. Preston. Trainer, H. Trotsek.
1975 5 2 1 0 $12,075
1974 13 2 2 6 $26,884
24 Apr75 7Kee 1⅛ :4711:12 1:49 sy 53 117 59 44 37 57¾ ArroyoH8 AlwS 84 MasterDerby123 HoneyMark 9
15 Apr75 7Kee 1 1/16 :47 1:11 1:423gd 6 115 56 54 23 25 ArroyoH5 Alw 88 MasterDerby123 RugglsFrry 6
22 Mar75 9FG 1⅛ :4611:1021:493ft 14 115 1020 914 911 98¼ BarrowT2 AlwS 88 MasterDrby123 ColonelPowr 11
14 Mar75 9FG 6 f :221 :46 1:104ft 1-2 ▲120 67¼ 54½ 22 11 BarrowT4 Alw 94 RugglesFrry120 ElectnSpecl 6
15 Feb75 6Hia 7 f :23 :4521:232ft 7 117 108¼ 79½ 32 1h BarrowT7 Alw 88 RgglsFerry117 BravestRman 11
Nov16-748CD 1 1:36 ft 5¾ 116 88½ 75 52½ 35¼ BarrowT2 HcpS 84 CircleHome116 MasterD'rby R'gl'sF'ry 9
Nov 6-748CD 7 f 1:25⅖sy 9 115 11181014 55 32½ BarrowT9 Alw 77 MasterD'rby122 W'yw'rdR'd R'gl'sF'y 11
Oct19-747Kee a 7 f 1:25⅘ft 8½ 122 109¾ 88½ 35 35½ BarrowT9 ScwS 88 Pack'rC'pt'n122 M'st'rD'by R'gl'sF'ry 11
Oct 9-747Kee 6 f 1:09⅗ft 5½ 115 65¾ 66½ 41½ 11½ BarrowT4 Alw 94 RugglesFerry115 Ga'ntBob Pack'rCa'n 6
Aug28-747AP 6 f 1:11⅗gd 2¼ ▲119 77 43½ 22½ 2¾ BarrowT6 Alw 84 CraftyD'ne119 R'gglesFerry DonOman 7
April 30 CD 5f ft 1:03⅖b April 23 Kee 3f ft :36b April 20 Kee 5f ft 1:04b

Dixmart 122 B. g (1972), by Swoon's Son—Liz Piet, by Piet.
Breeder, Copelan & Thornbury (Ky.).
Owner, C. O. Viar & R. Holthus. Trainer, R. Holthus.
1975 7 2 3 2 $29,800
1974 13 2 2 3 $11,085
22 Apr75 6Kee 7 f :23 :4541:23 ft 6½ 122 78 66½ 24 22 CampbllRJ1 Alw 89 Paris Dust 116 Dixmart 9
5 Apr75 7OP 170 :4611:1141:414ft 8 113 79 63¾ 2½ 1¾ CampbllRJ3 Alw 87 Dixmart 113 Doug 6
31 Mar75 5OP 6 f :22 :4541:112ft 6-5 ▲118 41¾ 52 41 32 CampbllRJ3 Alw 86 Jay'sGig114 BourrePadnah 9
26 Mar75 6OP 6 f :22 :4511:104ft 5¾ 113 32 23½ 22½ 2no CmpblRJ10 Alw 91 Pleasure Prize 113 Dixmart 10
11 Mar75 6OP 6 f :221 :4611:131sl 8¾ 112 86¾ 77½ 43 11½ CmpblRJ3 22500 79 Dixmart 112 Kayjo 11
4 Mar75 6OP 6 f :214 :4511:12 ft 3¼ 114 54 54¼ 3nk 2nk RiniA9 15000 85 Warrior Knight 112 Dixmart 10
18 Feb75 6OP 5½ f :222 :4641:053ft 4¾ 116 84 53¼ 41½ 36½ RiniA9 15000 83 BourrePadnh111 GrtRhythm 12
Oct19-745Haw 6½ f 1:16⅕ft 8-5e▲114 87½ 814 714 711 LivelyJ1 Alw 81 Str'teMiss114 J'dgeBol'm'r Hon'yM'rk 9
April 29 CD 6f ft 1:18b Mar 25 OP 3f ft :37⅖b Mar 20 OP 5f ft 1:02⅗b

Maurading 119 Gr. c (1972), by Warfare—Juliet, by Nearctic.
Breeder, Barrett M. Morris & Virginia M. Morris (Ky.).
1975 . 8 2 2 2 $32,450
1974 10 1 3 0 $7,955
Owner, Bromagen Cattle Co. Trainer, G. P. Bernis.

22 Apr75 6Kee 7 f :23 :4541:23 ft 3¾ 122 32 54½ 34½ 33 LouvereGE7 Alw 88 Paris Dust 116 Dixmart 9
5 Apr75 9OP 1⅛ :4641:1021:514ft 17 123 53½ 94½ 85½ 85½ McHrgeD7 AlwS 79 PrmisedCity126 BldChapeau 14
15 Mar75 9OP 170 :4721:1311:442gd 9½ 119 31 2h 41¾ 54¾ MelncnL2 HcpO 69 PromisedCity120 Me n'Mine 12
8 Mar75 7OP 170 :23 :4721:42 ft 4½ 117 1½ 1h 1h 1h MelanconL1 Alw 86 Maraudng117 CountryByJim 7
28 Feb75 8OP 6 f :213 :4511:111ft 4¾ 122 51¾ 44 53¾ 22¾ MelnconL8 Alw 86 PoorOldJoe 114 Marauding 8
14 Feb75 8OP 6 f :214 :4431:102ft 2½e*120 53½ 47 31 31 MelconL4 HcpO 92 King Jody 112 Untwine 11
7 Feb75 8OP 5½ f :221 :4621:06 gd 27 117 52½ 42½ 31½ 1¾ MelnconL4 Alw 88 Marauding 117 Peto'sFellow 12
24 Jan75 8LaD 6 f :231 :4821:142m 9-5 *1155 11½ 16 13 2½ WolfCG6 Alw Hot Paque 111 Marauding 6
Nov30-749FG 6 f 1:13⅗gd 68 112 42½ 33 58½ 511 Mel'onL6 HcpO 70 HoneyM'k117 RusticRuler MidniteR'o 14
April 28 CD 1m ft 1:45⅘b April 21 Kee 3f ft :37⅗b April 16 Kee 5f ft :59h

---

Naughty Jake 122 Dk. b. or br. c (1972), by Gallant Romeo—Matrona, by Terra Firma.
Breeder, S. Turner (Ky.).
1975 . 8 2 0 1 $25,650
1974 . 7 3 1 0 $17,675
Owner, Mildred Bachelor. Trainer, J. Bachelor.

29 Apr75 8CD 1 :4641:11 1:362ft 4½ 122 21½ 2½ 31½ 33½ VasqzG4 AlwS 94 RoundStake122 RushingMan 5
15 Apr75 7Kee 1 1/16 :47 1:11 1:423gd 9½ 123 33½ 43½ 55½ 412 VasquezG1 Alw 81 MasterDerby123 RugglsFrry 6
29 Mar75 7Lat 1 :48 1:1321:40 gd 1-3 *119 1½ 13 1½ 11 VasqzG3 AlwS 79 NaughtyJke119 PromndeLft 9
22 Mar75 5Lat 6 f :23 :4711:124sy 2-3 *122 26 23 11 14 VasquezG7 Alw 84 NaughtyJake122 ColonialPnt 7
20 Feb75 3Hia 1 1/16 :4631:11 1:424sy 5½ 117 711 511 48 49¾ ValdizanF1 Alw 79 CircleHome119 Administratr 7
29 Jan75 9Hia 7 f :222 :4441:22 ft 30 115 68 58 58 65½ ValdiznF5 AlwS 89 Ascetic 115 Ellora 11
18 Jan75 9Hia 6 f :22 :4431:101sy 74 115 75¾ 56½ 45 41¾ ValdiznF6 AlwS 90 Ricks Jet 114 Prevailer 11
Jan 9-759Crc 6½ f 1:19⅗ft 15 122 67 68¾ 67 45½ ValdizanF4 Alw 87 Strateaway113 Prevailer IrishRing 6
April 27 CD 3f ft :35h

Mr. Snow Cap 113 B. g (1972), by One More Chorus—Orange Ice, by Iceberg II.
Breeder, H. G. Tilson (Ky.).
1975 . 6 2 2 1 $9,210
Owner, Audley Farm Stable. Trainer, D. Smith.

24 Apr75 4Kee 6 f :22 :45 1:101sy 4 114 68 56½ 49 514 DelahyeE10 Alw 77 BearerBond112 CmmrclPilot 11
18 Apr75 6Kee 7 f :233 :4631:242ft 6-5 *112 21½ 2½ 2½ 12½ DelahsyeE2 Alw 84 Mr. Snow Cap 112 Easabaya 10
9 Apr75 7Kee 6 f :222 :4541:103ft 8-5 *114 43 43 21 2¾ DelahsyeE3 Alw 88 RushingMan118 Mr.SnwCap 9
12 Mar75 7FG 6 f :222 :4641:122ft 3-2 120 54¾ 44 31½ 2no DelahsyeE1 Alw 86 FlwlssFinish120 Mr.SnwCap 7
26 Feb75 8FG 6 f :214 :4531:111ft 1-2e*120 4¾ 1½ 21 34½ AndersnJR8 Alw 87 Tailor'sTack120 BoldChapau 9
16 Feb75 2FG 6 f :224 :4811:141sl 3-2 *120 1½ 11 12 15 DsyeE11 M10000 77 Mr.SnwCap120 BrtherBadBy 12
April 17 Kee 3f ft :35⅗b April 7 Kee 3f ft :36b March 28 FG 3f ft :37b

---

Victory Judge 113 B. c (1972), by Traffic Judge—Choiseul, by Victory Morn.
Breeder, R. C. Kyle (Can.).
1975 . 8 1 0 0 $1,452
1974 4 M 1 1 $1,050
Owner, Sacred Stable. Trainer, A. Battaglia.

17 Apr75 9GP Ⓣ a 1 1:392fm 90 114 813 811 813 823 RamosR6 Alw 61 TooCordial 114 StepForward 8
10 Mar75 9GP 7 f :22 :4411:213ft 239 110 55½101610231128 DennieD10 AlwS 68 GreekAnswer122 FashinSale 11
1 Mar75 6Hia 6 f :222 :4541:102ft 54 119 97¾ 810 914 913 ArroyoH7 Alw 78 SwingLbrSwing117 Zinglng 10
5 Feb75 8Hia 7 f :231 :4531:224ft 66 122 32½ 54½ 9171118 BrumfelcD9 Alw 73 Directory 117 Jimbosanda 11
29 Jan75 9Hia 7 f :222 :4441:22 ft 299 112 57 91511201117 ArroyoH11 AlwS 78 Ascetic 115 Ellora 11
18 Jan75 3Cwl 6½ :242 :4831:234m 2 *120 15 16 15 19 SaylerB5 Mdn 79 VictoryJudge120 ZperGgette 8
Jan10-758Cwl 5½ f 1:08⅖sy 5 105 614 511 54½ 41½ ClinchT1 Alw 81 Mike'sPal 116 PrinceArc NoDate 7
Jan 2-758Cwl 6½ f 1:25⅘m 13 116 63½ 31½ 31½ 818 GastonR6 Alw 53 Donda'sMir'e122 CoolItB'e Jan't'sDe't 10
Dec21-743Cwl a1 1:42⅗gd 2-3 *120 14 11 2h 35½ SaylerB1 Mdn 61 Cool ItBabe117 BrightM'ch V't'ryJ'ge 10
Dec 7-748Cwl 1 1/16 1:54⅕sy 29. 111 21½ 1h 1h 21½ SaylerB4 Alw 65 Clar'ceH'ry113 Vict'yJ'ge JimDanBob 6
April 21 GP 7f ft 1:28⅗h

Greek Answer 122 B. c (1972), by Northern Answer—Greek Victress, by Victoria Park.
Breeder, E. P. Taylor (Can.).
1975 5 3 0 1 $57,707
1974 . 11 5 2 2 $187,261
Ownr, W P. Gilbride. Trainer, F. H. Merrill.

26 Apr75 7CD 7 f :234 :4711:25 ft 1-3 *122 1½ 12½ 12 1¾ SolomneM7 Alw 82 Greek Answer122 Gatch 7
19 Mar75 9GP 1 1/16 :46 1:1011:424ft 6-5 *122 15 16 13 14 SolmneM6 AlwS 87 Greek Answer 122 Decipher 8
10 Mar75 9GP 7 f :22 :4411:213ft 3-5 *122 1½ 1½ 14 15 CstdaM11 AlwS 96 GreekAnswer122 FashinSale 11
29 Jan75 9Hia 7 f :222 :4441:22 ft 3½ 122 1½ 1½ 22 44¾ CastaM10 AlwS 90 Ascetic 115 Eliora 11
18 Jan75 9Hia 6 f :22 :4431:101sy 3-5 *122 1h 1h 2h 31 CstndaM4 AlwS 91 Ricks Jet 114 Prevailer 11
Oct19-748Bow 7 f 1:24⅘sft 2-3 *119 22½ 22 1h 2¾ Hin'j'saH6 AlwS 80 Gall'tBob113 Gr'kAnswer ParvaHasta 10
Sep15-748WO 1-70 1:42⅕ft 7-5 122 11½ 11 22½ 36½ C'st'daM7 HcpS 85 L'Enjol'r122 N'r t'eHighS'a G'kAnsw'r 11
Sep 2-748AP 6½ f 1:17⅘ft 3½ 122 12½ 11 11½ 1¾ C'st'daM2 ScwS 86 Gr'kAnsw'r122 Col'lP'w'r TheB'g'lPr'e 7
Au·24-748Sar 6½ f 1:13 ft 13 121 12½ 12 1½ 23¾ Cas'daM8 ScwS 92 F'lishPl's're121 G'kAnsw'r OurT'lism'n 8
Aug 5-746FE 6½ f 1:21⅘sl 2-5 *120 1h 2h 1h 48 GreenW2 AlwS 65 Col'sCl'rion115 OnaP'dSt'l'g P'sleyPal 8
Jly 21-746FE 6½ f 1:17 ft 1-3 *122 1½ 12 13 1¾ GreenW2 AlwS 94 Greek Answer 122 L'Enjoleur Hagelin 5
Jun28-746WO 6 f 1:10⅗ft 4-5 *120 2h 1½ 13 17 GreenW4 AlwS 90 Gr'kAnswer120 N'r t.HighSea R'lS'ari 6
Jun 9-746WO 6 f 1:10⅖ft 1-2 *114 1h 12 13½ 15½ GreenW7 AlwS 91 GreekAnswer114 Sgt.Hunt RunJay 7
April 21 CD 1m ft 1:41h

The key to this betting situation may have been more subtle than the First Leap-type pace play, but it is there for all to see. The favorite is breaking from a disadvantageous post position (or has to compete against a track bias or severe pace problem), and his past-performance history suggests he can ill afford to race under any handicap. The chief competition is easily identified and is set to race from a favorable post or has a track bias or favorable pace scenario in his corner.

Players who hope to win at this game must be able to downgrade horses with apparent good form who have little margin for error. Whenever such a favorite is encountered, the player should scan the rest of the field for logical threats who figure to benefit from the pace or the bias or whatever. If the chief competition is easily identified, or there are two or three legitimate upset threats, there will be an array of possibilities to play at overlayed prices.

What follows are additional past-performance profiles of vulnerable betting favorites from races run at Del Mar Racecourse during August 1993, while I was simultaneously conducting a 900-line handicapping seminar each day—partly to produce examples for this book.

High Mesa
Own: K C Stable & Martin
GONZALEZ S JR (96 9 9 15 .09) **$10,000**

Gr. g. 7
Sire: Relaunch (In Reality)
Dam: Buvette (To Market)
Br: Wimbledon Farm (Ky)
Tr: Mitchell Mike (28 9 9 1 .32)

L 114^5

Lifetime Record:	41	12	7	0	$118,875						
1993	6	4	0	0	$26,075	Turf	2	0	0	0	
1992	16	4	5	0	$46,550	Wet	1	0	0	0	
Dmr	4	1	1	0	$15,175	Dist	22	6	6	0	$57,125

17Jly93-5Hol	fst	6½f	:22^2	:45^1	1:09^3	1:16	Clm c-14000	90	7	1	2^{hd}	1^{hd}	12½	14½	Gonzalez S^5	LB 110 f	*.90	89-12	High Mesa110^{4½} Tod117^3 Emphatically117½		7
Handily, dropped whip 1/8; Claimed from Carr & Saip, Saip Jack Trainer																					
24Jun93-5Hol	fst	6f	:21^4	:44^4	:56^4	1:09^2	Clm 12500	92	3	4	2½	2½	1^1	1^{1½}	Gonzalez S^5	LB 112 f	5.60	93-07	High Mesa112^{1½} Dr. Hyde117¾ Earplug117^{1¾}	Driving	10
13Jun93-6Hol	fst	6f	:22^1	:45^1	:57^2	1:10^1	Clm 10000	85	7	1	3^3	3^{4½}	3^4	1^{hd}	Gonzalez S^5	LB 114 f	2.10	89-09	High Mesa114^{hd} Dr. Hyde117^1 Contented117^1	Wide backstretch	8
26May93-5Hol	fst	6f	:21^4	:45^1	:57^2	1:10	Clm 9000	85	7	1	3^{nk}	1½	1^{1½}	1^2	Gonzalez S^5	LB 110 f	25.30	90-11	High Mesa110^2 Father Six To Five115^{3½} Machote119½	Wide, driving	10
14May93-1Hol	fst	6f	:22	:45	:57	1:09^3	Clm 14000	63	3	5	3^{nk}	7^{4¾}	6^6	6^{11½}	Gonzalez S^5	LB 110 f	28.10	80-10	Screen Tale117^{2¾} Racer Rex117^3 Machote117^{no}	Brief speed	7
21Apr93-9GG	fst	6f	:22^1	:45^1	:57^3	1:09^4	Clm c-9000	71	2	3	1½	2^{hd}	6^{3¼}	5^{5½}	Gonzalez R M	LB 115 f	4.60	85-13	Fistylee117^{hd} Kleven Eleven117^2 Concave116^{2½}	Weakened	10
Claimed from Bautista Joe & Sharron, Matos Gil Trainer																					
27Nov92-1BM	fst	6f	:22^3	:45^3	:58	1:10^3	3↑ Clm 16000	63	2	1	1^{hd}	5^{1¾}	5^5	5^7	Gonzalez R M	LB 117	2.90	76-19	Plymeonemoretime119^2 SpdCrft117^1 ShrpEvnt117^4	Drifted out stretch	6
6Nov92-7BM	fst	6f	:22^2	:45	:57^1	1:10	3↑ Clm 12500	81	2	4	1^1	2½	2^3	2^2	Gonzalez R M	LB 117	2.10	84-20	Barry Chancy117^2 High Mesa117^{1½} Staff Meeting117	2nd best	7
10Oct92-6BM	fst	6f	:22^1	:44^4	:57^1	1:09^3	3↑ Clm 18000	77	6	9	9^{7½}	9^{9¼}	7^8	6^{5½}	Gonzalez R M	LB 115	*2.30	82-17	SlewOfDamascus117½ ShrpEvent119^{1½} Hrlen'sAgency117	Hopped start	9
13Sep92-9BM	fst	1	:23^1	:46^1	1:10	1:34^4	3↑ Clm 20000	80	7	1	1^{1½}	1^{hd}	2^2	4^{5¾}	Gonzalez R M	LB 119	*1.70	90-15	Aaron Commander117^5 Triple Alpha116^{nk} True Enough119	Weakened	7

WORKOUTS: ● Aug 4 Dmr 3f fst :35^2 H *1/29* Jly 29 Dmr 3f fst :35^3 H *4/39* Jly 10 Hol 4f fst :51^2 H *50/51* May 22 Hol 3f fst :37^3 H *16/26* May 8 Hol 4f fst :49^4 H *34/38* May 2 Hol 4f fst :46^2 H *2/37*

High Mesa went to the post at $1–1 odds and was a favorite to be played against in the first race of the August 19 card at Del Mar. Yes, trainer Mike Mitchell has a 32 percent win rate at Del Mar and was winning at a 25 percent clip for more than a year. Yes, one of Mitchell's patterns has been to drop a horse down below his claiming price and win, or allow the horse to be claimed, or both. But this is a very bad betting favorite, one that I would be willing to see beat me at $1–1 odds any day of the week.

Horses who have such sharp winning form, who were claimed recently by shrewd players of the claiming game, should not be trusted on the decline unless there is unmistakable evidence from the workout line, or from a private reliable clocker, or you personally have the skill to confirm physical health with a pre-race warm-up inspection at the track.

This horse has not worked in two weeks; he won for fun at $14,000 and is worth $20,000 if he is capable of repeating either of his last two races. Even Mitchell does not like to give away sharp horses when they can win for higher tags. To be dropping this horse so quickly, one thing is highly probable: High Mesa cannot reproduce either of the two most recent races. Something has gone wrong, or is about to go wrong. You may guess incorrectly a few of these situations but so what? At even

FIRST RACE

Del Mar

AUGUST 19, 1993

6 FURLONGS. (1.07³) CLAIMING. Purse $10,000. 3–year–olds and upward. Weights: 3–year–olds, 117 lbs. Older, 122 lbs. Non–winners of two races since July 1, allowed 3 lbs. A race since July 1, 5 lbs. Claiming price $10,000. (Maiden or races when entered for $8,500 or less not considered.)(Day 20 of a 43 Day Meet. Cloudy. 77.)

Value of Race: $10,000 Winner $5,500; second $2,000; third $1,500; fourth $750; fifth $250. Mutuel Pool $244,023.00 Exacta Pool $224,935.00

Last Raced	Horse	M/Eqt. A.Wt	PP	St	¼	½	Str	Fin	Jockey	Cl'g Pr	Odds $1
20Jun93 5Hol3	Diable Rouge	LB	5 117	1	3	2hd	21	21	1nk	Pincay L Jr	10000	10.00
1Aug93 2Dmr9	Midnight Leader	LBb	4 117	6	4	41	31	31½	21½	Nakatani C S	10000	13.50
2Aug93 1Dmr6	Bering Gifts	LB	5 117	9	9	10	91	6hd	3½	Lopez A D	10000	23.00
7Aug93 9Dmr8	Andimo	LBbf	6 117	5	10	5hd	5½	4hd	42½	Almeida G F	10000	5.80
29Jly93 10SR3	Some Call It Jazz	LBbf	4 112	10	8	9½	10	94	5hd	Fuentes J A5	10000	49.80
17Jly93 5Hol1	High Mesa	LBf	7 114	4	2	31	4hd	51½	6hd	Gonzalez S Jr5	10000	1.00
24Jly93 9Hol8	Irontree	LBbf	6 117	8	7	71	71½	72	7½	Sorenson D	10000	8.40
7Aug93 9Dmr6	Mega V.I.P.	LBf	4 119	3	6	83½	8hd	8hd	81½	Navarro V G	10000	23.90
26Dec92 5SA10	A World Of Kings	LB	4 117	7	1	1½	1½	1hd	912	Black C A	10000	17.80
13Nov92 7B M4	Roman Avie	LBbf	7 117	2	5	62½	62	10	10	Desormeaux K J	10000	7.40

OFF AT 2:02 Start Good. Won driving. Time, :22¹, :45², :57⁴, 1:10¹ Track fast.

$2 Mutuel Prices:

1–DIABLE ROUGE	22.00	9.80	7.40
7–MIDNIGHT LEADER		13.40	9.20
10–BERING GIFTS			8.00

$2 EXACTA 1–7 PAID $234.80

B. h, by Mamaison–Crimson Cameo, by Crimson Satan. Trainer Vienna Darrell. Bred by Horn E & Lillyan (Ky).

DIABLE ROUGE, racing along the inside rail all the way and a pace factor from the start, had the needed late response to prevail by a small margin. MIDNIGHT LEADER, close up early and wide down the backstretch, threatened late but could not quite get up. BERING GIFTS, far back early, entered the stretch five wide and was going fastest of all late. ANDIMO, off a bit awkwardly, moved up to get into contention before going a quarter and did not have the necessary punch in the final furlong. SOME CALL IT JAZZ, wide early while far back, came into the stretch six wide and found his best stride too late. HIGH MESA attended the early pace and weakened in the drive, then was not returned to be unsaddled when lame following the finish. IRONTREE, wide down the backstretch, was four wide into the stretch. MEGA V.I.P. was five wide into the stretch. A WORLD OF KINGS, an early pace factor, gave way. ROMAN AVIE, in contention early, was through after a half. DIXTON (5) WAS SCRATCHED BY THE STEWARDS ON THE ADVICE OF THE VETERINARIAN. ALL WAGERS ON HIM IN THE REGULAR. EARLY DOUBLE AND EXACTA POOLS WERE ORDERED REFUNDED AND ALL OF HIS TRIPLE SELECTIONS WERE SWITCHED TO THE FAVORITE, HIGH MESA (4).

Owners— 1, No Problem Stable & Williams; 2, Cannata Mr & Mrs Carl; 3, Moreno Robert B & Lisa; 4, Helstrom & Mevorach; 5, Adams Craig; 6, K C Stable & Martin; 7, Appleton Aynn & Thomas Jr; 8, O'Connor Karen & William; 9, King & Landsburg; 10, Fisher & Isom

Trainers— 1, Vienna Darrell; 2, Spawr Bill; 3, Feld Jude T; 4, Sinne Gerald M; 5, Adams Craig; 6, Mitchell Mike; 7, Harrington Mike; 8, Fenstermaker L R; 9, Cerin Vladimir; 10, Lloyd Kim

Midnight Leader was claimed by Carava & Zinner; trainer, Carava Jack.,
Bering Gifts was claimed by A D F Stables; trainer, Avila A C.,
High Mesa was claimed by Kaufman Cheryl; trainer, Marshall Robert W.

money you can afford the consequences. In the meantime, there must be at least one, maybe two or three horses in this race who are going to the post at inflated mutuels. The result chart is reproduced below.

The horse below is a variation on the same theme. This is another bad betting favorite who seems in great form. We should consider the obvious, which always is the key to evaluating horses who pose serious question marks.

San Berdou
Own: V H W Stables
GONZALEZ S JR (89 8 9 14 .09) $25,000
Dk. b or br g. 4
Sire: Superoyale (Raise a Native)
Dam: Tibouchina (Nodouble)
Br: Verne H. Winchell (Ky)
Tr: McAnally Ronald (22 3 4 2 .14)
112 5

Lifetime Record:	7 1 3 2	$25,850			
1993	7 1 3 2	$25,850	Turf	0 0 0 0	
1992	0 M 0 0		Wet	0 0 0 0	
Dmr	1 0 1 0	$4,400	Dist	3 0 2 0	$7,800

28Jly93- 4Dmr fst 6f :221 :452 :572 1:093 3↑ Clm 25000 101 10 1 1½ 1hd 1hd 2½ Gonzalez S5 B 110 5.00 90-07 Moscow M D119½ San Berdou110¾ Racer Rex1176½ Good effort 10
30Jun93- 6Hol fst 5½f :222 :452 :57 1:03 3↑ Md 25000 101 8 2 2½ 1hd 11½ 13 Gonzalez S5 B 117 *.60 97-12 San Berdou1173 Cutting Deep11712 Noble Year1176 12
Drifted out late, ridden out
10Jun93- 6Hol fst 5½f :22 :451 :571 1:033 3↑ Md 32000 79 4 4 32 32½ 31½ 32 Delahoussaye E B 122 *1.60 92-12 Icy Tactics116½ Moon Dream1161½ San Berdou1222½ Always close 11
26May93- 2Hol fst 6f :214 :45 :571 1:101 3↑ Md 40000 70 3 3 2hd 2½ 21½ 34¾ Black C A 122 3.40 84-11 Madeira Wine1152 Seattle Tudor1222¾ San Berdou1225 Weakened 7
21Apr93- 3Hol fst 6½f :22 :444 1:094 1:16 3↑ Md 45000 80 3 3 1½ 1½ 1½ 22½ Black C A B 120 2.50 86-11 Starlight Excess1202½ San Berdou120hd Seattle Tudor1155 Shown whip 9
17Mar93- 6SA fst 6½f :22 :45 1:094 1:162 Md 40000 77 3 2 1hd 1hd 2½ 25 Black C A 120 5.80 84-15 Collirio1205 San Berdou120½ Centennial Axe1186½ Battle for 2nd 12
17Feb93- 9SA fst 6½f :22 :444 1:10 1:17 Md 40000 42 2 1 11 11 11½ 615½ Black C A B 119 9.10 71-14 Big Gate117½ Starlight Excess1181¼ Collirio119hd Bolted midstretch 11
WORKOUTS: Aug 15 SA 5f fst 1:002 H 4/16 ● Aug 9 SA 4f fst :471 H 1/17 Jly 23 SA 5f fst 1:014 H 18/42 Jly 16 SA 5f fst 1:01 H 8/41 Jly 10 SA 4f fst :473 H 4/46 Jun 27 SA 4f fst :463 H 4/47

Why would Ron McAnally, a trainer of the highest magnitude, a trainer with two Eclipse Awards and countless champions, take a horse who had scored two straight victories with Beyer figures of 101 and 101 and leave him at the $25,000 claiming level? Isn't 101 par for the highest level of allowance competition, a hairsbreadth away from Grade 3 stakes? This horse has hit that number not once but twice and seems to be in peak form.

The for sale sign is lit up like a neon sign in a dark alley. It is telling you to beware and to look elsewhere for the winner of this race.

There is one more betting favorite to check out—also trained by Mike Mitchell. The date—August 5, 1993, and this is a one-mile race on the Del Mar turf course for $62,500 claiming fillies and mares. What is wrong with this horse?

Absolutely nothing!

Bright Ways
Own: Invader Stable & Ustin & Ustin
STEVENS G L (39 11 7 3 .28) $62,500
Dk. b or br f. 4
Sire: Procida (Mr. Prospector)
Dam: Incredible Idea (Youth)
Br: Mabee Mr-Mrs John C (Cal)
Tr: Mitchell Mike (9 3 3 0 .33)
L 116

Lifetime Record:	16 5 3 2	$139,925			
1993	7 1 2 1	$58,425	Turf	8 2 1 1	$62,775
1992	9 4 1 1	$81,500	Wet	1 0 1 0	$9,200
Dmr Ⓣ	2 1 0 0	$20,150	Dist Ⓣ	4 1 0 1	$30,975

3Jly93- 6Hol fm 1 Ⓣ :232 :463 1:103 1:352 ⒻClm c-50000 87 11 11 1110 115¾ 73 51½ Desormeaux K J LB 116 b *2.10 87-13 Don't Touch Lil116nk Summer Glory117nk Stolen Loot116hd 7 Wide stretch 11
Claimed from Golden Eagle Farm, Hess R B Jr Trainer
27May93- 3Hol fm 1 Ⓣ :222 :452 1:092 1:333 ⒻClm 95000 85 3 3 37 33 34 44¾ Stevens G L LB 114 b 4.00 92-02 Gumpher119½ Kalita Melody1163½ Paula Revere117¾ Not enough late 5
14May93- 7Hol fm 1⅛ Ⓣ :482 1:114 1:35 1:472 ⒻCnvnience H 60k 87 3 4 55 54½ 44 44 Delahoussaye E LB 116 b 2.50 83-12 Miss Turkana1171¾ Gumpher114no Certam De May1142½ No late bid 6
1Apr93- 3SA fm 1 Ⓣ :234 :471 1:111 1:354 ⒻClm 100000 94 1 2 1hd 1½ 12½ 31 Stevens G L LB 119 b *2.30 85-14 Misterioso115½ Paula Revere115½ Bright Ways1192¾ Overtaken late 8
24Feb93- 5SA gd 1⅛ ⊗ :474 1:13 1:373 1:502 ⒻAlw 44000N3X 96 3 1 11 12 14 15 Stevens G L LB 116 b 3.40 78-28 Bright Ways1165 Changed Tune118¾ Secretly1142 Ridden out 8
4Feb93- 8SA fm 1⅛ Ⓣ :464 1:102 1:352 1:473 ⒻAlw 44000N3X 85 3 3 32½ 31½ 2hd 23 Stevens G L LB 116 b 5.60 78-19 Sun And Shade1183 Bright Ways116½ Changed Tune1181¼ Jostled start 8
6Jan93- 8SA sly 1 1/16 ⊗ :232 :464 1:11 1:422 ⒻAlw 46000N3X 82 1 4 41¾ 3½ 11 21¾ Stevens G L LB 118 b 2.70 90-05 Potrichal1171¾ Bright Ways1185 Cafe West115hd Overtaken late 5
10Dec92- 8Hol fst 1 1/16 ⊗ :233 :47 1:114 1:434 3↑ ⒻAlw 37000N2X 87 5 3 41½ 21 2½ 11¼ Desormeaux K J LB 116 b 3.40 82-19 Bright Ways1161¼ Colours1181¾ Lyin To The Moon1141 Wide, ridden out 6
25Nov92- 5Hol fm 1 1/16 Ⓣ :234 :482 1:131 1:43 ⒻClm 57500 84 9 5 54 53¾ 32 1hd Desormeaux K J LB 116 b *2.10 80-16 Bright Ways116hd Chabeli1131¼ Gettin' Air116 Strong finish 10
27Aug92- 8Dmr fm 1 Ⓣ :233 :473 1:123 1:373 3↑ ⒻⓈAlw 35000 83 4 4 52¼ 52 1½ 11½ Desormeaux K J LB 115 b *1.90 83-17 BrightWys1151½ Gloriousness118no MountinsOfLune117 Boxed in 3/8-1/4 9
WORKOUTS: Jly 31 Dmr 4f fst :50 H 49/64 Jly 24 Dmr 5f fst 1:03 H 22/22 Jly 16 Hol 3f fst :382 H 18/21 Jun 29 Hol 4f fst :513 H 24/26 Jun 23 Hol 6f fst 1:132 H 3/17 Jun 12 Hol 4f fst :522 H 51/52

She loves the grass, loves Del Mar, has won at the distance, had a very wide trip in her last but still came home in 24 seconds flat including beaten-lengths adjustments. Today she is stepping up appropriately after Mitchell spent $50,000 to buy her from Bob Hess, Jr. Her workouts are slow, but she has three of them during the past 21 days and she rarely works fast. This is a nice filly with a good lifetime record in good form racing where she belongs.

She won by three to pay $4.00, which hardly is worth getting excited about, but in the modern age of exotic wagering, you will be amazed at what you can do with an honest favorite too. Bright Ways keyed a $2 trifecta in the fifth race that paid $127 with the second and fourth betting choices, and three separate triples that paid $50–1, $138–1 and $42–1, which involved another $1–1 favorite and second and third betting choices in the companion races.

Once in a while there will be no need to be that exotic, as value can be gleaned from a relatively simple exacta strategy first presented in the original *Betting Thoroughbreds*. It is a classic situation that regularly occurs and is a good starting point for players seeking to strengthen their exotic wagering, while catching overlays on solid horses who have been bet down below any reasonable price for a win bet. (More sophisticated wagering strategies are presented in Appendix D)

In some exacta situations, the betting public has trouble evaluating contenders for second money. If you have no such trouble, a check of the possible exacta payoffs on closed-circuit TV may lead to a maximum-limit play. On the other hand, the public sometimes concentrates its exacta play on the dominant race favorite linked to one other apparently fit horse. In such circumstances it pays to take a close look at this "second best" horse. If it lacks convincing credentials, if there are sound reasons to bet against it, a wheel on the rest of the field could produce exciting payoffs. Indeed, this phenomenon occurs many times over a season, and produces a betting pattern that is extraordinarily predictable. First revealed in the original *Betting Thoroughbreds*, it remains one of the most reliable exacta plays in the game. Hundreds of examples could be given here; none more dramatic than the one facing players lucky enough to have been at Belmont Park for the greatest performance in the history of thoroughbred racing, Secretariat's 1973 Belmont Stakes.

Going into the Belmont, Secretariat was lord and master of the three-year-old division, a solid 1–10 shot to become the first Triple Crown winner in twenty-five years. Unlike Carry Back, Northern Dancer, Kauai King, Canonero II, and Majestic Prince—the five horses that failed to complete the Derby-Preakness-Belmont sweep—Secretariat came up to the 1973 Belmont at the peak of his powers, working faster and more energetically for the race than for any other race in his life. The same could not be said for Sham, the second-best three-year-old of 1973.

Sham had tried Secretariat twice and had failed both times. In the Derby, Secretariat went very wide on both turns and with power in reserve outdrove Sham from the top of the stretch to the wire.

In the Preakness, while under no special urging, Secretariat made a spectacular move around the clubhouse turn—from last to first—passing Sham in the backstretch. For the final half of the race Pincay slashed his whip into Sham with wild fury. Turcotte, aboard Secretariat, never moved a muscle. But Sham never gained an inch. At the wire he was a tired horse.

Coming up to the 1973 Belmont, Sham had begun to show signs of wear and tear. He showed fewer workouts and they were not as brisk; this horse had been through a rough campaign. Five route races in top company in less than eight weeks. Trips to California, Kentucky, Maryland, and New York. Actually, the only thing keeping Sham in the Triple Crown chase was trainer Frank Martin's stubbornness. A more objective view of his chances in the Belmont said that he would never beat Secretariat and could even go severely off form.

These were the win odds quoted on the race:

Secretariat	$ .10–$1.00
Sham	$ 5.10–$1.00
Private Smiles	$14.30–$1.00
My Gallant	$12.40–$1.00
Twice a Prince	$17.30–$1.00

These were the exacta payoff possibilities as they were flashed on the closed-circuit TV system prior to post time:

Secretariat with Sham	$ 3.40
Secretariat with Private Similes	$24.60
Secretariat with My Gallant	$19.80
Secretariat with Twice a Prince	$35.20

Eliminating Sham from the exacta play meant an investment of $6 (three combinations) and a minimum payoff of $19.80 (My Gallant). What all this means is that the track was offering three horses and excellent payoffs to beat a tired Sham for second place. In fact, the payoffs were almost identical to the odds in the win pool, the odds being offered on each of these three horses to beat Sham *and* Secretariat. By conceding the race to Secretariat, the player had a chance to collect the same odds merely by beating Sham. Now that's what I call value.

Through the weakness of the second betting favorite and the availability of exacta wagering, an exciting but seemingly unplayable race turned into a very logical, very promising Prime Bet. In a very real sense, it was like being offered a bonus dividend for understanding the subleties of a great moment in racing history. It's times like that when a horseplayer knows he is playing the greatest game in the world.

105TH RUNNING—1973—SECRETARIAT

EIGHTH RACE
Belmont
JUNE 9, 1973

1 ½ MILES. (2:26⅗) 105th Running THE BELMONT $125,000 added. 3-year-olds. By subscription of $100 each to accompany the nomination; $250 to pass the entry box, $1,000 to start. A supplementary nomination may be made of $2,500 at the closing time of entries plus an additional $10,000 to start, with $125,000 added, of which 60% to the winner, 22% to second, 12% to third and 6% to fourth. Weights, Colts and Geldings 126 lbs. Fillies 121 lbs. Starters to be named at the closing time of entries. The winning owner will be presented with the August Belmont Memorial Cup to be retained for one year, as well as a trophy for permanent possession and trophies will be presented to the winning trainer and jockey. Closed Thursday, February 15, 1973 with 187 Nominations.
Value of race $150,200, value to winner $90,120, second $33,044, third $18,024, fourth $9,012. Mutuel pool $519,689, OTB pool $688,460.

Last Raced	Horse	Eqt	A	Wt	PP	¼	½	1	1¼	Str	Fin	Jockey	Odds $1
19May73 ^{8}Pim^{1}	Secretariat	b	3	126	1	1^{hd}	1^{hd}	1^{7}	1^{20}	1^{28}	1^{31}	Turcotte R	.10
2Jun73 ^{6}Bel^{4}	Twice A Prince		3	126	5	4^{5}	4^{10}	3^{hd}	2^{hd}	3^{12}	$2\frac{1}{2}$	Baeza B	17.30
31May73 ^{6}Bel^{1}	My Gallant	b	3	126	3	3^{3}	3^{hd}	4^{7}	3^{2}	2^{hd}	3^{13}	Cordero A Jr	12.40
28May73 ^{8}GS^{2}	Pvt Smiles	b	3	126	2	5	5	5	5	5	$4\frac{3}{4}$	Gargan D	14.30
19May73 ^{8}Pim^{2}	Sham	b	3	126	6	2^{5}	2^{10}	2^{7}	4^{8}	$4^{1\frac{1}{2}}$	5	Pincay L Jr	5.10

Time, :23⅗, :46⅕, 1:09⅘, 1:34⅕, 1:59, 2:24, (Against wind in backstretch.). Track fast.
New Track Record.

$2 Mutuel Prices:				
	2-(A)-SECRETARIAT	2.20	2.40	—
	5-(E)-TWICE A PRINCE		4.60	—
	(No Show Wagering)			

Ch. c, by Bold Ruler—Somethingroyal, by Princequillo. Trainer Laurin L. Bred by Meadow Stud Inc (Va).
IN GATE AT 5:38; OFF AT 5:38, EDT. Start Good. Won Ridden out.

SECRETARIAT sent up along the inside to vie for the early lead with SHAM to the backstretch, disposed of that one after going three-quarters, drew off at will rounding the far turn and was under a hand ride from Turcotte to establish a record in a tremendous performance. TWICE A PRINCE, unable to stay with the leader early, moved through along the rail approaching the stretch and outfinished MY GALLANT for the place. The latter, void of early foot, moved with TWICE A PRINCE rounding the far turn and fought it out gamely with that one through the drive. PVT. SMILES showed nothing. SHAM alternated for the lead with SECRETARIAT to the backstretch, wasn't able to match stride with that rival after going three-quarters and stopped badly.

$2.00 EXACTA (2–5) PAID $35.00

Appendix A
Guide to *Daily Racing Form* Past Performances

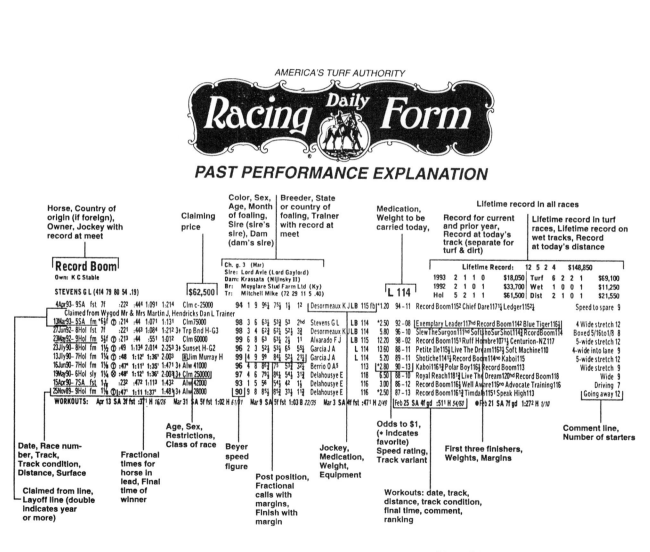

AMERICA'S TURF AUTHORITY

Racing Daily Form

PAST PERFORMANCE EXPLANATION

This past performance altered for illustrative purpose only

ABBREVIATIONS FOR TYPES OF RACES

Alw 15000	**ALLOWANCE RACE WITH NO RESTRICTIONS (Purse of $15,000)**
Alw 15000N1x	Allowance race for non-winners of a race other than maiden, claiming, or starter (Also used for non-winners of up to 5 races)
Alw 15000N1Y	Allowance race for non-winners of a race (or more, depending on number after N) in, or since, a specified time period
Alw 15000N2L	Allowance race for non-winners of two (or more) races lifetime
Alw 15000N$Y	Allowance race for non-winners of a specific amount of money one (or more) times in a specified time period
Alw 15000N1M	Allowance race for non-winners of one (or more) races at a mile or over in a specified time period
Alw 15000N1s	Allowance race for non-winners of one (or more) stakes lifetime
Alw 15000N1T	Allowance race for non-winners of one (or more) turf races

Clm 10000	**CLAIMING RACE (Entered to be claimed for $10,000)**
Clm 10000N2L	Claiming race for non-winners of two (or more) races lifetime
Clm 10000N1Y	Claiming race for non-winners of a race (or more, depending on number after N) in, or since, a specified time period
Clm 10000N1MY	Claiming race for non-winners of a race (or more) at a mile or over in a specified time period

OTHER CONDITIONS

Md Sp Wt	Maiden Special Weight race (for horses that have never won)
Md 32000	Maiden Claiming race (entered to be claimed for $32,000

Handicap 40k	**OVERNIGHT HANDICAP RACE (Purse of $40,000)**
OC 10000N	Optional Claiming race (entered NOT to be claimed)
OC 10000	Optional Claiming race (entered to be claimed)
Alw 8000s	Starter Allowance race (number indicates minimum claiming price, horse must have started for to be eligible)
Hcp 8000s	Starter Handicap race (number indicates minimum claiming price horse must have started for to be eligible)
Ky Derby–G1	Graded Stakes race, with name of race (North American races are graded in order of status, with G1 being the best)
PrincetonH 40k	Ungraded, but named Stakes race (H indicates handicap) Purse value is $40,000

SYMBOLS

▣	=	Inner dirt track
Ⓓ	=	Disqualified (symbol located next to odds and in company line)
DH	=	Dead-Heat (symbol located in company line if horses are among first three finishers)
▲	=	Dead-Heat (symbol used next to finish position)
3▲	=	Race for 3-year-olds and up
◆	=	Foreign race (outside of North America)
Ⓢ	=	Race for state-breds only
Ⓡ	=	Restricted race for horses who meet certain conditions
Ⓕ	=	Race for fillies, or fillies and mares
Ⓣ	=	Main turf course
🇹	=	Inner turf course
⊗	=	Race taken off turf
✳	=	About distance
+	=	Start from turf chute

TRACK CONDITION

DIRT TRACKS

fst	=	Fast
wf	=	Wet-Fast
gd	=	Good
sly	=	Sloppy
my	=	Muddy
sl	=	Slow
hy	=	Heavy
fr	=	Frozen

TURF & STEEPLECHASE

hd	=	Hard
fm	=	Firm
gd	=	Good
yl	=	Yielding
sf	=	Soft
hy	=	Heavy

WORKOUT LINE

●	=	Best of day/dist
B	=	Breezing
D	=	Driving
(d)	=	Worked around dogs
E	=	Easily
g	=	Worked from gate
H	=	Handily
tr.t	=	Training track
TR	=	Training race
3/25	=	Workout ranking

FINISH LINE

hd	=	Head
nk	=	Neck
no	=	Nose

EQUIPMENT & MEDICATION

b	=	Blinkers
f	=	Front bandages
B	=	Butazolidin
L	=	Lasix (furosemide)

'Points of Call' in Thoroughbred Charts

Following is a tabulation listing the "points of call" for the various distances in charts of thoroughbred racing:

3 Furlongs	PP	Start				Str	Fin
3½ Furlongs	PP	Start	¼			Str	Fin
4 Furlongs	PP	Start	¼			Str	Fin
4½ Furlongs	PP	Start	¼			Str	Fin
5 Furlongs	PP	Start	3-16	⅜		Str	Fin
5½ Furlongs	PP	Start	¼	⅜		Str	Fin
6 Furlongs	PP	Start	¼	½		Str	Fin
6½ Furlongs	PP	Start	¼	½		Str	Fin
7 Furlongs	PP	Start	¼	½		Str	Fin
7½ Furlongs	PP	Start	¼	½		Str	Fin
1 Mile	PP	Start	¼	½	¾	Str	Fin
1 Mile, 30 Yards	PP	Start	¼	½	¾	Str	Fin
1 Mile, 70 Yards	PP	Start	¼	½	¾	Str	Fin
1 1/16 Miles	PP	Start	¼	½	¾	Str	Fin
1 1/8 Miles	PP	Start	¼	½	¾	Str	Fin
1 3/16 Miles	PP	Start	¼	½	¾	Str	Fin

Note: In races at 1 1/4 Miles to 1 11/16 Miles, the Start call is eliminated and the ¼ mile call is substituted (as shown below):

1 1/4 Miles	PP	¼	½	¾	1	Str	Fin
1 5/16 Miles	PP	¼	½	¾	1	Str	Fin
1 3/8 Miles	PP	¼	½	¾	1	Str	Fin
1 7/16 Miles	PP	¼	½	1	1¼	Str	Fin
1 1/2 Miles	PP	¼	½	1	1¼	Str	Fin
1 9/16 Miles	PP	¼	½	1	1¼	Str	Fin
1 5/8 Miles	PP	¼	½	1	1⅜	Str	Fin
1 11/16 Miles	PP	¼	½	1	1⅜	Str	Fin

In races at 1 3/4 Miles or more, the first call is at the ½ mile (as shown below):

1 3/4 Miles	PP	½	1	1¼	1½	Str	Fin
1 13/16 Miles	PP	½	1	1¼	1½	Str	Fin
1 7/8 Miles	PP	½	1	1⅜	1⅝	Str	Fin
1 15/16 Miles	PP	½	1	1⅜	1⅝	Str	Fin
2 Miles	PP	½	1	1½	1¾	Str	Fin
2 Miles, 70 Yards	PP	½	1	1½	1¾	Str	Fin
2 1/16 Miles	PP	½	1	1½	1¾	Str	Fin
2 1/8 Miles	PP	½	1	1½	1¾	Str	Fin
2 3/16 Miles	PP	½	1	1½	1¾	Str	Fin
2 1/4 Miles	PP	½	1	1½	2	Str	Fin
2 5/16 Miles	PP	½	1	1½	2	Str	Fin
2 3/8 Miles	PP	½	1	1½	2	Str	Fin
2 1/2 Miles	PP	½	1	1½	2	Str	Fin

POINTS OF CALL & FRACTIONAL TIMES

Distance	1st call	2nd	3rd	4th	5th	Fractional Call Times			Finish
3½ f	start	1/4	—	str	finish	—	1/4	3/8	finish
4 f	start	1/4	—	str	finish	—	1/4	3/8	finish
4½ f	start	1/4	—	str	finish	—	1/4	1/2	finish
5 f	start	3/16	3/8	str	finish	—	1/4	1/2	finish
5½ f	start	1/4	3/8	str	finish	1/4	1/2	5/8	finish
6 f	start	1/4	1/2	str	finish	1/4	1/2	5/8	finish
6½ f	start	1/4	1/2	str	finish	1/4	1/2	3/4	finish
7 f	start	1/4	1/2	str	finish	1/4	1/2	3/4	finish
7½ f	start	1/4	1/2	str	finish	1/4	1/2	3/4	finish
1 mile	1/4	1/2	3/4	str	finish	1/4	1/2	3/4	finish
1 m 70 yds	1/4	1/2	3/4	str	finish	1/4	1/2	3/4	finish
1 1/16	1/4	1/2	3/4	str	finish	1/4	1/2	3/4	finish
1⅛	1/4	1/2	3/4	str	finish	1/2	3/4	mile	finish
1 3/16	1/4	1/2	3/4	str	finish	1/2	3/4	mile	finish
1¼	1/4	1/2	mile	str	finish	1/2	3/4	mile	finish
1⅜	1/4	1/2	mile	str	finish	1/2	3/4	mile	finish
1½	1/4	1/2	1¼	str	finish	1/2	3/4	1¼	finish
1⅝	1/4	1/2	1⅜	str	finish	1/2	mile	1¼	finish
1¾	1/2	mile	1½	str	finish	1/2	1¼	1½	finish
1⅞	1/2	mile	1⅝	str	finish	1/2	1¼	1½	finish
2 miles	1/2	mile	1¾	str	finish	1/2	1½	1¾	finish
2⅛	1/2	mile	1¾	str	finish	1/2	1½	1¾	finish

Conformation of Horse

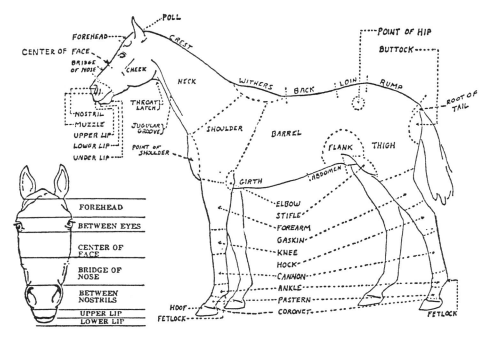

Abbreviations and Purse Value Index For North American Tracks

AC — (Agua) Caliente, Mexico—3
Aks — AKsarben, Neb.—7
Alb — Albuquerque, N. Mex—4
AP — Arlington Park, Ill.
(Arlington International Race Course)—19
Aqu — Aqueduct, N.Y.—28
ArP — *Arapahoe Park, Colo.—4
AsD — *Assiniboia Downs, Canada—4
Atl — Atlantic City, N.J.—7
Ato — *Atokad Park, Neb—1
BCF — *Brown Co. Fair, S.D.—1
Bel — Belmont Park, N.Y.—35
Beu — Beulah Park, Ohio—4
Bir — Birmingham Race Course, Ala.—6
BM — Bay Meadows, Cal.—14
Bmf — *Bay Meadows Fair, Cal.—10
Bml — Balmoral Park, Ill.
Boi — *Boise, Idaho
(Les Bois Park)—2
BnD — *Bandera Downs, Tex.—2
BRD — *Blue Ribbon Downs, Okla.—2
Cby — *Canterbury Downs, Minn.—3
CD — Churchill Downs, Ky.—24
Cls — *Columbus, Neb.—2
Crc — Calder Race Course, Fla.—13
CT — *Charles Town, W. Va.—3
CWF — *Central Wyo. Fair, Wyo.
DeD — *Delta Downs, La.—3
DeP — *Desert Park, Canada—1
Del — Delaware Park, Del.—6
Det — Detroit Race Course, Mich.—6
Dmr — Del Mar, Cal.—37
Due — Dueling Grounds, Ky.
ED — *Energy Downs, Wyo.
ElP — Ellis Park, Ky.—11
EP — *Exhibition Park, Canada—8
ErD — *Erie Downs, Pa.
Eur — *Eureka Downs, Kans.
EvD — *Evangeline Downs, La.—5
Fai — Fair Hill, Md.—6
FE — Fort Erie, Canada—6
Fer — *Ferndale, Cal.—3
FG — Fair Grounds, La.—9
FL — Finger Lakes, N.Y.—5
FMT — *Fair Meadows, Okla.
(Tulsa State Fair)—3
Fno — Fresno, Cal.—7
Fon — *Fonner Park, Neb.—4
Fox — *Foxboro Park, Mass.—5
FP — Fairmount Park, Ill.—4
Fpx — *Fairplex Park, Cal.—20
FtP — *Fort Pierre, S.D.—1
GBF — *Great Barrington Fair, Mass.—3
GF — *Great Falls, Mont.—2
GG — Golden Gate Fields, Cal.—16
Gil — *Gillespie County Fair, Tex.—2
GP — Gulfstream Park, Fla.—40
Grd — *Greenwood, Canada—18
GrP — *Grants Pass, Ore.—1
GS — Garden State Park, N.J.—8

Gtw — *Gateway Downs, Colo.—1
HaP — *Harbor Park, Wash.—1
Haw — Hawthorne, Ill.—13
Hia — Hialeah Park, Fla.—23
Hol — *Hollywood Park, Cal.—34
JnD — *Jefferson Downs, La—6
Kam — *Kamloops, Canada—1
Kee — *Keeneland, Ky.—33
Kin — *Kin Park, Canada—1
LA — *Los Alamitos, Cal.—10
LaD — *Louisiana Downs, La.—10
LaM — *La Mesa Park, N. Mex.—1
Lar — Nuevo Laredo, Mexico
Lga — *Longacres, Wash.—8
LnN — *Lincoln State Fair, Neb.—5
Lrl — *Laurel Race Course, Md.—15
Mar — *Marlboro, Md.—6
MD — *Marquis Downs, Canada—2
Mea — *Meadowlands, N.J.—16
MeP — *Metrapark, Mont.—2
Mex — *Mexico City, Mexico
(Hipodromo de las Americas)—N.A.
MF — *Marshfield Fair, Mass.—3
Mi — *Midway Downs, Okla.
Min — *Minnesota Downs, Minn.
Mnr — *Mountaineer Park, W.Va.—2
MPM — *Mt. Pleasant, Mich.—1
Mth — Monmouth Park, N.J.—18
Mus — *Muskegon, Mich.
Nmo — *Northampton, Mass.—3
NP — *Northlands Park, Canada—6
OP — Oaklawn Park, Ark.—19
Pen — Penn National, Pa.—4
Pha — Philadelphia Park, Pa.—10
Pim — Pimlico, Md.—16
Pla — *Playfair, Wash.—2
Pln — Pleasanton, Cal.—10
PM — *Portland Meadows, Ore.—2
PPM — Pikes Peak Meadows, Colo.—N.A.
PR — Puerto Rico (El Comandante)—N.A.
Pre — *Prescott Downs, Ariz.—3
PrM — *Prairie Meadows, Iowa—2
Qby — *Queensbury Downs, Canada
RD — *River Downs, Ohio—5
Ril — *Rillito, Ariz.
Rkm — Rockingham Park, N.H.—6
RP — Remington Park, Okla.—9
Rui — *Ruidoso, N. Mex—3
RWD — *Rollie White Downs, Tex.
SA — Santa Anita Park, Cal.—36
Sac — *Sacramento, Cal.—7
Sag — *Sagebrush Downs, Ore.
Sal — *Salem, Ore. (Lone Oak)—2
San — *Sandown Park, Canada—2
Sar — Saratoga, N.Y.—42
Sed — *Sedalia, Mo.
SFe — *Santa Fe, N. Mex.—4
SJD — *San Juan Downs, N. Mex.—1
SnD — *Sunflower Downs, Canada—1
Sol — *Solano, Cal.—9

Spt — *Sportsman's Park, Ill.—15
SR — *Santa Rosa, Cal.—10
Stk — Stockton, Cal.—7
StP — *Stampede Park, Canada—5
SuD — *Sun Downs, Wash.—1
Suf — Suffolk Downs, Mass.—6
Sun — Sunland Park, N. Mex.—3
SwF — *Sweetwater Fair, Wyo.
Tam — Tampa Bay Downs, Fla.—4
Tdn — Thistledown, Ohio—6
Tim — *Timonium, Md.—6
TP — Turfway Park, Ky.—14
TrM — *Trinity Meadows, Tex.—4
TuP — Turf Paradise, Ariz.—4
Veg — *Vegreville, Canada
Wds — *Woodlands, Kans.—1
WO — Woodbine, Canada—26
WRD — Will Rogers Downs, Okla.—2
Wyo — *Wyoming Downs, Wyo.—1
YM — *Yakima Meadows, Wash.—4

HUNT MEETINGS

Aik — Aiken, S. Carolina
AtH — Atlanta, Ga.
Avn — Avon, N.Y.
Bro — Brookhill, N.C.
Cam — Camden, S. Carolina
Cha — Charleston, S. Carolina
Clm — Clemmons, N. Carolina
Fax — Fairfax, Va.
FH — Far Hills, N.J.
Fx — Foxfield, Va.
Gln — Glyndon, Md.
GN — Grand National, Md.
GrM — Great Meadows, Va.
GV — Genesee Valley, N.Y.
Lex — Lexington, Ky.
Lig — Ligonier, Pa.
Mal — Malvern, Pa.
Mas — Mason Dixon, Ohio
Mgo — Marengo, Va.
Mid — Middleburg, Va.
Mon — Monkton, Md.
Mor — Morven Park, Va.
Mtp — Montpelier, Va.
Oxm — Oxmoor, Ky.
PmB — Palm Beach, Fla.
PmT — Pine Mountain, Ga.
Pro — Prospect, Ky.
PW — Percy Warner, Tenn.
RB — Red Bank, N.J.
SH — Strawberry Hill, Va.
SJm — St. James, Ill.
SoP — Southern Pines, N.C.
StL — St. Louis, Mo.
Try — Tryon, N.C.
Uni — Unionville, Pa.
War — Warrenton, Va.
Wil — Willowdale, Pa.

Tracks marked with (*) are less than one mile in circumference. N.A.—Not Available.

POST POSITIONS AND ODDS:
THE PROPER WAY TO SET UP A POST POSITION SURVEY

For the period involved, note at each distance charted: (1) the number of races from each post position, (2) the number of wins per post, and (3) the win percentage per post. A separate category should be maintained for the "outside post," for all races. *Optional*: At the same time, record the number of wire-to-wire winners.

A sample post position survey appears below:

POST POSITION
TURF RACES (1–1¹⁄₁₆ miles)

POST POSITION	STARTERS	WINS	WIN PERCENTAGE
1	69	18	26.1
2	69	12	17.4
3	69	8	11.6
4	69	8	11.6
5	69	7	10.1
6	68	10	14.7
7	54	1	—
8	43	3	—
9	21	1	—
10	5	1	—
11	2	0	0.0
12	1	0	0.0
outside	69	4	5.8

Wire-to-wire winners—20.3%

PERCENTAGE TABLE FOR COMPUTING A MORNING LINE

The following table provides a reference for computing a morning line. The percentage totals for the field should equal 118 to 125 points. This allows for the pari-mutuel tax.

ODDS	PERCENTAGE POINTS	ODDS	PERCENTAGE POINTS
1–5	83	2–1	33
1–4	80	5–2	28
1–3	75	3–1	25
1–2	67	7–2	22
3–5	62	4–1	20
2–3	60	9–2	18
3–4	57	5–1	16
4–5	55	6–1	14
even	50	8–1	11
6–5	45	10–1	9
7–5	41	12–1	8
3–2	40	15–1	6
8–5	38	20–1	4
9–5	35	30–1	3

Below is a sample morning line with percentage points.

HYPOTHETICAL RACE
3-YEAR-OLDS, 1961–1993
126 pounds, 1¼ miles

HORSE	ODDS	POINTS
Secretariat	6–5	45
Seattle Slew	7–2	22
Affirmed	5–1	16
Damascus	6–1	14
Spectacular Bid	8–1	12
Sunday Silence	15–1	6
Risen Star	20–1	4
Carry Back	30–1	3
Canonero II	50–1	2
		124 *points*

COMPUTING APPROXIMATE PLACE AND SHOW PAYOFFS

Short of using the most sophisticated electronic equipment, no player can hope to generate all possible place and show payoffs in a race. Place and show payoffs are determined by the order of finish itself, or more correctly, by the money bet in the place pool and the money bet in the show pool on each horse involved in the top two and three finishing positions. The player's best course is to compute the *lowest possible* place and show payoff—a single calculation—because the lowest possible payoff is statistically the most likely payoff. It is the one produced by the favorites in the race finishing in the money. The following example shows how this is done.

HORSE	PLACE POOL	SHOW POOL
Carry Back	$ 4,000	$ 2,500
Buckpasser	$ 8,500	$ 6,000
Count Fleet	$12,000	$ 7,000
Tom Fool	$ 9,000	$ 4,000
Native Dancer	$10,000	$ 5,000
Round Table	$ 5,500	$ 1,500
Swaps	$10,000	$ 8,000
Silky Sullivan	$ 1,000	$ 1,000
Totals	$60,000	$35,000

QUESTION: *How much will Native Dancer pay to place?*

ANSWER: Minimum payoff is computed in four steps.

STEP 1: Deduct 20 percent pari-mutuel takeout tax from place pool total (20 percent of $60,000, or $12,000). Net pool = $48,000.

STEP 2: Combine the amount of money bet on Native Dancer to place with the amount of money bet on the horse getting the most play in the race. In this case, Count Fleet with $12,000 is the favorite in the place pool; thus the combined total equals $22,000.

STEP 3: Subtract the $22,000 from the $48,000 net place pool to determine the amount of money available for profit. In this case, $48,000 − $22,000 = $26,000 profit.

STEP 4: Divide the $26,000 profit into two equal parts to determine the amount of profit available to Native Dancer place pool bettors. In this case

$$\frac{\$26,000}{2} = \$13,000$$

THUS: The odds on Native Dancer to place are $13,000 profit to $10,000 invested, or 13–10 ($1.30–$1.00). Native Dancer will pay a minimum place price of $4.60 (includes original $2 investment).

QUESTION: *How much will Tom Fool pay to show?*
ANSWER: Mimimum show payoff is computed in four steps.
STEP 1: Deduct 20 percent pari-mutuel takeout tax from show pool total (20 percent of $35,000, or $7,000). Net pool = $28,000.
STEP 2: Combine the amount of money bet on Tom Fool to show ($4,000) with the amount of money bet on the two horses getting the most play in the race. In this case, Swaps is getting $8,000; Count Fleet, $7,000. Thus the combined total for all three horses is $19,000.
STEP 3: Subtract $19,000 from the $28,000 net show pool to determine the money available for profit. In this case, $28,000 − $19,000 = $9,000 net profit.
STEP 4: Divide the net profit into three equal parts to determine Tom Fool's show pool profit. In this case

$$\frac{\$9,000}{3} = \$3,000$$

THUS: The odds on Tom Fool to show are $3,000 profit to $4,000 invested, or 3–4 ($.75–$1.00). Tom Fool will pay a minimum show price of $3.40 (includes breakage to nearest dime and original $2 investment).

With some practice, the place and show payoffs for any horse can be computed in this manner in a matter of seconds. *Hint:* Round off to convenient whole numbers.

HANDICAPPING AIDS

Throughout this book I have made reference to numerous improvements in handicapping information, including professional betting aids that have come into the game in recent years. While it is not my intention to make an unqualified endorsement for these products, I definitely can state that I have gained ground in my handicapping by using them in appropriate situations.

BLOODSTOCK RESEARCH INFORMATION SERVICES

BRIS is an online computer-linked database for horseplayers and breeders. It relies on *Daily Racing Form* data and produces many potentially useful charts and statistical surveys on jockeys, trainers, breeding tendencies and a wide assortment of esoteric facts. On off-track racing days and when horses attempt new distances, BRIS statistics are powerful handicapping aids. BRIS is based in Lexington, Kentucky, and can be reached by calling (800)-354-9353.

GORDON PINE'S PACE PARS

Published annually, this provides workable pace pars for every American racetrack. Cynthia Publishing, Studio City, CA, 91604.

HANDICAPPING NEWSLETTERS

Among many publications throughout the country, the *Northern California Track Record*, the *Handicappers Report for Southern California*, the *Insider's Edge* in Nebraska and the *Northwest Track Review* supply track bias and trip notes, race shapes, and pace figures for serious handicappers. Below is a sample page from the *Northern California Track Record*, published by Ron Cox and his associate editor Dan Montilion.

TRACK CONDITION: *FAST* DATE: *WEDNESDAY JUNE 24*

TRACK BIAS: Inside speed advantaged at all dirt distances.

1st RACE FINAL TIME W/VARIANT: 1:10-4 DIST: 6 Furlongs CLASS: Maiden Claiming 12,500 PURSE: 6,000
(93- 92- 96) 22-1   45-0   57-1   09-4 AGE: Males COND: Open

RACE SYNOPSIS: Compare with Cal bred at this level in second race. Solid rating.

2	NIJINSKY'S JOEY	0	(3/1)(Aime,Campbell) Barn seems to do well with first timers and layoff horses. Was bias aided but finished in hand and has to be considered vs. winners if he does not "bounce".
3	CIRCUS DANCER	2+	Serious improvement noted from the slower lanes. Should continue to improve at a route.
4	YASHIE	0	Made up a bit of ground while bias aided vs. a very good final fraction. However, has too many failures and goes for the very cold Offield barn.
5	RAGING REGAN	0	Needed race. Not on Lasix and was on the slower lanes and against the "shape". Router.
1	JUST JAMIE	X	Off one length slow from the rail. Was bias aided there-after. Hard to like 5 year old first time starters.
6	SEEME RUMBO	3/5	Was wide vs. the bias and can be excused.
7	DEFENSIVE PLAN	5/7	Far wide vs. bias but dropped out of it too early and seems an easy pass.

2nd RACE FINAL TIME W/VARIANT: 1:11-4 DIST: 6 Furlongs CLASS: Maiden Claiming 12,500 PURSE: 6,000
(95- 94- 91) 21-4   44-3   57-3   10-4 AGE: Males COND: Cal Bred

RACE SYNOPSIS: Compare with open company at this level in the first race. Good early pace for the level.

1	ASK LESTER	0	(9/1)(Belvoir,Keanel) Serious improvement in second lifetime try for Kaenal.Was bias aided early and off rail into lane. No reason to expect this type of improvement.
4	CAMELOT REMEMBERED	3	Dueled from the good lanes on the good pace and tired badly. Had been off 2 months and should improve in next and a paceless field would not hurt.
3	ANOTHER BLEND	2	Professional maiden. Runs fast enough to nibble at the purse.
2	ROBERT'S THRILL	0	Broke slow again. Seems his own worst enemy as he ran "green" again. Blinkers may help.
6	MIGHTY O.	3	Did nothing for Hansen in a race "shape" that should have aided closers. Was vs. bias.
7	SPIRIT OF DUBLIN	0	Far wide vs. bias while in need of the race. Should improve.
5	HI HO MY DADDY O.	3/5	Can't sprint. Bottom level route only hope. We'll still pass.

EXPANDED TRACK PROGRAMS

Here is a statistical page from *Post Parade*, the official track program of the New York Racing Association. *Post Parade* includes Equibase and for *Daily Racing Form* past performances along with feature stories by prominant writers and regular handicapping columns by Steve Crist and myself.

FACTS AND FIGURES IN NEW YORK
Performance Record For Current Meet Including Saturday

JOCKEY	Mounts	1st	2nd	3rd	% Win	% In Money	MAIN COURSE			TURF COURSE			FAVORITES			Avg Win Payoff
							Mts.	1st	% Win	Mts.	1st	% Win	Mts	1st	% Win	
Mike Smith	357	79	58	48	22.1	51.8	221	51	23.1	136	28	20.6	103	42	40.8	7.51
Jorge F. Chavez	317	57	34	31	18.0	38.5	199	32	16.1	118	25	21.2	35	14	40.0	13.72
Julie Krone	308	54	51	43	17.5	48.1	189	34	18.0	119	20	16.8	90	27	30.0	7.95
Robbie Davis	356	49	53	42	13.8	40.4	229	32	14.0	127	17	13.4	40	15	37.5	13.16
Jerry D. Bailey	243	46	37	37	18.9	49.4	147	26	17.7	96	20	20.8	69	22	31.9	10.19
Richard Migliore	244	38	38	35	15.6	45.5	165	29	17.6	79	9	11.4	37	12	32.4	10.88
Jose Santos	226	35	31	28	15.5	41.6	126	17	13.5	100	18	18.0	35	14	40.0	10.53
Chris Antley	276	33	39	42	12.0	41.3	158	16	10.1	118	17	14.4	40	15	37.5	11.00
Craig Perret	114	27	20	21	23.7	59.6	73	19	26.0	41	8	19.5	30	10	33.3	11.43
Eddie Maple	154	23	30	20	14.9	47.4	80	16	20.0	74	7	9.5	25	9	36.0	10.32
Frank Alvarado	192	23	20	27	12.0	36.5	129	17	13.2	63	6	9.5	12	3	25.0	19.65
John R. Velazquez	214	21	29	16	9.8	30.8	139	16	11.5	75	5	6.7	15	3	20.0	14.69

JOCKEY	2 YO's			3 & UP			Maiden			Claiming			Allowance			Stakes			Routes			Sprints		
	Mts	W%	$%	Mts	W%	$%	Mts	W%	$%	Mts	W%	$%	Mts	W%	$%	Mts	W%	$%	Mts	W%	$%	Mts	W%	$%
Mike Smith	26	26.9	50.0	331	21.8	52.0	64	21.9	42.2	148	25.0	53.4	113	21.2	55.8	32	12.5	50.0	206	20.9	53.4	151	23.8	49.7
Jorge F. Chavez	21	9.5	33.3	296	18.6	38.9	46	15.2	32.6	171	17.0	36.8	86	22.1	45.3	14	14.3	35.7	174	18.4	36.8	143	17.5	40.6
Julie Krone	20	10.0	45.0	288	18.1	48.3	58	10.3	43.1	119	18.5	48.7	102	17.7	48.0	29	27.6	55.2	171	15.8	46.2	137	19.7	50.4
Robbie Davis	26	7.7	50.0	330	14.2	39.7	72	9.7	38.9	148	16.2	42.6	114	15.8	40.4	22		31.8	192	14.1	34.9	164	13.4	47.0
Jerry D. Bailey	25	24.0	40.0	218	18.4	50.5	58	19.0	46.6	71	11.3	45.1	89	23.6	51.7	25	24.0	60.0	139	20.1	52.5	104	17.3	45.2
Richard Migliore	9		33.3	235	16.2	46.0	33	9.1	39.4	117	18.8	43.6	79	13.9	50.6	15	13.3	46.7	138	11.6	39.9	106	20.8	52.8
Jose Santos	18	22.2	50.0	208	14.9	40.9	49	16.3	40.8	82	12.2	40.2	73	19.2	43.8	22	13.6	40.9	138	17.4	39.1	88	12.5	45.5
Chris Antley	17	5.9	52.9	259	12.4	40.5	51	13.7	51.0	108	9.3	40.7	98	12.2	40.8	19	21.1	21.1	171	15.8	40.9	105	5.7	41.9
Craig Perret	14	14.3	50.0	100	25.0	61.0	34	29.4	64.7	14	14.3	57.1	52	25.0	59.6	14	14.3	50.0	68	22.1	58.8	46	26.1	60.9
Eddie Maple	14	21.4	28.6	140	14.3	49.3	44	11.4	36.4	50	26.0	52.0	51	7.8	54.9	9	11.1	33.3	97	12.4	48.5	57	19.3	45.6
Frank Alvarado	12	8.3	25.0	180	12.2	37.2	39	18.0	35.9	112	11.6	37.5	35	8.6	31.4	6		50.0	103	12.6	37.9	89	11.2	34.8
John R. Velazquez	17		17.6	197	10.7	32.0	50	8.0	28.0	100	11.0	34.0	56	8.9	30.4	8	12.5	12.5	109	9.2	33.0	105	10.5	28.6

TRAINER	Saddied	1st	2nd	3rd	% Win	% In Money	MAIN COURSE			TURF COURSE			FAVORITES			Avg Win Payoff
							Sadl'd	1st	% Win	Sadl'd	1st	% Win	Sadl'd	1st	% Win	
Gary Sciacca	115	30	7	13	26.1	43.5	59	9	15.3	56	21	37.5	16	9	56.3	14.28
Gasper S. Moschera	114	29	13	14	25.4	49.1	87	26	29.9	27	3	11.1	37	17	46.0	8.94
William I. Mott	78	23	9	13	29.5	57.7	46	13	28.3	32	10	31.3	25	10	40.0	6.74
H. Allen Jerkens	77	19	10	15	24.7	57.1	67	17	25.4	10	2	20.0	23	15	65.2	5.85
Flint S. Schulhofer	87	18	16	8	20.7	48.3	43	9	20.9	44	9	20.5	29	10	34.5	9.04
William Badgett Jr.	56	17	11	5	30.4	58.9	31	9	29.0	25	8	32.0	24	10	41.7	6.26
Michael E. Hushion	67	17	10	13	25.4	59.7	51	16	31.4	16	1	6.3	15	5	33.3	7.98
Peter Ferriola	96	14	20	15	14.6	51.0	90	14	15.6	6			30	6	20.0	7.96
Claude McGaughey III R.	59	14	12	10	23.7	61.0	49	12	24.5	10	2	20.0	22	12	54.6	5.90
Stanley R. Shapoff	80	14	9	10	17.5	41.3	62	11	17.7	18	3	16.7	4	1	25.0	17.59
Murray M. Garren	70	13	10	5	18.6	40.0	46	11	23.9	24	2	8.3	1			14.69
Robert Barbara	67	13	9	8	19.4	44.8	57	12	21.1	10	1	10.0	13	4	30.8	13.37

TRAINER	2 YO's			3 & UP			Maiden			Claiming			Allowance			Stakes			Routes			Sprints		
	Sdld	W%	$%	Sdld	W%	$%	Sdld	W%	$%	Sdld	W%	$%	Sdld	W%	$%	Sdld	W%	$%	Sdld	W%	$%	Sdld	W%	$%
Gary Sciacca	2	50.0	50.0	113	25.7	43.4	16	37.5	43.8	54	18.5	35.2	40	32.5	57.5	5	20.0	20.0	75	33.3	50.7	40	12.5	30.0
Gasper S. Moschera				114	25.4	49.1	7	14.3	14.3	90	26.7	50.0	17	23.5	58.8				66	21.2	50.0	48	31.3	47.9
William I. Mott	12	33.3	58.3	66	28.8	57.6	25	28.0	52.0	8	25.0	50.0	34	26.5	58.8	11	45.5	72.7	41	22.0	53.7	37	37.8	62.2
H. Allen Jerkens	10	20.0	80.0	67	25.4	53.7	17	29.4	82.4	19	21.1	47.4	29	13.8	41.4	12	50.0	75.0	27	33.3	59.3	50	20.0	56.0
Flint S. Schulhofer	7	28.6	42.9	80	20.0	48.8	37	16.2	43.2	7	28.6	42.9	27	29.6	51.9	16	12.5	56.3	64	21.9	51.6	23	17.4	39.1
William Badgett Jr.	5		20.0	51	33.3	62.7	12	16.7	41.7	20	30.0	55.0	21	42.9	71.4	3		66.7	33	30.3	63.6	23	30.4	52.2
Michael E. Hushion	1		100.0	66	25.8	59.1	2	50.0	100.0	42	28.6	52.4	22	18.2	72.7	1			24	16.7	41.7	43	30.2	69.8
Peter Ferriola				96	14.6	51.0				81	17.3	56.8	14		21.4	1			36	5.6	36.1	60	20.0	60.0
Claude McGaughey III R.	3	33.3	66.7	56	23.2	60.7	16	18.8	50.0				29	34.5	69.0	14	7.1	57.1	38	29.0	65.8	21	14.3	52.4
Stanley R. Shapoff	13	15.4	23.1	67	17.9	44.8	12	8.3	16.7	40	22.5	40.0	23	17.4	60.9	5		20.0	29	17.2	48.3	51	17.7	37.3
Murray M. Garren				70	18.6	40.0				43	25.6	44.2	25	8.0	36.0	2			52	15.4	38.5	18	27.8	44.4
Robert Barbara	8	12.5	62.5	59	20.3	42.4	4		25.0	46	19.6	45.7	14	21.4	50.0	3	33.3	33.3	17	29.4	35.2	50	16.0	48.0

Appendix B
Speed Figures

<hr>

After developing a few representative class par clockings at your favorite track (see Chapter 13), you may develop a workable parallel time chart along the lines of the following theoretical model. The model is the basic time chart for Aqueduct and is used as a starting point for Beyer figures in the *Daily Racing Form*.

THEORETICAL ONE-TURN SPEED FIGURE CHART

BEYER FIG.	5 FURLS.	5½	6 FURLS.	6½	7 FURLS.	1 MILE
131:	56.00	1:02.20	1:08.40	1:14.60	1:20.80	1:33.40
127:	56.20	1:02.40	1:08.60	1:14.80	1:21.00	1:33.80
124:	56.40	1:02.60	1:08.80	1:15.00	1:21.40	1:34.00
117:	56.80	1:03.00	1:09.40	1:15.60	1:22.00	1:34.60
113:	57.00	1:03.40	1:09.60	1:15.80	1:22.20	1:35.00
110:	57.20	1:03.40	1:09.80	1:16.20	1:22.40	1:35.40
109	57.20	1:03.40	1:09.80	1:16.20	1:22.50	1:35.50
108:	57.30	1:03.60	1:09.90	1:16.30	1:22.60	1:35.60
107:	57.40	1:03.70	1:10.00	1:16.40	1:22.70	1:35.70
106:	57.40	1:03.80	1:10:00	1:16.40	1:22.80	1:35.80
103:	57.60	1:04.00	1:10.20	1:16.60	1:23.00	1:36.00
100:	57.80	1:04.20	1:10.40	1:16.60	1:23.20	1:36.20
96:	58.00	1:04.40	1:10.80	1:17.20	1:23.60	1:36.60
93:	58.20	1:04.60	1:11.00	1:17.40	1:23.80	1:37.00
89:	58.40	1:04.80	1:11.20	1:17.80	1:24.20	1:37.40
86:	58.60	1:05.00	1:11.40	1:18.00	1:24.40	1:37.40
82:	58.80	1:05.40	1:11.80	1:18.20	1:24.80	1:38.00
79:	59.00	1:05.40	1:12.00	1:18.60	1:25.20	1:38.40

BEYER FIG.	5 FURLS.	5½	6 FURLS.	6½	7 FURLS.	1 MILE
75:	59.20	1:05.80	1:12.20	1:18.80	1:25.40	1:38.80
72:	59.40	1:06.00	1:12.40	1:19.00	1:25.60	1:39.00
68:	59.60	1:06.20	1:12.80	1:19.40	1:26.00	1:39.40
65:	59.80	1:06.40	1:13.00	1:19.60	1:26.40	1:39.80
62:	1:00.00	1:06.60	1:13.20	1:19.80	1:26.60	1:40.00
58:	1:00.20	1:06.80	1:13.60	1:20.20	1:26.80	1:40.40
55:	1:00.40	1:07.00	1:13.80	1:20.40	1:27.20	1:40.80
52:	1:00.60	1:07.20	1:14.00	1:20.60	1:27.40	1:41.00
49:	1:00.80	1:07.40	1:14.20	1:20.80	1:27.60	1:41.20
45:	1:01.00	1:07.80	1:14.40	1:21.20	1:28.00	1:41.60
42:	1:01.20	1:08.00	1:14.60	1:21.40	1:28.20	1:42.00
39:	1:01.40	1:08.20	1:15.00	1:21.60	1:28.40	1:42.40
35:	1:01.60	1:08.40	1:15.20	1:22.00	1:28.80	1:42.80

To assist interpolation to the nearest .10 seconds, clockings in .10 (¹⁄₁₀) seconds are represented on the Beyer Fig. lines 107–110 on the one-turn chart and 106–108 on the two-turn chart.

THEORETICAL TWO-TURN SPEED FIGURE CHART

BASIC BEYER FIG.	1 MILE	1 MILE 70 YDS.	1¹⁄₁₆ MI.	1⅛	1³⁄₁₆	1¼
133:	1:34.00	1:38.20	1:40.40	1:46.80	1:53.20	1:59.80
131:	1:34.20	1:38.40	1:40.60	1:47.00	1:53.40	2:00.00
129:	1:34.40	1:38.60	1:40.80	1:47.40	1:53.80	2:00.20
126:	1:34.60	1:38.80	1:41.20	1:47.60	1:54.00	2:00.60
124:	1:34.80	1:39.00	1:41.40	1:47.80	1:54.20	2:00.80
122:	1:35.00	1:39.20	1:41.60	1:48.00	1:54.40	2:01.00
120:	1:35.20	1:39.40	1:41.80	1:48.20	1:54.60	2:01.20
118:	1:35.40	1:39.60	1:42.00	1:48.60	1:55.00	2:01.60
116:	1:35.80	1:39.80	1:42.20	1:48.80	1:55.20	2:01.80
114:	1:35.80	1:40.00	1:42.40	1:49.00	1:55.40	2:02.00
112:	1:36.00	1:40.20	1:42.60	1:49.20	1:55.60	2:02.20
110:	1:36.20	1:40.40	1:42.80	1:49.40	1:55.80	2:02.40

BASIC BEYER FIG.	1 MILE	1 MILE 70 YDS.	1¹⁄₁₆ MI.	1⅛	1³⁄₁₆	1¼
108:	1:36.40	1:40.60	1:43.00	1:49.60	1:56.00	2:02.60
107:	1:36.50	1:40.70	1:43.10	1:49.70	1:56.20	2:02.80
106:	1:36.60	1:40.80	1:43.20	1:49.80	1:56.40	2:03.00
104:	1:36.80	1:41.00	1:43.40	1:50.00	1:56.60	2:03.20
103:	1:36.80	1:41.20	1:43.60	1:50.20	1:56.80	2:03.60
101:	1:37.00	1:41.40	1:43.80	1:50.40	1:57.00	2:03.80
99:	1:37.20	1:41.60	1:44.00	1:50.60	1:57.20	2:04.00
97:	1:37.40	1:41.80	1:44.20	1:50.80	1:57.40	2:04.20
95:	1:37.60	1:42.00	1:44.40	1:51.00	1:57.80	2:04.60
93:	1:37.80	1:42.20	1:44.60	1:51.20	1:58.00	2:04.80
92:	1:38.00	1:42.20	1:44.00	1:51.40	1:58.20	2:05.00
90:	1:38.20	1:42.40	1:44.80	1:51.60	1:58.40	2:05.20
88:	1:38.40	1:42.60	1:45.00	1:51.80	1:58.60	2:05.40
86:	1:38.60	1:42.80	1:45.20	1:52.00	1:58.80	2:05.60
83:	1:38.80	1:43.20	1:45.60	1:52.40	1:59.20	2:06.20
81:	1:39.00	1:43.40	1:45.80	1:52.60	1:59.40	2:06.40
79:	1:39.20	1:43.60	1:46.40	1:52.80	1:59.60	2:06.60
77:	1:39.40	1:43.80	1:46.20	1:53.00	1:59.80	2:06.80
75:	1:39.60	1:44.00	1:46.40	1:53.20	2:00.00	2:07.00
71:	1:40.00	1:44.40	1:46.80	1:53.60	2:00.40	2:07.40
69:	1:40.20	1:44.60	1:47.00	1:53.80	2:00.60	2:07.60
68:	1:40.40	1:44.80	1:47.20	1:54.00	2:00.80	2:07.80
67:	1:40.40	1:44.80	1:47.40	1:54.20	2:01.00	2:08.20
65:	1:40.60	1:45.00	1:47.60	1:54.40	2:01.20	2:08.40
63:	1:40.80	1:45.20	1:47.80	1:54.60	2:01.40	2:08.60
61:	1:41.00	1:45.40	1:47.80	1:54.80	2:01.80	2:08.80
59:	1:41.20	1:45.60	1:48.20	1:55.20	2:02.20	2:09.20
57:	1:41.40	1:45.80	1:48.40	1:55.40	2:02.40	2:09.60
55:	1:41.60	1:46.00	1:48.60	1:55.60	2:02.60	2:09.80

NOTE: *Variations between different racetracks may require an adjustment between the same Beyer figure on the one-turn and the two-turn chart. For instance, Tampa Bay Downs, which features an unusual seven-furlong chute (see Chapter 13), forces a .60 (³⁄₅) second-increase in the seven-furlong point values. At Santa Anita, point values are scaled 14 points higher in sprints and 9 points higher in routes, but all other values are the same.*

With par times and a practical parallel time chart, any player may begin making reasonably accurate speed figures and track variants by following three steps:

1. Convert all raw final clockings into their corresponding numbers on the chart.
2. Compare these numbers to par numbers for each class of race on the day in question.
3. Average the differences between the raw numbers and the par times.

THE NUTS AND BOLTS OF SPEED-FIGURE COMPUTATIONS

TRACK VARIANTS. To begin we will compare a day's worth of clockings to a set of class pars and the theoretical time charts. If, for example, we are at Aqueduct racecourse today and all the clockings were about one second faster than our class par research suggests, we might conclude that the track condition influenced the raw clockings accordingly. As a result we would be wise to *deduct* one second from the clockings earned by all horses who competed on this track to compensate for the speed of the racing surface. That is precisely what all the fuss is about—to measure how fast each horse has actually run. To do that we must negate the net effect of the racing surface on the actual clockings.

If the race has been run in 1:11 for a raw 93 and the class par is 85, then the variant for that race is −8 (8 points faster than par). At the end of a day's worth of main-track races, these differences should be compared. If they all seem to fall into a relatively compact range, the average obtained will be the variant for the day.

If the differences from par are scattered wildly above and below par, separate the routes from the sprints to see if that accounts for the unwieldy spread. Two separate variants may be the best way to treat this day, or perhaps the earlier races were different from the later ones.

As you proceed with this process every day, your work will get tighter and you will monitor the results of horses who return to the races to verify unusually high or low figures. As a rule of thumb, it is wise to be conservative in making ultrafast speed figures unless you have several levels of evidence to believe they are accurate. Had Faiz or a few of his racemates (see Chapter 13) failed in $7,500 claiming races in their next starts, I certainly would have had to adjust all my numbers for Canterbury Downs.

A SAMPLE DAY

BEYER FIG. PAR	CLOCKING IN BEYER FIGS.	VARIANT
88	91	−3 Sp.
83	88	−5 Sp.
85	89	−4 Rt.
106	106	0 Sp.
101	106	−5 Rt.
90	93	−3 Sp.
Turf	No fig.	No variant
1½ mi.	No fig.	No variant
111	115	−4 Rt.
94	97	−3 Rt.

STEP 1. After today's races, list and compare the final times with the par times for the appropriate distance and class. At Aqueduct, the par time for a $25,000 claiming race is 1:11.00 for six furlongs. On the parallel time chart that clocking is worth 93 Beyer figure points. A Grade 2, $100,000 sprint stakes on the card has been run in 1:22.80 for seven furlongs which is a Beyer figure of 106 and par is 106. What we seek to determine is if the relative speed of the track surface contributed to the raw clockings or slowed them down.

In the sample day above, we can see that the track is playing about three Beyer figure points fast at sprints and four at routes. Because the margin is so close, sprints and routes should be grouped together, for a variant of −3 points fast. A split variant only makes sense when there is a clear difference between the two different type races.

STEP 2. Deduct three Beyer figure points from the raw clockings to create the Beyer figure for each race winner. When we enter the net speed figures in our permanent record, we will note the variant and the adjusted speed figures in the following manner.

RACES

DATE	VARIANT	1	2	3	4	5	6	7	8	9	BIAS?
7/08	− 3fast	88	85	86r	103	103	T	I	112r	94r	DC. +

EXPLANATIONS:

Sprints: 3 races   − 8   total variant = − 3 average Sp. variant.

Routes: 4 races   − 16   total variant = − 4 average Rt. variant.

Average for all: − 24   divided by 7 ratable races = − 3.

Bias notations: DC: Deep closers (+, + +, + + + strength ratings)
             Spd: Early speed (+, + +)
             FR: Strong speed, front runners.
       Inside: I +, I + +.
     Outside: O +, O + +.

The interested handicapper should note these additional facts about speed figures.

- Variants for turf races may only be obtained by comparing the clockings to a completely different parallel time chart generated specifically for turf races. The basic mathematical relationships persist, of course, but the ratings will differ and some courses will require more than one set of time charts or point values. A single turf course really may be as many as five different turf courses with movable inside rails and different run-up distances. Some turf courses do not have electronic timing equipment.
- At the end of this appendix I have included a few sample Grade 3 turf pars to work with at selected tracks.
- It is unwise to include clockings from marathon distances, or extremely short sprints in variant calculations, although variants obtained from other races may be tentatively applied to such races pending further review.
- Class pars for New York and southern California tracks are found in Chapter 13.

- Adjustments for fillies and younger horses also are in Chapter 13.
- To obtain a rating for a horse who has finished behind the winner, consult the beaten-lengths chart in Chapter 13.

ADVANCED SPEED-FIGURE COMPUTATIONS

THE PROJECTION METHOD. After doing speed figures based on class pars for about 10 days to two weeks, you may downplay their importance and enter a brand new world that will sharpen your game. It is the world of making speed figures based on comparisons to the *projected clockings* of horses competing in each field.

No longer will you always seek to compare clockings to par times for the class. Instead you will examine a complete day's worth of races trying to find a cluster or two of relatively stable horses who appear to have performed as anticipated. The class pars will remain useful in cases where no such evidence presents itself or as a support mechanism to your projections.

For instance, if three or four horses who look as though they should have run a 93–92–92, respectively, and actually finished noses apart in a clocking rating an 88, that may be sufficient evidence to conclude the track was about four points slow. If another cluster of reliable horses validates the four-point spread, you have a solid basis for concluding a four-point variant. If, however, the second cluster projects 78 and the race is clocked in 70, I will also look at the class pars for each race to help reconcile the different projected variants. If the class par matches the first cluster but is six points slow for the second, I would make the variant for this day +5, as a logical compromise between the four points projected and the six points in the second class par.

When doing a variant for route races, you may encounter days when only one route was run and the projected, or par variant differs wildly from the variant you have obtained for sprints. Here, I would lean more on the projection based on information gleaned from the actual past performances. If the par is 92, but the projection says 87 and the clocking is 75, I would be inclined to trust the 87 and give this race a variant of +12, not 17 if my handicapping review of the actual horses suggested it. Otherwise, if projections seem very sketchy, I might take the median between the par and the projection to create a temporary par of 90 for the race and a tentative variant of +15.

If you have never attempted speed-figure projections before, you will be amazed how accurate your track variants can be. The trick is to use the class pars as a foundation while comparing actual clockings against the most reliable horses who ran that day.

Speed figures by projection is the ultimate method for measuring how fast a horse really ran; with some practical experience, it can be a laser tool for accurate variants. By a wide margin it has greater reliability than class par-based speed figures, or *DRF* track variants. It succeeds because it is based on the specific performances of the horses and therefore does not automatically mute the importance of significantly faster or slower races. While class pars will remain invaluable for many fundamental comparisons, projection-method speed figures are preferred by the vast majority of successful professional players in the game.

CLASS AND SPEED PARS ON SELECTED TURF COURSES

BAY MEADOWS. Grade 3 stakes par = 1:42.60 for 1 1/16 miles on its seven-furlong basic turf course using no chute.

GOLDEN GATE FIELDS. Grade 3 stakes par = 1:43.00 for 1 1/6 miles on basic turf course using an infield starting chute.

SARATOGA RACECOURSE. Grade 3 stakes par = 1:39.60 for 1 1/16 miles on 1-mile basic turf course.

SANTA ANITA. Six and one-half furlong downhill course, Grade 3 stakes par = 1:13.00; 1 mile on basic seven-furlong course = 1:33.40

Appendix C
Pace Figures

FRACTIONAL CLOCKINGS AND PACE PARS

To establish class pars for fractional clockings, procedures similar to those used to create class pars for speed figures are required. See Chapter 17 and the following two examples for details.

EXAMPLE: 15 Aqueduct races clocked in 1:11.20 during three months in 1992 produced a median ½-mile fractional split of 46.00. Seven-furlongs in 1:23.80 also produced a median ½ mile clocked in 46.00; 1⅛ miles in 1:52.40 produced a median six-furlong split of 1:13.80.

	½	¾	FINAL CLOCKINGS
Six furlongs:	46.00		1:11.20
Seven furlongs:	46.00		1:23.80
1⅛ miles:		1:13.80	1:52.40

Example: $25,000 claimers at Aqueduct produced the following median fractional clockings at six furlongs, seven furlongs, one mile, and 1⅛ miles.

$25,000 CLAIMING AT AQUEDUCT				
	¼	½	¾	FINAL CLOCKING
Six furlongs:	(22.40)	45.80		1:11.00
Seven furlongs:	(22.60)	46.10		1:23.80
1 turn mile:		46.30	1:11.40	1:37.00
1⅛ miles:		(48.40)	1:13.30	1:51.30

After conducting class par research for a few different class levels and clockings, you may use interpolation to extrapolate pars for every clocking at every distance.

NOTE: *With the assistance of a home computer, a relatively simple program can be written to extrapolate any par chart for any track using only two pace lines per distance. At the same time, an ingenious computer program has been written by Texas horseplayer, Joe Spira, which includes workable pace pars for most tracks and delivers my converted pace-speed numbers with minimum input. For details, see the resource listing in Appendix D. Below are some pace pars for various clockings at Aqueduct.*

SAMPLE AQUEDUCT PACE PARS

BEYER FIGURE			
110:	6f =	45.20	1:09.80
	7f =	45.40	1:22.40
	1 mi =	46.00	1:35.40
	1⅛ mi =	1:12.60	1:49.40
106:	6f =	45.30	1:10.00
	7f =	45.50	1:22.80
	1 mi =	46.10	1:35.80
	1⅛ =	1:12.80	1:49.80
100:	6f =	45.50	1:10.40
	7f =	45.70	1:23.20
	1 mi =	46.30	1:36.20
	1⅛ mi =	1:12.90	1:50.20
93:	6f =	45.80	1:11.00
	7f =	46.00	1:23.80
	1 mi =	46.60	1:37.00
	1⅛ mi =	1:13.20	1:51.20

The following is a complete list of six furlong pace pars for Aqueduct.

AQUEDUCT SIX FURLONG PACE PARS

¼ MI.	½ MI.		6 FURLS.		BEYER FIG.	CONVERTED SPEED PACE #
21.80.	44.40	=	1:08.20	=	131	112
22.00.	44.50	=	1:08.40	=	129	111
22.00.	44.60	=	1:08.60	=	126	110
22.10.	44.70	=	1:08.80	=	123	109
22.10.	44.80	=	1:09.00	=	120	108
22.10.	44.90	=	1:09.20	=	118	107
22.10.	45.00	=	1:09.40	=	115	106
22.20.	45.10	=	1:09.60	=	112	105
22.20.	45.20	=	1:09.80	=	109	104
22.20.	45.30	=	1:10.00	=	106	103
22.20.	45.40	=	1:10.20	=	103	102
22.30.	45.50	=	1:10.40	=	100	100
22.30.	45.60	=	1:10.60	=	98	99
22.30.	45.70	=	1:10.80	=	95	98
22.40.	45.80	=	1:11.00	=	92	97
22.40.	45.90	=	1:11.20	=	89	96
22.40.	46.00	=	1:11.40	=	86	95
22.40.	46.10	=	1:11.60	=	83	94
22.50.	46.20	=	1:11.70	=	81	93
22.50.	46.30	=	1:11.80	=	78	92
22.50.	46.50	=	1:12.20	=	75	91
22.60.	46.60	=	1:12.40	=	72	90
22.60.	46.70	=	1:12.60	=	70	89
22.60.	46.80	=	1:12.80	=	67	88
22.70.	46.90	=	1:13.00	=	64	87
22.70.	47.00	=	1:13.20	=	61	86
22.80.	47.10	=	1:13.40	=	59	85
22.80.	47.20	=	1:13.60	=	56	84
22.80.	47.30	=	1:13.80	=	53	83
22.90.	47.40	=	1:14.00	=	51	82
22.90.	47.50	=	1:14.20	=	48	81
23.00.	47.60	=	1:14.40	=	45	80
23.00.	47.70	=	1:14.60	=	42	79
23.10.	47.80	=	1:14.80	=	40	78
23.10.	47.90	=	1:15.00	=	37	77
23.20.	48.00	=	1:15.20	=	35	76
23.20.	48.10	=	1:15.40	=	33	75
23.30.	48.20	=	1:15.60	=	30	74
23.30.	48.30	=	1:15.80	=	28	73
23.40.	48.40	=	1:16.00	=	25	72

6½ AND SEVEN-FURLONG PACE LINES

¼	½	6½		7 FURLS.		BEYER FIG.		CONVERTED SPEED PACE #
22.60.	46.20.	1:18.00	=	1:24.80	=	89	=	96

AQUEDUCT ONE-TURN MILE

½-MI. SPLIT	6-FURL. SPLIT		1-MI.		BEYER FIG.	CONVERTED SPEED PACE #
45.00	1:09.40	=	1:33.40	=	131	112
45.80	1:10.20	=	1:35.00	=	113	105
46.00	1:10.60	=	1:35.60	=	105	102
46.40	1:11.20	=	1:36.60	=	95	99
46.60	1:11.60	=	1:37.40	=	89	96
47.00	1:12.00	=	1:38.40	=	79	92
47.20	1:12.20	=	1:39.00	=	72	90
47.80	1:13.00	=	1:40.60	=	55	84

NOTE: *A different chart is required for Belmont's one-turn races at one mile, 1¹/₁₆ miles and 1⅛ miles (1¼-mile races are started out of an angled chute set midway on the clubhouse turn). Belmont plays about 1.20 seconds faster than Aqueduct at the 1-mile distance, while the 1¹/₁₆-mile distance plays about .30 slower than a mathematically sound projection from Belmont mile clockings, due perhaps to run-up distance and soil composition in the straightaway chute.*

SAMPLE BELMONT PACE PARS FOR 1 MILE, 1¹/₁₆ MILES; 1⅛ MILES

½ MI.	¾ MI.		1 MI.	1¹/₁₆	1⅛ MI.		BEYER FIG.		CONVERTED PACE #
(45.70)	1:09.80		1:35.00			=	100	=	100
(46.40)	1:10.30	=		1:41.70		=	100	=	100
(46.80)	1:10.80	=			1:48.30	=	100	=	100

NOTE: *On my converted pace-speed number scale, 100 = 100 Beyer figures at all distances.*

TWO-TURN ROUTES

Two-turn routes require different parallel time charts, because the extra turn slows horses down, as observed in the difference between final clockings for one- and two-turn races at the one-mile distance.

SAMPLE PACE PARS FOR TWO-TURN 1⅛ MILES AT AQUEDUCT

½	¾	1⅛ MI.		BEYER FIG.		CONVERTED SPEED-PACE #
48.50	1:12.90	1:50.20	=	100	=	100
48.70	1:13.30	1:51.20	=	93	=	95
49.10	1:14.60	1:54.80	=	61	=	83

Using the above, the following is a generic, theoretical par chart. It may serve as a model for constructing par charts for two-turn distances at 1-mile and 1⅛-mile tracks.

AQUEDUCT AND THEORETICAL TWO-TURN PACE PARS

BEYER FIG.	½	¾	1 MI.	1 1/16	1⅛	CONVERTED SPEED-PACE #
109:	(48.30)	1:12.60	1:36.20	1:42.80	1:49.40	104
106:	(48.40)	1:12.80	1:36.60	1:43.20	1:49.80	102
100:	(48.50)	1:12.90	1:37.00	1:43.80	1:50.20	100
93:	(48.70)	1:13.30	1:37.80	1:44.60	1:51.20	95
82:	(48.60)	1:13.60	1:38.80	1:45.60	1:52.40	89
75:	(48.80)	1:13.80	1:39.60	1:46.40	1:53.20	85
61:	(49.10)	1:14.60	1:41.00	1:47.80	1:54.80	83

To plug in par times for another track, research one or two pace lines and note the differences at the ½- and ¾-mile calls for each distance. Churchill Downs is used as an example.

FOR CHURCHILL DOWNS: Deduct .30 for ½-mile *and* ¾-mile fractions at 1 1/16 miles; no adjustment to the pace pars for 1⅛ miles, although the 1⅛-mile distance runs about 1.00 second slower than Aqueduct's 1⅛-mile distance, or nine points slower on the Beyer speed figure scale. Please note that Churchill's one-mile race is a one-turn race and needs no adjustment compared to Aqueduct's one-turn mile.

For a much faster track, i.e., Santa Anita, pace pars must be compiled independently and we have seen enough differences in run-up distances, and so on, to know that fractional splits must be computed for each different distance to be relevant.

PAR TIMES AT SANTA ANITA: Santa Anita's six-furlong race is about .60 (⅗) seconds faster to the first ¼-mile call than the Aqueduct model and approaches .50 (⅖ +) seconds for the ½-mile call. The difference reverts to + .20 for the first ¼ and − .10 for the ½-mile call for seven furlongs because of the short run up to the starting beam for that distance at Santa Anita which slows up fractional splits.

SANTA ANITA SAMPLE PACELINES

100 NET BEYER FIGS. = 100 CONVERTED SPEED-PACE #'S

¼ MI.	½ MI.	6 FURLS.	7 FURLS.
21.60	44.60	1:09.60	
22.40	45.00		1:22.20

The following are Pace Pars for Santa Anita two-turn races. Each clocking is equal to 100 Beyer fig. and 100 converted speed-pace #.

½ MI.	¾ MI.	1 MI.	1 1/16	1⅛
46.10	1:10.20	1:36.00		
46.80	1:10.80		1:42.60	
47.00	1:11.00			1:49.20

Using the above, we can extrapolate the rest of Santa Anita's pace lines for a solid pace par chart. Obviously, adjustments in the opposite direction would be required for a slower track such as Calder. That is the process in a nutshell. And of course, the work is much, much easier when we store and sort information on our home computer.

MATHEMATICAL ERRORS IN FRACTIONAL CALL BEATEN LENGTHS

As cited in Chapter 16, there are severe errors built in to the assumption that one length = about 10 feet = ⅕ second. The proof of this may be gleaned through an examination of feet-per-second formulations as featured in the Sartin Methodology.

A horse covering ½ mile in 44 seconds is traveling 2640 feet in 44 seconds. This is 60.00 feet per second. If one length equals 10 feet as we have been told, then six lengths are being covered in one second.

A horse covering ¼ mile in 24.40 seconds is traveling 1320 feet in 24.20. This is 54.09 feet per sec. If one length = 10 feet, then 5.4 lengths are being covered in one second at this slow rate of speed.

The above error is compounded by the added fact that a horse length usually measures about 8.5 to 9.0 feet, as demonstrated repeatedly by researchers at the University of Pennsylvania's New Bolton Center for Equine Research.

If a length = 9.0 feet, than 6⅔ lengths will be covered in each second during a ½ mile clocked in .44 seconds (60 feet per second).

"TOO FAST" PRELIMINARY FRACTIONS FOR TWO-TURN ROUTES

The following table contains practical early "pace thresholds for late race meltdowns in route races. When any horse sets a preliminary pace faster than these swift clockings, it could explain a late race meltdown even when the ¾-mile fraction is in a neutral range. When it does not, the track should be examined for a possible speed bias and the horse should be examined very closely for future improvement.

Each preliminary fractional clocking scores within a range of 103–110 on my tighter, converted pace-speed number scale and are for 1¹⁄₁₆-mile races, except where noted. Other than top-level allowance races and good stakes, horses who go faster than these pars have gone too fast too early.

"TOO FAST" PRELIMINARY FRACTIONS IN ROUTES

Arlington International	22.40 and 46.20	(2-turn 1⅛)
Atlantic City Racecourse	22.70 and 46.90	(2-turn 1⅛)
Aqueduct Racetrack	23.20 and 47.60	(2-turn 1⅛)
Bay Meadows	22.40 and 46.00	
Belmont Park	22.60 and 46.00	(1-turn 1⅛)
Calder Racecourse	22.40 and 46.80	
Canterbury Downs (R.I.P.)	22.50 and 46.40	
Churchill Downs	22.60 and 46.80	
Del Mar Racecourse	22.30 and 45.70	
Fair Grounds Racetrack	22.70 and 46.60	
Golden Gate Fields	22.30 and 45.70	
Gulfstream Park	22.60 and 46.50	
Garden State Park	22.60 and 46.70	
Hollywood Park	22.20 and 45.40	(2-turn 1⅛)
Keeneland Racecourse	22.60 and 46.50	
Laurel Racecourse	22.70 and 46.80	(2-turn 1⅛)
The Meadowlands	22.20 and 45.90	
Monmouth Park	22.60 and 46.30	
Oaklawn Park	22.60 and 46.20	
Penn National Racecourse	22.60 and 46.40	
Philadelphia Park	22.60 and 46.40	
Pimlico Racecourse	22.50 and 46.20	
Pleasanton County Fair	22.30 and 46.20	
Santa Anita Park	22.00 and 45.80	
Saratoga Racecourse	22.50 and 46.70	(2-turn 1⅛)

Appendix D
Exotic Wagering Strategies

Betting strategy 101 says that a solid-looking horse coupled with several contenders in the daily double or exacta is a good betting strategy to boost profits in tandem with a win bet. Similarly, a horse properly used as an exacta key to win and/or run second with a handful of potential upset possibilities is another way to make good money even if the key horse turns out to be second best.

Every exotic wagering tool in this book is targeted toward players who wish to advance their skill. But casual players who concentrate their limited capital on daily doubles, exactas, trifectas, big triples and the Pick Six should expect a quick trip to Tap City.

Skilled players with considerable experience also face dangers. Some will forgo the win pool to focus on various exotic wagers, only to open the door to longer losing streaks that can drain an unprepared bankroll and psyche. The bottom line is this: Producing bonus profits from exotic wagering is license to continue. If the player is losing, or not winning as much as straight win play, the results must be accepted and play shifted toward more straightforward betting strategies matched to the player's level of skill. Exotic wagering experiments should be done privately, without actual money, *before* one attempts to include them into regular play.

Betting Strategies in Daily Doubles

1. *The Key Horse Wheel.* The basic strategy. To be used when a qualified prime bet occurs in a daily double race.

    STEP A: Buy $2 tickets on the key horse with all the horses in the second half of the daily double.

STEP B: Buy extra tickets using the key horse with the *lowest* payoff possibilities in the second half of the D.D.

STEP C: Buy extra tickets using the key horse with two or three *selected contenders* in the second half of the D.D.

The above steps frequently provide a balanced range of payoffs greater than the net payoff from a straight win bet on the key horse. The example below demonstrates a logical distribution of play involving such a key horse with a field of nine in the second half of the daily double.

Example of Key Horse Wheel

STEP A: $2 tickets on the KH with a, b, c, d, e, f, g, h, i. $18.

STEP B: $6 tickets on the KH with a, d, e (lowest payoffs). $18.

STEP C: $8 tickets on the KH with a, c, f (selected contenders). $24.

Totals: 30 daily double tickets bought = $60 investment.

NOTES: The KH-a combination was a $16 investment.

The KH-d and KH-e combinations were $8 investments.

The KH-c and KH-f combinations were $10 investments.

All the other combinations were $2 investments.

2. *A Partial Wheel.* Using the key horse with selected contenders in the second half of the D.D. To be used in tandem with a straight win on the key horse.

STEP A: Bet 50 percent of intended investment on the key horse to win.

STEP B: Buy multiple daily double tickets on the key horse with selected contenders in the second race.

This strategy is employed when there are very few probable contenders in the second half of the daily double.

Example of a Partial Wheel

STEP A: $30 win bet on the key horse.

STEP B: $10 daily doubles on KH-a, KH-c, and KH-f. $30.

Totals: $30 win + $30 in daily doubles = $60 investment.

3. *A Crisscross Saver.* Using the key horse *and* an alternate selection in the same race with selected contenders in the second half of the daily double. To be used in tandem with a win bet on the key horse.

STEP A: A 50 percent win bet on the KH.

STEP B: A partial wheel using the KH.

STEP C: A partial wheel using an alternate selection as a secondary KH.

To be used if there is a dangerous contender in the KH race and there are but a few legitimate contenders in the second half of the double.

Example of a Crisscross Saver

STEP A: $30 win bet on the KH.

STEP B: $6 D.D.s on KH-a, KH-c, and KH-f. $18.

STEP C: $4 D.D.s on Alt. Sel.-a, Alt. Sel.-c, and Alt. Sel.-f. $12.

Totals: $30 win bet + $18 KH D.D.s + $12.00 Alt. Sel. D.D.s = $60 investment.

4. *Daily Double–Exacta Combine.* Using the key horse in a partial D.D. wheel and in tandem with a crisscross, *plus* extra play on the KH in exactas if the opportunity is there.

STEP A: 50 percent win bet on KH.

STEP B: Partial D.D. wheel using the KH.

STEP C: Partial D.D. wheel using an alternate selection as a secondary KH.

STEP D: Exacta tickets using the KH to win over one, two, or three probable contenders for second place.

STEP E: Exacta tickets using the KH in the *place* position under one, two, or three probable contenders (including the alternate selection).

Example of Daily Double–Exacta Combine

STEP A: $30 win bet on the KH.

STEP B: $4 D.D.s on KH-a, KH-c, and KH-f. $12.

STEP C: $2 D.D.s on Alt. Sel.-a, Alt. Sel.-c, and Alt. Sel.-f. $6.

STEP D: $2 exacta tickets on KH over Alt. Sel., plus KH over two other probable contenders in the race. $6.

STEP E: $2 exacta tickets on KH in the *place* position under the alternate selection and two other probable contenders. $6.

Totals: $30 win bet + $12 KH D.D.s + $6 Alt. Sel. D.D.s + $6 + $6 in exactas = $60 investment.

Betting Strategies in Exactas

1. *The Key Horse Wheel.* Using a qualified prime bet as a key horse in exacta play.

   STEP A: Buy $2 exacta tickets on KH over the rest of the field.

   STEP B: Buy extra tickets on KH over the lowest payoff possibilities.

   STEP C: Buy extra tickets on KH over selected contenders. The example below is based on a ten-horse field.

   Example of Basic Strategy

   STEP A: $2 exacta tickets on KH over a, b, d, e, f, g, h, i, j. $18.

   STEP B: $6 exacta tickets on KH over a, KH over i, and KH over j. $18.

   STEP C: $6. exacta tickets on KH over d, e, f, j. $24.

   Totals: $18 for basic wheel + $18.00 (lowest payoffs) + $24 (selected contenders) = $60.

2. *Top and Bottom Wheel.* Using key horse as an exacta wheel in the win and place positions. For better value than straight win-place betting.

   STEP A: $2 tickets on KH over the field.

   STEP B: $2 tickets on KH under the field.

   STEP C: Extra tickets on KH over lowest possible payoffs.

   STEP D: Extra tickets on KH under lowest possible payoffs.

   STEP E: Extra tickets on KH over selected contenders.

   STEP F: Extra tickets on KH under selected contenders.

   Example of Top and Bottom Wheel

   STEP A: $2 tickets on KH over a, b, d, e, f, g, h, i, j. $18.

   STEP B: $2 tickets on KH under a, b, d, e, f, g, h, i, j. $18.

   STEP C: $2 tickets on KH over a, i, j. $6.

   STEP D: $2 tickets on KH under a, i, j. $6.

   STEP E: $2 tickets on KH over d, e, f, j. $8.

   STEP F: $2 tickets on KH under d, e, f, j. $8.

   Totals: $18 + $18 + $6 + $6 + $8 + $8 = $64 investment.

3. *A Partial Exacta Wheel.* Using key horse with selected contenders in exacta play. To be used in tandem with a straight win bet.

   STEP A: 50 percent win bet on KH.

STEP B: A partial exacta wheel.

STEP C: Saver exactas in the place position (optional).

Example of Partial Exacta Wheel

STEP A: $30 win bet on KH.

STEP B: $5 exacta tickets on KH over d, e, f, j. $20.

STEP C: $2 exacta tickets on KH under d, e, f, j. $8.

Totals: $30 win + $20 + $8 in exactas = $58 investment.

NOTE: Without saver exactas, STEP C, increase STEP B to $8 exactas.

4. *Straight Top and Bottom.* A partial wheel, using KH in the win and place positions with three (or fewer) selected contenders. To be used in tandem with a saver win wager.

STEP A: A 25 percent win wager.

STEP B: $10 exactas KH over three selected contenders.

STEP C: $5 exactas KH under three selected contenders. This strategy is only valuable when the contention is clearly defined.

Example of Straight Top and Bottom

STEP A: $15 win bet on key horse as a saver.

STEP B: $10 exactas on KH over d, f, j. $30.

STEP C: $5 exactas on KH under d, f, j. $15.

Totals: $15 win + $30 + $15 in exactas = $60 investment.

5. *Key Horse–Exacta Box.* Using key horse in all possible combinations with two or three other contenders in the same race.

STEP A: 50 percent win bet on key horse.

STEP B: KH in win position over three contenders.

STEP C: KH in place position under three contenders.

STEP D: Tickets on other contenders in all possible combinations with each other.

Example of Key Horse–Exacta Box

STEP A: $30 win bet on KH.

STEP B: $4 exactas on KH over d, f, j. $12.

STEP C: $4 exactas on KH under d, f, j. $12.
STEP D: $2 exacta box d, f, j. $12.

Totals: $30 win bet + $24 + $12 = $66 investment.

NOTE:　　If necessary to keep play at or below $60 total investment, reduce STEP A to $24.

6. *Seconditis Wheel.* Using key horse in a wheel underneath the rest of the field. To be used in tandem with a saver win wager.
STEP A:　20 percent win wager on key horse.
STEP B:　A full wheel using the KH underneath the rest of the field.
STEP C:　Extra tickets on lowest payoffs.
STEP D:　Extra tickets on selected contenders.
This strategy is extremely potent when the key horse is obviously sharp, but is burdened by a persistent history of finishing second.

Example of Seconditis Wheel
STEP A:　$12 win bet on key horse as saver.
STEP B:　$4 exactas on KH underneath a, b, d, e, f, g, h, i, j. $36.
STEP C:　$2 exactas on KH under a, i, j. $6.
STEP D:　$2 exactas on KH under d, f, j. $6.

Totals: $12 win bet + $36 + $6 + $6 in exactas = $60 investment.

Betting Strategies in Trifectas

There are many different ways to buy into the trifecta, including a complete win wheel of a key horse over the rest of the field and assorted boxes and partial wheels. The objective is to pick the correct 1–2–3 order of finish, which is far more difficult than picking a clear-cut winner or an exact 1–2 order of finish. But even so, and despite its reputation as a "sucker's bet," the trifecta sometimes offers intriguing possibilities, especially if play is kept in perspective as part of a sound betting strategy. The primary emphasis in such a strategy is on the win position. The trifecta is a profit booster, a home-run hitter's delight, but it can also be the quickest ticket to a losing season if the player fails to keep his eye on the ball.

1. *Partial Wheel.* Using key horse in the win position over a three-, four-, or five-horse box for the place and show positions. To be used in tandem with a realistic win wager on the KH.

   STEP A: 66 percent win bet on KH.

   STEP B: Partial wheel of KH over five selected contenders.

   At most tracks, it is possible to buy into the trifecta with $1 betting units, even though the full trifecta payoff is calculated on the basis of a $2 or $3 unit wager. Using this and other suggested strategies, it will cost $6 to partial wheel the KH over three horses, $12 to partial wheel the KH over four horses, and $20 to cover five horses under the KH.

Example of Partial Wheel

   STEP A: $40 win bet on KH.

   STEP B: Partial trifecta at $1 tickets of KH over a, d, e, f, j. $20

   Totals: $40 win bet + $20 trifecta = $60 investment.

   NOTE: If the KH wins, the trifecta is won if any two of the five selected contenders finish second and third.

2. *Partial Wheel Win and Place.* Using key horse in the win and place positions with four contenders. To be used in tandem with a realistic win wager.

   STEP A: 66 percent win bet on KH.

   STEP B: Partial wheel using KH in win position over four contenders.

   STEP C: Partial wheel using KH in place position with four contenders.

Example of Partial Wheel Win and Place

   STEP A: $40 win bet on KH.

   STEP B: $1 trifecta tickets KH over a, e, f, j box. $12.

   STEP C: $1 trifectas a, e, f, j box over KH over a, e, f, j box. $12.

   Totals: 40 win bet + $12 win trifectas + $12 place trifectas = $64 investment.

3. *Partial Wheel and Alternate.* Using KH in the win position in a partial wheel and using an alternate selection in another partial wheel. To be used in tandem with a win bet on key horse.

STEP A: 66 percent win bet on KH.

STEP B: Partial KH win wheel over four contenders.

STEP C: Partial alternate selection win wheel over four contenders.

Example of Partial Wheel and Alternate

STEP A: $40 win bet on KH.

STEP B: $1 trifecta tickets on KH over (a, e, f, j) box. $12.

STEP C: $1 trifectas on Alt. Sel. over a, e, f, KH box. $12.

Totals: $40 win bet + $12 KH win trifecta wheel + $12 Alt. Sel. trifecta wheel = $64.

NOTE: Hypothetically, the alternate selection in these examples is horse j.

4. *Full Wheel plus Place.* Using key horse to win and an alternate selection to place over the rest of the field. To be used in tandem with a win wager on KH.

STEP A: 66 percent win bet on KH.

STEP B: Playing the KH and Alt. Sel. on top of the rest of the field.

To be used only when the first two contenders seem very solid, a rare occurrence.

Example of Full Wheel plus Place

STEP A: $40 win bet on KH.

STEP B: $2 trifectas on KH with Alt. Sel. over a, b, c, d, e, g, h, i. $16.

Totals: $40 win bet + $16 in trifectas = $56 investment.

5. *Full Wheel plus Place and Show.* Using the key horse in the win position and using the alternate selection in the place and show positions. To be used in tandem with a win bet on KH.

STEP A: 66 percent win bet on KH.

STEP B: A full wheel using KH to win and Alt. Sel. to place.

STEP C: A full wheel using KH to win and Alt Sel. for show.

Example of Full Wheel plus Place and Show

STEP A: $40 win bet on KH.

STEP B: $1 tickets on KH over Alt. Sel. over a, b, c, d, e, g, h, i. $8.

STEP C: $1 tickets on KH over a, b, c, d, e, g, h, i, over Alt. Sel. $8.

Totals: $40 win bet + $8 + $8 trifecta wheels = $56 investment.

6. *Trifecta Box.* No key horse, but possible three- or four-horse trifecta box. To be used when there is no bona fide key horse and the pre-race favorite is distinctly eligible to go off form.
   STEP A: No win bet.
   STEP B: $1 tickets on a three-, four-, or five-horse box.

Examples of Trifecta Boxes

A three-horse box at $1 betting units involves 6 combinations.
A four-horse box at $1 betting units involves 24 combinations.
A five-horse box at $1 betting units involves 60 combinations.

NOTE: I do not recommend boxing trifecta contenders as a substitute for a prime bet. Such play is intended only for light action, or in special cases when the pre-race favorites are highly suspect.

7. *Double win key, spread format, plus optional exactas.* Two win keys, with two, three, four or more additional horses in the place position with two, three, four or more in the show position. A most effective strategy that maximizes opportunity at efficient cost. It is my personal favorite in numerous situations. Usually preferable when there is no prime bet, yet there may be two reasonable longshots, or a credible favorite and one reasonable longshot. It should be played in tandem with exactas and generally identifiable prospects for second and third, or random selections in chaotic races.
   • Two key horses +3 + 5 format. A spread format with two key horses in the win position, with three horses added in the place and show positions, plus exacta protection.
   STEP A: No win bet.
   STEP B: $4 exactas with the two key horses back and forth and $2 exactas using the two key horses over two or three secondary selections. Total cost $16–$20.
   STEP C: KH-a and KH-b, with KH-a, KH-b, c, d and e, with KH-a, KH-b, c, d and e. Total cost $24 at $1 trifecta units.
   • Two key horses +4 +6. Spread format with two key horses in

the win position, with two horses added in the place position, and two more added in the show position, plus exacta protection.

STEP A: No win bet.

STEP B: $6 exactas with the two key horses back and forth and $3 each over the two additional horses used in the place position. Total cost $24.

STEP C: KH-a and KH-b, with KH-a, KH-b, c, and d, with KH-a, KH-b, c, d, e and f. Cost $24.

Total cost $44, or $48.

THE PICK THREE AND PICK SIX

PICK THREE. The pick three is a daily double extended by one extra race. Accordingly, it tends to offer more pari-mutuel value than a straight three race parlay because the takeout occurs once, not three times. On the other hand the pick three is far more difficult than the daily double because the degree of difficulty is multiplied by the number of plausible contenders in the third extra race.

For instance, if horse A is a cinch to win the first race and horse B is a cinch to win the second, but six legit contenders seem plausible in the third, six tickets will be required to stablize the odds against cashing at the same level before the third race was included. The probable payoffs should be higher, of course, to reflect the new situation, but there will be no way to know the payoffs in advance because the pick three is a blind betting pool to be calculated after two of the winners are known. Given these circumstances, it is imperative for players to realize they need to develop situation standards before making pick three plays. I recommend playing the pick three only when the situation includes at least one of the following:

- A vulnerable heavy favorite.
- Two or more vulnerable morning line favorites.
- A prime bet candidate in one of the races, plus reasonable long-shots in one or more of the races.
- A strong track bias narrowing contention down to a few horses in each race.
- Any pick three which offers measurable value as a saver when played in tandem with a pick six, or prime bet play.

Pick three players use a wide spectrum of betting formats to properly distribute the bet. For instance, three horses in each race may be combined for a simple crisscross of all possible combinations for $54 using $2 units. (A,B,C × A,B,C × A,B,C = 27 combinations = $54.)

This is terribly inefficient. If you win, you will have only one winning combination and 26 losing combos and in most cases the wager will not reflect your opinions in any of the three races.

An alternative strategy using the same $54, plus $2 more for an extra logical ticket would be to select the three horses in order of preference in each of the three races and wager as follows:

A with A with A	=	$ 2
A with ABC with ABC	=	$18
ABC with A with ABC	=	$18
ABC with ABC with A	=	$18
	Total	$56

If your top horses win all three races, you hit the pick three four times. If your top horses win two of the races you hit it twice. If it wins one of the three races you hit it once.

Going a step further for better balance at $70 the bet would look like this:

A	with	A	with	A	×	4	tickets	=	$ 8
B	with	A	with	A	×	3	tickets	=	$ 6
A	with	B	with	A	×	3	tickets	=	$ 6
A	with	A	with	B	×	3	tickets	=	$ 6
A	with	A	with	C	×	2	tickets	=	$ 4
A	with	C	with	A	×	2	tickets	=	$ 4
C	with	A	with	A	×	2	tickets	=	$ 4
A	with	B	with	B	×	2	tickets	=	$ 4
B	with	A	with	B	×	2	tickets	=	$ 4
B	with	B	with	A	×	2	tickets	=	$ 4

A	with	B	with	C	×	1	ticket	=	$ 2
A	with	C	with	B	×	1	ticket	=	$ 2
A	with	C	with	C	×	1	ticket	=	$ 2
C	with	A	with	C	×	1	ticket	=	$ 2
C	with	C	with	A	×	1	ticket	=	$ 2
B	with	A	with	C	×	1	ticket	=	$ 2
B	with	C	with	A	×	1	ticket	=	$ 2
C	with	A	with	B	×	1	ticket	=	$ 2
C	with	B	with	A	×	1	ticket	=	$ 2
B	with	B	with	B	×	1	ticket	=	$ 2
							Total		$70

If your top pick wins all three races, you have hit the pick three four times. If your top pick wins two races you have hit it three times.

If your top pick wins one of the three races, you have hit it once or twice, depending on whether it is B or C that wins the other two races. If your second choice wins all three you hit it once. Optional with above:

C	with	B	with	B	×	1	ticket	=	$ 2
B	with	C	with	B	×	1	ticket	=	$ 2
B	with	B	with	C	×	1	ticket	=	$ 2
C	with	B	with	B	×	1	ticket	=	$ 2
C	with	C	with	C	×	1	ticket	=	$ 2
							Combined total		$80

If your secondary selections win all three races you still hit it once.

Beyond these basic, very sensible strategies, the most effective, most logical pick three play revolves around three tiers, as explained below.

THE THREE-TIER PICK THREE BETTING STRATEGY. Make a chart with your selections in order of preference for each of the three races. Put a + next to a

selection that qualifies as a prime bet play, or a solid single, put a −
next to the morning line favorite or probable favorite, place tentative
back-up selections in parentheses and #? to note the number of horses
in a wide open race where the selection order is weak. These charts will
prove very helpful and I recommend their use for pick six plays also.

PICK THREE BETTING CHART

SELECTION RANK

	1	2	3	4	ALL
Race 1	−A+	(b)	(c)		
Race 2	B	−a	c		
Race 3	a	b	−c	d	9?

The weakest "contender" on the betting chart is c in the third leg.
The best value horse in the matrix is B in the second race and the strongest win candidate is A in the first leg. Contender c in the third race
should be played against in all but one saver combination, involving the
strong win candidate in the first and the value win candidate in the
second. Also, the matrix suggests that the favorite in the second race
has no edge at all.

Every situation is different but the chart will help you weigh the play
in favor of your preferences and the chances to make a score. Here is the
way I would play the above chart for $86 to increase its payoff power:

$4 units	A	with	B	with	abc	=	$12
$4 units	A	with	B	with	abd	=	$12
$2 units	A	with	ac	with	abd	=	$12
$2 units	bc	with	B	with	abd	=	$12
$2 units	b	with	a	with	ab	=	$ 4
$2 units	A	with	B	with	*all*	=	$18
$2 units	bc	with	ac	with	ab	=	$16
							$86

If A wins first and B wins second, five hits with a or b; three hits with d in third leg; two hits with c in third leg; one hit with any other third-leg winner—plus numerous other payoffs with various backup combinations.

Unlike the daily double and exacta, scratches do not incur a refund or a consolation payoff in the pick three (or pick six). After the betting begins, the scratched selection automatically is moved to the race favorite. In California, the player is given an alternate selection in pick threes and pick sixes. When dead heats occur, the rules are terribly unfair in some states in which all winning tickets are treated alike instead of creating different sets of payoffs. (In 1991, I hit a pick three in northern California that involved a 20–1 shot in a dead heat with an odds-on favorite. Instead of getting more than $700 for a share of the pick three pool, I received $44, the same as bettors who used the favorite on their tickets. That's legal robbery.)

PICK SIX WAGERING STRATEGIES

There is no doubt that a matrix betting chart will prove useful to anyone attempting to design multi-tiered pick six tickets.

PICK SIX BETTING CHART

SELECTION RANK

	1	2	3	4	ALL
Race 1	− A +	(b)	(c)		
Race 2	B	− a	c		
Race 3	a	b	− c	d	9?
Race 4	A +	(b)			
Race 5	− C	A	B		
Race 6	a	b	c	d	

Using all contenders at equal strength, excluding the possible wheel in the third race:

$3 \times 3 \times 4 \times 2 \times 3 \times 4 = 964$ combinations $= \$1,928$

Using two singles, races 1 and 4, would produce a ticket:

$1 \times 3 \times 4 \times 1 \times 3 \times 4 = 144$ combinations $= \$288$

Using two singles from the above pick six, races 1 and 2, would produce a ticket:

$1 \times 1 \times 4 \times 2 \times 3 \times 4 = 96$ combinations $= \$192$

Using three possible singles in the above pick six, races 1, 2 and 4, would produce a ticket:

$1 \times 1 \times 4 \times 1 \times 3 \times 4 = 48$ combinations $= \$96$

Better coverage with no true singles, including the wheel of the third race will require a multiple-ticket strategy, the most formidable, most efficient way to play the pick six.

The example below includes a balanced combination of six tickets costing $612.

	1	2	3	4	5	6 =		
Ticket #1	A	Bac	abd	A	CAB	abc	=	$288
#2	bc	B	abd	A	CAB	abc	=	$108
#3	A	Bac	c	A	CAB	abc	=	$ 54
#4	A	B	abd	b	CAB	abc	=	$ 54
#5	A	B	efghi	A	CAB	ab	=	$ 60
#6	A	ac	ef	A	CAB	ab	=	$ 48
						Total		$612

Actual layouts will depend on how many potential singles there are among the top-rated contenders and how many logical back-up possibilities there are in each race, including the races with potential singles. At the bottom line all decisions must be funneled through the limitations of the player's bankroll.

Recommended Reading and Resources

BREEDING AND TRAINING

The Blood Horse Magazine, a weekly breeding and racing magazine, with annual reviews, published in Lexington, Kentucky.

Breeding the Racehorse, by Frederico Tesio, tr. by Marcese E. Spinola, British Book Center, 1973.

The Horse Traders, by Steven Crist, New York Times Publishing, 1988.

Maiden Stats, published annually by Bloodstock Research Information Services, Lexington, Kentucky. Includes win percentages for every foal's sire with first-time starters, first-timers on the turf or wet tracks and 2-year-old winners, plus the foal's Dosage Index and average winning distance of the sire's offspring and the most successful siblings produced by the dam.

Training Thoroughbred Horses, revised edition, by Preston M. Burch. The Blood Horse Library, 1973.

Typology of the Racehorse, by Franco Varola. J. A. Allen Sporting Book Center, 1974.

Whittingham, by Jay Hovdey, The Blood Horse Library, 1993.

HANDICAPPING

Ainslie's Complete Guide to Thoroughbred Racing, by Tom Ainslie. Simon and Schuster, 1968 and 1984.

Beyer on Speed, by Andrew Beyer, Houghton Mifflin, 1993.

Fast Track to Thoroughbred Profits, Mark Cramer, Lyle Stuart, 1984.

Figure Handicapping, James Quinn, William Morrow, 1993.

Modern Pace Handicapping, Tom Brohamer, William Morrow, 1991.

Money Secrets at the Racetrack, by Barry Meadow, TR Publishing, 1988.

Picking Winners, by Andrew Beyer, Houghton Mifflin, 1975.

Postures and Profiles, by Joe Takach, self-published, Elkins, PA. 1993.

Recreational Handicapping, James Quinn, William Morrow, 1986.

The Horseplayer magazine, excellent articles on the game, published in Beverly Hills, CA.

Thoroughbred Racing, State of the Art, by William Quirin, William Morrow, 1984.

Winning at the Races, Computer Discoveries in Thoroughbred Handicapping, by William Quirin, William Morrow, 1979.

VIDEOTAPES AND COMPUTER INFORMATION PROGRAMS

Body Language of the Racehorse, videotape, by Bonnie Ledbetter, Lawlor publishing, 1985.

Computer-Generated Pace and Speed Numbers Using Davidowitz Conversion Tables, by Joseph Spira, San Antonio, Texas. (210) 658–2091.

Handicapping Expo, 1990 and 1993. The complete library of video- and audio-tapes on handicapping subjects from the 1990 and 1993 Handicapping Expos. Symposiums on speed and pace; presentations on track bias, Triple Crown racing, betting strategies and most technical aspects of handicapping by Beyer, Brohamer, Cox, Davidowitz, McMannis, Quinn, Ragozin, Ruosso, and Sartin, among others. Lawlor Publishing, 1990 and 1993.

PC Dosage, A Comprehensive "Dosage" Computer Program, published by Blue Hen Software, Malibu, CA, 90265.

STATISTICS AND GENERAL RACING INFORMATION

The American Racing Manual, published annual by *Daily Racing Form.*

The Blood Horse, annual statistical review.

RACING HISTORY

The History of Thoroughbred Racing In America, by William H. Robertson, Bonanza Books, 1964.

In the Winner's Circle, by Joseph A. Hirsch and Gene Plowden, Mason Charter, 1974.

Secretariat: The Making of a Champion, by William Nack, Da Capo Press, 1975.

This Was Racing, by Joe H. Palmer, Henry Clay, 1973.

FICTION

Danger, by Dick Francis, Fawcett/Crest, 1986.

The King of The Nightcap, by William Murray, Bantam Books, 1990.